LEGAL REASONING
AND LEGAL WRITING

ASPEN PUBLISHERS

LEGAL REASONING
AND LEGAL WRITING

Structure, Strategy, and Style

SIXTH EDITION

Richard K. Neumann, Jr.
Professor of Law
Hofstra University

Wolters Kluwer
Law & Business

AUSTIN   BOSTON   CHICAGO   NEW YORK   THE NETHERLANDS

Aspen Publishers
Attn: Permissions Department
76 Ninth Avenue, 7th Floor
New York, NY 10011-5201

Printed in the United States of America

1 2 3 4 5 6 7 8 9 0

ISBN: 978-0-7355-7666-7

Library of Congress Cataloging-in-Publication Data

Neumann, Richard K., 1947-Legal reasoning and legal writing : structure, strategy, and style / Richard K. Neumann, Jr. — 6th ed.
  p. cm.
Includes index.
ISBN 978-0-7355-7666-7
1. Legal composition. 2. Trial practice—United States. 3. Law—United States—Methodology. I. Title.

KF250.N48 2009
808'.06634 — dc22
2009003050

About Wolters Kluwer Law & Business

Wolters Kluwer Law & Business is a leading provider of research information and workflow solutions in key specialty areas. The strengths of the individual brands of Aspen Publishers, CCH, Kluwer Law International and Loislaw are aligned within Wolters Kluwer Law & Business to provide comprehensive, in-depth solutions and expert-authored content for the legal, professional and education markets.

CCH was founded in 1913 and has served more than four generations of business professionals and their clients. The CCH products in the Wolters Kluwer Law & Business group are highly regarded electronic and print resources for legal, securities, antitrust and trade regulation, government contracting, banking, pension, payroll, employment and labor, and healthcare reimbursement and compliance professionals.

Aspen Publishers is a leading information provider for attorneys, business professionals and law students. Written by preeminent authorities, Aspen products offer analytical and practical information in a range of specialty practice areas from securities law and intellectual property to mergers and acquisitions and pension/ benefits. Aspen's trusted legal education resources provide professors and students with high-quality, up-to-date and effective resources for successful instruction and study in all areas of the law.

Kluwer Law International supplies the global business community with comprehensive English-language international legal information. Legal practitioners, corporate counsel and business executives around the world rely on the Kluwer Law International journals, loose-leafs, books and electronic products for authoritative information in many areas of international legal practice.

Loislaw is a premier provider of digitized legal content to small law firm practitioners of various specializations. Loislaw provides attorneys with the ability to quickly and efficiently find the necessary legal information they need, when and where they need it, by facilitating access to primary law as well as state-specific law, records, forms and treatises.

Wolters Kluwer Law & Business, a unit of Wolters Kluwer, is headquartered in New York and Riverwoods, Illinois. Wolters Kluwer is a leading multinational publisher and information services company.

for

Richard K. Neumann, Sr. and
Marjorie Batter Neumann,

who taught everything
on which this book is based

The power of clear statement is the great power at the bar.

—Daniel Webster
(also attributed to
Rufus Choate,
Judah P. Benjamin,
and perhaps others)

Summary
of Contents

Contents

III
OFFICE MEMORANDA 63

IV
ORGANIZING PROOF OF A CONCLUSION OF LAW 89

11. Varying the Depth of Rule Proof and Rule Application

103

12. Combining Proofs of Separate Conclusions of Law

113

13. Working with the Paradigm

125

V

GENERAL ANALYTICAL SKILLS   137

VI
GENERAL WRITING SKILLS   203

18. Paragraphing   205

19. Effective Style   215

20. Citations and Quotations   239

Contents

VII
LETTERS AND EXAM ANSWERS   265

21. Client Advice Letters   267

22. Demand Letters   273

23. How to Write Exam Answers   279

VIII
THE SHIFT TO PERSUASION 289

Preface

Students learn legal reasoning and legal writing better when the two are taught together than when they are taught separately. The act of writing forces the writer to test thought in order to express it fully and precisely, and thus complex analysis cannot be said to be complete until it becomes written and written well.

This text is designed to help students learn how to make professional writing decisions, how to construct proof of a conclusion of law, and how to develop their own processes of writing. The writing process is introduced in Chapter 6 and developed more fully in the remainder of the book.

Part I of the text introduces students to basic concepts of law as well as judicial opinions and methods of briefing them. Legal writing in general is introduced in Part II. Part III explains how to write an office memorandum. A chapter on client interviewing is included for those programs that provide an assignment's facts through a simulated interview. Parts IV, V, and VI explain analytical writing skills, including organizing proof of a conclusion of law, using authority, analyzing facts, and using paragraphing, style, and citations. Part VII covers lawyers' letters and law school examinations. Part VIII introduces advocacy skills. Appellate briefs are covered in Part IX; and oral argument in Part X.

On the inside covers of the book is a list of questions that students should ask themselves while working through successive drafts of a document. Each question represents a recurring problem in student writing — the sort that a teacher marks over and over again on student papers. Students can use these questions to make sure they have attended to likely problems. And teachers can use them to ease the burden of writing so many comments on student papers. Rather than write the same or a similar comment over and over again on students' papers, a teacher can circle problem passages and write a question number ("9-A," for example) in the margin. The inside front and back covers will give a page number in the text, where the student will find a complete explanation of the problem, what causes it, and how to fix it.

Richard K. Neumann, Jr.

January 2009

Acknowledgments

I am grateful to many people who generously contributed their thoughts to the development of this book in this or its earlier editions. Among them are Burton C. Agata, Lisa Aisner, Aaron Balasny, Kathleen Beckett, Sara Bennett, Barbara Blumenfeld, Ben Bratman, Susan L. Brody, Susan Bryant, Mark Carroll, Kimberly Klein Cauthorn, Robin Charlow, Kenneth Chestek, Barbara Child, Julie Close, Elizabeth W. Cohen, Leona Cunningham, Patti L. Dikes, Alice K. Duecker, Jo Anne Durako, Deborah A. Ezbitski, Peter M. Falkenstein, Neal R. Feigenson, Eric M. Freedman, William R. Ginsburg, John DeWitt Gregory, Marc Grinker, Donna Hill, Joseph Holmes, Sam Jacobson, Steven D. Jamar, Ellen M. James, Lawrence W. Kessler, Martha Krisel, Eric Lane, Jan M. Levine, Lisa Eggert Litvin, Ed McDougal, Douglas Miller, Juliet Neisser, Richard J. Peltz, Stuart Rabinowitz, John Regan, Linda A. Robinson, Jennifer Rosenberg, Kathryn A. Sampson, Terry J. Seligman, Carole Shapiro, Amy E. Sloan, Suzanne Spector, Judith Stinson, Grace C. Tonner, Marshall E. Tracht, Aaron D. Twerski, Ursula H. Weigold, Mary White, Grace Wigal, and Mark E. Wojcik, as well as the anonymous reviewers who examined the first edition manuscript for Little, Brown & Co. and those who responded to the questionnaires distributed by Little, Brown & Co. and Aspen Law & Business in preparation for each later edition.

I am also grateful for research assistance by Heather Canning, Elizabeth Hader, Shannon Hynes, Susan King, Vicky Ku, Ellen Leibowitz, Christine Lombardi, Courtney Murphy, Fusae Nara, Karen Nielsen, Colin Padgett, Rachael Ringer, Ashley Roberts, Edmire Saint-Pierre, Dan Wallach, and Carolyn Weissbach, supplemented by Darmin Bachu, Ann Carrozza, Nicole Gamble, Rori Goldman, Bill Kalten, Rachel Mallozzi, Beth Rogoff, Victoria Saunders, and Corey Wishner, together with the advice of Kellie Beach, Sharon Clarke, James Harris, Raj Jadeja, Lissa Mascio, Amee Shah, David Smith, and administrative assistance by Angela Wooden, Donna Posillico, Omayra Perez, Carla Alvarez, and Maureen Quinn.

Richard Heuser, Daniel E. Mangan, Carol McGeehan, Melody Davies, Betsy Kenny, Richard Audet, Nick Niemeyer, Cate Rickard, Lisa Wehrle, Kurt Hughes, John Burdeaux, and their colleagues at Aspen Law & Business and Little, Brown & Co. have had enormous insight into the qualities that make a text useful; their perceptiveness and creativity ultimately caused this book to become a different and far better text than it otherwise would have been.

Elliott Milstein and Joseph Harbaugh had much influence on the pedagogy that has shaped this book.

And Deborah A. Ezbitski, Lillianna Ezbitski Neumann, and Alexander Ezbitski Neumann inspired in countless ways.

Copyright Acknowledgments

Permission to reprint copyrighted excerpts from the following is gratefully acknowledged:

D. Binder & P. Bergman, *Fact Investigation: From Hypothesis to Proof* 92-96 (1984). Copyright © 1984 by the West Publishing Co.

Albert J. Moore, *Inferential Streams: The Articulation and Illustration of the Advocate's Evidentiary Intuitions.* Originally published in 34 UCLA L. Rev. 611, 625-27. Copyright © 1987 by the Regents of the University of California. All rights reserved.

E. Barrett Prettyman, *Some Observations Concerning Appellate Advocacy,* 39 Va. L. Rev. 285, 296 (1953). Copyright © 1953 by The Virginia Law Review Association.

J. Ramage & J. Bean, *Writing Arguments: A Rhetoric with Readings,* 4th ed., 10-11 (1998). Copyright © 1998 by Allyn & Bacon. Reprinted by permission.

LEGAL REASONING
AND LEGAL WRITING

I

INTRODUCTION TO LAW AND ITS STUDY

1 An Introduction to American Law

§1.1 The Origin of Common Law

At Pevensey, on the south coast of England, a man named William, Duke of Normandy, came ashore, together with ten thousand soldiers and knights, on a morning in late September 1066. Finding the town unsatisfactory for his purpose, he destroyed it and moved his people nine miles east to a coastal village called Hastings. A few days later, the English king, Harold, arrived with an army of roughly the same size. The English had always fought on foot, rather than on horseback, and in a day-long battle they were cut down by the Norman knights. According to legend, Harold was at first disabled by a random arrow shot through his eye and then killed by William himself, who marched his army north, burning villages on the way and terrorizing London into submission.

Although in December he had himself crowned king of England, William controlled only a small part of the country, and in the following years he had to embark on what modern governments would call campaigns to pacify the countryside. In 1069, for example, his army marched to York, executed every English male of any age found along the way, flattened the town, and then marched on to Durham, burning every farm and killing every English-speaking person to be found—all with the result that seventeen years later the survey recorded in Domesday Book revealed almost no population in Yorkshire. In the five years after William landed at Pevensey, one-fifth of the population of England was killed by the Norman army of occupation or died of starvation after the Normans burned the food supply. To atone for all this, William later built a monastery at Hastings. For nine centuries, it has been known as Battle Abbey, and its altar sits on the spot where Harold is said to have died.

The picturesque Norman castles throughout England were built not to defend the island from further invasion, but to subjugate and imprison the English themselves while William expropriated nearly all the land in the country and gave it to Normans, who became a new aristocracy. With the exception of a few collaborators, everyone whose native language was English became — regardless of earlier social station — landless and impoverished. Normans quickly occupied even the most local positions of power, and suddenly the average English person knew no one in authority who understood English customs, English law, or even much of the language. William himself never learned to speak it.

Pollock and Maitland call the Norman Conquest "a catastrophe which determines the whole future history of English law."[1] Although the Conquest's influences on English law were many, for the moment let us focus only on two.

The first concerns the language of law and lawyers. Norman French was the tongue of the new rulers, and eventually it became the language of the courts as well. The sub-language called Norman Law French could still be heard in courtrooms many centuries later,[2] even after the everyday version of Norman French had merged with Middle English to produce Modern English, a language rich in nuance because it thus inherited two entire vocabularies. As late as 1731, Parliament was compelled to enact a statue providing that all court documents "shall be in the English tongue only, and not in Latin or French."[3]

Law is filled with terms of art that express technical and specialized meanings, and a large proportion of these terms survive from Norman Law French. Some of the more familiar examples include *appeal, arrest, assault, attorney, contract, counsel, court, crime, defendant, evidence, judge, jury, plaintiff, suit,* and *verdict.* In the next few pages, you will also encounter *allegation, cause of action, demurrer, indictment, party,* and *plead.* And in the next few months you will come across *battery, damages, devise, easement, estoppel, felony, larceny, lien, livery of seisin, misdemeanor, replevin, slander, tenant,* and *tort.* (Begin now the habit of looking up every unfamiliar term of art in a law dictionary, which you should keep close at hand while studying for each of your courses.) Even the bailiff's cry that still opens many American court sessions — "Oyez, oyez, oyez!" — is the Norman French equivalent of "Listen up!"

Some words entered the English language directly from the events of the Conquest itself. In the course on property, you will soon become familiar with various types of *fees: fee simple absolute, fee simple conditional, fee simple defeasible, fee tail.* These are not money paid for services. They are

---

§1.1 1. Frederick Pollock & Frederick William Maitland, *The History of English Law Before the Time of Edward I* 79 (2d ed., Little, Brown & Co. 1899).

2. Blackstone called Norman Law French a "badge of slavery." William Blackstone, *Commentaries,* vol. 4, *416. Before the Conquest, courts were conducted in English, and law was written in English or Latin.

3. Records in English Act, 1731, 4 Geo II ch. 26.

forms of property rights, and they are descended directly from the feudal enfeoffments that William introduced into England in order to distribute the country's land among his followers. Even today, these terms appear in the French word order (noun first, modifiers afterward).

The second, and more important, influence concerns the way law is created. It is a comparatively modern invention for a legislature to "pass a law." (Lawyers say "enact a statute.") The embryonic medieval parliaments of England and Scandinavia instead made more specific decisions, such as when to plunder Visby or whether to banish Hrothgar. Although in some countries law might come from royal decree, in England before the Conquest it arose more often from the custom of each locality, as known to and enforced by the local courts. What was legal in one village or shire might be illegal (because it offended local custom) in the next. "This crazyquilt of decentralized judicial administration was doomed after 1066. From the time of the Norman Conquest, . . . the steady development in England was one of increasing dominance of the royal courts of justice over the local, customary-law courts."[4] The reason was that the newly created Norman aristocracy, which now operated the local courts, got into conflict with the Norman monarch over the spoils of power, while the English, defeated in their own country, began to find more justice in the king's courts than in their local lords' capricious enforcement of what had once been reliable custom.

Because communication and travel were so primitive, the "crazyquilt" pattern of customary law had not before troubled the English. Instead, it had given them an agreeable opportunity to develop, through local habit, rules that suited each region and village relatively well. For two reasons, however, the king's courts would not enforce customary law. The practical reason was that a judge of a national court cannot know the customary law of each locality. The political reason was that the monarchy's goal was to centralize power in itself and its institutions. Out of this grew a uniform set of rules, common to every place in the country and eventually known as the common law of England. Centuries later, British colonists in North America were governed according to that common law, and, upon declaring their independence, adopted it as each state's original body of law. Although a fair proportion of the common law has since been changed through statute or judicial decision, it remains the foundation of our legal system, and common law methods of reasoning dominate the practice and study of law.

In a medieval England without a "law-passing" legislature and with a king far too busy to create a body of law by decree, where did this common law come from? The somewhat oversimplified answer is that the judges figured it out for themselves. They started from the few rules that plainly could not be missing from medieval society, and over centuries—faced with new conditions and reasoning by analogy—they discovered other rules of common law, as though each rule had been there from the beginning, but hidden. The central tool in this process has been a rule called

---

4. Harry W. Jones, *Our Uncommon Common Law*, 42 Tenn. L. Rev. 443, 450 (1975).

stare decisis, Latin for "let stand that which has been decided," or, more loosely, "follow the rules courts have followed in the past." Those past decisions of courts are called *precedents.*

Eventually, the English parliament did become a law-passing legislature, a role later adopted by the United States Congress and the American state legislatures. That has left us with two ways in which law can be made (or, as lawyers would say, two sources of law). One is statutes enacted by legislatures together with other statute-like provisions. The other is common law and other judicial precedent.[5] (We will come back to this in §2.5).

Before we can look at law as a system of rules (in Chapter 2), you will need some background in how courts are structured.

§1.2 How American Courts Are Organized

Because the United States has a federal system of government, it has two different kinds of court systems. Each state has its own courts, enforcing that state's law, and in addition the federal government has courts throughout the country, enforcing federal law.[1] The Constitution allocates certain responsibilities to the federal government and reserves the rest to the states. State court systems tend to be organized as variations, from state to state, on similar themes, while the federal courts operate rather differently.

§1.2.1 State Courts

A very simple state court system might include one trial court in each county seat, together with an appellate court in the state capital to hear appeals arising out of the work of the trial courts. Although that was once the system in most states, so simple an organization would be unrealistic under modern conditions. Virtually every state now has several different kinds of trial court, and most now have more than one appellate court.

The usual pattern goes something like this: A trial court of *general jurisdiction*—called the Circuit Court, the Superior Court, the Court of Common Pleas, or something similar—will try all cases except those that fall within the *limited jurisdiction* of some specialized trial court. Specialized courts might include a Court of Claims to hear suits against the state government, a Probate Court to adjudicate questions involving wills

---

5. The doctrine of stare decisis is generally observed only in countries whose law is descended in one way or another from English law. For the most part, judicial precedent is *not* a source of law in continental Europe or in Latin America.

§1.2 1. As you will learn in the course on civil procedure, federal courts on occasion will enforce a state's law, and vice versa.

and inheritances, a Family Court to settle matters of support and child custody, a Juvenile Court to determine whether minors have committed crimes or are otherwise in need of special supervision, a Small Claims Court to decide (perhaps without lawyers) disputes where the value at stake is not large, a Magistrate's Court or the like to try some misdemeanors and other offenses, and a Housing Court to resolve litigation between landlords and tenants. Often these functions are merged. A Family Court, for instance, might have jurisdiction not only over support and custody, but also over matters that, in another state, would be adjudicated by a Juvenile Court. A Small Claims Court might not be a separate court, but instead a Small Claims Division of the court of general jurisdiction.

About two-thirds of the states have intermediate courts of appeal, which sit organizationally between the trial courts and the final appellate court. In some states, such as Pennsylvania and Maryland, the intermediate court of appeals hears appeals from every part of the state, while in others, such as California, New York, and Florida, the intermediate appellate court is divided geographically into districts, departments, or the equivalent, which function as coordinate courts of equal rank. In any event, a party dissatisfied with the result in an intermediate court of appeals can attempt to appeal — within certain limitations — to the highest court in the state.

The names of these courts are not consistent from state to state. In California and many other states, the Superior Court is the trial court of general jurisdiction, but in Pennsylvania the Superior Court is the intermediate court of appeal. In Maryland and New York, the Court of Appeals is the highest court in the state, but in many other states the intermediate appellate court has that name or a similar one. In New York, the trial court of general jurisdiction is called the Supreme Court, but in most states that is the name of the highest court in the state.

§1.2.2 Federal Courts

The federal court system is organized around a general trial court (the United States District Court); a few specialized courts (such as the United States Tax Court); an intermediate appellate court (the United States Court of Appeals); and the final appellate court (the United States Supreme Court).

The United States District Courts are organized into approximately one hundred districts. Where a state has only one district, the court is referred to, for example, as the United States District Court for the District of Montana. Some states have more than one district court. California, for instance, has four: the United States District Court for the Northern District of California (at San Francisco), the Eastern District of California (at Sacramento), the Central District of California (at Los Angeles), and the Southern District of California (at San Diego).

The United States Courts of Appeals are organized into thirteen circuits. Eleven of the circuits include various combinations of states: the Fifth

Circuit, for example, hears appeals from the district courts in Louisiana, Mississippi, and Texas. There is also a United States Court of Appeals for the District of Columbia and another for the Federal Circuit, which hears appeals from certain specialized lower tribunals.

The United States Supreme Court hears selected appeals from the United States Courts of Appeals and from the highest state courts where the state court's decision has been based on federal law. The United States Supreme Court does not decide questions of state law.

2 Rule-Based Reasoning[1]

§2.1   The Inner Structure of a Rule

At this moment the King, who had for some time been busily writing in
his notebook, called out "Silence!" and read from his book, "Rule Forty-
two. *All persons more than a mile high to leave the court."*
     Everyone looked at Alice.
     "*I'm* not a mile high," said Alice.
     "You are," said the King.
     "Nearly *two* miles high," added the Queen.

                                                        — *Lewis Carroll,*
                                                   Alice in Wonderland

A rule is a formula for making a decision.
     Some rules are *mandatory* ("any person who pays a fee of a hundred
rubles shall be entitled to a beach permit"), while others are *prohibitory*
("no person shall transfer more than two million pesos to another country
without a license from the Ministry of Finance") or *discretionary* ("the
curator of the Louvre may permit flash photographs to be taken when, in
the curator's judgment, no damage to art will result") or *declaratory* ("failure to pay the fare on the Konkan Railway is an offense"). Some appear to
be one kind of rule, but on examination turn out to be something else. For
example, the following seems mandatory: "a person in charge of a dog that
fouls the footway shall be fined ten pounds." But it would actually be
discretionary if some other rule were to empower the judge to suspend
sentence.

---

1. This term was suggested by Steven Jamar.

Every rule has three separate components: (1) a set of elements, collectively called a test; (2) a result that occurs when all the elements are present (and the test is thus satisfied); and (3) what, for lack of a better expression, could be called a causal term that determines whether the result is mandatory, prohibitory, discretionary or declaratory. (As you will see in a moment, the result and the causal term are usually integrated into the same phrase or clause.) Additionally, many rules have (4) one or more exceptions that, if present would defeat the result, even if all the elements are present.

Consider Alice's situation. She was confronted with a test of two elements. The first was the status of being a person, which mattered because at the time she was in the company of a lot of animals — including one with the head and wings of an eagle and the body of a lion — all of whom seem to have been exempt from any requirement to leave. The second element went to height — specifically a height of more than a mile. The result would have been departure from the court, and the causal term was mandatory ("*All* persons . . . *to* leave . . ."). No exceptions were provided for. Alice has denied the second element (her height), impliedly conceding the first (her personhood). The Queen has offered to prove a height of two miles. What would happen if the Queen were not able to make good on her promise and instead produced evidence showing only a height of 1.241 miles? (Read the rule.) What if the Queen were to produce no evidence and if Alice were to prove that her height was only 0.984 miles?

A causal term can be mandatory, prohibitory, discretionary, or declaratory. Because the causal term is the heart of the rule, if the causal term is, say, mandatory, then the whole rule is, too.

A mandatory rule requires someone to act and is expressed in words like "shall" or "must" in the causal term. "Shall" means "has a legal duty to." "The court shall grant the motion" means the court has a legal duty to grant it.

A prohibitory rule is the opposite: it forbids someone to act and is expressed by "shall not," "may not," or "must not" in the causal term. "Shall not" means the person has a legal duty not to act.

A discretionary rule gives someone the power or authority to do something. That person has discretion to act but is not required to do so. It is expressed by words like "may" or "has the authority to" in the causal term.

A declaratory rule simply states (declares) that something is true. That might not seem like much of a rule, but you are already familiar with declaratory rules and their consequences. For example: "A person who drives faster than the posted speed limit is guilty of speeding." Because of that declaration, a police officer can give you a ticket if you speed, a court can sentence you to a fine, and your state's motor vehicle department can impose points on your driver's license. A declaratory rule places a label on a set of facts (the elements). The rule's power is what that label permits people to do (the police officer to give you a ticket, and so on). Often the declaration is expressed by the word "is" in the causal term. But other words could be used there instead. And some rules with "is" in the causal term are not declaratory. You have to look at what the rule *does*. If it simply states that something is true, it is declaratory. If it does more than that, it is something else.

Below are examples of all these types of rules. The examples come from the Federal Rules of Civil Procedure, and you will study them later in the course on Civil Procedure. (Rules of law are found not just in places like the Federal Rules. In law, they are everywhere — in statutes, constitutions, regulations, and judicial precedents.)

If the rules below seem hard to understand at first, don't be discouraged. In a moment, you will learn a method for taking rules like these apart to find their meaning. For now, just read them to get a sense of how the four kinds of rules differ from each other. (The key words in the causal terms have been italicized to highlight the differences. In the prohibitory rule, the square brackets mean that the rule has been edited: words in the original have been replaced by the words in brackets.)

mandatory:	If a party is represented by an attorney, service under this rule *must* be made on the attorney unless the court orders service on the party.[1]
prohibitory:	The court *must not* require a bond, obligation, or other security from the appellant when granting a stay on an appeal by the United States, its officers, or its agencies, or on an appeal directed by a department of the federal government.[2]
discretionary:	The court *may* assert jurisdiction over property if authorized by a federal statute.[3]
declaratory:	A civil action *is* commenced by filing a complaint with the court.[4]

These rules might make no sense to a student who has just started law school. But within a few months, you will easily understand them as well as hundreds of other rules that are equally difficult. Here is a three-step method of figuring out what a rule means.

Step 1: Break the rule down into its parts. List and number the elements in the test. (An element in a test is something that must be present for the rule to operate.) Identify the causal term and the result. If there is an exception, identify it, and if the exception has more than one element, list and number them as well. (Exceptions can have elements, too; an exception's element is something that must be present for the exception to operate.) In Step 1, *you do not care what the words mean.* You only want

---

§2.1 1. Rule 5(b)(1) of the Federal Rules of Civil Procedure.
2. Rule 62(e) of the Federal Rules of Civil Procedure.
3. Rule 4(n)(1) of the Federal Rules of Civil Procedure.
4. Rule 3 of the Federal Rules of Civil Procedure.

to know the *structure* of the rule. You are breaking the rule down into parts small enough to understand when you do Step 2. Let's take the mandatory rule above and run it through Step 1. Here is the rule diagrammed:

elements in the test:

If
  (1) a defendant
  (2) located within the United States
  (3) fails to comply with a request for waiver
  (4) made by a plaintiff
  (5) located within the United States,

causal term:

the court shall

result:

impose the costs subsequently incurred in effecting service on the defendant

exception:

unless good cause for the failure is shown.

You do not need to lay out the rule exactly this way — and you certainly do not need to use boxes. You can use any method of diagramming that breaks up the rule so you can understand it. The point is to break the rule up visually so that it is no longer a blur of words and so that you can *see* *separately* the elements in the test, the causal term, the result, and any exception. When can you combine the causal term and result? You can do it whenever doing so does not confuse you. If you can understand the following, you can combine, at least with this rule:

> *causal term and result:*
>
> the court shall impose the costs subsequently incurred in effecting service on the defendant

Step 2: Look at each of those small parts separately. Figure out the *meaning* of each element, the causal term, the result, and any exception. Look up the words in a legal dictionary, and read other material your teacher has assigned until you know what each word means. You already know what a plaintiff and defendant are. If you look up "service" in a legal dictionary (see the result box above), you will learn that it is the delivery of legal papers. If you read other material surrounding this rule in Civil Procedure, you will learn that a "request for a waiver" (see element 4) is a plaintiff's request that the defendant accept service by mail and *waive* (give up the right to) service by someone who personally brings the papers to the defendant. The surrounding materials also tell you that the costs of service (see the result) are whatever the plaintiff has to pay to have someone hired for the purpose of delivering the papers personally to the defendant.

Step 3: Put the rule back together in a way that helps you *use* it. Sometimes that means rearranging the rule so that it is easier to understand. If when you first read the rule, an exception came at the beginning and the elements came last, rearrange the rule so the elements come first and the exception last. It will be easier to understand that way. For many rules — though not all of them — the rule's inner logic works like this:

What events or circumstances set the rule into operation?
(These are the elements in the test.)

When all the elements are present, what happens?
(The causal term and the result tell us.)

Even if all the elements are present, could anything prevent the result?
(An exception, if the rule has any.)

Usually, you can put the rule back together by creating a flowchart and trying the rule out on some hypothetical facts to see how the rule works. A flowchart is essentially a list of questions. You will be able to make a flowchart because of the diagramming you did earlier in Step 1. Diagramming the rule not only breaks it down so that it can be understood, but it also permits putting the rule back together so that it is easier to apply. The flowchart below comes straight out of the diagram in Step 1 above. (When you gain more experience at this — in a few months — it will go so quickly and seamlessly that Steps 1, 2, and 3 *will seem to merge into a single step.*) Assume that Keisha wants Raymond to pay the costs of service.

elements:

1. Is Raymond a defendant?
2. Is Raymond located within the United States?
3. Did Raymond fail to comply with a request for waiver?
4. Is Keisha a plaintiff who made that request?
5. Is Keisha located within the United States?

If the answers to all these questions are yes, the court shall impose the costs subsequently incurred in effecting service on Raymond — but only if the answer to the question below is no.

exception:

Has Raymond shown good cause for his failure to comply?

Step 3 helps you add everything up to see what happens when the rule is applied to a given set of facts. If all the elements are present in the facts, the court must order the defendant to reimburse the plaintiff for whatever the plaintiff had to pay to have someone hired for the purpose of delivering the papers personally to the defendant—unless good cause is shown.

The elements do not have to come first. If you have a simple causal term and result, a long list of elements, and no exceptions, you can list the elements last. For example:

Common law burglary is committed by breaking and entering the dwelling of another in the nighttime with intent to commit a felony therein.[5]

How do you determine how many elements are in a rule? Think of each element as an integral fact, the absence of which would prevent the rule's operation. Then explore the logic behind the rule's words. If you can think of a reasonably predictable scenario in which part of what you believe to be one element could be true but part not true, then you have inadvertently combined two or more elements. For example, is "the dwelling of another" one element or two? A person might be guilty of some other crime, but he is not guilty of common law burglary when he breaks and enters the restaurant of another, even in the nighttime and with intent to commit a felony therein. The same is true when he breaks and enters his own dwelling. In each instance, part of the element is present and part

---

5. This was the crime at common law. Because of the way its elements are divided, it does a good job of illustrating several different things about rule structure. But the definition of burglary in a modern criminal code will differ. A statute might break the crime up into gradations (burglary in the first degree, burglary in the second degree, and so on). A typical modern statute would not require that the crime happen in the nighttime, and at least the lower gradations would not require that the building be a dwelling.

missing. "The dwelling of another" thus includes two factual integers — the nature of the building and the identity of its resident — and therefore two elements.

Often you cannot know the number of elements in a rule until you have consulted the precedents interpreting it. Is "breaking and entering" one element or two? The precedents define "breaking" in this sense as the creation of a gap in a building's protective enclosure, such as by opening a door, even where the door was left unlocked and the building is thus not damaged. The cases further define "entering" for this purpose as placing inside the dwelling any part of oneself or any object under one's control, such as a crowbar. (These definitions are declaratory sub-rules. They are declaratory because they are statements rather than requirements, prohibitions, or grants of discretion. They are sub-rules because they exist only to explain parts of the main rule, the definition of burglary.) Can a person "break" without "entering"? A would-be burglar would seem to have done so where she has opened a window by pushing it up from the outside, and where, before proceeding further, she has been apprehended by an alert police officer — literally a moment too soon. "Breaking" and "entering" are therefore two elements, but one could not know for sure without discovering precisely how the courts have defined the terms used.

Where the elements are complex or ambiguous, an enumeration may add clarity to the list:

> Common law burglary is committed by (1) breaking and (2) entering (3) the dwelling (4) of another (5) in the nighttime (6) with intent to commit a felony therein.

Instead of elements, some rules have criteria or guidelines. These tend to be rules empowering a court or other authority to make discretionary decisions, and the criteria define the scope of the decision-maker's discretion. The criteria might be few ("a court may extend the time to answer for good cause shown"), or they might be many (like the following, from a typical divorce statute).

> Marital property [at divorce] shall be distributed equitably between the parties, considering the circumstances of the case and of the respective parties. . . . In determining an equitable disposition of property . . . , the court shall consider:
>
> (1) the income and property of each party at the time of marriage, and at the time of the commencement of the action;
>
> (2) the duration of the marriage and the age and health of both parties;
>
> (3) the need of a custodial parent to occupy or own the marital residence and to use or own its household effects;
>
> (4) the loss of inheritance and pension rights upon dissolution of the marriage as of the date of dissolution;
>
> (5) any award of maintenance . . . ;
>
> (6) any equitable claim to, interest in, or direct or indirect contribution made to the acquisition of such marital property by the party not having title, including joint efforts or expenditures and contributions and services as a

spouse, parent, wage earner and homemaker, and to the career or career potential of the other party;

(7) the liquid or non-liquid character of all marital property;

(8) the probable future financial circumstances of each party;

(9) the impossibility or difficulty of evaluating any component asset or any interest in a business, corporation, or profession, and the economic desirability of retaining such asset or interest intact and free from any claim or interference by the other party;

(10) the tax consequences to each party;

(11) the wasteful dissipation of assets by either spouse;

(12) any transfer or encumbrance made in contemplation of a [divorce] action without fair consideration;

(13) any other factor which the court shall expressly find to be just and proper.[6]

Only seldom would all of these criteria tip in the same direction. With a rule like this, a judge does something of a balancing test, deciding according to the tilt of the criteria as a whole, together with the angle of the tilt. If the criteria favor a party only slightly, she or he may get most of the marital property, but less than if the party had been favored overwhelmingly.

Criteria rules are a relatively new development in the law and grow out of a recent tendency to define more precisely the discretion of judges and other officials. But the more common rule structure is still that of a set of elements, the presence of which leads to a particular result in the absence of an exception.

§2.2 Organizing the Application of a Rule

Welty and Lutz are students who have rented apartments on the same floor of the same building. At midnight, Welty is studying, while Lutz is listening to a Radiohead album with his new four-foot speakers. Welty has put up with this for two or three hours, and finally she pounds on Lutz's door. Lutz opens the door about six inches, and, when he realizes that he cannot hear what Welty is saying, he steps back into the room a few feet to turn the volume down, without opening the door further. Continuing to express outrage, Welty pushes the door completely open and strides into the room. Lutz turns on Welty and orders her to leave. Welty finds this to be too much and punches Lutz so hard that he suffers substantial injury. In this jurisdiction, the punch is a felonious assault. Is Welty also guilty of common law burglary?

You probably say "no," and your reasoning probably goes something like this: "That's not burglary. Burglary happens when somebody gets into the house when you're not around and steals all the valuables. Maybe this will

6. N.Y. Dom. Rel. Law §236, Part B(5)(c) & (d) (McKinney 1999).

turn out to be some kind of trespass." But in law school a satisfactory answer is never merely "yes" or "no." An answer necessarily includes a sound *reason,* and, regardless of whether Welty is guilty of burglary, this answer is wrong because the reasoning is wrong. The answer can be determined only by applying a rule like the definition of burglary found on page 21. *Anything else is a guess.*

Where do you start? Remember that a rule is a structured idea: the presence of all the elements causes the result, and the absence of any of them causes the rule not to operate. Assume that in our jurisdiction the elements of burglary are what they were at common law:

1. a breaking
2. and an entry
3. of the dwelling
4. of another
5. in the nighttime
6. with intent to commit a felony therein.

To discover whether each element is present in the facts, simply annotate the list:

1. *a breaking:* If a breaking can be the enlarging of an opening between the door and the jam without permission, and if Lutz's actions do not imply permission, there was a breaking.
2. *and an entry:* Welty "entered," for the purposes of the rule on burglary, by walking into the room, unless Lutz's actions implied permission to enter.
3. *of the dwelling:* Lutz's apartment is a dwelling.
4. *of another:* And it is not Welty's dwelling: she lives down the hall.
5. *in the nighttime:* Midnight is in the nighttime.
6. *with intent to commit a felony therein:* Did Welty intent to assault Lutz when she strode through the door? If not, this element is missing.

Now it is clear how much the first answer ("it doesn't sound like burglary") was a guess. By examining each element separately, you find that elements 3, 4, and 5 are present, but that you are not sure about the others without some hard thinking about the facts and without consulting the precedents in this jurisdiction that have interpreted elements 1, 2, and 6.

The case law might turn up a variety of results. Suppose that, although local precedent defines Welty's actions as a breaking and an entry, the cases on the sixth element strictly require corroborative evidence that a defendant had a fully formed felonious intent when entering the dwelling. That kind of evidence might be present, for example, where an accused was in possession of safecracking tools when he broke and entered, or where, before breaking and entering, the accused had confided to another that he intended to murder the occupant. Against that background, the answer here might be something like the following: "Welty is not guilty of burglary because, although she broke and entered the dwelling of another in the nighttime, there is no evidence that she had a felonious intent when entering the dwelling."

Suppose, on the other hand, that under local case law Welty's actions again are a breaking and an entry; that the local cases do not require corroborative evidence of a felonious intent; and that local precedent defines a felonious intent for the purposes of burglary to be one that the defendant could have been forming—even if not yet consciously—when entering the dwelling. Under those sub-rules, if you believe that Welty had the requisite felonious intent, your answer would be something like this: "Welty is guilty of burglary because she broke and entered the dwelling of another in the nighttime with intent to commit a felony therein, thus meeting all the elements of common law burglary."

These are real answers to the question of whether Welty is guilty of burglary: they state not only the result, but the reason why.

§2.3   Some Things to Be Careful About with Rules

Rules must be expressed in terms of categories of actions, things, conditions, and people, and you have already had a taste of how slippery those kinds of definitions can be. Some of the slipperiness is there because precision takes constant effort, like weeding a garden. But some of it is there to give law the flexibility needed for sound decision-making. The language "in which law is necessarily expressed . . . is not an instrument of mathematical precision but possesses . . . an 'open texture.'"[1] That is because a rule's quality is measured not by its logical elegance—few rules of law have that—but by how well the rule guides a court into making sound decisions. A rule that causes poor decisions begs to be changed.

In addition, a given rule might be expressed in any of a number of ways. Where law is made through precedent—as much of our law is—different judges, writing in varying circumstances, may enunciate what seems like the same rule in a variety of distinct phrasings. At times, it can be hard to tell whether the judges have spoken of the same rule in different voices or instead have spoken of slightly different rules. In either situation, it can be harder still to discover—because of the variety—exactly what the rule is or what the rules are. All this may at first seem bewildering, but in fact it opens up one of the most fertile opportunities for a lawyer's creativity because in litigation each side is free to argue a favorable interpretation of the statements found in statutes and precedents, and courts are free to mutate the law through their own interpretations.

Ambiguity and vagueness can obscure meaning unless the person stating the rule is particularly careful with language. The classic example asks

---

§2.3   1. Dennis Lloyd & M. D. A. Freeman, *Lloyd's Introduction to Jurisprudence* 1139 (5th ed., Stevens 1985).

whether a person riding a bicycle through a park violates a rule prohibiting the use there of "vehicles." What had the rule-maker intended? How could the intention have been made more clear?

Even where the rule-maker is careful with language, a rule does not always express its purpose — or, as lawyers say, the policy underlying the rule. But the rule's policy or purpose is the key to unravelling ambiguities within the rule. Is a self-propelled lawn mower a prohibited "vehicle"? To answer that question, try to imagine what the rule-makers were trying to accomplish. Why did they create this rule? What harm were they trying to prevent, or what good were they trying to promote?

Not only is it difficult to frame a rule so that it controls all the rule-maker wishes to control, but once a rule has been framed, situations will inevitably crop up that the rule-maker did not contemplate or could not have been expected to contemplate. Would a baby carriage powered by solar batteries be a "vehicle"?

Finally, the parts of a rule may be so complex that it may be hard to pin down exactly what the rule is and how it works. And this is compounded by interaction between and among rules. A word or phrase in a rule may be defined, for example, by another rule. Or the application of one rule may be governed by yet another rule — or even a whole body of rules.

More than any others, two skills will help you become agile in the lawyerly use of rules. The first is language mastery, including an "ability to spot ambiguities, to recognize vagueness, to identify the emotive pull of a word . . . and to analyze and elucidate class words and abstractions."[2] The second is the capacity to think structurally. A rule is a structured idea, and the rule's structure is more like an algebraic formula than a value judgment. You need to be able to figure out the structure of an idea and apply it to facts.

§2.4   Causes of Action and Affirmative Defenses

The law cannot remedy every wrong, and many problems are more effectively resolved through other means, such as the political process, mediation, bargaining, and economic and social pressure. Unless the legal system focuses its resources on resolving those problems it handles best, it would collapse under the sheer weight of an unmanageable workload and would thus be prevented from attempting even the problem-solving it does well. Thus, a threshold task in law is the definition of wrongs for which courts will provide a remedy.

A harm the law will remedy is called a *cause of action* (or, in some courts, a *claim* or a *claim for relief*). If a plaintiff proves a cause of action, a court will order a remedy unless the defendant proves an *affirmative*

---

2. William L. Twining & David Miers, *How to Do Things with Rules* 120 (Weidenfeld & Nicolson 1976).

defense. If the defendant proves an affirmative defense, the plaintiff will get no remedy, even if that plaintiff has proved a cause of action. Causes of action and affirmative defenses (like other legal rules) are formulated as tests with elements and the other components explained in §2.1.

For example, where a plaintiff proves that a defendant intentionally confined him and that the defendant was not a law enforcement officer acting within the scope of an authority to arrest, the plaintiff has proved a cause of action called *false imprisonment.* The test is expressed as a list of elements: "False imprisonment consists of (1) a confinement (2) of the plaintiff (3) by the defendant (4) intentionally (5) where the defendant is not a sworn law enforcement officer acting within that authority." Proof of false imprisonment would customarily result in a court's awarding a remedy called *damages,* which obliges the defendant to compensate the plaintiff in money for the latter's injuries.

But that is not always so: if the defendant can prove that she caught the plaintiff shoplifting in her store and restrained him only until the police arrived, she might have an affirmative defense that is sometimes called a *shopkeeper's privilege.* Where a defendant proves a shopkeeper's privilege, a court will not award the plaintiff damages, even if he has proved false imprisonment. Again, the test is expressed as a list of elements: "A shopkeeper's privilege exists where (1) a shopkeeper or shopkeeper's employee (2) has reasonable cause to believe that (3) the plaintiff (4) has shoplifted (5) in the shopkeeper's place of business and (6) the confinement occurs in a reasonable manner, for a reasonable time, and no more than needed to detain the plaintiff for law enforcement purposes."

Notice that some elements encompass physical activity ("a confinement"), while others specify states of mind ("intentionally") or address status or condition ("a shopkeeper or shopkeeper's employee") or require abstract qualities ("in a reasonable manner, for a reasonable time, and no more than needed to detain the plaintiff for law enforcement purposes"). State-of-mind and abstract-quality elements will probably puzzle you more than others will. The plaintiff, for example, might be able to prove a confinement through a witness who saw a door being locked. And if the shopkeeper's own testimony is not good enough to prove her status, she can probably produce a license to do business at the place where the plaintiff says he was confined, or some other evidence tending to show that she operates a store. These elements are straightforward because the evidence that satisfies them can be seen, heard, or felt.

But how will the plaintiff be able to prove that the defendant acted "intentionally," and how will the defendant be able to show that she confined the plaintiff "in a reasonable manner, for a reasonable time, and no more than needed to detain the plaintiff for law enforcement purposes"? Because thoughts and abstractions cannot be seen, heard, or felt, the law has to judge an abstraction or a party's state of mind from the actions and other events surrounding it. If, for example, the plaintiff can prove that the defendant took him by the arm, pulled him into a room, and then locked the door herself, he may be able — through inference — to carry his burden of showing that she acted "intentionally." And through other inferences, the defendant may be able to carry her burden of proving the confinement to have been reasonably carried out if she can show that when she took the defendant by the arm, he had been trying to run from the store; that she called the police immediately; and that she turned the defendant over to the police as soon as they arrived.

§2.5   Where Rules Come From (Sources of Law)

In our legal system, the two main sources of law are statutes and case law.

Legislatures create rules through statutes. When we say, "There ought to be a law punishing people who text-message while driving," we vaguely imagine telling our state representative about the dangers of distraction behind the wheel and suggesting that she introduce a bill along these lines and persuade her colleagues in the legislature to enact it into law. Statute-like provisions include constitutions, administrative regulations, and court rules. Constitutions are created in varying ways, but every state has one in addition to the Constitution of the United States. Administrative regulations are promulgated by administrative agencies, and court rules are promulgated usually, but not always, by courts.

A large amount of our law is created by the courts in the process of enforcing it. That is because the courts, having created the common law (see §1.1), can change it, and periodically do, in decisions that enforce the law as changed. And it is also because legislatures do not really finish the job of legislating. Statutes have ambiguities, and often we do not know what a statute means until the courts tell us — through judicial decisions enforcing the statute. (You saw in §2.2 how that can happen.) Courts record their decisions in judicial opinions, which establish precedents under the doctrine of *stare decisis* (see §1.1). Lawyers use the words *cases, decisions,* and *opinions* interchangeably to refer to those precedents.

Thus, our two sources of law are statutes and judicial precedent. Statutes and opinions are hard to read and understand, and much of the first year of law school is devoted to teaching you the skills needed to interpret them. Statutes are explained in Chapter 16, and judicial opinions in Chapters 3, 4, and 15. We take on judicial opinions earlier because in the first few weeks of law school you will read many more judicial opinions than statutes.

Exercise.   Rule 11 of the Federal Rules of Civil Procedure

Exercise A. A provision from Rule 11(a) appears below. Decide whether it is mandatory, prohibitory, discretionary, or declaratory. Then diagram it. Finally, create a flowchart showing the questions that would need to be answered to determine when a court must strike a paper.

The court must strike an unsigned paper unless the omission is promptly corrected after being called to the attorney's or party's attention.

Exercise B. A provision from Rule 11(c)(1) appears below. Decide whether it is mandatory, prohibitory, discretionary, or declaratory. Then diagram it. Finally, create a flowchart showing the questions that would need to be answered to determine a sanctions issue under this provision.

If, after notice and a reasonable opportunity to respond, the court determines that Rule 11(b) has been violated, the court may impose an appropriate sanction on any attorney, law firm, or party that violated the rule or is responsible for the violation.

Exercise C. A provision from Rule 11(c)(1) appears below. Decide whether it is mandatory, prohibitory, discretionary, or declaratory. Then diagram it. Finally, create a flowchart showing the questions that would need to be answered to determine a joint responsibility issue under this provision.

Absent exceptional circumstances, a law firm must be held jointly responsible for a violation committed by its partner, associate, or employee.

Exercise D. A provision from Rule 11(a) appears below. Decide whether it is mandatory, prohibitory, discretionary, or declaratory. Then diagram it.

This rule does not apply to disclosures and discovery requests, responses, objections, and motions under Rules 26 through 37.

3 An Introduction to Judicial Decisions and Statutes

§3.1 The Anatomy of a Judicial Decision

An opinion announcing a court's decision can include up to nine ingredients:

1. a description of procedural events (what lawyers and judges did before the decision was made)
2. a narrative of pleaded or evidentiary events (what the witnesses saw and the parties did *before* the lawsuit began)
3. a statement of the issue or issues to be decided by the court
4. a summary of the arguments made by each side
5. the court's holding on each issue
6. the rule or rules of law the court enforces through each holding
7. the court's reasoning
8. dicta
9. a statement of the relief granted or denied

Most opinions do not include all of these things, although a typical opinion probably has most of them. Let us look at each of them in turn to see what they mean.

Opinions often begin with (1) a recitation of *procedural events* inside the litigation that have raised the issue decided by the court. Examples are motions, hearings, trial, judgment, and appeal. Although the court's description of these events may—because of unfamiliar terminology—seem at first confusing, you must be able to understand procedural histories because the manner in which an issue is raised determines the method a court will

23

use to decide it. A court decides a motion for a directed verdict, for example, very differently from the way it rules on a request for a jury instruction, even though both might require the court to consider the same point of law. The procedural events add up to the case's procedural posture at the time the decision was made.

Frequently, the court will next describe (2) the *pleaded events* or the *evidentiary events* on which the ruling is based. In litigation, parties allege facts in a pleading and then prove them with evidence. The court has no other way of knowing what transpired between the parties before the lawsuit began. If the procedural posture involves a motion to dismiss a pleading (see pages 8-9), that will have occurred before any evidence could be submitted, and the decision will be based on the allegations in the challenged pleading (usually a complaint). Otherwise, the court's knowledge of the facts will come from evidentiary events such as testimony and exhibits at trial or at a hearing, or perhaps affidavits and exhibits submitted in connection with a motion.

A court might also set out (3) a statement of the *issue or issues* before the court for decision and (4) a *summary of the arguments* made by each side, although either or both are often only implied. A court will further state, or at least imply, (5) the *holding* on each of the issues and (6) the *rule or rules of law* the court enforces in making each holding, together with (7) the *reasoning behind* — often called the *rationale for* — its decision. Somewhere in the opinion, the court might place some (8) *dicta*. (You will learn more about dicta in the next few months, but for the moment think of it as discussion unnecessary to support a holding and therefore lacking binding precedential authority.)

An opinion usually ends with (9) a *statement of the relief granted or denied*. If the opinion represents the decision of an appellate court, the relief may be an affirmance, a reversal, or a reversal combined with a direction to the trial court to proceed in a specified manner. If the opinion is from a trial court, the relief is most commonly the granting or denial of a motion.

An opinion announcing a court's decision is called *the court's opinion* or *the majority opinion*. If one or more of the judges involved in the decision do not agree with some aspect of the decision, the opinion might be accompanied by one or more *concurrences* or *dissents*. A concurring judge agrees with the result the majority reached but would have used different reasoning to justify that result. A dissenting judge disagrees with both the result and the reasoning. Concurrences and dissents are themselves opinions, but they represent the views only of the judges who are concurring or dissenting. Because concurrences and dissents are opinions, they contain some of the elements of a court's opinion. A concurring or dissenting judge might, for example, describe procedural events, narrate pleaded or evidentiary events, state issues, summarize arguments, and explain reasoning.

Exercise I.   Dissecting the Text of Roberson v. Rochester Folding Box Co.

Read *Roberson v. Rochester Folding Box Co.* below and determine where (if anywhere) each of these types of pronouncement occurs. Mark up the text generously and be prepared to discuss your analysis in class. Look up in a legal dictionary every unfamiliar word as well as every familiar word that is used in an unfamiliar way.

The majority opinion in *Roberson* discusses—and disagrees with—one of the most influential articles ever published in an American law review: Samuel Warren & Louis Brandeis, *The Right to Privacy*, 4 Harv. L. Rev. 193 (1890). Law reviews are periodicals that publish articles analyzing legal questions in scholarly depth. Almost every law review is sponsored by a law school and edited by students.

Like the cases reprinted in your casebooks for other courses, the version of *Roberson* printed here has been edited extensively to make it more readable. In casebooks and in other legal writing, certain customs are observed when quoted material is edited. Where words have been deleted, you will see ellipses (strings of three or four periods). Where words have been added, usually to substitute for deleted words, you will not see ellipses, but the new words will be in brackets (squared-off parentheses).

ROBERSON v. ROCHESTER FOLDING BOX CO.
64 N.E. 442 (N.Y. 1902)

PARKER, Ch. J. [The defendant demurred] to the complaint . . . upon the ground that the complaint does not state facts sufficient to constitute a cause of action. [The courts below overruled the demurrer.]

[We must decide] whether the complaint . . . can be said to show any right to relief either in law or in equity. [We hold that it does not show any right to relief.]

The complaint alleges that the Franklin Mills Co., one of the defendants, was engaged . . . in the manufacture and sale of flour; that before the commencement of the action, without the knowledge or consent of plaintiff, defendants, knowing that they had no right or authority so to do, had obtained, made, printed, sold and circulated about 25,000 lithographic prints, photographs and likenesses of plaintiff . . . ; that upon the paper upon which the likenesses were printed and above the portrait there were printed, in large, plain letters, the words, "Flour of the Family," and below the portrait in large capital letters, "Franklin Mills Flour," and in the lower right-hand corner in smaller capital letters, "Rochester Folding Box Co., Rochester, N.Y."; that upon the same sheet were other advertisements of the flour of the Franklin Mills Co.; that those 25,000 likenesses of the plaintiff thus ornamented have been conspicuously posted and displayed in stores, warehouses, saloons and other public places; that they have been recognized by friends of the plaintiff and other people with the result that plaintiff has been greatly humiliated by the scoffs and jeers of persons who have recognized her face and picture on this advertisement and her good name has been attacked, causing her great distress and suffering both in body and mind. . . .

[The] portrait . . . is said to be a very good one, and one that her friends and acquaintances were able to recognize; indeed, her grievance is that a good portrait of her, and, therefore, one easily recognized, has been used to attract attention toward the paper upon which defendant mill company's advertisements appear. Such publicity, which some find agreeable, is to plaintiff very distasteful, and thus, because of defendants' impertinence in using her picture without her consent for their own business purposes, she has been caused to suffer mental distress where others would have appreciated the compliment . . . implied in the selection of the picture for such purposes; but as it is distasteful to her, she seeks the aid of the courts to enjoin a further circulation of the lithographic prints containing her portrait made as alleged in the complaint, and as an incident thereto, to reimburse her for the damages to her feelings, which the complaint fixes at the sum of $15,000.

There is no precedent for such an action to be found in the decisions of this court. . . . Nevertheless, [the court below] reached the conclusion that plaintiff had a good cause of action against defendants, in that defendants had invaded what is called a "right of privacy" — in other words, the right to be let alone. Mention of such a right is not to be found in Blackstone, Kent or any other of the great commentators upon the law, nor so far as the learning of counsel or the courts in this case have been able to discover, does its existence seem to have been asserted prior to about the year 1890, when it was [theorized] in the Harvard Law Review . . . in an article entitled, "The Right of Privacy."

The so-called right of privacy is, as the phrase suggests, founded upon the claim that a man has the right to pass through this world, if he wills, without having his picture published, his business enterprises discussed, his successful experiments written up for the benefit of others, or his eccentricities commented upon either in handbills, circulars, catalogues, periodicals or newspapers, and, necessarily, that the things which may not be written and published of him must not be spoken of him by his neighbors, whether the comment be favorable or otherwise. . . .

If such a principle be incorporated into the body of the law through the [process of judicial precedent], the attempts to logically apply the principle will necessarily result, not only in a vast amount of litigation, but in litigation bordering upon the absurd, for the right of privacy, once established [through judicial precedent], cannot be confined to the restraint of the publication of a likeness but must necessarily embrace as well the publication of a word-picture, a comment upon one's looks, conduct, domestic relations or habits. [Thus, a] vast field of litigation . . . would necessarily be opened up should this court hold that privacy exists as a legal right enforceable in equity by injunction, and by damages where they seem necessary to give complete relief.

The legislative body could very well interfere and arbitrarily provide that no one should be permitted for his own selfish purpose to use the picture or the name of another for advertising purposes without his consent. In such event, no embarrassment would result to the general body of the law, for the rule would be applicable only to cases provided for by the statute. The courts, however, being without authority to legislate, are . . . necessarily [constrained] by precedents. . . .

So in a case like the one before us, which is concededly new to this court, it is important that the court should have in mind the effect upon future litigation and upon the development of the law which would necessarily result from a step so far outside of the beaten paths of both common law and equity [because] the right of privacy as a legal doctrine enforceable in equity has not, down to this time, been established by decisions.

The history of the phrase "right of privacy" in this country seems to have begun in 1890 in a clever article in the Harvard Law Review — already referred to — in which a number of English cases were analyzed, and, reasoning by analogy, the conclusion was reached that — notwithstanding the unanimity of the courts in resting their decisions upon property rights in cases where publication is prevented by injunction — in reality such prevention was due to the necessity of affording protection to . . . an inviolate personality, not that of private property. . . .

. . . Those authorities are now to be examined in order that we may see whether they were intended to and did mark a departure from the established rule which had been enforced for generations; or, on the other hand, are entirely consistent with it.

The first case is *Prince Albert v. Strange* (1 Macn. & G. 25; 2 De G. & S. 652). The queen and the prince, having made etchings and drawings for their own amusement, decided to have copies struck off from the etched plates for presentation to friends and for their own use. The workman employed, however, printed some copies on his own account, which afterwards came into the hands of Strange, who purposed exhibiting them, and published a descriptive catalogue. Prince Albert applied for an injunction as to both exhibition and catalogue, and the vice-chancellor granted it, restraining defendant from publishing . . . a description of the etchings. [The] vice-chancellor . . . found two reasons for granting the injunction, namely, that the property rights of Prince Albert had been infringed, and that there was a breach of trust by the workman in retaining some impressions for himself. The opinion contained no hint whatever of a right of privacy separate and distinct from the right of property. . . .

[In similar ways, the other English cases cited in the Harvard article do not actually support a common law cause of action for invasion of privacy.] In not one of [them] was it the basis of the decision that the defendant could be restrained from performing the act he was doing or threatening to do on the ground that the feelings of the plaintiff would be thereby injured; but, on the contrary, each decision was rested either upon the ground of breach of trust or that plaintiff had a property right in the subject of litigation which the court could protect. . . .

[Of the American cases offered in support of a common law right to privacy, none actually does so when the decisions are examined in detail.] An examination of the authorities [thus] leads us to the conclusion that the so-called "right of privacy" has not as yet found an abiding place in our jurisprudence, and, as we view it, the doctrine cannot now be incorporated without doing violence to settled principles of law by which the profession and the public have long been guided. [Thus, there is no common law right of privacy in New York.]

[That does not mean] that, even under the existing law, in every case of the character of the one before us, or indeed in this case, a party whose likeness is circulated against his will is without remedy. By section 245 of the Penal Code any malicious publication by picture, effigy or sign which exposes a person to contempt, ridicule or obloquy is a libel, and it would constitute such at common law. Malicious in this definition means simply intentional and willful. There are many [items], especially of medicine, whose character is such that using the picture of a person . . . in connection with the advertisement of those [items] might justly be found by a jury to cast ridicule or obloquy on the person whose picture was thus published. The manner or posture in which the person is portrayed might readily have a like effect. In such cases both a civil action and a criminal prosecution could be maintained. But there is no allegation in the complaint before us that this was the tendency of the publication complained of, and the absence of such an allegation is fatal to the maintenance of the action. . . .

The judgment of the Appellate Division and of the Special Term [is] reversed. . . .

GRAY, J. (dissenting). . . . These defendants stand before the court, admitting that they have made, published and circulated, without the knowledge or the authority of the plaintiff, 25,000 lithographic portraits of her, for the purpose of profit and gain to themselves; that these portraits have been conspicuously posted in stores, warehouses and saloons, in the vicinity of the plaintiff's residence and throughout the United States, as advertisements of their goods; that the effect has been to humiliate her . . . and, yet, claiming that she makes out no cause of action. They say that no law on the statute books gives her a right of action and that her right to privacy is not an actionable right, at law or in equity.

Our consideration of the question thus presented has not been foreclosed by the decision in *Schuyler v. Curtis,* (147 N.Y. 434). In that case, it appeared that the defendants were intending to make, and to exhibit, at the Columbian Exposition of 1893, a statue of Mrs. Schuyler, . . . conspicuous in her lifetime for her philanthropic work, to typify "Woman as the Philanthropist" and, as a companion piece, a statue of Miss Susan B. Anthony, to typify the "Representative Reformer." The plaintiff, in behalf of himself, as the nephew of Mrs. Schuyler, and of other immediate relatives, sought by the action to restrain them from carrying out their intentions as to the statue of Mrs. Schuyler; upon the grounds, in substance, that they were proceeding without his consent, . . . or that of the other immediate members of the family; that their proceeding was disagreeable to him, because it would have been disagreeable and obnoxious to his aunt, if living, and that it was annoying to have Mrs. Schuyler's memory associated with principles, which Miss Susan B. Anthony typified and of which Mrs. Schuyler did not approve. His right to maintain the action was denied and the denial was expressly placed upon the ground that he, as a relative, did not represent any right of privacy which Mrs. Schuyler possessed in her lifetime and that, whatever her right had been, in that respect, it died with her. The existence of the individual's right to be protected against the invasion of his privacy, if not actually affirmed in the opinion, was, very certainly, far from being denied. "It may be admitted," Judge Peckham observed, when delivering the opinion of the court, "that courts have power, in some cases, to enjoin the doing of an act, where the nature, or character, of the act itself is well calculated to wound the sensibilities of an individual, and where the doing of the act is wholly unjustifiable, and is, in legal contemplation, a wrong, *even though the existence of no property*, as that term is usually used, *is involved in the subject.*" . . .

[The majority misinterprets both the English and the American precedents.] Security of person is as necessary as the security of property; and for that complete personal security, which will result in the peaceful and wholesome enjoyment of one's privileges as a member of society, there should be afforded protection, not only against the scandalous portraiture and display of one's features and person, but against the display and use thereof for another's commercial purposes or gain. The proposition is, to me, an inconceivable one that these defendants may, unauthorizedly, use the likeness of this young woman upon their advertisement, as a method of attracting widespread public attention to their wares, and that she must submit to the mortifying notoriety, without right to invoke the exercise of the preventive power of a court of equity.

Such a view, as it seems to me, must have been unduly influenced by a failure to find precedents in analogous cases . . . ; without taking into consideration that, in the existing state of society, new conditions affecting the relations of persons demand the broader extension of . . . legal principles. . . . I think that such a view is unduly restricted, too, by a search for some property, which has been invaded by the defendants' acts. Property is not, necessarily, the thing itself, which is owned; it is the right of the owner in relation to it. The right to be protected in one's possession of a thing, or in one's privileges, belonging to him as an individual, or secured to him as a member of the commonwealth, is property, and as such entitled to the protection of the law. . . . It seems to me that the principle, which is applicable, is analogous to that upon which courts of equity have interfered to protect the right of privacy, in cases of private writings, or of other unpublished products of the mind. The writer, or the lecturer, has been protected in his right to a literary property in a letter, or a lecture, against its unauthorized publication; because it is property, to which the right of privacy attaches. . . . I think that this plaintiff has the same property in the right to be protected against the use of her face for defendant's commercial purposes, as she would have, if they were publishing her literary compositions. The right would be conceded, if she had sat for her photograph; but if her face, or her portraiture, has a value, the value is hers exclusively; until the use be granted away to the public. . . .

It would be, in my opinion, an extraordinary view which, while conceding the right of a person to be protected against the unauthorized circulation of an unpublished lecture, letter, drawing, or other ideal property, yet, would deny the same protection to a person, whose portrait was unauthorizedly obtained, and made use of, for commercial purposes. . . .

O'Brien, Cullen and Werner, JJ., concur with Parker, Ch. J.; Bartlett and Haight, JJ., concur with Gray, J.

If you found the *Roberson* decision distressing, that is not the end of the story. We will come back to *Roberson* at the end of this chapter and in the Exercise in Chapter 4.

A decision's *citation* is made up of the case's name, references to the reporter or reporters in which the decision was printed, the name of the court where the decision was made, and the year of the decision. For *Roberson,* all this information appears in the heading on page 31.

The case name is composed by separating the last names of the parties with a "v." If the opinion was written by a trial court, the name of the plaintiff appears first. In some appellate courts, the name of the appellant comes first, but in others the parties are listed as they were in the trial court. In a case with multiple plaintiffs or defendants, the name of only the first listed per side appears in the case name. That is why the *Roberson* opinion mentions two defendants, but only one appears in the case name.

Reporters are publications that print decisions, mostly from appellate courts. *Roberson* was decided by the New York Court of Appeals. Decisions of that court are published in North Eastern Reporter (abbreviated "N.E."). The decision you have just read begins on page 442 of volume 64. Thus, *Roberson* is cited to in the following form: *Roberson v. Rochester Folding Box Co.,* 64 N.E. 442 (N.Y. 1902). (In Chapter 20, you will learn more about constructing legal citations.)

§3.2   The Interdependence Among Facts, Issues, and Rules

Many facts are mentioned in an opinion merely to provide background, continuity, or what journalists call "human interest" to what would otherwise be a tedious and disjointed recitation. Of the remaining facts, some are merely related to the court's thinking, while others *caused* the court to come to its decision. This last group could be called the *determinative facts* or the *essential facts.* They are essential to the court's decision because they determined the outcome: if they had been different, the decision would have been different. The determinative facts lead to the rule of the case — the rule of law for which the case stands as precedent — and the discovery of that rule is the most important goal of case analysis. Of course, where several issues are raised together in a case, the court must make several rulings and an opinion may thus stand for several different rules.

The determinative facts can be identified by asking the following question: *if a particular fact had not happened, or if it had happened differently, would the court have made a different decision?* If so, that fact is one of the determinative facts. This can be illustrated through a nonjudicial decision of a sort with which you might recently have had some experience. Assume that a rental agent has just shown you an apartment and that the following facts are true:

A. The apartment is located half a mile from the law school.
B. It is a studio apartment (one room plus a kitchenette and bathroom).
C. The building appears to be well maintained and safe.
D. The apartment is at the corner of the building, and windows on two sides provide ample light and ventilation.
E. It is on the third floor, away from the street, and the neighbors do not appear to be disagreeable.
F. The rent is $500 per month, furnished.
G. The landlord will require a year's lease, and if you do not stay in the apartment for the full year, subleasing it to someone else would be dicult.
H. You have a widowed aunt, with whom you get along well and who lives alone in a house 45 minutes by bus from the law school, and she has oered to let you use the second floor of her house during the school year. The house and neighborhood are safe and quiet, and the living arrangements would be satisfactory to you.
I. You have made a commitment to work next summer in El Paso.
J. You have taken out substantial loans to go to law school.
K. You neither own nor have access to a car.
L. Reliable local people have told you that you are unlikely to find an apartment that is better, cheaper, or more convenient than the one you have just inspected.

Which facts are essential to your decision? If the apartment had been two miles from the law school (rather than a half-mile), would your decision be different? If the answer is no, the first listed fact could not be determinative. It might be part of the factual mosaic and might explain why you looked at the apartment in the first place, but you would not base your decision on it. (Go through the listed facts and mark in the margin whether each would determine your decision.)

Facts recited specifically in an opinion can sometimes be reformulated generically. In the hypothetical above, for example, a generic restatement of fact *H* might be the following: "you have a rent-free alternative to the apartment, but the alternative would require 45 minutes of travel each way plus the expense of public transportation." This formulation is generic because it would cover other specific possibilities that in the end would have the same effect. (Compare it to the original *H* above.) It could include, for example, the following, seemingly different, facts: "you are a member of the clergy in a religion that has given you a leave of absence to attend law school; you may continue to live rent-free in the satisfactory quarters your religion has provided, but to get to the law school, you will have to walk 15 minutes and then ride a subway for 30 minutes more, at the same cost as a bus."

A rule of law is a principle that governs how a particular type of decision is to be made — or, put another way, how certain types of facts are to be treated by the official (such as a judge) who must make a decision. Where a court does not state a rule of the case, or where it ambiguously states a rule, you might arrive at an arguably supportable formulation of the rule by considering the determinative facts to have caused the result. There is room for interpretive maneuver wherever you could reasonably interpret the determinative facts narrowly (specifically) or broadly (generically).

Notice how different formulations of a rule can be extracted from the apartment example. A narrow formulation might be the following:

> A law student who has a choice between renting an apartment and living in the second floor of an aunt's house should choose the latter where the student has had to borrow money to go to law school; where the apartment's rent is 500 per month but the aunt's second floor is free except for bus fares; where the student must work in El Paso during the summer; and where it is difficult locally to sublease an apartment.

Because this formulation is limited to the specific facts given in the hypothetical, it could directly govern only a tiny number of future decision-makers. It would not, for example, directly govern the member of the clergy described above, even if she will spend next summer doing relief work in Rwanda.

Although a decision-maker in a future situation might be able to reason by analogy from the narrow rule set out above, a broader, more widely applicable formulation, stated generically, would directly govern *both* situations:

> A student on a tight budget should not sign a year's lease where the student cannot live in the leased property during the summer and where a nearly free alternative is available.

An even more general formulation would govern an even wider circle of applications:

> A person with limited funds should not lease property that that person cannot fully use where there is a nearly free alternative.

32

The following, however, is so broad as to be meaningless:

> A person should not spend money in a way that would later lead to problems.

Reading opinions is not easy. "Cases do not unfold their principles for the asking," wrote Benjamin Cardozo. "They yield up their kernel slowly and painfully."[1] Kenney Hegland adds, "Reading law is a skill . . . which must be developed. . . . Usually, when we read, we are passive; it's like watching television. . . . Reading judicial opinions, [however,] you must be an active participant; you must take them apart"[2] until you figure out what makes each decision tick.

Often, courts do not explicitly state the issue, the holding, or the rule for which the case is to stand as precedent, and the determinative facts are not usually labelled as such. Whenever a court gives less than a full explanation, you must use what is explicitly stated to pin down what is only implied.

The determinative facts, the issue, the holding, and the rule are all dependent on each other. In the apartment hypothetical, for example, if the issue were different — say, "How shall I respond to an offer to join the American Automobile Association?" — the selection of determinative facts would also change. (In fact, the only determinative one would be fact K: "You neither own nor have access to a car.") You will often find yourself using what the court tells you about the issue or the holding to fill in what the court has not told you about the determinative facts, and vice versa.

For example, if the court states the issue but does not identify the rule or specify which facts are determinative, you might discover the rule and the determinative facts by answering the following questions:

1. Who is suing whom over what series of events and to get what relief?
2. What issue does the court say it intends to decide?
3. How does the court decide that issue?
4. On-what facts does the court rely in making that decision?
5. What rule does the court enforce?

In answering the fifth question, use the same kind of reasoning we applied to the apartment hypothetical: develop several different phrasings of the rule (broad, narrow, middling) and identify the one the court is most likely to have had in mind.

---

§3.2   1. Benjamin Nathan Cardozo, *The Nature of the Judicial Process* 29 (Yale U. Press 1921).

2. Kenney Hegland, *Introduction to the Study and Practice of Law* 72 (2d ed., West 1995).

Exercise II. Analyzing the Meaning of Roberson v. Rochester Folding Box Co.

What was the issue on appeal in *Roberson?* What rule did the appellate court enforce? What were the determinative facts? Be prepared to state and argue your conclusions in class.

§3.3   The Anatomy of a Statute

The *Roberson* decision was so unpopular that the following year the New York legislature enacted a statute providing exactly the relief that the *Roberson* court held was unavailable under the common law. The *Roberson* majority understood that that might happen. Recall the majority's words: "The legislative body could very well interfere and arbitrarily provide that no one should be permitted for his own selfish purpose to use the picture or the name of another for advertising purposes without his consent." The statute has been amended several times since enactment. Here is its current form:

New York Civil Rights Law §§ 50–51

§ 50.   Right of Privacy

A person, firm or corporation that uses for advertising purposes, or for the purposes of trade, the name, portrait or picture of any living person without having first obtained the written consent of such person . . . is guilty of a misdemeanor.

§ 51.   Action for Injunction and for Damages

Any person whose name, portrait, picture or voice is used within this state for advertising purposes or for the purposes of trade without the written consent first obtained as above provided [in § 50] may maintain an equitable action in the supreme court of this state against the person, firm or corporation so using his name, portrait, picture or voice, to prevent and restrain the use thereof; and may also sue and recover damages for any injuries sustained by reason of such use and if the defendant shall have knowingly used such person's name, portrait, picture or voice in such manner as is forbidden or declared to be unlawful by section fifty of this article, the jury, in its discretion, may award exemplary damages. . . .

(Although these sections are an improvement over *Roberson,* they still represent a narrow view of the right to privacy. In the Exercise in

Chapter 4, we will see how narrow it is. In many other states, the right to privacy protects against a wider range of harms.)

A judicial opinion always includes a story ("the facts"), and the rule of law for which the opinion stands is embodied in how the court uses rules of law to resolve the story. The New York Court of Appeals denied a remedy to Ms. Roberson, and, because of that decision's effect on her story, we know that—at the time of the decision—an advertiser in New York could use a person's picture in advertising without any legal obligation to get that person's permission or pay damages.

Statutes do not contain stories. Some statutes create things. If a state has a public university or a system of state parks or a public utility commission, those things were all created by statutes. A statute can also grant permission. It might, for example, grant to a state university the authority to open a law school. But the statutes that lawyers most frequently encounter either prohibit something or require it. And those statutes usually also provide remedies for violations, as § 51 does. Sometimes a statute will define certain conduct as a type of crime, and some other statute, found in a criminal code, will define the penalty. That is true of § 50.

Exercise III. Analyzing the Meaning of §§ 50 and 51 of the New York Civil Rights Law

Reading §§ 50 and 51 together as a single statute, what do they prohibit or require? If a person subject to New York law were to violate this prohibition or requirement, what might be the consequences? (List all the possible consequences.) In what ways did §§ 50 and 51 change the rule of *Roberson?*

4 Briefing Cases

§4.1 Introduction

In law school, the word *brief* can mean either of two things. Within a few months, you will learn how to write an *appellate brief,* which — despite its name — is a large and complex document, written to persuade a court to rule in favor of one's client.

Another kind of brief is a short analytical outline of a court's opinion. Students make these outlines to prepare for class, and you are about to write one now. (In law students' vernacular, you are about to *brief a case.*) The purpose of briefing is to figure out the logic through which the case was decided.

§4.2 How to Brief a Case

Just as no two lawyers share exactly the same thinking and working methods, no two law students brief in precisely the same way. Moreover, you will brief individual cases differently depending on the case's complexity and the course for which you are reading it.

Think of the briefing method set out below as a starting point. Adapt it as needed to the different sorts of opinions you study, and, as you go along, modify it also to suit the work habits you find most effective in the different classes for which you must prepare.

A brief might include, in outline form, the following items:

1. the title of the case, its date, the name of the court, and the place where the opinion can be found
2. the identities of the parties
3. the procedural history
4. the facts
5. the issue or issues
6. a summary of the arguments made by each side
7. the holding and the rule for which the case stands
8. the court's reasoning
9. the judgment or order the court made as a result of its decision
10. any comments of your own that may be useful but that are not covered by any other category

Each of these categories bears explanation.

1. Title, date, court, location of opinion.   This is the easiest part. For *Roberson,* a brief might begin as follows:

> **Case:**   *Roberson v. Rochester Folding Box Co.*
> (N.Y. Ct. App. 1902)
> page 29

If you were briefing a case researched in the library, however, you would use the citation (64 N.E. 442) in place of a page number in the text. The point is to identify the place where the opinion can be found.

2. Identities of parties.   This requires some thought: how do the identities of the parties frame the controversy? In *Roberson,* for example, you might write:

> **Parties:**   P = a person whose picture was used in advertising
> Ds = two companies that used that picture

Should you add that one of the defendants manufactured flour and the other apparently manufactured its packaging? Should you also add that the plaintiff did not consent to the use of her picture in advertising? If you believe those are mere background facts, then you would include them in your brief only if they are needed to make sense out of the story. On the other hand, if you believe that either the nature of the defendants' businesses or the plaintiff's nonconsent is important to the court's reasoning, then you should make sure that your brief records those facts. (Because these are matters of identity as well as events in the story, it really does not matter much whether you add them under "Parties" or under "Facts.")

3. Procedural history.   Here list the litigation events that are essential to the decision the court must make. Most published opinions are from appellate courts, and an appellate procedural history includes the trial court rulings appealed from. In *Roberson,* for example:

> **Proc. Hist.:** P sued to enjoin distribution of the picture and for damages. Ds demurred to complaint. Ct below held complaint stated a cause of action. Ds appealed.

4. Facts. Here write a short narrative limited to the determinative facts and whatever other details are necessary to make sense out of the story. Omit facts that neither are determinative nor are needed to make the story coherent. Do not just repeat the story you read in the case. Isolate and list the facts that the court considered important enough to emphasize.

5. The issue. Define the dispute before the court. Usually, the issue can be framed well in more than one way. But it can also be framed badly in more than one way. These statements of the issue in *Roberson* are technically correct but not very helpful:

> Did the complaint state a cause of action?
> Did the lower court correctly hold that the complaint stated a cause of action?

The *Roberson* court did have to decide whether the complaint stated a cause of action. But the first example tells us nothing about the real controversy. The second example is better because it is a little more precise. *Roberson* was an appeal, and appeals determine whether lower courts have erred. But we still do not know what all the fuss was about. This is much more helpful:

> **Issue:** Did New York recognize a common law right to privacy?

So is this:

> **Issue:** Could a plaintiff enjoin and get damages for the use of the plaintiff's picture in advertising where the plaintiff had not consented to that use?

These are the important questions that the *Roberson* court answered, and either would be fine in a brief for a law school class. They are the reasons why lawyers, judges, and law students would read the case a century later.

In framing issues, keep the following in mind:

First, refer to the governing rule, and if a particular element of that rule is in controversy, specify the element. You can refer to the rule explicitly ("Did New York at that time recognize a common law right to privacy?") or implicitly ("Could a plaintiff enjoin and get damages for the use of the plaintiff's picture in advertising where the plaintiff had not consented to that use?").

Second, it often helps to allude to enough of the determinative facts to make the issue concrete. The last example above refers to the picture, the advertising, and the lack of consent. That is enough here. Do not pack into the issue every one of a long list of determinative facts. Include only the most central ones. But when a court is faced with the question of whether to recognize a rule that it has not recognized before, a perfectly good issue can be framed without reference to facts because the real question — whether to change the law — can be bigger than the parties' facts, even though the facts are a significant part of the court's reasoning. That is why *both* of the last two examples above are good statements of the issue.

Finally, in some cases the procedural posture is important and should be part of the issue. But *Roberson* is not one of them. There, the real issue was whether New York would recognize a particular kind of cause of action. Although the court also had to decide whether a lower court had erred in refusing to dismiss the complaint, adding that aspect to the issue makes it needlessly complicated:

> Did the lower court err in overruling the demurrer on the ground that New York should recognize a common law right to privacy?

You will, however, read other cases in which the procedure is important enough that it should be stated in the issue.

6. *A summary of the arguments made by each side.* Do not go overboard. Record the *essential* points of each side's argument.

7. *The holding and the rule.* *Holding* and *rule* have overlapping meanings. *The rule of a case,* or *the rule for which a case stands,* is a principle that can be applied to decide other controversies in the future, like the rules examined in Chapter 2 and in §3.2. When discussing cases (but not statutes), *holding* can mean that, too. Or it can mean, in a narrower sense, the answer to the issue before the court, and often that issue is put in procedural terms.

In *Roberson,* you could say that the holding was that the complaint did not state a cause of action, or that the lower court erred in overruling the demurrer. The rule, of course, would be that New York did not recognize a common law right to privacy, or that in New York at that time a plaintiff had no remedy when someone else used the plaintiff's picture in advertising, even without the plaintiff's consent. And a great many lawyers, when referring to that rule, might call it the holding.

A law school professor who asks you for the holding of a case might want to know the procedural holding, or the rule, or both. Most probably, the professor wants to know the rule, and will be interested in the procedural holding only if the nature of the case makes it important. That is understandable: after all, we read these cases to learn about that rule and for little else.

If your formulation of the issue asks — as in *Roberson* — whether a certain principle is law, it might be enough just to list the issue and its answer:

Issue: Did New York recognize a common law right to privacy?

Holding: No.

That does represent the rule of *Roberson*. There is no need for a separate statement of the rule.

But another statement of the issue might call for a separate statement of the rule. That is particularly true when the issue is expressed with specifics about the facts or the procedure:

Issue: Could a plaintiff enjoin and get damages for the use of the plaintiff's picture in advertising where the plaintiff had not consented to that use?

Holding: No.

Rule: New York did not recognize a common law right to privacy.

Just as we formulated broad and narrow principles from the apartment hypothetical in §3.2, a case's rule can be stated narrowly or broadly, depending on how you conceptualize the determinative facts:

Narrow: At that time, a New York plaintiff could not enjoin and get damages for the use of the plaintiff's picture in advertising where the plaintiff had not consented to that use.

Broad: New York did not recognize a common law right to privacy.

As with the apartment example, the narrow rule would directly govern only a smaller number of future controversies, while the broader formulation will have a wider utility. (The common law right to privacy is not limited to advertising.) Part of a lawyer's creativity is discovering deeper meaning in an opinion by devising several alternative formulations of a rule. The art is to phrase the rule broadly enough that it has a reasonably general applicability, but not so broadly that it exceeds the principle that the court thought it was following. Within these limits, many opinions will afford several different but arguable ways to phrase a particular rule.

Sometimes a court provides a succinct statement of the rule. At other times, the court merely sets out the facts and issue and then, without saying much more, decides for one party or the other. In the first kind of opinion, the court's words provide one — sometimes the only — phrasing of the rule. In the latter, you must construct the rule yourself out of the determinative facts.

8. *The court's reasoning.* Here summarize the court's thinking, noting both the steps of logic the court went through and the public policies the court thought it was advancing through its decision.

9. *Judgment or order.* What did the court do as a result of its holding? Usually, it will be enough for you to write "reversed," "affirmed," "motion denied," or whatever judgment or order the court made.

10. *Comments.* Did the court write any instructive dicta? Do you agree or disagree with the decision? Why? Does the briefed case give you a deeper understanding of other cases you have already studied in the same course? Does material in a concurring or dissenting opinion add to your understanding?

─────────────────────

If an opinion resolves several issues, you will need to go through items 5 through 8 separately for each issue. For example, the middle of a brief of a two-issue decision might look something like this:

    Issue #1: . . .   arguments: . . .
                              holding: . . .
                              rule: . . .
                              reasoning: . . .
    Issue #2: . . .   arguments: . . .
                              holding: . . .
                              rule: . . .
                              reasoning: . . .

Read the entire opinion at least once before beginning to brief. You might work efficiently by making some temporary notes as you read, but you will waste effort if you start structuring your understanding — which is what briefing does — before you are able to see the decision *as a whole.*

A long-winded brief filled with the court's own words is far less useful than a short one in which you have boiled the opinion down to its essence. Briefs are a means, not an end: for you the hard work will be to understand what happened in the case and why, and the brief is only a repository for your analysis. You will waste effort if you spend too much time in writing and too little in thinking. In fact, if you do little more than edit the court's words into a brief, you have probably not understood the case. A better practice is to quote only those words that are truly essential to the case's meaning.

"You brief cases, not to get them right, but as a way of forcing yourself into the thick of things."[1] And "you learn law by struggling with it, not by memorizing it, not by buying commercial outlines."[2]

─────────────────────

§4.2   1. Kenney Hegland, *Introduction to the Study and Practice of Law* 85 (2d ed., West 1995).
   2. *Id.* at 58.

Exercise.   Briefing *Costanza v. Seinfeld*

Using the techniques described above, write out a brief of *Costanza v. Seinfeld.*[3]

COSTANZA v. SEINFELD
181 Misc. 2d 562, 693 N.Y.S.2d 897
(Sup. Ct., N.Y. County 1999)

Harold Tomkins, J.

A person is seeking an enormous sum of money for claims that the New York State courts have rejected for decades. This could be the plot for an episode in a situation comedy. Instead, it is the case brought by plaintiff Michael Costanza who is suing the comedian, Jerry Seinfeld, Larry David (who was the cocreator of the television program "Seinfeld"), the National Broadcasting Company, Inc. and the production companies for $100 million. He is seeking relief for violation of New York's Civil Rights Law §§ 50 and 51. . . .

The substantive assertions of the complaint are that the defendants used the name and likeness of plaintiff Michael Costanza without his permission, that they invaded his privacy, [and] that he was portrayed in a negative, humiliating light. . . . Plaintiff Michael Costanza asserts that the fictional character of George Costanza in the television program "Seinfeld" is based upon him. In the show, George Costanza is a long-time friend of the lead character, Jerry Seinfeld. He is constantly having problems with poor employment situations, disastrous romantic relationships, conflicts with his parents and general self-absorption.

. . . Plaintiff Michael Costanza points to various similarities between himself and the character George Costanza to bolster his claim that his name and likeness are being appropriated. He claims that, like him, George Costanza is short, fat, bald, that he knew Jerry Seinfeld from college purportedly as the character George Costanza did and they both came from Queens. Plaintiff Michael Costanza asserts that the self-centered nature and unreliability of the character George Costanza are attributed to him and this humiliates him.

The issues in this case come before the court [through] a preanswer motion to dismiss. . . . [P]laintiff Michael Costanza's claims for being placed in a false light and invasion of privacy must be dismissed. They cannot stand because New York law does not and never has allowed a common-law claim for invasion of privacy, *Howell v. New York Post Co.*, 81 N.Y.2d 115 (1993); *Freihofer v. Hearst Corp.*, 65 N.Y.2d 135 (1985). As the New York Court of Appeals explained,

> While legal scholarship has been influential in the development of a tort for intentional infliction of emotional distress, it has had less success in the

---

3. This case was suggested by Julie Close, together with Grace Tonner, Kenneth Chestek, and Jo Anne Durako.

development of a right to privacy in this State. In a famous law review article written more than a century ago, Samuel Warren and Louis Brandeis advocated a tort for invasion of the right to privacy. . . . Relying in part on this article, Abigail Marie Roberson sued a flour company for using her picture, without consent, in the advertisement of its product (*Roberson v. Rochester Folding Box Co.*, 171 N.Y. 538). Finding a lack of support for the thesis of the Warren-Brandeis study, this Court, in a four to three decision, rejected plaintiff's claim.

The *Roberson* decision was roundly criticized. . . . The Legislature responded by enacting the Nation's first statutory right to privacy (L. 1903, ch. 132), now codified as sections 50 and 51 of the Civil Rights Law. Section 50 prohibits the use of a living person's name, portrait or picture for "advertising" or "trade" purposes without prior written consent. . . . Section 50 provides criminal penalties and section 51 a private right of action for damages and injunctive relief.

Howell at 122-123. In New York State, there is [still] no common law right to privacy, *Freihofer v. Hearst Corp.* at 140, and any relief must be sought under the statute.

The court now turns to the assertion that plaintiff Michael Costanza's name and likeness are being appropriated without his written consent. This claim faces several separate obstacles. First, defendants assert that plaintiff Michael Costanza has waived any claim by [personally] appearing on the show. [This defense fails because the] statute clearly provides that written consent is necessary for use of a person's name or likeness, *Kane v. Orange County Publs.*, 232 A.D.2d 526 (2d Dept. 1996). However, defendants note the limited nature of the relief provided by Civil Rights Law §§ 50 and 51. It extends only to the use of a name or likeness for trade or advertising, *Freihofer v. Hearst Corp.*, at 140. The sort of commercial exploitation prohibited and compensable if violated is solicitation for patronage, *Delan v. CBS, Inc.*, 91 A.D.2d 255 (2d Dept. 1983). In a case similar to this lawsuit involving the play "Six Degrees of Separation," it was held that "works of fiction and satire do not fall within the narrow scope of the statutory phrases 'advertising' and 'trade,'" *Hampton v. Guare*, 195 A.D.2d 366 (1st Dept. 1993). The Seinfeld television program was a fictional comedic presentation. It does not fall within the scope of trade or advertising. . . .

Plaintiff Michael Costanza's claim for violation of Civil Rights Law §§ 50 and 51 must be dismissed. . . .

===========

After briefing a decision, ask yourself how it fits into the subject you are learning. Why did the editor of the casebook include the decision you briefed? What lesson does it teach you about the law? If the preceding decision or decisions involve similar issues, how does the one you have just briefed expand on what you learned from the others? What, for example, did you learn about the right to privacy from *Roberson*, and how does *Costanza* add to that? In other words, step back far enough to see the larger picture.

II

INTRODUCTION TO LEGAL WRITING

5 The Art of Legal Writing

§5.1 The Language as a Professional Tool

Contrary to the aphorism, a lawyer's stock-in-trade is neither time nor advice. It is words: writing them, speaking them, and interpreting them. That is true not only because legal work involves so much reading and writing, but—more importantly—because words are the most fundamental tool lawyers use to gain advantage for their clients. The constant question for a lawyer is how to use words to cause a result, whether in court, in negotiation, in drafting a contract or a will, or in writing an appellate brief.

Lawyers are fond of comparing words to surgeons' tools: "Words are the principal tools of lawyers and judges, whether we like it or not. They are to us what the scalpel and insulin are to the doctor."[1] Law is "one of the principal literary professions. One might hazard the supposition that the average lawyer in the course of a lifetime does more writing than a novelist. . . . He must use that double-edged tool, the English language, with all the precision of any surgeon handling a scalpel."[2] "Language is the lawyer's scalpel. If he cannot use it skillfully, he is apt to butcher his suffering client's case."[3]

Legal writing should give the viewer a quick and clear view, without distractions, of the idea behind it. Legal writing works well only if it transmits

---

§5.1 1. Zachariah Chafee, Jr., *The Disorderly Conduct of Words*, 41 Colum. L. Rev. 381, 382 (1941).

2. William L. Prosser, *English As She Is Wrote*, 7 J. Leg. Ed. 155, 156 (1954).

3. Irving R. Kaufman, *Appellate Advocacy in the Federal Courts*, 79 F.R.D. 165, 170 (1978).

thoughts with the clarity of Orwell's pane of glass.[4] If obscurity and other faults in your writing distract the reader's attention, you and your client will suffer for several reasons.

First, "[b]ad writing is not read."[5] The typical reader begins to resist and may not even finish reading because lawyers and judges are busy people who do not have time to wade through poor writing. Those readers will expect you to express difficult ideas so that they are quickly and fully understood. Second, a lawyer who writes badly is often assumed to be mediocre and unreliable. Judges and supervising lawyers are particularly quick to make that assumption. Third, the busy reader may misunderstand what you are trying to say. You might underestimate that danger. Most students are surprised to see how lawyers and judges make important decisions based on fast reading of complex documents.

In law and in law school, what counts is what *works*. Legal writing is put to practical tests in a real world. Office memoranda must provide everything needed to advise a client or plan litigation. Motion memoranda and appellate briefs must persuade judges to decide in the client's favor. And contracts, wills, opinions, statutes, and regulations must create or define legal rights and obligations. If these documents are to do their jobs, they must be able to withstand attack from what has been called the "reader in bad faith"—the opposing attorney who would like to distort an ambiguous phrase into something the writer never meant, the unsympathetic judge looking for a misstatement on which to base an adverse ruling, "and all the others who will want to twist the meaning of words for their own ends."[6] In law, good writing is strength. If other lawyers are better at it than you are, you will be at their mercy.

You are, of course, at somewhat of a disadvantage in the beginning because you have no firsthand experience with the type of reader you are writing for. Whether judge or supervisor, however, the typical reader of your future work is marked by five characteristics. First, the reader must make a decision and wants from you exactly the material needed for the decision—not less and not more. Second, the reader is a busy person, must read quickly, and cannot afford to read twice. Third, the reader is aggressively skeptical and will search for any gap or weakness in your analysis. That is not because lawyers are nasty people. Skepticism simply causes better decisions. Fourth, the reader will be frustrated by sloppiness, imprecision, inaccuracy, or anything that impedes the reader's decision-making process or hints that you might be unreliable. And fifth, the reader will be conservative about matters of grammar, style, citation form, and document format.

There are many different ways of doing any particular legal writing chore effectively—and many more of doing it badly. But there are also objective standards that can be used to separate writing that *works* from

---

4. "Good prose is like a windowpane." George Orwell, *Why I Write* (1947), in *The Orwell Reader* 390, 395 (Harcourt, Brace & World 1956).

5. Donald N. McCloskey, *The Writing of Economics* 3 (Macmillan 1987).

6. Henry Weihofen, *Legal Writing Style* 8 (2d ed., West 1980).

writing that does not. Although reasonable lawyers, teachers, and judges might disagree about a few small points, you will find among them a surprising amount of agreement about professional standards of writing. That should hardly be surprising, since all these people must use writing for similar practical purposes, and since all of them are familiar with the consequences of mediocre writing.

§5.2   Your Writing and Your Career

It really is true that "good writing pays well and bad writing pays badly"[1]—if bad writing pays at all.

An ability to write well can be essential to a young lawyer looking for a job. Employers will require you to submit writing samples. And when you scan employment announcements looking for your first job, you will see phrases like the following over and over: "seeks attorney with proven writing ability," "excellent research and writing skills required," "recruiting for associate with superb writing skills."

The American Bar Foundation has done surveys to identify the skills hiring partners look for in making hiring decisions and the skills young lawyers find most important in their early years of practice.[2] The hiring partners surveyed consider the quality of a job applicant's writing sample to be one of the top five factors in deciding whether to make a job offer.[3] The young lawyers said that written and oral communication are the most important skills in law practice.[4]

In essence, "excellent writing skills are a form of future job security."[5] A person who has supervised 400 lawyers at a major corporation puts it this way: "You are more likely to get good grades in law school if you write well. You are more likely to become a partner in your law firm, or receive comparable promotions in your law department or government law office."[6]

Why will employers care so much about your writing skills? "On [your] first day [as a lawyer] you will not be asked to give a talk on torts or property law. You will be given a set of facts and a legal issue about which you know almost nothing. You will be expected to find the law . . . and write a memo. . . . The finished product will be read by the person who signs your paycheck and who may rely upon your work to argue the issue in front of a judge."[7]

---

§5.2   1. Donald N. McCloskey, *The Writing of Economics* 2 (Macmillan 1987).

2. Bryant Garth & Joanne Martin, *Law Schools and the Construction of Competence,* 43 J. Legal Educ. 469 (1993).

3. *Id.* at 489.

4. *Id.* at 473.

5. Mark E. Wojcik, Perspectives, Fall 1994, at 7.

6. Richard S. Lombard (formerly general counsel at Exxon), remarks reprinted in *Lost Words: The Economical, Ethical and Professional Effects of Bad Legal Writing,* Occasional Paper 7 of the ABA Section of Legal Education Admissions to the Bar, at 54 (1993).

7. John McNeill, Perspectives, Fall 1994, at 7.

The demands of lawyerly writing come as a shock to many law students. You will need to learn new writing skills peculiar to law. And if you have had trouble with your writing in the past, now is the time to learn how to do it right. In fact, this is probably your *last* opportunity before your writing begins to affect your career.

Your goal now is to learn how to write so that *you cause things to happen.*

§5.3   Predictive Writing and Persuasive Writing

Much of what lawyers do in writing is either *predicting* or *persuading*.

Lawyers are regularly asked to predict what a court will do. For example, a newspaper might ask its attorneys whether, if it publishes a particular article, it will have to pay damages for defamation or invasion of privacy to some of the people mentioned in the article. If the answer is yes, the newspaper will want to know what changes in the article would prevent that. Clients also ask lawyers to investigate the value of litigating. After the article is published, a person mentioned in it might ask a lawyer whether a lawsuit against the newspaper is likely to succeed. In each of these situations, a client will make a decision relying on an attorney's prediction of how the courts will rule. If the newspaper is sued, lawyers on both sides will make further predictions in order to plan their litigation strategies.

For two reasons, lawyers record, in writing, their predictions and the reasoning behind them. The first is preservation for the future. Predictions tend to be used more than once. The same prediction (and the reasoning supporting it) might be used in deciding whether to sue, in drafting the complaint, in negotiating with opposing counsel, in planning the trial, and in pursuing an appeal—all of which may stretch over a period of years. In addition, two or more lawyers might work for the same client, and the lawyer who makes the initial prediction will need to record it in detail for supervisors and colleagues.

The second reason for reducing predictions to writing is that the act of writing improves the quality of the prediction. *The writing process and the thinking process are inseparable:* when an idea is spoken about, it might be half-formed, but if it is written about with care, it becomes fully developed. The number of variables to be considered can make predictive judgments so complex that an attorney is lost unless thoughts can be worked out on paper. It is not unusual for an attorney to start writing on the basis of a tentative prediction already made, only to find, after much writing—and rewriting—that the prediction "won't write" and must be changed.

Predictive writing is sometimes called objective writing, but objectivity only partly defines the genre. Any writing that makes a disinterested report of what the law is can be classified as objective. Predictive writing does more than that: it foretells how the law will resolve a particular controversy.

Suppose the newspaper publishes the article and is sued. Whenever in this litigation a court is asked to make an important decision, each party will submit documents intended to persuade the court to rule in that party's favor. This, not surprisingly, is called persuasive writing. The documents' intended audience is the judge (in the trial court) or the judges (on appeal) who will rule on the controversy, together with the law clerks or research attorneys who assist them. Persuasive writing contains *argument,* rather than prediction.

Persuasive writing and predictive writing have some things in common. For both, the typical reader is skeptical, busy, and cautious, and, in both situations, that person reads for the purpose of making a decision and expects the document to be useful.

But persuasive writing and predictive writing also differ in fundamental ways. The goal of predictive writing is to foretell what will really happen, whether pleasant or unpleasant. If the newspaper could become liable for damages, it might decide to do things before publication to limit its exposure if the editors are warned beforehand. And if a person mentioned in the article probably would not be awarded damages, he will want to know that before deciding whether to sue. In persuasive writing, on the other hand, the goal is to influence the court to make a favorable decision. Persuasive writing requires all the skills needed for predictive writing, but it requires others as well: strategic thinking, for example, and the ability to make compelling arguments.

§5.4 The Art Forms of Legal Writing

Predictive writing is done in *office memoranda.* Persuasive writing appears in two kinds of documents: *motion memoranda* submitted to trial courts and *appellate briefs*[1] submitted to appellate courts. Motion memoranda and appellate briefs become public records, kept in the court clerk's files. But an office memorandum is a confidential document not normally distributed outside the lawyer's office.

You can read an office memorandum in Appendix C; a motion memorandum in Appendix F, and two appellate briefs in Appendices G and H. These documents might seem imposing at first, but each of them is really a collection of parts. When you write the parts separately and then assemble them into a whole, the task is easier than it might at first seem.

Think of memoranda and briefs as manuals to guide the reader's decision making. Unlike essays, they are not read from beginning to end. The reader may open up a particular memorandum or brief on several different occasions, and the reader's purpose at any given time determines the portions of the document that will be read and the order in which they will be read. In that way, these documents are very much like your car's owner's manual.

---

§5.4 1. This is *not* the type of brief explained in Chapter 4.

The reader's need at the moment may be limited ("how do I change this flat tire?"), and it must be satisfied without having to read the entire document.

Lawyers write a wide range of other things too: contracts, wills, trusts, pleadings, motions, interrogatories, affidavits, stipulations, judicial opinions, orders, judgments, statutes, administrative regulations, and more. But instruction in these other forms of legal writing must wait until after you have learned much more about law and procedure and are able to enroll in upper-class drafting courses, clinics, and simulation courses.

6 The Process of Writing

§6.1 Writing in Four Stages

Writing happens in four stages: (1) analyzing the issues and the raw materials that can be used to resolve the issues and raw materials; (2) organizing them so that they can be written about; (3) producing a first draft; and (4) rewriting through several further drafts until the final product is achieved. *To some extent, these stages overlap.* You will, for example, continue to analyze while organizing, writing the first draft, and rewriting, although most of the analytical work comes at the beginning.

This chapter explores the four stages (in §§6.2-6.6) and concludes with a note on plagiarism (§6.7) and some general advice about writing (in §6.8). Students are most surprised by four things in this chapter and later:

1. The method of outlining taught in high school and college can stifle creativity and make it harder to write. A more fluid method — explained in §6.3 and §13.2 — is easier to use and leads to better writing.
2. The first draft is the *least* important part of writing (see §6.4).
3. Good *re*writing transforms the first draft into excellent writing (§6.6).
4. For *all* writers — even the ones who write best-selling novels that get turned into movies — writing is very hard work (§6.8).
5. Legal writing is hard to learn.

Let's talk about the last item on this list, and about your confidence in your writing. Learning a skill at a higher level of proficiency, with new requirements, can make you feel as though the competency you thought you had before has been taken away from you. Most students feel at least some of that while learning to write at the professional level. That feeling of doubt is sharpest near the beginning. But gradually—very gradually—it is replaced with a feeling of *strength*. By the end of law school instruction in writing, many students feel much stronger as writers than ever before because they have *become* stronger. For now, the important thing to remember is this: if in the weeks ahead you fall into doubt about your writing abilities, it is because you are learning a great deal very quickly. *It does not necessarily mean you are a bad writer. You might be a good one. Once you absorb what you are learning and start producing professional writing—and that will happen—your prior confidence will return and be stronger than before because you will now be reaching for mastery.*

Many law students and young lawyers report that while learning legal writing they felt discouraged, but that later they experienced a first moment of validation. That moment might have come late in a semester, when a legal writing teacher told them that they had done something really well. Or it might have come in a summer or part-time job, when a supervising lawyer complimented them on a well-written memo. Or it might have come in court when a judge leaned over the bench and said, "It was a pleasure to read your brief, counselor." That first moment of validation was the beginning of the recognition of *mastery*. Mastery was not yet complete; it would take much longer for that to happen. But it had begun.

Many students and young lawyers also say that they wished someone had told them while they were working so hard in legal writing that that moment of the beginning of mastery would *eventually* come. That is why I am telling you that if you are like most students—and even if you feel deeply discouraged along the way—that moment will eventually come.

§6.2   *Analyzing*

> [L]earning to write as a lawyer is another way to learn to think as a lawyer.
>
>   — Terrill Pollman

The writing process and the thinking process are inseparable. Or, as Donald McCloskey has put it, "writing is thinking."[1]

Analysis is deciding which authorities to rely on (Chapter 14), determining what the cases and statutes mean (Chapters 15 and 16), and how they govern the client's facts (Chapter 17). Students and lawyers usually print out or photocopy the authorities that research suggests might be relevant, and they mark them up while reading and rereading them, identifying the

---

§6.2   1. Donald N. McCloskey, *The Writing of Economics* 3 (Macmillan 1987).

most significant passages. It helps to outline the statutes (Chapter 2) and brief the cases (Chapter 4).

§6.3   Organizing

Good organization is crucial in legal writing. There are two reasons.

First, legal writing is a highly *structured* form of expression. As you learned in Chapter 2, rules of law are by nature structured ideas. And any effective discussion of them is also unavoidably structured and requires a well-organized presentation.

Second, legal writing is judged entirely by how well it educates and convinces the reader that your reasoning is correct. The final product must be designed so that it can be easily digested by the reader, and that cannot happen without good organization. In college, teachers criticize organization infrequently. But the reader of lawyerly writing is different from the reader for whom college essays are written. To the law-trained reader, unplanned writing resembles an irritating and inaccessible stream-of-consciousness, rather than something useful.

Students are told to outline but often resist doing it. Outlining seems like an arbitrary and useless requirement. If you dislike outlining, the problem may be that you were taught an outlining method that is unnecessarily rigid. Rigid methods of outlining demand that you draw an outline tree with roman numerals, capital letters, arabic numerals, lower-case letters, and italic numerals. That stifles creativity, and it is *not* the way effective writers write.

A fluid outlining method is simpler and *helps* you write. A fluid outline is a flexible collection of lists. Your raw materials (cases, facts, hypotheses, and so on) flow through it and into your first draft.

Chapter 10 explains the most effective methods of organizing analytical legal writing, and Chapter 13 explains how to make a fluid outline.

§6.4   The First Draft

Shitty First Drafts . . . All good writers write them. This is how they end up with good second drafts and terrific third drafts. . . . In fact, the only way I can get anything written at all is to write really, really shitty first drafts. . . . A friend of mine says that the first draft is the down draft — you just get it down. The second draft is the up draft — you fix it up. You try to say what you have to say more accurately. And the third draft is the dental draft, where you check every tooth. . . .

— Anne Lamott

Many students treat the first draft as the most important part of writing. But that is wrong: the first draft is actually the *least* important part. Analysis, organizing, and rewriting all do much more to cause an effective final product. And if you write on a computer, first-draft writing might not be separate from rewriting. That is because of the ease with which you can interrupt your first draft and go back to rewrite something you initially wrote only a few minutes ago.

Your only goal during the first draft is get things down on the page so that you can start rewriting. The first draft has no other value. Regardless of how many faults it has, the first draft accomplishes its entire purpose merely by coming into existence.

Do your first draft as early as you possibly can. The first draft may be the least important part of the writing process, but you cannot start rewriting until you have a first draft. And if you leave little time for rewriting, the document that might have been rewritten into something wonderful will only be okay, or less than okay.

§6.5   Overcoming Writer's Block

You start to work on your first draft, and nothing happens. You stare at the page or the computer screen, and it seems to stare right back at you. This does *not* mean you are an inadequate writer. Writer's block happens to everybody from time to time, even to the very best writers. What can you do to overcome it? Here are some strategies:

1. Do something unrelated for a while.   Prepare for class, do the dishes, or jog. While you are doing that, your unconscious will continue to work on the first draft. (This is called incubation.) After a while, ideas will pop into your conscious mind unexpectedly, and you will need to sit down and start writing again. But be careful: in law, you are usually writing against a deadline, and doing something else cannot go on for too long.

2. If the beginning is blocking you, start somewhere else.   The reader starts at the beginning, but you do not have to. A common cause of writer's block is starting to write at the beginning. The beginning of a document is often the hardest part to write. And in each part of the document, the first paragraph is often the hardest to write. One of the reasons is that if you are not sure exactly what you are going to say, you will not know how to introduce it. Sometimes the beginning of the document as a whole, and the beginning of each part of the document, can be written *in better quality*, as well as more easily, if you write them later in the process.

If you are not going to start writing at the beginning, where are you going to start? Look over your outline. Does something in the outline reach out to you because what you want to say about it is already forming in words in your mind? Even if it is a tiny part of your third issue, write it now. Later, you can go back and write the other issues. Some people write many small passages and then stitch them together to create the whole document, a process that word-processing software easily facilitates.

3. Rethink your outline. You might be blocked because your outline is unworkable. Just as pain tells you that something is wrong with your body, writer's block might be telling you that your outline does not give you a good structure on which to build the document. But do not rip up your outline just because you are blocked. You might have a fine outline and be blocked for other reasons.

4. Don't expect perfection in first drafts. If you are chronically blocked when you try to do first drafts, it might be because you expect yourself to produce, in one draft, a polished final version. That is expecting too much. Even well-known novelists cannot do that. Really bad first drafts are just fine. See §6.4, especially the Anne Lamott quote at the beginning of that section. Keep reminding yourself that the first draft is the *least* important part of writing. You can afford to write horribly in the first draft because you can fix everything during rewriting (§6.6).

5. Use writing to reduce your fear. The most effective way to reduce anxiety is to start writing early—long before your deadline—and to keep on working steadily until you are finished. If you start early, you will lose less sleep and be a happier writer. Many students procrastinate because they worry about writing. But procrastination increases anxiety and puts you further and further behind. The only way to break this cycle is to start writing so you can bring the task under control.

6. Separate yourself from distractions. If you are distracted by roommates or by the temptation to watch television or play computer games, leave the distractions in one place while you work in another.

§6.6 Rewriting

There is no such thing as good writing. There is only good rewriting.
— *Justice Louis Brandeis*

A clear sentence is no accident. Very few sentences come out right the first time, or the third.
— *William Zinsser*

A scrupulous writer, in every sentence that he writes, will ask . . . : What am I trying to say? What words will express it? What image or idiom will make it clearer? . . . Could I put it more shortly?
—*George Orwell*

In college, you might have completed assignments "by turning in what were basically first drafts, lightly edited to fix glaring errors."[1] As you will see in a moment, that will not work when you are creating a professional product.

A first draft is for the writer: you write to put your thoughts on the page. But in subsequent drafts, the focus shifts to the reader. How much will *this* reader need to be told? Will she or he understand what you say without having to read twice? Will this reader become convinced that you are right?

To answer these questions, impersonate — while you read your work — the reader for whom you are writing. Will this skeptical person see issues that you have not addressed? Will this busy person become impatient at having to wade through material of marginal value that somehow got into your first draft? Will this careful person be satisfied that you have written accurately and precisely?

You will do a better job of impersonating the reader if, between drafts, you stop writing for a day or two, clear your mind by working on something else, and come back to do the next draft both "cold" and "fresh." Obviously, that cannot happen if you put off starting the project and later have to put it together frantically at the last minute. To make sure that you have time to rewrite, start on an assignment as soon as you get it, and then pace yourself, working at regular intervals within the time allotted.

Do not be afraid to ax material from your first draft. The fact that you have written something does not mean that you have to keep it.

And do not be afraid to change your mind about your analysis of the law and the facts. Most writers have experienced the abandonment of an idea that felt valuable when thought about, sounded valuable when spoken, but nevertheless proved faulty when — in the end — it "wouldn't write." Most writers have experienced the obverse as well: sitting down to write with a single idea and finding that the act of writing draws the idea out, fertilizes it, causes it to sprout limbs and roots, to germinate, and to spread into a forest of ideas. The amount of understanding reflected in a good final draft is many times the amount that surfaced in the first draft because the writing process and the thinking process are inseparable, each stimulating and advancing the other. ("You do not learn the details of an argument until writing it in detail, and in writing the details you uncover flaws in the fundamentals."[2])

You produce a first draft by putting down on paper ideas so fragmentary that one might be ashamed of them. They might not even be quarter-baked — much less half-baked — but on paper they will at least be out in the open. At that point, a writer who is *satisfied* is engaged in self-delusion. But an undeluded writer will rewrite, and rewrite, and rewrite — and rewrite again. After a while, the product becomes moderately lucid and perhaps only then does the writer even begin to understand the ideas being written about.

---

§6.6   1. Steven V. Armstrong & Timothy P. Terrell, *Thinking Like a Writer* 9-18 (Clark Boardman Callaghan 1992).
   2. Donald N. McCloskey, *The Writing of Economics* 3 (Macmillan 1987).

While rewriting, use the lettered checklists on the inside front and back covers of this book to test your writing for good organization, paragraphing, style, and use of quotations. (If you are writing an office memorandum, a checklist on the inside back cover will also help you test your writing for predictiveness.) Use Appendix A (and a legal dictionary) to make sure that you are using legal terminology properly. Use Appendix B to check your writing for punctuation errors. And use the ALWD Citation Manual or the Bluebook to make sure that your citations are in proper form. (Chapter 20 of this book explains citation.)

And step back and consider your tone: does it make you sound like a responsible and prudent person — the kind of person the reader can rely upon?

Eventually, you will notice, after putting the writing through several drafts, that after a certain point the problems you are finding are mostly typographical errors and small matters of grammar, style, and citation. When that happens, you are working on the natural final draft, and the job is nearly finished. But do not rush this. Now that your attention is focused on details, make sure that they are right. In professional work, harsh consequences can grow out of small faults (such as misplaced commas and decimal points that turn ten thousand dollars into ten million dollars).

§6.7 *Plagiarism*

Plagiarism is using other people's words or ideas as though they were your own. You commit plagiarism if you lift words or an idea from *anywhere else* and put them into your own work without quotation marks (for words) and a citation (for words or ideas). Your teacher might have a policy or guidelines to help you avoid plagiarism, and all teachers punish plagiarism in one way or another.

You already know the ethical and moral reasons not to plagiarize because you heard them in college and high school. Here are two more reasons:

First, you will feel better about yourself if you do not steal words or ideas from someone else. You will have professional self-respect and pride in your own work only if you did the work yourself. And pride in your own work is one of life's pleasures.

Second, it is so easy to catch plagiarism that you should assume you will be caught and punished. For word plagiarism, all a teacher has to do is take some of your words and search for them in any of the legal research databases to find the case or article from which you got them. Many teachers routinely do that. Teachers can also electronically search other students' papers for words like yours. For idea plagiarism, a teacher who designed your assignment and grades the other students' papers knows where all the ideas came from. Even if you copy the detailed structure of your paper from another student, that can be plagiarism, and the teacher who grades both papers will notice it.

So don't plagiarize.

§6.8   Some General Advice about Writing

> Writing is easy. You just sit at a typewriter until blood appears on your
> forehead.
>
> — *Red Smith*

It is not *that* hard. But at times it can *feel* that way. If you know the
sensation Red Smith describes, that does not mean that you are a bad
writer. Red Smith was the leading sports journalist of his time. Every
day, millions of people opened their newspapers to read what he had
written the night before. Obviously, he was not a bad writer — and still
he knew that feeling. (So has nearly everybody else whose writing you
have ever enjoyed reading.)

Learning how to write like a lawyer is the beginning of learning how
to make professional decisions. Professional work differs from other methods of earning a living partly because a professional must constantly
decide — in very unclear situations — how to proceed. (We pay professionals like doctors and lawyers because they know how to figure that
out.) There is no easy, simple, cookbook-like formula for writing well.
When you write — and in every other part of the practice of law — you
will be confronted continually with a range of choices about what to do.
And your success as a lawyer will depend on your ability to understand the
choices available and to select wisely among them. Now is a good time to
start learning how.

As you write and rewrite, avoid the temptation to imitate unquestioningly whatever you happen to find in judicial opinions that appear in
your casebooks. Those opinions are in casebooks for what they tell you
about the law — not for what they tell you about how to write. In the last
decade or so, there has been a revolution in the way lawyers and judges look
at writing. Verbosity, obscurity, arcaneness, and disorganization that were
tolerated a generation ago are now viewed as unacceptable because they
make the reader's job harder and sometimes impossible. That means that
before you adopt a practice or device that you have seen in an opinion, you
should ask yourself *whether you are tempted to do so because it will
actually accomplish your purpose or because you feel safer doing what
a judge has done.* The latter is not a sound basis for a professional decision.
To get an idea of how things have changed since many of the opinions in
your casebooks were written, read the opening paragraphs below of two
decisions on the same issue.[1] One opinion is written in a style that was
once common, while the other has the clarity and forthrightness that supervisors and judges will expect of you:

---

§6.8   1. The issue is whether a person who stole mail after it has been delivered by the post
office violated the statute now at 18 U.S.C. § 1708 (2000), which penalizes stealing "from or out
of any mail, post office, or station thereof, letter box, mail receptacle, or any mail route or other
authorized depository for mail matter, or from a letter or mail carrier."

UNITED STATES v. ASKEY
108 F. Supp. 408 (S.D. Tex. 1952)

Counts 1 and 2 of the indictment charged defendant with violating 18 U.S.C. §1708. Counts 3 and 4 charged violation of 18 U.S.C. § 495. The court sustained a motion to dismiss Count 2 and submitted the remaining counts to a jury which found defendant guilty as charged. The court had carried defendant's motion for judgment of acquittal on Count 1 along with the case. After receiving the verdict, the court announced that the verdict would be set aside as to Count 1.

. . . There is no allegation that the letter, from which defendant abstracted the Treasury check, was a *mailed* letter or one which had been removed from some office, station, letter box, receptacle or authorized depository. The language . . . from the statute prohibits the abstracting or removing from "such letter," clearly referring back to the first part of the statute, dealing with letters *in the mails,* or taken from some post office, receptacle or depository. In other words, it would be no offense to remove the contents of a letter never deposited for mailing or transmitted through the mails. . . .

UNITED STATES v. PALMER
864 F.2d 524 (7th Cir. 1988)

About a month after settling into a house, Mildred Palmer found in her mailbox three envelopes addressed to Clifton Powell, Jr., the former occupant. Instead of returning the envelopes to the Postal Service, Palmer opened them. She found three checks (technically, warrants on Illinois's treasury) — no surprise, for the envelopes in which Illinois mails checks are distinctive. The district court described what happened next:

Richard Morrison was present when Palmer brought the mail into the house and knew she had received the state warrants. Palmer and Morrison discussed negotiating the warrants and getting the proceeds. Someone endorsed Clifton Powell, Jr.'s name without his authority on the reverse side of each warrant. The warrants were then delivered by Morrison to a man named Lawrence Armour, Sr. Armour had something which neither Palmer nor Morrison had: a bank account. For a fee Armour negotiated the three state warrants through his bank account and returned the balance of the proceeds to Morrison who shared them with Palmer.

. . . We must decide whether converting the contents of an envelope violates § 1708 when the envelope was delivered to an outdated address . . . .

Which opinion would you rather finish reading? Has one of these judges simply written out the material without seeming to think much about your needs as a reader? If so, what in the opinion prevents you from easily understanding what the judge is trying to say? If you understand the issue better from the other opinion, what did that judge do to make it easier for you? By the way, are you more curious about the outcome of one of these cases than you are about the other?

"When legalese threatens to strangle your thought process, pretend you're saying it to a friend. Then write that down. Then clean it up."[2]

2. Hollis T. Hurd, *Writing for Lawyers* 34 (Journal Broad. & Commun. 1982).

OFFICE
MEMORANDA

7 Office Memoranda

§7.1 Office Memorandum Format

> Form follows function.
> —*motto of the Bauhaus school of architecture*

This chapter describes the format of an office memorandum and the process of writing one. Chapters 9-17 explain the skills needed to analyze and organize the Discussion part of the memorandum: predicting legal consequences, organizing analysis, selecting authority, and analyzing precedent, statutes, and facts. Chapters 18-20 explain three skills—paragraphing, style, and using citations and quotations—that are particularly important during the rewriting process, as the memorandum evolves into a final draft.

An office memorandum might be read many times over a period of months or years by several different attorneys, including the writer, who may use it as a resource long after it is drafted. A memorandum might be written, for example, after a client has asked whether a lawsuit would be worth commencing. It would be used most immediately for advice to the client. If the result is a suit, some parts of the memorandum might be read again when the complaint is drafted. The memorandum might be consulted a third time when the attorney responds to a motion to dismiss; a fourth time while drafting interrogatories; a fifth time before making a motion for summary judgment; a sixth time before trial; and a seventh time in preparing an appeal.

Who should you imagine your reader to be? When you start working at a job, there will be nothing to imagine because most of the time your reader will be your supervisor. But in law school, your assignments are hypothetical. Imagine that you are writing to the typical partner or supervising attorney described in §5.1. This person will be busy and by nature skeptical and careful. She or he will be reading your memo for the purpose of making a decision and will probably be under some kind of pressure (especially time pressure) while reading.

Format varies from law office to law office and from case to case, but a typical office memorandum includes some combination of the following, often but not always in this order:

1. a memorandum heading
2. the Issue or Issues
3. a Brief Answer
4. the Facts
5. a Discussion
6. a Conclusion

In some offices and for some purposes, the Brief Answer might be combined with the Issue or Issues. In a relatively uncomplicated situation, the Brief Answer or the Conclusion (but not both) might be omitted.

The rest of this chapter is easier to follow if you look to the memorandum in Appendix C for illustration as you read the description below of each of these components.

The **memorandum heading** simply identifies the writer, the immediately intended reader, the date on which the memorandum was completed, and the subject matter.

The **Issue** (or Issues) states the question (or questions) that the memorandum resolves. The Issue also itemizes the inner core of facts that you think crucial to the answer. You can phrase the Issue either as a question about whether a legal test has been satisfied or how the law treats a particular problem ("Is driving at twice the speed limit the crime of reckless endangerment as well as the traffic offense of speeding?"). Or you can ask a question about how the courts would rule in a particular dispute ("Will the client be convicted of reckless endangerment for driving at twice the speed limit?").

The Issue includes a short list of crucial facts. The Issue printed in Appendix C asks about how the courts will rule in a case that is especially fact-sensitive. (Equity often is.) The one below asks how the law will treat a matter that is less fact-sensitive:

Will Donald Trump be able to get a trademark on the phrase "You're fired!"?

List real facts, not legal conclusions. The example above is limited to two facts: Donald Trump (the person who wants a trademark) and "You're fired!" (the thing he wants to trademark). They are facts and not law because you do not need to know any law to understand who and what they are. The following, on the other hand, does contain a legal conclusion:

> Will Donald Trump be able to get a trademark on the phrase "You're fired!" when others have already registered it and used it in ways that satisfy the Lanham Act definition of a trademark?

The Lanham Act's definition of a trademark is law. And saying that others have already used the phrase in ways that satisfy the Lanham Act definition of a trademark is a legal conclusion (also called a conclusion of law). To come to that conclusion, you would need to read section 45 of the Lanham Act and decide whether previous uses by others of the phrase satisfy the definition there. You do not list legal conclusions in the Issue because an issue is a question and a legal conclusion is part of the *answer* to that question. If Donald Trump cannot get a trademark, it will be because others have already beaten him to it. That is something you will decide later in the memo (in the Brief Answer, the Discussion, and the Conclusion).

The **Brief Answer** states the writer's prediction and summarizes concisely why it is likely to happen. This usually involves at least an allusion to the determinative facts and rules, together with some expression of how the facts and rules come together to cause the predicted result. (The complete analysis occurs in the Discussion.)

For the reader in a hurry, the Brief Answer should set out the bottom-line response in the most accessible way. Compare two Brief Answers, both of which respond to the following Issue:

Issue

Did the District Attorney act unethically in announcing an indictment at a press conference where the defendant's criminal record was recited, an alleged tape-recorded confession was played, ballistics tests on an alleged murder weapon were described, and the defendant was produced for photographers without the knowledge of her attorney?

Brief Answer (example 1)

Under DR 7-107(B) of the Code of Professional Responsibility, it is unethical for a prosecutor before trial to publicize, among other things, any criminal record the defendant might have, any confession she might allegedly have made, or the results of any tests the government might have undertaken. Under DR 1-102(A)(5), it is also unethical to engage in conduct "prejudicial to the administration of justice." That has occurred here if the press confe-rence — and particularly the presentation of the defendant for photographers — created so much pretrial publicity that the jury pool has been prejudiced. Therefore, the District Attorney violated DR 7-107(B) and may have violated Dr 1-102(A)(5).

Brief Answer (example 2)

Yes. Except for the production of the defendant for photographers, all the actions listed in the Question Presented are specifically prohibited by DR 7-107(B) of the Code of Professional Responsibility. In addition, if producing the defendant for photographers tainted the jury pool, it was unethical under DR 1-102(A)(5), which prohibits conduct "prejudicial to the administration of justice."

Example 1 is closer to the way you might think through the Brief Answer in a first draft. But to make it useful to the reader you would have to rewrite it into something like Example 2, which can be more quickly read and understood.

If the Issue and Brief Answer are both relatively simple, you can combine them. For example:

Will Donald Trump be able to get a trademark on the phrase "You're fired!"? No. Others have already registered it and used it in ways that satisfy the Lanham Act definition of a trademark.

Compare this to the example earlier in which the legal conclusion was wrongly incorporated into the Issue. The legal conclusion is part of the answer, not the question.

The **Facts** set out the events and circumstances on which the prediction is based. Usually, the Facts are a story narrative, but sometimes organizing them by topic works better (for example if different things happened in different places at the same time). Include dates only if they are determinative or needed to avoid confusion. A date could be determinative if the issue is based on time (such as a statute of limitations). See §3.2 on how to identify determinative facts.

One way to begin the fact statement is to introduce the most important character or characters (as in the example below). Another is to summarize the most important event or events ("Mr. Goslin deeded his home to his nephew, assuming he would be able to continue living there, and now the nephew is trying to force him to leave"). A third way of beginning is to state why the memo is being written. ("Mr. Goslin wants to know whether he can regain ownership, or at least exclusive possession, of his home"). Choose the method that would be most helpful in the case at hand to the reader who will probably make the most use of the memo.

Include all facts you consider determinative, together with any explanatory facts needed to help the story make sense. If your reader is already familiar with the factual background, this part of the memo might be abruptly short — much shorter than the fact statement in Appendix C — because your purpose will be to remind the reader about the essential facts, rather than to make a detailed record of them. For example, if over the past few days you and your supervisor have spent several hours working together on the Appendix C case — and your supervisor therefore is already familiar with the facts—you might use a condensed fact statement something like this:

> The client is elderly, retired, arthritic, and a widower. His only asset is his home, and he has no other place to live. His only income is from social security.
>
> Last year, when the client could no longer pay his mortgage, his nephew offered to make the remaining $11,500 in payments as they became due. Seventeen years ago, the client contributed $3,200 to the nephew's college tuition, but the nephew did not say he was now reciprocating.
>
> The client, without stating his purpose to anyone, then gave a deed to the house to the nephew. The client has told us, "At the time, it seemed like the right thing to do. He was going to pay the mortgage, and after a certain point—maybe after I'm gone—the place would become his. I didn't think it would end up like this." The nephew did not ask for a deed.
>
> A few weeks ago, the nephew unexpectedly moved into the house and ordered the client to move out. The client refused, and the nephew has become verbally and physically abusive.

For the reader who already knows the background, you can describe facts generically. For example, the fact statement above merely says that the client became unable to pay his mortgage, while the memo in Appendix C explains why and how that happened. The reader who is not intimately familiar with the case would want to know the facts in detail as they are given in Appendix C.

The **Discussion** is the largest and most complex part of the memorandum. It proves the conclusion set out in the Brief Answer. If the discussion is highly detailed or analyzes several issues, it can be broken up with subheadings to help the reader locate the portions that might be needed at any given time. When writing a Discussion, you will use rules to predict what a court will do; organize proof of your conclusion; select authority to back up your conclusion; work with precedent, statutes, and facts; and use citations and quotations. Chapters 9-17 and 20 explain how.

The **Conclusion** summarizes the discussion in a bit more detail than the Brief Answer does. The Brief Answer is designed to inform the reader who needs to know the bottom line but has no time to read more. The Conclusion is for the reader who needs and has time for more detail, but not as much as the Discussion offers. The Conclusion or Brief Answer can also provide an overview for the reader about to plunge into the Discussion.

Here and in the Brief Answer, choose carefully the words that will tell the reader how much confidence to ascribe to your predictions. Attached to many of your predictions will be the words "probably," "probably not," "likely," or "unlikely." If you think the odds are very high that you are right, you can say something like "almost certainly." If the Issue is framed as a question about whether a test has been satisfied ("Did the District Attorney act unethically . . . ?"), a simple "yes" or "no" will be understood as the equivalent of "almost certainly yes" or "almost certainly no," and you do not need to add the extra words.

Prediction can be expressed ("the client will almost certainly lose a lawsuit") or implied ("the client does not have a cause of action"). But make a prediction, not a guess. When you make a prediction conditioned on a fact not yet known, specify the condition ("if producing the defendant for television cameras tainted the jury pool, it was unethical").

Although the Brief Answer is limited to answering the Question Presented, the Conclusion is an appropriate place to explain what lawyering tasks need to be done next, to suggest methods of solving the client's problem, or to evaluate options already under consideration. If any of these things would be complicated, they can be accomplished in a **Recommendations** section added after the Conclusion.

§7.2   Writing an Office Memorandum

Some lawyers tend to write the Discussion before writing anything else; their reason is that the other components of the memorandum will be shaped in part by insights gained while putting the Discussion together. Other lawyers start by writing the Facts because they seem easier to describe. (Lawyers who write the Discussion first would say that they cannot start by writing the Facts because, until they have worked out the Discussion, they do not know which facts are determinative.) Another group of lawyers are flexible. They start with whatever component begins to "jell" first, and they often draft two or more components simultaneously.

As you put the memorandum through its final drafts, you will need to pay particular attention to paragraphing (see Chapter 18), style (Chapter 19), and citations and quotations (Chapter 20). Ask yourself the questions in the checklists in each of these chapters.

8 Initially Obtaining the Facts: Client Interviewing

§8.1 Introduction

Client representation usually starts with an interview. A person who wants legal advice or advocacy calls to make an appointment. The secretary finds a convenient time and, to help the lawyer prepare, asks what the subject of the interview will be. The person calling says, "I want a new will drawn" or "I've just been sued" or "I signed a contract to buy a house and now the owner won't sell." At the time of the appointment, that person and the lawyer sit down and talk. If the visitor likes the lawyer and is willing to pay for what the lawyer might do, the visitor becomes a client of that lawyer.

During that conversation, the lawyer learns what problem the client wants solved; the client's goals in getting it solved; and what the client knows factually about the problem. The lawyer also tries to get to know the client as a person and gives the client a reciprocal opportunity. Then or later, the lawyer and client also negotiate the retainer (the contract through which the client hires the lawyer), but here we focus on other aspects of the interview, especially fact-gathering.

This chapter is only an introduction to interviewing skills. At most schools, a much more thorough explanation comes in second-and third-year clinical and simulation courses.

§8.2   Lawyers and Clients

A client is not an item of work. You probably dislike it when a doctor treats you as a case of flu, rather than as a human being who has the flu. And the problem is more than unpleasantness: a doctor who treats you as a human being with symptoms of the flu might spend enough time with you to learn that you also have other symptoms, and that you therefore do not have the flu, but instead another disease, which should be treated differently. (If you have not yourself been a client, you can imagine much of how clients experience interviews with lawyers simply by remembering how you have experienced contact with other professionals, especially doctors.)

The opposite of treating the client as an item of work is "client-centered lawyering," a phrase that originated in a groundbreaking book by David Binder & Susan Price.[1] It means focusing our efforts around what the client hopes for (rather than what we think the client needs) and treating the client as an effective collaborator (rather than as a helpless person we will rescue). We have no special wisdom about what clients should want, and each client has to live with the results of our work long after the case has faded into the back of our memory. Clients are not helpless, and even if they were, only rarely could we rescue them. A better view is this: the client is a capable person who has hired you to help the client accomplish a particular goal.

If we really do center on the client, then we also should be able to respect the cultural, racial, ethnic, and gender differences that exist between us and our clients. That means that we recognize the differences and adapt to them, rather than assume that the client will adapt to us. For example, a lawyer might learn to listen for meaning that in the client's culture is implied, even though in the lawyer's own culture it might not be intended unless openly expressed. And we do this sincerely because insincerity is condescension. (If you doubt this, consider something else: it is good business to respect the cultural and gender differences between yourself and your clients. A very large amount of a lawyer's work comes through recommendations by satisfied clients, and clients whose differences have been respected sincerely are that much more likely to recommend.)

The client who is not experienced at hiring lawyers is very different from the client (usually a business person) who hires lawyers routinely. The inexperienced client may have more anxiety and may understand less about how lawyers work. The experienced client may have more sharply defined goals and may think of hiring the lawyer as bringing in a specialist to perform an already defined task.

And the client who wants help with a dispute (suing over an auto accident, for example) can be very different from the client who wants

---

§8.2   1. David A. Binder & Susan M. Price, Legal Interviewing and Counseling: *A Client-Centered Approach* (West 1977). A more recent version is David A. Binder, Paul B. Bergman & Susan M. Price, *Lawyers as Counselors: A Client-Centered Approach* (West 1991).

assistance completing a transaction (typically, negotiating a contract). If the transaction is important, the transactional client might be experiencing some stress, which might be replaced with happiness if the transaction is successful. But a dispute client has a much greater chance of feeling understandable stress, trauma, and anger.

Lawyers are obligated to keep clients' confidences secret. In most states, the obligation is defined by Rule 1.6 of the Model Rules of Professional Conduct: "A lawyer shall not reveal information relating to representation of a client." There are four exceptions: where "the client consents after consultation"; where a disclosure is "impliedly authorized in order to carry out the representation"; where "the lawyer reasonably believes [disclosure] necessary . . . to prevent the client from committing a criminal act that the lawyer believes is likely to result in imminent death or substantial bodily harm"; and where "the lawyer reasonably believes [disclosure] necessary" to protect the lawyer in a fee dispute, malpractice action, ethics investigation, or situation where the lawyer is being sued or prosecuted in connection with representation of the client. In some states, the Model Code of Professional Responsibility or a locally drafted ethics code provides a slightly different formulation.

§8.3 How to Interview

Suppose you are a client sitting in a lawyer's office. What furniture arrangement would help you open up to the lawyer? Some clients are perfectly willing to talk over a desk to a lawyer. Others would rather have something less formal, perhaps two chairs with a small table to the side. (Most lawyers' offices can accommodate all that and a desk as well.)

§8.3.1 How to Begin

In some parts of the country, "visiting" — comfortable chat for a while on topics other than legal problems — typically precedes getting down to business. In other regions, no more than two or three sentences might be exchanged first, and they might be limited to questions like whether the client would like some coffee.

When it is time to turn to business, the lawyer asks something like one of these:

> "How can I help you?"
> "Let's talk about what brings you here today."
> "My secretary tells me the bank has threatened to foreclose on your mortgage. You're probably worried. Where shall we begin?"

§8.3.2   How to Learn What the Client Knows

This section is only the barest introduction to fact-gathering techniques. At most schools, you can learn more in second- and third-year skills courses.

In your own mind, do not label the problem until you have heard most of the facts. A client who starts by telling you about a dispute with a landlord might have defamation and assault claims instead of a violation of a lease.

Do not leap in with questions as soon as the client has told you the nature of the problem. Give the client a full opportunity to tell you whatever the client wants to talk about before you intervene. Many clients want to make sure from the beginning that you hear certain things about which the client feels deeply. If you obstruct this, you will seem remote, even bureaucratic, to the client. And if you listen to what the client wants to tell you, you may learn a lot about the client as a person and about how the client views the problem.

In the beginning, encourage the client to present the facts in the way the client thinks best. After a while (sometimes pretty quickly), the client will want you to take the lead. Make sure you really do understand the chronology of events from beginning to end.

Then start exploring the various aspects of the problem in detail. On each topic, start with general questions ("tell me what happened the night the nuclear reactor melted down") and gradually work your way toward specific ones ("just before you ran from the control panel, what number on that dial was the needle pointing to?"). But do this gradually. If you jump too quickly to the narrow questions, you will miss a lot of information because it is the general questions that show you what to explore. Ask broad questions until you are not getting useful information anymore. Then go back and ask narrow questions about the facts the client did not cover. While the client is answering the broad questions, you can note on a pad the topics you will have to use narrow questions to explore later.

When you start exploring various aspects of the problem in detail, try to take up each topic separately. Too much skipping around confuses you and the client.

Word your questions carefully. How you ask has a lot to do with the quality and quantity of the information you get. A good question does not confuse, does not provoke resistance, and does not distort memory. One of the marks of an effective lawyer is the ability to ask the right question in the most productive way. What makes a question work well? First, it seeks information that really does need to be known. Second, a good question is phrased in a way most likely to produce valuable information. Some words help find information and encourage answers, while other words confuse, cloud memory, or provoke resistance. Third, a good question is asked in a useful sequence with other questions. Sometimes other questions have to be asked first, for example. And ask one question at a time. If you ask two at a time, only one of them will be answered.

Keep asking questions until you have all the details: when, where, who, how, and why. Get them precisely. "Last week" is not good enough. You need "Thursday, at about 11 A.M., in the truckstop parking lot." If the client tells you about a conversation, ask who else was present, what else was discussed, how long the conversation lasted, how it started, how it ended, what words each person present used, and so on. You are going to need these details to analyze the situation. Because in nonprofessional life vagueness and approximation are usually enough, young lawyers are too casual about these things. Experienced lawyers know that in representing clients only precision works.

Listen well. If you do not listen carefully, you might as well not have asked the question, and you will not know what to ask about next. The ability to listen well is as important in the practice of law as the ability to talk well. The popular image of a lawyer is of a person talking — to juries, to judges, to adversaries, to reporters. But in the end, the lawyer who succeeds is the one who also knows how to listen. Knowledge is strength, and in the practice of law one of the most important means of gaining knowledge is to listen carefully and precisely.

Some lawyers just want to get to the heart of the matter and quickly move on to other work, but they are in such a hurry that they leap onto the first important thing they hear, even if it is not in fact the heart of the matter. Instead, relax, let the client tell the story, and listen patiently and carefully.

Most clients will not mind if you take notes, but keep listening while you are writing.

§8.3.3 How to Conclude

Two agreements conclude the interview. One is the retainer through which the client hires the lawyer (and we are not covering that in this brief, introductory chapter). The other is an agreement on what each party will do — and not do — next. Here is a typical example: client will fax a copy of the lease by the end of today; the lawyer will check the law on constructive eviction and call the client tomorrow; in the meantime, the client will not speak to the landlord and will tell anybody who makes demands of the client to call the lawyer.

Clients often want the lawyer to predict immediately whether the client will win or lose. In nearly all instances, you cannot make that prediction. You might have to check the law, or the client might need to supply information or documents that were not brought to the interview. Nearly always, the client does not know all the facts, and you and the client will need to investigate them further. And you need to think about it. Hasty predictions are inaccurate more often than contemplated predictions are.

But clients want assurance. What can you give them? Usually, it is enough to explain what work you will do, adding or implying (whichever works better) that you take very seriously the problem and want to do something about it. Choosing a time when you will have an answer also helps.

9 Predictive Writing

§9.1 How to Predict

The prophecies of what the courts will do in fact, and nothing more pretentious, are what I mean by the law.

— *Oliver Wendell Holmes*

An office memo predicts how the law will treat the client. Sometimes this is done explicitly ("Ms. Rhee will probably be awarded damages for trademark infringement"), and sometimes it is done implicitly ("Ms. Rhee has a cause of action for trademark infringement"). The effect is the same.

If you had a law-related problem and needed to hire a lawyer, you would want that lawyer to start making predictions pretty quickly ("Will I win?" "Is it worth fighting for this?" "Can the other side get away with that?"). But the process of making those predictions would seem magical and mysterious. This chapter explains how to do it.

The difference between predictive writing and persuasive writing is explained in §5.3. Remember that a lawyer predicts for either of two reasons. One is so that a client can make a decision knowing how the law will respond ("if the client constructs her estate in this way, it will not be taxed"). The other is so that the lawyer can make a tactical or strategic decision ("this complaint will not be dismissed, but we will probably win on the evidence later").

How do you create a prediction about how a court will rule? Before beginning to write — and this is an example of the analytical process mentioned in §6.2 — develop arguments for each side on every issue. Think of the reasons why your client should win. And think of the reasons why the opposing party should win. (To predict which arguments will persuade a court, you need to know the arguments the court will hear.) Then, evaluate each argument by asking yourself how likely it is to persuade a judge. Bearing those evaluations in mind, how would a court rule on each issue? Then step back and consider the matter as a whole. In light of your predictions on the individual issues, how will the court decide the entire controversy?

For example, assume that, in the jurisdiction in question, the crime of common law burglary has been reduced to statute in the following form (and renamed burglary in the first degree):

> *Criminal Code § 102:* A person commits burglary in the first degree by breaking and entering the dwelling of another in the nighttime with intent to commit a felony therein.

And assume that the elements of burglary in the first degree have been statutorily defined as follows:

> *Criminal Code § 101(c):* A "breaking" is the making of an opening, or the enlarging of an opening, so as to permit entry into a building, or a closed off portion thereof, provided that neither owner nor occupant has consented thereto.
>
> *Criminal Code § 101(g):* An "entering" or an "entry" is the placing, by the defendant, of any part of his body or anything under his control within a building, or a closed off portion thereof, provided that neither owner nor occupant has consented thereto.
>
> *Criminal Code § 101(e):* A "closed off portion" of a building is one divided from the remainder of the building by walls, partitions, or the like so that it can be secured against entry.
>
> *Criminal Code § 101(f):* A "dwelling" is any building, or any closed off portion thereof, in which one or more persons habitually sleep.
>
> *Criminal Code § 101(n):* A dwelling is "of another" if the defendant does not by right habitually sleep there.
>
> *Criminal Code § 101(m):* "Nighttime" is the period between sunset and sunrise.
>
> *Criminal Code § 101(k):* "Intent to commit a felony therein" is the design or purpose of committing, within a building or closed off portion thereof, a crime classified in this Code as a felony, provided that the defendant had such design or purpose at the time both of a breaking and of an entering.

Assume further that the legislature has also enacted the following:

> *Criminal Code § 10:* No person shall be convicted of a crime except on evidence proving guilt beyond a reasonable doubt.
>
> *Criminal Code § 403:* An assault causing substantial injury is a felony.

Finally, assume — for the sake of simplicity — that none of these sections have yet been interpreted by the courts, and that you are therefore limited to the statute itself. (That is an unusual situation. More often, you will also be working with judicial decisions that have interpreted the statute.)

Let us take up Welty's facts from §2.2. A lawyer making a prediction might think about it in the following way:

> If we want to know whether Welty will be convicted of first-degree burglary, the controlling rule would be the test for first-degree burglary, which is set out in Criminal Code §102. It has six elements and no exceptions. [See §2.1.] And in section 101, the legislature has conveniently defined the elements. She is guilty only if each element is proved beyond a reasonable doubt (section 10). I'll make a list of the elements and annotate it by listing next to each element the facts relevant to it. [Lawyer does that.]
>
> The argument for a breaking is that when she pushed the door back, she enlarged an opening without Lutz's consent, and Lutz's apartment is a closed off portion of a building. The best argument against a breaking is that there is no proof beyond a reasonable doubt that she did not have permission from the owner, if Lutz is only a tenant. But that loses. There's no evidence that an owner knew anything of this, which makes it a speculative doubt and not a reasonable one.
>
> The argument that she entered is that she walked in. There is no contrary argument: she was in the apartment, and there's no evidence that she was pushed in by somebody else. Similarly, his apartment is plainly the dwelling of another, and this was at night.
>
> What she did next is a felony under section 403, but under section 101(k), she is not guilty of first degree burglary unless — at the time she pushed the door open and walked in — she already had the intent to hit him. The argument that she did is that she was already furious and walked right over and punched him, without hesitation. The contrary argument is that something else intervened after the breaking and entering and before the punch: Lutz turned on her and ordered her to leave, and she will testify that she "found this to be too much." That creates reasonable doubt that she had the intent to strike him at the time of the breaking and entering. She may have been angry when she pushed the door open and walked in, but anger does not necessarily include an intent to hit somebody.
>
> Okay, stepping back and looking at the overall picture, the prosecution will be able to prove every element but the last one. And since they will be missing an element, she will be acquitted.

This is how the lawyer might *think* through the process of prediction. If the lawyer were asked to record that prediction in the Discussion portion of an office memorandum, the lawyer might *write* something like the following. (Notice the organization.)

Welty will probably be acquitted of burglary in the first degree because the evidence does not show beyond a reasonable doubt that she had formed the intent to commit a felony when she broke and entered Lutz's apartment. Under section 102 of the Criminal Code, a person is guilty of burglary if he or she (1) breaks and (2) enters (3) the dwelling (4) of another (5) in the nighttime (6) "with intent to commit a felony therein." Under section 11, a defendant can be convicted only "on evidence proving guilt beyond a reasonable doubt."

> The first sentence expresses the ultimate conclusion that the entire Discussion is intended to support.
>
> The basic rule governing the controversy.
>
> In a longer Discussion, tell the reader the order in which you will address the issues; here some of that is implied.
>
> A rule of application that permeates the Discussion.

Although (as shown below) Welty broke and entered Lutz's dwelling in the nighttime, and although the assault she committed there is classified as a felony by section 403, the evidence does not prove beyond a reasonable doubt that she had formed the intent to assault Lutz when she broke and entered. Section 101(k) defines "intent to commit a felony therein" as "the design or purpose of committing, within a building or closed off portion thereof, a . . . felony, provided that the defendant had such design or purpose at the time both of a breaking and of an entering." When Lutz turned around and ordered her to leave while she was protesting his noise, she found this to be "too much" and punched him. A reasonable explanation for her intent is that it was formed after she was already in the room, and no words or action on her part show that she had the intent to punch Lutz before she actually did so. Although, in her rage, she might have contemplated an assault before or when she broke and entered, there is a difference between considering an act and having the "design or purpose of committing" it, and her actions before she struck Lutz show no more than an intent to complain.

> The determinative issue is considered first. Why consider first an element that the statute lists last? If one element is unprovable, it becomes the most important element because Welty can be convicted only if all the elements are proven. Why, then, bother to consider the other elements at all? You might be wrong about the element you think is dispositive, and the reader is entitled to a full accounting.
>
> A counter-analysis. (See §10.2.)

Welty's pushing open Lutz's apartment door was, however, a breaking, which section 101(c) defines as "the making of an opening, or the enlarging of an opening, so as to permit entry into a building, or a closed off portion thereof, provided that neither owner nor occupant has consented thereto."

> Notice how this paragraph begins with the writer's conclusion on the breaking issue, followed by the rule defining a breaking, an application of the rule to the facts, and more than one counter-analysis.

Lutz's apartment is a "closed off portion" of a building, which is defined by section 101(e) as "one divided from the remainder of the building by walls, partitions, or the like so that it can be secured against entry." Although Lutz's apartment is not described, it would be difficult to imagine an apartment that is not thus divided from the building in which it is located. During the incident in question, Lutz opened his front door about six inches after Welty knocked on it to complain of noise, and, when she walked into his apartment moments later, he immediately ordered her out. The initial opening of six inches would not have been enough to admit Welty, and Lutz's prompt order to leave shows beyond a reasonable doubt that he had not consented to her opening the door farther. And nothing suggests that Welty had consent from an owner of the apartment, who conceivably might have been someone other than Lutz.

Welty's walking into Lutz's apartment was an entry, which section 101(g) defines as "the placing, by the defendant, of any part of his body or anything under his control within a building, or a closed off portion thereof, provided that neither owner nor occupant has consented thereto." Welty walked into Lutz's apartment, and the circumstances do not show consent to an entry for the same reasons that they do not show consent to a breaking.

> This paragraph is structured like the preceding one, except that for economy it incorporates by reference the parallel analysis set out earlier.

The other elements are all substantiated beyond a reasonable doubt. First, Lutz's apartment is a dwelling. Section 101(f) defines a dwelling as "any building, or closed off portion thereof, in which one or more persons habitually sleep," and nothing suggests that Lutz does not habitually sleep in his own apartment. Additionally, that apartment is, to Welty, the dwelling of another, as defined by section 101(n), because nothing suggests that she herself habitually sleeps there. Finally, all these events transpired between sunset and sunrise, and therefore within section 101(m)'s definition of nighttime.

> On these facts, it is not easy to determine whether Welty broke or entered Lutz's apartment, or whether she intended, while doing so, to commit a felony inside. Above, a paragraph has justifiably been devoted to each of those issues. But the other elements are easier: a reader can quickly agree that Lutz's apartment is the dwelling of another and that the incident happened in the nighttime. Although the reader must be told enough about these elements to create confidence in the ultimate conclusion, the analysis can be compressed.

This is only one of many effective ways to organize an explanation of this material. When you write, resist the temptation to copy uncritically the style of this example. It might not be appropriate to your assignment or to your own approach to the analysis. In Chapter 10, you will learn how to expand this type of organization through a formula that can be varied in many ways to structure almost any kind of practical discussion involving the application of law to facts.

The issues here are not difficult, and the facts given were few. Even the earliest writing you do in law school will require both more extensive discussion and deeper analysis, using the skills of interpreting authority and analyzing facts that are explained in Chapters 14-17.

§9.2   How to Test Your Writing for Predictiveness

After you have written a first draft—and before you start on later drafts—ask yourself the following questions.[1]

9-A **Have you concentrated on solving a problem, rather than on writing a college essay?** A college essay is a forum for academic analysis—analysis to satisfy curiosity—rather than practical problem-solving. In a college essay, you can reason in any logical manner toward any sensible goal you select, even at whim. But legal writing is practical work, and, although curiosity is a valuable asset in problem-solving, it is not an end in itself. Rather, your Discussion must be directed toward resolving specific questions. Words not helpful in resolving those questions should be cut.

9-B **Have you edited out waffling?** Law exists to resolve disputes, and it does not have the leisure that other disciplines do to play in definitely with gray areas of analysis. (Historians have spent half a century trying to figure out whether it was necessary to drop a nuclear bomb on Hiroshima, and they will probably continue arguing about it forever. But if the issue were tried in court, the jury would have to decide it now.) Because of the law's need to decide, your thinking will be useful only if you take a position and prove it. Vague and mushy waffling represented by words like "seems to," "appears," and their synonyms makes a lawyer's advice less useful to clients and supervising attorneys. When you are disagreed with, lightning will not strike you down on the spot. On the contrary, supervisors and judges are grateful for forthrightness and impatient with hedging. (It is not waffling to say that "the plaintiff probably will win an appeal" or "is likely to win an appeal." No prediction can be a certainty.)

---

§9.2   1. When writing comments on your work, your teacher might refer to these questions by using the number-letter codes that appear next to each question here.

Have you told the reader whether your prediction is qualified **9-C** **in any way?** For precision, a prediction should at least imply the degree of accuracy ascribed to it by the writer. Is the underlying rule a matter of "settled law" and are the facts clear-cut? If the law is not settled, is that because different courts have interpreted it differently or because the authority is scanty? Is the prediction "iffy" or confident? Overt qualifications of accuracy are usually not necessary, since the prediction can be stated in a way that implies your degree of confidence in it. The implication comes not from "weasel words" like "seems to" or "perhaps" (see item 9-B), but instead from a precise statement of the variables on which the prediction is based ("The defendant will probably prevail unless . . .").

Have you accounted for gaps in the law? Occasionally, the **9-D** law has gaps — holes that have not yet been filled in by legislation or by precedent. Max Weber wrote that, unlike some of the legal structures of continental Europe, the English system of common law has never made a pretense of being a "gapless system of rules."[2] He might have added that one of the glories of the common law is the way it routinely fills in gaps by analogizing from precedent and by synthesizing different holdings into a new rule.[3] To an effective lawyer, gaps are creative opportunities to make new law while obtaining what a client wants. If the lawyer can persuade a court to rule for the client in a case of first impression in the lawyer's jurisdiction, the new precedent thus set fills part or all of a gap, and new law is thus made. Few things are more professionally satisfying to a litigator. On the other hand, students tend to want more certainty in the law and to view these gaps with terror because they make prediction difficult. One of the signs of growing self-confidence and maturity in a young lawyer is an increasing ability to feel comfortable with gaps in the law and to make reliable predictions in spite of them. For that to happen, each gap must be defined and explained, rather than glossed over. (See more in Chapters 14-16 on using authority to fill gaps.)

Have you accounted for gaps in the facts? You will also **9-E** encounter gaps in facts. What can you do when a critical or apparently critical fact cannot be learned before analysis must be committed to paper? Often you can figure out that the unknown fact is limited to a short list of possibilities, and you can analyze each of these possibilities in writing. For example, if the client is a defendant charged with burglary, he might not know whether the structure involved was used as a dwelling at the time of the alleged breaking and entry: the structure may be in a secluded location, and the owner may refuse to discuss the matter with anyone representing the client. Under local law, although breaking and entering a non-dwelling is undoubtedly criminal, it may be a lower degree of crime — with a less severe punishment — than burglarizing a dwelling. If a memorandum must be written now, you can explore both possibilities,

2. Max Weber, *On Law in Economy and Society* 62 (Edward Shils & Max Rheinstein trans., Simon & Schuster 1954).
3. These techniques are explained in Chapter 15.

and, when the fact is ultimately learned, the answer will already have been analyzed in writing. When this happens, the conclusion can be expressed either alternatively ("If the building turns out to be a dwelling, . . . But if not, . . .") or conditionally ("Unless the building turns out not to be a dwelling, . . ."). The factual gap and the possibilities that might fill it must be clearly identified. (Sometimes, the process of analyzing each possibility will lead you to discover that the unknown fact actually cannot affect the result because all the possibilities lead to the same answer.)

9-F **Have you refused to hide from bad news?** Good predictive writing squarely faces two sources of unhappiness. One is weaknesses in the client's case, and the other is arguments that might challenge your conclusion. No one is helped where a prediction turns out to be inaccurate because unpleasant possibilities have been avoided, and these kinds of avoidances are easily spotted by the typical reader, who has learned through experience that few legal conclusions are immune from attack, that every client's case has weaknesses, and that the client is always best protected when the complete situation is known from the beginning. That kind of reader is worried by writing that too easily reaches the conclusion that the client is in the right, as well as by writing that does not fully consider arguments that could challenge your conclusion. A writer shows maturity and dependability by exploring in depth both ideas that might put the client in the wrong and ideas that could show the writer to be incorrect. Predictive writing is frank and disinterested diagnosis. Advocacy has another time and place.

9-G **Have you ignored red herrings?** A student might feel obligated to discuss every fact, rule, case, and statute available so that the teacher does not think the student has done an incomplete job. "Why is that fact there if you didn't want us to talk about it?" a student might ask a teacher. Sometimes, it is there to test your ability to distinguish between that which is relevant and that which does not matter. Or it might be there merely to duplicate the mosaic of real life, in which the relevant and the irrelevant mingle freely. Because a lawyer is responsible for separating one from the other, you should be able, if asked, to explain how you differentiated between the relevant and the irrelevant. In your writing, address every true issue, but do not waste valuable time and space discussing things that will not affect how the controversy will be resolved.

Exercise I. Nansen and Byrd

Exercise I-A. With the aid of §§ 16 and 221(a) of the Criminal Code (below), break down the rule in § 220 into a list of elements and exceptions. Annotate the list by adding definitions for the elements (and for any exceptions you might come across). (Under each element you list, leave lots of white space. When you do the second part of this exercise, you will need room to write more.)

Criminal Code § 16: When a term describing a kind of intent or knowledge appears in a statute defining a crime, that term applies to every element of the crime unless the definition of the crime clearly indicates that the term is meant to apply only to certain elements and not to others.

Criminal Code § 220: A person is guilty of criminal sale of a controlled substance when he knowingly sells any quantity of a controlled substance.

Criminal Code § 221 (a): As used in section 220 of this code, "sell" means to exchange for goods or money, to give, or to offer or agree to do the same, except where the seller is a licensed physician dispensing the controlled substance pursuant to a permit issued by the Drug Enforcement Commission or where the seller is a licensed pharmacist dispensing the controlled substance as directed by a prescription issued by a licensed physician pursuant to a permit issued by the Drug Enforcement Commission.

Exercise I-B. You have interviewed Nansen, who lives with Byrd. Neither is a licensed physician nor a licensed pharmacist. At about noon on July 15, both were arrested and charged with criminal sale of a controlled substance. Nansen has told you the following:

Byrd keeps a supply of cocaine in our apartment. He had been out of town for a month, and I had used up his stash while he was gone. I knew that was going to bend Byrd completely out of shape, but I thought I was going to get away with it. I had replaced it all with plaster. When you grind plaster down real fine, it looks like coke. For other reasons, I had decided to go to Alaska on an afternoon flight on July 15 and not come back. Byrd was supposed to get back into town on July 16, and by the time he figured out what had happened, I would be in the Tongass Forest.

But on the morning of the 15th, Byrd opened the door of the apartment and walked in, saying he had decided to come back a day early. I hadn't started packing, yet — I wouldn't have much to pack anyway — but I didn't know how I was going to pack with Byrd standing around because of all the explaining I'd have to do. I also didn't want Byrd hanging around the apartment and working up an urge for some cocaine that wasn't there. So I said, "Let's go hang out on the street."

We had been on the sidewalk about ten or fifteen minutes when a guy came up to us and started talking. He was dressed a little too well to be a regular street person, but he looked kind of desperate. I figured he was looking to buy some drugs. Then I realized that that was the solution to at least some of my problem. I took Byrd aside and said, "This guy looks like he's ready to buy big. What do you think he'd pay for your stash?" Byrd looked reluctant, so I turned to the guy and said, "We can sell you about three ounces of coke, but we have to have a thousand for it." When the guy said, "Yeah," Byrd said, "Wait here" and ran inside the apartment building. A thousand was far more than the stuff was worth.

Byrd walked out onto the stoop with the whole stash in his hand in the zip-lock bag he kept it in, and while he was walking down the steps, about ten feet away from me and the guy who wanted to buy, two uniforms appeared out of nowhere and arrested Byrd and me.

The "guy" turned out to be Officer D'Asconni, an undercover policeman who will testify to the conversation Nansen has described. The police laboratory reports that the bag contained 2.8 ounces of plaster and 0.007 ounces of cocaine. When you told Nansen about the laboratory report, he said the following:

I didn't think there was any coke in that bag. What they found must have been residue. I had used up every last bit of Byrd's stuff. I clearly remember looking at that empty bag after I had used it all and wondering how much plaster to put in it so that it would at least look like the coke Byrd had left behind. I certainly didn't see any point in scrubbing the bag with cleanser before I put the plaster in it.

With the aid of Criminal Code § 221 (below), finish annotating your list of elements by writing, under each element, the facts that are relevant to that element.

Criminal Code § 221: As used in section 220, "controlled substance" includes any of the following: . . . cocaine. . . .

Exercise I-C. You have been asked to determine whether Nansen or Byrd is likely to be convicted of criminal sale of a controlled substance. The question is not whether Nansen or Byrd criminally sold a controlled substance, but whether either of them is likely to be convicted of doing that. To make that prediction, take into account § 10(a) of the Criminal Code.

Criminal Code § 10: No person shall be convicted of a crime except on evidence proving guilt beyond a reasonable doubt.

Using your annotated outline of elements, decide whether each element can be proved beyond a reasonable doubt, and whether any exceptions are satisfied. Then make your prediction. Finally, decide the order in which the elements would best be explored in the Discussion section of an office memorandum.

Exercise II.   The Hartleys and Debenture

Exercise II-A. Break down the rule in Contracts Code § 206 into a list of elements and exceptions. With the aid of § 210, do the same with the rule in § 209. Annotate the list by adding definitions for the elements (and for any exceptions you might come across). (Under each element you list, leave lots of white space. When you do the second part of this exercise, you will need room to write more.)

Contracts Code § 206: A contract made by an intoxicated person is voidable by that person if, at the time the contract was made, the other party to the contract had reason to know that the intoxicated party, because of the intoxication, was unable to understand the nature and consequences of the transaction.

Contracts Code § 209: A person who makes a contract because of duress can void the contract.

Contracts Code § 210: Duress occurs where a person makes a contract only because of an improper threat by the other party that causes the threatened person reasonably to believe that she or he has no reasonable alternative to the contract. In judging whether the threat caused such a belief and whether the belief was reasonable, all attendant circumstances shall be considered.

Exercise II-B. Your client is Megan Hartley. She married Troy Hartley six years ago. They have two children, twins born eight years ago and named Ariel and Jason. Troy is employed as an investment banker. Megan has a part-time job as a salesperson in an art gallery. Both have college degrees in liberal arts. Megan, who has never retained a lawyer before, has just hired you and wants to know her rights concerning the following situation:

Megan has explained to you that she and Troy have had marital difficulties. For the past two years, they have bickered often, and she cannot stand it when the bickering turns into shouting. On three occasions during those two years, Troy struck her, once on each occasion, in the face, at the end of a shouting match. The tension in this situation has caused Megan to drink, on average, a scotch or two a day. Troy does not drink.

When the Hartleys got married, Troy owned a German shepard and Megan owned an Akita. Because the two dogs did not get along, Megan gave the Akita to her brother. The shepard (whose name is Debenture) remained and has been a good watchdog. Although Debenture has never, to Megan's knowledge, bitten anyone, he bares his teeth and growls when Troy shouts, and this makes Megan nervous.

During the evening last Sunday, after a weekend of bitter arguing, Troy announced that he had had enough and was leaving. He quickly packed a bag and left.

Troy returned Monday evening and told Megan that he had consulted a lawyer, and that the lawyer had drafted a separation agreement. The agreement provided that Troy and Megan would live apart, beginning immediately, that they would have joint custody of the children, and that a divorce would be obtained as soon as possible. It provided that there would be no alimony, and in elaborate detail it divided up the couple's property. The agreement provided that it would become effective when signed by both parties. Troy had already signed it.

The art gallery where Megan works laid off half its staff on Monday morning. Megan was able to keep her job, but when she came home from work at six o'clock, she was depressed and worried about whether the gallery would close, throwing her out of work. She had one drink when she got home and another when Troy arrived a little more than an hour later. The children were with Megan's parents. At 7:30; she was drinking a third scotch when Troy put the agreement on the table and angrily demanded that she sign it. Debenture was sitting in the corner, and Megan could see him perk up and become more attentive as Troy's voice became louder.

Troy told Megan that if she did not sign the agreement, he would tell the court that her "artsy friends do drugs in front of Ariel and Jason." Troy added that no one would believe her if she were to deny these accusations because it would be her word against his and he would make a much better witness than she would. Angrily and in a very loud voice, Troy said that the court would therefore take the children away from her and give her none of their property. At this point, Troy was pounding the coffee table and Debenture was on his feet, staring at her very attentively.

Megan signed the agreement and asked Troy to leave immediately and to take Debenture with him. Troy left ten minutes later, taking his electronics equipment and laptop computer and Debenture. Megan made herself another scotch and phoned a friend. She asked the friend to come over and spend a few hours with her because she felt very worried.

Megan's friends do not "do drugs." She knows nothing about divorce law, and before consulting you, she had no idea whether Troy's predictions about divorce and the courts were accurate. (You believe that, in the absence of a separation agreement, a court would probably award Megan custody of the children, child support, and three to five years of alimony. You also believe that, in the absence of a separation agreement, a court would probably divide the property in a way that is more fair to Megan.)

Megan has a clear memory of what she saw and heard Monday night.

With the aid of Contracts Code § 201 and Domestic Relations Act § 401 (below), finish annotating your list of elements by writing, under each element, the facts that are relevant to that element.

> *Contracts Code § 201:* If a contract is voidable by one of the parties, that party need not obey the contract.
> *Domestic Relations Act § 401:* A separation agreement is a contract.

Exercise II-C. You have been asked to determine whether Irma can void the separation agreement. Using your annotated list of elements, decide whether each element is satisfied and whether any exceptions are satisfied. Then make your prediction. Finally, decide the order in which the elements would best be explored in the Discussion section of an office memorandum.

IV
ORGANIZING PROOF OF A CONCLUSION OF LAW

10

A Paradigm for Organizing Proof of a Conclusion of Law

§10.1 Why We Need to Organize Proof of a Conclusion of Law

Medwick is a first-year law student and a talented computer programmer. He is particularly good at creating web robots, which are also called bots.

A bot is software that searches for certain kinds of websites and then automatically does something—good or bad—on each site. Google uses bots to search and index websites. A website owner would want this because Google's indexing brings visitors to the site. A different bot, however, might be used to attack websites. For example, sites that sell concert tickets must defend themselves against bots attempting to buy up all the best seats.

In August, just before the start of the fall semester, Medwick created a bot that finds websites that allow people to post comments. Wherever it could, the bot would post a comment that was really an advertisement for a business that paid Medwick. The ads offered to sell things like out-of-print CD's, spare parts for vintage cars, or cheap vacations in Tahiti. The bot did everything automatically. Medwick activated it from his keyboard and studied Torts or Property for hours while the bot did its work. He planned to use the income to pay tuition.

Many websites require a visitor to agree to "Terms & Conditions," that typically appear in a little window or can be accessed through a link. Clicking on a button labeled "I Agree" or "I Accept" allows the visitor to use the site. Almost everyone clicks "I Agree" or "I Accept" without bothering to read the terms and conditions. A website's terms and conditions are a contract if a person using the website agrees to them. These are called clickwrap or click-through contracts. Clicking on "I Agree" or "I Accept" is the electronic equivalent of a signature on the last page of a contract.

In September, a process server walked into Medwick's Civil Procedure class and silently handed him some documents that looked like they had been drafted by a lawyer. This disrupted the class. After the process server left, the Civil Procedure teacher asked to see the documents. After looking at them for a few moments, she told the class that Medwick had been served with a summons and complaint, and that lawsuits begin that way. Medwick was stunned.

He is being sued by ExitRow.com, Inc., which operates a travel planning website. One part of the site has data on airlines, from which people can learn which airlines provide the most reliable service between any two cities. Another part has electronic bulletin boards where people can comment on travel issues such as improving security procedures and permitting cell phone calls during a flight.

The following sentence appears near the beginning of ExitRow.com's terms and conditions: "The User promises not to post advertising on this website or use the website for commercial purposes in any way." The terms and conditions can be viewed through a little window on ExitRow.com's home page. The only way into the site is through the home page, and the website blocks access to the rest of the site unless the user clicks on an "I Agree" button on the home page. Medwick had programmed his bot to click on every "I Agree" button it encountered. The bot cannot read or interpret contract language.

In its complaint, ExitRow.com requests damages for breach of contract and alleges that Medwick's bot posted hundreds of ads on its website. Medwick has hired your law firm to defend him. Your research shows that this dispute is governed by California law.

"I didn't agree to anything," Medwick told you. "I've never even seen their contract. I never promised not to advertise on their site. How could I agree to a contract I've never seen?"

Is Medwick bound to ExitRow.com's terms and conditions?[1]

Suppose you need to write out your legal analysis so that it could be read by another lawyer, either a supervising lawyer in your firm or a judge to whom you would argue this case. What will you say first? What will you say after that? How will you organize everything? And how much detail will you provide? Those questions are answered in this chapter and in Chapters 11 through 13.

§10.2 A Paradigm for Structuring Proof

A conclusion of law is a determination of how the law treats certain facts. In predictive writing, it can be expressed as a present statement ("Medwick is contractually bound by ExitRow.com's Terms and Conditions") or as a

---

§10.1 1. This fact pattern benefitted from suggestions by Kenneth Chestek and David Thomson.

prediction ("A court will probably hold that Medwick is contractually bound . . . "). In persuasive writing, it can be expressed as a present statement or as a recommendation to the court.

In both predictive and persuasive writing, you prove a conclusion of law by explaining the law and the facts in ways that convince the reader that your conclusion is the right one. Organizing what you say is essential to convincing the reader. This chapter and Chapters 11-13 explain how to organize.

A supervising lawyer who reads a predictive Discussion in an office memorandum does so in preparation for making a decision. So does a judge who reads persuasive writing in a motion memorandum or appellate brief. They will make different kinds of decisions. The lawyer will decide what to advise the client or how to handle the client's case. The judge will decide how to rule on a motion or appeal. But both look for a tightly structured analysis that makes your conclusion seem inevitable.

What do these readers need from you? The reader making a decision first needs to know what your conclusion is; then the main rule (or rules) on which your conclusion is based; next, proof and explanation that the rule exists and that you have stated it accurately; and then application of that and subsidiary rules to the facts. If all this turns out to be long and complicated, at the end of it you might restate the conclusion as a way of summing up.

Thus, to the reader who must make a decision, analysis is most easily understood if it is organized into the following formula — or into some variation of it.

To prove a conclusion of law:

1. State your conclusion.

2. State the primary rule that supports the conclusion.

3. Prove and explain the rule through citation to authority, description of how the authority stands for the rule, discussion of subsidiary rules, analyses of policy, and counter-analyses.

4. Apply the rule's elements to the facts with the aid of subsidiary rules, supporting authority, policy considerations, and counter-analyses; and

5. If steps 1 through 4 are complicated, sum up by restating your conclusion.

Acronyms have been used to help students remember this kind of formula. For example, *CRAC* stands for *C*onclusion, *R*ule, *A*pplication, and

Conclusion. A more complete acronym might be *CRuPAC:* Conclusion, *Rule,* Proof of Rule, Application, and Conclusion.[1]

What do the ingredients in this formula mean?

Your conclusion is the one you are trying to prove. Some examples are in the first paragraph of this section.

The rule is the principal rule on which you rely in reaching your conclusion. Other rules might also be involved, but this is the main one on which your analysis rests. For the conclusions quoted in the first paragraph of this section, the rule will be one that requires contemporaneous knowledge of a restraint.

Rule proof or *rule proof and explanation* is a demonstration that the main rule on which you rely really is the law in the jurisdiction involved. The reader needs to know for certain that the rule exists in the jurisdiction, and that you have expressed it accurately. Both can be done through citations to authority, such as statutes and precedent, together with explanations of how that authority stands for the rule as you have stated it, explanations of policy, and counter-analyses. (This chapter and Chapters 11-16 explain how to do all that.) Subsidiary rules sometimes help explain the main rule.

Rule application is a demonstration that the rule + the facts = your conclusion. Explain your logic and use authority to show that your result is what the law has in mind. (This chapter and Chapters 11-17 explain how.)

Sometimes authority that you use in rule proof might reappear in rule application, but for a different purpose. For example, suppose that *Alger v. Rittenhouse* held that a boat crew that caught a shark became its owner to the exclusion of the fisherman who hooked but lost the shark an hour before. (In your case, ranchers trapped in their corral a wild mustang that immediately jumped over the fence and ran onto your client's land, where it was captured by your client.) In rule proof, you can use *Alger* to prove that your jurisdiction has adopted the rule that wild animals become the property of the first person to reduce them to possession. In rule application, you can use *Alger* again — this time to show that your client satisfies that rule because her position is analogous to that of the boat crew.

A *subsidiary rule* is one that guides application of the main rule or works together with it in some way necessary to your analysis. In a criminal case, the main rule would set out the elements of the crime. Among the subsidiary rules would be the one that permits conviction of any crime only on evidence that establishes guilt beyond a reasonable doubt.

A rule's *policy* is the rule's reason for being. The law does not create rules for the fun of it. Each rule is designed to accomplish a purpose (such as preventing a particular type of harm). When courts are unsure of what a rule means or how to apply it, they interpret the rule in the way that would be most consistent with the policy behind it. Thus, policy can be used to show what the rule is (in rule proof) and how to apply it (in rule application).

Counter-analysis is a term used by law teachers, but not by many practicing lawyers. A *counter-analysis* evaluates the arguments that could reasonably be made against your conclusion. Do not waste the reader's time by evaluating marginal or far-fetched arguments. In predictive writing, the

§10.2   1. *CRuPAC* was suggested by Judith Stinson, Terrill Pollman, and Steve Epstein.

counter-analysis is an objective evaluation of each reasonable contrary argument, with an honest report of its strengths and weaknesses. You must report whether your conclusion can withstand attack. And you must consider the possibility that other analyses might be better than the one you have selected. Like authority and policy, counter-analyses can appear both in rule proof and in rule application—but for different purposes. (In persuasive writing in a motion memorandum or appellate brief, a counter-analysis is called a *counter-argument*. It does not objectively consider contrary points of view. It argues against them, stressing their weaknesses and showing their strengths to be unconvincing.)

You will find the paradigm formula to be flexible if you think of it as a tool to *help* you organize. It can be varied in many ways, although you should do so only for good reasons. This chapter explains why readers prefer that you organize your analysis this way. Chapters 11 and 12 explain how to vary the formula to suit your needs. Chapter 13 explains how to start using the formula and how to check your writing to see whether it is organized effectively.

The formula explained here is designed for practical writing in office and motion memoranda and in appellate briefs. Do *not* use it in this form when you take law school examinations. Instead, use the organization explained in Chapter 23.

§10.3 Why Readers Prefer This Type of Organization

Remember that all of your readers will be practical and skeptical people and will be reading your memorandum or brief because they must make a decision.

State your conclusion first because a practical and busy reader needs to know what you are trying to support before you start supporting it. If your conclusion is mentioned for the first time *after* the analysis that supports it (or in the middle of that analysis), some or all your reasoning seems pointless to the reader who does not yet know what your reasoning is supposed to prove. Effective writers usually state their conclusions boldly at the beginning of a Discussion or Argument ("The plaintiff has a cause of action because . . ."). This may take some getting used to. It is contrary to the way writing is often done in college. And most of us have been socialized since childhood to state a conclusion only after a proof—even in the most informal situations—to avoid appearing opinionated, arrogant, or confrontational.

Far from being offended, however, the reader who has to make a decision is grateful not to be kept in suspense. That kind of reader becomes frustrated and annoyed while struggling through sentences the relevance of which cannot be understood because the writer has not yet stated the proposition the sentences are intended to prove.

State the rule next because, after reading a conclusion of law, the skeptical law-trained mind instinctively wants to know what principles of law require that conclusion instead of others. After all, the whole idea of law is that things are to be done according to the rules.

Then prove and explain the rule because the reader will refuse to follow you further until you have established that the rule is really law the way you say it is and until you have educated the reader somewhat on how the rule works. The skeptical law-trained mind will not accept a rule statement as genuine unless it has been proved with authority. And you cannot apply a rule that the reader has not yet accepted and understood.

Apply the rule last because that is the only thing left. When you apply the rule to the facts, you complete the proof of a conclusion of law.

Along the way, counter-analyze opposing arguments because the skeptical law-trained mind will be able to think up many of those arguments and will want them evaluated. Almost *every* train of reasoning can be challenged with reasonable arguments. If you do not account for them, the reader will doubt you because it will look as though you are avoiding problems rather than solving them.

§10.4 Varying the Paradigm Formula to Suit Your Needs

The formula set out in §10.2 can be varied in three ways.

First, you can vary the sequence in which the components appear. (See §10.4.1 for how.)

Second, in rule proof and in rule application, you can vary the depth of your explanation to suit the amount of skepticism you expect from the reader. (See §10.4.2 and Chapter 11.)

Third, you can combine separately paradigmed analyses into a unified explanation of several issues and sub-issues. (See §10.4.3 and Chapter 12.)

§10.4.1 Varying the Sequence

In some situations, you might vary the sequence of the paradigm formula's components — for example, by stating the rule first and the conclusion second — although the order should not be illogical or confusing. Think long and hard before deciding to vary the sequence in the box on page 93, and, if you do vary it, you should be able, if asked, to give a good reason for doing so. In particular, *rule proof should be completed before rule application begins.* Variations in sequence usually do not work well in office memoranda. They are more likely to be useful in persuasive writing in motion memoranda and appellate briefs. Pages 314-315 explain why.

§10.4.2 Varying the Depth

In rule proof and explanation, some statements about the law are complicated and others are less so. You might need many pages to prove and explain a particular rule because many people might be skeptical about it ("*Pennoyer v. Neff* is still good law"). Or you might need only a few pages because what you say will easily be accepted.

The same is true about rule application. You need to write more analysis if the reader will be skeptical that the rule should be applied as you say, and you should write less if the reader will easily see the point.

Chapter 11 explains how to expand or contract analysis and how to decide when to expand or contract it.

§10.4.3 Combining Separately Structured Analyses

If you reach several conclusions or sub-conclusions, the reader will need a separately structured proof for each one.

For example, suppose you represent the plaintiff in a negligence lawsuit. Negligence has four elements: (1) a duty owed by the defendant to the plaintiff, (2) the defendant's breach of that duty, (3) an injury suffered by the plaintiff (4) proximately caused by the breach. To succeed at trial, you will need to prove all of the elements. If you are writing an office memorandum in which you predict success at trial, you will make four separate predictions:

1. We can prove a duty owed by the defendant to the plaintiff.
2. We can prove a breach of that duty.
3. We can prove that the plaintiff suffered an injury.
4. We can prove that the breach proximately caused the injury.

In the memo, you will say these more concisely, for example: "The breach proximately caused the injury." Each of these predictions is a separate conclusion of law, which will require its own separately paradigmed proof.

You can combine separately structured proofs like these into a single unified presentation that supports an overall conclusion ("The plaintiff has a cause of action for negligence"). Chapter 12 explains how.

Exercise I. *Changing Planes in Little Rock*

Wong sued Keating in an Arkansas state court. Wong has never lived in Arkansas, and none of the events that led to *Wong v. Keating* happened in Arkansas. The only time Keating has ever set foot on the ground in Arkansas was for 45 minutes while changing planes at the Little Rock airport. The only way for Keating to get to Shreveport, Louisiana, where she had a job interview, was to fly into Little Rock on one flight and then fly from Little Rock to Shreveport on another. During those 45 minutes, while Keating was walking in the airport from her incoming gate to her outgoing gate, a process server, acting on Wong's behalf, served Keating with a summons and complaint in *Wong v. Keating.* Keating moved to dismiss on the ground that Arkansas has no personal jurisdiction over her. Wong claims that service in Arkansas alone gives Arkansas personal jurisdiction over Keating.

Below is an analysis of this issue. Find the components of the paradigm for organizing proof of a conclusion of law. Find the writer's conclusion; the primary rule that supports that conclusion; proof and explanation of that rule; and application of that rule to the facts. Mark up the passage below to show where each of the components occurs. If you can find any counter-analyses or policy discussions, mark them, too. Finally, for each component, ask yourself whether the writer has told you enough. Are you confident that the writer is correct? If not, what kinds of additional information would you need?

Arkansas has personal jurisdiction over Keating. Under the Due Process Clause of the Fourteenth Amendment, a state is authorized to exercise personal jurisdiction over a defendant who is served with a summons while the defendant is voluntarily inside the state. *Burnham v. Superior Court*, 495 U.S. 604 (1990). That is true even if service of the summons is the only connection between the state and the plaintiff, the defendant, or the plaintiff's claim. It is true where the defendant does not reside in the state, is only traveling through the state, and has no connection to the state except for the trip during which the defendant was served. *Id.* It is also true where none of the events or circumstances alleged in the plaintiff's complaint happened in the state. *Id.*

The defendant in *Burnham* was a New Jersey resident who had traveled on business to southern California and then to northern California to visit his children. The plaintiff was the defendant's wife, who had him served in a divorce action while he was in northern California. Four justices of the Supreme Court joined in an opinion by Justice Scalia and held that, under precedent going back two centuries, a state has "the power to hale before its courts any individual who could be found within its borders." *Id.* at 610. Another four justices joined in an opinion by Justice Brennan and held that the defendant's presence in the state at the time of service was a purposeful availment that satisfies the minimum contacts requirements of *International Shoe*, 326 U.S. 310 (1945). The ninth justice (Stevens) concurred separately on the ground that both rationales are correct. Because there was no majority opinion, it is not settled which rationale supports the rule, although the rule had the unanimous support of all nine justices.

Regardless of the rationale, the effect here is that service on Keating in the Little Rock airport created personal jurisdiction in Arkansas. Keating was present in Arkansas at the moment of service. The process server's affidavit is evidence of that, and Keating concedes it. Moreover, she does not claim that she did not know she was in Arkansas or that she was in the state under duress. She bought her airline ticket knowing she would have to change planes in Little Rock, and her presence was therefore voluntary.

Keating argues, however, that she was not in Arkansas long enough to be subject to the state's jurisdiction, even if she was served in Arkansas. She points out that the *Burnham* defendant had traveled to California to conduct business there and visit his children, spending nights in hotels and purposely availing himself of the benefits of the state. Keating contends that this case is distinguishable from *Burnham* because her destination was Louisiana rather than Arkansas, and because she was on the ground in Arkansas for less than an hour and only for the purpose of getting to Louisiana.

This case cannot be distinguished from *Burnham*. The Scalia opinion stressed that the state's jurisdiction extends to any visitor, "no matter how fleeting his visit."

Id. at 610. And the Brennan rationale would treat using the Little Rock airport for a connecting flight as purposeful availment supporting minimum contacts because Keating gained a benefit from Arkansas. Any other result would represent unsupportable policy in an era of modern travel. There is no practical way to craft a rule that would clearly distinguish between a presence in the state that is too short for jurisdiction and a presence that is long enough, which is why the Supreme Court held in *Burnham* that any presence is enough, if the defendant is served while present.

Moreover, Keating's presence in Arkansas was not limited to her 45 minutes inside the airport. She could have been validly served while either of the airplanes on which she flew was on the tarmac or even in the air over Arkansas. Service of process on a passenger in an airplane that flew over Arkansas *but never landed in the state* has been sustained because at the moment of service the passenger was inside Arkansas, even though the passenger was not on the ground. *Grace v. MacArthur*, 170 F. Supp. 442 (E.D. Ark. 1959). The *Grace* court reasoned that there is no real difference between a passenger on an airplane that passes through Arkansas airspace and a passenger who travels through the state by train or bus without disembarking. *Id.* at 447.

Thus, Arkansas has jurisdiction over Keating, and her motion to dismiss should be denied.

Exercise II.   *What You See or What U See*

Here are the facts in *Cottrill v. Spears,* 87 Fed. Appx. 803, 804 (3d Cir. 2004):

[In 1995] Michael Cottrill and Lawrence Wnukowski met with . . . Britney Spears and her then-agent William Kahn. Kahn urged Cottrill and Wnukowski to write songs for Spears. . . .

On or about August 17, 1999, [four Swedish musicians] began working on a song originally entitled *Latin Song*, written for Zomba Recording Corporation's artist Spears. On October 28, 1999, Spears flew to Stockholm, Sweden to record songs for her upcoming album *Ooops! . . . I Did It Again*. While in Stockholm, Spears recorded the lyrics for *Latin Song*, which was retitled *What U See (Is What U Get)*. Spears departed Sweden on November 8, 1999. She never re-recorded the vocals for *What U See* after that date. The song continued to be mixed until May 2000, when it was copyrighted and released.

Wnukowski and Cottrill registered [their song *What You See Is What You Get*] with the United States Copyright Office on December 1, 1999. [*What You See* is Cottrill and Wnukoski's song title. *What U See* is the title on Spears's album.] Wnukowski and Cottrill did not distribute copies of the song until after it was copyrighted. Once copyrighted, Cottrill and Wnukowski forwarded the song to Kahn. Cottrill claims that he hoped Kahn would forward the materials to Steven Lunt, an employee of Zomba Records, then acting as Spears' agent. Kahn, however, denied ever having given the song to anyone after he received it from Cottrill and Wnukowski. He explained that he did not think it was a "good song." . . .

Below are two versions — Version A and Version B — of the court's reasoning. In each version, identify the court's conclusion, the primary rule the court relies on, rule proof and explanation, and rule application. Is each component in the best place? Is anything missing from either version? Which version does a better job of meeting your needs as a reader? Why?

Version A

Cottrill and Wnukowski bring this copyright infringement suit, claiming that the defendants infringed upon their song *What You See Is What You Get*. The District Court granted summary judgment for the defendants. The plaintiffs appeal from that decision.

The plaintiffs argue that, although they did not copyright their song *What You See* until after Spears had already recorded her vocals to the allegedly infringing song *What U See*, they adduced evidence to show that the defendants' access to the plaintiffs' song was meaningful. The plaintiffs point to the declaration of George Hajioannou, a musical technician, that it was possible to change the "instrumental and vocal track" of a piece of music using the software employed by the defendants to mix *What U See*. The plaintiffs reason that, because a change was possible, they are entitled to an inference that the defendants did change their song; *What U See*, after having access to *What You See*. We disagree. "Access must be more than a bare possibility and may not be inferred through speculation or conjecture." *Gaste*, 863 F.2d at 1066. By arguing no more than what is technically possible, the plaintiffs engage in speculation that the defendants altered *What U See* after December 1999. Speculation is no substitute for the kind of circumstantial evidence needed to preclude the entry of summary judgment.

Copying may be proved circumstantially by demonstrating (1) that the defendant had access to the allegedly infringed copyrighted work, and (2) that the allegedly infringing work is substantially similar to the copyrighted work. *Dam Things From Denmark v. Russ Berrie and Co., Inc.*, 290 F.3d 548, 561 (3d Cir. 2002).

To meet the first prong of *Dam Things*, the plaintiffs are not required to prove by direct evidence that the defendants gained access to the plaintiffs' work. Instead, access can be inferred by indirect evidence. *Boisson v. Banian, Ltd.*, 273 F.3d 262, 269 (2d Cir. 2001). The indirect evidence must simply show that there is a "reasonable possibility of access." *Gaste v. Kaiserman*, 863 F.2d 1061, 1066 (2d Cir. 1988). Thus, where there is a "relationship linking the intermediary and the alleged copier," access may be inferred. *Moore v. Columbia Pictures Indus., Inc.*, 972 F.2d 939, 942 (8th Cir. 1992).

Because the plaintiffs cannot show that the defendants had access to *What You See* prior to completing *What U See*, the District Court's grant of summary judgment was proper. We therefore affirm the District Court's grant of summary judgment in favor of the defendants.

Regardless of the means by which the plaintiffs allege that the defendants gained access to the infringed work, that access must be meaningful. The plaintiffs must show that the defendants had an "opportunity to view or to copy his work." *Moore*, 972 F.2d at 942. If the only opportunity to view the plaintiffs' work occurs after the defendants have completed their own work, then there can be no opportunity to copy the work, and thus no access for purposes of copyright law. See *Selle v. Gibb*, 741 F.2d 896, 901 (7th Cir. 1984). Here, Cottrill and Wnukowski failed to show that the defendants had meaningful access to the plaintiffs' song prior to the defendants recording the allegedly infringing song, *What U See.*

Version B

Cottrill and Wnukowski bring this copyright infringement suit, claiming that the defendants infringed upon their song *What You See Is What You Get.* The District Court granted summary judgment for the defendants. The plaintiffs appeal from that decision. We affirm because the plaintiffs have not shown that the defendants had meaningful access to *What You See.*

Copying may be proved circumstantially by demonstrating (1) that the defendant had access to the allegedly infringed copyrighted work, and (2) that the allegedly infringing work is substantially similar to the copyrighted work. *Dam Things From Denmark v. Russ Berrie and Co., Inc.*, 290 F.3d 548, 561 (3d Cir. 2002). The defendants concede that the songs are substantially similar. Thus, the only issue before us is whether the defendants had access to *What You See.*

To meet the first prong of *Dam Things* (the only one at issue here), the plaintiffs are not required to prove by direct evidence that the defendants gained access to the plaintiffs' work. Instead, access can be inferred by indirect evidence. *Boisson v. Banian, Ltd.*, 273 F.3d 262, 269 (2d Cir. 2001). The indirect evidence must simply show that there is a "reasonable possibility of access." *Gaste v. Kaiserman*, 863 F.2d 1061, 1066 (2d Cir. 1988). Thus, where there is a "relationship linking the intermediary and the alleged copier," access may be inferred. *Moore v. Columbia Pictures Indus., Inc.*, 972 F.2d 939, 942 (8th Cir. 1992).

Regardless of the means by which the plaintiffs allege that the defendants gained access to the infringed work, that access must be meaningful. The plaintiffs must show that the defendants had an "opportunity to view or to copy his work." *Moore*, 972 F.2d at 942. If the only opportunity to view the plaintiffs' work occurs after the defendants have completed their own work, then there can be no opportunity to copy the work, and thus no access for purposes of copyright law. See *Selle v. Gibb*, 741 F.2d 896, 901 (7th Cir. 1984). Here, Cottrill and Wnukowski failed to show that the defendants had meaningful access to the plaintiffs' song prior to the defendants recording the allegedly infringing song, *What U See.*

The plaintiffs argue that, although they did not copyright their song *What You See* until after Spears had already recorded her vocals to the allegedly infringing song *What U See*, they adduced evidence to show that the defendants' access to the plaintiffs' song was meaningful. The plaintiffs point to the declaration of George Hajioannou, a musical technician, that it was possible to change the "instrumental and vocal track" of a piece of music using the software employed by the defendants to mix *What U See*. The plaintiffs reason that, because a change was possible, they are entitled to an inference that the defendants did change their song, *What U See*, after having access to *What You See*. We disagree. "Access must be more than a bare possibility and may not be inferred through speculation or conjecture." *Gaste*, 863 F.2d at 1066.

By arguing no more than what is technically possible, the plaintiffs engage in speculation that the defendants altered *What U See* after December 1999. Speculation is no substitute for the kind of circumstantial evidence needed to preclude the entry of summary judgment.

Because the plaintiffs cannot show that the defendants had access to *What You See* prior to completing *What U See*, the District Court's grant of summary judgment was proper. We therefore affirm the District Court's grant of summary judgment in favor of the defendants.

11 Varying the Depth of Rule Proof and Rule Application

§11.1 Introduction

Chapter 10 explained a paradigm for structuring proof of a conclusion of law. This chapter explains how to vary two parts of that paradigm — rule proof and rule application — in terms of depth.

Depending on the situation, rule proof and rule application can be very short, very long, or somewhere in between. In one instance, rule proof might need only a sentence, while rule application might require three pages. In another instance, the reverse might be true. Or each of them might be four or five pages long — or four or five sentences long. How can you tell how much depth is needed? Ask yourself three questions:

First, how much explanation will convince the reader that the conclusion is correct? That depends on the reader's level of skepticism, which in turn depends on how important the issue is to the decision the reader must make, and on how complicated the reader will think the issue to be.

Second, how much explanation will prevent the reader from studying independently the authorities you rely on? The second question poses what might be called the need-to-read test: you have not explained enough if your reader would find it hard to agree with you without actually studying the authorities you have cited. A reader's need to go to the books is predicated on the context. A reader is more likely to feel that need with a critical, difficult, or obscure point than with a simple, peripheral, or routine one. A reader's need to know more is particularly great for authority that is the only support or the central basis for your conclusion.

Third, how much explanation would tell the reader those things needed to make an informed decision? Put another way, if the reader were to go to the books, would the reader be startled to find the things you have left out? Part of your job *is* to leave things out. The reader is counting on you to cut out the things that do not matter. But do not leave out so much that the reader is deprived of some of the information on which a decision would have to be based.

Do not explore an issue in more depth than a reader would need. Remember that the reader is a busy person, almost as intolerant of too much explanation as of too little. If you include much detail about peripheral issues or about routine propositions with which the reader will easily agree, the reader feels stuck in quicksand.

Be careful. Most students underestimate the skepticism of readers. If you have no idea how much to explain, err on the side of making a more complete explanation until you have gained a better sense of what must be fully proven and where proof can be at least partially implied.

Rule proof and rule application can each be explored in a way that is *conclusory*, *substantiating*, or *comprehensive*. The rest of this chapter explains how.

§11.2   Conclusory Explanations

A conclusory explanation does no more than allude to some basis for the deduction made by the writer. Here is an example:

> Medwick is contractually bound to ExitRow.com's Terms and Conditions because he programmed his bot to click on the "I Agree" button on ExitRow.com's website. A contract is formed by an objective manifestation of agreement, even if a party does not read the contract before agreeing to it. *Marin Storage & Trucking, Inc. v. Benco Contracting & Eng'g, Inc.*, 107 Cal. Rptr. 2d 645, 651 (Ct. App. 2001). Programming a bot to click on an "I Agree" button is analogous to signing a contract without reading it.[1]

Here the rule is clearly set out, but the only proof of it is a citation to a decision, without any explanation of the court's reasoning or of the facts

---

§11.2   1. In this chapter's examples, the citations are in the format used in office memoranda and therefore include only an unofficial West reporter. A document submitted to a California state court, however, would need a parallel cite to an official California reporter as well. See ALWD Citation Manual rules 12.4 and 12.6(e) and Bluebook B5.1.3 and rules 10.3.1 and 10.4. (Chapter 20 explains citation rules in detail.) Thus, in a motion memo or appellate brief submitted to a California court, the citation in this example would change to *Marin Storage & Trucking, Inc. v. Benco Contracting & Eng'g, Inc.*, 89 Cal. App. 4th 1042, 1049, 107 Cal. Rptr. 2d 645, 651 (2001). (The official reporter is Cal. App. 4th. The unofficial West reporter is Cal. Rptr. 2d.) Because this chapter's examples are all written as though they were in an office memo, the official reporter is omitted from them.

there adjudicated. The conclusion is also plainly stated, but the only rule application is an allusion to a single fact: Medwick programmed his bot to click on the "I Agree" button on ExitRow.com's website. In addition, there are no counter-analyses and no discussion of policy.

A conclusory explanation is appropriate only where the reader will easily agree with you, or where the point is not important to your analysis. In those situations, a detailed analysis would seem tedious to the reader. Elsewhere, however, a conclusory explanation would deprive the reader of information essential to the decision the reader must make. For example, from the example above, a supervising lawyer could not decide how to advise Medwick. At the very least, the lawyer would want to know the facts of *Marin Storage & Trucking,* how they are analogous to website click-through agreements, the court's reasoning in *Marin,* and whether any cases decide whether bots can create contracts.

§11.3   Substantiating Explanations

A substantiating explanation goes more deeply into the writer's reasoning but still does not state the analysis completely:

> Medwick is contractually bound to ExitRow.com's Terms and Conditions. A contract is formed by an objective manifestation of agreement, even if a party does not read the contract before agreeing to it. *Marin Storage & Trucking, Inc. v. Benco Contracting & Eng'g, Inc.*, 107 Cal. Rptr. 2d 645, 651 (Ct. App. 2001). In *Marin,* a party was bound when its employees signed contractual documents without reading them. In website click-through contracting, a person agrees to a website's terms and conditions if he programs a bot to do something that he knows the website will interpret as agreement. *Register.com, Inc. v. Verio, Inc.,* 356 F.3d 393 (2d Cir. 2004). Medwick programmed his bot to click on "I Agree" and "I Accept" buttons automatically wherever the bot found them, which is what the bot did on ExitRow.com's website. That is analogous to signing a contract without reading it.

This passage provides more rule proof and more rule application. But it is not comprehensive.

A substantiating explanation is appropriate where the reader needs more than a conclusory explanation, but where the point being made is not central to your analysis. It is not appropriate where the reader will probably be aggressively skeptical. The substantiating passage above would not, for example, satisfy the lawyer who must make difficult decisions about how to handle Medwick's case.

§11.4   Comprehensive Explanations

A comprehensive explanation includes whatever analyses are necessary to satisfy an aggressive skepticism. Rule proof and rule application can be augmented with further detail about the law and the facts, with added or expanded counter-analyses, and with policy discussions sufficient to give the skeptical reader confidence that the law's goals would be achieved through your conclusion:

Medwick is contractually bound to Exit-Row. com's Terms and Conditions because he programmed his bot to agree to them.	The writer's conclusion.
A contract is formed by an objective manifestation of agreement, even if a party does not read the contract before agreeing to it. *Marin Storage & Trucking, Inc. v. Benco Contracting & Eng'g, Inc.*, 107 Cal. Rptr. 2d 645, 651 (Ct. App. 2001). Marin often supplied construction cranes to Benco at building sites. *Id.* at 649. After each day, Marin's crane operator wrote the number of crane-usage hours on a form and handed it to a Benco employee, who confirmed the hours and signed the form. *Id.* At the top of the form were the words "Work Authorization and Contract," and at the bottom was the sentence "This is a contract which includes all terms and conditions stated on the reverse side." *Id.* There was no evidence that any of the Benco employees who signed the form ever read the reverse side. *Id.* at 649-650. The court held that Benco's employees objectively manifested agreement when they signed a document with words warning that it was contractual. *Id.* at 651. Whether they read the terms of the contract was irrelevant. *Id.*	The main rule. Rule proof begins.
The Restatement takes the same position: "where an offer is contained in a writing either the offeror or the offeree may, without reading the writing, manifest assent to it and bind himself without knowing its terms." Restatement (Second) of Contracts, §23, comment b (1979). The policy behind this rule is to protect a party who relies on the agreement from a later	Policy is introduced.

argument by the other party that no contract exists because the other party had not read or understood it. *Id.* comment e.

Medwick is an experienced programmer and knows that websites often require users to agree contractually to terms and conditions. He could have visited ExitRow.com's website personally and read ExitRow.com's Terms and Conditions. Instead, he programmed his bot to click on "I Agree" and "I Accept" buttons automatically wherever the bot found them, which is analogous to signing a contract without reading it.

No California court has decided a contract case involving a bot. But in a diversity case applying California law the Second Circuit held that a website visitor is not bound to a contract the visitor has not read unless the website informs the visitor that a particular action constitutes agreement to that contract and the website allows the visitor to read the contract before agreeing to it. *Specht v. Netscape Communications Corp.*, 306 F.3d 17 (2d Cir. 2002). Netscape claimed that the plaintiffs had agreed to all of its contract by downloading Netscape's software. *Id.* at 23. Although the website gave notice of some contract terms, a visitor would have had to search the site exhaustively to discover others, including the ones at issue in the lawsuit. *Id.* at 23-24. The Second Circuit held that the plaintiffs were not bound by the additional terms because "a reasonably prudent Internet user in circumstances such as these would not have known or learned of [their] existence." *Id.* at 20.

But in a later diversity case also applying California law, the Second Circuit held that a person agrees to a website's terms and conditions if he programs a bot to do something that he knows the website will interpret as agreement. *Register.com, Inc. v. Verio, Inc.*, 356 F.3d 393 (2d Cir. 2004). Verio programmed its bot to visit Register.com's website several times a day and collect web addresses, to which Verio then sent marketing solicitations. *Id.* at 396-397.

Rule application begins.

A counter-analysis begins.

To show why *Specht* does not control, the writer explains the most analogous case.

Register.com's website contained this notice: "By submitting a . . . query, you agree
that . . . under no circumstances will you
use this data to . . . support the transmission
of mass unsolicited, commercial advertising
or solicitation via email." *Id.* at 397. The
court held that because Verio's bot had
been programmed to collect web addresses
despite the notice, Verio was contractually
obligated not to use them for email marketing. The court distinguished its earlier decision in *Sprecht* on the grounds that in that
case Netscape had designed its website so
that visitors would not have known they
were agreeing to additional terms. *Id.* at 402.

    Register.com is the only case that applies
California contract law to bots. Like Verio,
Medwick programmed his bot to behave in a
way that a website would interpret as agreement to the site's terms and conditions. He
thus agreed to and is bound by those terms
and conditions.

A wrap-up restating the
conclusion.

§11.5   Cryptic Explanations

    Beginning students sometimes write explanations so cryptic as to be less
than conclusory. The writer of a passage like the following has tried to put
too much into a small bottle:

> Medwick is contractually bound to ExitRow.com's Terms and Condi-
> tions. *Marin Storage & Trucking, Inc. v. Benco Contracting & Eng'g,
> Inc.*, 107 Cal. Rptr. 2d 645, 651 (Ct. App. 2001).

A cryptic explanation is never enough — even in a situation where a conclusory explanation would suffice — because a cryptic explanation omits
any statement of the rule on which the conclusion is to be based.

Exercise.   Punitive Damages and Bedbugs

    This Exercise is divided into Exercise A and Exercise B, below. To do either
exercise, you will need the facts in *Matthias v. Accor Economy Lodging*, 347
F.3d 672 (7th Cir. 2003). Here they are, in the court's words:

>   . . . The plaintiffs . . . were guests [in the defendant's Motel 6] and
> were bitten by bedbugs, which are making a comeback in the U.S. as

a consequence of more conservative use of pesticides. . . . The jury . . . awarded each plaintiff $186,000 in punitive damages though only $5,000 in compensatory damages. . . .

. . . In 1998, EcoLab, the extermination service that the motel used, discovered bedbugs in several rooms in the motel and recommended that it be hired to spray every room, for which it would charge the motel only $500; the motel refused. . . . By the spring of 2000, the motel's manager "started noticing that there were refunds being given by my desk clerks and reports coming back from the guests that there were ticks in the rooms and bugs in the rooms that were biting." She looked in some of the rooms and discovered bedbugs. . . .

Further incidents of guests being bitten by insects and demanding and receiving refunds led the manager to recommend to her superior in the company that the motel be closed while every room was sprayed, but this was refused. . . .

. . . By July, the motel's management was acknowledging to EcoLab that there was a "major problem with bed bugs" and that all that was being done about it was "chasing them from room to room." . . . Rooms that the motel had placed on "Do not rent, bugs in room" status nevertheless were rented.

It was in November that the plaintiffs checked into the motel. They were given Room 504, even though the motel had classified the room as "DO NOT RENT UNTIL TREATED," and it had not been treated. . . .

Although bedbug bites are not as serious as the bites of some other insects, they are painful and unsightly. Motel 6 could not have rented any rooms at the prices it charged had it informed guests that the risk of being bitten by bedbugs was appreciable. . . .

Exercise A: Below is the court's explanation for its conclusion that Motel 6 is liable for an intentional tort. Is the court's explanation conclusory, substantiating, comprehensive, or cryptic? Did the court choose an appropriate level of explanation? (Should it have explained less or more or neither?) To answer these questions, you need to know why the court reached this conclusion. A plaintiff who has proved that a defendant has committed an intentional tort, such as fraud or battery, is eligible for punitive damages. In this appeal, the defendant raised two punitive damages issues. The first is this one (was the plaintiff eligible for punitive damages?). The second, which you will reach in Exercise B, is whether the trial court's punitive damage award was too large.

[Motel 6's] failure either to warn guests or to take effective measures to eliminate the bedbugs amounted to fraud and probably to battery as well (compare *Campbell Iv. A.C. Equipment Services Corp.*, 242 Ill. App. 3d 707, 610 N.E.2d 745, 748-49, 182 Ill. Dec. 876 (Ill. App. 1993); see Restatement (Second) of Torts, supra, § 18, comment c and e), as in the famous case of *Garratt v. Dailey*, 46 Wn.2d 197, 279 P.2d 1091, 1093 — 94 (1955), appeal after remand, 49 Wn.2d 499, 304 P.2d 681 (Wash. 1956), which held that the defendant would be guilty of battery if he knew with substantial certainty that when he moved a chair the plaintiff would try to sit down where the chair had been and would land on the floor instead. See also *Massachusetts v. Stratton*, 114 Mass. 303 (Mass. 1873). There was, in short, sufficient evidence of "willful and wanton conduct" within the meaning that the Illinois courts assign to the term to permit an award of punitive damages in this case.

Exercise B: Below is the court's explanation for its conclusion that the trial court did not award excessive punitive damages. Is the court's explanation conclusory, substantiating, comprehensive, or cryptic? Did the court choose an appropriate level of explanation? (Should it have explained less or more or neither?)

> . . . In arguing that $20,000 was the maximum amount of punitive damages that a jury could constitutionally have awarded each plaintiff, the defendant points to the U.S. Supreme Court's recent statement that "few awards [of punitive damages] exceeding a single-digit ratio between punitive and compensatory damages, to a significant degree, will satisfy due process." *State Farm Mutual Automobile Ins. Co. v. Campbell*, 538 U.S. 408 (2003). The Court went on to suggest that "four times the amount of compensatory damages might be close to the line of constitutional impropriety." *Id.* . . . Hence the defendant's proposed ceiling in this case of $20,000, four times the compensatory damages awarded to each plaintiff. The ratio of punitive to compensatory damages determined by the jury was, in contrast, 37.2 to 1.
>
> The Supreme Court did not, however, lay down a 4-to-1 or single-digit-ratio rule—it said merely that "there is a presumption against an award that has a 145-to-1 ratio," . . . and it would be unreasonable to do so. We must consider why punitive damages are awarded and why the Court has decided that due process requires that such awards be limited. The second question is easier to answer than the first. The term "punitive damages" implies punishment, and a standard principle of penal theory is that "the punishment should fit the crime" in the sense of being proportional to the wrongfulness of the defendant's action, though the principle is modified when the probability of detection is very low (a familiar example is the heavy fines for littering) or the crime is potentially lucrative (as in the case of trafficking in illegal drugs). Hence, with these qualifications, which in fact will figure in our analysis of this case, punitive damages should be proportional to the wrongfulness of the defendant's actions. . . .
>
> England's common law courts first confirmed their authority to award punitive damages in the eighteenth century, see Dorsey D. Ellis, Jr., *Fairness and Efficiency in the Law of Punitive Damages*, 56 S. Cal. L. Rev. 1, 12-20 (1982), at a time when the institutional structure of criminal law enforcement was primitive and it made sense to leave certain minor crimes to be dealt with by the civil law. And still today one function of punitive-damages awards is to relieve the pressures on an overloaded system of criminal justice by providing a civil alternative to criminal

prosecution of minor crimes. An example is deliberately spitting in a person's face, a criminal assault but because minor readily deterrable by the levying of what amounts to a civil fine through a suit for damages for the tort of battery. Compensatory damages would not do the trick in such a case, and this for three reasons: because they are difficult to determine in the case of acts that inflict largely dignatory harms; because in the spitting case they would be too slight to give the victim an incentive to sue, and he might decide instead to respond with violence — and an age-old purpose of the law of torts is to provide a substitute for violent retaliation against wrongful injury — and because to limit the plaintiff to compensatory damages would enable the defendant to commit the offensive act with impunity provided that he was willing to pay, and again there would be a danger that his act would incite a breach of the peace by his victim.

When punitive damages are sought for billion-dollar oil spills and other huge economic injuries, the considerations that we have just canvassed fade. As the Court emphasized in *Campbell*, the fact that the plaintiffs in that case had been awarded very substantial compensatory damages — $1 million for a dispute over insurance coverage — greatly reduced the need for giving them a huge award of punitive damages ($145 million) as well in order to provide an effective remedy. Our case is closer to the spitting case. The defendant's behavior was outrageous but the compensable harm done was slight and at the same time difficult to quantify because a large element of it was emotional. And the defendant may well have profited from its misconduct because by concealing the infestation it was able to keep renting rooms. Refunds were frequent but may have cost less than the cost of closing the hotel for a thorough fumigation. The hotel's attempt to pass off the bedbugs as ticks, which some guests might ignorantly have thought less unhealthful, may have postponed the instituting of litigation to rectify the hotel's misconduct. The award of punitive damages in this case thus serves the additional purpose of limiting the defendant's ability to profit from its fraud by escaping detection and (private) prosecution. If a tortfeasor is "caught" only half the time he commits torts, then when he is caught he should be punished twice as heavily in order to make up for the times he gets away. . . .

All things considered, we cannot say that the award of punitive damages was excessive. . . . The judicial function is to police a range, not a point. . . .

Combining Proofs of Separate Conclusions of Law

§12.1 Introduction

If you reach several conclusions or sub-conclusions, the reader will need a separately structured proof for each one. You can combine separately structured proofs for several conclusions or sub-conclusions into a single unified presentation.

You will need to do this in four situations: where more than one element of a rule is in dispute (see §12.2); where more than one claim or defense is at issue (§12.3); where there are alternative ways of proving a single conclusion (§12.4); or where there are other separate but related issues (§12.5).

§12.2 How to Organize Where More Than One Element Is at Issue

If you must resolve all the elements of a rule, you will have an ultimate conclusion for the rule as a whole, together with a sub-conclusion for each element:

Ultimate Conclusion on the Ultimate Issue	"The client has a cause of action for negligence because Bevens injured the client by driving while talking on a hand-held cell phone."

**Sub-
Conclusions
on Sub-Issues**

Element #1: "As a driver, Bevens owed a duty of
care to others on the road, including
the client."

Element #2: "Bevens breached that duty by
talking on a hand-held cell phone
while driving."

Element #3: "The client suffered injuries in an
auto accident."

Element #4: "The accident and the injuries were
proximately caused by Bevens's
breach of the duty of care."

If this analysis were to be written out, the opening or *umbrella* passage
would state the conclusion ("The client has a cause of action for negligence") and the essence of the reason ("because Bevens injured the client
by driving while talking on a hand-held cell phone"). The opening paragraph
would also recite the *rule* on which it is based (the elements of negligence).
If the rule is settled law, it might be proved in the opening paragraph with
little more than a citation to authority. Otherwise, *rule proof* would supply
whatever else is needed to show that the underlying rule is law (and perhaps
to show generally how the rule is expected to work, if that would help).

Then would follow separate, paradigm-structured discussions for the elements. Each element is a sub-issue for which you have a sub-conclusion
(shown above). Each element would have to be defined through a rule that
provides a definition (*a declaratory or definitional rule*); the definition
would have to be proved through authority (*rule proof*); and the facts
would have to be analyzed in light of the definition (*rule application*).

The umbrella passage would be a single paragraph in a simple situation and
a few paragraphs in a complicated one (for example, if the underlying rule is
hard to prove). The umbrella passage would at first seem to be an incomplete
paradigm structure because it would *not include rule application and definitions of the elements.* But this paragraph or these paragraphs actually function
as an umbrella paradigm structure that covers, organizes, and incorporates
the subordinate, structured proofs of each of the elements. (For illustrations,
see pages 80-81 or the Discussion in the office memo in Appendix C.)

The umbrella passage also sets out a road map for what follows. It at least
implies to the reader what issues you will consider, their relative importance
or unimportance, and sometimes the order in which you will consider them.

After the umbrella passage, the most dispositive issues or sub-issues
usually—but not always—should be addressed first. Here, if you were to
determine that the client has no cause of action because talking on a hand-
held cell phone did not proximately cause the accident, you could analyze
the fourth element (proximate cause) before you analyze the others. The
fourth element would be the most important one because it would resolve
the ultimate issue (whether the client has a cause of action).

If you believe, however, that *all* the elements can be proven, you could
instead analyze them in the order in which they appear in the rule. That

might be easier for the reader to follow if no element takes vastly more space than another to explain. But the situation might be different if one element were to consume, for example, three-quarters of the Discussion. There, the reader might be able to follow the analysis more easily if you were to dispose of the other elements first to set up the context.

You might be tempted to focus on one element, conclude that it is not satisfied in the facts, and then ignore the other elements as moot on the theory that the one you have analyzed disposes of the whole controversy. That will not work because it might turn out that you are wrong about the element you believe to be dispositive. Here, for example, you cannot ignore the other elements of negligence just because you believe that the fourth element (proximate cause) is not satisfied. If you turn out to be wrong, the reader of predictive writing is entitled to know what will happen with the other elements.

How do you know when you have found a rule defining an element? Sometimes a court (or a statute) simply tells you what an element means ("Proximate cause is . . . "). At other times, the court does not define the element; it just identifies the facts it considered important and then announces that the element has or has not been satisfied. There, you will need to formulate the rule yourself, using the process explained in §3.2.

(The next three paragraphs discuss difficult material. They will not help you write your first office memo. But read them carefully later when you review this chapter while writing a document to be submitted to a court, such as a motion memo or appellate brief.)

All of this can become more complicated where a procedural rule interacts with a substantive rule. Substantive rules create rights and liabilities from events that occur in everyday life. You have been studying or will soon study substantive rules in the courses on Contracts, Torts, Property, and Criminal Law. Procedural tests govern how lawyers work in litigation and how judges and juries make decisions. You are studying some procedural rules in Civil Procedure and will study others later in Evidence and Criminal Procedure. The two most frequent ways in which procedural and substantive rules interact are where the application of a substantive rule is governed by a procedural test and where a procedural test incorporates a substantive rule.

Where the application of a substantive rule is governed by a procedural test: When a procedural test and a substantive test are used together, the procedural test tells us how to apply the substantive test to the facts. An example happens in every criminal case: the defendant is guilty only if the prosecution proves each element of the crime beyond a reasonable doubt. The umbrella is the rule defining the crime, and the sub-issues are the elements of the crime. The procedural rule (requiring proof beyond a reasonable doubt) is not part of this structure. But, inside each issue, you use it to measure whether the substantive element has been satisfied. For example, if the issue is whether the defendant is guilty of common law burglary, the sub-issues are, "Is there proof beyond a reasonable doubt that the defendant *broke* a building?" and "Is there proof beyond a reasonable doubt that the defendant *entered* a building?" and "Is there proof beyond a reasonable doubt that the building was a *dwelling*?" and so on (see §9.1).

Where a procedural test incorporates a substantive rule: For example, in federal courts a party is entitled to summary judgment if (1) there is no genuine issue of material fact and (2) the party is entitled to judgment as a matter of law.[1] The second element incorporates all substantive rules on which a judgment would rest — such as the rule defining the cause of action. These two elements would be separate issues under the umbrella of the test for summary judgment. The elements of the substantive rules would be sub-issues under the second element of the test for summary judgment ("entitled to judgment as a matter of law"). There would be an umbrella (the second element, covering the elements of the substantive tests) within an umbrella (the procedural test as a whole). This happens *only* where a procedural rule incorporates a substantive test, most often with a summary judgment or a preliminary injunction. An example appears in Appendix F.

§12.3 How to Organize Where More Than One Claim or Defense Is at Issue

Suppose your supervising attorney wants to know whether the client will be awarded damages in a tort case. You need to figure out whether the client has a cause of action (one issue or collection of issues). And you anticipate that the defendant will raise the affirmative defenses of comparative negligence (another issue or collection of issues) and sovereign immunity (yet another). Although this is a more complex situation than the one where several elements of a single rule are in dispute, it is handled in the same way (see §12.2). You build an umbrella paradigm structure, and underneath it you prove the sub-conclusions through separate, subordinate paradigm-structured analyses. The ultimate conclusion might, for example, be that the client will not be awarded damages because, although she has a cause of action (the first sub-conclusion) and was not comparatively negligent (the second sub-conclusion), the claim falls within the defendant's sovereign immunity (the third sub-conclusion). Thus:

Ultimate Conclusion on the Ultimate Issue	The client should be awarded damages.
Sub-Conclusions on Sub-Issues	Sub-Issue #1: The client has a cause of action for negligence.
	Sub-Issue #2: She committed no comparative negligence (an affirmative defense).
	Sub-Issue #3: Sovereign immunity does not prevent recovery here (another affirmative defense).

§12.2   1. F.R. Civ. P. 56. See §26.2.3.

Because negligence has four elements, the first sub-issue could be divided further into separate proofs of each of those four elements.

§12.4 How to Organize Alternative Ways of Proving a Single Conclusion

In the first year of law school, this typically occurs in a moot court assignment where the jurisdiction has no rule on point, where it could choose between or among competing rules, and where you could argue that either of two or more competing rules will—independently of one another—justify the conclusion. It, too, is handled through the umbrella paradigm structure explained in §12.2:

Ultimate Conclusion on the Ultimate Issue	The judgment below should be reversed.
Sub-Conclusions on Sub-Issues	Sub-Issue #1: This court should adopt rule X. Sub-Issue #2: Under rule X, the judgment should be reversed. Sub-Issue #3: Even under rule Y (the competing rule), the judgment should be reversed.

§12.5 How to Organize Where There Are Other Separate but Related Issues

There are still other ways in which separate issues might need to be resolved to support a single conclusion. Suppose someone sues your client, and your supervising attorney wants to know whether that lawsuit can be dismissed on forum selection grounds (on grounds that it was brought in the wrong court). You will have to resolve some or all of the following issues: Does this court have subject matter jurisdiction over this kind of case? Does this court have personal jurisdiction over our client? Is this court the right venue for this lawsuit?

If your conclusion is that the lawsuit was brought in the right court, you will, in fact, have to show that the court has subject matter and personal jurisdiction and that venue is proper. To do that, you will use the same umbrella paradigm structure explained in §12.2:

Ultimate Conclusion on the Ultimate Issue	This lawsuit is not dismissible on forum selection grounds.

Sub-Conclusions on Sub-Issues

Sub-Issue #1:   This court has subject matter jurisdiction.

Sub-Issue #2:   This court has personal jurisdiction over our client.

Sub-Issue #3:   Venue is proper in this court.

§12.6   How to Start Working with Multi-Issue Situations

All of these different ways to organize can seem confusing when you first think about them. But with some practice, they will become second nature. Many students do feel confused at this point, but within a few weeks, they begin to gain confidence in organizing this way. And within a year or two, most students instinctively think in structured proofs. This section provides some suggestions for getting to that point.

While researching and planning your writing, ask yourself how many issues you have. If you have a hard time identifying issues, ask yourself how many conclusions of law a court would need to make to rule in your favor. Then ask how many conclusions of law a court would need to make to rule in the other side's favor. Now consolidate those two lists to produce a list of issues. When you had two lists (before consolidating them), many issues will have been listed twice because they were flip sides of each other. When you consolidate, you will often merge two issues into one. The advantage of making two lists is that it helps you avoid overlooking an issue. When you look at only your side of the case, you sometimes miss an issue that the other side will raise.

Now, figure out what kind of issues you have. Is an issue part of the cause of action, part of a defense, part of a procedural requirement, or something else? This will help you figure out which of the structures described in §§12.2 through 12.5 to use.

Choose one of the multi-issue structures explained in this chapter, and adapt it to your case. Start a document on your computer and type a list of every conclusion of law you will make in your memorandum or brief, like the lists in §§12.2 through 12.5. Organize the conclusions logically — for example, elements of a cause of action first, then defenses. Treat this as the beginning of an outline. In the next chapter, §13.1 explains how to complete this outline and turn it into a memo or brief.

Use roadmap paragraphs to explain your umbrella paradigm to the reader. A roadmap paragraph lists the conclusions you will reach. It maps out your discussion so the reader knows what to expect. If the document is a long one (such as an appellate brief), the roadmap paragraph tells the reader where to find the analysis supporting each conclusion. In a shorter document, your headings inside the document will do that. In a roadmap paragraph, you state your ultimate conclusion ("The client should be awarded damages," for example) and then state the sub-conclusions that support that ultimate conclusion. If some elements of a test are at issue and others are not, the roadmap paragraph is the place to make that clear. Most judges say that a well-written roadmap paragraph is very important or essential in helping them understand what you are trying to say.[1] Here is a typical roadmap paragraph, which you might use to introduce the discussion outlined in §12.3:

> The plaintiff should be awarded damages. The evidence supports all four of the elements of negligence. The defendant owed a duty to the plaintiff to keep the loading dock clear and breached that duty by leaving explosive materials on the loading dock overnight. The plaintiff's injury, destruction of the warehouse, is uncontested. It was proximately caused by the breach when the materials exploded. Although the defendant pleaded the defense of comparative negligence, there is no evidence to support it. And sovereign immunity has been waived by § 419 of the Highways Code.

Use headings to show your reader where your analysis of each issue begins. Lawyers and judges will not read your work from beginning to end. They will read parts of it at a time, and headings help them find the parts they need. If you are writing a predictive memo, look at the way headings are used in Appendix C. If you are writing a persuasive memo or a brief, you will write point headings, which are explained in Chapter 28.

Exercise. After the Night in the Bar

In *Vincent v. Williams*, 279 Ill. App. 3d 1, 664 N.E.2d 650, 652 (1st Dist. 1996), the plaintiff sought what the court called "his day in court after a tough night in a Chicago bar." Vincent claimed that Jayson Williams and Charles Barkley (professional basketball players) "falsely accused Vincent of threatening Williams with a knife. Vincent was arrested and charged with aggravated assault. The [criminal]] case was stricken on leave to reinstate when Williams and Barkley failed to appear in court." *Id.* Vincent then sued Williams and Barkley for malicious prosecution, false imprisonment, and defamation. The trial court granted Williams and Barkley's motions to dismiss these claims. Vincent appealed that decision. The Illinois Appellate Court's opinion adjudicating that appeal appears below.

How many separately structured proofs of a conclusion of law are in the Appellate Court's opinion? In which of them is one or more elements of the claim at issue? (In each instance, how many elements of the claim are at issue?) In which structured proofs is an affirmative defense at issue? Make a diagram, like the ones earlier in this chapter, to show what the court did. Consider each structured proof. Are you told everything you need to know in the sequence in which you need to know it while you are reading? Could the opinion, or any part of it, have been organized better?

---

§12.6   1. Kristen K. Robbins, *The Inside Scoop: What Federal Judges Really Think about the Way Lawyers Write*, 8 J. Leg. Writing Inst. 257, 273 (2002).

[I.] Malicious Prosecution

The trial court dismissed the malicious prosecution claim for failure to state a cause of action . . . . To state a cause of action for malicious prosecution, one must allege facts showing: (1) the commencement or continuance of an original or criminal judicial proceeding by the defendant; (2) termination of the prosecution in favor of the plaintiff in a manner indicative of the innocence of the plaintiff; (3) the absence of probable cause for such proceeding; (4) the presence of malice; and, (5) damages resulting to the plaintiff. . . . *Joiner v. Benton Community Bank*, 82 Ill. 2d 40, 411 N.E.2d 229, 44 Ill. Dec. 260 (1980).

Vincent's aggravated assault case was stricken on leave (SOL). This, said the court, was not a disposition in Vincent's favor for the purposes of a malicious prosecution claim.

Now, on appeal, Vincent argues that the trial court's decision "ignores . . . the modern reality" that an SOL is the manner in which cases are disposed of when the prosecution cannot make a case.

Vincent's argument ignores the "long line of cases" that has held, since 1862, that striking a case from the docket with leave to reinstate is not a legal termination in favor of the defendant. See *Khan v. American Airlines*, 266 Ill. App. 3d 726, 732, 639 N.E.2d 210, 203 Ill. Dec. 171 (1994).

Vincent relies on *Rich v. Baldwin*, 133 Ill. App. 3d 712, 479 N.E.2d 361, 88 Ill. Dec. 748 (1985), as support for his position. In *Rich* the court held that the dismissal of a criminal charge, on defense counsel's motion, for failure to try the accused within the statutory period, constituted a termination in the accused's favor.

But the *Khan* court distinguished *Rich*. When a case is stricken on leave to reinstate, said the court, it is not terminated. *Khan*, 266 Ill. App. 3d at 732. A plaintiff whose case is stricken on leave must obtain a final determination in his favor by bringing a motion for discharge on speedy trial grounds. Failing to do so, the plaintiff failed to meet his burden of proving a favorable final determination. *Khan*, 266 Ill. App. 3d at 733.

We note plaintiff does not contend, nor does the record reflect, that he made a demand for immediate trial when the case against him was dismissed. In the absence of a demand for immediate trial, the statutory period for bringing a criminal charge to trial does not begin to run. 725 ILCS 5/103-5(b) (West 1992); *People v. Garrett*, 136 Ill. 2d 318, 555 N.E.2d 353, 144 Ill. Dec. 234 (1990) . . . .

Public policy favors the exposure of crime, and courts should encourage and protect citizen cooperation by "narrowly circumscribing" the circumstances in which malicious prosecution actions may be brought. *Misselhorn v. Doyle*, 257 Ill. App. 3d 983, 629 N.E.2d 189, 195 Ill. Dec. 881 (1994).

We find that the trial court did not err in dismissing the malicious prosecution claim for failure to state a cause of action.

[II.] False Imprisonment

. . . Vincent alleged that Williams and Barkley conspired together to fabricate a fictitious story about Vincent threatening Williams with a knife. This story, Vincent said, was a cover-up for Williams' unprovoked attack on Vincent. When the police came to the bar to investigate a report of a fight, Williams and Barkley, in furtherance of their plot, informed the police of this fictitious threat. Based upon this information, Vincent said, the police were induced to arrest him. In his complaint, Vincent alleged that, "as a direct and proximate result of the defendants' false and malicious statements, [Vincent] was arrested, charged with aggravated battery, and confined in jail for approximately twelve hours before he was released on bail." . . .

To state a cause of action for false imprisonment, the plaintiff must allege that his personal liberty was unreasonably or unlawfully restrained against his will and that defendant(s) caused or procured the restraint. *Meerbrey v. Marshall Field & Co.*, 189 Ill. App. 3d 1085, 545 N.E.2d 952, 137 Ill. Dec. 191 (1989). An unlawful arrest by an officer caused or procured by a private person is the same as an arrest by the private person. *Dutton v. Roo-Mac, Inc.*, 100 Ill. App. 3d 116, 426 N.E.2d 604, 55 Ill. Dec. 458 (1981); *Mangus v. Cock Robin Ice Cream Co.*, 52 Ill. App. 3d 110, 367 N.E.2d 203, 9 Ill. Dec. 769 (1977). For liability to attach to the private person, however, the arresting officer must have relied solely on the information given to him by the private party when making the arrest. *Dutton v. Roo-Mac, Inc.*, 100 Ill. App. 3d at 119-20.

It is clear to us that Vincent's complaint, on its face, states a cause of action for false imprisonment. Defendants, however, challenge the factual allegation that they caused or procured Vincent's arrest. They argue that the trial court, by taking judicial notice of the police report that had been attached to plaintiff's prior complaint (but later withdrawn), could find that the officer did not arrest Vincent based solely on information given by them. This report indicated that two female witnesses gave the investigating police officers the "same info" given by the defendants.

In support of their argument, defendants rely on *Weimann v. County of Kane*, 150 Ill. App. 3d 962, 502 N.E.2d 373, 104 Ill. Dec. 110 (1986). In *Weimann*, the court held that a reviewing court could take judicial notice of records of proceedings in its own or other courts which contained easily verifiable facts "as an aid in the efficient disposition of litigation." *Weimann*, 150 Ill. App. 3d at 969. The court then took judicial notice that an arrest warrant had been issued against the plaintiff. Because there had been a warrant, the court found that Weimann's complaint for false imprisonment against the county sheriff's office was properly dismissed for failure to state a cause of action.

"Judicial notice may be taken of factual evidence where the facts are capable of immediate and accurate demonstration by resort to easily accessible sources of indisputable accuracy." *In re Marriage of DeBow*, 236 Ill. App. 3d 1038, 602 N.E.2d 984, 177 Ill. Dec. 89 (1992). The police report should not have been judicially noticed in this case.

This police report is not a "source of indisputable accuracy." It is an inadmissible hearsay document of unproved verity. Furthermore, the report was attached to a prior complaint that had been withdrawn by plaintiff. Strictly speaking, the report was not a part of the second amended complaint. It should not have been considered. See *W.P. Iverson & Co. v. Dunham Mfg. Co.*, 18 Ill. App. 2d 404, 425-26, 152 N.E.2d 615 (1958) (an amendment, complete in itself, which does not refer to or adopt a prior pleading, supersedes it, and the original pleading ceases to be a part of the record, being in effect abandoned or withdrawn).

But even if judicial notice of this document were taken, it would not negate Vincent's allegation that defendants caused or procured his arrest. The report merely indicates that two other witnesses gave the police the "same info" given by defendants. The report does not say whether the witnesses' statements were based on direct observation of the incident or exactly what information they corroborated. This hearsay report, vague and general, should not be a substitute for direct, testimonial evidence. Whether the two other witnesses actually saw Vincent assault Williams with the threat of a knife is a matter that may be taken up in other proceedings in this case.

For this reason, the plaintiff's factual allegation that defendants, in conspiracy with one another, falsely and maliciously caused or procured his arrest are sufficient to withstand the section 2-615 motion. The trial court's order dismissing [the false imprisonment claim] is reversed.

[III.] Defamation

[A.] Publication to the police

The trial court did not state on the record its reasons for dismissing [the defamation claim] with regard to the statements made to the police officers. This is probably because the trial court had already dismissed the defamation claim in Vincent's first amended complaint on the basis of absolute immunity.

In the second amended complaint, Vincent made no new allegations with respect to statements made to the police that would take this claim outside the trial court's original ruling that the statements were subject to absolute privilege. On review, we assume that the trial court's ruling on the defamation claim in the second amended complaint was the same as before, i.e., that absolute privilege applied.

It has long been held that statements made to law enforcement officials, for the purpose of instituting legal proceedings, are granted absolute privilege. See *Starnes v. International Harvester Co.*, 184 Ill. App. 3d 199, 204, 539 N.E.2d 1372, 132 Ill. Dec. 566 (1989), and the cases cited in that decision. In *Starnes* the court rejected the argument that when a claim of malice is made, a qualified, rather than an absolute, privilege applies. When absolute privilege attaches, no action for defamation lies, even where malice is alleged. *Weber v. Cueto*, 209 Ill. App. 3d 936, 568 N.E.2d 513, 154 Ill. Dec. 513 (1991).

In this case, the statements that Vincent claims to be defamatory are the statements alleging Vincent's criminal activity, which Williams and Barkley reported to the police during the investigation of the fight. These statements are cloaked with absolute privilege and the trial court properly dismissed the claim.

[B.] Publication to the news media

Vincent's original complaint was filed in July 1992. The defamation count in that complaint sought redress for publication only to Chicago police officers. In January 1994 Vincent filed his second amended complaint in which he alleged, for the first time, that defamatory statements were made by defendants to "members of the news media."

In *Zielinski v. Schmalbeck*, 269 Ill. App. 3d 572, 646 N.E.2d 655, 207 Ill. Dec. 89 (1995), the court noted that actions for slander, libel, or for publication of matter violating the right of privacy must be commenced within one year of the time that the cause of action accrued. 735 ILCS 5/13-201 (West 1992).

Vincent is unable to avoid the operation of the applicable limitations period. He claims on appeal, as he did in the trial court, that the new allegation related back to the original complaint. This argument was specifically rejected by the trial court. In doing so, the trial court correctly held that the decision in *Weber v. Cueto*, 253 Ill. App. 3d 509, 624 N.E.2d 442, 191 Ill. Dec. 593 (1993), is directly on point.

In *Weber*, the court stated that "the controlling factor" to be determined when deciding whether a count relates back is "not whether the amended action seeks the same remedy; rather, the court must determine that the two actions or remedies, even though different, require the same proof." *Weber*, 253 Ill. App. 3d at 516. The court then went on to find that a claim of defamation by publication to the newspapers did not relate back to a claim of defamation to authorities because the two claims did not require the same proof. Publication to the newspapers would not be subject to a defense of privilege, as was the publication to authorities. *Weber*, 253 Ill. App. 3d at 520.

Based on *Weber*, the allegation of publication to the news media could not relate back to the original complaint. The claim, having been filed for the first time in 1994, in the second amended complaint, was not timely. The trial court properly dismissed it on that basis.

Conclusion

We affirm the circuit court order dismissing [the malicious prosecution and defamation claims] of Vincent's complaint as to both Williams and Barkley. The order dismissing [the false imprisonment claim] is reversed and remanded for further proceedings.

13 Working with the Paradigm

§13.1 Using the Paradigm to Outline and to Begin Your First Draft

Think of the paradigm formula for organizing proof of a conclusion of law (from Chapters 10, 11, and 12) as a tool to *help* you organize. It will also keep your material from getting out of control. Here it is again:

To prove a conclusion of law:

1. State your conclusion.

2. State the primary rule that supports the conclusion.

3. Prove and explain the rule through citation to authority, description of how the authority stands for the rule, discussion of subsidiary rules, analyses of policy, and counter-analyses. (*This is rule proof and explanation, or simply rule proof.*)

4. Apply the rule's elements to the facts with the aid of subsidiary rules, supporting authority, policy considerations, and counter-analyses. (*This is rule application.*)

5. If steps 1 through 4 are complicated, sum up by restating your conclusion.

This section describes one method of starting to work with the formula. It is only a suggestion for the first time you write. If you develop a different procedure that works better for you, use that instead.

In the method described here, you label everything so that you know where it goes and then just plug it into whatever variant of the formula best fits your situation. The first time you try this, it might seem a little awkward if you have never done anything like it before. But the second or third time, it might feel natural because it fits the way people instinctively work and because it takes less effort than other methods of organizing.

Begin by figuring out how many issues and sub-issues you have. Each one will be analyzed through a separate paradigm structure.

For each issue or sub-issue, identify the rule that is central to and governs the answer. (You might also use other rules, but for the moment focus on the rule that — more than any other — compels your answer.)

Now, inventory your raw materials. *For each issue or sub-issue,* sort everything you have into two categories: rule proof and rule application. Some methods of sorting seem to work better than others. Dividing your notes into two piles, for example, does *not* seem to work very well.

A better method is to go through your notes and write "RP" in the margin next to everything that you might use to prove that your rule really is the law and "RA" next to everything that might help the reader understand how to apply the rule. Some ideas or authorities might do both and get a notation of "RP/RA." If you have several issues or sub-issues, you can work out a method of marking them separately, such as "#3RP" for "rule proof on issue 3" or "#1RA" for "rule application on issue 1." If you have photocopied cases or printed them out, write these notations next to each part of the case that you will use. Go through your facts, too, marking the ones that are important enough to talk about during rule application. If you have been thinking about ideas that are not in your notes, write them down and note where they go.

Now, think about how all these things add up. If you have not yet drawn a conclusion, do it now. If you decided previously on a conclusion, check it against your raw materials to see whether it still seems like the best conclusion.

Ask yourself whether a reasonable argument could be made against any part of your analysis. If so, make a note of it and of where it goes. Decide whether the argument is so attractive that it would probably persuade a judge. And decide exactly *why* a judge would — or would not — be persuaded. If you decide that the argument is likely to persuade, modify your analysis accordingly. (If you cannot find any arguments at all that might work against your analysis, you may be avoiding problems that other people will later see.)

You have now completed most of the analytical process described in §6.2. And your notes are now complete enough to be organized into an outline based on some variation of the paradigm formula.

To make the fluid outline described in §6.3, just assemble everything. *For each issue or sub-issue,* take a piece of paper and write four abbreviated headings on it (for example: "concl" or "sub-concl," "rule," "RP," and "RA").

(You can do this on a computer instead, if you feel more comfortable typing than writing.) Under "concl" or "sub-concl," write your conclusion or sub-conclusion for that issue in whatever shorthand will remind you later of what your thinking is (for example: "no diversity—Wharton/citizen of Maine"). Under "rule," do something similar. Under "RP," list your raw materials for rule proof. For each item listed, do not write a lot—just enough so that you can see at a glance everything you have. If you are listing something found in a case you have photocopied, a catch-phrase and a reference to a page in the case might be enough (for example: "intent to return—*Wiggins* p.352"). Under "RA," do the same for rule application. Make sure that everything you have on that issue is listed in an appropriate place on that page.

Assume that for rule proof on a certain issue you have listed six resources (cases, facts, and so on). You have not yet decided the order in which you will discuss them when you prove the rule. In most situations, the decision will be easier and more apt if you do *not* make it while outlining. The best time to decide is just before you write that issue's rule proof in your first draft. (*You do not need to know exactly where everything will go before you start the first draft.*) When you decide, just write a number next to each item ("1" next to the first one you will discuss, and so on).

When you write the first draft (§6.4), you probably will not use everything that you previously marked into one category or another. Inevitably, some material will not seem as useful while you are writing as it did when you were sorting, and you will discard it.

Keep track of what you are doing by checking off or crossing out each item in the outline as you put it into the first draft. When everything has been checked off or crossed out, you have completed the first draft of your Discussion in an office memorandum (or Argument if you are writing a motion memorandum or appellate brief).

So far, you have concentrated on making sure that all worthwhile raw materials get into your first draft. During rewriting, your focus will change. While you rewrite (§6.6), look to see where things are. If you find conclusions at the end of analysis, for example, move them to the beginning. While rewriting, ask yourself the questions in §13.2.

§13.2   Rewriting: How to Test Your Writing for Effective Organization

A well-organized presentation of analysis is immediately recognizable. Issues and sub-issues are handled separately, and each issue is clearly resolved before the next is taken up. Inside each issue and each sub-issue, the material is organized around the elements of the controlling rule or rules, and not around individual court decisions. Rule proof is always completed before rule application begins. Each issue and each sub-issue is explored through a well-chosen variation of the formula explained in this chapter.

The reader is given neither too little nor too much explanation, but instead is able to read quickly and finish confident that the writer's conclusion is correct. Authority is discussed in the order of its logical importance, not necessarily in the chronological order in which it developed. Finally, the writer's organization is apparent throughout: the reader always knows where he is and how everything fits together. These things all come from sound *architecture:* from a wisely chosen building plan that the writer can explain and justify if asked to do so.

To figure out whether you have accomplished these things, ask yourself the following questions after you have written a first draft.[1]

13-A **For each issue, have you stated your *conclusion*? If so, where?** State it precisely, succinctly, and in such a way that the reader knows from the very beginning what you intend to demonstrate. Some lawyers express a prediction openly ("Kolchak will not be convicted of robbery"), while others imply the prediction by stating the conclusion on which it is based ("The evidence does not establish beyond a reasonable doubt that Kolchak is guilty of robbery").

13-B **For each issue, have you stated the *rule* or rules on which your conclusion is based? If so, where?** If the cases on which you rely have not formulated an explicit statement of the rule, you might be tempted just to describe the cases and let the reader decide what rule they stand for. If you feel that temptation, you probably have not yet figured out yourself exactly what the rule is. And if you have not done it, the reader will not do it for you. Formulate a credible rule, and prove it by analyzing the authority at hand. (See Chapters 2, 15, and 16.)

13-C **For each issue, have you *proved* the rule? If so, where? And do you explain the rule proof in an appropriate amount of depth?** Is your rule proof conclusory, substantiating, or comprehensive? How did you decide how much depth to use? If you were in the decision-maker's position, would you need more rule proof? Less? Is policy accounted for? (If the rule seems arbitrary, the reader will resist agreeing that it is the correct one to use. The reader will more easily agree if you at least allude to the policy behind the rule and the social benefits the rule causes.) Have you counter-analyzed attractive arguments that might challenge your choice or formulation of the rule?

13-D **For each issue, have you *applied* the rule to the facts? If so, where? And do you explain the rule application in an appropriate amount of depth?** Is your rule application conclusory, substantiating, or comprehensive? How did you decide how much depth to use? If you were in the decision-maker's position, would you need more rule application?

---

§13.2   1. When marking up your work, your teacher might refer to these questions by using the number-letter codes that appear next to each question here.

Less? Is policy accounted for? Have you counter-analyzed attractive arguments that might challenge your application of the rule?

Have you completed rule proof before starting rule application? | 13-E |
If you let the material get out of control, the result may be a little rule proof, followed by a little rule application, followed by a little more rule proof, followed by a little more rule application—and so on, back and forth and back and forth. Finish proving the rule before you start applying it. If you start to apply a rule before you have finished proving it, the reader will refuse to agree with what you are doing.

Have you varied the sequence of the paradigm formula only where truly necessary? | 13-F | If you have varied the sequence of the components of the formula, why? Was your goal more valuable than any clarity you might have sacrificed by varying the sequence? (It might have been, but your decision should be a conscious one.)

Have you organized a multi-issue presentation so that the reader understands how everything fits together? | 13-G | If you have combined separately structured explanations, did you identify separate subconclusions? Are the combined paradigms covered by an umbrella paradigm? Is the result crystal-clear to the reader? If not, how could it be made so? (If you are writing a persuasive motion memorandum or appellate brief, see §26.3.)

Have you organized around tests and elements, rather than around cases? | 13-H | Your goal is not to dump before the reader the cases you found in the library. The law is, after all, the rules themselves, and a case merely proves a rule's existence and accuracy. The cases are raw materials, and your job is not complete until you have built them into a coherent discussion organized around the applicable tests and their elements. A mere list of relevant cases, with discussion of each, is not helpful to a decision-maker, who needs to understand how the rules affect the facts. This fault is called case-by-case-itis. It is easy to spot in a student's paper: the reader sees an unconnected series of paragraphs, each of which is devoted to discussion of a single case. The impression made is sometimes called "show-and-tell" because the writer seems to be doing nothing more than holding up newly found possessions. A student not making this mistake might use five cases to analyze the first element of a test, one case—if it is dispositive—to analyze the second, three for the third, and so on, deploying cases where they will do what is needed.

Have you avoided presenting authority in chronological order unless you have a special need to do so? | 13-I | The reader wants to know what the current law is and how it governs the facts at hand. Although a little history might be useful somewhere in the discussion, you will waste the reader's time if you begin with the kind of historical background typical of a college essay. Unless there is some special need to do otherwise, present authority in the order of its logical importance, not the order in which it came to be.

13-J | Have you collected closely related ideas, rather than scattering them? If there are three reasons why the defendant will not be convicted, list them and then explain each in turn. The reader looking for the big picture cannot follow you if you introduce the first reason on page 1; mention the second for the first time on page 4; and surprise the reader with the third on page 6. If you have more than one item or idea, listing them at the beginning helps the reader keep things in perspective. It also forces you to organize and evaluate your thoughts. Sometimes, in the act of listing, you may find that there are really fewer or more reasons — or whatever else you are listing — than you had originally thought.

Exercise I.   Griggs and the Anti-Bandit (Checking Organization During Rewriting)

This exercise is designed to help you spot organizational problems in your own writing so that you can fix them during the rewriting process.

Griggs has been charged in Maryland with a version of theft called possession of stolen goods, specifically a BMW floor mat and an Anti-Bandit automobile CD player. He told Officer Ochs that he had driven onto the shoulder of a rural road after realizing that he was lost, and that he had attempted to turn around by backing up his van a few feet into the woods, where it became stuck in the mud. According to Griggs, he got out, tried to rock the van out of the mud, and noticed the mat and the Anti-Bandit lying on the ground. The Anti-Bandit comes with a handle and is designed to be removed from the car and carried away at the owner's convenience. Griggs says that he did not notice, 50 feet further into the woods, a BMW stripped of tires, battery, and the like. (The police have found nothing else taken from the BMW.) Griggs says that he worked the mat under one of his rear wheels to gain traction, and that, when his baby woke up in the back seat and started crying, he slid the Anti-Bandit into his dashboard (from which his own had been stolen some weeks before) and started playing the song from *SpongeBob SquarePants,* which his daughter finds soothing. Appearing just as Griggs was about to drive away with the mat and the Anti-Bandit in his van, Officer Ochs believed none of this and placed Griggs under arrest.

Pretend that you have been asked to determine whether Griggs is guilty of possessing stolen property. The passage below is your first draft. You wrote it last week and then set it aside so that, after clearing your mind, you could see it as a reader would when you start to rewrite (see §6.6). Your first task now is to decide whether your first draft is well organized, and if it is not, what needs to be fixed. Using the questions in §13.2, read the passage below, looking for organizational effectiveness. You might find this easier if you mark it up, dividing it into the components of the paradigm. Is everything there? Do they appear in an effective sequence (§10.4)? Is the depth enough to allay a reader's skepticism (Chapter 11)? If yes, what convinces you? If not, what causes doubt? If you would need to know more in order to be convinced, what should have been included? Does this passage combine separately proved conclusions of law (Chapter 12)? If yes, is it done effectively and introduced with a roadmap paragraph (§ 12.6). In general, how would you reorganize this passage? Be prepared to discuss your thinking in class.

In Maryland, a person is guilty of possessing stolen property — a version of theft — if that person (1) possesses stolen personal property; (2) either knows "that it has been stolen" or believes "that it probably has been stolen"; and (3) "intends to deprive the owner of the property," or "willfully or knowingly uses, conceals, or abandons the property in a manner that deprives the owner of the property," or "uses, conceals, or abandons the property knowing that the use, concealment, or abandonment probably will deprive the owner of the property." Md. Code Ann. § 7-104(c)(1) (2002).

At about 1 A.M. Officer Ochs found Griggs in possession of the floor mat and the Anti-Bandit. Both were later shown to have come from a BMW that was stolen between 9 and 10 o'clock earlier that evening. Griggs admitted that the radio and floor mat were not his. Hence, Griggs was in exclusive possession of a stolen radio and a stolen floor mat, and, since they were recently stolen, the possession element is satisfied.

In *Carroll v. State*, 6 Md. App. 647, 252 A.2d 496 (1969), the defendant met an acquaintance on a deserted back road and purchased a car engine from him at substantially below market value. While driving off with the engine in his truck, the defendant was arrested. On appeal, he argued that because he had no direct knowledge that the property was stolen, his conviction should be reversed. The Court of Special Appeals rejected this argument and held that a defendant's knowledge of a property's stolen character can be proved by evidence showing that under the circumstances the defendant "knew or could reasonably have suspected that the property in his possession was stolen." *Id.*, at 650, 252 A.2d at 498. Exclusive possession of stolen property can lead to the same inference, even where the defendant denies knowing that the property was stolen. *Burns v. State*, 149 Md. App. 526, 817 A.2d 885 (2003). Because of the prosecution's obligation to prove guilt beyond a reasonable doubt, a conviction can be based solely on circumstantial evidence only where "the circumstances, taken together . . . exclude every reasonable hypothesis or theory of innocence." *Mills v. State*, 3 Md. App. 693, 697, 241 A.2d 166, 168 (1968). Therefore, Griggs knew that the BMW floor mat and the Banzai Anti-Bandit radio were stolen property or believed that they probably were, satisfying the knowledge element.

In *Carroll*, the defendant intended to deprive the true owner of the engine because the defendant planned on installing it in his own car. Here Griggs's actions show a similar intent. First, he had the radio and floor mat in his van. Second, he had used the Anti-Bandit to quiet his baby and the floor mat to free his van from the mud. Third, although Griggs told Officer Ochs that he "hadn't had a chance" to decide what he intended to do with these items eventually, he had started the van's engine and was beginning to drive off. Therefore, Griggs's actions satisfy the deprivation element. "Deprive" means to withhold property of another (1) permanently; (2) for a period that results in the appropriation of a part of the property's value; (3) with the purpose to restore it only on payment of a reward or other compensation; or (4) to dispose of the property or use or deal with the property in a manner that makes it unlikely that the owner will recover it. Md. Code Ann. § 7-101(c) (2002). Although a defendant is presumed innocent and the prosecution must prove guilt beyond a reasonable doubt, "the trier of facts in a criminal case . . . is not commanded to be naive and to believe without scrutiny every glib suggestion or farfetched fairy tale." *Berry v. State*, 202 Md. 62, 67, 95 A.2d 319, 321 (1952).

Therefore, Griggs will be convicted of theft in the form of possessing stolen goods.

Exercise II.   Teddy Washburn's Gun (Analyzing and Organizing)

This exercise takes you through the ground work needed to make a prediction and helps you organize raw materials — rules, facts, statutes, cases — into an outline that tracks the components of the paradigm. After the fact narrative below, you will find two statutes and three cases, followed by questions for you to answer.

Facts

In his prime, Gorilla Morrell was often on the bill at Friday Night Wrestling. Now he is reduced to hanging around Washburn's Weights Room & Gym, which is next door to Washburn's Bar & Grill. Gorilla is good for Teddy Washburn's business because customers in the Weights Room try to take Gorilla on. When this happens, customers from the Bar wander into the Weights Room to watch. There they order more drinks, which Washburn passes through a hole he has cut through the wall. Afterward, Gorilla, his adversary, and the spectators tend to adjourn back to the Bar, where the spirit of conviviality usually leads to games of billiards accompanied by further orders of food and drink.

Washburn has let Gorilla build up a bill of $283.62, dating back over several weeks. Last night, they had words over the matter. Gorilla took a swing at Washburn, who came out from behind the bar and chased Gorilla out into the street. There Gorilla took another swing at Washburn, and Washburn, demanding his money, pulled out a gun (which he bought and for which he has a license).

Gorilla grabbed for the gun, but it fell out of Washburn's hand, sliding five or six feet along the sidewalk and coming to rest at the feet of Snare Drum Bennett, a mechanic who was returning from work. Bennett happened onto this scene only in time to hear Washburn demand money and to see him pull out the gun and have it knocked from his hand.

Bennett, Washburn, and Gorilla looked at the gun, then at each other, and then at the gun again. Finally, Bennett crouched down, picked up the gun, checked to make sure the safety was on, and put it in her coat pocket. "Washburn," she said, "you haven't paid *me* yet for the front end work I did on your car."

"I will," said Washburn.

"It's $575," said Bennett, "and it's been three weeks. I think you should go back inside. You ought to pay your own debts before you accuse other people of welshing out on you."

"How can I pay you," exclaimed Washburn, "if he won't pay me?"

"That's your problem," said Bennett, "I'm holding on to the gun. You can't seem to handle it right now, and I want my money."

At that point, Gorilla clobbered Washburn in the face and sent him staggering. Bennett turned around, walked a half-dozen steps, and began to turn into a dark alley. Washburn started to get up, called out "Hey, you!" and took a step in Bennett's direction. Bennett took the gun from her coat, pointed it at Washburn, smiled, and said, "Back off, bucko."

Washburn froze, and Bennett walked into the alley. As soon as she was out of sight, she dropped the gun into an open but full trash dumpster. The dumpster belongs to a grocery store and is about five feet inside the alley, which in turn is about twenty feet from the front door of Washburn's bar.

An hour or so later, the police came to Bennett's home and arrested her for robbing Washburn of his gun. Bennett told them where she had dropped it. The police went straight to the dumpster but found nothing inside, not even the trash that had muffled the gun's fall.

Statutes

Criminal Code § 10: No person shall be convicted of a crime except on evidence proving guilt beyond a reasonable doubt.

Criminal Code § 302: A person commits robbery by taking, with the intent to steal, the property of another, from the other's person or in the other's presence, and through violence or intimidation. A person does not commit robbery if the intent to steal was formed after the taking.

Cases

BUTTS v. STATE

The defendant had worked for the Royal Guano company for two and a half days when he was fired. He demanded his wages but was told that he would have to wait until Saturday, which was payday. He was ordered off the premises and left. After a few hours, he returned with a gun, found the shift foreman, and demanded his wages again. The foreman told him to come back on Saturday. (The company agrees that it owed the defendant wages, but insists that he wait until payday to receive them.) When the foreman refused, the defendant showed the gun and demanded again. The foreman then paid the amount the defendant requested.

An intent to steal is an intent to deprive the owner permanently of his property. There is no intent to steal if the defendant in good faith believes that the property taken is the defendant's own property and not the property of somebody else.

The defendant could reasonably have supposed that he was entitled to his pay when his connection with the company was severed. He was wrong because the money was the property of the company until the company paid it to him. But he acted in good faith and therefore did not have the intent to steal (although he may be guilty of crimes other than robbery).

GREEN v. STATE

We reverse the defendant's conviction for robbing Mrs. Lillie Priddy.

Although there was evidence that the defendant assaulted Mrs. Priddy, that alone does not prove robbery. Mrs. Priddy testified as follows: She was walking along a road and came upon the defendant, who struck her so that she lost consciousness. After a minute or two, her mind cleared, and she saw the defendant standing in the road and her purse on the ground about five feet from each of them. The contents of the purse were spilled out on the ground. She kicked him and ran, never seeing her purse again.

The issue is whether there was a "taking" sufficient to support a charge of robbery. A taking is the securing dominion over or absolute control of the property. Absolute control must exist at some time, even if only for a moment.

If Mrs. Priddy was unconscious, she could not know whether the defendant ever had control of her purse, or whether it simply fell to the ground and was later taken away by someone else. None of its contents were found in the defendant's home. The testimony showed a very violent assault and battery upon her by the defendant, but does not establish a robbery.

STATE v. SMITH & JORDAN

The defendants overpowered and disarmed the complainant of his knife. He had surprised them after they broke into his gas station. With the complainant's knife (but not the complainant), they got into their car and drove off. Later, the police found the defendants standing by their wrecked car. The complainant's knife was on the ground nearby. The defendants were convicted of robbery.

To convict for robbery, the defendant must have intended permanently to deprive the complainant of the taken property. If a defendant takes another's property for the taker's immediate and temporary use with no intent permanently to deprive the owner of his property, he is not guilty of robbery.

It would be unreasonable to assume that the defendants, fleeing from arrest for the crime of breaking into the gas station, had any expectation of returning the knife. They would have been captured if they had tried. For the purpose of decision here, we assume that defendant took the knife "for temporary use" and that after it had served the purpose of escape, they intended to abandon it at the first opportunity lest it lead to their detection. That, however, would leave the complainant's recovery of his knife to mere chance and thus constitute a reckless exposure to loss that is consistent with an intent permanently to deprive the owner of his property. In abandoning it, the defendants put it beyond their power to return the knife. When, in order to serve a temporary purpose of one's own, one takes property (1) with the specific intent wholly and permanently to deprive the owner of it, or (2) under circumstances which render it unlikely that the owner will ever recover his property and which disclose the taker's total indifference to his rights, one takes with the intent to steal.

Analyzing and Organizing

Exercise II-A: You have been asked to determine whether Bennett is likely to be convicted of robbing Washburn of his gun. Make a list of the issues.

Exercise II-B: For each issue, take a separate piece of paper and, using the process described in §13.1, answer the following questions:

1. What rule from the cases above disposes of the issue? (If you cannot find a rule that would dispose of the issue, say so. If that is true, it means that additional authority is needed from the library.)
2. What passages from these authorities prove the rule?
3. What facts in Bennett's story would be determinative for the issue?
4. What passages from these authorities would guide you in applying the rule to those determinative facts? (If you find none for a given issue, say so. Again, if you are right, more authority is needed.)

Exercise II-C: In Exercise II-B, you started creating an outline from which to write. If there are any holes in this outline, list them. How will you fill them in?

V

GENERAL ANALYTICAL SKILLS

14 Selecting Authority

§14.1 Introduction

You need authority both in rule proof — to show that your formulation of the rule accurately states the law — and in rule application — to show that your resolution of the facts conforms to what the law intends. This chapter explains how to select the best available authority. Chapters 15 and 16 explain how to use the two most important kinds of authority: case law and statutes.

Courts use a complicated set of preferences to determine which authority they will follow. A hierarchy (explained in §14.2) ranks authorities so that, in the event of conflict, one can be chosen over another. There are special problems with dicta (§14.3), with precedent from other jurisdictions (§§14.4-14.5), and with the selection of nonmandatory precedent (§14.6).

A special problem — addressed at several points in this chapter — involves filling gaps in the law. A gap exists where the jurisdiction whose law governs a particular case does not have all of the legal rules needed to decide the case. (See question 9-D on page 83.)

For example, suppose that the courts in four states have decided through precedent to adopt a newly invented cause of action. Suppose further that the courts of ten other states have held that in those states no such cause of action exists. The remaining 36 states have large gaps in their law on this subject because in each of them there is no local authority on point. If, in any of those 36 states, we bring a suit based on this new cause of action, the courts will have to fill the gap by deciding whether to recognize it locally.

A gap can also occur where the jurisdiction seems to have the rules needed but the local case law does not provide clear and complete guidance on how those rules should govern certain categories of facts. For example, suppose that local authority (precedent or statutory) has enunciated a rule and definitively explained its policy. But suppose our case's facts are on the margin and we are not sure whether the rule should reach that far, and if so, how. We would know a lot more if we consulted cases in other jurisdictions with similar rules, if those cases have considered whether and how to apply the rules to facts like ours.

Gaps routinely occur in every jurisdiction's law because law-makers cannot foresee every type of controversy that the law could be called upon to resolve. When a currently litigated case is affected by a gap, the lawyers involved propose methods of deciding the case that might, through precedent, fill the gap at the same time. (Section 14.5 explains how.) In fact, gaps are also routinely filled as the law continually reshapes itself through precedent.

§14.2 The Hierarchy of Authority

You will be able to follow the hierarchy of authority more easily if you visualize it this way:

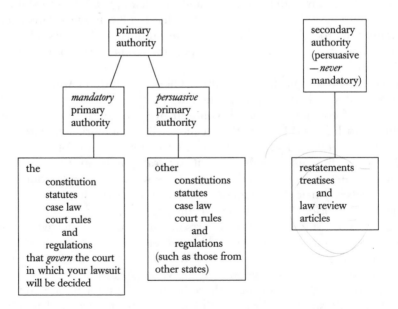

There are two kinds of authority. *Primary authority* includes decisions, statutes, and statute-like materials such as constitutions, court rules, and administrative regulations. (For brevity, we can refer to statutes and statute-like materials collectively as "enactments.") Treatises, law review articles, and other commentaries on the law are *secondary authority*. Primary authority is produced by a legislature, a court, or some other governmental entity with the power to make or determine law. Secondary authority, on the other hand, is only a description of what a private person or a private group believes the law to be; the author of secondary authority may be knowledgeable but lacks the power to create law.

Primary authority is in turn subdivided into two varieties. *Mandatory authority* — which must be obeyed — includes enactments of the government whose law controls the question to be resolved, as well as the decisions of the appellate courts to which an appeal could be taken from the trial court where the issue is being or could be litigated. (Before reading the rest of this chapter, you might want to review §1.2 on how courts are organized.) *Persuasive primary authority* — which need not be obeyed — has been produced by a governmental entity empowered to make law, but not by the entity whose law controls the matter at issue.

Within a state or the federal government, some mandatory authority outranks other mandatory authority. A constitution prevails over an inconsistent statute, and either a constitution or a statute trumps an inconsistent court rule or regulation promulgated by an administrative agency. That is basic civics: a constitution is the fundamental law creating a government in the first place; a legislature can enact only those kinds of statutes allowed by a constitution; and an administrative agency is still more subservient and is allowed to regulate only to the extent permitted by statute. Moreover, later enactments prevail over earlier ones of the same rank. A later statute, for example, prevails over an earlier one, but not over an earlier constitutional provision. In addition, a constitution or a statute will prevail over an inconsistent common law precedent. And case law made by higher courts prevails over inconsistent case law made by lower courts. Finally, later decisions prevail over inconsistent earlier ones from the same court.

Persuasive primary authority occurs in four forms: (1) decisions by appellate courts whose law does not control the dispute in question (for example, a decision from another state); (2) decisions by coordinate appellate courts, to which an appeal could not be taken from the trial court where the issue would be or is being litigated (an example is given in the next paragraph); (3) decisions made by trial courts anywhere; and (4) dicta in any decision.

A precedent is not mandatory merely because it was made by an appellate court in the jurisdiction where a present controversy is being or would be litigated. To be mandatory, a decision must have been made by an appellate court to which the matter at hand could be or already has been appealed. For example, the United States Court of Appeals for the Sixth Circuit hears appeals from federal trial courts in Kentucky, Michigan, Ohio, and Tennessee, while the coordinate court for the Third Circuit decides appeals from federal trial courts in Delaware, New Jersey, and Pennsylvania. An opinion by the Sixth Circuit is mandatory authority to a United States District Court in Ohio, because the Sixth Circuit can reverse, on appeal, a decision of that trial court. The same opinion is mandatory to the Sixth Circuit itself, which is bound by its own prior decisions. But that opinion is only persuasive authority to a United States District Court in Philadelphia, because the Third Circuit — not the Sixth — hears appeals from federal trial courts in Pennsylvania. And that opinion is only persuasive authority in the Court of Appeals for the Third Circuit (a coordinate court to the Sixth Circuit) and in the Supreme Court of the United States (which is superior to all the circuits).

Decisions by the United States Supreme Court, on the other hand, are mandatory in every federal court because the Supreme Court has the power ultimately to reverse a decision by any federal court.[1] But decisions of the United States Supreme Court are mandatory authority in a state court only on issues of federal law because the United States Supreme Court has no jurisdiction to decide matters of state law.

Secondary authority.   In contrast to primary authority, which may be either mandatory or persuasive, secondary authority is always persuasive and never mandatory. The most significant forms of secondary authority are (1) restatements, which are formulations of the common law drafted by scholars commissioned by the American Law Institute; (2) treatises written by scholars; and (3) articles and similar material published in law reviews. If secondary authority is both on point and needed to fill a gap in the law, a court is most likely to be influenced by a restatement. On an issue not considered by the restatements, the most influential secondary authority will usually be a treatise or article written by a renowned scholar.

Since 1923, the American Law Institute has commissioned restatements in contracts, property, torts, and several other fields in an attempt to express some consensus about the common law as it has developed in the 50 states. When a restatement is no longer up-to-date, it is superseded by a second or third version. Thus, the Restatement (Third) of Property replaced the Restatement (Second) of Property. A restatement consists of a series of black-letter law rules organized into sections, to which commentary is appended. Although some states' courts are relatively unimpressed by restatements, other states give special respect to one or another of the restatements. You can find out whether a state's courts defer to a particular restatement by checking the manner and frequency with which the restatement is cited in the state's decisions.

The authoritativeness of a treatise depends on the reputation of its author and on whether the treatise has been kept up-to-date. Some of the outstanding treatises have been written by Wigmore (evidence), Corbin

---

§14.2   1. The Supreme Court's refusal to grant a writ of certiorari in a particular case is not precedent. A petition for certiorari is a request for permission to appeal to the Supreme Court. The overwhelming majority of these petitions are denied simply because the Supreme Court cannot possibly decide the thousands of cases annually that various parties want to appeal to the nation's highest court. The Court itself has held that "the denial of a writ of certiorari imports no expression of opinion upon the merits of the case." *United States v. Carver,* 260 U.S. 482, 490 (1922). On the other hand, if you cite to a decision below from which the Supreme Court has "denied cert.," in some situations you must incorporate the denial into the citation as part of the case's "subsequent history." See §20.3.1.

(contracts), Williston (contracts), and Prosser and Keeton (torts). Some treatises are multivolume works; some are in a single volume; some double as hornbooks; some are hardbound with pocket parts or other annual supplements; and some are in looseleaf binders for easier updating.

Law reviews print two kinds of material: articles (written by scholars, judges, and practitioners) and comments and notes (written by students). If an article is thorough, insightful, or authored by a respected scholar, it may influence a court and may therefore be worth citing. Most articles, however, do not fit that description, and an article's publication should not be taken to mean that it will be influential.[2] Only in the most unusual of circumstances does a student comment or note influence a court. But even where law review material will not be influential (and therefore would not be worth citing), it might nevertheless stimulate your thinking, and its footnotes can help you find cases, statutes, and other authority.

Legal encyclopedias, legal dictionaries, digests, and *American Law Reports* are *not* authority. They are not written by scholars, and their only function is to collect cases and to summarize parts of them. The definitions in legal dictionaries are taken from opinions, often verbatim. Not only is the true authority the decision itself, but the dictionary rarely uses a case from the jurisdiction where your issue arises. Legal encyclopedias discuss more complex material but suffer from the same fault. Although digests and *American Law Reports* are more exhaustive, the true authority is still the cases they cite.[3]

§14.3 How Courts Use Dicta

A dictum is not a holding and thus cannot be controlling authority, no matter what court it comes from. Once, after hearing an argument based on dictum from *Marbury v. Madison* — the single most important decision in American constitutional law — the Supreme Court held that

> general expressions [that] go beyond the case . . . may be respected, but ought not to control the judgment in a subsequent suit. . . . The reason . . . is obvious. The question actually before the Court is investigated with care, and considered

---

2. A respected appellate judge writes, "My experience teaches . . . that too few law review articles prove helpful in appellate decision making. They tend to be too talky, too unselective in separating the relevant from the irrelevant, too exhaustive, too exhausting, too hedged, too cautious about reaching a definite conclusion. When they do, they strive too hard for innovation or shock effect at the expense of feasibility or practicality." Patricia M. Wald, *Teaching the Trade: An Appellate Judge's View of Practice-Oriented Legal Education,* 36 J. Leg. Ed. 35, 42 (1986).

3. Years ago, lawyers and judges were in the habit of citing to legal encyclopedias and dictionaries, even though they were not authority, and you will see that done occasionally in opinions printed in your casebooks. That practice is no longer considered acceptable. Today lawyers and judges seek real authority, and if you cite to a legal dictionary or encyclopedia, the reader will doubt you, and you risk creating an impression of sloppiness.

in its full extent. Other principles which may serve to illustrate it, are considered in their relation to the case decided, but their possible bearing on [future] cases is seldom completely investigated.[1]

If that is so, why do courts write dicta in the first place?

Sometimes it adds clarity to an opinion. A court may want, for example, to make clear what the case is *not* ("if the plaintiff had presented evidence of injury to his reputation, he might be entitled to damages"). Or the court may wish to illustrate the possible ramifications of its decision ("when a minor is at the controls of a power boat — or for that matter an automobile or an airplane — she is held to the standard of care expected of a reasonable adult"). Occasionally, a court will add dicta to justify an apparently harsh decision ("although these facts constitute a cause of action for defamation — which the plaintiff did not bring — they do not substantiate the invasion of privacy cause of action asserted in the complaint") or to make a suggestion to a lower court on remand ("although the parties have not appealed on the question of appropriate damages, that issue will inevitably arise in the new trial we order, and we believe it necessary to point out . . .").

Sometimes a dictum is inadvertent. A judge might get a bit carried away or might formulate the issue or the rule or the determinative facts so that it is not clear whether a particular comment is really within the scope of the decision. Even when a judge is careful in defining the issue, rule, and determinative facts, readers might reasonably disagree about whether a particular comment is necessary to the resolution of the issue at hand.

If a court decides an issue on two independent grounds, either of which would alone have been sufficient, neither is dictum. Both were the basis of the decision, even if only one would have been needed.

A dictum can never be mandatory authority. But if the court that wrote the dictum can reverse the court in which the current matter is now being litigated, the dictum, though still not mandatory, becomes especially influential.

It is not wrong to use a dictum, but it is wrong to use it inappropriately. Although a dictum can be used to supplement reliance on unclear or incomplete holdings, it can never take the place of a holding, and it is inappropriate to treat it as though it could. And where a dictum is used, it must be identified as such or the result can be viewed as an attempted deception.

§14.4   How Courts React to Foreign Precedent

Lawyers and judges sometimes use the term "foreign law" to mean law from another state. It may help here to use four phrases not common among lawyers and judges. For brevity, we can call the court that authored a precedent the "precedential court," and we can use the expression

§14.3   1. *Cohens v. Virginia,* 19 U.S. 264, 399-400 (1821).

"decisional court" for the court that has been or could be asked to adjudicate a current controversy in which the precedent might be used.[1] Where the courts are in different states, we can refer to one as the "precedential state" and the other as the "decisional state."

Cases from other jurisdictions are consulted only for guidance and only where a gap appears in local law. Although some courts prefer to fill a gap by analogizing to existing local law, most courts are curious about foreign precedent when local law does not settle the question. Even then, a decisional court will not be influenced by foreign holdings that are inconsistent with policies embedded in the decisional court's own local law.

A decisional court will not be persuaded merely because a court in another state has taken a particular position. Although a court might be impressed because a doctrine is the rule of a majority of states that have decided the matter, or because there is a trend among recent decisions toward or away from a rule, a court will nevertheless reject a rule it believes unwise. In determining the majority and minority rules and any recent trend, a court considers the number and importance of states that have taken a particular position, not the number of decisions. A precedential state's law becomes settled only when so held by that state's highest court. Until a precedential state's highest court has ruled, the opinion of a lower court, while significant, is only a tentative expression of that state's law on the point.

Precedent interpreting statutes in other jurisdictions is treated somewhat differently from precedent interpreting the common law. That is because decisions interpreting statutes are not free-floating authority for what the law is in some generalized sense: they are authority for the meaning of specific words found in specific statutes, and they have no life independent of the words interpreted. If, for example, a statute were to be repealed, the cases interpreting it would no longer represent current law.

Opinions interpreting a statute from another state can be persuasive authority, but only if the other state's statute is similar to your statute. If the two are *identical,* precedent from the other state can be particularly persuasive. Two statutes can be virtually identical even if there are minor differences in wording that do not affect the statutes' meaning. Where the substance of the statutes is different, precedent from the other state has more limited value. If the two statutes take radically different approaches to solving the same problem, precedent from the other state usually has little or no value.

Precedent interpreting the other state's statute can have a strong impact where your statute is derived from the other one, especially where the foreign precedent predates enactment of your statute. Less weight is given to foreign precedent that interprets the original statute *after* the derivative version was enacted in your state, but even then the foreign precedent can be persuasive.

---

§14.4   1. These terms come from James Hardisty, *Reflections on Stare Decisis,* 55 Ind. L.J. 41, 45 (1979).

Where your statute is derived from a model or uniform statute, such as the Uniform Commercial Code, courts can easily see the persuasiveness in precedent interpreting other states' enactments of it. But states often make changes in uniform statutes when enacting them. Be sure that the other state's version of the model statute is not materially different from your statute's version. A local court can also be persuaded by the commentaries written by the drafters and published with the model statute.

Of course, if your state has no statute on the subject, precedent interpreting statutes from other states has no value at all. If your state treats the issue as one of common law, the only foreign precedent it will consider will be precedent based on other states' common law.

§14.5 How to Use Foreign Precedent and Other Nonmandatory Authority to Fill a Gap in Local Law

There are two steps. First, lay a foundation for reliance on nonmandatory authority by defining a gap in local law (§14.5.1). Then use nonmandatory authority to fill the gap (§14.5.2).

§14.5.1 Laying the Foundation

Because foreign law is used only to help fill gaps in local law, you can use it *only after laying a foundation* for it. A foundation is laid when you define the gap and specify how local law does not dispose of the controversy.

A particularly deep gap occurs where the issue is one of "first impression" in the decisional state, which means that the appellate courts there have never before had occasion to resolve it. If some local courts have ruled, the issue is no longer one of first impression, but a gap would still exist if the rulings are all from nonmandatory courts. (The law is still not settled.) If those courts have ruled infrequently or are in disagreement, the gap is deep, and foreign precedent may have a significant role in resolving it. If, however, the lower courts have ruled often and agree with each other, the gap is shallower, and the role of foreign precedent is limited to providing context for a discussion of whether the jurisdiction's highest court will or should overrule the lower courts despite the consensus below. (Wherever a gap is shallow, an evaluation of foreign authority is only a sideline to a main discussion of local cases.)

Another possibility is that local cases, even from the highest court in the jurisdiction, may be so infirm from age or poor reasoning that foreign precedent can again provide context for a discussion of whether the decisional jurisdiction will or should change course. But be careful: a precedent is not infirm just because it is old or just because you or your client do not like its reasoning. Age weakens a precedent when society has so changed that the precedent no longer represents public policy on the matter in question. And a precedent can be damaged by its own reasoning if doubted by a significant body of thought among judges and scholars.

Still another possibility is that local cases might have come very close to the issue but without directly resolving it. Because analogies to and syntheses of local authority are often capable of disposing of the issue, this kind of gap is probably not deep, and the role of foreign precedent is limited to noting whether the resulting analogy or synthesis is consistent with what has happened elsewhere. Analogy and synthesis are explained in Chapter 15.

If other states have statutes on the question and the decisional state has none, that is not necessarily a gap in the law. The decisional state's courts might hold that when its own legislature declined to enact such a statute, the legislature's inaction was, in effect, a determination decision that the decisional state's law will not include the provisions adopted elsewhere.

To lay the foundation, do three things: (1) state the issue precisely, (2) explain what local law has decided, and (3) show how that does not resolve the dispute (define what local law has not decided). The following is the first of three examples that lay a foundation very concisely:

> No appellate court in this state has decided whether the sale of a newly built home implies a warranty of habitability, and the legislature has enacted no statute that would resolve the issue. However, a common law warranty of habitability has been recognized, as a matter of common law, in a growing number of states. . . .

Here, the gap is total: there are no statutes and no case law. But it is usually not this clear cut. For example, there might be cases that have nibbled around the edges of the issue; or cases to which analogies could be made; or cases setting out public policy; or even a case that gives the false impression of having resolved the question. If so, the foundation is not complete until you have explained—in as much detail as the reader would need to agree with you—why the issue is still open.

> No reported decision has determined whether a violation of §432 [a state statute] is negligence per se. But Colorado and Arizona [neighboring states with similar conditions] have enacted similar statutes. [*Here, add an explanation of the statutes sufficient to convince the reader that they really are similar.*] Courts in those states have held. . . .

Here, we have a statute, but the courts have not yet decided a certain aspect of its meaning (whether a violation is negligence per se). The foundation would not be complete until the similarity of the Colorado and Arizona statutes has been demonstrated.

> The Second District Court of Appeal has permitted this type of jury instruction, but the Fourth District considers it so confusing to the jury that it is reversible error unless clarified by other instructions. [*Here, add explanations of the Second and Fourth District cases.*] It is also

reversible error in the federal courts and in most of the states that have
considered the issue. . . .

In this example, there are in-state cases, but they disagree with each other.
To complete this foundation — and before discussing the out-of-state author-
ity — the Second and Fourth District cases would have to be explained.
  The following is *not* a foundation:

Kansas [the decisional state] has not addressed this issue.

We are not told what the issue is. Nor are we told what Kansas has done. Are
there no analogous precedents? Is there nothing in Kansas law that would
set out local public policy on the question? (Unless shown otherwise, the
reader will suspect that there are analogous cases and expressions of public
policy, but that the writer either did not find them or is not willing to talk
about them.)
  Do not lecture the reader on basic principles of the hierarchy of authority
("since there are no reported decisions in this state on this issue, it is
necessary to look to the law of other jurisdictions"). The reader long ago
learned that that is the standard way of filling local gaps.

§14.5.2 Filling the Gap

A gap in the decisional state's common law can be filled by relying on
precedent from other jurisdictions and on the views of scholarly commentators. If the gap centers on the meaning of an unclear statute, the gap can
be filled only by relying on foreign precedent that interprets similar statutes
elsewhere and on scholarly commentators who discuss the same or similar
statutes.
  Once the foundation has been laid, describe precisely the topography of
foreign precedent. Synthesize it into a pattern where possible, and analogize
where necessary (see Chapter 15). It is not enough to cite to some scattered
out-of-state cases with analogous facts. The decisional court is free to ignore
nonmandatory authority, and it will do so unless you can show that the
foreign precedents fit nicely into the gap in local law. *The snuggest fit occurs
where the policy behind the foreign cases coincides with established public
policy in the decisional state.* The focus usually should be on the case law.
The views of commentators generally play a secondary role.
  If a large number of jurisdictions have ruled on the question, the reader
will need to know which is the majority or plurality rule and which rule is
favored by the recent trend of decisions. This can be supported only by a
precise statement of the score: the number of jurisdictions that have
adopted the majority or plurality rule; the number of jurisdictions that
have adopted other rules; and the number of jurisdictions that have
switched since a date that you have selected in order to define the trend.
  If the issue is crucial to your analysis, the score should in turn be supported by a citation for each jurisdiction. (If the issue is federal and has not

been settled by Supreme Court precedent, you will need to account for each of the 13 federal circuits.) It may be powerful to say that 31 states have adopted the position you believe to be correct, but there are three inherent risks in trying to back up that kind of claim by citing to a law review article or judicial opinion that collects the citations on which you rely. First, the law review article or opinion may be a few years old, and in the interim the list of states may have shrunk or grown. Second, readers depend on you to report what *you* have found, rather than secondhand information that you have not yourself verified. Third, the reader who wants to check your authority will want to know directly from your writing where to find it, and that reader will not want to trace your research through second and third sources. This is one of the very few situations in which a string citation, a footnote, or both are acceptable in a memorandum or brief. A string citation lists many cases or statutes. In a string cite, one case per jurisdiction is usually enough.

But in an office memo, if the matter is peripheral to your analysis, you may be able to prove the score through a citation to a *recent* precedent or article or an annotation in *American Law Reports* (using the up-date in the pocket part), if either of them tabulates the scores and cites cases. (As readers, judges are less flexible. In a memo or brief submitted to a court, the score always must be proved the long way, by a citation for each jurisdiction.)

§14.6   How to Select Nonmandatory Precedent

So many opinions have been published that they occupy millions of pages in thousands of volumes of reporters, filling shelf after shelf in law libraries. The mass is so large that computers are increasingly used to keep track of it. After you have isolated those opinions that touch on the subject to be written about, how do you choose, first, the opinions to rely on and, second, those to emphasize?

If you have found mandatory authority, it will have to dominate your analysis. If local but not mandatory precedent is to be considered, or if you need to refer to foreign precedent, you must make some difficult choices unless the available precedent is so sparse that the only option is to discuss it all. Since your goal is to predict a court's action (or, in a motion memo or appellate brief, to persuade a court to act), your criteria for selecting nonmandatory precedent will have to be the same criteria the courts use.

The task would be easier if courts were to adopt uniform and well-defined rules on the selection of nonmandatory precedent on which to rely, but any such rules would deprive judges of some of the flexibility and creativity so valuable to judicial decision-making. Instead, without having made any overt rules on the subject, most courts, in most cases, apply a relatively uniform set of criteria. Generally, courts are impressed as follows, in approximately this order of priority:

First: whether a precedent is on point with the issue before the decisional court, or, if not on point, whether a sound analogy or synthesis makes it useful anyway. If the opinion is easily distinguished, or if a synthesis would be logically faulty, the decisional court will not be influenced.

Second: the quality of the precedent's reasoning. Is the logic of the holding sound? Is it based on a reasonable interpretation of other authority? Is it based on public policy agreeable to the decisional court? Even long-standing precedent will not persuade if it does not make good sense.

Third: the identity of the precedential court. Is it the highest court in its jurisdiction? Is it a court with recognized expertise or leadership in the field (such as the New Jersey and California supreme courts in negligence law)? Is it a court that has in the past influenced the courts of the decisional state? Is it in a state where the relevant conditions are similar to those prevailing in the decisional state? Is it a court philosophically compatible with the decisional court? (California negligence decisions, for example, are not influential in New York.)

Fourth: the treatment of the precedent (or the rule it stands for) in other reported opinions. Is the precedent or rule discussed with approval or with skepticism? Is it part of a general trend or widely accepted body of law? Or is it a lonely straggler that the rest of the law seems to be leaving behind? Do courts seem to be looking for excuses not to enforce the rule the precedent stands for? (If in its own state the precedent has been overruled — even if only impliedly — this criterion becomes, of course, the most important.)

Fifth: the clarity with which the holding is expressed. If the rationale for the holding is unstated or vaguely stated, the opinion is, to that extent, less probative of what the law is.

Sixth: when the precedent was decided. Judges are predisposed to treat newer opinions as more authoritative than substantially older ones, simply because changing social conditions can make a rule inapt. On the other hand, a holding so new as not to have been tested through experience may be treated a little warily at first. A rule adopted only by a minority of states may be especially persuasive if the recent case law shows a trend toward it, making it the "emerging trend."

Seventh: positions taken by judges in the precedential court. Was the decision unanimous? If not, was the dissent well reasoned and eloquent or written by a respected judge? For that matter, was the majority opinion written by an influential judge?

Exercise.   The Hierarchy of Authority

You are working on a case that is now being litigated in the United States District Court for the District of Nevada. You have been asked to find out whether a defendant who made and lost a motion to dismiss for insufficient service of process can subsequently move to dismiss for failure to state a claim on which relief can be granted. You have found the following authority, all of which squarely addresses your issue. Although the logic and wording of each authority will, of course, affect its weight, make a preliminary ranking of the following authorities solely from the information provided here. (If you are not familiar with the boundaries of the federal circuits, see the map facing the title page in any volume of Federal Reporter, Second Series. Nevada is in the Ninth Circuit.)

Catdog v. Amundsen — 4th Circuit, 2004
Great Basin Realty Co. v. Rand — Nevada Supreme Court, 1998
Matthewson's treatise on Federal Courts (published last year)
Wilkes v. Jae Sun Trading Corp. — 9th Circuit, 1973
Pincus v. McGrath — United States Supreme Court, 1949
Rule 12 of the Federal Rules of Civil Procedure (effective 1938)
Barking Pumpkins Records, Inc. v. Sepulveda — California Supreme Court, 2005
Garibaldi v. City of Boulder — 10th Circuit, 2003
Ott v. Frazier — 7th Circuit, 1931

15 Working with Precedent

§15.1 Eight Skills for Working with Precedent

Perhaps once in a blue moon, a lawyer might find that an issue is entirely resolved by mandatory precedent on point—precedent from a mandatory appellate court that has decided the same issue on mirrored facts. More often, the law is less certain, and the lawyer must construct an answer from more tangential precedent, using at least some of eight skills. They are (1) ranking precedent according to the hierarchy of authority and the principles that are derived from it; (2) formulating rules along a continuum from the broadest to the narrowest interpretations arguable from the facts and wording of precedent; (3) analogizing; (4) distinguishing; (5) eliciting policy; (6) synthesizing fragmented authority into a unified whole; (7) reconciling conflicting or adverse authority; and (8) testing the result of the first seven skills for realism and marketability to the judicial mind.

Chapter 14 explained the *hierarchy of authority* and the principles that are derived from it. This chapter explains the other skills.

§15.2 Formulating a Variety of Rules from the Same Precedent

In §3.2, you learned something about *formulating rules along a continuum from the broadest to the narrowest interpretations.* Start by

153

generating several different formulations of a case's rule, using the techniques explained in §3.2.

Then figure out which formulation is most likely to be adopted by a court. Be careful. You cannot do whatever you please. In predictive writing, formulate the rule as you believe the courts are most likely to in the case you are trying to predict. And in persuasive writing, select a formulation that both favors your client and is likely to be accepted as valid by the court you are trying to persuade. In addition, if the rule has been stated over and over again in many mandatory decisions and in pretty much the same wording, you do not have much room for interpretive maneuver.

§15.3   Analogizing and Distinguishing

An *analogy* shows that two situations are so parallel that the reasoning that justified the decision in one should do the same in the other. When a court is persuaded by an analogy to precedent, the court is said to "follow" the precedent. *Distinguishing* is the opposite of analogy: a demonstration that two situations are so fundamentally dissimilar that the same result should not occur in both. Analogizing and distinguishing have been two of the most important intellectual tools in the slow and gradual construction and evolution of the common law. Both help find and state the rule for which a precedent stands, together with something about how that rule is to be applied. Distinguishing does so by showing what the rule is not and how it is not to be applied. There are three steps in analogizing or distinguishing. First, make sure that the issue in the precedent is the same one you are trying to resolve. Second, identify the precedent's determinative facts. Do not look for mere coincidences between the precedent and the current case; look instead for facts that the precedential court treated as crucial and on which it really relied. Finally, compare the precedent's determinative facts to the facts you are trying to resolve. Although you should strongly consider what the precedential court has said about its reasoning, your conclusion need not necessarily be one that was within the stated or even conscious contemplation of the precedential court, since a court cannot always predict every one of the reasonable consequences of each precedent it sets. Your conclusion should, however, be the most logical and plausible one that is consistent with the heart of the precedential court's reasoning and with public policy.

§15.4   Eliciting Policy from Precedent

Policy is elicited from precedent that explains the underlying goals that the rules involved are intended to advance. "It is revolting," Justice Holmes once wrote, "to have no better reason for a rule of law than that so it was laid down in the time of Henry IV. It is still more revolting if the grounds upon which it was laid down have vanished long since, and the rule simply persists from blind imitation of the past."[1] A court needs confidence that its decisions are consistent with the law's goals. Thus, legal analysis persistently asks what the rules are meant to accomplish, whether the proposed result would accomplish that, and whether the rules and the result would create more problems than they would solve. And where a jurisdiction has no settled rule and therefore must choose between or among competing rules, the rule selected must be one that is consistent with the jurisdiction's policies. Although you may find policy openly stated in precedent, more often it might be implied through the court's reasoning.

§15.5 Synthesis and Reconciliation

Synthesis is binding together several opinions into a whole that stands for a rule or an expression of policy. By focusing on the reasoning and generic facts that the cases have in common, synthesis finds and explains collective meaning that is not apparent from the individual cases themselves.

A passage does not explain a synthesis merely because several cases are mentioned, one after another. It is not a synthesis to describe Case A, describe Case B, describe Case C, describe Case D, and then stop. That is nothing more than an amplified list: the raw materials have been held up to view, but they have not been sewn together.

To turn it into a unified whole, step back and ask yourself what the cases really have in common under the surface. Identify the threads that appear in all four cases, tie the threads together, and organize the analysis around the threads themselves (rather than around the individual cases). The reader cares more about the threads than about the cases, and an individual case is important only to the extent that it teaches something about a thread. It may turn out that Case B sets out the most convincing proof of whatever is in question; Cases A and D agree and are the only out-of-state cases to have decided the issue; and Case C is a much older decision standing for the same rule but on reasoning that is less complete than that expressed in Case B. An effective synthesis might explain Case B in full; use Cases A and D to show that foreign authority agrees; and then use Case C not at all (or only if needed to fill in a remaining gap). Make the synthesis clear to the reader. First, state it in an opening sentence that includes the synthesized rule or statement of policy:

> Although the Supreme Court has not ruled on the question, the trend in the Courts of Appeal is to hold that such a prosecution is dismissable where any of four kinds of government misconduct has occurred: . . .

§15.4   1. O. W. Holmes, *The Path of the Law,* 10 Harv. L. Rev. 457, 469 (1897). (See §11.6.)

A synthesis like this could take several pages to prove because, typically, no case will consider more than one form of misconduct.

Second, organize your explanation around some variation of the formula for structuring proof of a conclusion of law (see §10.1), and use the techniques of forceful writing (see §19.3) to show the reader how the synthesis fits together. Remember that the reader will most easily understand the synthesis in the reverse of the order in which you developed it. Although in developing the synthesis in a first draft you might start from the case details and work up to a synthesized rule or statement of policy, things will be most clear to the reader in later drafts if you reorganize so that you start with the synthesized rule or policy and work down to the supporting details.

Finally, read over your explanation while pretending to be someone who does not know the cases or your synthesis. If the structure of your synthesis is not instantly clear to that kind of reader, find the problem and fix it.

Some syntheses are illustrated in the memoranda and briefs in Appendices C and F through H. (See the marginal notes there.)

Reconciliation: If two decisions seem on the surface to be in conflict, you might be able to demonstrate that the conflict does not exist because on closer examination the two decisions actually stand for the same rule, espouse the same policy, or can be harmonized in some other way. Used in that way, reconciliation has much in common with synthesis. Similarly, a precedent might seem on the surface to conflict with a decision that would be favorable to your client in a current case. There you might be able to demonstrate that the seemingly adverse precedent does not actually conflict with the decision your client would prefer — and in some respects even supports a decision in your client's favor. (But the converse might also happen: if the precedent seems on the surface to be helpful to your client, your adversary might be able to demonstrate that it really stands for something entirely different and actually hurts your client and helps your adversary.) Reconciliation often uses other skills. For example, the seemingly adverse precedent might lose its adversity if it turns out to be distinguishable. Or it might actually reflect favorable policy.

§15.6   Testing for Realism and Marketability

The last skill is that of *testing the result of your reasoning for its realism and marketability to the judicial mind.* Whatever other skills you might use in assembling your analysis, step back from what you are doing and ask yourself whether the result will seem reasonable and just to the typical judge. The experience of adjudicating creates what Roscoe Pound called "the trained intuition of the judge,"[1] an instinct for how the law ought to treat each set of facts. If the result of your reasoning would strike the judicial mind as unrealistic and unreasonable, that mind will reject what

§15.6   1. Roscoe Pound, *The Theory of Judicial Decision,* 36 Harv. L. Rev. 940, 951 (1923).

you have done, even if you have used all the other skills well. (If you do everything else you are taught in law school but omit testing for reasonableness and marketability, your analysis will be *formalistic* because it will do no more than comply with the forms of the law.) Because the law is hardly ever certain, a judge can always fold back your reasoning and make other analogies, build other syntheses, and so forth — or, worse, adopt the analogies, syntheses, and other constructs proposed by your adversary. Karl Llewellyn wrote that "rules *guide,* but they do not *control* decision. There is no precedent that the judge may not at his need either file down to razor thinness or expand into a bludgeon."[2]

The skill of testing for realism and marketability requires that you have some understanding of how the judicial mind operates. That may take a long time to come to know fully, but you are learning it now through the decisions you read in casebooks and through the writing you do in this course. Although lawyers often write arguments based on equity, justice, and reasonability, they *never write down for others to read* the kind of testing described here. It is easy to see why: how could you reduce to writing a test for realism? If a lawyer concludes that the result of her or his reasoning would offend the judge's trained intuition, the lawyer simply starts over again and builds another analysis.

Exercise I.   Emil Risberg's Diary (A "Confidential or Fiduciary Relation"?)

Facts

Returning from an expedition across the Arctic ice cap in the nineteenth century, Emil Risberg and his companions became stranded at the northern tip of Greenland. After several weeks they all died of scurvy and exposure. A few years later, their hut was found, their bodies were buried at sea, and their possessions were returned to their families. Emil Risberg's widow received, among other things, his diary.

Risberg had measured the group's geographic position every day during the expedition, and he recorded those measurements, as well as a mass of other detail, in his diary. His measurements showed that he and the group he led had travelled farther north than anyone else had gone at the time. The diary brought Risberg much posthumous fame, and it was not until early in the twentieth century that any explorer got closer to the north pole. The diary was passed on in Risberg's family through inheritance. Four years ago, when the diary became controversial, it was owned by Risberg's great-granddaughter, Olga Risberg.

The controversy began when a researcher named Sloan announced that Risberg had faked his measurements and that he could not possibly have gotten as far north as the diary showed. Sloan supported his argument with a large amount of scientific evidence involving things like the ocean currents that shift the ice pack and the distances that can be travelled in a day over ice. Olga Risberg took this very badly.

2. K. N. Llewellyn, *The Bramble Bush* 180 (Oceana 1930).

Within a month or two, she went to the officers of the New York Geographical Society, whom she had never met before, and gave them the diary, together with a letter that contained the following sentence:

> I donate my great-grandfather's diary to the Society because I believe the Society is best situated to evaluate the measurements recorded in it and to establish once and for all that Emil Risberg went where he claimed to have gone.

No officer of the Society signed a contract obligating it to do the study in exchange for the gift. The Society had not asked Olga Risberg to make a gift of the diary, and no one at the Society said anything to her about conducting a study or about her motivation for the gift. At the time, the diary had an appraised value of $15,000.

At the time of the gift, the diary was not virtually Olga Risberg's only asset. She was and is an architect living in a suburb of Minneapolis. The total value of her home, car, and savings greatly exceeded (and still greatly exceeds) $15,000.

The Society did nothing to evaluate the diary. Two years ago, Olga demanded that the Society either resolve the controversy or return the diary to her. The Society replied in a letter that, among other things, stated the following:

> When you donated the diary to the Society, you expressed some hope that it would be evaluated. But the Society made no promise — orally or in writing — to study the controversy surrounding the diary. If and when our board of directors chooses to go ahead with a study, we will do so, but you made a gift, which we accepted without conditions.

Sloan has just died. In his papers are notes showing that he had faked his own measurements, that he had started the controversy to build his reputation, and that all along he had believed that Risberg's diary was accurate. Olga has been besieged with offers to buy the diary from people who were unaware that she had donated it to the Society. All of the offers are well into six figures.

Olga Risberg is your client. She wants the Society either to complete very soon an objective and thorough study or to reconvey title to the diary back to her so that she can either sell it or have somebody else do the study. She will be satisfied with either, and she is willing to sue to get it.

You have concluded that the gift cannot be set aside on the grounds of fraud. You are now exploring whether Olga Risberg will be able to persuade a court to impose a constructive trust on the Society's title to the diary. You have learned from *Sharp v. Kosmalski* that the elements of a constructive trust are "(1) a confidential or fiduciary relation, (2) a promise, (3) a transfer in reliance thereon and (4) unjust enrichment."

All four elements are at issue because the Society concedes none of them. In practice, you would consider each element separately. For these exercises, we will focus on the first element alone, leaving the others until later. In other words, the issue for the moment is whether the relationship between Olga Risberg and the Society was "confidential or fiduciary."

From your library research, the three cases reproduced below are most closely on point. Because all of them are New York appellate cases that are not inconsistent with each other, we will not focus on problems of out-of-state authority and inconsistent authority.

Exercise I-A. Read *Sharp v. Kosmalski*, below, and answer these questions: For the Risberg dispute, how does *Sharp* fit into the hierarchy of authority (§14.2)? Is it mandatory? On the question of what a "confidential or fiduciary relationship" means, what rule or rules does *Sharp* reasonably stand for, along a range from broad to narrow (§15.2)? What policy or policies does it stand for (§15.4)?

SHARP v. KOSMALSKI
351 N.E.2d 721 (N.Y. 1976)

GABRIELLI, J. . . .

Upon the death of his wife of 32 years, plaintiff, a 56-year-old dairy farmer whose education did not go beyond the eighth grade, developed a very close relationship with defendant, a school teacher and a woman 16 years his junior. . . . Plaintiff came to depend upon defendant's companionship and, eventually, declared his love for her, proposing marriage to her. Notwithstanding her refusal of his proposal of marriage, defendant continued her association with plaintiff and permitted him to shower her with many gifts, fanning his hope that he could induce defendant to alter her decision concerning his marriage proposal. Defendant was given access to plaintiff's bank account, from which . . . she withdrew substantial amounts of money. Eventually, plaintiff . . . executed a deed naming her a joint owner of his farm . . . . [N]umerous alterations . . . were made to plaintiff's farmhouse in alleged furtherance of "domestic plans" made by plaintiff and defendant.

In September, 1971, while the renovations were still in progress, plaintiff transferred his remaining joint interest to defendant. . . . In February, 1973, . . . defendant ordered plaintiff to move out of his home and vacate the farm. Defendant took possession of the home, the farm and all the equipment thereon, leaving plaintiff with assets of $300.

Generally, a constructive trust may be imposed "[w]hen property has been acquired in such circumstances that the holder of the legal title may not in good conscience retain the beneficial interest" [citations omitted]. In the development of the doctrine of constructive trust as a remedy available to courts of equity, the following four requirements were posited: (1) a confidential or fiduciary relation, (2) a promise, (3) a transfer in reliance thereon and (4) unjust enrichment [citations omitted].

. . . The record in this case clearly indicates that a relationship of trust and confidence did exist between the parties and, hence, the defendant must be charged with an obligation not to abuse the trust and confidence placed in her by the plaintiff. . . .

. . . Even without an express promise . . . courts of equity have imposed a constructive trust upon property transferred in reliance upon a confidential relationship. In such a situation, a promise may be implied or even inferred from the very transaction itself. As Judge Cardozo so eloquently observed: "Though a promise in words was lacking, the whole transaction, it might be found, was 'instinct with an obligation' imperfectly expressed *(Wood v. Duff-Gordon, 222 N.Y. 88, 91)*" *(Sinclair v. Purdy, 235 N.Y. 245, 254 . . .). . . .*

. . . Indeed, in the case before us, it is inconceivable that plaintiff would convey all of his interest in property which was not only his abode but the very means of his livelihood without at least tacit consent upon the part of the defendant that she would permit him to continue to live on and operate the farm. . . .

The salutary purpose of the constructive trust remedy is to prevent unjust enrichment. . . . A person may be deemed to be unjustly enriched if he (or she) has received a benefit, the retention of which would be unjust. . . . This case seems to present the classic example of a situation where equity should [impose a constructive trust in response to] a transaction pregnant with opportunity for abuse and unfairness. . . .

Exercise I-B. Read *Sinclair v. Purdy*, below, and answer these questions: For the Risberg dispute, how does *Sinclair* fit into the hierarchy of authority (§14.2)? Is it mandatory? On the question of what a "confidential or fiduciary relationship" means, what rule or rules does *Sinclair* reasonably stand for, along a range from broad to narrow (§15.2)? What policy or policies does it stand for (§15.4)?

SINCLAIR v. PURDY
139 N.E. 255 (N.Y. 1923)

CARDOZO, J. . . . Elijah F. Purdy [owned a half] interest in real estate in the city of New York. . . . Elijah was a clerk of what was then known as the Fifth District Court. His ownership of real estate subjected him to constant importunities to go bail for those in trouble. The desire to escape these importunities led him to execute a deed conveying his undivided half interest to his sister Elvira [who already owned the other half]. . . . The relation between [brother and sister] was one of harmony and affection, and so continued till the end. . . . There is evidence of repeated declarations by Elvira that, though the [whole] title was in her name, a half interest was his. . . . Elijah died at the age of 80 in 1914. [A niece, who would have inherited from Elijah, brought this suit to establish a trust in favor of Elijah—and thus in favor of the niece—over the property deeded to Elvira.]

. . . The sister's deposition shows that her brother disclosed his plan to her before the making of a deed. . . . It was an expedient adopted to save him the bother of going upon bonds. She does not remember that she made any promise in return. He trusted, as she puts it, to her sense of honor. A little later she learned that the title was in her name.

We think a confidential relation was the procuring cause of the conveyance. The grantor could not disclose the trust upon the face of the deed. If he had done so, he would have defeated the purpose of the transfer, which required that title, to outward appearance, be vested in another. He found, as he thought, in the bond of kinship a protection as potent as any that could be assured to him by covenants of title. . . . "The absence of a formal writing grew out of that very confidence and trust, and was occasioned by it." [Citation omitted.]

In such conditions, the rule in this state is settled that equity will grant relief. [Citations omitted.] . . .

. . . Here was a man transferring to his sister the only property he had in the world. . . . He was doing this, as she admits, in reliance upon her honor. Even if we were to accept her statement that there was no distinct promise to hold it for his benefit, the exaction of such a promise, in view of the relation, might well have seemed to be superfluous. . . . Though a promise in words was lacking, the whole transaction, it might be found, was "instinct with an obligation" imperfectly expressed (*Wood v. Duff-Gordon*, 222 N.Y. 88, 91). It was to be interpreted, not literally or irrespective of its setting, but sensibly and broadly with all its human implications. . . .

Exercise I-C. Read *Tebin v. Moldock* (two opinions), below, and answer these questions: For the Risberg dispute, how does *Tebin* fit into the hierarchy of authority (§14.2)? Is it mandatory? On the question of what a "confidential or fiduciary relationship" means, what rule or rules does *Tebin* reasonably stand for, along a range from broad to narrow (§15.2)? What policy or policies does it stand for (§15.4)?

TEBIN v. MOLDOCK
241 N.Y.S.2d 629 (App. Div. 1963)

BREITEL, J.P. . . . Plaintiffs are the son, sister and two brothers of a New York decedent, all of whom are residents of Poland. Defendant is decedent's niece, and a native-born American. Decedent emigrated to the United States from Poland in 1913. She died in 1956, a widow, leaving only plaintiff son as a surviving descendant. The action was to impose a constructive trust, in favor of plaintiffs, of certain funds deposited in savings institutions, and a multiple dwelling. The assets had once belonged to decedent but she, in the last five years of her life, had transferred them to defendant niece. . . .

[We hold that] a constructive trust [must] be imposed on the . . . assets of decedent in the hands of defendant niece. While the evidence does not establish fraud or undue influence, it does inescapably establish that the assets were transferred on certain promises to hold for the benefit of the son, which promises were made in a confidential relationship. These promises were relied upon, and for their breach equity is bound to provide appropriate relief.

Hermina Tebin, the decedent, was born in Poland in 1882. She married there, but later separated from her husband, left her two sons with her parents, and emigrated to the United States in 1913. One son died in 1920 without issue. The other, who was born in 1904, is the first-named plaintiff in this action.

Since coming to this country decedent lived in New York, earned her livelihood as a midwife, acquired the lower east side multiple dwelling in which she lived, and accumulated cash funds in the amount of about $19,000. During this period of over 40 years, she saw her son in Poland once when she travelled there in 1928, and stayed for some two months. She maintained an intermittent correspondence with him throughout and until the end of her life. . . .

In 1920, decedent brought her sister Aniela to the United States. . . . Defendant niece is Aniela's daughter, whom decedent knew as a growing child, befriended and assisted as a young woman training for an educational career, and who, in decedent's later years, handled her moneys and affairs when illness and age closed in.

[Decedent's health began to deteriorate in 1947. In 1951, she gave bank accounts and a deed to the multiple dwelling to the niece, who signed an] agreement [providing] that decedent should retain the use, free, of her apartment, and receive for her life the net income from the property less a management fee to the niece. The [agreement] recited that the niece was the sole and entire owner of the property.

In August, 1951 decedent made a will in which the niece was named as the sole beneficiary of her estate. It contained the following clause: "Third: I have given certain oral instructions to my said niece, with respect to my son Kazimierz Tebin, and having full faith and confidence in her honesty and integrity, I feel certain that she will carry out my instructions. Nonetheless, in the event that she fails to carry out my instructions, it shall be a matter for her own conscience and not otherwise."

As decedent's end approached, the niece handled more and more of the aunt's affairs, faithfully, and paid all her expenses of living, hospitalization and medical services, out of the funds theretofore transferred to the niece. After the aunt's death, the niece from the same sources paid the funeral expenses. . . .

Presently, the niece holds the real property and about $14,000 of roundly $19,000 transferred to her.

Plaintiffs assert that the niece and her mother frightened decedent with the representation that if any assets were ever received by the son, he being in a Communist country, the assets would be taken from him and that Stalin would kill him. . . .

Plaintiffs also claim that the assets were transferred to the niece on her promise that she would hold them for decedent's son and advance funds as he needed and could profitably use them.

The niece and her mother assert that the relation between the decedent and her son was not a close one, the decedent often complained of the greediness of the son and his persistent and exclusive interest in receiving remittances and gifts. Moreover, it is asserted that the niece was to send moneys to the son only in her exclusive discretion and judgment, and never in excess of $25 in any one month. . . .

In July, 1952 decedent came to Mr. Solon, a lawyer, and retained him to recover her property. . . . Decedent had told Mr. Solon the Stalin story and that she had transferred the assets to the niece to provide her lifetime needs and take care of her son. While there were some ensuing conversations about bringing a lawsuit nothing further was done to prosecute the matter. . . .

The niece testified that decedent told her: "that she was an older woman, that she wanted someone . . . who would look after her needs while she was alive [and] that all during her lifetime [her son] had always written to her and asked her to help, and that since she was giving me everything she had, she thought that he probably would, after her death, seek me out and ask me for help, and she asked me to see that he never got his hands on any lump sum of money. That is why she was giving it to me. But she knew that if he would write to me and ask me for help, and if I felt that he needed it, that I would help him." . . .

In August, 1952 decedent wrote to her son in Poland:

> I was very sick with my heart [because] Aniela and her daughter Janina scared me by telling me that if I leave my estate to you Stalin will take it away from you after I die and that . . . you may be shot to death. So I gave all to Janka — $14,000 and a house and now they are trying to commit me to an insane asylum so they could keep everything for themselves. I will try to have you come here and take it all back because they stole it from me by fraud and they bribed the lawyer.
>
> Keep this letter so that you could appear as a witness if necessary. . . .

It is evident . . . that a secret agreement had been effected between aunt and niece for the benefit of the aunt during her lifetime, and the son. . . .

[A constructive trust will be imposed where] the one who entrusted property did so because of certain understandings, and the one to whom the assets are given acquiesced even in silence (e.g., *Sinclair v. Purdy*, 235 N.Y. 245, 253-254 . . .). . . .

In dealing with the problem of a secret trust or the breach of a confidential relationship the ordinary rules imposed by the Statute of Frauds . . . are not applicable. Equity in this area has always reached beyond the facade of formal documents, absolute transfers, and even limiting statutes on the law side. . . .

Accordingly, the judgment . . . should [provide] for a constructive trust in [the son's] favor. . . .

TEBIN v. MOLDOCK
200 N.E.2d 216 (N.Y. 1964)

Per curiam. . . . The judgment should be modified to limit the scope of the constructive trust imposed on defendant Janina Moldock to an obligation to pay $25 a month for the benefit of Kazimierz Tebin. . . . [W]e conclude the record supports a finding that defendant, occupying a relationship of confidence and trust with decedent, undertook to devote a small part of the property given to her for the benefit of plaintiff. On the basis of defendant's own testimony this would approximate $25 a month. No such breach of confidence or of fiduciary obligation, either before or after decedent's death, has been established as would warrant forfeiture by defendant of the major interest in decedent's property which it was clearly decedent's intent that defendant should have.

Exercise I-D. Is there a way of synthesizing some or all of these cases so that they stand for a unified view of the law (§15.5)? Do not feel bound to your previous answers about the rules and policies that each case stands for. When you think about the three together, you might — or might not — see a bigger picture.

Exercise I-E. Now that we know what the rule is, what are the determinative facts in Olga Risberg's case (§3.2)? List them.

Exercise I-F. Based on your answers to Exercises I-A through I-E, how do you think a court would rule on the issue of whether Olga Risberg and the Society had a "confidential or fiduciary relationship" (§9.1)? This is your tentative prediction.

Exercise I-G. Step back a bit and think about the tentative prediction you made in Exercise I-F. Will it seem reasonable, just, and realistic to the judicial mind (§15.6)? Are there troublesome facts that would bother a judge? If so, why should your prediction stand? What counter-arguments could challenge your prediction (page 102)? Will they overcome your analysis? Why or why not?

Exercise I-H. Considering the results of Exercise I-G, how will the court resolve the issue of whether Olga Risberg and the Society had a "confidential or fiduciary relationship"? This is your final prediction.

Exercise II.   QKast (The Partial Breach Issue)

Facts

QKast is a hot hip-hop group with overtones from blues and soul, which performs against visual backgrounds with fog and laser effects. They appeared on July 25 in the new Nutmeg Dome in Bridgeport, Connecticut. This was the ninth of 16 concerts in QKast's North American tour, which began in June in Milwaukee. After the first concert was highly praised on MTV, all of the remaining performances — except Bridgeport — were sold out within hours after the time tickets became available.

Your client is the Bridgeport Cultural Authority (BCA), which owns the Nutmeg Dome and is now involved in a contract dispute with the Corvo

Construction Company. BCA contracted with Corvo to build the Nutmeg Dome. Among other things, the contract required (in paragraph 4) that Corvo build the Dome "so as to be ready for full use on or before the first day of July" of this year. Paragraph 51 of the contract provided as follows: "Because of the difficulty of determining lost income in the entertainment industry, in the event of Corvo's failure to perform its obligations according to the schedule set out herein, Corvo shall be liable to BCA in the amount of two thousand dollars for each day of delay."

The Dome consists of an auditorium and the offices and facilities needed to run it. BCA moved into the offices on July 1, and the July 25 concert was the first event scheduled in the Dome. The offices constitute six percent of the cubic feet in the building.

Corvo concedes that, due to its own fault, the electrical and ventilation systems were not installed according to the specifications set out in paragraphs 23 and 28 of the contract. Corvo further concedes that, as a result, it would have been unsafe to use QKast's fog effects on July 25 and that there was inadequate electricity behind the stage on that date to use the group's laser effects.

These problems became apparent before the concert, and the local media reported throughout July that QKast might not be able to use its usual fog and laser effects. Eighteen hundred tickets went unsold, and BCA's profit from these tickets would have been $22,000. After the performance, QKast's guitarist told MTV.

> Yo, man, what's up with that? No self-respecting band would play a gig in this place. Can you imagine just standing around on the stage and not being able to get down, no equipment, no nothing? C'mon, man, our performances usually be off the meter. They must think we're some rookies. This Dome is just wack!

On July 27, Corvo was able to complete the work to BCA's satisfaction. BCA believes that public confidence in the Nutmeg Dome is less that it would have been had Corvo performed on time, and that, to an unpredictable extent, it may become harder to book performances and to sell tickets than it otherwise would have been. BCA believes that performers' agents who might have considered booking into the Dome will now be reluctant to do so.

Before BCA decided to build the Dome, it studied the revenue generated by similar structures in other cities of comparable size. The study showed that these buildings have, on average, 12 to 15 bookings a month, of which two or three are concerts and the rest sports, conventions, and community events. The profitability of a booking varies considerably, depending on the nature of the events. But the average net daily income of the buildings studied was $1,500. Net income is profit after all expenses (mortgage, salaries, etc.) have been paid. (Average daily income is 1/365 of annual income—*not* the average income generated by each event.)

You are *not* being asked to determine the rights of the QKast: They might sue, too, but your client is BCA.

BCA wants to recover from Corvo liquidated damages of $52,000 (26 days at $2,000 per day). You are worried that where breach was only partial—Corvo delivered on time a building that was usable for some but not all purposes—liquidated damages might be held so disproportionate to BCA's injury that they would constitute an unenforceable penalty. The issue is thus whether a partial breach can be remedied through liquidated damages.

From your library research, the three cases reproduced below are most closely on point.

Exercise II-A. Read *Banta v. Stamford Motor Co.*, below, and answer these questions: For the BCA-Corvo dispute, how does *Banta* fit into the hierarchy of authority (§14.2)? Is it mandatory? What rule or rules does *Banta* reasonably stand for, along a range from broad to narrow (§15.2)? What policy or policies does it stand for (§15.4)?

BANTA v. STAMFORD MOTOR CO.
92 A. 665 (Conn. 1914)

PRENTICE, C.J. [Stamford Motor Co. contracted with Banta to build him a yacht for $5,500] to be paid in installments as the work of construction progressed. [If the yacht was not delivered by September 1, 1911, the contract provided that Stamford Motor should pay Banta $15 in liquidated damages] for each day of delay. The boat was [delivered on] November 25, 1911.

[Stamford Motor refused to pay Banta $15 per day of delay, for which Banta now sues.]

The boat was . . . intended by the plaintiff for use by him in cruising in Chesapeake Bay during the months of October and November, and later for a pleasure trip in Florida waters. [Stamford Motor knew this. Banta was unable to cruise in Chesapeake Bay. At the time, it would have cost $15 a day to rent a comparable yacht. Banta] did not rent another boat. . . .

[Stamford Motor argues that the daily rate payable for delay is so disproportionate as to constitute a penalty and not liquidated damages. A predetermined damages provision in a contract is really a penalty if its purpose is to insure timely performance by putting the tardy party in fear. But such a provision is liquidated damages if its purpose is to compensate the other party for loss due to delay.]

"[P]arties are allowed to . . . fix beforehand the amount to be paid as damages for a breach . . . but the courts [will not enforce such a provision if the amount is so excessive that it is actually a penalty. When, on the other hand,] the amount of damages would be uncertain or difficult of proof, and the parties have beforehand expressly agreed upon the amount of damages, and that amount is not greatly disproportionate to the presumable loss, their expressed intent will be carried out." [Citation omitted.]

[To determine whether a sum agreed to be paid in the event of breach is an unenforceable penalty or enforceable liquidated damages, the law does not compare that sum with the loss the plaintiff actually suffered, but instead with the loss that the parties] might reasonably have antici- pated at the time the contract was made. [Banta is therefore] under no obligation to show actual damage suffered commensurate with the $15 a day rate. . . .

[Because Banta's injury was the loss of pleasure for a period of time, it would be difficult for a court to calculate an amount of money that would compensate for that loss. The parties agreed beforehand on an amount that would do that. And no fact suggests that this amount was greatly disproportionate to the possible loss which the parties imagined at the time they made the contract. Banta is entitled to liquidated dam- ages of $15 per day of delay.]

Exercise II-B. Read *Hungerford Construction Co. v. Florida Citrus Exposi- tion, Inc.*, below, and answer these questions: For the BCA-Corvo dispute, how does *Hungerford* fit into the hierarchy of authority (§14.2)? Is it mandatory? What rule or rules does *Hungerford* reasonably stand for, along a range from broad to narrow (§15.2)? What policy or policies does it stand for (§15.4)? Is there a similar rule in Connecticut?

HUNGERFORD CONSTRUCTION CO. v. FLORIDA CITRUS EXPOSITION, INC.
410 F.2d 1229 (5th Cir.)

BELL,, Circuit Judge.

[This diversity case concerns] the construction of a building at Winter Haven, Florida . . . which was to serve as an exhibition center for the citrus industry. [The roof leaked, and acoustical plaster inside] was dam- aged. The damaged plaster was replaced by the contractor but sub- sequent leaks left it in a discolored condition. . . .

. . . The building owner was awarded [damages based on] a . . . pro- vision in the contract [that provided for] liquidated damages in the amount of $200.00 per calendar day of delay [after the scheduled com- pletion date. T]he building was delivered to the owner [on time and] was in continuous use thereafter. The owner contended that the liquidated damages clause was nevertheless applicable because of loss of secondary use due to the roof leak. . . .

. . . The building was to be used by the owner mainly for a year round office and for a citrus festival during February and March. [The owners also hoped to rent it for exhibitions, and to charge the public for tours of the structure.]

[We conclude that under Florida law this liquidated damages clause is an unenforceable penalty clause if used] as a basis for damages for loss of secondary use under the facts here.

"[T]he courts . . . allow [parties] to agree upon such a sum as will prob- ably be the fair compensation for the breach of a contract. But when they go beyond this, and . . . stipulate . . . a sum entirely disproportionate to the measure of liability which the law regards as compensatory, the courts will refuse to give effect to the stipulation and will confine the parties to such actual damages as may be pleaded and proved." [Citation omitted.]

[Here, t]he evidence as to loss of secondary use was entirely speculative. One auto show may have been lost but there is no evidence as to the amount of rent which would have been realized out of this transaction or whether the loss occurred during the period in suit. The only other loss of use claimed was in the form of a daily admission charge to the public to see the building and its contents. [But there is no evidence that a significant number of people would actually have wanted to tour this building. This is] entirely disproportionate to the sum of $200.00 . . . per day. . . .

Exercise II-C. Read *Sides Construction Co. v. City of Scott City*, below, and answer these questions: For the BCA-Corvo dispute, how does *Sides* fit into the hierarchy of authority (§14.2)? Is it mandatory? What rule or rules does *Sides* reasonably stand for, along a range from broad to narrow (§15.2)? What policy or policies does it stand for (§15.4)? Is there a similar rule in Connecticut?

SIDES CONSTRUCTION CO. v. CITY OF SCOTT CITY
581 S.W.2d 443 (Mo. Ct. App. 1979)

Greene, Judge.

Plaintiff [contracted to build a swimming complex for] defendant city. The contract provided [that if construction was completed after the scheduled delivery date, the plaintiff would be liable for liquidated damages of $50 per day of delay.]

[T]he contract provided that [the liquidated damages were intended to compensate the city and the public] "for loss to the Owner and the public due to the obstruction of traffic, interference with use of existing or new facilities, and increased cost of engineering, administration, supervision, inspection, etc. . . ."

[The work was completed five and a half months late. The defendant deducted $50 per day from its payments to the plaintiff, which claims] that the liquidated damages provision in the contract was, in reality, a penalty since defendant failed to show that it sustained any actual damages by plaintiff's failure to complete the contract [on time].

The right to stipulate for liquidated damages for delay in completing construction of public works is generally recognized, and the stipulated amount may be recovered, if reasonable. Provisions for fixed per diem payments for delay in the performance of such contracts are usually construed as stipulations for liquidated damages, and not as penalties, where the actual damages are uncertain or are difficult of ascertainment, and where the stated sum is a reasonable estimate of probable damages or is reasonably proportionate to actual damages.

. . . Although we doubt . . . that any proof of actual damages were necessary to bring the liquidated damages provision to life, the defendant has shown damage by the necessity of having to hire additional engineering personnel to inspect the project; by being inconvenienced by the regrading of the parking lot; and, by the loss of interest on its capital investment during the delay period in question.

It is true that the precise amount of such damages is difficult to ascertain. That is why a liquidated damages provision in a construction contract is beneficial to both parties. It protects the owner from a future laborious recitation of item by item damage, and it protects the contractor from a potential lump sum claim of substantial sums of money in the event of breach of the completion provision. Here, . . . the amount of liquidated damages . . . was not greatly disproportionate . . . , and should not be considered as a penalty. . . .

Exercise II-D. Which of these cases is mandatory authority for this issue? Does the mandatory authority tell you everything you need to know about Connecticut law to make a prediction? If not, we have a gap in local law (§§14.1-14.6). How can we use nonmandatory authority to fill it (§§14.3-14.6)?

Exercise II-E. Is there a way of synthesizing two (or all three) of these cases so that they stand for a unified view of the law (§15.5)? Do not feel bound to your previous answers about the rules and policies that each case stands for. When you think about the three together, you might — or might not — see a bigger picture.

Exercise II-F. If the cases cannot be synthesized, can they at least be reconciled (§15.5)? They might not stand together for a unified view of the law (synthesis), but then again, they might not be inconsistent either.

Exercise II-G. If synthesis or reconciliation is unlikely, will one or more of the cases be disregarded because they are distinguishable from BCA's facts or because of the hierarchy of authority (§§14.2, 14.6)?

Exercise II-H. Now that you have identified the controlling rules, what are the determinative facts in the BCA-Corvo dispute (§3.2)? List them.

Exercise II-I. Based on your answers to Exercises II-A through II-H, how do you think a court would rule if BCA were to sue Corvo (§9.1)? This is your tentative prediction.

Exercise II-J. Step back a bit and think about the tentative prediction you made in Exercise II-I. Will it seem reasonable, just, and realistic to the judicial mind (§15.6)? Are there troublesome facts that would bother a judge? If so, why should your prediction stand? What counter-arguments could challenge your prediction (page 102)? Will they overcome your analysis? Why or why not?

Exercise II-K. Considering the results of Exercise II-J, how will a court rule if BCA sues Corvo? This is your final prediction.

16 Working with Statutes

§16.1 Ten Tools of Statutory Interpretation

Interpretation is the art of finding out . . . what [the drafter] intended to convey.

—Francis Lieber

I don't care what their intention was. I only want to know what the words mean.

—Oliver Wendell Holmes

These two quotations might seem to express contradictory approaches to interpreting any source of law. The first focuses on what the lawmaker intended to do, and the second on what the lawmaker did. The first approach might use any reliable evidence of intent, but the second concentrates on the words actually used.

The search for meaning or intent begins with the words of the statute. At one time, nearly every jurisdiction in the United States followed the "plain meaning" rule, which permits inquiry into other evidence of legislative intent only where the words of the statute do not plainly convey meaning. In recent decades, however, a number of courts have modified or abandoned the plain meaning rule and now search outside the statute for evidence of intent even where the statutory wording seems clear and unambiguous. Those courts that still adhere to the plain meaning rule do so because they believe legislative intent can most efficiently be established by finding meaning in the words of the statute itself and by inquiring further only when those words are ambiguous. Those courts that examine other evidence of intent even when the statutory words are clear do so because they believe that the words' meaning is not good enough if other evidence shows that the legislature intended something else. (Are you beginning to understand the tension between what words mean and what their author intended them to mean? If the legislature wanted to communicate one thing but instead communicated another, which message should a court choose to receive—the one sent or the one intended to be sent?)

Aside from reading the statute, what kind of inquiry could a court make? You might think that the sensible thing would be to ask the legislature what it had in mind. But most state legislatures are made up of between 100 and 200 voting members, and Congress includes 100 Senators and 435 Representatives. Even if a group could have a collective state of mind, a legislature is just too large to be able to tell you what it, as a group, was thinking in some earlier year when it enacted the statute you are interested in. In addition, legislatures consider such a staggering number of bills that most members are not likely to have clear memories of what they thought a bill meant when they voted for or against it. And even on the day of a vote, most legislators have no more understanding of a bill than they can get from a quick reading of it or—more likely—from reading a short synopsis of it. Finally, many questions of statutory interpretation arise long after enactment, when few of the enacting legislators are still in office or even alive.

How, then, can the meaning be found? Where the meaning of a statute has not been settled, courts use ten tools:

1. the *wording* of the statutory section at issue;
2. any *statutory* context that might indicate the legislature's intent: other sections of the same statute, other statutes addressed to the same subject matter, the heading of the section at issue, and the statute's title and preamble (if any);
3. the historical context: the *events and conditions* that might have *motivated* the legislature to act;
4. the context created by announcements of *public policy* in other statutes and in case law;
5. *interpretations of the statute by lower or collateral courts* (if the statute has been comprehensively interpreted by *higher* courts, its meaning would be settled through mandatory authority, and none of these tools would be needed);
6. the statute's *legislative history,* which consists of the documents and records created by various parts of the legislature during the course of enactment;
7. a collection of maxims known as the *canons of statutory construction;*
8. *comparison with parallel statutes in other jurisdictions,* focusing on judicial interpretation of those statutes, as well as the circumstances in which they were enacted;

9. *interpretations of the statute by administrative agencies* charged with enforcing the statute; and
10. *interpretations of the statute by scholars* who are recognized experts in the field.

Beginners sometimes overlook the possibility that terminology in a particular section of a statute may be defined in another section of the same statute, or even in a definitions section that applies to an entire code. In addition, a relatively mundane word is sometimes defined, for the purposes of the statute, in a surprising way. And a term may have different meanings in different statutes. As versatile as the English language is, the number of ideas needing to be expressed seems to exceed the number of concise words and phrases available to be symbols for them, and some expressions have to do double or triple duty.

For example, section 6-201 ("Franchises") of the Administrative Code of the City of New York defines "the streets of the city" as

> streets, avenues, highways, boulevards, concourses, driveways, bridges, tunnels, parks, parkways, waterways, docks, bulkheads, wharves, piers, and public grounds or waters within or belonging to the city

while section 16-101(3) ("Department of Sanitation") defines "street" to include any

> street, avenue, road, alley, lane, highway, boulevard, concourse, driveway, culvert and crosswalk, and every class of road, square and place, and all parkways and through vehicular park drives except a road within any park or a wharf, pier, bulkhead, or slip by law committed to the custody, and control of the department of ports and terminals.

Why might a wharf be a "street" for one purpose, but not for another? In section 6-201, the word "street" is a symbol for a place where activity might require getting a franchise from the city. In section 16-101(3), the same word is a symbol for a place for which the Department of Sanitation has the responsibility for cleaning, sweeping, sanding, and removing ice, snow, and garbage. In each case, the statute would be unreadable if the idea were fully described every time it is mentioned.

Do not focus solely on a rule's phrasing while ignoring the policies underlying the rule. The result is an overly mechanical application, often far from the contemplation of the legislature or the policies the rule is meant to advance. Remember that words are merely symbols for concepts, and that interpretation is the art of seeing through the words to locate the ideas represented. Courts will not mechanically apply a statute in a literal way if that would undermine the approach the legislature has taken to solving the problem in dispute.

Although legislative history is often resorted to and would seem to be the most direct evidence of the legislature's purpose, it is sometimes viewed with suspicion. It is often incomplete, especially with state statutes, and,

because of the chaotic nature of legislative work, it can be internally contradictory. It is also vulnerable to manipulation by legislators who may not
share the views of a majority of their colleagues. And the collective intent of
a legislature (or any other large group of people) may simply be more a
metaphysical idea than something ever provable through evidence. On the
other hand, some portions of the typical legislative history tend to be
viewed by the courts as particularly reliable. Those are the reports of the
committees that considered and reported the bill and the floor comments of
the sponsors of the bill, except as to amendments not considered by the
committees and not endorsed by the sponsors.

Although scholars have criticized many of the canons of construction,
courts continue to use them regularly. It is certainly true, as Judge Posner
has pointed out, that the courts have no way of knowing whether legislators
have enacted a particular statute with the canons in mind, or even whether
legislators have ever heard of the canons of construction.[1] It is also true, as
Karl Llewellyn showed, that canons tend to be inconsistent with one another and that courts may invoke them to justify decisions rather than to
help in making decisions.[2] On the other hand, few scholars would reject all
the canons, and some canons are never criticized, such as these:

- A statute is to be construed in light of the harm the legislature meant
  to remedy.
- Statutory words and phrases are to be construed in the context of the
  entire statute of which they are a part.
- Statutes on the same subject (in Latin, *in pari materia*) are to be
  construed together.
- Where possible, statutes are to be construed so that their constitution-
  ality is preserved.
- Penal statutes are to be narrowly construed.
- Statutes in derogation of the common law are to be narrowly construed.

In a less certain category are canons — many of which contradict each
other — on whether repeals by implication are favored; on whether the
expression of one thing in a statute necessarily excludes another not mentioned; on the construction to be given to words of permission and to words
of command; on whether words and phrases judicially construed in other
contexts before enactment are to be given the same meaning in a statute; on
the effect of grammar on interpretation; on the effect of statute titles, section headings, and preambles on interpretation; on the treatment to be
given to legislative history; on the effect of interpretations by administrative
agencies; on the effect of judicial interpretations in which the legislature, by
not amending, might have acquiesced; and on a host of other issues.

Canons are rules of a sort and must be proved with authority, usually
case law to be found in the digests under the topic heading of "Statutes." But

---

§16.1   1. Richard A. Posner, *Statutory Interpretation — in the Classroom and in the
Courtroom,* 50 U. Chi. L. Rev. 800, 806 (1983).
    2. Karl N. Llewellyn, *The Common Law Tradition: Deciding Appeals* 521-35 (Little, Brown
& Co. 1960).

be careful: the lawyer hurling a canon as an epithet is apt to find a contradictory one thrown right back. A convincing argument is instead a thoughtful and thorough analysis of the statute. Canons play a part in that, but not the largest part.

Let us examine two decisions from a single litigation to see seven of the ten tools in operation.

McBOYLE v. UNITED STATES
43 F.2d 273 (10th Cir. 1930)

PHILLIPS, Circuit Judge.

William W. McBoyle was convicted and sentenced for an alleged violation of the National Motor Vehicle Theft Act, section 408, title 18, U.S. Code. The indictment charged that on October 10, 1926, McBoyle caused to be transported in interstate commerce from Ottawa, Ill., to Guymon, Okl., one Waco airplane, . . . which was the property of the United States Aircraft Corporation and which had theretofore been stolen; and that McBoyle then and there knew it had been stolen. . . .

In the movies, when you hear someone say, "They've crossed the state line—call the FBI," this is the kind of statute that creates federal jurisdiction.

The primary question is whether an airplane comes within the purview of the National Motor Vehicle Theft Act. This act defines the term "motor vehicle," as follows:

> The term "motor vehicle" when used in this section shall include an automobile, automobile truck, automobile wagon, motor cycle, or any other self-propelled vehicle not designed for running on rails.

Counsel for McBoyle contend that the word "vehicle" includes only conveyances that travel on the ground; that an airplane is not a vehicle . . . ; and that, under the doctrine of ejusdem generis, the phrase "any other self-propelled vehicle" cannot be construed to include an airplane.

A canon of construction: Where general language follows a list of specific examples, the general language's meaning is limited to the same nature [ejusdem generis] as the specific, unless there are clear indications to the contrary.

[In a passage deleted here, the court traces various meanings ascribed to the word "vehicle" in both legal and popular usage, quoting authorities that define a vehicle as an object that travels and carries things or people. One of the definitions specifies that a ship is a vehicle; according to

The court focuses on the words of the statute and considers the canon of ejusdem generis only long enough to decide that the court's interpretation of the statute would not offend the canon.

another, a vehicle carries things or people, "especially on land."]

Both the derivation and the definition of the word "vehicle" indicate that it is sufficiently broad to include any means or device by which persons or things are carried or transported, and it is not limited to instrumentalities used for traveling on land, although the latter may be the limited or special meaning of the word. We do not think it would be inaccurate to say that a ship or vessel is a vehicle of commerce.

An airplane is self-propelled [and] is designed to carry passengers and freight from place to place. It runs partly on the ground but principally in the air. It furnishes a rapid means for transporation of persons and comparatively light articles of freight and express. It therefore serves the same general purpose as an automobile, automobile truck, or motorcycle. It is of the same general kind or class as the motor vehicles specifically enumerated in the statutory def inition and, therefore, construing an airplane to come within the general term, "any other self-propelled vehicle," does not offend against the maxim of ejusdem generis.

Furthermore, some meaning must be ascribed to [Congress's use of the] phrase "any other self-propelled vehicle" [immediately after Congress had specifically listed] all of the known self-propelled vehicles designed for running on land. . . .

We conclude that the phrase, "any other self-propelled vehicle," includes an airplane. . . .

Are you convinced by the court's interpretation of the statutory wording?

COTTERAL, Circuit Judge (dissenting). I feel bound to dissent on the ground that the National Motor Vehicle Theft Act should not be construed as relating to the transportation of airplanes.

A prevailing rule is that a penal statute is to be construed strictly against an offender and it must state clearly the persons and acts denounced. [Citations omitted.]

Another *canon of construction.* The dissenter will soon try to link this one up with *ejusdem generis.*

It would have been a simple matter in enacting the statute to insert, as descriptive

Now the dissenter takes on the *words of the statute,* but in a way words, airplanes, aircraft, or flying machines. If they had been in the legislative mind, the language would not have been expressed in such uncertainty as "any other self-propelled vehicle not designed for running on rails." The omission to definitely mention airplanes requires a construction that they were not included. Furthermore, by excepting vehicles running on rails, the meaning of the act is clarified. These words indicate it was meant to be confined to vehicles that *run,* but not on rails, and it did not extend to those that *fly*. . . .

The rule of ejusdem generis has special application to this statute. General words following a particular designation are usually presumed to be restricted so as to include only things or persons of the same kind, class, or nature, unless there is a clear manifestation of a contrary purpose. [Citation omitted.] The general description in this statute refers to vehicles of the same general class as those enumerated. We may assume an airplane is a vehicle, in being a means of transportation. And it has its own motive power. But is an airplane classified generally with "an automobile, automobile truck, automobile wagon, or motor cycle"? Are airplanes regarded as *other types of automobiles* and the like? A moment's reflection demonstrates the contrary.

Counsel for appellant have referred us to debates in Congress when the act was pending as persuasive of an interpretation in his favor. [Citations to the Congressional Record omitted.] . . . The discussions of the proposed measure are enlightening . . . in showing that the theft of automobiles was so prevalent over the land as to call for punitive restraint, but airplanes were never even mentioned.

It is familiar knowledge that the theft of automobiles had then become a public menace, but that airplanes had been rarely stolen if at all, and it is a most uncommon thing even at this date. The prevailing mischief sought to be corrected is an aid in the construction of a statute. [Citation omitted.]

the court did not. The dissenter asks what Congress could have written into the statute but chose not to.

The dissenter turns to the *canon* considered in the court's opinion.

Because this question was not addressed in the reports of the committees that drafted the statute, the only relevant *legislative history* is the floor debates. Floor debates are a notoriously unreliable form of legislative history because they can include remarks by legislators who took no part in drafting the statute in committee, who might not have thought much about it, and who may not even have read it. But here the floor debates reveal surprising evidence of legislative intent: no legislator complained about a need to do something about airplane theft.

Finally, the dissenter takes up the *historical context.*

McBOYLE v. UNITED STATES
283 U.S. 25 (1931)

Mr. Justice HOLMES delivered the opinion
of the Court. . . . The question is the meaning of the word "vehicle" in the phrase "any
other self-propelled vehicle not designed
for running on rails." No doubt etymologi-
cally it is possible to use the word to signify
a conveyance working on land, water or air,
and sometimes legislation extends the use
in that direction, e.g., land and air, water
being separately provided for, in the Tariff
Act [of] 1922 [citation omitted]. But in
everyday speech "vehicle" calls up the picture of a thing moving on land. Thus in Rev.
Stats. §4, intended, the Government suggests, rather to enlarge than to restrict
the definition, vehicle includes every contrivance capable of being used "as a means
of transportation on land." And this is repeated, expressly excluding aircraft, in
the Tariff Act [of] 1930 [citation omitted].
So here, the phrase under discussion
calls up the popular picture. For after including automobile truck, automobile
wagon and motor cycle, the words "any
other self-propelled vehicle not designed
for running on rails" still indicate that a
vehicle in the popular sense, that is a vehicle running on land, is the theme. It is a
vehicle that runs, not something, not commonly called a vehicle, that flies. Airplanes
were well known in 1919, when this statute
was passed; but it is admitted that they
were not mentioned in the reports or in
the debates in Congress. It is impossible
to read words that so carefully enumerate
the different forms of motor vehicles and
have no reference of any kind to aircraft,
as including airplanes under a term that
usage more and more confines to a different
class. The counsel for the petitioner have
shown that the phraseology of the statute
as to motor vehicles follows that of earlier
statutes of Connecticut, Delaware, Ohio,
Michigan and Missouri, not to mention

*While dissecting the words of the
statute,* Holmes considers the
statutory context.

Historical context and *legislative
history* are considered together.

Again, Holmes simultaneously
uses two tools—this time
legislative history and *comparison with parallel statutes.* The
point is that Congress seems to
have modelled the Act on statutes
that clearly are not addressed to
aircraft theft. The most telling
comparison—and perhaps the
most enjoyable for its irony—is
with a *city's* traffic regulations,
which certainly could not have
been meant to penalize the
stealing of airplanes.

the late Regulations of Traffic for the District of Columbia [citation omitted], none of which can be supposed to leave the earth.

. . . When a rule of conduct is laid down in words that evoke in the common mind only the picture of vehicles moving on land, the statute should not be extended to aircraft, simply because it may seem to us that a similar policy applies, or even upon the speculation that, if the legislature had thought of it, very likely broader words would have been used. [Citation omitted.]

Judgment reversed.

As important as *policy* is, it also has its limitations. Here Holmes notes that his court is permitted to construe the statute only to accomplish the goal Congress had selected for it—and not some other goal the court might think equally valid.

_____

What idea or ideas—and which tools of statutory construction—most persuaded the Supreme Court to see the statute differently from the way the Tenth Circuit saw it?

Missing from these opinions are the three tools that use interpretations of the statute by others: by lower or collateral courts, by administrative agencies, and by scholars expert in the field. Each tool's absence has an explanation. First, the judges themselves tell us why they have no cases on point to guide them: airplane theft seems to have been exceedingly rare at the time. Second, no administrative agency would have had a reason to interpret the statute because no administrative agency was charged with enforcing it. And finally, no law review articles seem to have analyzed the statute helpfully.

Parenthetically, Congress later amended the statute so that it now penalizes anyone who "transports in interstate or foreign commerce a motor vehicle, vessel, *or aircraft,* knowing the same to have been stolen."[3] Having learned something from *McBoyle* about how overly specific wording can make a statute like this at least partly obsolete, Congress later defined "aircraft" so that the statute could adapt to changing technology: "'Aircraft' means any contrivance now known *or hereafter invented* . . . for flight in

_____

3. 18 U.S.C. § 2312 (2000) (emphasis added). An adjacent section penalizes anyone who knowingly "receives, possesses, conceals, stores, barters, sells, or disposes of any motor vehicle, vessel, *or aircraft,* which has crossed a State or United States boundary after being stolen." 18 U.S.C. § 2313(a) (2000) (emphasis added). (Stealing a vehicle or an airplane would, of course, be punished under the law of the state where the theft took place. But once a stolen vehicle or airplane is moved out of state, it will be much harder for the local authorities to prosecute the thieves or those who received the stolen property from them. To make available the resources of the federal government, Congress made it a separate federal offense to move such stolen property across state lines.)

the air."[4] Although the amendment was enacted when airplanes were still powered by piston engines and propellers rather than by jets, it probably penalizes the act of knowingly moving a stolen space shuttle across a state line.

§16.2 How to Present Statutory Analysis in Writing

Writing about a statutory question focuses on the words of the statute because the words are what is to be interpreted. The crucial term or phrase should appear, inside quotation marks, when you state the issue, your conclusion, the rule on which you rely, and the most important steps of logic in the analysis:

> If regularly scheduled boat service is considered one of the "streets of the city" within the meaning of section 6-201, would the Interborough Repertory Theatre need to get a franchise to offer entertainment on evening cruises using the theater's own boat?

But your obligation to tell the reader the *rule* on which you rely usually cannot be satisfied merely by quoting the statute in unedited form. Because statutes are drafted to govern wide ranges of factual possibilities, a rule expressed entirely in statutory language may need to be reformulated for practical application. If, for example, you are asked to determine whether moving a stolen "boat" across a state line violates the National Motor Vehicle Theft Act, you will not be able to express the controlling rule by quoting the statutory sentence on which your reasoning will be based: "The term 'motor vehicle' when used in this section shall include an automobile, automobile truck, automobile wagon, motor cycle, or any other self-propelled vehicle not designed for running on rails."

For the purpose of resolving your issue, that sentence does not fully communicate the governing rule. It does not even contain a list of elements. A far more useful formulation, supportable by the interpretative case law (*McBoyle*), would be something like this: "For the purposes of the Act, a 'motor vehicle' is a conveyance that is 'self-propelled,' that operates primarily on land, and that does not run on rails." This is so much easier to apply: A boat does not run on rails; it might be self-propelled; but, it hardly ever transports things or people across land. What the reader needs is a statement of the rule that is *embodied* in the statute.

Do not be careless, however, when you reformulate the statutory language into a useful expression of a rule: you want something that you can apply to facts, but you also want something that accurately pronounces the statute's meaning. If you oversimplify or distort, trouble awaits. It helps to use the key phrases of the statute. "Self-propelled" is a key phrase here because not all boats are that. A barge, pushed by a tug, is not self-propelled.

---

4. 18 U.S.C. § 2311 (2000) (emphasis added).

Exercise I. Plagiarism and the Board of Bar Examiners

Hardy and Tisdale were enrolled in a law school course in which students write and submit papers. They were given identical assignments. Tisdale wrote a draft of the first half of his paper before Hardy did, and Hardy asked to see it. That was forbidden by the course rules because the assignment's due date had not yet arrived. Tisdale showed Hardy what he had written anyway and let Hardy borrow the computer disk on which Tisdale's work was stored.

Hardy copied Tisdale's work onto a disk of his own. He then changed as many of the words as he could. When he was finished, the first half of two papers had approximately the same organization, although about 80% of the words were different — similar, but different.

Tisdale and Hardy then got into an argument in which one of them said unkind things about Nirvana and the other said unkind things about Garth Brooks. They stopped speaking to each other. Tisdale wrote the rest of his paper on his own. Hardy went to the library to find what he would need for the second half of his paper. On the due date, they submitted their papers.

But a paper derived from another can never really be purged of all noticeable traces of the original. The teacher instantly recognized the similarity between the first half of Hardy's paper and the first half of Tisdale's. In the second half of Hardy's paper, the teacher noticed phrases in Hardy's paper that did not "sound like" him. The teacher had a vague memory of having seen those phrases previously somewhere else. (To design assignments and to keep up in their field, teachers read cases, articles, and books constantly.) The teacher logged onto LEXIS and then onto WESTLAW, typing in the suspect phrases from Hardy's paper and asking for all the sources in which they appeared. (In this way, a teacher can easily check a student's paper for plagiarism.) The teacher found a number of instances where Hardy had copied passages word for word from sources he did not cite and without quote marks around the copied words.

When confronted with all this, Hardy claimed that by changing most of the words in Tisdale's draft he had not misrepresented someone else's work as his own, and that the plagiarism in the second half of his paper was not deliberate. He said that while researching he must have written down the phrases in question, then misplaced the cites, and later assumed that the words in his notes were his own. The teacher rejected that explanation and gave Hardy a failing grade for the course. The law school suspended him for a year. (Tisdale was also punished, but it is Hardy who poses the issue in this Exercise.)

Hardy tried to transfer to another law school. But law schools do not consider transfer applications from students who are in trouble for academic dishonesty. After a year, Hardy returned to the law school that had suspended him. Last spring, he graduated. He has applied for admission to the Wisconsin bar.

In every state, an applicant for admission to the bar must prove to the bar examiners that she or he has the type of character needed to practice law. After passing the bar examination, the applicant must fill out a detailed character questionnaire and submit supporting documents, including an affidavit from the applicant's law school. A false, misleading, or incomplete answer on the questionnaire is itself grounds for denying the application for admission. Every state's questionnaire asks, among other things, whether the applicant has ever been accused of academic dishonesty, and the law school's affidavit must answer the same question.

On his questionnaire, Hardy described what he had done and what the school had done. And in its affidavit, the law school reported — as it must — the same thing.

After admission to the bar, a lawyer can be professionally disciplined if the lawyer commits professional misconduct in violation of the state's code governing lawyers' ethics. In most states, one agency reviews the character of bar applicants, and a different agency investigates complaints of unethical conduct by lawyers. Admission to the bar and discipline of already-admitted attorneys are two separate processes, although the two share some underlying purposes.

(As a practical matter, a failing grade in a course can seriously damage a student's chances of finding a desirable job. Character trouble with the bar examiners or suspension from law school would make a student an extremely unattractive job applicant. For an admitted attorney, the same is true of professional discipline, even if the discipline falls short of disbarment or suspension.)

The statute-like provisions governing admission to the bar are usually found in a state's court rules as well as in the bar examiners' own rules. A state's ethics code, too, is often found in the state's court rules.

Your research has focused on the following: (1) two Wisconsin Supreme Court Rules governing admission to the bar, (2) two Wisconsin Board of Bar Examiners Rules, and (3) four cases, each interpreting a statute or court rule (quoted within the case). One of the cases is from Wisconsin. It interprets an attorney disciplinary rule rather than a rule governing admission to the bar.

Will Hardy be admitted to the Wisconsin bar?

WISCONSIN SUPREME COURT RULES

SCR 22.46.   Character and fitness investigations of bar admission applicants

(1) . . .

(2) . . . the applicant shall make a full and fair disclosure of all facts and circumstances pertaining to questions involving the applicant's character and fitness. Failure to provide information or misrepresentation in a disclosure constitutes grounds for denial of admission.

SCR 40.06.   Requirement as to character and fitness to practice law

(1) An applicant for bar admission shall establish good moral character and fitness to practice law. The purpose of this requirement is to limit admission to those applicants found to have the qualities of character and fitness needed to assure to a reasonable degree of certainty the integrity

and the competence of services performed for clients and the maintenance of high standards in the administration of justice . . . .

(3) An applicant shall establish to the satisfaction of the board that the applicant satisfies the requirement set forth in sub. (1) . . . . The board shall decline to certify the character and fitness of an applicant who knowingly makes a materially false statement of material fact or who fails to disclose a fact necessary to correct a misapprehension known by the applicant to have arisen in connection with his or her application . . . .

(5) The dean of a law school in this state shall have a continuing duty to report to the board any information reflecting adversely upon the character and fitness to practice law of an applicant for bar admission . . . .

RULES OF THE WISCONSIN BOARD OF BAR EXAMINERS

BA 6.01

Standard of character and fitness. A lawyer should be one whose record of conduct justifies the trust of clients, adversaries, courts and others with respect to the professional duties owed to them. A record manifesting a deficiency in the honesty, diligence or reliability of an applicant may constitute a basis for denial of admission. The Supreme Court Rules place on the applicant the burden of producing information sufficient to affirmatively demonstrate the character and fitness appropriate for bar admission.

BA 6.02

Relevant conduct. The revelation or discovery of any of the following should be treated as cause for further inquiry before the Board decides whether the applicant possesses the character and fitness to practice law . . . (b) academic misconduct . . . .

In re SCRUGGS
475 N.W.2d 160 (Wis. 1991)

PER CURIAM
[Respondent is a lawyer admitted to the bar of this state.]

[Before he was admitted, and as a third-year law student applying to a law firm for a job, respondent] provided the firm with what purported to be a copy of his law school transcript, showing a grade point average of 3.2. In fact, the transcript was not that of [respondent] . . . It appears from the record that [respondent] submitted the transcript of a fellow student on which he had substituted his own name and biographical information. After he was hired by the firm, [he] made several false, erroneous and inaccurate statements to [the firm,] concerning . . . his law school grade point average.

After his employment with that firm was terminated[, he made similar misrepresentations when applying for another job.] . . .

[At least some of this conduct occurred after respondent was admitted to the bar.]

The referee [who heard the evidence] concluded that [respondent] engaged in conduct involving dishonesty, fraud, deceit and misrepresentation in violation of SCR 20:8.4(c).[1] . . .

. . . [We suspend respondent's] license to practice law for two years.

In re ZBIEGIEN
433 N.W.2d 871 (Minn. 1988)

PER CURIAM:

[The petitioner has graduated from law school and has applied for admission to the bar of this state.]

[In a law school seminar in products liability, the petitioner submitted a draft paper that] was plagiarized in large part from the works of other authors. Nearly all of the first 12 pages were taken verbatim or nearly verbatim from a number of law review articles without proper citation in the endnotes. In addition, some endnotes were taken from other sources in such a way as to give the appearance that they were petitioner's own work. Several other portions of the paper were paraphrased or had words or phrases omitted or substituted for the originals as they appeared in various published sources. Again, no proper citation was given. . . . [The petitioner received] a course grade of "F". . . .

[The petitioner] admitted the extensive plagiarism . . . both in the form of direct quotes not properly indented and footnoted and paraphrased passages not appropriately credited to the original sources. [He said that his computer printer had not been printing properly, and he did not proofread the paper as it came out of the printer because at the time his wife was disabled from an auto accident, and his teenage son had ran away from home.] . . .

The [State Board of Law Examiners, however,] found that not only had petitioner plagiarized a substantial amount of text and footnotes taken verbatim, or nearly verbatim, from various published sources without proper identification [and] that the alleged computer problems did not explain away the plagiarism. . . .

Petitioner appeals from that determination. . . .

Rule II.A of the Minnesota Rules of the Supreme Court for Admission to the Bar provides that an applicant must establish good character and fitness to the satisfaction of the Board.

"Good character" is defined as "traits that are relevant to and have a rational connection with the present fitness or capacity of an applicant to practice law." Definition 4, Minn. R. Admis. Bar (1986). . . .

---

§16.2 1. SCR 20.8.4 provides: "It is professional misconduct for a lawyer to: . . . (c) engage in conduct involving dishonesty, fraud, deceit or misrepresentation."

Plagiarism, the adoption of the work of others as one's own, does involve an element of deceit, which reflects on an individual's honesty. . . . The petitioner clearly plagiarized large sections of his paper. [Plagiarism] is an affront to honest scholars everywhere and to other members of [a law school] class whose legitimate pursuits would be weighed against this appropriated material. Petitioner was guilty of this act. . . .

It is the view of this court that [this] petitioner's conduct, wrongful though it was, does not demonstrate such lack of character that he must be barred from the practice of law. He has been punished [already in practical terms because the Board's investigation has delayed his admission to the bar] for over a year. [In dealing with law school officials and when testifying before the Board, the petitioner was filled with genuine remorse and shame.] We . . . believe that this conduct will not be repeated. We hold that, under the facts and circumstances of this case petitioner will not be barred from the practice of law. . . .

KELLEY, J (dissenting):
. . . When this court admits an applicant to the practice of law, it certifies to the public that . . . it knows of no reason why the applicant-admittee does not possess the character which the profession demands of all admitted attorneys in this state. We judge an applicant's character by the standard that it must reflect those traits of integrity, honesty and trustworthiness necessary for a lawyer to possess when he or she represents clients, when dealing with professional peers, and when appearing before the courts. Yet, in this case, notwithstanding that we know that this petitioner has . . . recently engaged in outright dishonesty by plagiarizing and claiming as his own the intellectual works of others with no attempt at appropriate attribution of source, the majority would conclude, even as it condemns the petitioner's conduct, that he has been "punished" enough by the delay in his admission. . . .

[D]enial of admission . . . has not as its purpose punishment but rather protection of the public and the integrity of the legal system. . . .

Even though I would deny the petition, I would not foreclose forever, petitioner's admission to the Bar. I would, however, require that he prove that after a reasonable period of time had elapsed he then . . . demonstrates that from the experience he has learned to conduct his affairs in a manner that this court can, with confidence, certify to the public that his character does reflect traits of integrity and trustworthiness.

In re LAMBERIS
443 N.E.2d 549 (Ill. 1982)

SIMON, J:
[The respondent is a lawyer admitted to the bar of this state.]

In writing a thesis which he submitted to [a law school] in satisfaction of a requirement for a [post-J.D.] master's degree in law, the respondent [while a member of the bar] "knowingly plagiarized" . . . [i]n preparing pages 13 through 59 of his 93-page thesis [by using two books' words] substantially verbatim and without crediting the source . . . .

The purpose for which respondent used the appropriated material . . . displays a lack of honesty which cannot go undisciplined, especially because honesty is so fundamental to the functioning of the legal profession . . . .

[Under] DR 1-102(A)(4) of the [Illinois Code of Professional Responsibility] "[a] lawyer shall not *** engage in conduct involving dishonesty, fraud, deceit, or misrepresentation." . . .

Having decided that the respondent's conduct warrants some discipline, we must decide whether to impose disbarment, suspension or censure. The Hearing Board recommended censure; the Review Board recommended suspension for six months; and the Administator argues here for disbarment . . . .

[I]n the 10 years since respondent entered private practice, no client has ever complained about his conduct, professional or otherwise . . . .

[Although] the respondent's conduct undermined the honor system that is maintained in all institutions of learning[, the law school involved] has already . . . expelled [him], an act which will also undoubtedly ensure that the respondent will be hereafter excluded from the academic world.

In view of the respondent's apparently unblemished record in the practice of law and the disciplinary sanctions which have already been imposed by [the law school], we choose censure as the most appropriate discipline for the respondent.

In re WIDDISON
539 N.W.2d 671 (S.D. 1995)

GILBERTSON, J:

[The applicant has graduated from law school and applied for admission to the bar of this state.]

[During his] second year of law school, he wrote and submitted a casenote for law review publication [which] included . . . material from secondary sources which he had failed to cite . . . . The faculty advisor . . . assigned [the applicant] a failing grade in the law review course . . . .

[After the applicant took the final exam in the course on Worker's Compensation, the professor discovered two students' examination answers] were strikingly similar . . . . [T]he professor assigned a failing grade to each examination[, one of which was the applicant's].

[The applicant] has the burden of proving by clear and convincing evidence his qualifications for admission to practice law in this state . . . . One of those qualifications is that he "be a person of good moral character." SDCL 6-16-2. SDCL 16-16-2.1 defines "good moral character" as including, but not limited to, "qualities of honesty, candor, trustworthiness, diligence, reliability, observance of fiduciary and financial responsibility, and respect for the rights of others and for the judicial process."

That statute also provides that "*[a]ny* fact reflecting a deficiency of good moral character may constitute a basis for denial of admission." SDCL 16-16-2.1 (emphasis added). Good moral character is a prerequisite to practice law in every state. . . .

"The state bears a special responsibility for maintaining standards among members of the licensed professions" such as attorneys at law. [citations omitted] . . . The same zeal to protect the public from the unfit within the bar must also be applied to the unfit who would seek to enter the bar. . . .

[The applicant] has not met his burden of proving good moral character. [We affirm the order denying his application for admission to the bar], with leave to reapply at a future date provided [the applicant] is able to rectify his character deficits and show he has gained an understanding of, and the ability to put into practice, the qualities of honesty, candor, and responsibility required [of lawyers].

Exercise II. *The Ironwood Tract*

Fourteen years ago, Palo Verde Development Corporation purchased a deed to an Arizona parcel known as the Ironwood tract. The tract is unimproved terrain and has never been fenced or built upon. It is one mile from a paved road and 65 miles from downtown Phoenix. Today, the nearest residential development is Verde River Estates, nine miles from the tract, toward Phoenix along the same road. From the date of the purchase until this past September, no employee of Palo Verde had set foot on the tract.

Palo Verde built Verde River Estates during the last two years. When the last units were sold in September, the company sent a surveying team to the Ironwood tract, but they were chased off the land by Homer Chesbro, whose Black Canyon Ranch adjoins the Ironwood tract. Chesbro bought the Ranch eleven years ago from a person who told him that he was buying both the Ranch and the tract. Although the metes and bounds description in Chesbro's deed does not include the tract, that and most of the rest of the deed is in language that nonlawyers would find incomprehensible. For the past eleven years, Chesbro and his employees have grazed cattle on the Ironwood tract two or three times a month throughout the year. The land cannot support more grazing, and the soil will not support farming or other intensive agriculture, although luxury housing could be built on it.

Chesbro had no idea that Palo Verde had a deed to the property. At the same time, Palo Verde did not know that Chesbro was using the tract or that he thought his deed included it.

If Chesbro claims that he acquired title by adverse possession, will Palo Verde succeed in an action to eject him and quiet its own title? Your research has uncovered three statutes and five cases.

<h2>ARIZONA REVISED STATUTES</h2>

<h3>§12-521.   Definitions</h3>

A. In this article, unless the context otherwise requires:

1. "Adverse possession" means an actual and visible appropriation of the land, commenced and continued under a claim of right inconsistent with and hostile to the claim of another.

2. "Peaceable possession" means possession which is continuous, and not interrupted by an adverse action to recover the estate . . . .

<h3>§ 12-526.   Real Property in Adverse Possession and Use by Possessor; Ten-Year Limitation . . .</h3>

A. A person who has a cause of action for recovery of any lands, tenements or hereditaments from a person having peaceable and adverse possession thereof, cultivating, using and enjoying such property, shall commence an action therefor within ten years after the cause of action accrues, and not afterward . . . .

<h3>§ 12-527.   Effect of Limitation on Title</h3>

When an action for recovery of real property is barred by any provision of this article, the person who pleads and is entitled to the bar shall be held to have full title precluding all claims.

[These sections are descended from provisions in the Arizona Civil Code of 1901. The Arizona Supreme Court has held that what is now § 12-527 provides a cause of action through which a person who occupies land through adverse possession can obtain title to it after the requisite number of years have passed. *Work v. United Globe Mines*, 100 P. 813 (Ariz. 1909), *aff'd*, 231 U.S. 595 (1914). Because the Arizona statutes reproduced above were modelled after Texas statutes, the *Work* court relied on a Texas case, *Moody v. Holcomb*, which interpreted those Texas statutes. *Moody* was decided before 1901. Compare *Work* to the first two cases below, *Arizona Superior Mining Co. v. Anderson* and *State v. McDonald*. Added together, these three cases tell you how the Arizona courts will react to the other out-of-state cases in this exercise.]

<h2>ARIZONA SUPERIOR MINING CO. v. ANDERSON</h2>
262 P. 489 (Ariz. 1927)

Ross, C.J. [The parties disagree over whether this case should be tried in Pima County or Maricopa County. The relevant Arizona statute is ambiguous.]

Counsel . . . have directed our attention to decisions [interpreting similar statutes in other states, but we are free to disregard precedent from states where] the language of the statute . . . is different from the language of our statute. [The situation is different where the other state's statute is the one from which our statute is drawn. In adopting our statute] from another state, we took it with the construction theretofore placed upon it [by the courts of that state].

STATE v. McDONALD
352 P.2d 343 (Ariz. 1960)

MURRY, J. [The issue is whether the plaintiff can be made to pay the fees and expenses of the defendant's expert witnesses. The governing Arizona statute, A.R.S. § 12-1128, is ambiguous.]

A.R.S. § 12-1128 was adopted from California [in 1901. After that date, two California cases interpreted the original California statute to mean] the usual costs attending trial allowed by statute. [Citations omitted.] . . .

Although we are not bound to follow the interpretation [afterward] placed on a statute by [the] state from which our statute [had earlier been] adopted, it is persuasive. [Citation omitted.] . . .

ADAMS v. LAMICQ
221 P.2d 1037 (Utah 1950)

WOLFE, J. This action was commenced by the appellant to quiet title to an eighty acre tract of land in Duchesne County, Utah. . . .

[T]he respondents claimed title to the land . . . by virtue of seven years' adverse possession[, during which they used the land as a winter range for sheep].

The . . . tract in question consisted of unbroken and unimproved brush lands suitable only for grazing. . . . The property was [not inclosed by a fence. T]he respondents during the winter grazed all of the eighty acres . . . , entering thereon in November and remaining until April, at which time they moved their sheep onto higher grazing lands in Colorado for the summer and early autumn. The respondents did not leave anyone upon or in charge of the eighty acres during the summer months while they were away. . . .

. . . Sec. 104-2-9, Utah Code Annotated 1943, provides: "For the purpose of constituting an adverse possession . . . , land is deemed to have been possessed and occupied in the following cases: . . . (3) Where, although not inclosed, it has been used for the supply of fuel, or of fencing timber for the purposes of husbandry, or for pasturage, or for the ordinary use of the occupant." (Italics added.)

In *Kellogg v. Huffman*, 137 Cal. App. 278, 30 P.2d 593, it was held under Sec. 323, subd. 3, Cal. Code Civ. Proc., which is identical to Section 104-2-9, subd. 3, quoted above, that pasturing during the entire grazing season of each year during which feed is available, if done to the exclusion of others, is a sufficient use and occupation of land, which is reasonably fit for grazing purposes only, to constitute the occupation and possession necessary to establish title by adverse possession. . . .

Thus we conclude that the respondents . . . had continuously claimed, occupied, and used [the property] for at least seven years prior to the commencement of this action. . . .

KELLOGG v. HUFFMAN
30 P.2d 593 (Cal. Ct. App. 1934)

BARNARD, P.J. This is an action to quiet title to 160 acres of land in the Kettleman Hills in Fresno county. . . . This property was rough and arid and was situated in what was, until about 1929, a sparsely settled country used only for grazing purposes. . . .

The appropriate portion of section 323 of the Code of Civil Procedure reads as follows: ". . . For the purpose of constituting an adverse possession . . . land is deemed to have been possessed and occupied in the following cases: . . . (3) Where, although not inclosed, it has been used for the supply of fuel, or of fencing-timber for the purposes of husbandry, or for pasturage, or for the ordinary use of the occupant."

. . . To establish adverse possession it is only necessary that land be put to such use as can reasonably be made thereof, and such a use is sufficiently continuous if, during the required time, it be so used at all times when it can be used for the purpose to which it is adapted. [Citations omitted.] It is well settled in this state that pasturing during the entire grazing season of each year during which feed is available, if done to the exclusion of others, is a sufficient use and occupation of land, which is reasonably fit only for pasturage purposes, to constitute the occupation and possession necessary to establish a title by adverse possession. [Citations omitted.] . . . ". . . It is sufficient that the use is in accordance with the usual course of husbandry in the locality." [Citation omitted.]

[There was ample evidence of adverse possession through use of the land for grazing purposes.]

DE LAS FUENTES v. MACDONELL
20 S.W. 43 (Tex. 1892)

GAINES, J. This was an action on trespass to try title. . . .

Appellants . . . complain that the court erred in sustaining the defendant's plea of the statute of limitations of five years. . . . The [land] was never inclosed [by fences]. It is fit only for grazing purposes. There have never been any houses upon it. No part of it has ever had any inclosures upon it, except small pens, made of posts and brush, for the purpose of penning sheep. These were renewed every year . . . . The land was used for "grazing and lambing purposes." How many sheep were kept upon it does not appear. One witness states that in 1871 there were 13,000 sheep upon the land. . . . Cattle belonging to others were permitted to graze upon the land. . . . There have been several cases decided in this court in which the effort has been made to show an adverse possession of land by merely grazing cattle and horses upon it, but it has uniformly been held that the possession was not sufficient to meet the requirements of the statute. [Citations omitted.] [T]he mere occupancy of land by grazing live stock upon it, without substantial inclosures or other permanent improvements, is not sufficient to support a plea of limitation under our statutes. Uninclosed land, in this state, has ever been treated as commons for grazing purposes; and hence the mere holding of live stock upon it has not been deemed such exclusive occupancy as to constitute adverse possession. . . . There must be "an actual occupation of such nature and notoriety as the owner may be presumed to know that there is a possession of the land" [citation omitted]; "otherwise, a man may be disseised without his knowledge, and the statute of limitations run against him, while he has no ground to believe that his seizure has been interrupted" [citation omitted]. We think the testimony insufficient to show adverse possession. . . .

17 Working with Facts

§17.1   What Is a Fact?

Consider the following statements:

1. *The plaintiff's complaint alleges* that, at a certain time and place, the defendant struck the plaintiff from behind with a stick.
2. At trial, *the plaintiff's principal witness testified* that, at the time and place specified in the complaint, the defendant struck the plaintiff from behind with a stick.
3. At the conclusion of the trial, *the jury found* that, at the time and place specified in the complaint, the defendant struck the plaintiff from behind with a stick.
4. At the time and place specified in the complaint, *the defendant struck* the plaintiff from behind with a stick.
5. At the time and place specified in the complaint, the defendant *brutally* struck the plaintiff from behind with a stick.
6. At the time and place specified in the complaint, the defendant *accidentally* struck the plaintiff from behind with a stick.
7. At the time and place specified in the complaint, the defendant *committed a battery* on the plaintiff.

Which of these statements expresses a fact?

Number 7 plainly does not: it states a *conclusion of law* because battery is a concept defined by the law, and you can discover whether a battery occurred only by consulting one or more rules of law. Numbers 5 and 6, however, are a little harder to sort out.

193

Statement 6 includes the word *accidentally*. The defendant might have wanted to cause violence, or he might have struck the plaintiff only inadvertently and without any desire to do harm. With both possibilities, an observer might see pretty much the same actions: the stick being raised, the stick being lowered, the collision with the back. There might be small but perceptible differences between the two — the defendant's facial expression, for example, or the words spoken immediately before and after the incident. But even those differences might not occur. A cunning defendant intent on harm, for example, can pretend to act inadvertently. The difference between the two possibilities is in what the defendant might have been thinking or feeling when he struck the plaintiff. If we say that the defendant struck the plaintiff "accidentally," we have inferred what the defendant was thinking at the time. That is a factual inference. (It would be a conclusion of law if it were framed in terms that the law defines, such as "intention to cause a contact with another person.") An inference of fact is not a fact: it is a conclusion derived from facts.

Statement 5 contains the word *brutally,* which is a value-based and subjective *characterization.* If one is shocked by the idea of a stick colliding with a human being — regardless of the speed and force involved — even a gentle tap with a stick might be characterized as brutal. (Conversely, an observer who is indifferent to suffering and violence might call repeated lacerations with a stick "playful.") And a friend of the plaintiff or an enemy of the defendant might construe whatever happened as "brutal," while an enemy of the plaintiff or a friend of the defendant might do the reverse. Assuming that we have not seen the incident ourselves, we should wonder whether the word *brutally* accurately summarizes what happened, or whether it instead reflects the value judgments and preferences of the person who has characterized the incident as brutal. A characterization is not a fact; it is only an opinion about a fact.

We are left with statements 1 through 4. Do any of them recite a fact? There are two ways of answering that question. Although the two might at first seem to contradict each other, they are actually consistent, and both answers are accurate, although in different ways.

One answer is that statements 1, 2, and 3 are layers surrounding a fact recited in statement number 4: number 1 is an allegation of a fact; number 2 is evidence offered in proof of the allegation; number 3 is a conclusion that the evidence proves the allegation; and number 4 is the fact itself. This is an answer that might be reached by a perceptive lay person who has noticed what you now know to be a sequence inherent to litigation: the party seeking a remedy first alleges, in a pleading, a collection of facts that, if proven, would merit a remedy, and that party later at trial submits evidence to persuade the finder of fact that the allegations are proven. Notice that this first answer is built on the ideas that a "fact" is part of an objective, discoverable truth and that the purpose of litigation is to find that truth.

The other answer is that numbers 1 through 4 all recite facts, the first three being procedural events inside a lawsuit. This answer is derived from the requirement, inherent to litigation, that the decisions of the finder of fact be based not on an objective "truth" that occurred out of court, but instead on whether *in court* a party has carried her or his burdens to make certain allegations and to submit a certain quantum of evidence in support of those allegations. Because it is not omniscient, a court cannot decide on the basis of what is "true." In a procedural sense, litigation is less a search for truth than it is a test of whether each party has carried burdens of pleading, production, and persuasion that the law assigns to one party or another. Because of the adversary system, the court is not permitted to investigate the controversy: it can do no more than passively weigh what is submitted to it, using as benchmarks the burdens set out in the law. Thus, if a party does not allege and prove a fact essential to that party's case, the court must decide that the fact does not exist. And this is so even if the fact does exist. That is why experienced lawyers tend to be more confident of their abilities to prove and disprove allegations than they are of their abilities to know the "real" truth about what happened between the parties before litigation began.

Both answers are correct, but their value to you will change as time goes on. Right now, the first answer gives you a model of how facts are processed in litigation. But soon the second answer will become increasingly important. That is because, as you learn lawyering, you will have to learn the ways in which the law compels lawyers to focus on whether a party can carry or has carried a burden of pleading, production, or persuasion.

The nonexistence of a fact can itself be a fact. For example, consider the following:

8. At trial, no witness has testified that the defendant struck the plaintiff deliberately or that the plaintiff suffered any physical or psychological injury or even any indignity.

Here, the absence of certain evidence is itself a fact. Consequently, the defendant might be entitled to a directed verdict because some things have not been proved.

Facts have subtleties that can entangle you if you are not careful. Beginners tend to have difficulties with four fact skills: (1) separating facts from other things; (2) separating determinative facts from other kinds of facts; (3) building inferences from facts; and (4) purging analysis of hidden and unsupportable factual assumptions. When you have mastered these skills, you will be able to make reasoned decisions about selecting and using facts. The last few pages have explained the first skill, and Exercise I at the end of this chapter develops it further. The remainder of this chapter considers each of the other skills in turn.

§17.2 Identifying Determinative Facts

Facts can be divided into three categories. The first category is made up of facts that are essential to a controversy because they will determine the court's decision: if a change in a fact would have caused the court to come to a different decision, that fact is determinative. The second is a category of explanatory facts that, while not determinative, are nevertheless useful because they help make sense out of a situation that would otherwise seem disjointed. The third category includes coincidental facts that have no relevance or usefulness at all: they merely happened. Part of life's charm is that all three categories of facts — the relevant and the irrelevant — occur mixed up together in a disorderly mess. But lawyers have to separate out the determinative facts and treat them as determinative.

You have already started learning how to do that in this and other courses, mostly through the analysis of precedent. When, for example, you are asked to formulate the rule of a case, you have begun to develop the habit of isolating the facts the court considered determinative and then reformulating those facts into a list of generalities that — when they occur together again in the future — will produce the same result that happened in the reported opinion. But when you look at a given litigation through the lens of an opinion, you are looking at it *after* a court has already decided which facts are determinative: you are explicating the text of the opinion to learn what the court thought about the facts. We are concerned here with another skill: looking at the facts at the *beginning* of the case, before they are even put to a court, and predicting which the court will consider determinative.

Recall Welty's experience with Lutz, which you first considered in Chapter 2:

> Welty and Lutz are students who have rented apartments on the same floor of the same building. At midnight, Welty is studying, while Lutz is listening to a Radiohead album with his new four-foot speakers. Welty has put up with this for two or three hours, and finally she pounds on Lutz's door. Lutz opens the door about six inches, and, when he realizes that he cannot hear what Welty is saying, he steps back into the room a few feet to turn the volume down, leaving the door open about six inches. Continuing to express outrage, Welty pushes the door completely open and strides into the room. Lutz turns on Welty and orders her to leave. Welty finds this to be too much and punches Lutz so hard that he suffers substantial injury. In this jurisdiction, the punch is a felonious assault. Is Welty also guilty of common law burglary?

Common law burglary is the breaking and entering of the dwelling of another in the nighttime with intent to commit a felony therein. Whichever way a court rules, the size of the opening between Lutz's door and the door frame is going to be one of the determinative facts because the size of the opening helps to determine whether, at the moment Welty walked in, Lutz's dwelling was surrounded by the kind of enclosure that can be broken. Depending on one's theory, Lutz's activities before Welty knocked on the door could be either explanatory or determinative: they help make sense out of the situation, but they also help explain Welty's actions and intent, which go to other elements of the test for burglary. But you have not been told that Lutz only recently got into hard rock and that previously he had been a devotee of country music; those facts are omitted because they are purely coincidental and do not help you understand the issues.

Of the four fact skills considered in this chapter, isolating the determinative facts is probably the one that seems most obvious from your law school work generally. The first few months of law school are designed to teach two things that are the heart of this skill: rule analysis and a heightened sense of relevance.

§17.3   Building Inferences from Facts

> The main part of intellectual education is . . . learning how to make facts live.
>
> —*Oliver Wendell Holmes*

We will continue a bit further with Welty and Lutz.

One of the elements of burglary is the intent to commit a felony within the dwelling. In the jurisdiction where Welty and Lutz live, that element can be satisfied only if a defendant had that intent at the time that any breaking and entering might have occurred. If the defendant formed the intent for the first time after entering the dwelling, the element is not satisfied. Assuming for the moment that Welty broke and entered Lutz's apartment when she opened the door further and walked in, did she—at the instant she stepped inside—intend to commit a felony there?

Your response may be "Well, let's ask Welty—she's the one who would really know." But things are not so easy. If you are the prosecutor, you may find that the police have already asked her that question and that she has refused to answer or has given an answer that the police consider self-serving. In fact, one rarely has direct evidence of a person's state of mind: people do not carry electronic signboards on their foreheads on which their thoughts can be read at moments the law considers important. Instead, as the prosecutor you would have to prove Welty's state of mind through the surrounding circumstances—for example, through the things she did or did not do, as well as the things she knew other people had or had not done. Although her state of mind would be easier to determine if she had appeared at Lutz's door with an arsenal of weaponry—or, in another situation, with safecracking tools—inferences can be built from circumstances even without such dramatic displays of intent.

Even if you are Welty's defense lawyer and can freely ask her when she formed an intent to hit Lutz, you might not be much better off than the prosecutor. She might tell you something like the following:

> I don't know when I decided to punch him. I had to listen to his loud music on his four-foot speakers for two or three hours while I was trying to study for civil procedure. At least once or twice during that time, I thought that it might

be nice to punch his lights out, but I don't know that I had decided then to do it. When I knocked on his door, I thought, "This guy had better be reasonable, or else" — but at that instant I don't know whether I was committed to punching him. When I pushed the door open and stepped inside, I thought, "This joker might learn a little respect for the rest of us if something very emphatic happened to him — something that might help him remember in the future that other people have needs and that he shouldn't be so self-centered." Even then, I wasn't certain that I was going to do anything except try to reason with him. And when he ordered me out, I decked him. Nobody told me that I was supposed to make sure that my thoughts fit into this "state of mind" thing you're telling me about. I have no idea when I "formed an intent" to hit him. I can only tell you what my thoughts were at each step in the story. You're the lawyer. You tell me when I "formed an intent."

Now the problem is something else: a party's thoughts do not mesh nicely with the law's categories of states of mind. Welty's sequence of emotions somehow culminated in an action, but there seems to have been no magical moment at which anger crystallized into a decision that the law might recognize as "intent." A defense lawyer handles this problem in the same way that a prosecutor deals with the absence of direct evidence: each lawyer will build inferences from the circumstances surrounding Welty's actions. As Welty sees the arguments unfold, she might conclude that the law is doing strange and perhaps arbitrary things in categorizing her thoughts. But the law must have a way of judging states of mind, and it relies heavily on circumstances.

Albert Moore has used the term inferential stream to refer to the sequence of circumstantial conclusions that can grow out of a fact or piece of evidence.[1] Circumstantial evidence does not necessarily lead to only one stream of inferences. Consider the evidence in *Smith v. Jones,* where Smith claims that Jones caused an accident by running a red light:

> Jones testifies that his two children, ages five and six, were arguing in the back seat of his car just before the accident occurred. [This] is circumstantial propositional evidence that Jones entered the intersection against the red light because there is a series of valid generalizations that connects this evidence to the factual proposition in question. These generalizations might be stated as follows:

> *Generalization 1:* People driving with children arguing in the back seat of the car sometimes pay attention to what is happening in the back seat.
> *Generalization 2:* People who are paying attention to what is happening in the back seat of the car are sometimes momentarily distracted from what is happening on the road in front of them.
> *Generalization 3:* People who are momentarily distracted from what is happening on the road in front of them sometimes enter an intersection against the red light.
> *Conclusion:* Jones entered the intersection against the red light.

---

§17.3   1. Albert J. Moore, *Inferential Streams: The Articulation and Illustration of the Advocate's Evidentiary Intuitions,* 34 UCLA L. Rev. 611 (1987).

Based on the foregoing, one might conclude that this circumstantial evidence tends to prove only that Jones entered the intersection against the red light. One could also, however, conclude that this evidence tends to disprove that Jones entered the intersection against the red light. This conclusion might be based on the following analysis:

Generalization 4: People driving with children arguing in the back seat are sometimes conscious of the presence of children in the car.
Generalization 5: People who are conscious of children in their car sometimes drive cautiously.
Generalization 6: People who drive cautiously sometimes pay close attention to the road.
Generalization 7: People who pay close attention to the road sometimes do not enter an intersection against the red light.
Conclusion: Jones did not enter the intersection against the red light.

In *Smith v. Jones,* therefore, the evidence that Jones' children were arguing in the back of the car just before the accident, by itself, may tend to prove or disprove that Jones entered the intersection against the red light, depending on which set of generalizations is viewed as more reliable and accurate. . . . Thus, circumstantial propositional evidence may "cut both ways" in two situations: when the same evidence tends to prove or disprove the same factual proposition; or when it tends to prove one factual proposition while also tending to disprove another.[2]

§17.4   *Identifying Hidden and Unsupportable Factual Assumptions*

As David Binder and Paul Bergman have pointed out, "[i]f in medieval times there was 'trial by combat,' then today we have 'trial by inference.'"[1] Your adversary and the court will mercilessly challenge your inferential streams, looking for weaknesses in the way they were put together. Consequently, you must purge your analysis of hidden assumptions that will not stand up to scrutiny when exposed. Consider the following:

Detective Fenton Tracem rushes breathlessly into the office of the local prosecutor, Les Gettem, eager to persuade Les to issue an indictment. Fenton describes the evidence he has uncovered:

> Les, we've got a good case for bank robbery against Clyde. The gun the robber used and dropped at the door was originally purchased by Clyde. The owner of A-1 Guns can definitely identify Clyde as the purchaser and the teller can identify the gun. Moreover, the day after the $10,000 was taken, Clyde deposits $7,000 cash in a bank account using the fictitious name of Dillinger. A teller at the bank can definitely identify Clyde. Then later that day, Clyde buys a $1,500 gold watch and

2. *Id.* at 625-27.
§17.4   1. David A. Binder & Paul Bergman, *Fact Investigation: From Hypothesis to Proof* 82 (West 1984).

pays for it in cash. The owner of A-2 Jewelry can also identify him. Finally, the next day — two days after the robbery — Clyde moves out without giving Ness, his landlord, his two neighbors, Capone and Siegel, or the post office his new address. Ness, Capone, Siegel and the post office clerk are all willing to testify. Les, we're rock-solid on this one.

The detective has disgorged a mass of circumstantial evidence which appears in the aggregate to be quite convincing. The prosecutor cannot, however, be content to rely on this presentation. In order to analyze the probative value of the evidence, Gettem must first expressly articulate the generalization which links each item of evidence to an element.

[E]xpressly articulating generalizations is the key to determining just how strong a piece of evidence is.

Consider, therefore, the generalization the prosecutor might articulate for the first piece of evidence, that the gun used and dropped by the robber was originally purchased by Clyde. The generalization might be something like, "People who have purchased a gun subsequently used in a robbery are more likely to have participated in the robbery than people who have not."[2]

How accurate is this generalization? See what happens when you compare it with *either* of two strings of other generalizations. Here is the first one: "Robbers do not feel morally compelled to pay for what they acquire, and because guns can be stolen, a robber does not have even a practical need to pay for a gun." This is the second string: "Robbers tend to plan their crimes with at least some amount of forethought; some forethought would cause a robber to foresee the possibility of losing control of a gun during the robbery; other forethought would cause a robber to foresee that a gun legally purchased from a merchant might be traced back to the robber; Clyde is bright enough to have come to both of these foresights." Both strings seem more believable than "People who have purchased a gun subsequently used in a robbery are more likely to have participated in the robbery than people who have not" — and *either* string might overcome and negate the generalization on which the detective relies.

> In the beginning years of practice, one must force oneself to articulate explicitly the generalizations on which one relies, for it is not a skill practiced in everyday life. In fact, there is a word for people who state the generalizations underlying all inferences they make: bores. But in the privacy of one's office, one should expressly identify the premises on which one relies [because] by articulating the underlying generalization one can consciously consider the question of how strongly it is supported by common experience.
>
> This point may be seen more clearly if one asked to evaluate another of Det. Tracem's pieces of evidence without the aid of an expressed generalization. "The day after the $10,000 was taken, Clyde deposits $7,000 cash in a bank account using the fictitious name of Dillinger." As D.A. Les Gettem, one is asked how strongly suggestive of Clyde's guilt this piece of evidence is. . . .
>
> . . . If your answer is something like, "The evidence is strongly indicative of guilt" (or "isn't too probative of guilt"), you have had a knee-jerk reaction to

---

2. *Id.* at 92-93.

the evidence. Undoubtedly some accumulation of common experience was implicit in whatever conclusion you reached. But unless the common experience is crystallized in an explicitly stated generalization, one has no focal point for considering how uniformly common experience supports the gen- eralization.

If your conclusion did include a generalization, it may have been something like, "People who deposit $7,000 in a bank account under a fictitious name are likely to have gotten the money illegally." With this generalization explicitly stated, one has a basis for gauging with some degree of accuracy the probative value of the fictitious bank account evidence. One has an explicit premise which can be tested according to one's own and a factfinder's probable views as to how the world operates. . . .

There are other reasons for articulating generalizations. Their articulation may bring to mind potential exceptions. . . . [O]ne method of testing the degree to which common experience uniformly supports a generalization is to add "except when" to a generalization, and see how many reasonable exceptions one can identify. . . .

[For example, consider] a generalization that one might make in Clyde's case: "People who move without leaving a forwarding address are usually trying to avoid detection." By adding "except when," one sees that this generalization is subject to many exceptions and is therefore less likely to be persuasive. People may be trying to avoid detection, except when they simply forget to leave a forwarding address, or except when they do not yet know the permanent address to which they will be moving, or except when they will be moving around for a time and will not have a permanent address.[3]

As Binder and Bergman point out, only bores recite for the benefit of others all the generalizations underlying their inferences. Thus, when you build and test your own inferences, you will not commit to paper much of the analysis Binder and Bergman describe. As they suggest, it is thinking reserved for the privacy of your own office.

But things are different when you attack your adversary's inferences. If Clyde becomes your client, you might argue that a directed verdict should be — or, on appeal, should have been — granted because a rational jury would not be able to find guilt beyond a reasonable doubt. In a supporting memorandum or in an appellate brief, you might write, "The evidence that he moved without leaving a forwarding address does not tend to prove guilty flight. It could just as easily prove that he forgot to leave a forwarding address, or that he did not yet know his new permanent address when he moved, or that he would be moving around for a time without a permanent address."

Exercise I.   The Menu at the Courthouse Cafe

The following appear on the menu at the Courthouse Cafe. Decide what is a fact, what is a characterization, and what is a conclusion of fact. (If part of an

---

3. *Id.* at 93-96.

item is factual and part is not, decide exactly where the fact ends and the non-fact begins.)

Hot, steaming coffee
Healthful oat bran muffins
Pure beef hot dogs
Garden-fresh vegetables
Hand-picked huckleberries
Home-made huckleberry pie
Delicious peanut butter ice cream

Exercise II.   Welty's State of Mind

Complete the first part of this exercise before doing any portion of the second.

1. Develop whatever streams of inferences are necessary to determine Welty's state of mind from the facts given earlier in this chapter. Write out each fact on which you rely and each inference in the stream flowing from that fact.

2. You are now no longer the person who completed the first part of this exercise. You are somebody else, and you have been hired to attack each of the inferential streams developed in the first part of the exercise. Write down every hidden assumption you can find in those inferential streams, and decide whether each assumption is probable enough to support the inferences that flow from it.

VI

GENERAL WRITING SKILLS

18

Paragraphing

§18.1 How Paragraphing Reveals Your Organization

Before law school, you might have paragraphed by writing until you seemed to have written a lot, stopping, starting a new paragraph, and then going through the cycle again and again. But in law, paragraphs put together that way will confound and annoy readers who must find your meaning quickly.

Most readers unconsciously use paragraph divisions to learn how a writer's thoughts fit together. They assume that each paragraph substantiates or explores a separate and distinct idea or subject. They also assume that the first or second sentence in each paragraph states or implies that idea or subject and, if necessary, shows how it is related to matters already discussed. To the extent that you frustrate these assumptions, your writing will be less helpful to the reader and therefore less influential.

Paragraphing has three goals. The most obvious is to break your material up into digestible chunks. The second is to help you discipline yourself to confront and develop each theme inherent in the material. The third is to tell the reader where she or he is in your logic, how that place was arrived at, and where you are headed—in other words, to make your organization apparent. If the reader feels lost or does not immediately know what the paragraph's thesis or topic is or how it differs from that of the preceding paragraph, there is something wrong with the paragraph's length or structure or with the wording of individual sentences. As you will see in §18.4, the paragraph's first sentence is the one most often botched.

How can you tell the difference between a paragraph that accomplishes these goals and one that does not? An effective paragraph has five characteristics. First, it has *unity:* it proves one proposition or covers one subject. Material that is more relevant to other propositions or subjects has been removed and placed elsewhere. Second, an effective paragraph has *completeness:* it includes whatever is necessary to prove the proposition or cover the subject. Third, an effective paragraph has *internal coherence:* ideas are expressed in a logical sequence that the reader is able to follow without having to edit the paragraph mentally while reading. Fourth, an effective paragraph is of *readable length:* it is neither so long that the reader gets lost nor so short that valuable material is underdeveloped or trivialized. Fifth, an effective paragraph *announces or implies its purpose* at the outset: its first or second sentence states its thesis or topic and, if necessary, makes a transition from the preceding material.

Ineffective paragraphing is related to incomplete analysis. When you set out to fix problem paragraphs, you will often find yourself fixing analytical problems as well.

§18.2   Probative Paragraphs and Descriptive Paragraphs

Some paragraphs merely *describe* conditions or events; they convey information without analysis. But in legal writing, most paragraphs are expected to do more than that: they *prove* propositions that help resolve issues. In descriptive writing, the paragraph states information, and the first or second sentence tells the reader the paragraph's topic or theme, to the extent that is not already evident from the context. But in probative writing, the paragraph exists to prove its first or second sentence, which states the paragraph's *thesis.*

A topic is merely a category of information ("weather in Death Valley"), but a thesis is a proposition capable of proof or disproof ("the climate of Death Valley is brutal"):

Descriptive	Probative
In January in Death Valley, the average high temperature is about 65°, and the average low is about 37°. Spring and fall temperatures approximate summer temperatures elsewhere. In April and in October, for example, the average high is about 90°, and the average low about 60°. July is the hottest month, with an average high of	The climate in Death Valley is brutal. At Furnace Creek Ranch, the highest summer temperature each year reaches at least 120° and in many years at least 125°. The highest temperature recorded in Death Valley — 134° — is also the highest recorded in the Western Hemisphere and the second highest recorded anywhere on

about 116° and an average low of about 87°. The highest temperature ever recorded in Death Valley was 134° on July 10, 1913. Average annual rainfall is about 1 1/2 inches. earth. (The highest is 136° — in the Sahara.) In the summer sun, a person can lose four gallons of perspiration a day and — in 3% humidity — die of dehydration.

A confused reader of descriptive writing might ask, "What is this paragraph about?" But a confused reader of probative writing asks instead, "What is this writer trying to prove?"

Probative and descriptive writing can occur in the same document. In college writing, you might typically have written many descriptive paragraphs setting out an abundance of raw data and then concluded with a short passage expressing one or more inferences that the data supported.[1] Although the document as a whole might tend to support the inferences, probative writing in college tends to be limited to the final passage — if it occurs even there.[2] But in a Discussion (or Argument in a motion memorandum or appellate brief), the writing should be largely probative, with only occasional digressions into description. Some other parts of a memorandum or brief, however, are predominantly description. The best examples are the Statement of Facts in an office memorandum and the Preliminary Statement in a motion memorandum or appellate brief.

§18.3 Thesis Sentences, Topic Sentences, and Transition Sentences

A probative paragraph states its thesis in its first or second sentence, and that sentence is the *thesis sentence*.[1] A descriptive paragraph does the same with its *topic* unless the topic is implied by the context. Although in descriptive writing a topic can often be implied, in probative writing the thesis should be expressly stated. (Remember that a practical reader needs to know your purpose in saying things before you start saying them.) With either type of paragraph, a *transition sentence* helps show the reader

---

§18.2 1. In law that kind of organization will frustrate your readers to the point of impatience. The law-trained reader needs to learn *at the beginning* what you intend to prove and needs to be told, at *each* step along the way, *how* the data support the proposition you are trying to prove.

2. Unless the reader is told *how* the data support the inference, the writing is not probative. A mere recitation of data is not a proof. Proof is an explanation of *how* the data support the inference.

§18.3 1. In college, "thesis sentence" is sometimes used to refer to a sentence that sums up the meaning of an entire essay. Here, it has a different meaning.

how the paragraph is connected to the material before it or the material after it.[2]

Thesis, topic, and transition sentences can be worked into a paragraph in several different ways. A transition sentence most often appears at the beginning of a paragraph, less often at the end (as a bridge into the next paragraph), rarely in the middle, and not at all if a transition is unnecessary. The first sentence in a paragraph can often do double duty. It might state a thesis or topic and—perhaps in a dependent clause—make a transition. Or a transition sentence at the beginning of a paragraph can imply a topic while making a transition from the previous paragraph. If the paragraph begins with a transition sentence that does not also state a thesis or state or imply a topic, the paragraph's second sentence can express either. Where a paragraph's thesis or topic is complex, the paragraph might end with a closure sentence that ties up loose ends.

§18.4   The Two Most Common Ways of Botching the Beginning of a Paragraph

The two most common ways of botching the beginning of a paragraph are (1) omitting entirely any statement of the thesis or topic, and (2) using a topic sentence to begin a probative paragraph (which should have a thesis sentence instead). Either problem can force a judge to read the paragraph two or three times to figure out its purpose, unless that is clear from the context.

1. *Botching the beginning by omitting any statement of the thesis or topic:* The habit of announcing or alluding to a paragraph's purpose at the beginning is a kind of self-discipline. Because it forces you to articulate the paragraph's reason for being, it will encourage you—especially during rewriting—to limit the paragraph to one thesis or topic (unity), to do whatever is necessary inside the paragraph to prove that thesis or cover that topic (completeness), and to express the ideas in the paragraph in a sequence appropriate to the thesis or topic (coherence). If a statement of the topic or thesis is missing, that often means that you do not yet know what the paragraph is supposed to accomplish—which can lead to conversations like this:

(a) Instructor identifies a murky paragraph in student writing.
(b) Instructor asks student, "Tell me in a sentence what you are trying to say in this paragraph."

2. This paragraph (in the text above) is descriptive. Its topic is the three kinds of sentences that tell a reader a paragraph's purpose and relationship to its surroundings. Although the paragraph could have begun with a sentence expressing that, the topic sentence was omitted on the grounds that it would have blocked the flow into the paragraph; that too many announcements of paragraphs' topics can become tedious; and that this paragraph's purpose is implied by the context. From your point of view as the reader, was that the best writing decision? Does the context make the topic clear enough without a topic sentence? Or would you rather have been told at the beginning what the paragraph is about?

(c) Student reads paragraph — ponders — and, generally, comes up with a one-sentence statement.

(d) Instructor says, "Well, would it help the reader if you *said that* at the front end of the paragraph?"

(e) Light bulb flashes over student's head.

(f) Instructor then asks, "Now if that's your main idea, how does *this* sentence [indicating one whose function is unclear] tie in to that idea?"

(g) If the student suggests a function, the instructor asks, "Is there any way you could make that function clearer to the reader?"

(h) If the student does not see a function, the instructor asks, "Does that sentence belong in the paragraph?"

As the author of this familiar scene concludes, "There is no reason why you, the writer, cannot carry on that conversation inside your own head as you [rewrite]."[1]

2. *Botching the beginning by using a topic sentence to begin a probative paragraph:* Consider this probative paragraph, which begins with an unhelpful topic sentence:

> The federal bank robbery statute penalizes obtaining anything of value from a bank "by force and violence, or by intimidation." 18 U.S.C. § 2113 (2000). Several cases have defined the term "intimidation." For example, a defendant takes by intimidation when he hands a bank teller a note reading "Put all your money in this bag and nobody will get hurt." *United States v. Epps,* 438 F.2d 1192 (4th Cir. 1971). The same is true where a defendant, while holding his hand in his pocket to suggest that he has a weapon, hands a teller a note reading, "This is a holdup." *United States v. Harris,* 530 F.2d 576 (4th Cir. 1976). And even where a teller never sees a weapon, intimidation is proved where a defendant produces a note stating, "I have a gun. Give me all the bills or I will shoot you." *United States v. Jacquillon,* 469 F.2d 380 (5th Cir. 1972), *cert. denied,* 410 U.S. 938 (1973).

This is *not* a descriptive paragraph. Its purpose is to prove a definition of "intimidation." But the first sentence does not tell you what the definition is and therefore it is not a thesis sentence. The first sentence announces only a topic — the federal bank robbery statute — and thus does not communicate what the paragraph is meant to prove. In fact, *no* sentence in the paragraph sets out the definition that the paragraph is intended to prove. To the reader who needs to know what "intimidation" is, a paragraph like this one is frustrating to the point of impatience. Not only does the reader need to know exactly what you are trying to prove, but she or he needs to know it *before proof begins.* Most of the problem could be solved with an accurate thesis sentence like this:

> Under the federal bank robbery statute, 18 U.S.C. § 2113 — which penalizes obtaining anything of value from a bank "by force and

§18.4   1. Peter W. Gross, *California Western Law School's First-Year Course in Legal Skills,* 44 Alb. L. Rev. 369, 389–90 (1980).

violence, or by intimidation"—the courts have defined "intimidation" as conduct reasonably calculated to produce fear, even in the complete absence of physical violence. . . .

The last fourteen words of this sentence give the whole paragraph meaning because they synthesize the holdings of the cases into a definition that the paragraph proves to be accurate.

Once you have replaced a topic sentence with a thesis sentence, some rewording and reordering of other sentences might be needed to give the paragraph coherence—to show, in other words, *how* the rest of the paragraph proves the thesis. Notice how the earlier version has been changed here so that it seems to flow straight from the new thesis sentence:

> Under the federal bank robbery statute, 18 U.S.C. § 2113—which penalizes obtaining anything of value from a bank "by force and violence, or by intimidation"—the courts have defined "intimidation" as conduct reasonably calculated to produce fear, even in the complete absence of physical violence. For example, even where a teller never actually sees a weapon, intimidation is proved where a defendant produces a note stating, "I have a gun. Give me all the bills or I will shoot you." *United States v. Jacquillon,* 469 F.2d 380 (5th Cir. 1972), *cert. denied,* 410 U.S. 938 (1973). More vaguely expressed threats are treated the same way. A defendant takes by intimidation when he hands a bank teller a note reading, "Put all your money in this bag and nobody will get hurt." *United States v. Epps,* 438 F.2d 1192 (4th Cir. 1971). And the result is the same even where the threat is entirely implied—for example, where a defendant, while holding his hand in his pocket to suggest that he has a weapon, hands a teller a note reading, "This is a holdup." *United States v. Harris,* 530 F.2d 576 (4th Cir. 1976).

If your prior writing experience has primarily been descriptive—and that is true of most law students—you will have to discipline yourself to see the difference between a descriptive paragraph and a probative one. And you will have to be careful to begin a probative paragraph with a thesis sentence. You will probably find that this kind of self-discipline forces you to make your meaning more clear to the reader throughout the paragraph—and that consequently you will analyze more deeply.

Both of these problems occur for pretty much the same reason. When you begin a probative paragraph with a topic sentence—or when you write a paragraph that has no thesis or topic sentence at all—in all likelihood you did not know when you began to write the paragraph what you intended to prove or describe within it. In a first draft, there is nothing wrong with that. The purpose of a first draft, after all, is to get the material out in the open so that you can finish analyzing it. But during rewriting, when you find a topic sentence atop a probative paragraph—or when you find a paragraph with no thesis or topic sentence at all—that is often a clue that you have not yet begun to articulate *even to yourself* what you are trying to accomplish in the paragraph. But this problem is miraculously easy to solve: merely asking yourself "What am I trying to prove here?" often produces almost instantly a thesis sentence that gives the whole paragraph meaning and relevance.

§18.5 How to Test Your Writing for Effective Paragraphing

In first drafts, paragraphs are seldom put together well. Instead, the work of paragraphing generally occurs during re-writing, when you should be trying to find paragraphs that do not accurately reflect the structure of your analysis. To identify the paragraphs in need of rehabilitation, ask yourself the following questions.[1]

Have you told the reader, near the beginning of each paragraph, the paragraph's thesis (if the paragraph is probative) or its topic (if the paragraph is descriptive)? | **18-A** |
If the reader does not learn the paragraph thesis or topic at the beginning, the reader will have to read the paragraph two or three times to figure out its purpose. The only time you are exempt from this requirement is where the topic or thesis is clearly implied by the context.

Have you gotten rid of throat-clearing introductory sentences, which bump into the paragraph's thesis or topic backward? | **18-B** |
For example:

> The district court considered this question in *Pickett.* There, the court showed limited patience with the way the parties referred to themselves and each other. It did agree to call one defendant Guitar Maker Oswald Who Lives in Germany. But it refused to call another The Artist Formerly Known as Prince, or even just "the Artist," and it refused to allow that defendant to use his guitar symbol in place of his name in the captions of pleadings and motions. Instead, the court just called him Nelson.

You can combine the first two sentences into a single thesis or topic sentence that goes straight to the point:

> In *Pickett,* the district court showed limited patience with the way the parties referred to themselves and each other. . . .

Have you given each paragraph a unified purpose? | **18-C** |
Prove one proposition or cover one subject. Remove and place elsewhere material that is more relevant to other propositions or subjects.

---

§18.5   1. When marking up your work, your teacher might refer to these questions by using the number-letter codes that appear next to each question here.

18-D Within each paragraph, have you expressed your ideas in a logical and effective sequence? Where a paragraph is confusing but nothing is wrong with its size or with the wording of individual sentences, the problem is usually that the paragraph lacks internal coherence. That happens when ideas within the paragraph are presented in a sequence that makes it hard for the reader to understand them or how they fit together to prove the thesis or illuminate the topic.

18-E Have you broken up paragraphs that were so large that the reader would have gotten lost? Although there are no set rules on paragraph length, paragraphs that wander aimlessly or endlessly do not accomplish the goals of paragraphing. Where that happens, you have probably tried to develop two or more complex and separable themes in a single paragraph, perhaps without being aware of it. The cure is to identify the individual themes and then break up the material accordingly into digestible chunks (which become separate paragraphs).

18-F Have you rewritten paragraphs that were so short that no thesis or topic is developed? Generally, one- and two-sentence paragraphs are ineffective unless you have a special reason for emphasizing something or for separating out uncomplicated material. One- or two-sentence paragraphs can be used to good effect in clearing up matters that are preliminary (such as identifying the procedural posture) or ancillary (such as identifying issues that are not presently before the court). When used carefully, short paragraphs can also emphasize some memorable aspect of the material. In many other situations, however, a short paragraph leaves the reader hungry for a more satisfying explanation of some important point. If a paragraph is so short that no thesis or topic is developed, ask yourself whether (1) you might have missed the complexities of the thesis or topic, or (2) the thesis or topic might be so simple that it does not merit treatment in a separate paragraph because it is actually part of some other thesis or topic.

18-G Have you shown the reader how each paragraph is related to the surrounding material (unless the relationship is implied by the context)? There are several ways of doing this. The paragraph can begin with a transition sentence. Or it can begin with a sentence that both makes a transition and states a thesis or topic. Or the last sentence of the preceding paragraph can build a bridge between the two paragraphs: that sentence can raise an expectation, for example, that the second paragraph satisfies.

Exercise I.   The First Weeks of Law School (Probative and Descriptive Paragraphs)

Write two paragraphs—one descriptive and the other probative—about the first weeks of law school.

Descriptive paragraph: Summarize what happened during your first weeks in law school. Describe only things you saw, heard, read, and wrote. Do not try to prove any belief you might have about the first weeks of law school.

Probative paragraph: The opening sentence of this paragraph should be "The first weeks of law school are hard" (or "puzzling" or "exciting" or "cruel" or "challenging" or any other characterization you choose) "because" — and here you complete the sentence by stating whatever you believe to be the cause of your characterization. The rest of the paragraph should prove the thesis expressed in this sentence.

Exercise II.   *Maldonado's Citrus Croissants (Thesis and Topic Sentences, Paragraph Coherence)*

Is the paragraph below probative or descriptive? What is the thesis or topic? Is it adequately expressed in the first or second sentence? If not, write an appropriate thesis or topic sentence or find a sentence already in the paragraph that states its thesis or topic. Within the paragraph, are ideas expressed in a logical sequence so that you do not have to edit the paragraph mentally while reading? If you believe the sentences in the paragraph should appear in a different order, rearrange them and write out separately your reasons for doing so. Decide whether any sentence's wording should be altered to improve the flow from sentence to sentence and from idea to idea. (Each sentence is preceded by a letter in brackets so that you can refer to it in class without having to read the sentence aloud.)

> [A] A matter of general knowledge within an industry lacks a trade secret's novelty or uniqueness and therefore is not protectable as a trade secret. *Wright v. Palmer,* 11 Ariz. App. 292, 464 P.2d 363 (1970); Restatement of Torts §757 comment *b* (1939). [B] If an examination of a product "completely disclose[s]" the process through which it was made, that process by definition is not a secret. Restatement §757 comment *b*. [C] Maldonado's Citrus Croissants recipe is not a trade secret. [D] Although the recipe for Citrus Croissants was unique and novel and had not been developed by any other baker, anyone in the baking industry could have purchased Citrus Croissants from a store and discovered their ingredients and baking process through reverse engineering, a relatively time-consuming and expensive process. [E] Thus, the recipe could have been discovered, although not easily. [F] Since the recipe could have been disclosed through marketed croissants, it does not constitute a trade secret.

Exercise III.   *Escape from Prison (Paragraph Unity, Coherence, and Length)*

Is the paragraph below limited to proving a single proposition or covering a single subject? If not, what material is extraneous? Is the paragraph of appropriate size? If you believe it is too long, how should the problem be solved? Are the ideas expressed in a sequence that enables you to understand the meaning of the paragraph without reading it twice? If not, what sequence would be better? Edit the paragraph in light of your answers to these questions. Add any thesis, topic, or transition sentences that you think are needed. Bring your work to class and be prepared to explain your thinking. (Each sentence is preceded by a letter in brackets so that you can refer to it in class without having to read the sentence aloud.)

[A] A prisoner who leaves a prison without permission is guilty of a crime of escape. [B] Until relatively recently, the defense of necessity was not available in California to a prisoner who claimed that prison conditions were so intolerable as to require escape. [C] An early case, for example, affirmed a conviction for escape, conceding that "if the facts were as stated by the defendant, he was subjected to brutal treatment of extreme atrocity" in a "remote" mountain prison camp far from any authorities to whom he might complain. *People v. Whipple*, 100 Cal. App. 261, 266, 279 P.2d 1008, 1010 (2d Dist. 1929). [D] And a more recent case affirmed a conviction where the defendant offered evidence that other prisoners had threatened to kill him, and that prison guards had refused to protect him. *People v. Richardson*, 269 Cal. App. 2d 768, 75 Cal. Rptr. 597 (1st Dist. 1969). [E] Both *Whipple* and *Richardson* cited 1 Hale P.C. 611 for the proposition that escape from prison can be excused only to avoid death as immediate as that threatened when the prison itself is engulfed in fire. [F] But drawing on decisions from other jurisdictions, the Court of Appeal for the Fourth District has held that, through a "limited defense of necessity," a prisoner can defeat a prosecution for escape if the prisoner can demonstrate (1) that she or he was "faced with a specific threat of death, forcible sexual attack or substantial bodily injury in the immediate future," (2) that a complaint to the authorities would have been futile or not possible, (3) that the same was true regarding resort to the courts, (4) that the prisoner used no "force or violence" in escaping, and (5) that the prisoner surrendered to the authorities "when he [had] attained a position of safety from the immediate threat." *People v. Lovercamp*, 43 Cal. App. 3d 823, 831-32, 118 Cal. Rptr. 110, 115 (4th Dist. 1974). [G] Even under this test, Victor Minskov does not have a defense to the charge of escape. [H] He had been beaten twice by a group of prisoners who threatened to attack him as long as he remained in the same prison. [I] He scaled the prison wall at 4 A.M. immediately after the second beating and while being chased by the same group. [J] After the first beating, he had complained to prison guards, who laughed at him, and during the second beating his cries for help brought no response. [K] The courts would not have been able to protect him from such an assault, and he used no force or violence in escaping. [L] But after leaving the prison he hid under an assumed name for 16 months and was finally captured at the Los Angeles airport trying to leave the country. [M] Thus, he will not be able to show that he complied with the last element of the *Lovercamp* test by surrendering to the authorities upon attaining "a position of safety from the immediate threat."

19 Effective Style

§19.1 *Clarity and Vividness*

English has more synonyms and near-synonyms than almost any other language. English was created through the merger of two languages, Anglo-Saxon and Norman French, and it has borrowed liberally from other languages, especially Latin and Greek. Because it has such a huge vocabulary, English can express with precision a very wide range of nuance if you can find the "right" word. But with so many similar words to choose from, it is easy to choose the "wrong" one — the word that blurs meaning, rather than sharpening it.

Many people feel compelled to go straight for the "wrong" word because some words are considered to have a higher status than others. Important-sounding words tend to be less vivid and less precise than simple and straightforward ones. We feel important when we write, "The victim *indicated* that the defendant had held the gun," but we haven't said as much as we should have. Did we mean "The victim *said* that the defendant had held the gun"? Or did we mean "The victim *pointed* at the defendant when asked who had held the gun"? If the reader really wants to know what happened, *indicated* obscures the truth rather than communicating it. The simpler word often says more than the more dignified one. And the dignified word is often euphemistic and fuzzy rather than crisp and vivid.[1]

You might be tempted to try to sound like a lawyer but fail to *communicate* like one — for example by writing *ingested* (an impressive but vague

§19.1   1. Both tendencies are described in George Orwell's most famous essay, *Politics and the English Language*.

215

word) instead of something that would tell exactly what happened, such as *ate, drank,* or *swallowed.* Judges and senior lawyers want to read straightforward English. They will be frustrated and confused by pretentiously vague writing, which they will treat as evidence of a writer's mediocrity. Law depends on clarity, precision, and readability.

In one experiment, appellate judges and their law clerks were asked to appraise material written in a contorted style that might be called "legalese," while other judges and their law clerks were asked to evaluate the same material rewritten into straightforward "plain English." They thought the original legalese "substantively weaker and less persuasive than the plain English versions."[2] And the judges and law clerks assumed that the traditional legalese had been written by lawyers working in low-prestige jobs.[3]

Please do not write like this:

> the above captioned appeal is maintained by the defendant as a direct result of

Instead, write like this:

> the defendant appeals because

The longer version ("the above captioned appeal . . .") might sound fancy, but a reader will not as easily understand it. Figure out exactly what should be said and then say precisely that.

To understand the importance of clarity in law, remember two things. First, you must prove everything you say, because the law-trained mind considers every unsupported assertion to be the equivalent of an untruth. Second, no matter how important the issue, your reader will be able to spare only a very limited amount of time to ponder what you write. The more time that must be spent trying to figure out what you are saying, the less time the reader will have left to think about your message and to consider agreeing with it. Where poor writing obscures the message or makes the reading troublesome, you may get rejection even where you should have gotten agreement. "[A] cardinal principle of good writing [is] that no one should ever have to read a sentence twice because of the way it is put together."[4]

When it comes to clarity, *you will never get the benefit of doubt.* As Donald McCloskey puts it, the reader is always right: "If the reader thinks something you wrote is unclear, then it is, by definition. Quit arguing."[5]

---

2. Robert W. Benson & Joan B. Kessler, *Legalese v. Plain English: An Empirical Study of Persuasion and Credibility in Appellate Brief Writing,* 20 Loyola L.A. L. Rev. 301, 301 (1987).
3. *Id.* at 301-02.
4. Wilson Follett, *Modern American Usage* 480 (Warner Books 1974).
5. Donald McCloskey, *The Writing of Economics* 7 (Macmillan 1987).

§19.2 *Conciseness*

> The present letter is a very long one simply because I had no time to make it shorter.
>
> *—Pascal*

First drafts are not lean. Rewriting is the discipline of exercise and diet that trims a passage down to something easily read and understood. And conciseness is important in legal writing for three reasons. First, concise writing is by nature more clear and often more precise. Second, the typical reader of legal writing has no time to spare and either will resent inflated verbiage or will simply refuse to read it. And third, something about legal work paradoxically creates a temptation to swell a simple expression into something ponderous and pretentious.

For example, compare two versions of the same analysis[1]:

It is important to note that, at the time when the parties entered into the agreement of purchase and sale, neither of them had knowledge of the cow's pregnant condition.

When the parties agreed to the sale, neither knew the cow was pregnant.

Because of the fact that the cow, previous to the contract, had not become pregnant, despite planned and observed exposure to bulls whose reproductive capacities had been demonstrated through past experience, the seller had made the assumption that the cow would not be able to produce offspring.

The seller had assumed that the cow was infertile because she had not become pregnant when he tried to breed her with known stud bulls.

Due to the fact that the seller had made a statement to the buyer describing the cow's opportunities to reproduce and the failures thereof, there would have been, in the buyer's thinking, no purpose to any further investigation or inspection he might have considered making.

Because the seller had told the buyer about the cow's history, the buyer did not investigate further.

---

§19.2   1. The facts, though not the words, in these examples are derived from *Sherwood v. Walker,* 33 N.W. 919 (Mich. 1887), a classic mutual mistake case that appears in most Contracts casebooks and is discussed in all of them.

For these reasons, the contract did not include a provision for an upward modification in the payments to be made by the buyer to the seller in the event that the cow should later prove to be capable of reproduction.

Thus, the contract did not provide for an increase in the purchase price if the cow should turn out to be fertile.

How did the verbose rough draft on the left become the concise, finished product on the right?

First, some sentences were rewritten so that a person or a thing did something. Although the verbose draft is weighted down with modifiers, the concise version focuses on well-chosen nouns and verbs, and many modifiers became unneeded because their meaning has been incorporated into nouns and verbs (and sometimes into more succinct modifiers):

the cow's pregnant condition	*became*	the cow was pregnant
despite planned and observed exposure to bulls whose reproductive capacities had been demonstrated through past experience	*became*	when he tried to breed her with known stud bulls
there would have been, in the buyer's thinking, no purpose to any further investigation or inspection he might have considered making	*became*	the buyer did not investigate further

Second, words and phrases were eliminated if they could not justify themselves:

It is important to note that	*was deleted because the "importance" is communicated by the sentence's placement and, ironically, by the rewritten version's brevity*
previous to the contract	*was deleted because it is communicated by the context*

Third, each word and phrase was weighed to see if the same thing could be said in fewer words:

at the time when	*became*	when
entered into the agreement of purchase and sale	*became*	agreed to the sale

neither of them	*became*	neither
had knowledge of	*became*	knew
Because of the fact that	*became*	because
had made the assumption	*became*	assumed
would not be able to produce offspring	*became*	was infertile
Due to the fact	*became*	Because
had made a statement to	*became*	told
describing the cow's opportunities to reproduce and the failures thereof	*became*	about the cow's history
For these reasons	*became*	Thus
include a provision for	*became*	provide for
an upward modification in the payments to be made by the buyer to the seller	*became*	an increase in the purchase price
in the event that	*became*	if
the cow should later prove to be capable of reproducing	*became*	the cow should turn out to be fertile

Be careful, however, not to edit out needed meaning. In the material above, it would be folly to eliminate so much verbiage that a reader would not know that the cow was pregnant when sold; that the parties did not know of the pregnancy at the time; how each party became ignorant; that the contract did not provide for an adjusted price; and why it did not do so. But not all meaning is needed: "an upward modification in the *payments* to be made by the buyer to the seller" tells us that the money was to be paid in installments, but that meaning does not survive into the rewritten version because it has nothing to do with the issue under discussion.

§19.3 *Forcefulness*

Forcefulness is not a writer's version of table-pounding. Instead, forceful writing leads the reader through ideas by specifying their relationships with one another and by identifying the ideas that are most important or compelling.

Specifying relationships. Transitional words and phrases, such as the following, can very economically show relationships between ideas:

accordingly	in fact
additionally	(in order) to
although	in spite of
analogously	in that event
as a result	instead
because	moreover
but	nevertheless
consequently	not only . . . , but also
conversely	on the contrary
despiteon	the other hand
even if	on these facts
even though	rather
finally	similarly
for example	since
for instance	specifically
for that reason	such as
furthermore	there
hence	therefore
here	thus
however	under these circumstances
in addition (to)	while
in contrast	

Some transitional words and phrases are stronger than others. Be careful to select those that accurately represent the relationship at hand and that claim neither too little nor too much.

For example, some words are better than others at showing causation. *Because* and *since* do a much better job than *as* and *so*. Both *as* and *so* can confuse a reader who sees them used much more often — and much more effectively — to join contemporaneous events ("the muggles gasped *as* Harry flew past on his Nimbus 2000") or to emphasize the abundance of some fact ("they were *so* astonished that . . ."). In describing causation in a rough draft, you might use *as* or *so* just to get onto the page a sentence that is forming in your mind:

> The magistrate who issued the arrest warrant was able to evaluate the reasonableness of Det. Bloom's conclusion that the defendant was hiding in his friend's home, so the arrest warrant was sufficient authority, under the rule of *Commonwealth v. Sadowski,* for the police to search that home.

But in rewriting, you should notice that the limp, little word *so* will not catch the reader's attention the way *because* would. To figure out how to rewrite the sentence, first decide whether you want to emphasize the facts (the first example below) or the conclusion you draw from them (the second below).

> Because the magistrate who issued the arrest warrant was able to evaluate the reasonableness of Det. Bloom's conclusion that the defendant was hiding in his friend's home, the arrest warrant was sufficient authority, under the rule of *Commonwealth v. Sadowski,* for the police to search that home.

> The arrest warrant was sufficient authority, under the rule of *Commonwealth v. Sadowski,* for the police to search the home of the defendant's friend because the magistrate who issued the warrant was able to evaluate the reasonableness of Det. Bloom's conclusion that the defendant was hiding there.

The word *since* is an acceptable synonym for *because,* especially in passages where one word or the other must be used several times. But "since" is the weaker of the two, and it causes confusion if the reader does not know immediately from the context whether it refers to causation or to time:

> Because the defendant spent the marital assets on extravagances, the plaintiff has no money for attorney's fees.

If this had begun with "since," you would not have known until near the end of the sentence whether the dependent clause introduced causation or marked a point in time ("Since the defendant spent . . .").

Some words and sentence structures show contrast better than others do. Consider this:

> The Court of Appeal has held that the objection is waived if not made at trial, but it has also held that, even without an objection, a conviction should be reversed where a prosecutor's conduct was as inflammatory as it was here.

The word *but,* buried in the middle of a long sentence, only weakly alerts the reader that one idea (the rule about waiver) is being knocked down by another (the exception for inflammatory prosecutorial conduct). Everybody writes this kind of thing in rough drafts, but it should be recognized and cured during rewriting:

> Although the Court of Appeal has held that the objection is waived if not made at trial, it has also held that, even without an objection, a conviction should be reversed where a prosecutor's conduct was as inflammatory as it was here.

Although tells the reader from the very beginning of the sentence that the first clause, however damning, will be shown, before the sentence is over, not to matter. Because it comes at the beginning of a sentence or clause, and because it is the larger and less commonly used word, *although* will usually show contrast more clearly than *but.* If handled carefully, however, *but* can still do the job well:

> The Court of Appeal has held that the objection is waived if not made at trial. But it has also held that, even without an objection, a conviction should be reversed where a prosecutor's conduct was as inflammatory as it was here.

This solves the problem in a different way. The sentence has been broken in two, and the new second sentence begins with *But.* (Despite common belief, no rule of grammar forbids starting a sentence with a conjunction.)

Where several ideas are discussed collectively, you can lead the reader forcefully if you make that clear, perhaps through some sort of textual list. The list need not be diagrammed. In fact, it is usually more economical to incorporate a list into the text with a transition sentence ("There are four reasons why . . ."), followed by sentences or paragraphs coordinated to the transition sentence ("First . . ." or "The first reason . . .").

You can show logical relationships through the structure of your sentences:

> The amended court rule provides for attorney sanctions, *which eliminates the need to rely on any inherent powers the court might or might not have to punish attorneys whose procedural misconduct multiplies the court's work.*

Here, the italicized[1] dependent clause, when joined to the rest of the sentence, aggressively ties together the ideas that sanctions are now provided for by court rule and that the court therefore need not face the difficult issue of whether it has an inherent power to punish (even without a court rule).

Identifying the ideas that are most important or compelling. There are several ways of accomplishing that. One is simply to say it:

> This attorney's most reprehensible act was to make a motion for a preliminary injunction where his clients were not in any way threatened with harm.

Other methods are more subtle. You can put an emphasized idea at the beginning of a sentence, paragraph, or passage, where it will be most quickly noticed. Or you can arrange a series of sentences so that the shortest and simplest of them conveys the emphasized idea:

> This attorney served and filed a pleading alleging extremely unlikely facts without making any factual investigation and under circumstances

---

§19.3 1. Italics appear in these examples only to identify parts of the sentences for discussion, not to suggest that you italicize (or underline) for emphasis. Although italics or underlining for emphasis can be effective if done sparingly and carefully, it is too easily overdone and seldom has the desired effect on a reader.

indicating that his clients' only motive for litigation was harassment. He made numerous frivolous motions, including one for a preliminary injunction where his clients were in no way threatened with harm. He has now brought an appeal without any basis in statute or precedent, and he has submitted a record and brief not in compliance with the court's rules. *He has thoroughly disregarded the professional obligations of an attorney.*

Notice the differences in tone between the last example and the two that preceded it. The paragraph quoted immediately above might be appropriate for a brief in which an adversary urges that the attorney be punished or that a punishment meted out below be sustained; it might also be appropriate to an opinion in which a court justifies a punishment. The tone is one intended to convince. Although the two preceding examples address the same subject, they are expressed in a more objective tone in which analysis is reported without advocacy (although those two examples might also appear in a persuasive or justifying document to provide a foundation for other, more rhetorical statements).

Forcefulness helps all legal writing, simply to help the reader understand what is important and how ideas are related. But a rhetorical tone is reserved for documents intended to persuade or justify and is inappropriate where you are asked, in predictive writing, to report how the law will resolve a given set of facts. Predictive writing is not advocacy.

§19.4   Punctuation and Other Rules of Grammar

In re HAWKINS
502 N.W.2d 770 (Minn. 1978)

[The Lawyers Professional Responsibility Board petitioned the court for an order disciplining the respondent lawyer for unethical conduct.]

The referee . . . found that respondent's failure to comply with [certain court rules] and his repeated filing of documents rendered unintelligible by numerous spelling, grammatical, and typographical errors were sufficiently serious that they amounted to incompetent representation. . . .

It is apparent to us that [respondent's] repeated disregard of [court rules], coupled with the incomprehensibility of his correspondence and documentation, constitutes a violation of Rule 1.1 of the Minnesota Rules of Professional Conduct.[1] . . .

. . . Public confidence in the legal system is shaken when lawyers disregard the rules of court and when a lawyer's correspondence

---

§19.4   1. [*Court's footnote.*] Rule 1.1 . . . provides as follows: "A lawyer shall provide competent representation to a client. Competent representation requires the legal knowledge, skill, thoroughness and preparation reasonably necessary to the representation."

and legal documents are so filled with spelling, grammatical, and typographical errors that they are virtually incomprehensible. . . .

Respondent . . . is hereby publicly reprimanded for unprofessional conduct [and ordered, among other things, to participate in a program of writing instruction].

In another case, a trucking company and the Interstate Commerce Commission battled for 19 years over the confusion caused by the absence of a single comma in an administrative order.[1] And in another case, the Maine Supreme Court had to write a two-thousand word decision to untangle the mess created by two commas that somehow ended up in the wrong place in a statute.[2]

Correct punctuation makes writing clear and easier to understand. It is not mere decoration. A lawyer cannot excuse a poorly punctuated sentence by arguing that the reader would be able to understand it if she or he would think about it. A lawyer's job is to make meaning so plain that the reader need not read the sentence twice.

Punctuation and other grammar skills have an important effect on your credibility and reputation. Readers — including readers of law school examinations — will question your analytical abilities and general competence if you do not observe the accepted rules of English grammar. "Where lumps and infelicities occur," the novelist John Gardner wrote, "the sensitive reader shrinks away a little, as we do when an interesting conversationalist picks his nose."[3]

If you have not already mastered the rules of punctuation and of grammar generally, do so now. Appendix B summarizes the more important rules of punctuation. Make sure that you understand *every* rule in Appendix B: your law school writing will be scrutinized for solid grammar in a way that you might not have experienced before.

§19.5   How to Test Your Writing for Effective Style

> In any language, it is a struggle to make a sentence say exactly what you mean.
>
> —*Arthur Koestler*

In first drafts — even by the best writers — style is usually pretty awful. Effective style is really achieved through rewriting, as you spot style

---

1. *T. I. Mccormack Trucking Co. v. United States*, 298 F. Supp. 39 (D.N.J. 1969).
2. *Sawyer v. State*, 382 A.2d 1039 (Me. 1978).
3. John Gardner, *The Art of Fiction: Notes on Craft for Young Writers* 99 (Knopf 1984).

problems and fix them. While rewriting, ask yourself the following questions.[1]

Have you used nouns and verbs that let the reader see the action? Consider these examples:

19-A

wrong:	In *Smith,* there was no withdrawal of the guilty plea, based on the court's determination of a lack of evidence of coercion.
right:	In *Smith,* the court denied the defendant's motion to withdraw her guilty plea because she submitted no evidence that the plea had been coerced.
wrong:	There is a possibility of action in the near future by the EPA to remove these pesticides from the market.
right:	The EPA might soon prohibit these pesticides.

In the "wrong" examples, you can barely tell who has done what to whom because the pontifical tone obscures the action, and because the nouns and verbs are vague and lazy. They do not stand out, take charge, and create action. The "right" examples are more vivid and easier to understand. You immediately know what is going on and do not have to read the same words twice.

In law, people do things to other people and to ideas and objects. The only way you can describe that is with nouns and verbs that are straightforward and often fairly plain and simple. As with so many other legal writing problems, rewriting is the key to solving this one. Your early drafts might have sentences like the "wrong" example above, but your final drafts should more closely resemble the "right" one. Here is how to do it:

Nouns: As you rewrite, figure out who is doing things and make those people and organizations the subject of sentences and clauses. Grammatically, only the subject gets to act. In the examples above, the main event was what the court did, which is why the court had to become the subject of the sentence. But the defendant did something, too, (or, more accurately, failed to do something), and she thus became the subject of a clause inside the sentence.

Verbs: As you rewrite, do two things: (*1*) Wherever possible, replace the verb *to be* with a verb of action. The verb *to be* includes "is," "are," "am," "was," "were," and "will be." They do a good job of describing condition or status ("the defendant is guilty"). But they are not verbs of action. In fact, they obscure action. Consider ways of eliminating variations on *there is* (such as *there were* and *it is*). Sometimes these constructions are helpful or even unavoidable ("there are four reasons why the plaintiff will not be able to recover . . . ."). At other times, however, they hide your message in a

---

§19.5   1. When marking up your work, your teacher might refer to these questions by using the number-letter codes that appear next to each question here.

fog of pretentious verbiage. (*2*) Replace *nominalizations* with real verbs. A nominalization is a phrase that is built around a noun but is asked to do a verb's work. "The search *was a violation of* the defendant's rights" should become "the search *violated* the defendant's rights." The nominalized phrase *was a violation of* is weaker and wordier than the blunt and vivid verb *violated.* The same problem occurs when you ask an adjective to do a verb's job ("was violative of"). Some other examples:

cross out	*and replace it with*
is able to	can
enter into an agreement	agree
make the argument that	argue that
make the assumption that	assume that
is aware of	knows
is binding on	binds
give consideration to	consider
make a determination	determine
make an objection	object
make payment to	pay
make provision	provide

19-B **Have you used verbs that communicate the precise relation-ship between subjects and objects?** For example:

wrong: The court *dealt with* common law larceny.

What did the court do to larceny? Define it? Define only one of the elements? Clarify the difference between larceny and false pretenses? Decide that there is no longer an offense by that name because the legislature has replaced it with the statutory crime of theft? The sentence would be much better with a verb that tells the reader precisely what happened.

wrong: The defendant *indicated* that he was interested in buying hashish.

How did he do that? By nodding affirmatively when asked if that was his desire? By asking "Is hashish sold in this neighborhood?"? By saying "I want to buy some hash"? (Depending on the surrounding facts and on local law, a court might treat these three possibilities very differently.)

wrong: The Freedom of Information Act *applies* to this case.

Does the Act require that the document at issue be published in the Federal Register? Does it require that the document be given to anyone who asks for a copy? Does it require that the document be available for photocopying, but not at government expense? Or does it give the government permission to refuse to do any of these things? We would know more if *applies* were replaced with a verb or a verbal phrase that communicates exactly what the Act really does.

> **wrong:**   Section 452(a) *involves* the Rule Against Perpetuities.

Here, *involves* communicates only that § 452(a) has some connection with the Rule Against Perpetuities. Has § 452(a) codified the Rule? Modified it? Abolished it?

The four verbs illustrated here—"deal with," "indicate," "apply," and "involve"—rarely communicate a precise relationship between a subject and an object.

Have you brought the reader to the verb quickly?   Consider this:

19-C

> The defendant's solicitation of contributions through an organization with a misleading name, immediate deposit of the funds in a bank account in the Bahamas, and eventual use of the money to buy a vacation home in his own name constitutes fraud.

The verb is what ties an English sentence together. In fact, an English sentence is incomprehensible until the reader has identified both a subject *and* a verb. And the most easily understood sentences bring the reader to the verb as quickly as possible. The example above cannot be understood in a single reading because it is "front-loaded." You do not reach the verb and object ("constitutes fraud") until after plowing through a subject that is 39 words long.

Sentences like that are caused by automatically making whatever you want to talk about the subject of the sentence. "What shall I talk about next?" you ask yourself and then write down the answer. That becomes the subject of a sentence, no matter how unreadable the result. In first drafts, you cannot avoid doing this, but in later drafts you should recognize the problem and correct it.

There are two easy ways to fix a front-loaded sentence. The first is to find a way to make the subject simple, thus bringing the reader to the verb quickly:

> The defendant committed fraud by soliciting contributions through an organization with a misleading name, immediately depositing them in a Bahamian bank account, and eventually using the money to buy a vacation home in his own name.

The other cure, sometimes a little less effective, is to break the original sentence in two:

> The defendant solicited contributions through an organization with a misleading name, immediately deposited them in a Bahamian bank

account, and eventually used the money to buy a vacation home in his own name. This was fraud.

You will lose control of your sentences if you just let them happen. Each sentence must be *built* if it is to communicate well.

19-D **Have you put the verb near the subject and the object near the verb?** A sentence is hard to understand if you insert a clause or phrase between a subject and a verb or between a verb and an object:

> Grateful Dead Productions, despite the Dead's reputation for tolerating and even encouraging bootleg tapings of concerts when they were still giving them, has several times sued for copyright infringement when the band's albums have been bootlegged.

The solution is to move the clause or phrase to the end or to the beginning of the sentence, leaving the subject and verb (or the verb and object) relatively close together.

move phrase or clause to the END of the sentence   Grateful Dead Productions has several times sued for copyright infringement when the Dead's albums have been bootlegged, despite the band's reputation for tolerating and even encouraging bootleg tapings of concerts when they were still giving them.

move phrase or clause to the BEGINNING of the sentence: Despite the Grateful Dead's reputation for tolerating and even encouraging bootleg tapings of concerts when they were still giving them, Grateful Dead Productions has several times sued for copyright infringement when the band's albums have been bootlegged.

The clause or phrase should begin the sentence only if you want to emphasize it.

19-E **Have you used transitional words and phrases to show how ideas are related?** Beginners often underestimate the reader's need to be told explicitly how ideas fit together or contrast with one another. You can do this economically with transitional words and phrases. See the ones listed in §19.3.

19-F **Have you streamlined unnecessarily wordy phrases?** Good rewriting pares a convoluted phrase down to something straightforward:

cross out	*and replace it with*
because of the fact that	because
during such time as	during
for the purpose of	to
for the reason that	because

in the situation where	where
in the case of	in
in the event that	if
make a motion	move
subsequent to	after
take into consideration	consider
until such time as	until
with regard to	regarding
with the exception of	except

Have you deleted throat-clearing phrases (also known as "long windups")? Phrases like the following waste words, divert the reader from your real message, and introduce a shade of doubt and an impression of insecurity: `19-G`

It is significant that . . .

The defendant submits that . . .

It is important to note that . . .

The next issue is . . .

Of the two examples below, why would the plaintiff's attorney feel more comfortable writing the first than the second?

The plaintiff submits that the judgment should be reversed because . . .

The judgment should be reversed because . . .

The unnecessary words in the first example shift emphasis from the idea propounded and to the obvious but irrelevant fact that the writer is the one doing the propounding. (But it is *not* ineffectual to begin an attack on an adversary's argument by beginning with phrasing like "Although the defendant has argued. . . .")

Have you broken up or streamlined unnecessarily long sentences? They obscure meaning. If a sentence is too `19-H` long to be understood easily on the first reading, express the sentence's ideas in fewer words, or split the sentence into two (or more) shorter sentences, or do both. If you decide to reduce the sentence's verbiage, see questions 19-A, 19-F, and 19-G and review §19.2. If you decide to break up the sentence, be sure to avoid the "sing-songy" style described in question 19-I.

Have you rewritten sentences so that none are "sing-songy"? For example: `19-I`

The defendant solicited contributions through an organization with a misleading name. He immediately deposited the funds in a bank account in the

Bahamas. Eventually, he used them to buy a vacation home in his own name. This was fraud.

These are four simple sentences, three of them beginning with a subject. The passage sounds naive and probably will bore the reader. The cause is a tendency to write down one thing at a time, without describing the relationships between or among the things mentioned. At its most extreme, the result is a series of simple sentences, all beginning with the subject.

There are two kinds of cure. One is to focus on the relationships, especially causal ones, using some of the transitional words and phrases listed in §19.3:

> Not only did the defendant solicit contributions through an organization with a misleading name, but he immediately deposited the funds in a bank account in the Bahamas. Moreover, he used them to buy a vacation home in his own name. Therefore, he has committed fraud.

The other cure is to vary three things periodically: the types of sentences (some simple, some compound, some complex); the lengths of sentences (some long, some short, some medium); and the way sentences begin (some with the subject, some with a prefatory word or phrase, some with a dependent clause). Closely related material can be combined into fewer sentences, where the sentence structure itself can demonstrate relationships between ideas:

> Having solicited contributions through an organization with a misleading name and deposited them in a Bahamian bank account, the defendant used the funds to buy a vacation home in his own name. This was fraud.

This example uses a subordinate sentence element ("Having solicited . . . bank account") to achieve the desired effect.

You can avoid the sing-songy effect by understanding and using the full range of sentence structures available in English.

19-J | **Have you avoided the passive voice unless you have a good reason for using it?**   In the active voice, the subject of the sentence acts (*"Maguire sued Schultz"*), but in the passive voice the subject of the sentence is acted upon (*"Schultz was sued by Maguire"*). The passive voice has three disadvantages: it is often more verbose; it tends to vagueness; and it is usually weaker and more boring to read. Most sentences should be in the active voice.

But the passive may be the more effective voice where you do not know who acted, where you think the identity of the actor is not important, or where you want to deemphasize the identity of the actor. For example, compare the following:

Ms. Blitzstein's aid-to-dependent-family benefits have been wrongfully terminated fourteen times in the last six years.

The Department of Public Welfare has wrongfully terminated Ms. Blitzstein's aid-to-dependent-family benefits fourteen times in the last six years.

Here the passive is actually more concise. Depending on the context, the passive might not be vague because the reader might be likely to know that the Department is the only agency capable of terminating aid-to-dependent-family benefits, or at least that the Department is being accused of doing so in this instance. And, again depending on the context, the passive sentence may be the stronger and more interesting of the two. If the reader is a judge who is being asked to order the Department to stop this nonsense, the passive will be the stronger sentence because it emphasizes the more appealing idea. (Generally, a judge is more likely to sympathize with a victim of bureaucratic snafus than to condemn a government agency for viciousness or incompetence.)

Sometimes, the passive voice is a good way of avoiding sexist pronouns. See question 19-S.

Have you avoided placing modifiers so that the reader will wonder what they modify? When people talk, modifiers sometimes | **19-K** | wander all over sentences, regardless of what they are intended to modify. But in formal writing, more precision is required. These sentences all mean different things:

The police are authorized to arrest *only* the person named in the warrant.
[*They are not authorized to arrest anyone else.*]

The police are authorized *only* to arrest the person named in the warrant.
[*They are not authorized to torture or deport him.*]

The police are *only* authorized to arrest the person named in the warrant.
[*They have the right to arrest him, but they do not have to. The warrant gives them some discretion.*]

Only the police are authorized to arrest the person named in the warrant.
[*Civilians are not so authorized.*]

Make sure that the modifier's placement communicates what you really want to say, and do not assume that a busy reader will be willing or even able to figure out the meaning from the context.

19-L Have you used parallel constructions when expressing a list? Even implied lists should be expressed in some sort of consistent structure. Each item or idea must be phrased in the same grammatical format. Consider the following:

> This attorney should be disbarred because of his neglect of a matter entrusted to him, for pleading guilty to the felony of suborning perjury, and because he disclosed a client's confidences without the client's consent.

Here, the first listed item is expressed as a noun possessed by a pronoun ("his neglect"); the second as an unpossessed gerund ("for pleading"); and the third as a dependent clause, complete with subject, verb, and object ("because he disclosed confidences"). Although the first and third items are preceded by the word "because," the second is not. Isolated from the others, each form alone would be grammatical. But the inconsistencies among them make the whole sentence sound inarticulate. That would not have been true if each item in the list were expressed in the same format:

> This attorney should be disbarred because he neglected a matter entrusted to him, pleaded guilty to the felony of suborning perjury, and disclosed a client's confidences without the client's consent.

19-M Have you used terms of art where appropriate? Where an idea peculiar to the law is usually expressed through a term of art, that term should be used because it conveys the idea as precisely as the law can manage and because it often makes long and convoluted explanations unnecessary. Do not write "the plaintiff asked the court to tell the defendants to stop building the highway." It is much more precise to write "the plaintiff moved for an order preliminarily enjoining. . . ."

But do not confuse terms of art with legal argot. A term of art is the law's symbol for an idea that usually cannot be expressed with precision in any other way. Legal argot, on the other hand, has no special meaning peculiar to the law. It is just pretentious wording used for everyday concepts by a writer who wants to sound like a lawyer but succeeds only in a hollow way. (See question 19-O.)

19-N Have you edited out inappropriately used terms of art? Terms of art ought to be used only to convey the precise meaning the law holds for them. Where you use a term of art (perhaps because it sounds lawyer-like) but do not really intend to communicate the idea the term of art stands for, the reader will assume that you do not know what you are talking about.

19-O Have you edited out imitations of lawyer noises? Said noises found in and about a lawyer's writing have heretofore caused, resulted in, and led to grievous injury with respect to said lawyer's readers, clients, and/or repute, to wit: by compelling the aforesaid readers to suffer confusion and/or consternation at the expense of the aforementioned clients and consequently rendering said repute to become null, void, and nugatory.

Good legal writing and good writing in other fields have the same characteristics of clarity and smoothness in reading. Thinking like a lawyer is not the same as imitating lawyer noises. Expressions like "to wit," "hereinbefore," and "aforesaid" are argot — not terms of art (see question 19-M) — and they do not convey anything that ordinary English cannot communicate more clearly and less awkwardly. The most influential memos and the most persuasive briefs are written in the real English language. For example:

just fine:	Elvis has left the building.
bad:	Elvis has departed from the premises.
worse:	It would be accurate to say that Elvis has departed from the premises.
meaningless:	Elvis has clearly and unequivocably left the building.
meaningful:	There is uncontroverted evidence that Elvis has left the building.

Why is "clearly and unequivocably" meaningless? Elvis could not *un*clearly or equivocably leave the building. Either he has left, or he has not. Writing something like "clearly and unequivocably" pounds the table without adding meaning. But "uncontroverted evidence" is meaningful because it says that there is evidence that Elvis has left and no evidence that he has not, which would easily justify a judicial finding of fact. We expect to read in the next sentence about the 27 witnesses who will testify that they saw Elvis go through the stage door, step into a stretch limousine, and disappear into the night.

Have you edited out contractions and other conversational language? | **19-P**
They might be appropriate in an informal letter to a client, but they have no place in other lawyerly documents.

Have you edited out inappropriate abbreviations? | **19-Q**
In formal documents, a lawyer does not write "the N.C. Supreme Court has held. . . ." Spell words out unless the abbreviation is generally used at least as often as the full name (for example, "NAACP" and "FCC"). Otherwise, abbreviate only in citations.

Have you avoided rhetorical questions? | **19-R**
They do not work. Your job is to lead — not jab — the reader.

Have you avoided sexist wording? | **19-S**
In the way all languages evolve, English is now shedding many centuries of sexist

phrasing. Perhaps a decade or two from now, English might settle into phrasings that are both gender-neutral and fluid. In the meantime, writers must struggle a bit.

The thorniest problem is English's use of the pronouns *he, his,* and *him* to refer generally to people of either sex. The problem would not exist if English had a pronoun that meant "any person," regardless of sex. But English lacks that. The ersatz pronoun *s/he* irritates most readers. The ritual incantations *he or she, his or her,* and *him or her* are wordy and, if repeated often, tedious.

The best solution is to eliminate the need for a pronoun. If that cannot be done, recast both the pronoun *and* its noun in the plural. Often, that also makes the writing more concise:

> To calendar a motion, an attorney must file *his* moving papers with the clerk.

pronoun replace with "the"

> To calendar a motion, an attorney must file *the* moving papers with the clerk.

actor made plural

> To calendar motions, attorneys must file *their* moving papers with the clerk.

actor eliminated from sentence

> A motion is calendared by filing the motion papers with the clerk

With these sentences, the most concise solution is to eliminate the actor entirely and cast the sentence in the passive voice. But that may not be true in other situations. And even here, the most concise solution might not be the best one. If the sentence is meant to warn the kind of lawyers who forget to file their moving papers, that point is lost if the attorneys themselves are not even mentioned.

As a last resort, you might fall back on *he or she, his or her,* or *him or her.* But these phrases pose another problem. Suppose the sentence reads this way:

> To calendar a motion, an attorney must file his or her moving papers with the clerk.

Our eye hits the word *his,* and we imagine a male attorney, maybe in a dark blue suit, handing documents over a counter to a court clerk. (For most readers, words create images — and the more specific the words, the more detailed the image.) Our eye continues through the words *or her,* and for a split-second we allow for the possibility that this attorney with moving papers might be female. We do this for a split-second because the other image got there first (and maybe because of assumptions about sex-based roles and certain kinds of jobs). And after that split-second is over, we go back to thinking about moving papers and clerks and what happens when things are not calendared properly — and if we are imagining anything, it is probably still the male lawyer in the blue suit.

Why not solve this problem by reversing the pronouns so that we write instead *she or he, her or his,* and *her or him?* Elsewhere in this book, that has been done in the few places where it would be impractical to use one of the better pronoun solutions (eliminating the need for a pronoun or making the pronoun plural). Reversing the pronouns is not commonly done in lawyers' writing, but there is no reason why it could not be. A reasonable reader who sees it for the first time in your writing will probably understand that you are trying to write in a fair-minded way. If your reader is unreasonable (and more than a few readers are), your problems are bigger and need more immediate attention than any pronouns you might use. With an unreasonable or potentially unreasonable reader, do not make the situation worse by reversing the pronouns in a way the reader may not have seen before.

Sex-biased nouns are usually easier to avoid. The "reasonable man" in negligence law can as easily be the "reasonable person"; a "juryman" is better as a "juror" anyway; and, depending on the context, "manpower" might be replaced with "effort," "personnel," "workers," or something else. Some nouns, such as "businessman," are harder, however. Unless sex truly matters ("the corporation specializes in the manufacture of businesswomen's clothing"), it is sexist to refer to a woman in business as a "businesswoman." (She is a person in business. What does her sex have to do with it?) Unless the awkward term "businessperson" gains acceptance, the only solution is to rephrase the sentence so that you do not need a word like "businessman" or "businesswoman."

Exercise I.   Kalmar's Driveway (Clarity and Conciseness)

Rewrite the following sentences around nouns and verbs that describe action. Make sure that each sentence is of comprehensible length. Eliminate throat-clearing phrases, and replace nominalizations, unnecessary passives, and unnecessarily wordy constructions. (See §§19.1, 19.2, and 19.5.) You will find this easier if you read the whole exercise before starting to rewrite.

1. It is evident that Kalmar is likely to be convicted of accepting a bribe because all the elements of bribery are susceptible of proof beyond a reasonable doubt.

2. A person is guilty of accepting a bribe if that person is an employee of the government and "requests or receives from any other person anything of value, knowing it to be a reward or inducement for an official act," Crim. Code § 702, and a conviction may occur only if evidence is presented by the prosecution that persuades the finder of fact beyond a reasonable doubt that the defendant is guilty.

3. The initial element that can be established is that Kalmar is an employee of the government.

4. The facts indicate that in his capacity as Roads Commissioner, Kalmar had occasion from time to time to purchase, on behalf of the government, quantities of cement, asphalt, and other road construction materials from Phelps, who caused these materials to be delivered to road-repair sites on trucks owned by Phelps.

5. Kalmar had need for a new driveway at his own home, and he made a request to Phelps for a recommendation of a contractor who would do a good job at a reasonable price.

6. Phelps told Kalmar that she would look into the matter, but, without Kalmar's knowledge, a new driveway was built at his home by her employees the next day.

7. The circumstances fit into a pattern showing that Kalmar had knowledge that he was being offered a reward or inducement by Phelps for official acts directly relating to his job, and although the statute does not specify that a defendant must know at the time the thing of value is actually delivered or physically taken that it is a reward for official acts, Kalmar both accepted and continued to receive the bribe when, according to the facts, he did not undertake any effort to compensate Phelps for the cost of the driveway.

8. Because the cost involved is such that it could not have been accidentally overlooked by Kalmar, there can be no innocent explanation for the fact that he had an opportunity every day to see that he had a new driveway for which nothing had been paid, and there is therefore no reasonable doubt about his guilt.

Exercise II.   Smolensky at the Plate (Clarity and Forcefulness)

Rewrite the following to bring the reader to the verb quickly and use transitional words and phrases to show how ideas are related. Avoid "sing-songy" sentences and make sure that subjects, verbs, objects, and modifiers are appropriately placed. (See §19.1, 19.3, and 19.5.) You will find this easier if you read the whole exercise before starting to rewrite.

1. Vargas, when Smolensky, who was batting, turned around and attacked him with a baseball bat, was playing catcher.

2. In *Crawford v. Bender*, the Court of Appeals held that a person who engages in a sport, has an opportunity to know beforehand of the types of bodily contact customary in that sport, and suffers an injury as a result of such a contact, cannot recover damages.

3. Some physical contact is inevitable in athletics. Assault is not inevitable and is prohibited by the rules of virtually every team sport.

4. Vargas participated in the game of baseball. He consented to those bodily contacts that are customary in baseball or permitted by the rules of the game. Baseball players are rarely beaten with baseball

bats. In the past, Vargas has only been hit with a bat by accident. League Rule 19 specifically prohibits "striking another player."

5. To hold that Vargas will not be able to recover when Smolensky will not be able to offer any evidence that would show that Vargas intended to consent to be attacked with a bat would be inconsistent with the rule of *Crawford*.

20 Citations and Quotations

§20.1 Why Legal Citation Is Complicated

Legal writing has unique citation rules. Your typical reader will need very specific information about each authority you cite and will need it expressed in "citation language" that can be quickly skimmed and understood. A properly constructed citation conveys a large amount of information in a very small space. Bad citation form, on the other hand, is instantly noticed and causes a reader to suspect that the writer is sloppy and therefore unreliable.

From a citation, a reader expects to learn the following:

1. *where* the authority can be found: the names of publications and volume, page, section, or paragraph numbers, as well as
2. some basic facts affecting the authority's *weight:* identity of courts and jurisdictions together with dates, subsequent histories, and explanatory parentheticals.

These are communicated through *citation grammar:* words, abbreviations, and numbers that, when expressed in proper order, have precise meaning for the reader.

Two books codify the most commonly followed rules of legal citation: the ALWD Citation Manual and the Bluebook. Your teacher has probably assigned one or the other of these books. You do *not* need to consult both unless your teacher tells you to. They address the same citation issues, and most of the time their rules will produce identical citations.

Two kinds of tasks confront you in using the ALWD Citation Manual or the Bluebook: finding the applicable citation rule in the book you are using (which can be like statutory research) and discovering its meaning (which can be like statutory interpretation). The research is not as hard as it looks. Fortunately, both books have very good indices. If the index does not produce what you need, try the table of contents instead.

Do not imitate citation forms you see in casebooks or in the library without first making sure that they satisfy the requirements of the cite book you are using. You will read many citations that would violate rules found in one or both of the citation books. Some states follow unique citation rules of their own. Several publishers of reporters, digests, and annotation and looseleaf services have developed their own citation styles, which differ from both ALWD and Bluebook rules. And some important citation traditions have been changed through one or both books in recent years, which means that material published earlier might have used citation formats no longer considered acceptable.

§20.2   Touring the ALWD Citation Manual and the Bluebook

If you are using the ALWD Citation Manual, read §20.2.1. If you are using the Bluebook, read §20.2.2.[1]

§20.2.1   The ALWD Citation Manual

ALWD stands for the Association of Legal Writing Directors. The third edition of the ALWD Citation Manual is divided into the following parts which you can follow in the Manual's table of contents:

Part 1 explains how to use the Manual and how to get your word-processing software to work well with citations.

---

§20.2   1. If you are using the ALWD Manual, you might encounter lawyers and judges who use "bluebook" as a verb ("Have you bluebooked your citations?"). To bluebook means to make sure your cites are in proper form, regardless of whether you use the ALWD Manual or the Bluebook. Usually, the ALWD Manual and the Bluebook prescribe the same citation form, and lawyers and judges generally cannot tell the difference between a citation created from the ALWD Manual and a citation created from the Bluebook. Lawyers and judges use "bluebook" as a verb just as you might ask for a "kleenex" or talk about "xeroxing" when it does not matter who manufactured the tissue or the photocopy machine. Lawyers and judges might also ask, "Have you shepardized your cases?" Shepard's is a series of red-covered books that show whether a precedent has been overturned by later decisions. Few people use them any more. Lexis now owns the Shepard's name and uses it for the Lexis service that accomplishes the same thing on a computer. Westlaw calls its competing service Key-Cite. Lawyers and judges use the verb "shepardize" in part because they may have gone to law school when the only way to make sure a case was still good law was to open up the red Shepard's books. Although lawyers and judges will ask whether you have shepardized, they usually will not care which service you use to verify your precedents.

Part 2 (rules 1 through 11) explains some basics such as typeface, abbreviations, citing to pages and sections, and full and short-form citation formats.

Part 3 governs citations to specific types of authority, including cases (rule 12) and statutes (rule 14).

Part 4 (rules 38 through 42) governs electronic sources such as Lexis, Westlaw, and websites.

Part 5 (rules 43 through 46) explains matters common to all citations, regardless of the type of authority involved. Examples include citation placement, signals, and explanatory parentheticals.

Part 6 (rules 47 through 49) explains quotations.

The appendices provide citation rules for each jurisdiction (appendices 1 and 2), the standard abbreviations used in legal writing (appendices 3-5), and a sample memo illustrating cite forms (appendix 6). From appendix 1, you can learn the citation form for each jurisdiction's statutory code, the names and abbreviations of the reporters to which a particular court's decisions must be cited, and even a few details about the history of a jurisdiction's court system. (Federal courts are listed at the end, after Wyoming.) Appendix 2 reproduces individual states' court rules on citation.

On the inside back cover of the ALWD Manual is a locator showing where you can find the rules on the major kinds of authority. On the inside front cover is a locator showing the pages on which you can find Fast Formats, which illustrate citations to various kinds of authorities.

§20.2.2 The Bluebook

The eighteenth edition of the Bluebook is divided into the following parts, which you can follow in the Bluebook's table of contents.

The blue pages near the front explain how to adapt Bluebook rules for practical writing in briefs and memoranda. The Bluebook began as a guide for law review editors, and the blue pages were added later to translate Bluebook rules for use in memoranda and briefs.

Citation rules are on white pages in the middle of the Bluebook. Rules 1 through 9 govern general citation issues, such as introductory signals (rule 1.2), short-form cites (rule 4), and quotations (rule 5). Rules 10 through 21 govern citations to specific types of authority, such as cases (rule 10) and statutes (rule 12).

The Bluebook has two numbering systems. The white pages contain rules, which are numbered. The blue pages at the front of the Bluebook contain supplementary explanations, but they are numbered as though they were rules. For example, citing to the Federal Rules of Civil Procedure is covered by both B6.1.3 (blue pages) and rule 12.8.3 (white pages). To resolve a citation problem, you might need to check both the blue pages and the white pages. You might find what you need in the white pages, in the blue pages, or in both. But if the white pages tell you to do one thing and the blue pages tell you to do another, follow the blue pages.

The tables—in the back of the book on white paper with a blue border—provide special citation rules for each jurisdiction (tables 1-4) and the standard abbreviations used in legal writing (tables 5-17). From table 1, you can learn the citation form for each state's statutory code, the names and abbreviations of the reporters to which a particular court's decisions must be cited, and even a few details about the history of a state's court system. Tables 6 through 16 show you how to abbreviate things like the names of cases, courts, and law reviews. (Some tables also appear at the end of the blue pages, but you will not use them often.)

On the inside back cover of the Bluebook are quick reference examples drawn from the blue pages. These can be helpful when you are writing your own citations. (On the inside front cover are quick reference examples for law review footnotes, but you will not need them during the first year of law school.)

§20.3   Citation to Specific Types of Authority

You will understand the rest of this chapter more easily if you read the relevant citation rule, in the book your teacher has assigned, when the rule is mentioned here. (Ignore references in this chapter to the book your teacher has *not* assigned.)

§20.3.1   Citation to Cases

A case citation has up to six components, which must appear in the following order:

1. the *case name*	ALWD rule 12.2 and appendix 3 Bluebook B5.1.1, rule 10.2, and table 6

2. reference to the
    reporter or *reporters*,
    with volume and
    page numbers
	ALWD rule 12.4 and appendix 1
	Bluebook B5.1.2,
	    rule 10.3, and table 1

3. identification of the *court*	ALWD rule 12.6 Bluebook B5.1.3 and rule 10.4
4. the *date* of the decision	ALWD rule 12.7 Bluebook B5.1.3 and rule 10.5

5. the *subsequent history*
    (if any)
	ALWD rule 12.8
	Bluebook B5.1.5 and
	    rule 10.7

For example:

Gussin v. Nintendo of Am., Inc., 62 F.3d 1433 (Fed. Cir. 1995)

Here are the citation's component parts:

1. **case name**   *Gussin v. Nintendo of Am., Inc.*

2. **reporter**   62 F.3d 1433
   reference

3. **court**   Fed. Cir.

4. **date**   (1995)

5. **subsequent**   [none to report in this cite]
   history

"Am." and "Inc." are abbreviations for "America" and "Incorporated" (ALWD appendix 3; Bluebook table 6). "F.3d" is the third series of Federal Reporter (ALWD appendix 1, last entry; Bluebook table 1). *Gussin* is found in volume 62 beginning at page 1433. "Fed. Cir." is the Federal Circuit of the United States Courts of Appeals (ALWD appendix 4; Bluebook rule 10.4(a)). *Gussin* has some subsequent history, but not of the kind that ALWD rule 12.8 or Bluebook rule 10.7 would require you to report in a citation you would write more than two years after the decision (see pages 245-246 for why).

Case name: The rules on what you must include or omit from case names, and how things are to be abbreviated, might seem overly detailed and counter-intuitive. With *Gussin,* for example, many students would naturally have abbreviated "Incorporated" but would just as naturally have spelled out "America." ALWD rule 12.2 and appendix 3 and Bluebook rule 10.2 and table 6 tell you exactly what to do. But a minor mistake here — spelling out a word like "America," for example — is easily overlooked by most readers. Spelling out "Incorporated," on the other hand, will strike your reader as naive.

Reporter reference: *Gussin* appears in only one reporter, called Federal Reporter, 3d Series. It is in volume 62 and on page 1433. U.S. Supreme Court cases and many state cases appear in more than one publication. Reporters can be official or unofficial. An official reporter is published by a government; an unofficial reporter by a private publisher, most often West. For the U.S. Supreme Court, the official reporter is United States Reports (abbreviated U.S.), and the unofficial reporters are Supreme Court Reporter (S. Ct.) and Lawyers' Edition (L. Ed.). ALWD appendix 1 and Bluebook table 1 show, for each state, whether there is an official reporter; in which West regional reporter or reporters the state's decisions appear; and how to abbreviate the relevant reporters.

In office memoranda, cite to a single reporter, preferably the one published by West (ALWD rule 12.4; Bluebook rule 10.3.1(b)). In documents to be submitted to courts — generally motion memoranda and briefs — do the same unless a local court rule requires that you parallel cite to an official reporter (ALWD rule 12.4; Bluebook B5.1.3 and rule 10.3.1). The ALWD Manual reproduces the local citation rules in appendix 2. If you parallel cite, the official reporter comes first:

> *Joe's Pizza, Inc. v. Aetna Life & Cas. Co.*, 236 Conn. 863, 675 A.2d 441 (1996).

In two senses, the U.S. Supreme Court is an exception to these practices. First, the preferred source is the official reporter — U.S. — and not one of the unofficial ones (ALWD rule 12.4(c); Bluebook table 1). The two unofficial reporters — Supreme Court Report and Lawyer's Edition — have tables in every volume that allow you to find an opinion there even if you know only the official citation. Second, the ALWD Manual and the Bluebook disagree about whether to parallel cite with U.S. Supreme Court cases. The Bluebook permits only one source, preferably the official one (see table 1). The ALWD Manual prefers only one source, again the official, but permits parallel citing to the unofficial reporters if you want to (ALWD rule 12.4(c)(2)).

Court: Four aspects of ALWD rule 12.6 and Bluebook rule 10.4 sometimes prove troublesome for beginners. First, do *not* specify the court if the citation includes a reporter that publishes the decisions of only one court. Such a reporter "clearly indicates" (ALWD rule 12.6(e)) or "unambiguously convey[s]" (Bluebook rule 10.4) the name of the court. Most commonly, it will be an official state reporter that bears only the name of the state and publishes the decisions of the state's highest court. Both of the citations below satisfy the requirement to identify the court:

> *Joe's Pizza, Inc. v. Aetna Life & Cas. Co.*, 236 Conn. 863, 675 A.2d 441 (1996).

> *Joe's Pizza, Inc. v. Aetna Life & Cas. Co.*, 675 A.2d 441 (Conn. 1996).

Second, because the reader needs to know exactly which court rendered the decision, it is not enough merely to name the *type* of court: the *specific* court itself must be identified. Thus, "U.S. Ct. App." does not tell the reader which of the 13 federal circuits was responsible for the decision. One of the approved abbreviations (such as "8th Cir.") must be used instead. Similarly, "U.S. Dist. Ct." is not sufficient for the United States District Court for the Eastern District of Pennsylvania; "E.D. Pa." tells the reader exactly which court made the decision.

Third, although ALWD rule 12.6 and Bluebook rules 10.4 and 10.5 do not explicitly allow it, you can omit the court or the date from the citation when the same information is included in the preceding text:

> As long ago as 1897, the New York Court of Appeals held that . . . *People v. Conroy*, 151 N.Y. 543, 45 N.E. 946.

(Including the date twice here would waste space and seem picayune to the reader.) If a decision's weight depends in some *significant* way on the identity of the court or the date, you can stress either or both of those things in the text before the reader gets to the cite. In the example above, if the rule you state is a surprising one and likely to excite skepticism, you might want to relax the reader a bit by making clear at the outset that you are relying on top-quality authority. Or you might want to do it where it is important for the reader to understand that you are relying on a long and well-established line of cases, or — at the opposite extreme — that, although the rule you state is an antique, it was enforced just last year by an appellate court in your jurisdiction.

Finally, the ALWD Manual and the Bluebook disagree about whether to identify the geographic subdivision of an intermediate state court in a cite. Bluebook rule 10.4(b) prohibits identification of the subdivision of an intermediate state court except where that is "of particular relevance." But the geographic subdivision is often "of particular relevance" in states where the intermediate appellate court is segmented geographically — such as New York and California — because the geographic subdivision can affect the authoritative value of the decision. It might be mandatory authority in that subdivision but of lesser weight elsewhere in the same state. State law will tell you the extent to which that is true. ALWD rule 12.6(b)(2) requires that you identify geographic subdivisions of state intermediate appellate courts if that information affects the weight of authority. This problem does not arise, of course, in states such as Pennsylvania and Maryland, where the intermediate appellate court sits as a single court hearing appeals from all parts of the state.

Date: This is simple. Just give the year unless the case is published only in one of the temporary forms specified in ALWD rule 12.7(c) or Bluebook 10.5(b).

Subsequent history: The subsequent history includes only the result of appeals from the decision cited to. Many decisions are not appealed and thus have no subsequent history. Where there is a subsequent history, the years of both lower and appellate decisions are included if they are different. If both decisions date from the same year, that year is listed only at the end of the citation and not elsewhere. ALWD rule 12.10(b) and Bluebook rule 10.7.2 govern the situation where the case name changed during the appeal.

There is an exception to the obligation to report subsequent history, and that involves denials of petitions to the U.S. Supreme Court for writs of certiorari. "Cert," as lawyers call it, is a kind of permission to appeal to the Supreme Court. The overwhelming majority of these petitions are denied. Because in denying them the Supreme Court makes no decision on the merits of the case, the only reason to report cert denials in a citation is to tell the reader that there is no longer any possibility of reversal by the Supreme Court.

Cert would normally have been granted or denied within two years after the decision below, and ALWD rule 12.8(a)(7) and Bluebook rule 10.7 require that you report denials of certiorari petitions as subsequent history only if you are writing within two years after the cited decision. After the Federal Circuit's decision in *Gussin,* the Supreme Court denied cert. Under the cert denial exception to the obligation to report subsequent history, your cite would look like this:

> **if you had**   *Gussin v. Nintendo of Am., Inc.,* 62 F.3d 1433
> **written your**   (Fed. Cir. 1995), *cert. denied,* 517 U.S. 1166
> **cite in 1997:**   (1996)

> **if you write**   *Gussin v. Nintendo of Am., Inc.,* 62 F.3d 1433
> **your cite today:** (Fed. Cir. 1995)

The *prior* history is cited to only in the circumstances described in ALWD rule 12.9(a) and Bluebook rule 10.7, second paragraph.

§20.3.2 Citation to Statutes

A citation to a statute currently in force has four components:

1. the *name* of the statute as it was originally enacted—but only if the statute is still known by that name;

2. the *section* being cited to, as numbered in the *original* enactment—but only if the statute is still known by its enacted name;

3. a reference to the *current codification,* providing title, article, chapter, and section numbers, as required by ALWD rules 14.2 and 14.4 and appendix 1 or Bluebook rules 12.1, 12.2.1, 12.3.1, and table 1; and

4. the *date* (and supplement, if any), as determined under ALWD rules 8 and 14.2(f) and Bluebook rule 12.3.2.

For example, this citation

> Wilderness Act, § 2(b), 16 U.S.C. § 1131(b) (2006)

is made up of the following parts:

1. **statute name**   Wilderness Act

2. **section in**   § 2(b)
    original
    enactment

3. **current**   16 U.S.C. § 1131(b)
    codification

4. **date of code**   (2006)

The third component is the most important. The rest of the citation is built around it. Here, "U.S.C." stands for United States Code. The Code is divided into 50 titles, and the number that precedes "U.S.C." is the title number. The number that follows it is the section number. If you wanted to find this statute in the library, you would locate the Code, find a volume that includes title 16, and open it to a page where § 1131(b) appears.

Most statutes are no longer known by the names under which they were originally enacted. Sometimes, that is because the statute has been recodified so many times over the years that its original enacted name has been forgotten. Just as often, the statute was a routine enactment in the first place and never had a name, or at least not one worth remembering. Where the section being cited to in the code is thus no longer identified with the session law in which it was originally enacted, the citation consists only of the third and fourth components:

18 U.S.C. § 4 (2006)

Citation to specific sections of a statute is regulated by ALWD rule 6 and Bluebook rules 3.3 and 6.2(c). In citations, always use a section symbol ("§") rather than the word "section." When you refer to a statute outside a citation—making what is called a textual reference to the authority—ALWD rule 6.11 allows you to use either the section symbol or the word "section." Bluebook rules 6.2(c) and 12.9(c) are confusing about which to use in textual references. The section symbol can begin a citation sentence (a sentence made up only of citations) but never a textual sentence, which should begin with a word. Add a space between the section symbol and the number that follows.

Readers will expect to see the "§" symbol, even though it is not on your keyboard and even if you are not sure how to make one with your word-processing software. WordPerfect and Microsoft Word can both put section symbols into your documents.

§20.4 Rules Governing All Citations

Authority can be referred to in three different ways: a full citation ("*Daubert v. Merrell Dow Pharm., Inc.*, 509 U.S. 579 (1992)"), a short-form citation ("*Id.* at 586"), or a textual reference ("In *Daubert,* the Supreme Court ruled . . .").

Full citations: A full citation should be used whenever you first mention an authority and wherever clarity would be promoted by communicating all the information found in a full citation. Generally, the worst place for a full citation is near the beginning of a sentence:

Under California Civil Code § 1597, "[e]verything is deemed possible except that which is impossible in the nature of things."

Here you have to climb over the citation just to find out what the rest of the sentence is about. Either of the following would be better:

state the proposition for which the authority stands before citing	"Everything is deemed possible except that which is impossible in the nature of things." Cal. Civil Code §1597 (West 1982).
if the source of the authority should be emphasized, refer to it briefly when introducing the proposition	A California statute provides that "[e]verything is deemed possible except that which is impossible in the nature of things." Cal. Civil Code § 1597 (West 1982).

This example is statutory. A case would be handled the same way, except that the last example above might begin, "The California Supreme Court has held. . . ."

Short-form citations: These may be used at any time after authority has been introduced with a complete citation, except where a short form would cause confusion. Confusion would occur, for example, if a short-form citation were to appear many pages after the full citation. The most frequently used short-form citations are governed by the following rules:

	ALWD	*Bluebook*
generally	rule 11.2	B5.2 and rule 4
cases	rule 12.21	rule 10.9
statutes	rule 14.6	rule 12.9

Beginners tend to encounter two problems with short-form citations. One arises from the once permitted but now prohibited practice of using *"supra"* with primary authority (ALWD rule 11.4(b)(4); Bluebook B8.2 and rule 4.2). Since so much previously published material follows the old rule, ALWD rule 11.4(b)(4) and the second sentence of Bluebook rule 4.2 are sometimes overlooked by students.

The other problem is that Bluebook B8.2 and rule 4.1 are often misunderstood. (ALWD rule 12.21 is more clear.) The ALWD and Bluebook rules amount to the same set of principles: Short-form citations to cases include the name of only the first party, or, if the first party is a frequent litigant — such as "United States," "California," or "State" — the name of the opposite party instead. If the citation should refer to a specific page in the decision, the following information is added: volume number, name of reporter, and the page referred to (the last preceded by "at"). The first page number of the decision does not appear in a short-form citation. In this example, both official and unofficial reporters are cited to:

Joe's Pizza, 236 Conn. at 869, 675 A.2d at 445.

Just to show you what is missing in a short-form cite, here is the full citation:

Joe's Pizza, Inc. v. Aetna Life & *Cas. Co.,* 236 Conn. 863, 869, 675 A.2d 441, 445 (1996).

Sometimes you can omit the case name from a short-form citation. ALWD rule 12.21(c) allows you to do so if at least some of the case name appears in the sentence preceding the short-form cite:

The *Joe's Pizza* court relied on § 59 of the Second Restatement of Judgments. 236 Conn. at 869, 675 A.2d at 445.

Bluebook rule 10.9(a)(i) allows you to omit the case name from a short-form citation "if the reader will have no doubt about the case to which the citation refers."

If the immediately preceding citation is to the same case, use *Id.* in a short-form cite instead of the name of the first party, even if the preceding citation is also in short form. (In legal citation, *Id.* means the same thing that *Ibid.* means in college textbooks.) When using *Id.,* be careful to show any ways in which the second citation refers to something different from the first. Thus, where "*Id.* at 414" is followed simply by "*Id.,*" the reader has *in both instances* been referred to page 414. If you want the second cite to refer to page 598, it should be "*Id.* at 598" and not just *Id.*

Where "*Id.*" is used and you need to specify a page number inside the case, omit the name and volume number of the first reporter cited. But that is not true where a party's name is used. All of the following are proper short-form cites:

Id., at 869.
Id., at 869, 675 A.2d at 445.
Joe's Pizza, 236 Conn. at 869, 675 A.2d at 445.

Textual references: A textual reference is the mention of authority in text without the formalities of either a long- or short-form citation. There are two textual references in the following sentence, one to a case and the other to a statute:

In *Sanders,* the Supreme Court held that 5 U.S.C. §§701-706 do not provide . . .

A textual reference, if written unambiguously, is an appropriate device when discussing authority that you have earlier cited in full. Textual references are governed by ALWD rule 43.1(d) and by Bluebook rules 10.9(c) and 12.9.

Citation sentences and clauses: Citations, whether full or short form, are arranged in citation sentences and clauses according to ALWD rule 43.1(a) and Bluebook B2 and rule 1.1. Where an authority supports an entire sentence of your text, you must put the citation in a separate citation sentence:

> A defamation defendant enjoys an absolute privilege for expressions of mere opinion. *Gertz v. Robert Welch, Inc.,* 418 U.S. 323 (1974).

On the other hand, where an authority supports only part of a sentence, the citation is interpolated into the textual sentence as a citation clause:

> A defamation defendant enjoys an absolute privilege for expressions of mere opinion, *Gertz v. Robert Welch, Inc.,* 418 U.S. 323, 339-40 (1974), and it is a question of law, to be determined by the court and not the jury, whether a statement at issue is one of fact or of opinion, *Information Control Corp. v. Genesis One Computer Corp.,* 611 F.2d 781, 783 (9th Cir. 1980).

This is a densely packed sentence, full of citation clutter, but it is one that many lawyers would write. You probably found it a bit hard to climb over the *Gertz* cite so you could get to the rest of the sentence. You can fix all this by writing sentences that have no cites inside them. An occasional textual reference to authority is not a problem. It is the mass of a complete citation that distracts the reader. Write textual sentences that do not include full citations and insert citation sentences between the textual sentences. Thus:

> A defamation defendant enjoys an absolute privilege for expressions of mere opinion. *Gertz v. Robert Welch, Inc.,* 418 U.S. 323, 339-40 (1974). It is a question of law, to be determined by the court and not the jury, whether a statement at issue is one of fact or of opinion. *Information Control Corp. v. Genesis One Computer Corp.,* 611 F.2d 781, 783 (9th Cir. 1980).

Where several authorities are cited for the same point, the order in which they appear in citation sentences and clauses is governed by ALWD rule 45 and Bluebook rule 1.4.

Citing to specific parts of an authority: For the following, see the rules listed:

	ALWD	*Bluebook*
volumes	rules 12.3 (cases) and 22.1 (books)	rule 3.2(a)
supplements	rule 8	rule 3.2(a)
sections	rule 6	rules 3.3, 6.2(c)
pages	rule 5	rule 3.2(a)

A citation that directs a reader to a specific page in an authority is called a "pinpoint cite" or a "jump cite." A quotation *must* be cited to a specific page.

Where you refer to only part of an opinion — even without quoting — a reader is entitled to know which pages you have in mind (ALWD rules 5.2, 12.5; Bluebook B10.3 and rule 3.3). A few opinions are too short to need pinpoint citing. For most lawyers, an opinion that covers two pages in a West reporter is probably short enough to justify dispensing with a pinpoint cite unless you are quoting. For many lawyers, an opinion that covers four pages needs a pinpoint cite.

Abbreviations: Four provisions of ALWD rule 2 and Bluebook rule 6.1 might seem perplexing in the beginning. First, no space appears between initials or between initials and numbers, although a space must appear between an initial or number abbreviation and something longer. Thus:

wrong:	S.W. 3d
	Cal.4th
	F.Supp.2d
right:	S.W.3d
	Cal. 4th
	F. Supp. 2d

Second, in abbreviations of the names of law reviews, you must add a space between initials that stand for the name of a place or institution and initials that stand for other things. Thus:

wrong:	N.C.L. Rev.
	N.Y.U.L. Rev.
right:	N.C. L. Rev.
	N.Y.U. L. Rev.

(North Carolina is, of course, a place, and New York University is an institution.)

Third, the ALWD Manual and the Bluebook differ on one abbreviation practice. Bluebook rule 6.1(b) and table 6 provide that where an abbreviation is formed by deleting part of the middle of a word and leaving part of the beginning and end, an apostrophe is inserted where the deletion was made, and the abbreviation does not end in a period. But ALWD appendix 3 and rule 12.8(a) abbreviate some of these words with periods and others with apostrophes. Thus:

	ALWD	*Bluebook*
Association	Assn.	Ass'n
Commission	Commn.	Comm'n
Department	Dept.	Dep't
Government	Govt.	Gov't
International	Intl.	Int'l
Society	Socy.	Soc'y

But:

	ALWD	*Bluebook*
affirmed	aff'd	aff'd
reversed	rev'd	rev'd

Fourth, both the ALWD Manual and the Bluebook abbreviate "second" and "third" as "2d" and "3d" — and *not* "2nd" and "3rd."

Signals: If needed, your purpose in citing an authority can be communicated through signals, which are formulaic words or abbreviations that introduce the citation. The accepted signals and their definitions are set out in ALWD rule 44 and Bluebook B4 and rule 1.2. Signals help compress massive amounts of information in law review footnotes and in other kinds of scholarly writing, including the seminar papers you might write in the second or third year of law school. A signal is *not* used where the authority directly supports the statement you are citing it for (ALWD rule 44.2(a)(1); Bluebook 1.2(a)). Nor is a signal needed where your own discussion of the authority makes clear why you are citing to it (see the way cites are handled in Appendices C, F, G, and H in this book).

In practical writing — memos and briefs written in law offices for other lawyers and for courts — there are two reasons for you to avoid signals unless they are truly necessary. First, signals cannot communicate the type of precise information needed by the reader of a brief or memorandum. A person who must make a decision based in part on your writing needs to know not only what an authority stands for but also *exactly* how that is relevant to the decision to be made. In briefs and memoranda, your own discussion of the authorities does that much better than signals can.

Second, every Bluebook edition since 1947 has changed the definitions of signals in one way or another.[1] The most troublesome example occurred in the 16th edition, which reversed the meaning of the signal *see* so that after 1996 it meant the exact opposite of what it had meant before. This was almost universally criticized, and even the House of Representatives of the Association of American Law Schools expressed disapproval. In the 17th edition, published in 2000, the Bluebook editors reverted to the definition that was in the 15th edition.

After all this, many readers no longer recall the precise definitions of what signals are supposed to communicate. When you write, you can consult the Bluebook or the ALWD Manual for the hypertechnical meaning of a signal. But your reader is not going to do that. Practical, decision-making readers do not have time for it, and they expect you to make your message clear at first glance without making them decode the signals you are using.

If you really need to use a signal, there is a solution to the definitions problem. The solution is endorsed explicitly by the Bluebook in rule 1.2(e) and implicitly permitted by the ALWD Manual. It is called using signals as

---

§20.4   1. Carol M. Bast & Susan Harrell, *Has the Bluebook Met Its Match? The ALWD Citation Manual,* 92 L. Lib. J. 337, 339 n. 8, 341 (2000).

verbs. When signals are used as verbs, they are not italicized, and cryptic abbreviations like *Cf.* and *e.g.* are replaced with ordinary words in the English language. For example:

signal: *See, e.g., In re Burger Boys, Inc.,* 94 F.3d 755 (2d Cir. 1996); *In re Orion Pictures,* 4 F.3d 1095, 1101 (2d Cir. 1993).

verb: See, for example, *In re Burger Boys, Inc.,* 94 F.3d 755 (2d Cir. 1996); *In re Orion Pictures,* 4 F.3d 1095, 1101 (2d Cir. 1993).

To the reader, there is nothing to decode in "See, for example." Even in memoranda and briefs, the best practice, in most instances, is to *explain* the authority on which you rely rather than to use signals, even as verbs. A reader who must make a decision needs to know the details of your thinking.

Parentheticals: Two types of parentheticals appear in legal citations. The first is an integral part of the citation and provides required information, such as the court and year for a case (ALWD rules 12.6 and 12.7; Bluebook rules 10.4 and 10.5) or the year for a statute (ALWD rule 14.2(f); Bluebook rule 12.3.2).

The second type is an *explanatory parenthetical* that provides information you could express outside the cite but for economy want to compress into the citation (ALWD rule 46; Bluebook rule 1.5). For cases, see ALWD rule 12.11 or Bluebook rule 10.6. For statutes, see ALWD rule 14.2(h) or Bluebook rule 12.7. Some of this information is technical comment on the authority and is usually better placed in a citation parenthetical unless you want it emphasized in the text:

in citation: *Carey v. Population Services Int'l,* 431 U.S. 678, 691-99 (1977) (plurality opinion).

emphasized in text: Although a majority of seven justices struck down that portion of the statute which prohibited distribution of nonprescription contraceptives to persons under the age of 16, only four justices supported the rationale now urged in this court. *Carey v. Population Services Int'l,* 431 U.S. 678, 691-99, 702-03, 707-08, 713-16 (1977).

You will run into trouble, however, if you go overboard trying to express the *substance* of an authority in explanatory parentheticals:

Carey v. Population Services Int'l, 431 U.S. 678, 691-99 (1977) (holding that state statute prohibiting distribution of nonprescription contraceptives to persons under 16 years old is unconstitutional because sexual activity may not be constitutionally deterred by increasing its hazards).

Not only is this explanatory parenthetical awkward and hard to read, but it oversimplifies and inevitably misrepresents the material in order to pack it into parenthetical form.

If the material is complicated and important to the issue, explain it in text. Use an explanatory parenthetical only for information that is simple and not an important part of your discussion or argument. And resist the temptation to use explanatory parentheticals to avoid the hard work of explaining complicated and important authority.

Typeface: You are already used to two typefaces. This sentence—and most of this book—is in roman, which most people think of as ordinary type. *This sentence is in italics, or slanted type.* Typeface is governed by ALWD rule 1 and Bluebook B13. You need to know two things.

First, the following should be in italics: case names, signals, *id.,* cross-references (*supra, infra*), and phrases introducing subsequent history (*aff'd, rev'd,* and so on). Before people wrote on computers, they had to underline rather than italicize because typewriters could not shift back and forth between ordinary type and italics. (The examples in the Bluebook blue pages underline rather than italicize, even though virtually all law school and law office writing is now done on computers.) All word processing software will italicize. Italics look much more professional than underlining.

Second, the Bluebook was designed primarily to govern citing in law review footnotes, and, except for the blue pages, the rules and examples in the Bluebook are aimed at the needs of people who write, edit, and read law review articles and their footnotes. The blue pages were added afterward to translate Bluebook rules for use in memoranda and briefs. The Bluebook—but *not* the ALWD Manual—requires that in law review footnotes certain sources, such as books, be printed in large and small capitals. Large and small caps never appear in memoranda and briefs. Before computers, typewriters could not produce them, and they look awful in the middle of your text. ALWD rule 1.3(5) and Bluebook B13 provide for ordinary roman and italics instead. If you are using the Bluebook, do not be confused by the large and small cap examples that appear throughout the Bluebook white pages. Instead, follow B13 in the blue pages. If you are using the ALWD Manual, you can forget this problem because the ALWD Manual does not require large and small caps for anything.

Local citation rules: Several states have a few rules of their own governing one or another aspect of citation in documents to be submitted to courts. Most commonly, these rules require that decisions be cited to the local official reporter as well as to a West reporter, but there are other provisions as well. As long as you are writing documents that will be submitted to your teacher only (and not to a real court), you need not worry about these local citation rules unless your teacher tells you to consult them. But later—in a law school clinical program or in a law office—when you first begin preparing documents that really will be filed in court, you will have to make sure that your citations conform to local practice.

All of the local citation rules are reproduced in appendix 2 of the ALWD Manual. If you are using the ALWD Manual, just check appendix 2 when you start writing documents that really will be submitted to a court. If you are using the Bluebook, table BT2 in the blue pages refers to local citation rules but does not reproduce them.

§20.5 Quotations

Beginners have many more problems with quotations than they think they will. This section explains the complex rules on quotation format. Section 20.6 of this book explains how to avoid faults like overquoting, unnecessarily long quotations, and quoting out of context.

ALWD rules 47 through 49 and Bluebook rule 5 govern the format of quotations. Here are the most essential requirements:

Use brackets to enclose additions and substitutions that you place inside quotation marks, including the transformation of a lowercase letter into a capital or vice versa (ALWD rule 48; Bluebook rule 5.2). Parentheses and brackets convey different messages, and you cannot substitute one for the other. On your computer keyboard, brackets are at the right end of the row under the numbers.

If you incorporate a quote beginning with a capitalized word into a sentence of your own, the capital letter must be reduced to a lowercase letter unless the capital denotes a proper name. For example:

wrong: The court held **that** "**Not** so long ago, in a studio far, far away from the policymakers in Washington, D.C., George Lucas conceived of an imaginary galaxy," but his trademark is not infringed when politicians refer to a proposed missile defense system as Star Wars. *Lucasfilm Ltd. v. High Frontier,* 622 F. Supp. 931, 932, 935 (D.D.C. 1985).

right: The court held **that** "[n]ot so long ago, . . ."

If you add or delete italics, or if you omit citations from a quote, you must communicate that in a parenthetical following the citation (ALWD rule 48; Bluebook rule 5.2). This shows the correct format:

In order to obtain the names of a defamation defendant's confidential sources, a plaintiff must prove that she or he has "*independently* attempted to obtain the information elsewhere and has been unsuccessful." *Silkwood v. Kerr-McGee Corp.,* 563 F.2d 433, 438 (10th Cir. 1977) (emphasis added).

Under ALWD rule 49 and Bluebook rule 5.3, if you delete words (other than a citation) from a quote, you must indicate that by an ellipsis (". . ."). When the final words of a sentence are omitted, the sentence ends with *four* periods — three for the ellipsis and one to end the sentence. There are two exceptions. First, where you incorporate a quotation into a sentence of your own composition — as in the Star Wars and *Silkwood* examples above — do not place an ellipsis at the beginning or the end of the quotation. Incorporating the quote into your own sentence suggests that you might have omitted something. Second, do not place an ellipsis at the beginning of a quotation, even if you intend the quote to stand on its own as a complete sentence (ALWD rule 49.3(b)(2); Bluebook rule 5.3). If the quote is not incorporated into a sentence you have written and if the first letter of the quote was not capitalized in the original, capitalize that letter and place it in brackets to indicate an alteration (ALWD rule 48.1; Bluebook rule 5.3(b)).

ALWD rule 47.5(a) requires that a quotation as long as 50 words or four lines of *typed* text (not text as printed in the book you are citing from) be put in a single-spaced, indented quotation block. Bluebook rule 5.1 requires the same thing if the quote is 50 words or more. If you are using the Bluebook, you have to count the words and not just the lines.

A block quote should *not* begin and end with quotation marks (ALWD rule 47.5(a); Bluebook rule 5.1(a)). The indentation alone tells the reader that it is a quote. And the citation to the quote's source does *not* appear in the quotation block (ALWD rule 47.5(c); Bluebook rule 5.1(a)). The cite goes instead in your text, at the beginning of the next line you write. The first example below is wrong on *both* counts:

wrong: Judge Kozinski disagreed:

> "Where does [Vanna] White get this right to control our thoughts? The majority's creation goes way beyond the protection given a trademark or a copyrighted work, or a person's name or likeness. . . . For better or worse, we *are* the Court of Appeals for the Hollywood Circuit. Millions of people toil in the shadow of the law we make, and much of their livelihood is made possible by the existence of intellectual property rights." *White v. Samsung Electronics Am., Inc.,* 989 F.2d 1512, 1519, 1521 (9th Cir. 1993) (Kozinski, J., dissenting) (emphasis in original).

Thus, . . .

right: Judge Kozinski disagreed:

> Where does [Vanna] White get this right to control our thoughts? The majority's creation goes way beyond the protection given a trademark or a copyrighted work, or a person's name or likeness. . . . For better or worse, we *are* the Court of Appeals for the Hollywood Circuit. Millions of people toil in the shadow of the law we make, and much of their

> livelihood is made possible by the existence of intellectual property rights.
>
> *White v. Samsung Electronics Am., Inc.,* 989 F.2d 1512, 1519, 1521 (9th Cir. 1993) (Kozinski, J., dissenting) (emphasis in original). Thus, . . .

But many block quotations should not exist in the first place. See question 20-A in §20.6.

§20.6 How to Test Your Writing for Effective Use of Quotations

While writing—and rewriting—ask yourself the following questions.[1]

Have you quoted and cited every time you use the words of others? The words of others must have quotation marks **20-A** around them and a citation to the source. If you do not do this, you will be treated as a plagiarist. It does not matter whether you did it out of sloppiness or out of an intent to deceive. (And an idea that you get from a written source must be attributed to that source with a citation, even if you express the idea in your own words.)

Have you quoted only the essential words? Generally speaking, quoted words should not appear in your work unless they fit **20-B** into at least one of the following categories:

1. words that must be *interpreted* in order to resolve the issue;
2. words that are so closely identified with the topic under discussion that they are *inseparable* from it;
3. words that, *with remarkable economy,* put the reader in touch with the thinking of a court, legislature, or expert in the field; or
4. words that are *the most eloquent and succinct conceivable* expression of an important idea.

Beginners are too quick to think that words, merely because they are printed in a book, can satisfy the third or fourth criterion. That kind of awe causes a student to write a sentence like the following:

> The court relied on "[w]ell-established jurisprudence of our sister states . . . holding that baseball is a strenuous game involving danger to . . . players . . . and that one who, with full knowledge of this danger, attends . . . and places himself in a position of danger, assumes the risks

§20.6 1. When marking up your work, your teacher might refer to these questions by using the number-letter codes that appear next to each question here.

inherent in the game." *Gaspard v. Grain Dealers Mut. Ins. Co.,* 131 So. 2d 831, 834 (La. Ct. App. 1961).

Although the writer of the sentence above did some editing, the only words really worth quoting are the ones used below:

> Relying on "[w]ell-established" precedent in other states holding baseball to be a dangerous game, the court concluded that anyone who knows of that danger and nevertheless plays baseball "assumes the risks inherent in the game." *Gaspard v. Grain Dealers Mut. Ins. Co.,* 131 So. 2d 831, 834 (La. Ct. App. 1961).

The most convincing descriptions of authority are written almost entirely in your own words, punctuated with very few and very short quotations that convey the essence of the court's approach.

Block quotations are especially troublesome. A busy reader will skim over or refuse to read large quotations because their experience tells them that only a few of the quoted words really matter, and that it may take too much effort to find them. Readers feel that block quotations are obstacles that have to be climbed over. The more of them you use, the more quickly a reader will refuse to read any of them. And judges and supervising attorneys view large quotations as evidence of a writer's laziness. They think that your job is to find the essential words, isolate them, and concisely paraphrase the rest. When you throw a big block quotation at a reader, you are asking the reader to do some of your work.

How do you cut a block quotation down to size? Assume that you have written the following in a first draft:

> Although in *Roth* the Supreme Court held that a government could, without satisfying the traditional clear-and-present-danger test, restrict public distribution of obscene material, it came to the opposite conclusion when faced with a statute that punished private possession of obscene materials in one's own home:
>
>> It is true that in *Roth* this Court rejected the necessity of proving that exposure to obscene material would create a clear and present danger of antisocial conduct or would probably induce its recipients to such conduct. . . . But that case dealt with public distribution of obscene materials and such distribution is subject to different objections. For example, there is always the danger that obscene material might fall into the hands of children . . . or that it might intrude upon the sensibilities or privacy of the general public.
>
> *Stanley v. Georgia,* 394 U.S. 557, 567 (1969). A number of the Court's later right-to-privacy rulings have been based in part on *Stanley.*

First drafts are full of passages like this, and in a first draft they cause no real harm. But in later drafts, you should realize that the block quote will repel the reader. Ask yourself "Why do I want this quote? What words inside it satisfy one or more of the four criteria?"

The answer might be that no words in the quote satisfy those criteria, but that the quote does contain ideas that you want the reader to know about. If so, rewrite all of it in your own words. If you do this well — and it requires effort — your words will be better than anyone else's because your words will *fit* better.

On the other hand, the answer might be that some words are too valuable to give up. Here, "might fall into the hands of children" creates an image that economically reflects the Court's thinking (criterion 3), and "intrude upon the sensibilities or privacy of the general public" sets out a standard that will need to be interpreted (criterion 1). Isolate words like that, and rewrite everything else, condensing in the process. You might come up with something much more readable, like this:

> Although in *Roth* the Supreme Court held that a government could, without satisfying the traditional clear-and-present-danger test, restrict public distribution of obscene material, it came to the opposite conclusion when faced with a statute that punished private possession of obscene materials in one's own home. In *Stanley v. Georgia*, 394 U.S. 557 (1969), the Court struck down such a statute and distinguished *Roth* because publicly distributed pornography "might fall into the hands of children" or "intrude upon the sensibilities or privacy of the general public." *Id.* at 567. A number of the court's later right-to-privacy rulings have been based in part on *Stanley*.

This is shorter; it flows better; and it makes the meaning much more clear than the block quote did. The reader's attention is taken straight to the essential words, which stand out when integrated into your own text.

To accomplish this kind of thing, you do *not* need to be a better writer than a Supreme Court justice was. The justice who wrote *Stanley* had the task of justifying a significant decision of constitutional law. The writer of the passage above had a smaller job: explaining, as concisely as possible, the difference between *Roth* and *Stanley*. The smaller job simply takes fewer words.

At the opposite extreme is the problem of too many short quotations, rather than quotations that are too long, although the effect on the reader is similar. This is called snippetizing, and it might take the form of a quote from and cite to case A, followed by a quote from and cite to case B, followed by a quote from and cite to case C, and so on, without substantial discussion of any of the cases or of the ideas expressed in the quotes. Strings of snippet quotations give the reader the feeling of sliding over the surface of complex ideas, which the writer refuses to explain.

A writer whose quotations are too long or too many is sometimes called a "cut-and-paste artist" because the product is not really writing at all. Little thought goes into it, and readers have no confidence in it. What they want is your analysis, which comes only with hard mental work — not finding quotable words and typing them into your document.

20-C Have you been careful not to quote out of context? "Sentences out of context rarely mean what they seem to say, and nobody in the whole world knows that better than the appellate judge. He has learned it by the torturing experience of hearing his own sentences read back to him."[2]

20-D Have you quoted accurately? You see language in a case that you want to quote. You type it into your draft, but—although you do not realize it at the time—some of the words you type into your document are not the same as those that appear in the case. Supervisors, judges, and teachers can easily spot this. When they do, they will lose some confidence in you because it suggests that you have not been careful. We all tend, at least a little bit, to rewrite quotes unconsciously into our own style while copying them. The only way to prevent this is to proofread your paper with the sources in front of you. If you photocopied or printed out the sources, do not throw them away until after you proofread. Otherwise, proofread in the library.

20-E Have you placed quotation marks exactly where they belong? The most common problems are (1) omitting the quotation marks that close a quotation, even though the opening quotation marks are included ("Where does the quote end?" writes the teacher in the margin); (2) omitting the quotation marks that open a quotation, even though the closing marks are present ("Where does the quote begin?" asks the teacher); and (3) where there is a quote within a quote, forgetting to change the double quotation marks of the original to single marks.

20-F Have you been careful not to quote from a headnote? A court's opinion is limited to the text appearing in the reporter *after* the name of the judge who wrote it. The one- or two-sentence headnotes that appear between the case's name and the opinion itself are supplied by the publisher and are not written by the court. Those headnotes may be useful in research, but they are not part of the opinion and have no authoritative value, even if they resemble parts of the opinion. Moreover, the headnotes are written in a distinct style, instantly recognizable by the experienced reader. For example:

> That portion of award of double costs and attorney fees imposed upon counsel would be imposed upon counsel personally, even though client was responsible for pursuing litigation, where client received bad legal advice.[3]

This is typical of headnote style. Every "the," "a," and "an" has been omitted. More important, the sentence is so terse that a reader has only the barest idea of what the court might actually have decided. The reader

---

2. E. Barrett Prettyman, *Some Observations Concerning Appellate Advocacy,* 39 Va. L. Rev. 285, 295 (1953).

3. Publisher's headnote to *Thorton v. Wahl,* 787 F.2d 1151, 1152 (7th Cir. 1986).

will instantly spot the difference, feel cheated of a real description of the case, and think the writer lazy and unreliable.

Exercise I.   The First Amendment (Quotations)

1. You are in the midst of writing a memorandum involving the right-of-assembly clause—and no other part of the First Amendment. You intend to quote the words to be interpreted. This is the text of the entire amendment:

> Congress shall make no law respecting an establishment of religion, or prohibiting the free exercise thereof; or abridging the freedom of speech, or of the press; or the right of the people peaceably to assemble, and to petition the Government for a redress of grievances.

Using words from the Amendment, complete the following sentence: "The First Amendment provides . . . "

2. Do the same for a memorandum involving the freedom-of-speech clause.

Exercise II.   Suing Presidents (Citations and Quotations)

Correct the following passage for inappropriate use of quotations and citations. Correct every error you can find, adding and subtracting to the citations as necessary. Be prepared to explain your work in class.

1	The rivalry between Thomas Jefferson and John Marshall continued
2	during the trial of Aaron Burr in Richmond for treason—a trial presided
3	over by Marshall as Circuit Justice. To aid in his defense, Burr moved for an
4	order compelling production of certain documents in the possession
5	of Jefferson or of other people whom Jefferson supervised. John C. Yoo,
6	*The First Claim: The Burr Trial, United States v. Nixon, and Presidential*
7	*Power,* 83 Minnesota Law Review 1435, 1446-47 (1999). Jefferson passion-
8	ately asserted a privilege not to be summoned into court to testify—a
9	privilege smaller than the one that Bill Clinton was to assert 188 years
10	later. "To comply with such calls," Jefferson wrote to the federal prosecu-
11	tor, "would leave the nation without an executive branch" because any
12	litigant might thus haul a President away to some far part of the country.
13	Yoo at 1451-52. Jefferson instead offered to testify "by way of a depo-
14	sition." In other words, he thought he should not have to go to
15	Richmond but volunteered to put himself under oath if the lawyers and,
16	presumably, the judge (in this case, Marshall) would come to him in
17	Washington.
18	Clinton asserted an immunity while President against lawsuits alleging
19	liability for nonofficial conduct because the burdens of private litigation
20	would interfere with the duties of the Presidency. The Supreme Court
21	had earlier held in *Nixon v. Fitzgerald,* 457 U.S. 731, that Presidents and
22	former Presidents are immune from civil liability for their *official* acts. But
23	in *Clinton v. Jones,* 520 U.S. 681, 117 S.Ct. 1636, 137 L.Ed.2d 945 (1997),
24	the Supreme Court held that a person can be at the same time both

25   a President and a defendant in a lawsuit alleging nonofficial liability.
26   As a result, the lawyers and the judge did go to Washington so that
27   President Clinton could testify in a deposition (just as Jefferson had vol-
28   unteered to testify).
29   John F. Kennedy was a private litigant while President. He was sued
30   in 1960, while he was a presidential candidate, over an auto accident.
31   *Clinton*, 520 U.S. 681, 692. After he was inaugurated in 1961, he
32   moved for a stay, arguing that as long as he was Commander in Chief of
33   the Armed Forces — as all Presidents are under U.S. Const., art II, sec-
34   tion 2 — he was relieved from the obligation to defend against private
35   lawsuits by the Soldiers' and Sailors' Civil Relief Act of 1940, 50 U.S.C.
36   501-525. After the motion was denied, Kennedy settled with the plain-
37   tiffs. *Id.*
38   Two other Presidents were at least technically private litigants while in
39   office, although their participation in the lawsuits was insignificant.
40   Theodore Roosevelt had been sued and the case dismissed before he
41   became President, and while he was President the dismissal was affirmed
42   on appeal. *People ex rel. Hurley v. Roosevelt,* 71 N.E. 1137 (1904).
43   The same thing happened to Harry Truman. *DeVault v. Truman,* 354
44   Mo. 1193 (1946).
45   Incidentally, Judge Susan Webber Wright, who presided over Clinton's
46   deposition, had been his student when Clinton was a law professor in the
47   early 1970's. NY Times, July 11, 1994.

Exercise III.   *Disqualifying Judges (Citations and Quotations)*

Correct the following passage for inappropriate use of quotations and citations. Correct every error you can find, adding and subtracting to the citations
as necessary. Be prepared to explain your work in class.

1   By modern standards, *Marbury v. Madison* should have been decided
2   without the participation of Chief Justice John Marshall, who wrote the
3   Court's opinion. Marshall was President John Adams's last secretary of
4   state. 2 ALBERT J. BEVERIDGE, THE LIFE OF JOHN MARSHALL 485-564 (1919).
5   "Until nine o'clock of the night before Thomas Jefferson's inauguration,
6   Adams continued to nominate officers, including judges, and the Senate
7   to confirm them. Marshall, as Secretary of State, signed and sealed the
8   commissions." Beveridge at 560. In fact, when Marshall signed the commis-
9   sions, he was both secretary of state *and* Chief Justice. When Marshall was
10   sworn in as Chief Justice five weeks earlier, Baker, *John Marshall: A Life in*
11   *Law* 354 (1974), Adams asked him to continue to serve as secretary of state
12   during the remaining weeks of the Adams administration. 2 Beveridge,
13   *supra,* at 558-59.
14   After working, as secretary of state, into the evening of March 3, 1801,
15   to finish the paperwork on Adams's last judicial appointments, Marshall,
16   as Chief Justice, administered the oath of office to Jefferson at noon the

17   next day. 2 Beveridge, p. 562. When James Madison, Jefferson's secre-
18   tary of state, took office a few hours later, he found on his desk — which
19   had been Marshall's desk until midnight the evening before — four un-
20   delivered commissions for Federalists nominated and confirmed by
21   the Senate as justices of the peace in the District of Columbia. One of
22   them had been made out to Marbury. Madison refused to turn them
23   over, and all four sued to get their commissions. *Marbury v. Madison* at
24   137-38.
25   Today, federal law requires that "Any justice, judge, or magistrate of
26   the United States shall disqualify himself in any proceeding in which his
27   impartiality might reasonably be questioned." Title 28 U.S.C. § 455(a).
28   Judicial ethics require the same thing. ABA Code of Judicial Conduct,
29   Canon 3(E) (1990, as amended 1997) ("A judge shall disqualify himself
30   or herself in a proceeding in which the judge's impartiality might reason-
31   ably be questioned").
32   " . . . we join our sister circuits in concluding that a showing of an *appearance*
33   of bias or prejudice sufficient to permit the average citizen reasonably to ques-
34   tion a judge's impartiality is all that must be demonstrated to compel recusal
35   under section 455." *U.S. v. Heldt*, 668 F2d 1238, 1271 (1981) (emphasis in
36   original), *cert. denied*, 456 US 926, 102 SCt 1971, 72 LE2d 440 (1982).
37   Moreover, a federal judge "shall also disqualify himself in the following
38   circumstances: (3) Where he has served in government employment . . .
39   or expressed an opinion concerning the merits of the particular case
40   in controversy. . . ." 28 U.S.C. § 455(b)(3) (2000).

Note: Below is the full text of 28 U.S.C. § 455(a) and (b)(3):

   (a)   Any justice, judge, or magistrate of the United States shall disqualify
himself in any proceeding in which his impartiality might reasonably be questioned.
   (b)   He shall also disqualify himself in the following circumstances: . . .
   (3)   Where he has served in governmental employment and in such
capacity participated as counsel, adviser or material witness concerning
the proceeding or expressed an opinion concerning the merits of the particular case in controversy. . . .

VII
LETTERS AND EXAM ANSWERS

21 Client Advice Letters

§21.1 The Letters Lawyers Write

Most of the letters you will write as a lawyer will fit into one or another of these categories:

Client advice letters convey in writing your advice to the client. This chapter explains client letters in §21.2, and a relatively simple example is given in Appendix D. Client letters are about halfway between a conversation with the client and an office memo. They record the essence of what you would say to the client in a meeting in your office. And often they summarize an office memo.

If the client is an individual, most advice should be given, at least preliminarily, in person or over the telephone. Advice given by letter can be cold. Conversation, on the other hand, promotes questions as well as brainstorming together with the client about how to solve the problem. But a client letter can usefully supplement advice given in person. For example, if a client has a complicated or difficult decision to make, the client might want a written explanation to refer to while thinking things over.

If the client is an organization, a larger proportion of the advice will be given by letter. For the most part, the problems are more complex, and the people in the organization need conversation less because they are more experienced than individual clients are at dealing with the problems at hand.

Demand letters are sent not to clients, but to people who are making clients unhappy (or to their lawyers). Typically, a demand letter recites what the other person has been doing to the client's detriment, explains how this violates the client's rights or the other person's obligations, and states what action the client will take if the other person does not stop. Demand letters are explained in Chapter 22.

Housekeeping letters are sent by one lawyer to another or by a lawyer to a client. For example, from lawyer to lawyer, in litigation: "This letter memorializes our understanding, reached by telephone today, that the depositions scheduled for February 17 are rescheduled for March 8." Another example, from lawyer to lawyer, in a business transaction: "Enclosed is a draft of the contract. Please note sections 11.01 and 16.19, which . . . ." And still another, from lawyer to client: "Enclosed are a set of interrogatories put to us by the defendant. Please collect any information you might have that could answer interrogatories 9 through 23. I will call you in a few days so we can decide how to respond."

§21.2 Client Advice Letters

The tone of a client letter should be professionally precise and at least implicitly supportive. If you are explicitly sympathetic, it should not sound fake or forced. In choosing a tone, ask yourself four questions: What does the situation call for? What would this client want from a professional? What are you comfortable with in terms of your own style? And how do you want to present yourself to clients? The second question — what this client would want from a professional — may be the most complex. Consider the client's level of sophistication (education, occupation, experience with lawyers). And consider the client's feelings. Is the client experiencing anxiety, grief, or anger? Even in positive situations, such as buying property, happiness can be mixed with anxiety. Or is this transaction, from the client's point of view, pure business? It probably is if the client is an organization or a business person, if you have been hired on a matter the client considers routine, and if the client has a lot of experience with lawyers.

Contractions ("don't," "won't") are fine in a letter, though not in a memo or brief.

The format of a client advice letter resembles in some ways the format of an office memo: issue (and often a brief answer), facts, discussion, conclusion (see Chapter 7). If the letter is complex, you might use headings to break it up, although you would adapt the wording in the headings to the client and the situation. The client advice letter in Appendix D is simple enough to need only a few headings. Here are the parts of a client advice letter, each of which you can see in the letter in Appendix D:

1. The beginning formalities.   First is the letterhead (which is already printed on the law office's stationery); the date; the client's name and address; and the salutation ("Dear Mr. Vargas:" — always with a colon, never a comma). If the client is an organization, a "Re:" reference might be helpful. It comes between the client's address and the salutation; is flush to the right margin; and might include a number that would help the client identify its own records on the matter. Here is an example:

Monica Naguchi
Standard Insurance Co.
4 Cornell Street
Claremont, CA 91711

RE: Cucamonga Forwarders, Inc.
your file # 98-326

Dear Ms. Naguchi:

2. One or two opening paragraphs, stating the problem about which the client has sought your advice and a brief summary of what your advice will be. This corresponds to the issue and brief answer in an office memo. If you have bad news, this is where the client will learn that it is bad. Think long and hard about the words you will use to convey that bad news. Reading words on a page can be a cold experience for the client.

3. One or a few paragraphs reviewing the key facts on which the advice is based, as the lawyer understands those facts. You might think it wastes words to tell the client the client's own facts, but there are several good reasons for doing so.

First, if you have misunderstood any of the facts and the client knows better, the client can correct what is wrong. Many lawyers add a sentence asking the client to do that ("If I have described any of the facts inaccurately, please call me").

Second, a fact recitation limits the advice in the future to the facts recited, and that can be important if the facts change. A tenant who does not have a claim against the landlord for a filthy lobby might have one next week if the lobby ceiling caves in.

Third, you might recently have learned of some facts the client does not yet know about. If so, describe the newly found facts in ways that tell the client they are new ("Since we last spoke, I have discovered that the 1986 deed was never properly recorded in the county clerk's office").

And finally, a fact recitation is a good, professional transition into the advice itself.

4. The advice, which can be structured in either of two ways. If the client wants to know how the law treats a certain situation — "Would I win a lawsuit against the railroad?" or "Would my company violate the law if we were to import this product?" — you will predict how a court would rule or you will report the client's or other people's rights and obligations.

On the other hand, if the client must make a decision, you will counsel in the letter by suggesting the options from which the client can choose and, for each option, explaining the things that might make it attractive or unattractive. In the advice portion of the letter, list the options and explain their *advantages, costs, risks, and chances of success.* When you estimate risks and chances of success, you are making predictions. Costs are not limited to money. The cost of suing includes not only legal fees and other litigation expenses, but also the time and energy the client would have to invest in the lawsuit and the stress most litigants suffer while the suit is in progress.

Be especially careful about the words used to communicate the degree of confidence you have in the accuracy of your advice. When you write "we have a reasonably good chance of winning at trial," you might mean that you believe the client will probably win although the risk of loss is significant. But many clients would read those words to mean that victory is nearly assured. That is because it is only human for a client who has suffered a wrong to assume that forces of justice will resolutely correct it. Do not, through vagueness, imply unjustified optimism. Find ordinary, everyday words that the client you are writing to will understand exactly as you mean them.

Conversely, if the news truly is bad, do not cushion it so much that the client will not appreciate it. Do not say "our chances in litigation are problematic" if what you really mean is "it is very unlikely that such a lawsuit would succeed."

A good client letter can be understood by a lay person in one reading. It will take serious work on your part to accomplish that. Use as little lawyer talk as possible. If a term of art has a pretty good equivalent in ordinary English, use the equivalent even if it does not convey 100 percent of the meaning of the term of art (80 percent is good enough unless the missing 20 percent is relevant to the client's situation). If you use a term of art, define it. Do not assume that a client can understand what you could get another law student to understand.

When you translate lawyer talk into ordinary English, do it respectfully. For example, you might imagine writing the letter to one of your grandparents. This is not just good communication. It is also good business. People do not easily like or trust a stereotyped lawyer who talks in legalese, but they can like and trust a genuine human being who does a good job of being their lawyer.

Write simply but do not oversimplify. If the law is settled, in flux, or unclear, it might help to explain that. Discuss authority only if it is central to the issue, such as a recent Supreme Court case that changes everything you have told the client in the past.

Reciting the law can be cold and confusing ("in this state, tax must be paid by the property owner on each lien against real property recorded in the county clerk's office"). Describing its effect on the client is warm and often eliminates the need to recite the law ("if you refinance the mortgage on your home, you will have to pay $1,250 in mortgage tax").

Unlike the reader of virtually everything else you write as a lawyer, your client assumes that you know the law, which means that you do not have to recite rules of law or cite and explain authority as thoroughly as you would in a memo or a brief. But you do have to know what you are talking about. Lawyers are not perfect at predicting, but if you are so wrong as to not know what you are talking about, you will lose clients and learn a lot about the details of malpractice law.

Organize the material in any way that will help the client understand it. Often that is not through the paradigm formula described in Chapter 10. You are not writing for the skeptical senior partner or judge to whom everything must be proved. You are writing for a lay person who will not easily understand what you know. (But sometimes your explanation might be so detailed as to need headings.)

5. One or two closure paragraphs: Sum up your advice in two or three sentences. Specify what can or should be done next, who should do it, and when it should be done. If the client needs to make a decision, set the stage for that. Invite the client to telephone you, or if extended conversation might be needed, suggest that the client make an appointment to see you. On the other hand, if the advice is negative ("although your competitors behaved badly, they did nothing illegal"), closure might be limited to an offer to answer questions if the client would like to call.

This is also a good place to note the extent to which your advice is conditioned on facts not yet known or events that have not yet happened. In some law offices, the closure paragraphs include boilerplate sentences pointing out that the advice is limited to the facts recited earlier and to current law, which might change, and so on. Other offices do not include this kind of thing on the assumption that it alienates clients.

6. The ending formalities: your signature over your typed name and under a parting comment like "Sincerely Yours" or whatever words are customary in your office. (Most readers never notice the parting comment or care, unless you say something completely inappropriate.)

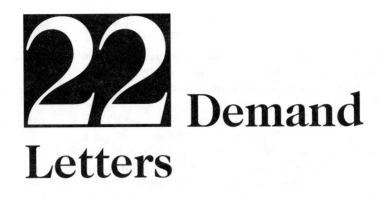# 22 Demand Letters

§22.1 Why and How Lawyers Write Demand Letters

Lawyers write demand letters to persuade somebody else to do something ("resume shipping my client's most recent album under the contract") or to stop doing something ("cease using the hip-hop group name that infringes on my client's trademark"). To persuade, you will do three things in the letter: (1) state your client's position on the facts and the law, (2) tell the other side what you expect them to do, and (3) give them incentives to comply with your demand.

You have three or four audiences.

The first, obviously, is the person to whom the letter is addressed. The recipient might be a lay person; or, if you know the other side has a lawyer, you will write to the lawyer directly.

Second, even if you write to a lay person, assume that she or he will show the letter to a lawyer who will advise the recipient on whether to comply with your demands. That means you must persuade two people: the lay person to whom you wrote the letter and the lawyer who will advise that person. You will say some things to persuade the lay person and other things to persuade the lawyer. This will be a challenge because if you write entirely lawyer-to-lawyer, you will confuse the lay person, and if you write entirely for a lay audience, you will omit things needed to persuade the lawyer.

The third audience is anybody else to whom the recipient might show your letter. That could include other people who know your client and will think badly of her or him if you write an abusive letter. It could include the media if the matter is newsworthy. And it could include a judge or jury if a lawsuit is later filed. You can assume that the recipient will show the letter to anybody, and that the recipient will eagerly do that if it could hurt your client. If you say anything ill advised in the letter, the recipient will use it against you.

The fourth audience is your client. Good lawyerly practice is to send to your client a copy of any document you generate on the client's behalf. A demand letter might be the first time that you give voice to the client's grievance, and a client hires a lawyer to speak in ways the client cannot. This can be satisfying for you and the client. But it also creates two risks. First, do not raise the client's hopes that the letter will solve the problem. Sometimes it will, and sometimes it will not. Second, in the letter, do not posture to have an effect on the client. Your target is the other side. Stay focused on the goal of persuading them. You will be less persuasive if you try at the same time to impress the client.

Sometimes the law governing your client's claim requires that a demand letter be sent before suing, and that the demand letter contain certain things. When that is true, add those requirements to the guidelines in this chapter.

Sometimes you will send something that looks like a demand letter when you really are not making a demand. For example, you might be giving the other side notice that your client is unilaterally exercising a right ("my client terminates the contract because you have not fulfilled the requirements of section 22.06").

§22.2   Strategy: Persuading through a Letter

How will you persuade the reader to comply with your demand?

Develop the most convincing possible position on both the facts and the law. You want the reader to believe that if the dispute were put to a court or other authority, you would win. If the other side does not fear that you would win, you have very little leverage.

Explain carefully why the law favors your client. Because long letters might be scanned rather than read, you have to make this explanation very concise, while still expressing the important and persuasive parts of your position. And if the letter will be addressed to a lay person, explain in a way that educates both that person and the lawyer on the other side.

Look at things from the reader's point of view. What will most likely persuade this particular reader—not readers in general—to do what you want? If the client knows the opposing party, ask what the client knows about the opposing party's goals and the approaches that are most likely— and least likely—to persuade the opposing party. (You do not want to make arguments that the other side will consider weak or so deeply offensive that the offense prevents the other side from conceding anything.)

Anticipate the arguments the opposing side will make. Demonstrate in the letter why those arguments fail. If you do not do this, the letter is a waste of your time and effort because the other side will simply retort that their arguments are better than your arguments. The only way you can persuade is to undermine their confidence in their own justifications.

Be firm but reasonable. You must be firm to cause the other side to worry. But be reasonable to enhance your credibility with all of your audiences. The other side knows that letter-writers who make extreme and unrealistic statements are often unpersuasive in court. A demand letter with a bullying tone can fail to persuade for that reason alone. It can also damage the writer's position later when the recipient shows the letter to a judge or jury. Assertiveness has a chance of working. Bullying does not.

Write in a professional tone. Do not insult or demean the other side or show anger or sarcasm. Belligerence does not persuade. You have to show that the other side did something they should not have done (or failed to do something they should have done). But you can do that *in substance* while avoiding, or at least minimizing, an accusatory tone. Give professional respect: your message is that the other side is wrong, but most of the time your message does not need to be that they are bad people. If you accuse them of being bad people, they are much less likely to give you what you want. Do not accuse them of having the worst of motives unless you are convinced you can prove it and the law would *require* you to prove it in court. Simply express a professional view of how the law treats these facts.

Write in simple, clear, concise language. Professionalism persuades, but lawyer babble has little or no effect on the reader. Write in simple, straightforward words so that you are easily understood.

Accusatory adjectives and adverbs have no effect on the reader of a demand letter. Words like "scandalous" and "outrageous" might actually cause the other side to laugh. But if the governing legal rule contains a term like bad faith or negligence, you must use that term and show how the facts satisfy it.

Appeal to the reader's self-interest. Try to think of realistic ways in which they actually might be better off if they do what you want—in addition to avoiding your consequences.

If the other side would be receptive to moral arguments, make them. But before you make moral arguments, ask yourself whether the other side has moral arguments of its own to counter yours. That should not deter you from making moral arguments. But be prepared for it.

If the client has a continuing relationship with the opposing party—for example, if the dispute involves a contract between them and the contract will not terminate until years from now—consider the client's need to avoid damaging that relationship. What is the client's goal in that relationship and how might the letter advance and avoid undermining that goal? For this and other reasons, you might show the letter to the client before sending it.

§22.3   Legal Ethics and Demand Letters

The rules of professional ethics place limits on what you can say in a demand letter.

You may not "make a false statement of material fact or law."[1] You are not allowed to imply that you are disinterested.[2] You are also not allowed to give advice to opposing parties, except to suggest that they consult a lawyer of their own.[3] Many states do not permit lawyers to threaten criminal prosecution in civil matters, although the ABA Model Rules of Professional Conduct no longer make this prohibition.

You may not communicate with a lay person if you know that person is represented by a lawyer.[4] But if you do not know who the lawyer is, you can write to the lay person directly and suggest that she or he show the letter to the lawyer. If you are writing to an organization that is often involved in litigation, you can probably omit the suggestion that they show the letter to their lawyer (they will do it automatically).

§22.4   Structure of a Demand Letter

1. The beginning formalities.   For the letterhead, address, and salutation, see §21.2. In the first paragraph, state whom you represent and give enough information about the dispute so the reader will know why you are writing.

2. The facts.   Include all the facts that are germane—but *only* the ones that are truly germane. If you include every little fact, the other side will not get the point. In other words, be complete but say no more than necessary. If you want the reader to pay attention to every word, use the minimum number of words needed to get the point across.

Make sure your facts are perfectly accurate. Do not stretch the facts or ignore facts that favor the other side. Any inaccuracy will give the other side an excuse to respond that your analysis and your demand are wrong because you are wrong about the facts. If you anticipate that the other side will dispute one of your facts or assert some facts of their own, address that at some point in the letter, either here in the facts or later when you analyze the law. You might show how your evidence on the disputable fact is overwhelming. Or you might explain that even if the fact that other side might assert is true, it makes no difference legally and does not change your analysis.

---

§22.3   1. Rule 4.1(a) of the ABA Model Rules of Professional Conduct.
2. Rule 4.3 of the ABA Model Rules of Professional Conduct.
3. Drafters' comment to Rule 4.3 of the ABA Model Rules of Professional Conduct.
4. Rule 4.2 of the ABA Model Rules of Professional Conduct.

Honest mistakes account for much more of what goes wrong in life than stealing and lying do. If you do not know why the other side did what it did, do not speculate. Describe only what *happened*. Do not talk about what the other side intended unless the legal test you would have to satisfy in court requires it.

3. The law. Show how the law favors your client. Explain the key concepts, but add only the essential details. Again, if you want the reader to pay attention to every word, use the minimum number of words needed to get the point across. If you are writing to a lay person, explain the law in language the lay person will understand, without oversimplifying.

Should you refer to specific statutes and cases? A lawyer usually will not be persuaded without them. The same will be true for a lay person who regularly deals with legal issues (such as an insurance company adjuster). But other lay people might not understand what you are talking about if your letter is filled with citations they cannot understand. If the letter will be sent to a lay person, and if you have two or three cites, you might leave them in the text. But if you have a lot of citations, you might consider putting them in footnotes, where they will be seen by a lawyer but will not distract a lay person. (But do not put citations in footnotes in a memorandum or appellate brief.)

4. The demand and the consequences of failing to comply. A very thin line separates threats from stating what will happen if the other side does not satisfy your demand.

threat:	If you do not resume deliveries by the close of business on May 15, we will sue for damages and ruin your business.
stating consequences:	If you do not resume deliveries by the close of business on May 15, the only way my client will be able to protect itself will be to sue for damages equal to its business losses. Those losses have been small through today's date, but they will become huge beginning on May 15.

Threats anger readers and make them want to fight back. Threats can also offend third parties like judges and juries. You are writing to make the other side afraid of something, and they will not experience that fear unless you specify the consequences of not complying with your demand.

The best strategy is to depersonalize the consequences by de-emphasizing your role in them. Do not say "we will sue for damages and ruin your business." If they were to comply, they would feel humiliated. For that reason alone, they could refuse to concede. Try to find a way for them to concede with dignity.

Characterize the consequence as something you will be forced to do ("the only way my client will be able to protect itself will be to sue for damages equal to its business losses"). And attribute the severity of the consequence to something out of your control ("Those losses have been small through today's date, but they will become huge beginning on May 15").

Or you could describe what the law will do and mention what you will do only in that context. Suppose you represent Ms. Metzger, who tells you that the fumes from a restaurant under her apartment are nauseating. You might end a letter to the restaurant owner by saying this:

> Thus, in all the reported decisions in this state, neighbors like Ms. Metzger have always won, and often the courts have forced restaurants to move or close. For that reason, we will have no choice but to sue unless by July 31 you have installed the filtration equipment required by city ordinance 63-179.

As in this example, the demand should be precise. Say exactly what the consequences will be.

The consequences are meaningless unless you set a clear deadline. If you set no deadline or a vague one ("immediately"), the other side will probably ignore your letter. You will lose credibility if your deadline is unreasonable. If the letter quoted above was received on July 25, the restaurant owner might be unimpressed for two reasons. First, compliance would be extremely difficult in less than a week. And second, an unreasonable deadline would make you look like an unrealistic person, and that could make your letter unpersuasive.

5. The ending formalities.   See §21.2.

23 How to Write Exam Answers

§23.1 How Exam Answers Differ from Other Forms of Legal Writing

A supervising lawyer or a judge reads your work for the purpose of deciding what to do in the client's case. But a teacher reads your exam answers to decide something else: how much you have learned in the course. Many students assume that teachers want to know how well students have memorized rules of law. But that is only part of it. A teacher is also interested — and often *much more* interested — in your understanding of how to use the rules and what the law is trying to accomplish with them.

To get credit for what you know about these things, you can structure your exam answers in a way that reveals what the teacher needs to know about you.

Compare a law school examination to a computerized cash register in a grocery store. The cashier places each item above an electronic "eye" that "sees" the item's universal product code and rings up the price. If the cashier does not hold an item at exactly the proper angle, the eye sees nothing and registers nothing. The cashier is able to try again and again and, if necessary, can even ring up a purchase manually. Like the electronic eye, the teacher will give you credit for what you show in the proper form, but, unlike the cashier, you get only one chance.

§23.2   Answering Essay Questions

The traditional law school examination question contains a story, which you are asked to analyze in terms of the field of law covered by the course. This is called an essay question, even though a good answer to it could not accurately be called an essay.

You are graded on how well you identify the real issues in the story, identify the governing rules, state those rules accurately, and apply the rules to the facts. The teacher is less interested in your conclusions than in the analytical skills and understanding you display in arriving at and explaining those conclusions. In answering an essay question, the most effective organization is one that clearly shows the things the teacher is grading: issue spotting, knowledge of legal rules, and the ability to analyze and solve a legal problem in depth. (As you will see in a moment, that will differ from the paradigm formula described in Chapter 10.)

There are many effective methods of producing an answer to an essay question. Here is one:

Start by reading the question once from beginning to end without using a pen for any reason. Just read, so that you see the big picture. Then read the question again, underlining important things or making notes in the margin. Then read it a third time — but while doing so, make a list on scratch paper of all the issues you see in the question. (Leave plenty of blank space between issues.) Whenever you see a fact relevant to a particular issue, make a note of that fact under the issue in your list of issues.

For each fact, ask yourself why it is there. There are only four possible reasons why a particular fact is in the story: (1) it creates or helps to create an issue because it is inconsistent with another fact or appears to be in-consistent with the law; (2) it helps to resolve an issue because it shows whether the elements of a rule have been satisfied; (3) it is there to tempt you into making a mistake; or (4) it has no legal value and just helps to tell the story. Often reasons overlap. A fact might help create an issue and also provide raw material for resolving it. Or it might create an issue and tempt you into answering incorrectly.

How can a fact tempt you? Every teacher knows of analytical mistakes that some students will make from an incomplete understanding of the subject of the course. For example, on a civil procedure exam, suppose that the summons and complaint are served on the defendant in a way that does not satisfy any formula in Rule 4 of the Federal Rules of Civil Procedure, but the defendant gets copies of the summons and complaint anyway, reads them, and thus understands that the plaintiff is suing her. In the sentence before this one, everything after the word "but" was put there to tempt you into making a mistake. Teachers call facts like these "red herrings." Some students will reason that the failure to follow Rule 4 does not matter because the defendant got notice anyway. But that is not the law. If you fall for the red herring, you will answer incorrectly and get a low score on this issue. But if you recognize it to be a red herring, you will answer that the failure to follow Rule 4 is fatal even if the defendant obtained the summons and complaint through other means. When you later write your answer, use "even if" or similar language to show the teacher that you spotted the red herring and did not fall for it. To get full credit, explain why the red herring does not change your conclusion.

If—while *reading* the question—you assign to each fact one or more reasons for being in the story, you will more likely recognize the true issues in the question (reason 1) and use the facts appropriately to resolve issues (reason 2). And you will be less likely to fall into a trap after falling for a temptation to make a mistake (reason 3).

Now focus on your scratch paper list of issues. Look at each issue individually. What rules are necessary to resolve it? Make a note of each rule in the blank space under the issue. What policy considerations would help resolve the issue? Make a note of them as well. If you think of anything else relevant to the issue, make a note of that as well. In what sequence should the issues be discussed in your answer? Write "1" next to the one that should be discussed first, "2" next to the one that should come second, and so on.

You have just made an outline of your answer. Under exam conditions, you do not have time to make an extensive formal outline, but the one that grew out of your list of issues will be good enough.

Most teachers will tell you, in one way or another, approximately how much time you should spend answering each question on the exam. Do not be afraid to spend a third to half that time reading the question and making an outline. If you do that well, you will have everything you need to write a good answer.

Now write. For each issue, use the following permutation of the paradigm formula described in Chapter 10:

1. Since the teacher is more interested in your issue-spotting ability than in your conclusion, start by stating the *issue.* You could express the issue as a question ("Does the buyer's email message satisfy the statute of frauds?"). Or instead you could express the issue by stating how you resolve it ("The buyer's email message satisfies the statute of frauds"). Either method will do the job.

2. The governing *rule* or *rules* should normally follow. Use some judgment about this. If the rule is very basic—such as the four elements of negligence—it might not be necessary to state it because if you do a good job of applying a rule that the whole class knows, the teacher could reasonably conclude that you know it, too. But usually the teacher is specifically trying to find out whether you know a rule. If on a Civil Procedure exam, you realize that the court plainly lacks subject matter jurisdiction but the defendant has not moved to dismiss on that ground, the teacher is trying to find out whether you know that defects in subject matter jurisdiction can never be waived.

3. Proof of a rule is usually not necessary (because the teacher is in part testing your ability to remember rules that have been more or less

proven in class) and often not possible (because the facts on final exams are frequently set in mythical jurisdictions or no jurisdiction at all). However, in some subjects dominated by uniform or federal statutes, the teacher may be willing to give you a little credit if you are able to refer to specific sections of a code, although such a teacher will not give you credit for good citation form.

4. Having stated the rule, *analyze* the issue by *applying* the rule to the facts. Use additional rules as you need them. You can show intellectual depth by explaining how your analysis is consistent with the policy behind these rules. You can also show intellectual depth by including a counter-analysis. With big issues, you usually cannot get full credit without policy discussions and counter-analyses.

5. If you have not already done so, state your *conclusion* before moving on to the next issue.

Students have traditionally tried to remember this formula by calling it "IRAC": *I*ssue, *R*ule, *A*nalysis/application, *C*onclusion. Your answer to each essay question will include several IRAC-structured discussions — one for each issue you identify. But limit the IRAC formula to exam-taking: it does not work well in office memoranda, motion memoranda, or appellate briefs.

As you use each fact, rule, or policy consideration, cross it off the checklist on your scratch paper. Do the same for each issue as you finish it. When you have finished the last issue, go on to the next exam question. (If you have time after answering all the questions, go back and proofread what you wrote.)

Your goal is to accumulate the largest number of points when the teacher grades your answer. (Remember the cash register.) Teachers give points for spotting issues and resolving them in a professional way. If you understand that, you will also understand the two biggest causes for losing points. One is failing to spot issues. If you miss an issue entirely, the teacher cannot give you any points at all.

The other big cause for losing points is failure to explain your reasoning fully. If you identify the issue, state your conclusion on that issue, and then move on to something else, many teachers will give you only a fraction of the points available for that issue, even if your conclusion is absolutely correct. That fraction can be very small. If an issue is worth 15 points, a teacher might give you only three to five points for stating a correct answer and doing nothing more. The proportion of points allocated to your reasoning tends to grow if the issue is a big one and tends to shrink if it is a small one. If the issue is worth only three points, you might get one point for spotting it, one point for resolving it, and one point (only a third of the total) for giving a reason. Teachers' practices on things like this differ widely, and some teachers do not assign a specific number of points to each issue. But if you assume that all teachers grade this way, you are less likely to miss points for not giving reasons.

To get the remaining points, you have to explain why you are right. A good explanation of your reasoning lays out the steps in your logic in a lawyerly manner, using the rules and policies covered during the course. (That is not the same as writing down every thought you have on the subject.) Why are you right? How do the law and facts support that conclusion? What other conclusions did you reject? Why are they inferior? Use facts that support your arguments. If facts could be used to challenge your arguments, show why those challenges should not succeed. Support your reasoning with policy, and show why contrary policy would not change your answer.

And decide. In law, it is a cop-out to go back and forth and then stop ("the plaintiff could argue this, and the defendant could argue that"), which some teachers call ping-ponging. Who will or should win? Why?

§23.3 Other Types of Questions

There is a non-story variant of the essay question. The teacher might describe a proposed statute and ask you to comment on it. There are no characters and no plot. Here, a good answer might in fact resemble an essay. Figure out how the proposal would alter the way the law functions, and decide whether that would be a good idea or a bad one, remembering the policy considerations that were stressed in class and in the casebook. Then write an answer in which you state your conclusion and substantiate it by analyzing the proposal in policy terms.

Some law school exams include short-answer questions. Several of them might be based on a single set of facts. Each question poses a specific and narrowly framed inquiry, such as "Did the defendant waive defects in personal jurisdiction?" You are given a small space — perhaps enough for a paragraph — in which to give your answer and the reasons for it.

Some exams include multiple-choice questions. To answer them effectively, it helps if you know how multiple-choice questions are created. A teacher thinks up a fact pattern, adds a question ("Did the manufacturer breach the contract's anti-delegation clause?"), supplies the correct answer, and then adds three or four wrong answers to produce a list of answers from which you choose.

People who make their living giving multiple-choice exams — like the SAT and the LSAT — call the wrong answers "distractors" because they are meant to distract and fool you. An effective distractor sounds right, often using phrases or concepts you heard and read often during the course. But the distractor will contain a flaw that makes it ultimately wrong. The flaw could be that although the distractor is literally true, it does not really explain what the law will do; the correct answer does that. Or the distractor might be partly right and partly wrong. Or it might be incomplete — right as far as it goes, but it does not solve the problem. Or it might be all wrong but dressed up in lawyer-like language so that it sounds good anyway. To identify a distractor, look for the flaw. And think carefully about it. Do not make a quick, snap decision. Ask yourself, "What could be wrong here?" You have to understand the law to eliminate a distractor.

How do you identify the correct answer? You have to know the law precisely, and you have to know exactly how to apply it to facts. You really have to know the material.

You can use two methods to choose the correct answer to a multiple-choice question. You can identify the correct answer because you really know it to be correct. Or you can identify all the distractors, thus identifying the correct answer by process of elimination. You are much better off if you use both methods. Use one to make a tentative selection of the correct answer. Use the other method to check and confirm your choice.

You can eliminate the distractors by finding the wrong idea in each one. But to be sure that the only alternative left standing really is the correct answer, you need to examine it carefully to make sure that it really is based on an accurate understanding of the law and that the reasoning in it is also right. You know that you have answered correctly when you know both why the answer you have chosen is right and why the other alternatives are really distractors.

§23.4   General Suggestions for Taking Exams

Start preparing for exams long before the end of classes. The best preparation is to make your *own* course outline during the semester from your class notes and from the portions of the text covered by the teacher. The act of making the outline is an irreplaceable self-teaching experience. In structuring the course outline, the casebook's table of contents is more helpful than you might suppose. The table of contents collects the casebook's chapter and section headings, and those headings are the beginning of an outline.

Many students make flow charts instead of, or in addition to, an outline. A flow chart poses a series of questions to ask yourself so you can determine where the facts suggest a particular type of issue. For example, if you need to figure out whether a state has personnel jurisdiction over a particular defendant, start by asking these questions:

1. Does the defendant reside in the forum state?
   (If yes, that state has general jurisdiction over her — jurisdiction to adjudicate any claim against her.)
2.(a) Does the forum state's long-arm statute cover both the claim and the defendant?
2.(b) Does the defendant have minimum contacts with the foreign state? *(Here, you could add subsidiary questions that would help you figure out whether the defendant has minimum contacts. For example, did the defendant purposefully avail herself of something beneficial involving the forum state?)*

2.(c)   Does the claim arise out of those contacts?
        (If the answer to questions 2(a), (b), and (c) is yes, the forum state has long-arm jurisdiction over the defendant.)

3.   Was the defendant served with the summons and complaint while she was in the forum state?
        (If yes, the forum state has tag jurisdiction over her.)

4.   Has the defendant agreed contractually to submit to jurisdiction in the foreign state?
        (If yes, . . .)

To help remember these questions, many students make a chart or a diagram, drawing arrows to show the sequences in which the questions should be asked.

Teachers differ from one another on examination philosophy, and most teachers tell their classes something of their own views on examinations and grading. Take seriously what each teacher tells you.

During the examination, budget your time carefully. One of the tragedies of the examination room is the student who spends so much time on one question that the others cannot be handled adequately.

Read the instructions carefully. Before beginning to answer a question, be sure that you understand the role you have been assigned. Are you being asked to analyze objectively the rights and liabilities of various characters in a story? To state the legal advice you would give to one of the characters if that person were your client? To make arguments on behalf of one character and against others? To write a judicial opinion? *Do exactly what you are instructed to do.* Do it completely. And do not do anything else. The teacher will give you credit only for doing what you were instructed to do.

Do not waste time writing about background matters unless they truly help you resolve the issues in the exam. Most teachers will give you credit only for finding issues and analyzing them. Do not start your answer by repeating the facts. (But do *use* the facts later in your answer by applying the rules to them.) And do not give the historical evolution of the rules you are using unless the evolution is needed to substantiate the position you are taking. If you are given the wording of a statute or if you are taking an open-book exam, you will waste time and get no credit if you hand-copy the statute into your exam book. Instead, refer to the statute and explain how it supports your conclusion.

Your goal is not to find the largest number of issues in each question. It is to identify the issues actually in the question—no more and no less. You will, of course, lose credit for missing issues. But many teachers will also reduce your grade if you "find" issues that are not reasonably suggested by the facts. Even if your teacher does not do that, you waste time if you resolve nonexistent issues.

Analyze every genuine issue, even if you believe that your analysis of one issue would make all the others moot. Not only must you do that in law practice anyway, but you cannot get full credit on examinations without doing it.

Some issues are worth more—often *much* more—than other issues. A one-hour, 33-point essay question might include a five-point issue, an 18-point issue, a six-point issue, and a four-point issue. Some students will spend no more time or space on the 18-point issue than on the others. That can be a disastrous mistake. The big issue is worth 18 points because it is hard. It takes more thought and writing to resolve a big and difficult issue than to resolve a small and easier issue. If you treat all these issues as worth the same amount of effort, you will probably lose most of the points available for the big issue. (Some teachers do not assign specific point values to issues, but they will still penalize a student who gives no more effort to a tough issue than to an easy one.) How can you tell which issues are the big ones? Smaller issues are more easily resolved. Big issues are tougher puzzles and often require several steps of logic.

Many—perhaps most—big issues can reasonably be resolved in more than one way. Remember that the teacher is most interested in the quality of your reasoning (and often less interested in the result of that reasoning). It is not unusual for two students to get full credit for a given issue while coming to opposite conclusions about it. They deserve full credit because both conclusions are reasonable and arguable, and because both students supply knowledgeable and perceptive supporting analyses. But that does not mean that you can adopt any conclusion you please. Some conclusions are more reasonable and easier to prove than others. And some issues on an exam have only one correct answer (usually when the teacher wants to know whether you have understood some very basic concept in the course).

It is, however, never enough to state the arguments for each side and then waffle or avoid stating a conclusion. Take a position and support it with analysis. That is what lawyers are paid to do and what your teachers hope you are learning how to do.

If you make an assumption in answering a question, say so. A sloppy student mushes over a gap in the facts without realizing that the gap is there. A precise student recognizes the gap, defines it exactly, and offers a resolution of the issue while taking the gap into account. (But make assumptions only where there truly is a relevant gap in the facts, which does not happen very often on exams. Do not invent far-fetched facts of your own that distort the question the teacher wants you to answer. The teacher will see that as an attempt to avoid facing the hard aspects of the exam.)

Use terms of art properly. Misuse of a term of art implies that the student's knowledge of the subject is superficial.

Teachers justifiably hate gimmicks in exam answers. Simply write down—in a business-like manner—what the teacher must see if you are to get credit.

The teacher will give you credit only for what is plainly written in the examination booklet. You will get no credit for things that you know but do not expressly state. And you will get no credit for things that you expressly state in handwriting that the teacher cannot read.

Finally, learn from your examinations. Most teachers will let you read your examination after final grades are posted. Many are willing to talk with you individually about what you did well or badly. Some provide written post-mortems (sometimes called model answers) that explain the issues on the exam. Take advantage of all of these things. Sometimes, you will learn more about the subject matter of the course (which may be tested again on the bar examination and in any event will help you later as a lawyer). And sometimes you will learn how to write examination answers more effectively.

VIII
THE SHIFT TO PERSUASION

24

Developing a Persuasive Theory

§24.1 Introduction

Persuasive writing aims to convince judges to do what your client wants. Whether you are writing a motion memorandum or an appellate brief, the ability to persuade centers on three skills: developing a persuasive theory (explained in this chapter), developing persuasive arguments (see Chapter 25), and working within a procedural posture (see Chapter 26).

§24.2 Strategic Thinking

There are 55 reasons why I shouldn't have pitched him, but 56 why I should.

—*Casey Stengel, New York Yankees manager, on why he started Ed Lopat in the final game of the 1952 World Series*

My main objection to Lou was that he managed by hunch and desperation. You ask Casey Stengel why he made a certain move and he will tell you about a roommate he had in 1919 who demonstrated some principle Casey was now putting into effect. You ask Lou and he will say, "The way we're going, we had to do *something*." If there is a better formula for making a bad situation worse, I have never heard it.

—*Bill Veeck, owner of the Cleveland Indians, on why he wanted to fire manager Lou Boudreau and hire Casey Stengel in 1946*

A strategy is a plan for reaching a goal.

In litigation writing, a lawyer develops strategies by identifying goals (such as persuading a court to adopt rule X or to find fact Y) and then by generating a list of possible methods of accomplishing each goal. In imagining these alternative strategies, the lawyer asks him- or herself, "What would *cause* a court to decide in my favor?" After predicting each strategy's risks and chances of success, the lawyer selects the best one for each goal.

If you are asked why you did a particular thing and can answer only "I guess it seemed like a good idea at the time," people will assume that you did not really think through the problem. In post-mortems of your work, a supervising lawyer or a teacher might ask you a litany of questions about strategy:

What was your goal?
What was your strategy?
What other possible strategies did you consider and reject?
For each rejected strategy, why was it inferior to the one you did choose?
What led you to believe that the strategy you chose would actually achieve the ultimate goal?
Did you do all the things necessary to execute the strategy you chose?
Did you do anything that impeded that strategy?
If the goal was not achieved, why not?

Supervisors and teachers ask these questions because a lawyer's job is *to make desired things happen.* The supervisor or teacher will be trying to make sure that your planning is free of the kinds of thinking that prevents strategy, such as overlooking opportunities, relying on unrealistic assumptions, and engaging in wishful thinking and other forms of self-deception.

The first sophisticated strategic decisions that you will make in law are the development of a theory that will persuade a court to rule in your client's favor (explained in this chapter) and the development of arguments to support that theory (explained in Chapter 25). Later in this chapter, you will learn what theories are and how they work. But first, let us consider the creative process through which all effective strategy decisions are made.

§24.3 Professional Creativity

Effective professional work usually progresses through the six stages of the creative process:[1]

1. *Problem-identification*: Identifying a problem that must be solved or some other situation in which a decision must be made.

---

§24.3 1. *See, e.g.,* Teresa M. Amabile, *The Social Psychology of Creativity* 79-81 (Springer-Verlag 1983); Silvano Arieti, *Creativity: The Magic Synthesis* 15-18 (Basic Books 1976); John Dewey, *How We Think* 12-15 (Heath & Co. 1933); Graham Wallas, *The Art of Thought* 80-82 (Harcourt, Brace & Co. 1926). (Researchers use different names for these stages. The ones used here were mostly suggested by Steven Jamar.)

2. *Gathering and evaluating information and raw materials*: Learning about the relevant law and facts in a fairly open-ended manner.
3. *Solution-generation*: Thinking up the largest reasonable number of potential solutions.
4. *Solution-evaluation*: Testing potential solutions to see how well they would work.
5. *Decision:* Comparing the evaluated solutions and choosing the most effective one.
6. *Action:* If the decision is a prediction, action means reporting it and the reasons for it in an office memorandum. If the decision is selection of a strategy, action means using the strategy in a motion memorandum or an appellate brief.

Frequently, these stages overlap, and at least some parts of them occur unconsciously. You might, for example, find yourself thinking up arguments (which is a form of *solution-generation*) while reading cases in the library (*gathering and evaluating information and raw materials*). And you might unexpectedly make a decision — perhaps while washing dishes or driving car — on the basis of some unconscious solution-evaluation that occurred during the preceding hours or days.

When you predict, you realize that you need to know what courts will do (*problem-identification*), and you read cases and statutes in the library (*gathering and evaluating information and raw materials*), develop arguments for each side (*solution-generation*), test each argument for the likelihood of its adoption by a court (*solution-evaluation*), formulate a prediction based on the most likely arguments (*decision*), and record that prediction in an office memorandum (*action*).[2]

You are now learning another level of lawyerly analysis: strategizing. And the process here follows a similar pattern. When you create a strategy, you notice a need to cause a particular event (*problem-identification*), and you find the helpful and harmful authorities and facts (*gathering and evaluating information and raw materials*), think up the largest reasonable number of competing strategies (*solution-generation*), assess each strategy for its effectiveness (solution-evaluation), choose the most effective strategy (*decision*), and execute it in a motion memorandum or appellate brief (*action*).

These sequences of thought all rest on habits of *disciplined curiosity*. Problem-identification, for example, requires the ability to spot quickly what John Dewey called a "forked-road situation . . . that is ambiguous, that presents a dilemma, that proposes alternatives"[3] — a place, in other words, where your thinking can make a difference and cause things to happen. Problem-identification thus is the opposite of passivity, which always sends you down the easier or more obvious road without considering the one less often taken.

---

2. See §8.1.
3. John Dewey, *How We Think* 15 (Heath & Co. 1933).

Solution-generation and solution-evaluation pose the greatest challenges for students, in part because they require contrary skills. To think up the largest number of reasonable alternatives for solution-generation, you must be willing to look below the surface of the facts and law for deeper possibilities and meaning. (See §6.2 for an example.) Solution-generation requires temporarily suspending judgment. That is because workable ideas tend to arrive in one's mind mixed together with unworkable ones. The poet Schiller wrote that solution-generation becomes blocked "if the intellect examines too closely the ideas already pouring in. . . . Regarded in isolation, an idea may be insignificant, and venturesome in the extreme, but it may acquire importance from an idea which follows it. . . . [People who are ineffective at solution-generation] reject too soon. . . ."[4]

The key is to avoid premature judgment, to defer evaluation until after you have developed an array of alternatives. This can be constricted by snap evaluation of ideas as soon as they are expressed, by verbal aggression (yours or other people's), by a desire to conform, or by what Kenney Hegland calls the "fear of making a fool of yourself."[5] Lon Fuller, the great contracts scholar, wrote that solution-generation does not easily happen when you ask yourself "anxiously at every turn that most inhibitive of questions, *'What will other people think?'*"[6]

Paradoxically, solution-evaluation needs the qualities that would impoverish solution-generation: ruthless skepticism, fear that an idea might truly be foolish, a pragmatic sense of the realistic, a precise ability to calculate risk. The trick is to turn those qualities off while thinking up solutions and then to turn them back on once you have assembled a full range of solutions and are ready to start evaluating them. During solution-generation, you will do best if you think with intellectual freedom and a tolerance for chaos, but during solution-evaluation you must become a completely different kind of person, viewing things with the cold-blooded realism of a person who must take responsibility for success or failure. The critical thinking on which solution-evaluation depends is taught aggressively throughout the law school curriculum. But because solution-generation and solution-evaluation depend on contrary qualities, you must be careful not to let that critical skepticism — of which we teach so much — overwhelm your ability to imagine the widest range of possibilities.

Only rarely does a person come to law school already skilled at both solution-generation and solution-evaluation. Most students need substantial improvement in both, but — because those two stages require such contrary states of mind — you might start off with more ability at one than the other. There are, however, many effective ways of generating and evaluating solutions. As you become a professional, you will develop styles of generating and styles of evaluating that best make use of the person you are, taking advantage of your strengths while controlling your weaknesses.

---

4. Quoted at Morris I. Stein, *Creativity as Intra- and Inter-Personal Process,* in *The Creative Encounter* 21-22 (Rosemary Holsinger, Camille Jordan & Leon Levenson eds., Scott, Foresman & Co. 1971).

5. Kenney F. Hegland, *Trial and Practice Skills* 181 (West 1978).

6. Lon L. Fuller, *On Teaching Law,* 3 Stan. L. Rev. 35, 43 (1950) (emphasis in original).

§24.4 Theories: Of the Case, of the Motion, of the Appeal

To make their decisions, judges need more than raw information about the law and the facts. They make decisions by *choosing between theories,* and you will lose if your adversary's theory is more attractive than yours is.

Think back to the last major decision you had to make — perhaps the choice of a career, the selection of a law school, a decision about where to live, or the purchase of a car or an appliance. If your decision-making was conscious and deliberative — as judges hope their decisions are — you can probably recall an idea — or a small number of related ideas — that caused you to choose one career over another, one law school over another, and so forth. And if your decision-making was conscious and deliberative, there was probably a moment when you first identified and appreciated this idea (or small group of ideas). At that moment, you probably also realized that one of the alternatives had become inevitable. Some people who specialize in sales work call this moment the "selling point" because the decision to buy becomes inevitable once the selling idea is fully appreciated by the buyer.

Persuading is selling, and judges have accurately been described as "professional buyers of ideas."[1] Judges have their selling points, and both lawyers and judges use the word *theory* to refer to the collection of ideas that, in a given case, a lawyer offers for purchase. At trial, each lawyer propounds a *theory of the case.* Where the court is to decide a motion or an appeal, the phrases *theory of the motion* or *theory of the appeal* might be used instead. Each lawyer proposes a theory, and the court chooses between them, or — if neither theory is satisfactory — the court may fashion one of its own, often causing unhappiness to both sides.

A theory, then, is an idea on which a decision can be based. A persuasive theory is a view of the facts and law — intertwined together — that justifies a decision in the client's favor and motivates a court to make that decision. A persuasive theory "explains not only *what* happened but also *why*" through a compelling story that "has both rational and psychological appeal" and thus is "persuasive both to the mind and to the heart."[2]

For example, if Welty is prosecuted for burglarizing Lutz's apartment (see pages 80-81), the prosecution's theory of burglary might be that Lutz's conduct did not imply permission to break the threshold and enter the apartment, and that Welty's actions show beyond a reasonable doubt that — when she stepped into the apartment — she had already formed an intent to assault Lutz.[3] To prove the element of a breaking, for example, the prosecutor might point to four facts: (1) Lutz opened the door only six inches, (2) he

§24.4   1. Girvan Peck, *Strategy of the Brief,* Litigation, Winter 1984, at 26, 27.

2. David Binder & Paul Bergman, *Fact Investigation: From Hypothesis to Proof* 140, 184 (West 1984).

3. The other elements of common law burglary would not be hard to prove: Welty did, in the nighttime, enter the dwelling of another. See §8.1.

never told Welty she could enter, (3) his only reason for stepping away from the door was to turn down the volume on his stereo so that he could hear what Welty was already saying while she was outside the apartment, and (4) as soon as Lutz discovered that Welty had entered the apartment, he ordered her to leave. To prove the element of "intent to commit a felony therein," the prosecutor might focus—in a way you have already explored in Chapter 9—on Welty's anger at the time she entered the apartment.

On the other hand, Welty's attorney might develop the theory that the evidence creates reasonable doubt about whether she broke through a threshold to get into Lutz's apartment and about whether, at the instant she walked through the door, she intended to strike him. To substantiate this theory, Welty's attorney might argue that there was nothing to break once the door was open; that Lutz's actions could reasonably have been understood by Welty to have implied permission to enter and continue the conversation inside the apartment; and that Welty's actions before she was ordered to leave are consistent with an innocent intent to persuade Lutz to behave in a more neighborly fashion. If believed, this theory should cause an acquittal on the charge of burglary.[4]

You might see something of how hard adjudicating is by putting yourself in the position of the judge and jury in this case, and by considering the consequences if you make a mistake: either an innocent person could be punished or a person could go free despite evidence of guilt beyond a reasonable doubt. You might also understand some of the difficulties of advocacy by putting yourself in the position of each of the lawyers and asking yourself how you would go about persuading the decision-makers both to adopt your theory *and to reject your adversary's theory.*

§24.5   Characteristics of a Persuasive Theory

A theory is worth arguing if it stands a significant chance of being adopted by the judge or jury who must adjudicate the dispute. The more a theory satisfies the following criteria, the greater its chances of adoption.

1. Does the theory "[a]ccount for or explain all of . . . the undeniable facts"?[1]   When a judge or jury first looks at the case, if your theory is inconsistent with an undeniable fact, one of the two will be considered wrong—and it will not be the undeniable fact. Beyond that point, ambiguous evidence and debatable inferences are usually resolved in

4. For the separate charge of assault, the lawyer might have to ask some questions to develop a further theory: for example, if Welty struck Lutz because she thought he had become so angry that he might strike her, she might—to the charge of assault (but not burglary)—argue self-defense.

§24.5   1. David M. Malone & Peter T. Hoffman, *The Effective Deposition* 53 (2d ed., NITA 1996).

whatever way is most consistent with the evidence that cannot be questioned. When the time for decision arrives, the adjudicator's natural tendency is to say, "Let's start with what we *do* know."

2. Does the theory "explain away in a plausible manner as many unfavorable facts as it can"?[2]   It is not enough to build on the evidence you like. Your theory should also explain why the evidence you *dislike* should not prevent a decision in your favor. Is it overcome by other evidence in your favor? Does it prove facts that are not as important under the law as other facts that your evidence has proved?

3. Does the theory "[e]xplain why people acted in the way they did"?[3]   If your theory does not do that, some significant part of the case will still seem mysterious to the judge or jury. As long as that mystery remains, a judge or jury will feel that your theory hasn't "solved" the controversy. If a theory assumes that the actors behaved differently from the way people normally do in similar circumstances, the theory is not persuasive unless it includes a compelling reason for the difference. Theories that impute deceit to disinterested witnesses, for example, are less attractive than those that suggest honest but faulty abilities to observe and remember. Innocent misunderstandings are much more common in life than lying or stealing.

4. Is the theory "supported by the details"?[4]   "Detail . . . on contested key facts enhances the believability of the story"[5] at the heart of your theory. If the case turns on whether a certain car was green or yellow and your star witness testifies that it was green but says nothing about whether it was a station wagon or a sedan, whether the driver was male or female, or whether the day was sunny or rainy, a judge or jury can naturally conclude that the witness has an unreliable memory.

5. Does the theory have a solid basis in law?   Are your interpretations of the statutes and cases reasonable? When a court examines your legal arguments using the tools and skills explained in Chapters 14, 15, 16, and 25, will the court be persuaded?

6. Is the theory "consistent with common sense and . . . plausible"?[6] All other things being equal, a simple theory is more down-to-earth than a complex one, although even a simple theory must address all the facts. A theory has a commonsense appeal if its internal logic is consistent, if it is realistic, if its explanations are compatible with the judge or jury's experiences in life, and if it reflects their values and the values of the community to which they feel responsible. The most easily sold theories are those

2. George Vetter, *Successful Civil Litigation* 30-31 (Prentice-Hall 1977).
3. David M. Malone & Peter T. Hoffman, *The Effective Deposition* 53 (2d ed., NITA 1996).
4. *Id.*
5. *Id.*
6. *Id.*

that are based on easily believable interpretations of the evidence and the authorities; that would lead to reasonable results; that do not ask a judge or jury to believe that people have behaved in improbable ways; and that ask for narrow decisions rather than earth-shaking ones.

Like any other kind of consumer, a judge buys only when struck with a feeling of confidence that the purchase will turn out well, without causing injustice or embarrassment on appeal or before the public. Like most people who have had substantial opportunity to observe human nature, judges can be astute at surmising how various kinds of people would behave under given circumstances. And like most people with substantial responsibilities, judges see the world as a place that works well when people are reasonable, rather than extreme. Judges feel safer when they can make narrow decisions, rather than earth-shaking ones, because narrow decisions are less likely to create new problems and controversies. (A judge would much rather find that your client is not guilty on the facts than hold that the statute defining the crime is unconstitutional.)

A theory that sells in an appellate court has a flavor different from one that seems attractive to a trial court. That is because trial judges and appellate judges do not see their work in precisely the same way. A trial court is a place of routine, and trial judges want to make decisions the way they are usually made and not in ways that would greatly disturb the world. Although trial judges sometimes try to avoid the full impact of appellate authority, the rulings of the courts to which a trial judge's decision could be appealed are like orders from a superior, and the trial judge needs and wants to know — through those rulings — what the supervising courts expect. In contrast, appellate judges are conscious of their responsibility to see the bigger picture and to keep the law as a whole fair and reasonable, even if that requires modifying the common law now and then to fit changes in society. Judicial circumspection and the doctrine of stare decisis keep these changes in direction to a minimum, however, and appellate courts generally presume the decision below to be correct, reversing only if deeply troubled by what happened in the lower court. Generally, theories presented to high appellate courts are more policy-oriented than theories presented to trial courts.

§24.6   Developing a Theory

Luck is the residue of design.

—Branch Rickey

Before the memorandum in Appendix C was written, Goslin undoubtedly showed his lawyer a deed that, on its surface, seemed to give the nephew every right to have Goslin and his belongings removed. A lawyer who lacks the skill of theory design might say something like this to such a client: "Well, Mr. Goslin, you made a mistake. In future, don't give a deed without securing some rights for yourself, either by making a collateral contract or by taking payment for your equity. In the meantime, I think you'll have to move out."

Another—and better—lawyer might look under the surface for possibilities: at the time of the deed, did Goslin believe he was giving up all his property rights? Did he think he was going to continue to live in the house? Had the nephew said or done anything that would show that the nephew thought Goslin was making a gift or was going to move out? Is there anything in the history of this uncle and this nephew on which some sort of reliance theory might be based? Since people do not usually negotiate with their relatives at arm's-length or with written contracts, and since people can turn on each other even in family relationships, might some part of the law go so far as to enforce understandings between relatives, even if those understandings have never been spoken or written down? Notice the technique: first, open doors to factual possibilities; then find out how the law treats those possibilities and discover whether there is evidence to prove them.

A theory will not spring forth in final form from your mind. Instead, a germ first occurs and then grows as new information is learned and more law researched. Although research guides the growth of the theory, the theory also guides the course of the research, each filling in the gaps of the other. Sometimes, there is rapid progress; at other times, it may be painfully slow. More than at any other time in legal writing, this is when you depend on the creative process described in §24.3.

How do you develop a theory?

First, narrow your focus to the issues. What will really matter to the court? Every case has some aspects that have distressed the client or the attorney but will be greeted in court with profound boredom. Certain kinds of suffering—for good reasons or bad—have no effect whatever on the typical judge. Some suffering can be dismissed on the ground that it is too small to merit judicial intervention, or that it is as much the client's own fault as anybody else's, or that it represents problems courts cannot solve. Conversely, every case has some aspects that both client and attorney would like to forget but will nevertheless strongly influence a judge. The client might have suffered a wrong, for example, but only while doing something that judges find grossly unacceptable. Or the other side might enjoy one of the traditional advantages in court: it might, for instance, be engaged in one of those industries that courts like to protect. Every theory has to take these kinds of things into account. Identifying them corresponds very roughly to the problem-identification stage of professional creativity mentioned in §24.3.

Second, list your case's strengths and weaknesses and the other side's strengths and weaknesses. What are your best facts? Conversely, what facts make you worry? What are your best and worst authorities and rules of law? And the human equities of the situation? Be realistic about the people in the courthouse and the way they are likely to deal with your case. This is part of the gathering and evaluating information and raw materials stage of professional creativity described in §24.3.

Third, think of a way of looking at the case that, if believed, would make your client the winner. This is solution-generation from §24.3.

Fourth, compare your theory to the criteria for effectiveness explained in §24.5. To the extent your theory falls short of effectiveness, can you fix it? This is solution-evaluation from §24.3. If your theory is ineffective and cannot be fixed, go back to solution-generation and develop another one.

Finally, once you have an effective theory, write the memo or brief that will present it. This combines the decision and action stages from §24.3.

It can help to develop contradictory theories together — to develop, in other words, your adversary's most likely theory while creating your own. If you look at the case as your adversary will see it and if you hypothetically work up a theory for your adversary to argue, you will be able to identify the weaknesses in your theory. Otherwise, you will look at the controversy one-sidedly, and your theories will reflect wishful thinking and be too one-dimensional to withstand attack.

§24.7   Imagery and Story-Telling

A picture held us captive.

> — *Wittgenstein*

Imagery has a powerful effect in theory development. Thinking in images — in other words, focused daydreaming — helps to find new ways of looking at things that would otherwise be iron-bound givens.

A truck runs off the highway, through a farmer's fence, and over the farmer's cow. The truck driver's insurance company wants to pay as little as possible for this cow, and the farmer, of course, wants more.

The insurance company's lawyer wants to treat the cow as "a unit of livestock" or "a farm asset." The insurance company is better off litigating this as a question about how much money the farmer is entitled to for the replacement of a machine-like object that consumes grass as fuel to produce milk and an occasional calf. The farmer's books can be gone over to determine the productivity of this object, its acquisition costs, depreciation, useful life remaining at the time of its destruction, etc.

The farmer's lawyer, on the other hand, wants to know if the cow had any other value. The lawyer asks the farmer some questions. "That wasn't just any cow," replies the farmer.

> That was Bessie! She was the only Guernsey cow left in this county. She didn't give that thin milk you get out of a Holstein that people buy in the grocery store. She gave the thickest, most flavorful milk you ever tasted. We didn't sell it to the dairy. We drank it ourselves and made the best butter and cheese out of it. And Guernseys are smaller cows. They're friendly, like pets, and Bessie was like part of our family.

The persuasive weight of each of these theories is in the imagery of what we *see*. The farmer's lawyer wants us to see a big pair of Guernsey eyes in a head that is nudging the farmer with affection — a loss to the farmer's family that includes but is greater than the loss of a grass-to-milk machine. The insurance company's lawyer wants us to see the farmer's balance sheet, where a certain item of livestock is carried as an asset valued at a certain number of dollars. In any writing that grows out of this controversy, the farmer's lawyer probably will not mention Bessie's head nudging the farmer, and the insurance company's lawyer probably will not mention the balance sheet — because those things are not, strictly speaking, relevant to the legal controversy. But if they are good writers, these lawyers will include enough relevant detail so that we will see these scenes anyway because they are implied.

If you develop an eye for revealing detail, your theories will much more quickly come to life as vivid, compelling stories. Vividness not only helps the reader remember the story (and the theory it embodies), but it makes the story and the theory more believable. Imagery makes a theory real.

Exercise.   Escape from Prison? (Developing a Theory)

Orville Bradwyn is charged with the crime of escape from prison. The state's sole witness was Benjamin Tunmeyer, a prison guard, who testified as follows.

Q: Please tell the court what you observed and did at 6:30 in the evening on the sixth of July.

A: I was checking prisoners in the dinner line. Prisoners are required to be in there at that time, and any prisoner who has not shown up for dinner is considered missing. The defendant did not appear. I then checked his cell. Some material had been put in his bed, bunched up so that it looked like somebody was asleep there. His radio had been left on. But he was gone.

Q: What did you do?

A: We searched the grounds outside the prison. We didn't find the defendant there, so we searched inside the prison — first the perimeter, and then the inside of buildings and containers where someone might hide. We finally found him in the laundry room at 7:39 P.M.

Q: What did he have with him?

A: All of his clothing.

Q: Does the prison wash the laundry of any other institution?

A: Yes, we do the laundry for the state hospital down the road. It's done in the same laundry room where we found the defendant.

Q: How is the hospital's laundry transported to and from the prison?

A: By truck. The hospital's truck brings in it in the morning and picks it up at about 8 P.M.

Q: Are prisoners permitted in the laundry room in the evening?

A: No prisoner is allowed in that room after 5 P.M. Hiding in one of the hospital's laundry bags is an obvious way to escape from the prison.

Q: What precautions are taken to prevent that?
A: At 5 P.M., a guard makes sure all prisoners assigned to work in the laundry have left, and then the door is locked. In addition, the guard opens up each laundry bag that goes to the state hospital and makes sure it has only laundry in it. Then he locks up the room and locks another door on the corridor leading to the laundry room. Nobody is inside those doors until the hospital's truck arrives about three hours later.
Q: What guard was assigned that responsibility on the night in question?
A: Me. I sent out all the prisoners and satisfactorily inspected the state hospital's bags. Then, I locked the doors and left.
Q: Was Mr. Bradwyn assigned to work in the laundry?
A: Yes. But he was not scheduled to work in the laundry room on the day in question.

Cross-examination:

Q: Are you familiar with Mr. Bradwyn's reputation among other prisoners and among corrections officers?
A: He is an exceptionally tidy person.
Q: Were there any prior occasions on which you and Mr. Bradwyn had shouting matches?
A: Yes. It's almost impossible to inspect his cell. He starts yelling the minute you touch any of his things. He says he doesn't like them moved.
Q: What was the defendant doing when you found him?
A: He was washing his clothes. No, actually, he was drying them. They were in the dryer.
Q: What items of clothing were in the dryer?
A: Both of his prison uniforms — prisoners are issued two — socks, undershirts, undershorts. They were still wet.
Q: What did you find when you searched Mr. Bradwyn's cell?
A: Letters from his family, personal photographs, letters from his lawyer, an address book.
Q: Before dinner, prisoners are free to move about outside their cells; aren't they?
A: Yes.
Q: And the same is true after dinner, isn't it?
A: Until 7:30.

After this testimony, the prosecution rested. Bradwyn moved to dismiss on the ground that the prosecution had presented insufficient evidence to convict.

Develop two theories that satisfy the criteria in §24.5. One theory should support Bradwyn and his motion. The other should support the prosecution and oppose the motion. Use the method outlined in §24.6.

The relevant statute and cases interpreting it appear below:

CRIMINAL CODE § 745

If any person committed to prison shall break and escape therefrom or shall escape or leave without authority any building, camp, or any place whatsoever in which he is placed or to which he is directed to go or in which he is allowed to be, he shall be deemed guilty of an escape and shall be punished by imprisonment for a term not to exceed five years, to commence immediately upon the expiration of the term of his previous sentence.

STATE v. HORSTMAN

The crime of escape is established by proof that the defendant was confined in a prison and escaped from such confinement or departed without authority from a place to which she or he was duly assigned. Unauthorized departure is the gravamen of the offense.

STATE v. CAHILL

While incarcerated, the defendant was placed in solitary confinement for fighting with another prisoner. A guard inadvertently left the cell door unlocked. The defendant got out and was apprehended on top of the prison wall.

The defendant argues that the evidence does not prove that he committed the crime of escape because there is no evidence that he escaped from the custody of the Department of Prisons. He argues that, at most, he is guilty of the lesser crime of attempted escape.

The crime of escape was complete, however, when the defendant got out of his cell. The crime can be committed without leaving the prison as a whole. It is enough that the defendant left a place where he was confined within the prison.

STATE v. LIGGETT

The defendant was incarcerated and assigned to work in the prison shop manufacturing auto license plates. On the day in question, the defendant was reported absent from his shift in the license plate shop. After a prolonged search, he was found inside a machine in the prison cannery, using a pillow, and reading a novel.

The evidence does not prove beyond a reasonable doubt that the defendant committed the crime of escape. He failed to report for work in one part of the prison and, without authorization, spent the time in another part. That might violate prison rules and merit internal prison discipline, but it is not the crime of escape.

Developing Persuasive Arguments

§25.1 What Is an Argument?

Arguments are the primary tool lawyers use to persuade people to do things. *An argument is a group of ideas arranged logically to convince a reader or listener to do a particular thing or to adopt a particular belief.*

That would *not* include excited utterances from drivers after a fender-bender in a parking lot. The drivers might sound argumentative, but they are really ventilating anger, neither of them having any hope of persuading the other. Nor does it include the pushy expression of one's view on news, fashion, sports, or gossip. In daily life, many people are eager to state their opinions. But they seem to do it just so that you know what they think — and not with the intent of changing your mind.

Uncapitalized, "argument" means a contention designed to persuade. Capitalized, it means the largest portion of a motion memorandum or appellate brief. There might be many arguments in an Argument.

In designing an argument, your initial question should be "What will make the reader or listener want to agree with me?" A good argument will *affect* the audience. It leads readers or listeners through reasoning so convincingly that, at the end, they are pleased to be persuaded.

Arguments can be expressed ("the defendant committed negligence by running a red light and hitting my client's car") or implied, usually by reciting the facts in a way that suggests the argument ("my client entered the intersection with a green light and was hit sideways by the defendant, whose light was red"). This chapter explains how to make expressed arguments in the Argument portion of a motion memorandum or a brief.

305

Chapters 29 and 30 explain how to make implied arguments in a Statement
of the Case and in a Question Presented.

Most disputes are two-sided in the sense that each side can make credible
arguments, and it takes real work for the judge or jury to choose between
them. Here is an example from a nonlitigation setting: hypothetical testimony before a Congressional committee on whether to impose a tariff on
shoelaces:[1]

A new and stiff tariff should be
imposed on imported shoelaces.
We do not ask for a ban on the
import of foreign shoelaces. All we
ask for is a chance to compete fairly.
Foreign shoelace manufacturers pay
their workers only a small fraction
of what workers in our shoelace fac-
tories are paid, and that is why their
shoelaces are so much cheaper than
ours. Unless imported shoelaces are
taxed on the boat or at the border,
they will become so cheap that our
own domestic shoelace manufacturers will be driven into bankruptcy. Our own hard-working
employees will lose their jobs,
leaving their families destitute and
adding to the unemployment problem. And if our own domestic
shoelace manufacturing industry
disappears,   our   country   will
become completely dependent on
imported shoelaces. If imported
shoelaces were cut off in war or
other   national   emergency,   we
would have no source of new
shoelaces, which means that eventually most shoes would become un-
wearable. Every soldier has to lace
up boots to go into combat. Most of
the office and factory workers have
to tie shoelaces to get to work in the

Imported shoelaces should not
be subject to a tariff. The American consumer already pays too
much for shoelaces. If they are
so essential that everyone needs
them, they should cost less. We
cannot artificially protect every
domestic industry that faces
hard foreign competition. If we
tried, the cost of living to the
American consumer would go up
because it is impossible for people
to live without buying imported
goods. A tariff might save some
American jobs, but it would
destroy others because some people make their living importing
shoelaces. If the American shoelace manufacturers cannot compete without the help of a tariff,
their industry should become
extinct and its people and capital
directed toward some business
that Americans really can do better or cheaper than foreign produ-
cers. And the country is not going
to be brought to its knees because
it doesn't have shoelaces. It is
extremely difficult to imagine
any national emergency that
could cut off a supply of imported
shoelaces. And if a national
emergency ever did that, it

---

§25.1 1. A tariff is a tax on imported products. It makes the import more expensive when
sold to the consumer. Arguments like these have been made whenever Congress has considered
tariff and trade bills. (The examples here were vaguely inspired by testimony regarding the 1962
Trade Expansion Act but not about shoelaces.) This is a hypothetical. Please do not assume that
imported shoelaces are now specially taxed, or that the domestic shoelace industry has any
trouble competing with imports, or that a domestic shoelace industry even exists. The parallel
block quotes are just examples of how arguments work against each other.

morning. Without shoelaces every domestic industry would eventually come to a halt. Please do not let our domestic shoelace industry become extinct.

would also cut off the supply of so many other imports that shoelaces would be the least of our worries.

If a controversy is *evenly* two-sided, the person who must choose the winner—usually a court, but here a legislature—will have a hard time deciding because the arguments on each side are attractive. Your job is to make your arguments better than the adversary's, or to make the adversary's arguments worse by finding their weak points, or—preferably—to do both of these things. This chapter explains how.

§25.2 What Judges Expect from Written Argumentation

You already know some things about how judges think: in our system of litigation the lawyers (and not the judge) frame the issues, develop the theories and arguments, and adduce the evidence. Judges are busy people who view any assertion skeptically and who must make many decisions in short periods of time. Thus, they need complete but concise arguments that can be quickly understood.

In addition, there is so much litigation now that courts are increasingly dependent on written arguments submitted by attorneys. Many—perhaps most—appeals today are decided without oral argument and without any other personal contact between attorneys and judges. On appeal, the written brief bears the primary burden of persuading the court. A similar evolution is occurring in trial courts. It is not unusual today for a judge to complete a case without a trial, without a hearing, without an oral argument, without a conference in chambers, and solely on the basis of the attorneys' written submissions in connection with a motion to dismiss or a motion for summary judgment.

Judges are evaluated on their skill at the *art* of judging—not on whether they know all the law. Although judges know a great deal about rules of procedure (which they use constantly), they usually know much less about individual rules of substantive law (which come up less often). And in most courts judges cannot specialize in particular areas of substantive law: they must decide any case you bring before them. Unless a case turns on parts of the law about which a judge has thought deeply lately, the judge depends on the attorneys to explain what the law is and how it governs the case. And a judge knows nothing at all about the facts of a case except for what can be learned through the attorneys and their evidence.

Judges will want you to *teach* them your case. Think of a motion memorandum or appellate brief as a *manual on how to make a particular decision* (and — by implication — on how to write the opinion that justifies that decision). A lawyer who can show the court how the decision should be made, laying out all the steps of logic, stands a much better chance of winning.

If done in a respectful tone, this is not as presumptuous as you might think. If you have prepared properly, you will know much more about the decision than the judge will. But teach the court without insulting its intelligence, and do so in the clearest and most concise manner possible. Judges find it hard to rule in your favor if you are condescending or waste their time.

§25.3   *Argumentation Techniques*

> A carefully prepared, carefully stated, lawyer-like written argument is a work of art and a joy forever.
>
> —*E. Barrett Prettyman*

A convincing argument is not just a random collection of stray comments that sound good for the client. Those kinds of comments might be useful raw materials, but they become an argument only when they coalesce into a coherent presentation that influences the audience. Here is how to do it:

1. Design a compelling theory and back it up with compelling arguments.
2. Include both motivating arguments and justifying arguments.
3. Limit your contentions to those that have a reasonable chance of persuading the court.
4. Organize to emphasize the ideas that are most likely to persuade.
5. Make your organization obvious.
6. Give the court a clear statement of the rule or rules on which the case turns.
7. Rely on an appropriate amount of authority with appropriate amounts of explanation.
8. Explain exactly and in detail how the law governs the facts.
9. To the extent they advance the theory, make the facts and people involved come alive on the written page.
10. "Tell the judge exactly what will happen in the real world if he decides for you or for your opponent."[1]

---

§25.3   1. Hollis T. Hurd, *Writing for Lawyers* 61 (Journal Broad. & Commun. 1982).

11. Reinforce the theory with carefully chosen wording.
12. Confront openly your weaknesses and your opponent's strengths.
13. Enhance your credibility through careful editing and through the appearance of the memorandum or brief.
14. Make it easy for the judge to rule in your favor.

Each of these techniques requires strategic decisions on your part. If you think these decisions through carefully, you should be able to explain your work by answering the litany of strategy questions in §24.2.

You will find the following material easier to understand if you read the motion memorandum in Appendix F before continuing here.

1. Design a compelling theory and back it up with compelling arguments. Until you provide proof, a judge will not believe anything you say. In litigation writing, proof is a well-argued theory that compels a decision favorable to your client. You can develop a theory through the process described in §§24.6-24.7. And the quality of your theory can be measured by the criteria set out in §24.5. But even a good theory does not sell unless it is argued.

A persuasive argument is neither extravagant nor belligerent. To a judge, extreme statements sound unreliable. Because judges are experienced, professional skeptics, they are rarely fooled by inaccurate or farfetched statements, and when they find such a statement in an argument, in their view a dust of untrustworthiness settles over the theory and the lawyer involved. Judges usually have what Hemingway, in another context, called "a built-in, shock-proof, shit detector."[2] Because you cannot afford to be seen as unreliable, you need to be similarly equipped so that you can examine — with a judge's skepticism — each statement you contemplate making. In addition to the skills explained here, it helps to have a mature and thorough understanding of human nature (some of which can be acquired in law school, even if it is not listed in the catalog).

A good theory and good arguments are reasonable and accurate, appear reliable, and make your client's victory appear *inevitable* — either because the higher courts will reverse any other result, or because it is the only right thing to do, or both. The feeling of inevitability is a judge's selling point. It is reached by laying out for the judge every step of logic so that the advocate's conclusion becomes more and more irresistible as the argument proceeds. A judge knows when the selling point approaches, because the job of deciding seems to grow easier.

2. Include both motivating arguments and justifying arguments. Both are needed to persuade.

A motivating argument is one that causes a judge to *want* to decide a case in a particular way. It causes the judge to feel that any other decision would be unjust. Motivating arguments tend to be centered on facts or a

---

2. *Writers At Work: The Paris Review Interviews, Second Series* 239 (George Plimpton ed., Penguin 1965).

combination of facts and policy. Greatly oversimplified, the following are the primary motivating arguments in the sample motion memorandum and appellate briefs in the appendices:

> **Appendix F:** The defendant created a risk of irreversible harm to the health of 130 children by mishandling a toxic substance which he could have handled safely using well accepted techniques.
>
> **Appendix G:** The defendant was only following her doctors' treatment plan for a recognized illness, and the law should leave her alone.
>
> **Appendix H:** The defendant and his friends had misrepresented their true identities, and a crime-ridden society is threatened when people do that.

(In all three appendices, notes in the margins show you where motivating arguments are being made.)

A justifying argument is one that shows that the law either requires or permits the result urged by the arguer. Justifying arguments are centered on legal rules or on a combination of rules and policy. Again oversimplified, the following are the main justifying arguments in the sample motion memo and briefs in the appendices:

> **Appendix F:** The evidence satisfies the test for summary judgment in a negligence case.
>
> **Appendix G:** The defendant was not disguised within the meaning of the statute. And if she was, the statute would violate the constitutional right to privacy.
>
> **Appendix H:** The defendant was disguised within the meaning of the statute. And the statute does not violate the constitutional right to privacy.

The first year of law school is designed, among other things, to teach you how to make justifying arguments. (You probably understood something of motivating arguments even before you came to law school, although you will learn more about making them.)

In judicial opinions, justifying arguments are usually developed in much detail while motivating arguments are only hinted at. The hints are found most often in the court's recitations of the facts. Have you had the feeling, while reading the first few paragraphs of an opinion, that you knew how the case would be decided before the court had told you — and even before the court had begun to discuss the law? If so, it was probably because you noticed in the fact recitation clues about which facts had motivated the court.

Why do you need both motivating arguments and justifying arguments? A motivating argument alone is not enough because even a motivated judge is not supposed to act without a solid legal justification. Judges understandably want to feel that they are doing a professional job of judging, and they can be reversed on appeal if they fail to justify their actions within the law.

And a justifying argument alone is not enough because, in a large number of cases, a justifying argument, without more, will not persuade. The law can usually be interpreted in more than one reasonable way. When a judge is given a choice between two conflicting justifying arguments, each of which is reasonable, the judge will take the one she or he is motivated to take. (Judges are, after all, human.) Remember what Karl Llewellyn wrote: "rules *guide*, but they do not *control* decision. There is no precedent the judge may not at his need either file down to razor thinness or expand into a bludgeon."[3] (See §15.6.)

Many beginners have more difficulty developing motivating arguments than they do with justifying arguments. Before starting law school most of us have already had a fair amount of experience justifying our own beliefs. But that is not the same as getting inside another person's thinking and *causing* her or him to *want* to do something. To motivate, we need to learn not only a new argument style, but also a new *process* of creating arguments. That is because the process of creating justifying arguments is different from the process of creating motivating arguments.

> [In a college course, Kathleen wrote a paper on the] question "Is American Sign language (ASL) a 'foreign language' for purposes of meeting the university's foreign language requirement?" Kathleen had taken two years of ASL at a community college. When she transferred to a four-year college, the chair of the foreign languages department at her new college would not allow her ASL proficiency to count for the foreign language requirement. ASL isn't a "language," the chair said summarily. "It's not equivalent to learning French, German, or Japanese."
>
> Kathleen disagreed, so [in a different course she decided to write a paper on this issue]. While doing research, she focused almost entirely on subject matter, searching for what linguists, brain neurologists, cognitive psychologists, and sociologists had said about the language of deaf people. Immersed in her subject matter, she was [not very] concerned with her audience, whom she thought of primarily as her classmates and the professor [who taught the class in which she was writing the paper. They] were friendly to her views and interested in her experiences with the deaf community. She wrote a well-documented paper, citing several scholarly articles, that made a good case to her classmates (and the professor) that ASL was indeed a distinct language.
>
> Proud of the big red A the professor had placed on her paper, Kathleen returned to the chair of the foreign language department with a new request to count ASL for her language requirement. The chair read her paper, congratulated her on her good writing, but said her argument was not persuasive. He disagreed with several of the linguists she cited and with the general definition of "language" that her paper assumed. He then gave her some additional (and to her fuzzy) reasons that the college would not accept ASL as a foreign language.[4]

---

3. K. N. Llewellyn, *The Bramble Bush* 180 (Oceana 1930).

4. John D. Ramage & John C. Bean, *Writing Arguments: A Rhetoric with Readings* 10-11 (4th ed., Allyn & Bacon 1998).

This is a common experience when justifying insights are used in an attempt — often unsuccessful — to influence real-world decision-making. The ideas that made sense in the library and sounded wonderful to colleagues are ignored by the person who makes a decision, whether that person is an administrator (as here) or a judge.

It would be easy for Kathleen to dismiss the chair of the foreign language department as a nincompoop, but for two reasons she cannot and should not do that. First, she cannot get around the fact that he has the power of decision. The only way she can get her ASL work to count for the foreign language requirement is *to change his mind.* For this issue, he is the judge.

Second, he might have sincere concerns that deserve to be addressed. Does Kathleen know what they might be? At this point, she does not. Her paper focused on the issue itself, and the only audience she imagined was a friendly one. She avoided thinking about the unfriendly audience, even though the skeptical audience — the department chair — is the only one that can make the decision. We would like to forget about the skeptical audience, but if we want action, we have to *concentrate* on that audience.

How can Kathleen find out what the department chair's concerns might be? How can she address them?

> Spurred by what she considered the chair's too-easy dismissal of her argument, Kathleen decided . . . to write a second paper on ASL — but this time aiming it directly at the chair of foreign languages. Now her writing task falls closer to the persuasive end of our continuum. Kathleen once again immersed herself in research, but this time it focused not on subject matter (whether ASL is a distinct language) but on audience. She researched the history of the foreign language requirement at her college and discovered some of the politics behind it (an old foreign language requirement had been dropped in the 1970's and reinstituted in the 1990's, partly — a math professor told her — to boost enrollments in foreign language courses). She also interviewed foreign language teachers to find out what they knew and didn't know about ASL. She discovered that many teachers [inaccurately] thought ASL was "easy to learn," so that accepting ASL would allow students a Mickey Mouse way to avoid the rigors of a real foreign language class. Additionally, she learned that foreign language teachers valued immersing students in a foreign culture; in fact, the foreign language requirement was part of her college's effort to create a multicultural curriculum.
>
> This new understanding of her target audience helped Kathleen totally reconceptualize her argument. She condensed and abridged her original paper. . . . She added sections showing the difficulty of learning ASL (to counter her audience's belief that learning ASL was easy), and literature (to show how ASL met the goals of multiculturalism), and showing that the number of transfer students with ASL credits would be negligibly small (to allay fears that accepting ASL would threaten enrollments in language classes). She ended her argument with an appeal to her college's public emphasis (declared boldly in its mission statement) on eradicating social injustice and reaching out to the oppressed. She described the isolation of deaf people in a world where almost no hearing people learn ASL and argued that the deaf community on her campus could be integrated more fully into campus life if more students could "talk" with them [in their own language]. Thus, the

ideas included in her new argument, the reasons selected, the evidence used, the arrangement and tone all were determined by her primary focus on persuasion.[5]

Kathleen's first paper was limited to justifying arguments because it did no more than provide a logical rationale that could support a decision in her favor — if the department chair were inclined to rule as she wanted. It lacked motivating arguments because it did not address the concerns of the department chair.

The second paper included both kinds of arguments and thus was good lawyering. She got inside the decision-maker's thinking and showed him that his own values and needs would benefit from doing what she wanted. Purely justifying arguments remained — because they are needed to justify a decision in her favor — but they receded in importance and were joined by policy arguments with which the department chair could sympathize as well as arguments that addressed genuine practical problems that had made him skeptical.

3. Limit your contentions to those that have a reasonable chance of persuading the court. You might be tempted to throw in every good thing you can think of about your theory and every bad thing about your adversary's theory, assuming that all this cannot hurt and might help. That is "shotgun" writing, and it hurts more than it helps. Instead, focus sharply on the strong contentions. Develop them fully, and leave out the weak ones. As Holmes put it: "strike for the jugular and let the rest go."[6] That creates a document that is more compact but explores more deeply the ideas on which the decision will be based.

A good argument begins by subduing the judge's skepticism into a general feeling of *confidence* that the theory can be relied on, and then, on that foundation of confidence, it builds a feeling that your client is the *inevitable* winner. Weak contentions interfere with this. They excite skepticism, rather than quieting it. If a judge believes that you have indiscriminately mixed unreliable contentions with seemingly attractive ones, the judge's natural temptation is to dismiss the whole lot as not worthy of confidence, for the same reason that a person considering the purchase of a house justifiably suspects the integrity of the entire structure after cracked beams are found in the attic. Just as it is the builder's job to select only sturdy materials, so it is the lawyer's job — and not the judge's — to separate out the weak ideas before the memorandum or brief is submitted. A judge has neither the time nor the inclination to delete all the suspect material and then reassemble the remainder into something sturdier.

When you determine whether a contention has a reasonable chance to persuade, you are, of course, making a predictive judgment. A "reasonable chance" does not mean certainty and, in a case where you have nothing better, might not even mean probability. To be worth making,

---

5. *Id.* at 11.
6. Oliver Wendell Holmes, *Speeches* 77 (Little, Brown & Co. 1934).

however, a contention should have the capacity to seem tempting and attractive to a judge.

4. Organize to emphasize the ideas that are most likely to persuade.

Remember that you will make both motivating arguments and justifying arguments. Justifying arguments can be organized through the paradigm formula you have already learned because they are proofs of a conclusion of law. Motivating arguments, on the other hand, are more often appeals to a human sense of justice or pragmatic policy needs. When you add motivating arguments, you may vary the paradigm formula in radical ways (many of which would not work in predictive writing). In part, that is because motivating arguments should be introduced very early in a presentation, preferably in the first paragraph.

To merge motivating and justifying arguments, do this: First, write a justifying argument structured in the paradigm format you have already learned (Chapters 10-13). Then start adding motivating arguments wherever they seem relevant to what you have already written. Finally, write an opening paragraph that sums up your motivating arguments. (This is illustrated in the memorandum in Appendix F and in the appellate briefs in Appendices G and H. See the notes in the appendix margins.) With more experience, you will be able to write motivating and justifying arguments at the same time, or even to write the motivating argument before you write the justifying argument.

The opening paragraph that introduces the motivating argument should precede all statements of rules, proof of those rules, and rule application. Word for word, the opening paragraph is the most powerful argumentative passage you can write. It is worth rewriting and rewriting again many times until it introduces your motivating arguments in the most persuasive way.

Why is it so important to introduce the motivating arguments first? There are several reasons. Most importantly, it tracks the way many judges think. They act on what motivates them (unless it cannot be justified). Motivation is established first, the need to justify afterward. Moreover, early impressions tend to color how later material is read, and, like most people, a judge reads most carefully at the beginning. In addition, because judges are so busy, they expect the strongest material first. If they find themselves reading weak material early, they assume that nothing better follows and stop reading altogether.

(You probably read a newspaper in the same way: you expect the most important or most entertaining material near the beginning of a story, and when you have had enough, you stop reading and go on to something else. Newspaper editors know that, and newspaper stories are written with the least valuable material at the end, so that readers can decide how much of a story to read. Just as your method of reading a newspaper would be thrown off if the most valuable material were strewn randomly throughout the story, so a judge's method of reading a memorandum or a brief would become muddled if the strongest arguments might appear anywhere.)

Thus, judges will expect you to get immediately to the point. A judge quickly becomes impatient with long prefatory passages of historical background because that kind of material usually does not help in making a decision. (Even in a constitutional case where the issue is the drafters' intent one or two centuries ago, the historical material is part of the argument, not a preface to it.) An argument—and even a predictive memorandum—written in the style of a law review article is considered especially offensive because law review writing aims to be densely encyclopedic and is not focused to assist decision-making.

Michael Fontham has said that the "best strategy is to strike quickly, establish momentum, and maintain the advantage through a forceful presentation of contentions selected for their persuasive effect."[7] Focus the reader's thoughts on the ideas that can cause you to win.

In general, the most persuasive sequence is to present first the issues on which you are most likely to win; within issues, to make your strongest arguments first; and, within arguments, to make your strongest contentions and use your best authority first.

For example, if your adversary must prove that a five-element test has been satisfied, and if you think that your adversary's proof is weakest on element number three, do not argue the elements in the order in which they are listed in the controlling statute. Argue number three first because as far as you are concerned, it is the controlling element. (Your adversary, however, might do either of two things. She might argue them in exactly the order listed in the statute, to build a feeling of cumulating persuasion. Or if some elements are extremely easy to prove, she might get them out of the way first and then concentrate on the ones where the battle is concentrated.)

Sometimes, however, the logic of the dispute requires that the strongest material be delayed to avoid confusing the court. Some arguments are simply hard to understand unless preceded by less punchy material. In these situations, you must weigh your need for clarity against your need to show merit from the start.

5. Make your organization obvious. You cannot afford to let the judge grope for clues about how your contentions are related to each other. Instead, use the techniques of forceful writing[8] to help the judge see your focus. Very soon after you begin to discuss each issue, tell the judge exactly what your theory is. Use a thesis sentence to state each contention before you begin to prove it. And use transitional words and phrases to show how your contentions are cumulative:

There are three reasons why . . . First, . . . Second, . . . And finally, . . .

Not only has the defendant violated . . . , but she has also . . .

6. Give the court a clear statement of the rule or rules on which the case turns. That rule might not be exactly as stated in the cases to which you cite. In fact, the cases might enforce the rule without stating

---

7. Michael R. Fontham, *Written and Oral Advocacy* 108 (Wiley 1985).
8. See §19.3.

it at all, and you might have to figure out what the rule is from the court's reasoning, particularly the way it treats the facts. (See §3.2.)

The judge who reads your Argument needs what Karl Llewellyn called the advocate's "own clean phrasing of the rule," together with "a passage which so clearly and rightly states and crystallizes the background and the result that it is *recognized* on sight as doing the needed work and as practically demanding to be lifted into the opinion."[9] Particularly in appellate courts, judges know that they will have to write an opinion justifying their decision, and that the opinion should be as convincing as possible to the parties, to the bar, to the public, and to any still higher court to which the decision could be appealed. That is a hard task where a gap in the law must be filled. The judge who asks in oral argument in a gap-filling case, "Counselor, what rule would you have us enforce?" really wants to know how — if the lawyer prevails — the court should word the second component of the paradigm formula when it writes the opinion.

As you already know, for any given rule, the authority can usually be interpreted to support several different formulations from broad to narrow. In choosing one formulation over another, balance two separate factors. First, out of any given set of authority, some rule formulations are more likely than others to be accepted by a court. And second, some formulations more logically support the client's position. The trick is to find a formulation that does both.

7. Rely on an appropriate amount of authority with appropriate amounts of explanation.
To rule in your favor, a court would need to believe that you have provided sufficient authority, although the typical judge is unwilling to tolerate an exhaustive explanation of every case you cite. How do you steer a middle course between underciting and overciting and between underexplaining and overexplaining?

Begin by predicting the amount of citation and explanation a skeptical but busy judge would need. Then carefully study the available authorities. Place in a "major authority" category those that are likely to *influence* the court and in a "peripheral" category those that are merely somewhat related to the issue. Think in terms of cause and effect: if you had to make the judge's decision, which authorities would be most likely to have an effect on you, *even an effect adverse to your client's position*? Those are the authorities you must discuss, and many of them are best discussed in detail. Peripheral authorities should eventually be discarded unless they are needed to fill holes in your argument not settled by the major authorities.

The quantity of authority and the volume of explanation will depend on how much is needed to clarify the issue involved, how disputed that issue is, and how important it is to your theory. At one extreme, an idea may be so complex, so disputed, and so critical that it must be supported by a comprehensive explanation, filling many pages, of major authorities. At

9. Karl N. Llewellyn, *The Common Law Tradition: Deciding Appeals* 241 (Little, Brown & Co. 1960) (emphasis in original).

the other extreme, if the court is apt to be satisfied with a mere conclusory explanation, you should limit citation to one or, at the very most, two cases. If an idea is undisputed and routine, such as an uncontested procedural test, it should be enough to cite, with little or no explanation, the most recent decision from the highest court in the jurisdiction that has invoked the test. (For example, notice how the test for summary judgment is proved in the memorandum in Appendix F.)

The point is to give the court confidence that you are right without tiring its patience.

8. Explain exactly and in detail how the law governs the facts. A court rules for one party over another not merely because the law is abstractly favorable, but, more importantly, because the law and facts *combine* favorably. The judge often reaches the selling point only where the law and facts are finally combined — woven together — to show that what the writer wants is inevitable. Beginners sometimes devote so much attention to the law that they overlook the final step of arguing the facts — weaving the law into the facts to show the court precisely how the decision should be made. After all the work of explaining the law, a beginner might assume that the application to the facts is obvious, but it hardly ever is. Do not assume that merely mentioning the facts is enough: *show* the court exactly how the determinative facts require the decision you seek.

9. To the extent they advance the theory, make the facts and people involved come alive on the written page. As the judge looks at the facts of your case, you want her or him to see more than a chronological recitation of events. Instead, you want the judge to see something that reveals character and causation. An illustration of the difference between those two things is from E. M. Forster's classic lectures on fiction.[10] When we read "The king died, and then the queen died," we might see in the mind's eye either no image or at best an image of stick-like figures without personality. But when we read "The king died, and then the queen died of grief," we see instead an image of at least one real human being: she may be wearing fairytale-like clothing, but she is genuinely suffering as real people do.

When a judge, reading an argument, visualizes stick figures or no image at all, the case seems boring and unimportant, and the judge is not motivated to rule in your favor. But the judge begins to take sides if she or he can visualize real people doing real things to each other.

Before you begin to write, make a list on scratch paper of the determinative facts. You will have to discuss those facts to make your argument, and that is where your opportunities occur. For each fact, ask yourself what the fact illustrates about the *people* involved: does it show who is an innocent victim, who is predatory, who is inexcusably foolish, and so forth. For each fact, ask yourself further what the fact illustrates about *what happened*:

10. E. M. Forster, *Aspects of the Novel* 86 (Harcourt Brace 1927).

does it show the events to have been accidental, caused by one person's carelessness, the result of another's greed and cunning, and so on. Only by knowing what each fact reveals can you tell the client's story in a compelling way.

When you describe these facts in your writing, do not characterize them with emotion-laden words. Although a fact is determinative because the law coldly makes it so, a judge can form a human reaction to it, simply because judges prefer to make decisions that are fundamentally fair. On the other hand, a judge's professional self-image is naturally offended by an argument that reads like political oratory or a story in a tabloid newspaper. *Vividness* is not the same as luridness, which demeans an argument and the judge who reads it. If a fact will seem compelling to a court, that fact will speak for itself. All you will need is a calm description of the fact, in simple words and with enough detail to make the picture vivid. When reading the Argument in the memorandum in Appendix F, you may have thought that the painter was irresponsible — but the writer never called him that. Instead, the writer simply described what happened so that *you* formed that opinion. (Forster did not say that the queen loved the king. He only told you why she died.)

10. *"Tell the judge exactly what will happen in the real world if he decides for you or for your opponent."* [11]   In a trial court, that usually means showing the judge how the parties have been affected by the dispute, how they would be affected by the relief you seek, or how in some other way what you seek is fundamentally fair.

In an appellate court, where precedent makes law, it also means showing the court how you should prevail from a policy standpoint. Not only must you show the court that your client deserves individually to win, but you also must demonstrate that what you want makes sense in other cases as well because the decision will become precedent. If a court must choose between competing rules, for example, you should spend more than a little effort showing that the rule you urge is better than others. Even where the law is settled and the question is how to apply it, a court is still less likely to rule in your favor if the court lacks confidence that what you want is, in a very general sense, a good idea.

Prove policy with authority. Some policy is openly announced in decisions and statutes, but more often it is implied. For example, courts everywhere like solutions that are easily enforceable, promote clarity in the law, are not needlessly complex, and do not allow true wrongdoers to profit from illegal acts. Other policy considerations may differ from state to state. In Arizona, for example, public policy disfavors solutions that interfere with development of land for homes and industry, while in Vermont policy prefers conservation, the environment, and preservation of agriculture. Some states favor providing tort remedies even at some risk to judicial efficiency, although in others the reverse is true. Still other policy considerations differ

---

11. Hollis T. Hurd, *Writing for Lawyers* 61 (Journal Broad. & Commun. 1982).

from era to era. Some activities once greatly favored in the law—such as the building and operation of railroads in the nineteenth century—now enjoy no special treatment, while other things—such as a woman's reproductive control over her own body—are now protected in a way they once were not.

Lawyers tend to introduce policy-based arguments with phrasings like the following:

> This court should reject the rule urged by the defendant because it would cause . . .

> Automobile rental companies [or some other category of litigants] should bear the risk of loss because . . .

> Not only is the order requested by the plaintiff not sanctioned by this state's case law, but such an order would violate public policy because . . .

Remember, however, that policy arguments are used to reinforce argument from authority. Only where authority is unusually sparse should policy arguments play the predominant role in a theory.

11. Reinforce the theory with carefully chosen wording.   Choose words in part for the effect they should have on the reader. Simple, concrete words can paint the pictures on which your theory is based. In the memorandum in Appendix E, notice how facts are described almost entirely in short, everyday words with very specific meanings. And notice how the word *toxic* is used to remind the reader that although lead paint seems innocuous, it is not.

Readers see scenes where writers have given concrete descriptions to build on. The knack is, first, to isolate the very few facts that are essential to the scene because they will motivate the reader or are determinative under the law, and then to describe those facts in words that are simple and concrete enough for the desired image to come quickly into the reader's mind. This is not simple and concrete:

> Where contamination has occurred, lead dust can be ingested by young children through frequent and unpredictable hand-mouth contact during play.

This is:

> If the floor inside a building or the soil outside is contaminated with lead dust, young children can literally eat lead because they frequently and unexpectedly put their hands and other things in their mouths while playing.

Did you see a more vivid image when you read the second example?

You can do harm with words that claim too much. The first example below is actually less persuasive than the second:

> It is obvious, therefore, that the defendant clearly understood the consequences of his acts.

> Therefore, the defendant understood the consequences of his acts.

In the first example, "It is obvious" and "clearly" supply no extra meaning. Instead, they divert the reader's attention from the message of the sentence. Judges assume that expressions like these are used to cover up a lack of logical proof.

Your references to the parties should be clear to the reader, but the way you refer to the parties can also advance your theory. For example, suppose Eli Goslin, the client in the office memo in Appendix C, were to sue Herbert Skeffington. (The office memo explains why.) In a later motion memorandum or appellate brief, the plaintiffs lawyer would refer to his client with dignity as "Mr. Goslin." Even if his neighbors might know him to treat people and pets vilely and to have vicious opinions that offend all decent-minded folk, he is a sympathetic figure in litigation as long as the court knows him to be "Mr. Goslin," the elderly widower who only wants to live out his last days in his own home. And Goslin's lawyer might frequently refer to Herbert Skeffington as "the nephew" or "the defendant," with no dignity other than his role as nephew and with no personality other than what he reveals about himself through the way he treats his uncle. While he is the shadowy "nephew," it is easier to think him capable of deceit, greed, and cold-bloodedness. But if the judge were to think of him as Mr. Skeffington — and to think of the other interlopers as Mr. Skeffington's wife Amelia and their children Wendy and Tom, aged respectively eight and four — it is a little harder to think ill of them.

It can work the opposite way, too. In the motion memo in Appendix F, the plaintiff's lawyer always refers to the defendant with dignity as "Mr. Raucher." The defendant's conduct is criticized, but he is never demeaned personally. And this refusal to demean can make his conduct look more starkly unacceptable because the issue is cleanly what he did and not him. That is not so in Goslin's situation: the issue there really is the nephew and his character.

But your first obligation when referring to parties is to do so in a way the court will understand. In general, you have three ways: by name ("Trans-Continental Airlines"), generically by the party's out-of-court role ("the airline"), or by the party's in-court role ("the defendant").

Once the reader knows who has sued whom, the clearest references are by name. (Most modern courts write their own opinions that way.) If you represent a person in conflict with a large organization, it might help humanize your client to use the client's name while referring to the opponent generically ("Ms. DiMateo asked the airline for an earlier flight"), but only after introducing the organization by name and telling the reader that you will be using a generic designation: "Ms. DiMateo sued Trans-Continental

Airlines ('the airline') afterf. . . ." But if Trans-Continental has a terrible reputation for service, its name might do more than a generic reference to create sympathy for your client.

In trial courts, the parties' in-court roles ("plaintiff," "defendant") are usually clear to the reader but lifeless. Appellate courts, on the other hand, will become confused if you refer to the parties as "the appellant" or "the appellee," and many prohibit it, preferring instead references to the parties' roles in the trial court ("plaintiff," "defendant") or their out-of-court roles ("the taxpayer," "the employee").[12]

12. Confront openly your weaknesses and your adversary's strengths. Hiding from problems will not make them go away in the night. You have to confront and defeat them. "Be truthful in exposing . . . the difficulties in your case," an appellate judge has written. "Tell us what they are and how you expect to deal with them."[13] If you do not do that, the court will assume that you have no arguments worth making on the subject.

Ask yourself four questions. First, which cases and statutes favor your adversary? Second, which facts work to your adversary's advantage? Third, what are your adversary's strongest arguments? (Your adversary *does* have strong arguments; otherwise, the case would not be worth litigating.) And fourth, what will your adversary say to fight against your arguments? The answers to these questions identify your adversary's strengths. After you know what those strengths are, read §25.5 to find out what to do about them.

13. Enhance your credibility through careful editing and through the appearance of the memorandum or brief. Help the judge to trust you. Understandably, judges do not trust easily. Their decisions are important ones, and you will always face at least one opposing attorney with another theory to sell. A judge will more readily trust you if you appear to be careful, thorough, and professional. For that reason, a document is more persuasive if its appearance is flawless.

A well-written memo or brief can earn warm gratitude and respect from a judge.[14] Where one side in a case has produced fine writing and the other has done the opposite, a court can draw invidious comparisons and be influenced accordingly:

> If counsel for Phipps had asked us to direct dismissal of the complaint, we
> might well have done so, as we could do even [now] in the absence of such a

12. *See, e.g.*, Rule 28(d) of the Federal Rules of Appellate Procedure.

13. Roger J. Miner, *Twenty-five "Dos" for Appellate Brief Writers*, 3 Scribes J. Leg. Writing 19, 24 (1992).

14. "We express our appreciation to Ellen M. Burgraff, Esq., . . . for her excellent brief and argument in this case." *Swanger v. Zimmerman*, 750 F.2d 291, 294 n. 3 (3d Cir. 1984). "As Mr. Nevin [appellant's lawyer] says in his excellent brief . . ."*United States v. Moore*, 109 F.3d 1456, 1465 (9th Cir. 1997). "The court expresses its appreciation to appellant's counsel for submitting excellent briefs on this appeal." *Johnson v. Stark*, 717 F.2d 1550, 1551 n. 2 (8th Cir. 1983). "We commend assigned counsel for his excellent briefs and argument." *United States v. 4492 South Livonia Rd.*, 889 F.2d 1258, 1271 (2d Cir. 1989).

request. [Citations omitted.] However, in light of counsel's inadequate and intemperate brief, . . . we shall not do so. In contrast, we compliment counsel for Mrs. Lopez on her excellent and helpful brief. . . .[15]

Beginners in law often underestimate how much bad writing upsets judges. To give you a flavor of how strongly judges feel about this, read the explanatory parentheticals in the footnote attached to this sentence.[16]

Edit out every form of intellectual sloppiness: inaccuracies; imprecision; incorrectly used terms of art; errors with citations and other matters of format and layout; mistakes with the English language, its spelling and punctuation; typographical errors; and empty remarks that do not advance the argument (such as rhetorical questions and irrelevant histories of the law). Any of those would suggest a lawyer who cannot be relied on — and judges will be quick to draw that inference.

14. Make it easy for the judge to rule in your favor. "The first rule of advocacy is to make your argument understandable."[17] Judges are overburdened with so many cases that you must assume a certain amount of fatigue. If a memorandum or brief is frustrating, it will be ignored. Instead, submit a document that is easy to read and use. Think about the problems a judge would have with the document, and solve them before submission. Not only should the writing be clear, concise, and focused sharply on the issue at hand, but the type should be easy to read; margins should be large enough that each page does not look oppressively dense; and headings should look like headings (and not like part of the text). A visually inviting document is more likely to be read with care.

---

15. *Lopez v. Henry Phipps Plaza South, Inc.*, 498 F.2d 937, 946 n. 8 (2d Cir. 1974).

16. The following are only a few of the many cases in which judges have embarrassed or punished lawyers for poor writing or violating court rules on briefs or memoranda: *Kano v. National Consumer Coop. Bank*, 22 F.3d 899, 899 (9th Cir. 1994) (ordering a lawyer to pay sanctions of $1,500 for violating page limit, double-spacing, and typeface rules); *DCD Programs, Ltd. v. Leighton*, 846 F.2d 526, 528 (9th Cir. 1988) (suspending a lawyer for misrepresenting the record below); *Jorgenson v. Volusia County*, 846 F.2d 1350, 1351 (11th Cir. 1988) (affirming the district court's punishing lawyer "for failing to cite adverse, controlling precedent"); *Gardner v. Investors Diversified Capital, Inc.*, 805 F. Supp. 874, 875 (D. Colo. 1992) ("The amended complaint . . . is replete with misspellings, grammatical aberrations, non sequiturs. . . ."); *P. M. F. Services, Inc. v. Grady*, 681 F. Supp. 549, 550-51 n. 1 (N.D. Ill. 1988) ("With callous disregard for the reader, plaintiff's counsel" refers to the parties in confusing ways and "uses possessives without apostrophes, leaving the reader to guess whether he intends a singular or plural possessive, etc. Such sloppy pleading and briefing are inexcusable"); *Green v. Green*, 261 Cal. Rptr. 294, 302 n. 11 (Cal. App. 1st Dist. 1989) (ordering appellant to pay appellee's attorney's fees in part because of "the slap-dash quality of [his] briefs"); *In re Hawkins*, 502 N.W.2d 770, 770-72 (Minn. 1993) (publicly reprimanding lawyer and ordering him to attend remedial instruction because of, among other things, "his repeated filing of documents rendered unintelligible by numerous spelling, grammatical, and typographical errors"); *Slater v. Gallman*, 339 N.E.2d 863, 865 (N.Y. 1975) (imposing costs on appellant because of a verbose and unfocused brief); *Frazier v. Columbus Bd. of Educ.*, 638 N.E.2d 581, 582 (Ohio 1994) (dismissing appeal because appellant's jurisdictional memo exceeded page limit).

17. *American Iron & Steel Institute v. Environmental Protection Agency*, 115 F.3d 990 (D.C. Cir. 1997).

§25.4   *Argumentation Ethics*

The rules of professional ethics place limits on what you are permitted to do in argument.

First and most basically, a lawyer is forbidden to "[k]nowingly make a false statement of law or fact" to a court.[1] The whole system of adjudication would break down if lawyers did not speak honestly to courts.

Second, a lawyer is required to inform a court of "legal authority *in the controlling jurisdiction* known to the lawyer to be *directly adverse* to the position of the [lawyer's] client and not disclosed by opposing counsel."[2] The system of adjudication would suffer immeasurably if courts could not depend on lawyers to give a full account of controlling law. (Section 25.5 explores ways to comply with this requirement while least damaging your case.)

Third, a lawyer is not permitted to advance a theory or argument that is "frivolous" except that a lawyer may make a "good faith argument for an extension, modification or reversal of existing law."[3] In a legal system like ours, where "the law is not always clear and never is static," the rules of ethics permit a lawyer to advance theories and arguments that take advantage "of the law's ambiguities and potential for change."[4] But a frivolous theory or argument—one that stands little chance of being adopted by a court—is unfair to courts and to opposing parties because it wastes their time, effort, and resources.

Separate court rules—procedural, rather than ethical in nature—also punish lawyers who make frivolous arguments. In federal trial courts, for example, every "written motion, or other paper" must be signed by an attorney, whose signature certifies "that to the best of the [signer's] knowledge, information, and belief, formed after inquiry reasonable under the circumstances . . . the claims, defenses, and other legal contentions therein are warranted by existing law or by a nonfrivolous argument for the extension, modification, or reversal of existing law or the establishment of new law."[5] Where that standard is violated, the court has the power to impose monetary fines on the offending lawyer.[6] Similar rules govern in appellate courts.[7]

---

§25.4   1. Rule 3.3(a)(1) of the Model Rules of Professional Conduct.

2. Rule 3.3(a)(2) of the Model Rules of Professional Conduct.

3. Rule 3.1 of the Model Rules of Professional Conduct.

4. Comment to Rule 3.1 of the Model Rules of Professional Conduct.

5. Fed. R. Civ. P. 11.

6. *Id.*

7. For example: "If a court of appeals determines that an appeal is frivolous, it may . . . award just damages and single or double costs to the appellee." Fed. R. App. P. 38.

§25.5   How to Handle Adverse Authority and Arguments

Adverse authority will not go away just because you ignore it: if the court does not find it, opposing counsel probably will. There are, in fact, a number of reasons for you to address adverse authority. First, as you have just read, the ethical rules require it. Second, a lawyer who ignores adverse authority is seen by courts as unreliable and unpersuasive, while a lawyer who speaks with candor is more easily trusted and respected by the bench. Third, a lawyer who ignores adverse authority throws away the opportunity — often the only opportunity — to give the court reasons for not following it. The first reason applies only to authority within "the controlling jurisdiction," but the others apply to any adverse authority that can be predicted to influence the court, even precedent from other jurisdictions.

If the authority is a statute, court rule, or administrative regulation, you must show that the provision was not intended to govern the controversy, or that it was intended to govern it but without harm to your client. Although it may seem tempting to argue that a statute you do not like is unconstitutional, courts rarely sustain such attacks. In fact, if a statute or similar provision is susceptible to more than one meaning, courts are obliged to choose one that would not violate a controlling constitution. You should frontally attack a statute only if there is significant doubt — shared by respected lawyers — about its validity.

If the adverse authority is precedent, consider distinguishing it, focusing on significant — and not merely coincidental — differences between the precedent and your case. Be careful. The differences on which you rely should be important enough to impress a skeptical judge. Hypertechnical discrepancies and minor factual variations will not persuade because they seem arbitrary rather than a basis for a just decision. Another approach might be to reconcile the precedent with your case, showing that — although the precedent seems superficially adverse — its underlying policy would actually be furthered by the ruling you want from the court. Still another approach is to attack the precedent head-on, challenging its validity on the grounds that it is poorly reasoned or that changes in society or in public policy have made it unworkable. Although the doctrine of stare decisis does not absolutely forbid the overruling of precedent, a frontal attack on mandatory case law is nearly always an uphill fight, to be attempted only when there is very serious doubt — again shared by at least some respected lawyers — about the precedent's viability. In general, do not ask a court to overrule mandatory authority if you can win through distinguishing, reconciliation, or some other skill of precedent analysis. Judges simply prefer distinguishing and reconciling precedent to overruling it. But things are different where local law has a gap and where the challenged authority is not mandatory: if a judge must choose between competing out-of-state rules, he or she will not be able to decide without rejecting at least some precedent as ill-founded.

With both precedent and statutes, you might consider taking more than one approach, arguing in the alternative—but only if neither alternative would weaken the persuasive force of the other. It is not illogical, for example, to argue, first, that a statute was not intended to govern the facts before the court and, alternatively, that, if the statute is interpreted otherwise, it should be held unconstitutional. (For an example, see the brief in Appendix G.) It is illogical, however, to argue, first, that the statute was not intended to govern the facts and, alternatively, that it should be construed to provide a benefit to the client.

Attack an opposing argument if it has been made by your adversary, or if there is a reasonable possibility that the court might think of it and be persuaded by it: Otherwise, the court will assume that you have no defense to such an argument. But make your own arguments first. You will win more easily if the court's dominant impression is that you deserve to win, rather than that your adversary deserves to lose. A defensive tone can undermine an otherwise worthwhile argument. And your theory will be more easily understood if you argue it before you attack opposing arguments.

If you are responding to a memorandum or brief that your adversary has already propounded,[1] you know most of the arguments that threaten you because they will appear in the document to which you are responding. The court might itself think up other arguments not mentioned by your adversary. Even if an argument has not been mentioned by your adversary, attack it if it has a reasonable chance of occurring to and persuading the court. (In nonresponsive writing, where you will not see your adversary's writing before submitting your own, use this criterion for all opposing arguments.)

How much emphasis should you give to an attack on an adverse argument or authority? Give it as much emphasis as necessary to convince the judge not to rule against you. Little treatment is necessary if the point is minor and if the argument or authority is easily rebutted. You will, of course, need to say more if the point is more significant or if your counter-analysis is more complex. You cannot reduce the force of adverse arguments and authorities by giving them minimal treatment in your own writing: they have lives and voices of their own.

Beginners often have difficulty writing the transition and thesis sentences that introduce attacks on opposing arguments. In responsive writing, it is enough to refer to what opposing counsel has said and then to get on with the counter-argument. Here are some examples:

> The plaintiff misconstrues § 401(d)(1). Four other circuits have already decided that § 401(d)(1) provides for X and not, as the plaintiff contends, for Y. [*Follow with an analysis of the circuit cases.*]

---

§25.5 1. The attorney going forward—the movant in a trial court or the appellant on appeal—submits a memorandum or brief. Then the opposing attorney submits an answering memorandum or brief. The first attorney may complete the exchange with a reply memorandum or brief. This is called *responsive* writing. In some situations—usually in trial courts—the attorneys submit their documents simultaneously each without having seen the other's writing. Most law school persuasive writing assignments are *non*responsive.

> No appellate court has held to the contrary, and the few district court decisions cited to by the plaintiff are all distinguishable. [*Follow with an analysis of the district court cases.*]

> The legislative history also demonstrates that Congress intended to provide for X and not for Y. [*Follow with an analysis of the legislative history.*]

These opening sentences are written so that opposing counsel's contention is surrounded by the writer's counter-contention and the beginning of the counter-contention's proof. The effect is to argue affirmatively and not defensively. This is much weaker:

> The plaintiff has argued that § 401(d)(1) provides for Y, but . . .

In nonresponsive situations—where you suspect but do not actually know which arguments your adversary will make—begin simply by denying the contention while emphasizing your counter-contention:

> Section 401(d)(1) provides for X and not for Y.

The following sounds defensive and almost silly:

> Opposing counsel might argue that § 401(d)(1) provides for Y, but . . .

Opposing counsel might never argue it, but it may occur to the judge or to the judge's law clerk.

Both in responsive and in nonresponsive writing, a dependent clause can be useful in thesis and transition sentences:

> Although the House Judiciary Committee report states that its bill would have provided for Y, § 401(d)(1) more closely tracks the bill drafted in the Senate Judiciary Committee. Both that committee's report and the conference committee report flatly state that § 401(d)(1) provides for X.

Be careful, however, not to use a dependent clause to make a relatively minor problem look like a major one. For example, compare

> Although a few district courts have held that § 401(d)(1) provides for Y, every circuit that has faced the question has held the contrary.

with

> Every circuit that has faced the question has held that § 401(d)(1) provides for X. [*Analysis of circuit cases.*] The few district court cases to the contrary are distinguishable.

Exercise I.   The Shoelaces

Go back to the shoelace arguments on pages 306-307. Imagine that you are a member of Congress and will have to vote on this matter soon. You have to choose between these two sets of arguments. Does one of them persuade you? Why? Does one (or both) leave holes that bother you—and therefore make you hesitate? If the answer to that question is yes, why? What could fill the gap? Why does the gap exist?

Exercise II.   The Painter and the Preschool

Remember that a judge begins to take sides if she or he can visualize real people doing real things to each other. In the memorandum in Appendix F, how and where are the mental images created? Find the passages that put them into your mind. What did the writer do to help you see them?

26 Handling the Procedural Posture

§26.1 Why Procedural Postures Matter

The procedural posture is the procedural event or events—such as a motion—that places an issue before the court. For example, if you were asked to give the procedural posture in the trial court in *Roberson v. Rochester Folding Box Co.* (on page 25), a reasonable answer might begin like this: "The defendants demurred to the complaint, in essence asking that it be dismissed."

In trial courts, an attorney requests a judicial order by making a motion for it, and most procedural postures are defined in terms of the motion that has been made. Each type of motion is governed by rules that govern how the motion is to be decided. If you move for summary judgment, for example, you must satisfy the test for summary judgment, and your arguments ought to be designed to satisfy that test.

In a motion memorandum or an appellate brief, the procedural posture governs the arguments you can make. It also governs how you use and describe facts. That is because courts see the facts through filters that differ from one posture to another.

§26.2 Types of Procedural Postures

Trial court motions fall into four very generalized categories: (1) motions that challenge the quality of an adversary's allegations (in a pleading);

329

(2) other motions that challenge the manner in which the litigation began; (3) motions that challenge the quality of a party's evidence; and (4) a large catch-all category of miscellaneous case management motions. When a trial court's decision is appealed, the case moves into yet another procedural posture, where the trial judge's decision is evaluated according to a standard of review.

Rules governing how motions are decided may differ from state to state. Check the rules that govern the court for which you are writing a memorandum or brief, as well as the precedent interpreting those rules. That takes time and thought in the library. Guessing about local rules frequently leads to grief.

§26.2.1 Motions Challenging the Quality of a Party's Allegations

The *burden of pleading* is a party's obligation to allege, in its pleading, facts that, if proven, would entitle the party to the judgment it seeks. In a civil case, the plaintiff's complaint must allege facts that, if proven, would constitute a cause of action. If a defendant pleads a counterclaim or an affirmative defense in the answer, that answer must allege facts that, if proven, would substantiate a counterclaim or affirmative defense. And in a criminal case, the government's indictment or information must allege facts that, if proven, would be a crime.[1]

In a civil action, a defendant can, before answering a complaint, move to dismiss it for failure to state a cause of action. Because this motion tests the sufficiency of allegations (and nothing more), the record is limited to the four corners of the complaint. The question is not whether either party has proved anything. Instead, the court assumes — for the purpose of the motion only — that the factual allegations in the complaint can be proven, and the court then decides whether, if proven, those allegations would amount to a cause of action. If the court concludes that they could not, it strikes the cause of action from the pleading. If the court strikes all the causes of action pleaded in a complaint, the complaint itself is dismissed and the litigation is terminated unless the plaintiff can serve and file an amended complaint with additional or reformulated allegations that would survive a motion to dismiss.

Similarly, a plaintiff can move to dismiss a counterclaim or an affirmative defense pleaded in the defendant's answer. And in a criminal case a defendant can move to dismiss one or more counts in the indictment or information, or the entire indictment or information.

Because, at this stage in litigation, no evidence has been submitted, lawyers do not describe the "facts" alleged in the pleadings as things that actually happened. Until it receives evidence later in the case, the court has

---

§26.2 1. Criminal defendants do not file written answers to indictments or informations. Criminal defendants cannot constitutionally be required to make statements about the events at issue. Instead, a criminal defendant pleads only "guilty" or "not guilty," orally in court and without saying more.

no idea whether the alleged "facts" happened, and the "facts" therefore are described purely as allegations:

> Although the plaintiff has alleged that the defendant struck him from behind with a stick, he has not alleged that the defendant intended to cause him injury.

In this procedural posture, you cannot accurately write the following:

> Although the defendant struck the plaintiff from behind with a stick, the defendant did not intend to cause the plaintiff injury.

We will find out later—after evidence has been produced—whether the defendant struck the plaintiff or intended to cause injury.

There is an exception to all this. If the defendant admits, in the answer, an allegation made in the complaint, the allegation is considered established without need of evidence. The event alleged and admitted might be described as a fact ("The defendant struck the plaintiff") because the admission makes it as good as proved. Or it might be described as a conceded allegation ("The defendant admits that he struck the plaintiff").

§26.2.2 Motions Challenging Other Aspects of the Way in Which the Litigation Began

A defendant might move to dismiss an action on the ground that the court lacks jurisdiction over the subject matter, or that it lacks personal jurisdiction over the defendant, or that venue is improper, or that the summons did not include all the information required, or that it was improperly served, or that some persons who must be made parties have not been,[2] and so on.

Like motions challenging the quality of allegations, these seek dismissal of the action, and they are made after the plaintiff serves a summons and complaint and before the defendant serves an answer.[3] (Actually, an answer would be served only if the motion is denied.) But these motions are different in one important respect: they are not limited to the contents of the complaint. In fact, the contents of the complaint might be irrelevant to the motion. If the defendant asserts that the summons was improperly served, for example, the court would ignore the contents of the complaint and would instead hear testimony from the server and from the defendant about how the summons was delivered to the defendant.

---

2. See Rule 12(b)(1)-(5) and (7) of the Federal Rules of Civil Procedure.
3. Several of them are waived unless made during that period. *See, e.g.,* Rule 12(b) and (h) of the Federal Rules of Civil Procedure.

§26.2.3 Motions Challenging the Quality of a Party's Evidence

These include (1) motions for summary judgment; (2) motions for directed verdict (or in federal courts, motions for judgment as a matter of law); and (3) motions for judgment notwithstanding the verdict (in federal courts, renewed motions for judgment as a matter of law[4]). In contrast to the motions testing allegations in pleadings, these require the court to decide whether a party has sustained a burden to produce evidence. There are also (4) motions for a new trial, which are analytically different from the other three (and therefore explained near the end of this section).

Do not confuse the *burden of production* with the *burden of persuasion*. The burden of persuasion is the obligation to persuade the trier of fact that a particular allegation ultimately is true. The burden of production (often called the burden of going forward) is the threshold obligation to satisfy the judge (even in cases where the actual trier of fact is a jury) that the party who must shoulder the burden can provide enough evidence about a particular allegation to make it worth putting the question to the trier of fact.

The law has good reasons to avoid putting an issue to a trier of fact unless the party with the burden of production has at least a threshold quantum of evidence. First, putting a question to a trier of fact, in a trial or hearing, is expensive and time-consuming. Second, it might also be unnecessary. The only purpose of a trial is to ascertain the facts from conflicting evidence. If the evidence is not really in conflict, the court can adjudicate without a trial. Third, there are certain risks where the trier of fact is a jury. Although the right to trial by jury is one of the foundations of common law procedure — treasured as a vehicle for limiting the authority of government — jurors with no training in law are so capable of misunderstandings that many of the rules of evidence and procedure are designed to limit what juries can see, hear, and decide.

Although the difference between a burden of persuasion and a burden of production may seem technical, it is important in practice and in practical legal writing. A beginner may be confused not only because the two burdens at first seem similar, but also because the term *burden of proof* is occasionally but confusingly applied to both burdens collectively. You will be able to differentiate between them, however, if you remember some of the basic concepts of each burden.

You already know all of the following: when a civil case is tried, the plaintiff has the burden of persuading the fact finder of the existence of facts that substantiate each element of a cause of action pleaded in the complaint. The defendant can try to prevent the plaintiff from carrying

---

4. In federal courts since 1991, motions for directed verdict have been known as motions for judgment as a matter of law, and motions for judgment notwithstanding the verdict have been known as renewed motions for judgment as a matter of law. See Rule 50 of the Federal Rules of Civil Procedure. Despite the change of terminology, these motions continue to function just as they did when they were called by their traditional names. In state courts, they will still be known by the traditional names unless the state amends its rules to conform with the federal practice.

that burden, or the defendant can raise one or more affirmative defenses, or the defendant can do both. A defendant who pleads an affirmative defense assumes the burden of persuading the fact finder of the existence of facts that substantiate each element of that defense. In criminal cases the prosecution must carry a burden of persuasion as to every element of the crime, and the defendant assumes a similar burden for each element of any asserted affirmative defense. The trier of fact determines whether these burdens have been carried, and the trier does so only at the end of the trial. The trier of fact should find against a defendant if the plaintiff or prosecution has carried its burden of persuasion and if the defendant has not done so with an affirmative defense. But the trier of fact should find for a defendant if the defendant has substantiated an affirmative defense, even if the plaintiff or prosecution has carried all its burdens. In any event, if the trier of fact is a jury, the result is a verdict, and if the trier is a judge, the result is the judge's findings of fact.

The concept that may now seem odd to you is that the parties might not even be allowed to try to carry these burdens of persuasion unless they have already shown that they can satisfy their burdens of production. The burden of production requires the party shouldering it to come forward with a minimum, threshold quantum of evidence, defined by the relevant rules of procedure and by the case law interpreting those rules. The question of whether a party has carried a burden of production is generally put to a judge through one of the three motions that challenge the quality of the other party's evidence.

Motions for summary judgment,[5] for directed verdict,[6] and for judgment notwithstanding the verdict[7] exist so that parties, lawyers, and judges can avoid, where possible and appropriate, the effort and expense of trial, as well as the perils of juries. A motion for summary judgment can be made before trial. A motion for a directed verdict can be made during trial, after the adversary has rested (finished presenting evidence) and before the jury has begun to deliberate. And a motion for judgment notwithstanding the verdict is made — as its name suggests — after the jury has returned a verdict. In criminal cases, there are no summary judgments, and only the defendant can move for a directed verdict or for judgment notwithstanding the verdict.

Although these motions are governed by different procedural rules, all three are decided according to approximately the same logic: the motion should be granted if the opposing party has failed to satisfy a burden of production and if the law is such that the movant is entitled to a favorable judgment.

Measuring whether a party has satisfied a burden of production requires taking into account the amount of evidence that would be required at trial to carry a burden of persuasion. In the overwhelming majority of civil

---

5. See Rule 56 of the Federal Rules of Civil Procedure.
6. See Rule 50(a) of the Federal Rules of Civil Procedure (motion for judgment as a matter of law).
7. See Rule 50(b) of the Federal Rules of Civil Procedure (renewed motion for judgment as a matter of law).

actions, the party charged with a burden of persuasion must satisfy it by a *preponderance of the evidence:* by evidence showing more likely than not that the alleged facts are true. A few burdens of persuasion are heavier and must be carried by *clear and convincing evidence.* And in criminal cases, the prosecution must prove guilt *beyond a reasonable doubt,* which is the heaviest burden known to the law.

For example, if a party must at trial prove a fact by clear and convincing evidence, that party will lose one of these motions unless she or he can produce (in response to a summary judgment motion) or has already produced (at trial before one of the other motions is made) evidence that would give a reasonable jury a basis for deciding that the fact has been proved by clear and convincing evidence. The burden of production would be less onerous in a case where the burden of persuasion is a preponderance of the evidence. And it would be more onerous in a case where the burden of persuasion is proof beyond a reasonable doubt.

Although motions for summary judgment occur often in civil practice, they may at first perplex you. The judgment is "summary" because there is no trial. The evidence is not put before the court through testimony in a courtroom, but instead through the parties' written submissions, which can include affidavits, deposition transcripts, exhibits, and answers to interrogatories. In virtually every American jurisdiction, the moving party is entitled to summary judgment if none of the material facts are genuinely disputed and if that party is entitled to judgment as a matter of law.[8]

Be careful: although this seems like a simple, two-element test, it has some deceptive subtleties. First, a fact is not material merely because it is logically connected to the controversy. A fact is material in this sense only if it is truly determinative or, put another way, capable "of *altering the outcome* of the litigation."[9]

Second, a fact is not genuinely disputed just because the parties have different opinions about it. On a motion for summary judgment, an alleged fact is genuinely at issue only if the evidence would support a decision for either party. If a reasonable jury could go one way or the other, then the case deserves a trial and deliberation by a trier of fact, even if we could make a good prediction about what the trier of fact would decide. Notice the difference: for summary judgment, it does not matter whether the verdict might be predictable; what matters is whether it is possible for rational jurors to disagree with each other about how to interpret the evidence.

Third, most motions for summary judgment are made by defendants, challenging plaintiffs to show that they have sufficient evidence to carry the plaintiffs burden of producing evidence at trial. In federal courts and in most states, a plaintiff who does not have evidence to do that will lose the motion and the case (which is right because that plaintiff would be doomed at trial anyway). Thus, it is really the *non*moving party who must demonstrate a genuine dispute about a material fact.[10] Some states do not follow

8. *See, e.g.,* Rule 56 of the Federal Rules of Civil Procedure.

9. *Rivera-Muriente v. Agosto-Alicea,* 959 F.2d 349, 352 (1st Cir. 1992).

10. *See Celotex Corp. v. Catrett,* 477 U.S. 317 (1986); *Anderson v. Liberty Lobby, Inc.,* 477 U.S. 242 (1986); *Matsushita Elec. Industrial Co. v. Zenith Radio Corp.,* 475 U.S. 574 (1986).

this principle. They instead require the moving party (usually the defendant) to prove that each material fact is not disputed. You can rarely figure out the jurisdiction's practice on this point by reading its rules of procedure. (It would not be clear from reading Rule 56 of the Federal Rules of Civil Procedure, for example.) You need to look carefully at the jurisdiction's recent cases on summary judgment.

Finally, the second element of the test for summary judgment incorporates the relevant substantive rules at issue — primarily the rules defining the cause of action and any affirmative defenses — because the only way a court can determine whether a party is entitled to judgment as a matter of law is to apply the substantive rules that define the parties' rights and obligations. If you move for summary judgment in a products liability case, the second element incorporates every part of the law of products liability that happens to be relevant to your case.

Unlike the three motions just described, the motion for a new trial does not test whether a party has carried a burden of production. A new trial can be granted on two kinds of grounds: (1) the jury's verdict is seriously tainted through procedural faults such as erroneously admitted evidence or inaccurate jury instructions, or (2) the verdict was against the overwhelming weight of the evidence. The first category obviously does not test the quality of a party's evidence. The second does but by examining the extent to which a burden of persuasion (rather than a burden of production) has been carried. A new trial is not granted merely because the judge would have come to a different verdict if she or he had been the trier of fact. But it can be granted if the overwhelming weight of the evidence is on one side of the case and the jury returned a verdict for the other side.

In any of these procedural postures, a description of the facts is framed in terms of the evidence submitted:

> The plaintiff testified that he was struck in the back and that the defendant was the only person who was behind him at the time. The defendant does not deny that he struck the plaintiff or that he used a stick to do it. Aside from the stick, the only evidence that might conceivably show that the defendant intended to cause injury is a letter, dated two days before the incident, in which the defendant complained that the plaintiff "had better keep his cattle off my land or I'll have to do something."

Notice how each fact is connected with evidence so that the reader can judge whether the evidence really proves it. That is because the provability of facts is at issue. In these procedural postures, the only facts that can accurately be stated without any reference to evidence are those that are "true" because the parties do not disagree about them.

§26.2.4 Miscellaneous Case Management Motions

These are housekeeping motions, used to manage the progress of litigation, such as motions in discovery; motions for preliminary injunctions; and
suppression motions in criminal cases. What makes these motions different
from the ones you have just read about is that the granting of a management
motion does not terminate the litigation; instead, management motions
regulate the litigation's progress. Burdens of production and burdens of
persuasion are so effective at helping a court structure its decision-making
that they are used not just to award judgments, but also to decide many of
these motions as well.

For example, before trial, a criminal defendant who gave the police a
statement might move to suppress it, arguing that the police wrongfully
obtained the statement by failing to inform him of his constitutional
right to remain silent. If the court grants the motion, the statement
cannot be used as evidence at trial. At or before the hearing on the
motion, the defendant must carry a burden of production by submitting
at least some evidence that he made a statement. That is a relatively
easy burden for the defendant to satisfy, especially because the prosecution is not likely to deny it. Once the burden of production has been
met, however, the prosecution must shoulder a much heavier one: the
prosecution must show beyond a reasonable doubt that the defendant
was warned, in language he could understand, that he need not say anything to the police, that anything he says may be held against him, that
he has a right to have an attorney present during interrogation, and that
if he cannot pay for an attorney, one would be appointed for him at
government expense.[11]

Because these miscellaneous motions are generally decided on the basis
of evidence, the facts are described in the same way as with motions for
summary judgment, for directed verdict, and for judgment notwithstanding
the verdict.

§26.2.5 Appeal

On appeal, a standard of review is applied to the decision below. Standards of review are explained in §33.3.

§26.3 *Writing in a Procedural Posture*

(You will understand this section more easily if you read Appendix F
first.)

---

11. *See Miranda v. Arizona*, 384 U.S. 436 (1966).

Because most of a legal education is spent studying the substantive law of torts, property, and so on, you might tend to view issues in the abstract ("should the plaintiff win?"). But judges see issues in terms of the motion context in which issues are raised.

If, for example, a plaintiff moves for summary judgment, you are wrong if you define the issue as whether the plaintiff should win the case. The issues the judge will see are whether there is a material dispute of fact and whether the plaintiff is entitled to judgment as a matter of law (the test for summary judgment). Compare the following Questions Presented:

> Is a painting contractor negligent where he power-sands large amounts of lead paint from the exterior of a building and thus spreads lead paint debris over most of an adjacent preschool, which is then closed and deleaded at great expense because of the overwhelming scientific evidence that lead is toxic?

> Is a painting contractor negligent *as a matter of law where it is undisputed* that he power-sanded large amounts of lead paint from the exterior of a building and thus spread lead paint debris over most of an adjacent preschool, which was then closed and deleaded at great expense because of the overwhelming scientific evidence that lead is toxic?

The italicized words in the second example are not throw-away jargon. They reflect the test for summary judgment and are the core of the decision the court must make. If any of the itemized facts is disputed, the first element of the test for summary judgment is not satisfied. If on those undisputed facts, the painter's negligence is not so clear as to be a matter of law, the second element is not satisfied. (For a reason why it might not be that clear, see page 465.)

Similarly, on appeal the question is not whether the appellant should have won in the trial court, but instead whether the trial court's ruling was error as defined by the applicable standard of review.[1]

Because the procedural posture and the rules governing it control the way the judge will make the decision, you must show the judge how to decide within those procedural rules. How can you do that in writing?

First, remember that in a motion or appeal the threshold rule is *not* the rule of substantive law that provides the remedy sued for. The threshold rules are procedural. In a trial court, the threshold rules are the rules that govern how the motion is to be decided. On appeal, the threshold rules are the ones that govern the trial court's decision plus the appellate court's standard of review.

For example, the memorandum in Appendix F has been submitted by Tulta Preschool, Inc., in support of a motion for a summary judgment. In deciding the motion, the court will evaluate the record in terms of the elements of the test for summary judgment: whether there is a genuine

---

§26.3   1. See §33.3.

dispute about a material fact and whether on the undisputed facts the movant is entitled to judgment as a matter of law. That test is invoked very early in Tulta Preschool's Argument.

Second, some but not many procedural tests contain an element that incorporates the underlying substantive rules on which the litigation as a whole is based (causes of action, affirmative defenses, and so on). In the test for a summary judgment, that happens through the element requiring entitlement to judgment as a matter of law.[2] In the test for a preliminary injunction, it is done through the element requiring likelihood of success on the merits. In these situations, the court makes a procedural decision, but part of that decision is substantive.

Third, organize your paradigm variations around the procedural test. If the procedural test incorporates a substantive test, the substantive test operates as a sub-rule. To see how that is done, read carefully the Argument in Appendix F, which includes several paradigmed proofs inside the organization of an umbrella paradigm. The umbrella structure — through which the entire Argument is organized — is built on the test for a summary judgment. The elements of this test are proved through a distinct paradigmed proof:

> *Umbrella paradigm:*   proof, supplied element by element (below) that Tulta Preschool is entitled to summary judgment on the question of liability

A. (first element of the test for summary judgment) paradigmed proof that "there is no genuine issue as to any material fact"

B. (second element of the test for summary judgment) paradigmed proof that "the moving party is entitled to judgment as a matter of law" on a claim for negligence:

　　1. paradigmed proof of Raucher's duty to Tulta

　　2. paradigmed proof that Raucher breached that duty

　　3. paradigmed proof that his breach caused Tulta's injury

　　4. paradigmed proof that Tulta suffered an "actual injury"

Because the second summary judgment element (entitlement to judgment as a matter of law) incorporates a rule of substantive law (the test for negligence), proof of the second summary judgment element includes separate paradigmed proofs for each element of the test for negligence. Or, looked at

2. See §26.2.3 and Appendix F.

from the opposite direction, each negligence element is proved inside a larger paradigmed proof (entitled to judgment as a matter of law), which is in turn inside yet another paradigmed proof (the test for summary judgment).

Although that may all sound complicated, it is the precise sequence of logic that a judge would go through in order to decide whether Tulta Preschool should be granted a summary judgment. The judge would have to decide whether Tulta Preschool has proved each of the elements of the test for summary judgment — including all the elements of negligence, which is incorporated into the element of entitlement to judgment as a matter of law. An argument carefully organized in this way can systematically demolish a judge's skepticism because it demonstrates, element by element, how a party has carried — or, if you are arguing the other side, failed to carry — a burden.

Finally, do not go overboard in citing to authority for the procedural test. Most procedural tests are so commonly invoked that judges know them by heart. A conclusory explanation[3] is usually sufficient for rule proof. (And that is all that was needed at the beginning of Tulta Preschool's Argument in Appendix F. Can you find the sentence and cite where it happens?) You should provide more only in two situations. The first is where authority will help you guide the court in rule application. (Can you find where that is done at Tulta Preschool's Argument?) And the second is where the parties disagree about the proper formulation of a procedural rule. That does not happen often.

§26.4 Researching to Account for Your Case's Procedural Posture

You are looking for two kinds of rules:

First, you are, of course, searching for the rules that govern the *substance* of the controversy — definitions of causes of action, crimes, affirmative defenses, and other forms of rights and obligations like the ones you have already studied in the courses on torts, property, contracts, and criminal law. This is by far the larger research task in nearly all instances. Second, you are looking for the *procedural* rules that govern how the court's decision is to be made. Some examples are

1. rules setting out the tests for granting various motions ("Summary judgment is appropriate if there is no genuine issue of material fact and if the moving party is entitled to judgment as a matter of law");
2. rules controlling how the court must evaluate the record before it on the motion to be decided ("In deciding a motion for summary judgment, the court views the evidence in the light most favorable to the party opposing the motion");

---

3. See §11.2.

3. if an appeal has been taken, the rule defining the standard of review in the appellate court ("On appeal, a grant of summary judgment is reviewed de novo").

A court evaluates the record differently for different types of motions. And the standard of review differs from one kind of appeal to another.

Much time will be saved in the library if you first identify the type of motion involved and then look in the procedural statutes and court rules and in the digests for procedural rules that govern the motion's disposition. For any given motion, you will probably find part of the procedural law in a statute or court rule and the rest in interpretive case law.

If you find the procedural rules in a procedural statute or court rule, the language may be subtle, but it will not be terribly hard to recognize. The section heading alone will usually announce that you have arrived at the right place. In case law, when a court mentions the rules governing how a motion is to be decided, it usually does so immediately after reciting the facts and immediately before beginning the legal analysis (just as it was done in Tulta Preschool's memorandum[1]). That is because the procedural rules are a threshold through which the court must pass in order to begin the analysis. This is typical of the kind of language you will find:

> A complaint should not be dismissed for failure to state a claim unless it appears beyond a doubt that plaintiffs can prove no set of facts in support of their claim which would entitle them to relief. [Citations omitted.] The allegations of plaintiffs' complaint must be assumed to be true, and further, must be construed in [the plaintiffs'] favor. [Citations omitted.] The issue is not whether plaintiffs will ultimately prevail, but rather whether they are entitled to offer evidence in support of their claims. [Citation omitted.][2]

The first sentence is the test that must be satisfied before the motion can be granted. The rest are some of the rules that govern how the court is to evaluate the record before it on this particular type of motion.

§26.4   1. See Appendix F.
2. *United States v. Aceto Agric. Chems. Corp.*, 872 F.2d 1373, 1376 (8th Cir. 1989).

27 Motion Memoranda

§27.1 Motion Memorandum Format

When a motion is made, each party submits a memorandum of law. A defendant moving for an order dismissing a complaint, for example, submits a document that might be titled "Memorandum in Support of Defendant's Motion to Dismiss." The opposing party's document might be titled "Memorandum in Opposition to Defendant's Motion to Dismiss." This chapter describes the format of a motion memorandum and the process of writing one.

Like the reader of an office memorandum, the judge (and the judge's law clerk) may look at each memorandum more than once. Depending on the judge's work habits and on the nature of the motion, at least some part of the memorandum might be read once in preparation for a hearing or oral argument on the motion, again while deciding the motion, and a third time while writing an opinion. Thus, you cannot assume that a memorandum will be read from front to back or at one sitting.

And you cannot assume that a long memorandum will be read in its entirety. To the judge, your case is one of dozens or hundreds on a docket that might be overwhelming. In an uncongested court, a trial judge has an attention span of ten to 15 minutes. In a congested one, the judge's attention span might be less than five minutes. All of this means that you have to make your point both quickly and well, or lose.

The format of a motion memo is often more flexible than that of an office memo or an appellate brief. Few court rules govern the content of motion memos, and customs among lawyers differ from one jurisdiction to the next. The following *might* be found in a motion memo, although very few memos include them all:

1. a cover page
2. a Table of Contents, if the memo is long or if you want to gain the persuasive effect of showing all the point headings and sub-headings in one place
3. a Table of Authorities — *but only if* the memo is long and many authorities have been cited
4. a Preliminary Statement, also called an Introduction or Summary or a Statement of the Case
5. *in complex and unusual situations,* a Question (or Questions) Presented, also called Issue Presented or just Issue
6. a Statement of the Case, also called Statement of Facts or just Facts
7. an Argument, broken up by point headings
8. a Conclusion
9. an indorsement (and, in some courts, the attorney's signature)

In practice, you can shape the format to suit your case and the most persuasive way to present your theory. Some motions, for example, do not lend themselves to a Question Presented, and it is often omitted. Most memoranda do not have or need a Table of Authorities. In especially short memoranda, you might omit the Table of Contents, but usually that would be a mistake because it deprives you of an opportunity to summarize your theory by putting all your point headings and sub-headings on one or two pages. (See Chapter 28.)

(The rest of this chapter is easier to follow if you look to the memorandum in Appendix F for illustration as you read the description below of each of these components.)

The **cover page** includes a caption and title, which correspond to the memorandum heading at the beginning of an office memorandum. The caption identifies the court and the parties, specifying their procedural designations (plaintiff, defendant, etc.). In a criminal case, the prosecution is called, depending on the jurisdiction, "State," "Commonwealth," "People," or "United States," and no procedural designation follows those terms in the caption. (The prosecution is not a "plaintiff.") The title identifies the memorandum and the purpose of its submission ("Memorandum in Opposition to Defendant's Motion to Dismiss").

The **Table of Contents** begins on the page after the cover page. If a **Table of Authorities** is included (and it usually is not), it appears on the first page after the Table of Contents. The tables are put together and paginated just as they would be in an appellate brief. They are explained in Chapter 32 (on appellate brief writing) because they are often omitted from law school memorandum assignments. (See pages 396-397.) Although it is optional, a Table of Contents can help you persuade by compiling all your point headings and sub-headings in one place so the reader can see a broad overview of your Argument (see Chapter 28). Some lawyers add a Table of Contents to a medium- or large-sized motion memo to gain that advantage. A Table of Authorities, however, is needed only in an exceptionally large motion memo, approaching the size of an appellate brief.

The **Preliminary Statement** or **Introduction** or **Summary** briefly sets out the case's procedural posture by identifying the parties (to the extent that is necessary); explaining the nature of the litigation; and describing the motion before the court and the relief sought through the motion. If it can be done very concisely, the Preliminary Statement might also summarize the parties' contentions, emphasizing the writer's theory of the motion. The point is to tell the judge why the matter is before the court and to define the type of decision the judge is being asked to make. That can usually be done in less than a page.

Although a persuasive **Question Presented** or **Issue** is at least superficially similar to the Issue in an office memorandum, here the Question should persuade as well as inform. A convincing Question Presented is — for the small number of words involved — one of the most difficult drafting tasks in legal writing. Chapter 30 explains how to do it. Most motion memoranda do not include a Question Presented. It is appropriate and effective in complicated or unusual situations where you want the court to understand, in a concise way, the exact issue presented by the motion to be decided. Put another way, most lawyers omit Questions Presented from a motion memo unless they can think of a good strategic reason for including it. Questions Presented do appear, however, in nearly all appellate briefs.

The **Statement of the Case** or **Statement of Facts** corresponds to the Facts in an office memorandum, but there are differences in substance and in drafting technique. Chapter 29 explains how to write a Statement of the Case.

The **Argument** corresponds to the Discussion in an office memorandum, but here the goal is to persuade as well as to explain. An Argument is organized into *points,* each of which is a single, complete, and independent ground for relief. Each point has a heading and may be divided by subheadings, all of which are reproduced verbatim in the table of contents. Chapter 28 explains how to construct point headings and sub-headings. The Argument is the most complex component of a motion memorandum, but you have already learned many of the skills required. Chapters 10-17 explain how to organize proof of a conclusion of law and use authority and facts. Additionally, you will need to know how to develop theories (Chapter 24) and arguments (Chapter 25); and how to work with a procedural posture (Chapter 26). Focus on your best arguments and your best authorities. Your reader does not have time for smaller stuff.

In a motion memorandum, the **Conclusion** is intended only to remind the reader of what you seek (or oppose), with an allusion to your theory, if that can be compressed into one or two sentences. Although a Conclusion in a persuasive document is shorter than a Conclusion in an office memorandum, it cannot persuade if it is cut to the bone. Compare the following:

Conclusion

For all these reasons, this court should preliminarily enjoin construction of the logging roads here at issue.

Conclusion

Thus, the Forest Service's authorization of these logging roads violates the National Environmental Policy Act, the Administrative Procedure Act, and the enabling legislation of the Forest Service. The
harm would be irreparable, and an injunction would promote the public interest. This court should therefore preliminarily enjoin the Forest
Service from building the roads.

The second example does a much better job of reminding the court, in just a
few sentences, of precisely what the writer wants and why it should be done.

The **indorsement,** like the signature in an office memorandum, appears
under a line reading "Respectfully submitted." The indorsement, however,
is entirely typewritten and includes the attorney's name, an indication
of which party the attorney represents, and the attorney's office address
and telephone number. In some jurisdictions, the attorney also signs the
memorandum.[1]

§27.2 Writing a Motion Memorandum

As with office memoranda, lawyers differ about which part of a
motion memorandum they draft first. But virtually every lawyer modi-
fies her or his habits somewhat from document to document, simply
because a practice that works well in one instance might not work well
in another.

Many lawyers start by writing the Preliminary Statement because it is not
hard to do and is a convenient way to get going. Then they turn to the heart
of the job, which is the Statement of the Case and the Argument.

Some lawyers write the Argument before they write the Statement of the
Case because writing the Argument shows them what to do with the facts.
Other lawyers might write the Argument and the Statement of the Case
simultaneously. Some might outline the Statement of the Case while writing
the Argument.

Some lawyers write the point headings and sub-headings before starting
to write the Argument. Others might write an outline of the Argument and
gradually convert the outline into headings and sub-headings. (Even in a
finished memorandum, the headings and sub-headings *are* an outline of the
Argument.)

§27.1   1. *See, e.g.,* Rule 11 of the Federal Rules of Civil Procedure.

The Question Presented is usually best written after the Argument and the Statement of the Case. The Question Presented compresses into a very small space ideas that are usually developed while writing the Argument and Statement.

The Conclusion, the Tables, and the indorsement are best done last. The cover page can be done any time.

While putting the memorandum through further drafts, ask yourself the questions in the checklists on the inside front and back covers.

28 Point Headings and Sub-Headings

§28.1 How Points and Headings Work

In a motion memorandum or appellate brief, the Argument is divided into points. Each point is given a heading and may be divided by sub-headings. You will understand this chapter more easily if, before reading it, you read the point headings and sub-headings in the Tables of Contents of the memorandum in Appendix F and the briefs in Appendices G and H.

A point is an independent, complete, and free-standing ground for a ruling in your favor on a Question Presented. (If you are writing a memo without a Question Presented, focus instead on the issue or issues before the court.) If only one ground would support a favorable ruling on the Question, you have only one point for that Question and only one point heading, although the point itself could be broken up into sub-headings to the extent that would help the reader. If, on the other hand, you have two or more favorable theories, each of which could stand alone as a *complete* and *independent* ground for relief, each theory is a separate point and is to be summarized in a separate heading.

How could you have more than one complete and independent reason for a ruling in your favor? Take a motion to dismiss at the commencement of an action. As they would appear in the Table of Contents, the movant's point headings might read as follows:

> I. The complaint should be dismissed
>   for failure to state a cause of
>   action.

II.   The action should be dismissed
      because the summons was improperly
      served on the defendant.

III. The action should be dismissed on
      the ground of res judicata.

VI.   The action should be dismissed on
      the ground that the plaintiff's time
      to sue has expired.

If true, any one of these should justify granting the motion. A complaint that fails to set out a cause of action should be dismissed even if properly served and even if the action is not barred by res judicata or the statute of limitations. An action should be dismissed if the summons was not properly served, even if the complaint does state a cause of action — and so on.

Sub-headings can be used to develop a point heading:

I.   **The complaint should be dismissed for fail-
      ure to state a cause of action.**

      A.   *The plaintiff claims only that the defen-
           dant School District did not "adequately"
           teach him.*

      B.   *Virtually every jurisdiction that has con-
           sidered the question has refused to recog-
           nize a tort of "educational malpractice."*

      C.   *Because an education is the result of the
           efforts of both student and teachers, a fail-
           ure to learn cannot be attributed solely to
           the school.*

      D.   *A tort of "educational malpractice" would
           disrupt the public schools.*

           1.   Scarce educational resources would be
                diverted to pay damages or insurance
                premiums.
           2.   A litigious atmosphere would interfere
                with teaching and learning.

II.   **The action should be dismissed
      because the summons was improperly served
      on the defendant.**

The numbering and lettering sequence is the same as with a formal outline:

    I. [point heading]

        A. [sub-heading]

             1. [secondary sub-heading]

             2. [secondary sub-heading]

        B. [sub-heading]

    II. [point heading]

A solitary sub-heading is inappropriate. If you find yourself with an "A" but no "B," either create a "B" or incorporate the substance of "A" into the point heading itself.

Before completing your research, you can start to outline the Argument by rough-drafting the point headings and sub-headings. In fact, your rough draft of the headings can be part of your outline.

When you set up headings and sub-headings in a Table of Contents and in an Argument, study the examples in Appendices F, G, and H for format. In the Argument (but not in the Table of Contents, where they are printed verbatim), point headings appear in bold print. In both places, all headings and sub-headings are single-spaced. In the Argument, headings and sub-headings are centered with extra margins on both sides and white space above and below. Headings and sub-headings should be obvious to a reader who is skimming. That reader does not easily notice this amid surrounding text:

I. The complaint should be dismissed for failure to state a cause of action.

But a better layout on the page has a more arresting effect:

        I. The complaint should be dismissed for failure to state a cause of action.

If you have only an inch or two left at the bottom of a page in the Argument, do not put a heading there; put it instead at the top of the next page. For the same reason that newspaper headlines do not appear at the bottom of a newspaper page, point headings and sub-headings look silly if they appear at the bottom of an Argument page without any text underneath.

§28.2   How to Evaluate Your Headings and Sub-Headings for Effectiveness

The effectiveness of your point headings and sub-headings can be judged by the following criteria:

1. When collected in the Table of Contents, the headings and sub-headings should lay out a complete and persuasive outline of your theory.
2. Each point should be an independent, complete, and freestanding ground for a ruling in your favor.
3. Headings and sub-headings should not assume information that a judge would lack when reading the Table of Contents.
4. The sub-headings should be neither too many nor too few.
5. Each heading and sub-heading should be a single sentence that can be immediately understood.
6. Each point heading should identify the ruling you want.
7. The controlling rules should be identified in the headings or sub-headings.
8. The one, two, or three most determinative facts should at least be alluded to in either the headings or sub-headings.
9. Headings and sub-headings should be forceful and argumentative.

1. When collected in the Table of Contents, the headings and sub-headings should lay out a complete and persuasive outline of your theory.   Many judges read the point headings in the Table of Contents before reading any other part of the memo or brief. The point headings are thus your opportunity to introduce and outline your theory. Although the reader would have to study the Argument to learn how the theory works, the headings—when read together in the Table of Contents—should lay out the significant steps of logic on which the theory is based, outlining a paradigm-structured argument, with rule proof and rule application and perhaps with policy arguments and counter-analyses. (Notice how that is done with the headings and sub-headings in §28.1.) If you draft the headings after you write the Argument, be sure that the headings and sub-headings present a complete and coherent picture of your theory when they are isolated in the Table of Contents. When you compile the headings and sub-headings in the Table of Contents, you may find that you have to redraft them because only then might you discover gaps or inconsistencies not apparent when the headings are scattered in the Argument.

Look at the Tables of Contents of the memorandum in Appendix F and in the briefs in Appendices G and H. Read the headings and sub-headings there as a judge would on first opening each document. From the headings, can you understand each writer's theory? Why or why not?

2. Each point should be an independent, complete, and free-standing ground for a ruling in your favor. A careless beginner might write four or five "point" headings for material that will yield only one or two genuine points. This is caused by confusing a point with a contention. Check yourself in the following way: if you have several point headings, look at each one in isolation. If the court were to believe everything you say in and under that heading, but were to believe absolutely nothing else in the Argument, would you win? If the answer is no, the "point" cannot stand on its own, and you have fewer points than you thought you did. You have a real point only if the court can make some ruling in your favor based on what is in and under that heading alone.

Beginners sometimes make the opposite error of grouping several points under one heading. This happens most often where the writer's adversary is the one charged with a burden of pleading, production, or persuasion. If the adversary must carry a burden for several elements, the failure to support any element creates a complete and independent ground for a ruling against the adversary (and therefore a separate point).

For example, in the memorandum in Appendix F, the plaintiff is entitled to summary judgment if (1) there is no genuine dispute of a material fact and (2) the plaintiff is entitled to judgment as a matter of law. The plaintiff has only one point because he must prove both these elements to win. But the defendant can win if either element is missing. If the defendant contests both elements, he will have two separate points because either of them would support a decision against the plaintiff.

3. Headings and sub-headings should not assume information that a judge would lack when reading the Table of Contents. Put yourself in the judge's position. When turning to the Table of Contents for the first time, the judge knows nothing of the case. How would you react to this heading?

> I. **The motion to quash because of the first amendment should be denied.**

Quash what? What does the First Amendment have to do with this? The following is better:

> I. **The motion to quash a deposition subpoena should be denied because the subpoena does not violate the journalist witness's first amendment right to maintain the confidentiality of his sources.**

4. The sub-headings should be neither too many nor too few. For each point, the number of sub-headings should equal the number of *significant* steps of logic inherent in the argument. For example, the

351

failure-to-state-a-cause-of-action point on page 348 depends on the following steps of logic:

- The complaint alleges only educational malpractice. Because the complaint cannot be interpreted to allege any other kind of claim, it can survive a motion to dismiss only if this state were to recognize a cause of action for educational malpractice.
- The idea of recovering for educational malpractice has been scorned by other courts.
- Such a tort is impractical because a court would not be able to determine how much of the fault was the student's and how much was the school's.
- Such a tort would damage schools by disrupting the educational process.

These are the very steps represented in the sub-headings on page 348. More sub-headings would have fragmented the argument so much that the reader would not quickly see how it fits together. Fewer sub-headings would have hidden the logic.

5. Each heading and sub-heading should be a single sentence that can be immediately understood.   What does this heading mean?

> I.   Because this state's shield law
>   provides no explicit protection for the
>   media against revealing nonconfidential
>   information or sources and because the
>   legislative history is silent, the scope of art. 9,
>   section 765 is limited to protecting only
>   confidential information or sources, and this
>   court should therefore quash a subpoena that
>   sought information that the movant,
>   a newspaper reporter, had obtained
>   through conversations in which he
>   had not promised to keep his
>   informants' identities in confidence.

A monster like this has two parents. One is the urge to put everything in the point heading and save nothing for the sub-headings. The other is simple verbosity: even more than elsewhere, conciseness is a real premium in a heading. Rewriting can produce something like this:

> I.   The deposition subpoena should be quashed
>   because the evidence sought is not confidential
>   and is therefore not protected by this state's
>   media shield law.

  A. *Art. 9, Section 765 permits a litigant to ob-*
   tain information that the media has not
   treated as confidential.

  B. *The appellant journalist concedes that he did*
   not promise confidentiality to his sources.

6. Each point heading should identify the ruling you want. A point heading fails this criterion if it leaves a judge wondering "What do you want me to do?" In a trial court, you can tell the judge what you want by identifying the order or judgment that you argue should be granted or denied. (On appeal, you can do the same thing by identifying the order or judgment appealed from and by calling it either correct or erroneous — which implies whether you want it affirmed or reversed.) To all of the following headings (from three different cases), a judge's reaction would be "What do you want from me?":

Case A: I. **The parties never formed a
    contract to merge.**

Case B: I. **The complaint states a cause of
    action.**

Case C: I. **The evidence sought is not
    protected by a privilege.**

In a trial court, the following would at least tell the judge what you want:

Case A: I. **The defendant's motion for summary
    judgment should be granted because
    the parties never formed a contract
    to merge.**

Case B: I. **The complaint states a cause of
    action and should not be dismissed.**

Case C: I. **The motion to quash should be
    denied because the evidence sought
    is not protected by a privilege.**

Later, if there were an appeal, the following headings would do the same job. Notice how each heading identifies the ruling appealed from:

Appeal A: I. **Because the parties never formed a
    contract to merge, the circuit court
    should have granted the defendant's
    motion for summary judgment.**

Appeal B: I.   **The complaint states a cause of action, and the district court erred in dismissing it.**

Appeal C: I.   **The superior court properly refused to quash a subpoena for evidence not protected by a privilege.**

Be careful about two things. First, this criterion applies only to *point* headings, not sub-headings. Second, the examples above satisfy this criterion *but not the next two.*

7. *The controlling rules should be identified in the headings or sub-headings.*   A reader who must make a decision is not influenced until the governing rules are set out. Notice how the sub-headings below do that:

Case A: I.   **The defendant's motion for summary judgment should be granted because the parties never formed a contract to merge.**

       A.   *In an action for breach of contract, a defendant is entitled to summary judgment where the plaintiff is not able to produce evidence of the existence of a contract.*

Case B: I.   **The complaint states a cause of action and should not be dismissed.**

       A.   *This state has recognized the tort of wrongful discharge.*

Case C: I.   **The motion to quash should be denied because the evidence sought is not protected by a privilege.**

       A.   *The First Amendment does not protect evidence in the possession of a journalist where the journalist did not obtain it under a promise of confidentiality and where the evidence cannot be obtained elsewhere.*

Be careful: the examples above satisfy this criterion *but not the next one.*

8. *The one, two, or three most determinative facts should at least be alluded to in either the headings or sub-headings.*   This is what pins down for the reader how the rules entitle you to what you want. Notice how sub-headings *B* (and in the last example *B* and *C*) do that:

Case A: I.   **The defendant's motion for summary judgment should be granted because the parties never formed a contract to merge.**

           A.   *In an action for breach of contract, a defendant is entitled to summary judgment where the plaintiff is not able to produce evidence of the existence of a contract.*

           B.   *The written contract was never signed, and there was no evidence of an oral understanding that could survive the Statute of Frauds.*

Case B: I.   **The complaint states a cause of action and should not be dismissed.**

           A.   *This court has recognized the tort of wrongful discharge.*

           B.   *The complaint alleges that the plaintiff was discharged solely because he questioned the defendant employer's corrupt contributions to political campaigns.*

Case C: I.   **The motion to quash should be denied because the evidence sought is not protected by a privilege.**

           A.   *The First Amendment does not protect evidence in the possession of a journalist where the journalist did not obtain it under a promise of confidentiality and where the evidence cannot be obtained elsewhere.*

           B.   *This journalist did not promise his source confidentiality, and his source did not request it.*

           C.   *The evidence sought cannot be obtained elsewhere because the journalist's source has died.*

Each of the examples above reflects a paradigm-structured argument, with a conclusion, a rule, an implied rule proof, and an express rule application. (Rule proof can be implied because the reader will understand that where a rule is stated in a heading, the proof will appear in the Argument under that heading.)

9. Headings and sub-headings should be forceful and argumentative.   Each heading and sub-heading should state an essential idea in an assertive way and show how that idea fits into your theory. The two faults to avoid are topic headings and headings with a tone of weakness or neutrality. These headings are topical:

> Disruption in the public schools.
>
> Absence of a contract to merge.
>
> Wrongful discharge.
>
> Confidentiality.

But these are argumentative:

> The public schools would be disrupted if this court were
> to recognize a tort of educational malpractice.
>
> The parties made no contract to merge.
>
> The complaint states a cause of action
> in wrongful discharge.
>
> The journalist neither promised confidentiality
> nor was asked for it.

(If you use headings in fact statements, however, they usually must be topical. Argumentative headings belong in the Argument, not in the fact statement. See the fact statement in Appendices F, G, and H.)

Statements of the Case

§29.1 How a Statement of the Case Works

> There is nothing more horrible than the murder of a beautiful theory by a brutal gang of facts.
>
> —*La Rochefoucauld*

"It may sound paradoxical," wrote Justice Jackson, "but most contentions of law are won or lost on the facts."[1] And in a motion memorandum or an appellate brief, the judge learns of the facts in the Statement of the Case, which has two purposes. The ostensible purpose is to summarize the factual record relevant to the decision the court has been asked to make. The ulterior purpose is to imply your motivating arguments[2] through the way the facts are presented. (Motivating arguments, after all, grow out of the facts.)

You will understand this chapter more easily if, before continuing here, you read the Statements of the Case in the motion memorandum in Appendix F and in the appellate briefs in Appendices G and H.

Statements of the Case are subject to some rather strict rules.

You must recite in the Statement all facts that you mention elsewhere in your motion memorandum or appellate brief. You must also recite in the statement all facts on which your adversary relies. The judge is entitled to a place in the document where all the legally significant facts can be seen together.

---

§29.1   1. Robert H. Jackson, *Advocacy Before the Supreme Court: Suggestions for Effective Case Presentations,* 37 A.B.A. J. 801, 803 (1951).
  2. See pages 309-313.

You must provide a citation to a page in the record for every fact in the Statement. (See §29.4) The judge is entitled to an easy method of checking what you say.

You are not allowed to argue, analyze law, draw factual inferences, or even characterize[3] the facts. It is called a *Statement* of the Case because the facts are *stated* there and analyzed elsewhere. Inferences and characterizations of facts belong in the Argument because they are argument. (You are, however, allowed to report the inferences witnesses drew and the characterizations they spoke. And you are allowed to state inferences that your adversary is certain not to contest because an undisputed inference will be treated as a fact.)

You are not allowed to discuss facts that are outside the record. (See §29.4) A Statement of the Case describes only procedural facts: allegations in pleadings, testimony, other evidence, and so on. Other facts must be excluded, a process called *limiting the Statement to the record.* It is called a Statement of the *Case* because the only facts allowed are the ones that have been put before the court through appropriate procedural means. (It could more accurately be called a "Summary of the Record," although nobody uses that term.) However, the *absence* from the record of a particular allegation or piece of evidence can itself be a fact. And you can describe such a gap in the record ("no witness identified the defendant") if it demonstrates that the opposing party has failed to carry some burden of pleading, production, or proof.

Finally, you are not allowed to misrepresent the facts, either overtly or by omission. (See §29.3)

If you cannot argue, characterize, or state inferences in a Statement of the Case, how can you persuade there? The most effective Statements of the Case persuade through organization that emphasizes favorable facts and through word choice that affects the reader while saying nothing that the adversary could reasonably claim to be inaccurate. In other words, a persuasive Statement of the case is *descriptive in form but probative in substance.*

Consider two examples, each the beginning passage of a Statement of the Case. Assume that the plaintiffs are suing a backcountry hiking guide for negligence after the guide led them into disaster. (Citations to the record have been deleted.)

On June 11, the plaintiffs asked in Stove Pipe Springs whether there was a backcountry guide who could lead them through certain parts of Death Valley. After some discussion, they hired the defendant to take them on a full-day hike the next day.

The climate in Death Valley is one of the hottest and driest known. The highest temperature recorded each year reaches at least 120° and in many years at least 125°. The highest temperature recorded in Death Valley — 134° — is also the highest recorded

---

3. See §17.1.

When they started out, the defendant carried a compass and map. Each plaintiff carried sunglasses, a large-brim hat, and a quart of water.

At trial, a climatologist testified about the climate in Death Valley. Occasionally, winter temperatures fall below freezing, but there is no water to freeze. Spring and fall temperatures approximate summer temperatures elsewhere. July is the hottest month, with an average high of about 116° and an average low of about 87°. The highest temperature ever recorded in Death Valley was 134°. (The highest recorded on earth was 136°.) Reports by early explorers of temperatures above 150° have not been confirmed or repeated through official measurements. Average annual rainfall is about 1½ inches, and the number of days on which precipitation falls in an average year is eight.

in the Western Hemisphere and the second highest recorded anywhere on earth. (The highest was only two degrees hotter and was recorded in the Sahara desert.) The rainfall is only 1½ inches per year—the lowest in the Western Hemisphere—and in a few years no rain falls at all.

In the summer sun there, a person can lose four gallons of perspiration a day and—in 3% humidity—die of dehydration unless the lost water is quickly replaced. A person becomes delirious after two gallons are lost. At that heat and humidity, unprotected wood can split open spontaneously.

The defendant advertised himself as a professional and experienced backcountry guide. He was hired by the plaintiffs and then took them into Death Valley for a full-day hike on a June day with a quart of water each.

After reading the example on the right you are prepared to believe that this hike was madness, and that the guide was responsible for it. But in early drafts, many beginners instinctively produce a Statement like the one on the left, which does not convince you that the guide did anything alarming. It fails because it is descriptive *both* in form *and in substance.* After you complete your first-draft Statement, your goal will be to rewrite it until you have something that more closely approximates the example on the right, which is descriptive in form but *probative* in substance.

How did the example on the right persuade you?

First, you were given no marginal facts—such as the temperatures in other months or the unverified reports by explorers—that would have obscured the information that is critical. You were not even told the precise date because only the month or season matters. And each fact was given a prominence corresponding to the fact's value.

Second, the writer selected facts that would illustrate the theory: you will lose four gallons of water a day in such a place. After two gallons, you will become delirious. This was a full-day hike. The plaintiffs had a quart of water each. The defendant claimed to be a professional and experienced guide. As each of these facts is added, the logic of the theory unfolds.

Third, the relationship between each fact and the theory was pointed out to you. You were told, for example, why these temperatures should have suggested caution to the guide: they were "the highest recorded in the Western Hemisphere and the second highest recorded anywhere on earth," and the only higher temperature "was recorded in the Sahara desert."

Finally, you were given the kind of vivid details that make a theory come alive: the delirium, for example, and the wood splitting open. (See §24.7.)

But the example on the right appears to be nothing more than a description of the relevant facts. Nothing in it could reasonably be challenged as untrue by an adversary. Each fact is objectively verifiable in the record. The only characterization ("one of the hottest and driest known") was testified to by an expert witness (the climatologist). And—most importantly—the writer never expressed inferences. *You drew all of them yourself.*

In the movie *Amistad*, a renowned lawyer and former President is asked how to win the freedom of Africans who were kidnapped into slavery and landed in Connecticut. "In a courtroom," he says, "whoever tells the best story wins." (A strategy based on that insight wins the case.)

Litigators become story-tellers. That does not mean that they recite facts. Facts are just a collection of events and circumstances. Reciting them is usually boring. A *story*, on the other hand, touches us in the heart and in the mind because the people in it come alive so that we sympathize with one, are offended by another, worry about a third, are impressed with a fourth, and so on. A litigator has to *find* the story in the facts and develop it so that it affects the reader (§29.2 shows how). Finding the story means figuring out how the facts can come together to make a plot—like the plot of a short novel—that touches the reader.

Law school does a good job of teaching analysis and argument. But equally important to a litigator is the ability to find a story in the facts and then tell it in a persuasive way. When you are writing a Statement of the Case, you can develop your story-finding and telling skills by explaining the story to a friend who does not know the case you are working on. As you tell the story orally, it will improve if you consciously try to use the techniques described in §29.2. Then, when you are satisfied with it, write the Statement of the Case.

§29.2 How to Tell Your Client's Story Persuasively

> If you want to win a case, paint the Judge a *picture* and keep it simple.
>
> —*John W. Davis*

Here is how to paint the picture in the Statement of the Case:

1. Reflect your theory throughout the Statement.
2. Breathe life into the facts by telling a compelling story about people.
3. Choose the method of organization that tells the story most persuasively.

4. Start with a punch.
5. Focus on facts that would show that you have satisfied a procedural burden (or that your adversary has failed to do so).
6. Emphasize favorable facts.
7. Neutralize unfavorable facts.
8. Humanize your client.

1. Reflect your theory throughout the Statement. Tightly focus the 'Statement of the Case on facts that advance your theory. If the Statement wanders aimlessly and indiscriminately through the facts, the reader will not grasp your theory and may not even understand the story.

Every word should be selected to make the theory more clear. In the Statement in Appendix G, you learn that the defendant "suffers from gender dysphoria syndrome," while the prosecution's Statement in Appendix H instead says the defendant "planned to undergo surgery" to alter gender. Do these phrasings advance the theories? How? When referring to the defendant, the prosecution's Statement uses the words "he," "him," and "her." The defendant's Statement, on the other hand, uses feminine pronouns and calls the defendant "*Ms.* Bresnahan." Is any of that unethical?[1] Would the court be misled? Has either attorney risked credibility? Or do these phrasing reflect legitimate differences in the parties' theories?

If you focus the Statement in this way, it might be surprisingly short. For example, consider the following from one of Cardozo's opinions (surely, a model of brevity):

> A radiator placed about ten or twelve inches from the edge of an unprotected hoistway and parallel thereto fell down the shaft and killed a man below.[2]

After reading this we are prepared to hold liable whoever was careless enough to have put the radiator there, whoever knocked it over, and whoever failed to put a protective screen over the top of the shaft. Just tell us who they are so we can enter a judgment against them. Imagine the facts *not* mentioned: why the radiator was put there, where it came from, where it was supposed to go afterward, why the man was below, and so on. None would have advanced the theory, and all would have distracted the reader.

Throughout the Statement, the reader should be conscious—from the way the facts are cast—of whom you represent. If the reader wonders about that, even for a paragraph or two, you have probably written an unpersuasive Statement.

2. Breathe life into the facts by telling a compelling story about people. You can make the story come alive by setting out the facts that show who has behaved properly and who has not, letting the facts

§29.2 1. See §§25.4 and 29.3.
2. *DeHaen v. Rockwood Sprinkler Co.*, 179 N.E. 764, 765 (N.Y. 1932).

themselves make your case. A simple narrative with vivid nouns and verbs does this best. For example, *Hatahley v. United States*[3]

> involved, on its face, cold jurisdictional and legal problems: Were rights under the Taylor Grazing Act, a federal law, affected by a state law regulating abandoned horses? Had there in any event been compliance with the state statute's terms? Did the Federal Torts Claims Act cover intentional trespasses within the scope of federal agents' authority? The injuries for which redress were sought were the carrying off of horses and mules belonging to the plaintiffs, who were Navaho Indians.
>   . . . Here is how the facts were set forth in [the plaintiffs'] brief:
>
> > The animals were rounded up on the range and were either driven or hauled in trucks to a Government-owned or controlled corral 45 miles away. Horses which could not be so handled were shot and killed by the Government's agents on the spot. [T]he horses were so jammed together in the trucks that some died as a result, and, in one instance, the leg of a horse that inconveniently protruded through the truck body was sawed off by a federal employee. . . . (Fdg. 23, 25; R. 33-34.) Later, the animals were taken in trucks to Provo, Utah, a distance of 350 miles, where they were sold to a glue factory and horse meat plant for about $1,700 — at about 3 cents a pound (R. 93, 293) — no part of which was received by petitioners (Fdg. 24; R. 34).[4]

The Supreme Court held that "[t]hese acts were wrongful trespasses not involving discretion on the part of the agents, and they do give rise to a claim compensable under the Federal Tort Claims Act."[5] On this fact description, does the result surprise you?

After reading the Statement of the Case for the movant or for the appellant, the judge should be left with the feeling that something is unacceptably wrong with what has happened. The movant or the appellant, after all, wants the judge to *do* something about the facts. But after reading the Statement of the Case of an appellee or a party opposing a motion, the judge should instead believe the facts are fair and just — or at least that they are not so unjust as to call for judicial intervention. One way to arouse those feelings is to show how the facts are vividly, even interestingly, just or unjust. Can you still see in your mind trucks, horses, a corral, a man with a saw? Does that scene sum up what *Hatahley* was all about?

3. Choose the method of organization that tells the story most persuasively.
The first step in organizing a Statement of the Case is to make a list of the facts that are — according to your theory — determinative. Add explanatory facts only if needed to avoid confusion or to tell the story coherently. Omit the coincidental facts. (See §17.2 for more on determinative facts, explanatory facts, and coincidental facts.)

Include dates only if they are determinative or are needed to avoid confusion. Beginners tend to include every available date because dates are the

---

3. 351 U.S. 173 (1956).
4. Frederick Bernays Wiener, *Briefing and Arguing Federal Appeals* 58-59 (Bur. of Natl. Affs. 1967). (The references to "Fdg." and to "R." are citations to the record. Section 29.4 explains what a record is and how to cite to it.)
5. *Hatahley*, 351 U.S. at 181.

easiest of all facts to state. But irrelevant dates clutter up the Statement and thus obscure the truly important facts. And if time is not an issue, they can mislead the reader by implying that it is. For example, where the first sentence in a Statement is "The summons and complaint were served on February 1, 1988," the reader will get the impression that the controversy is about a statute of limitations or some other issue involving time.

Include the identity of a witness only if that truly adds to the story. Identifying all the witnesses by name clutters up the Statement and gets in the way of the story you want to tell. For instance, the identity of a witness could be valuable if the fact is an admission ("the plaintiff himself admitted that he was not wearing his seat belt"); if the witness is impressively authoritative ("four professors of engineering testified about why the dam collapsed"); or if the fact is part of the witness's state of mind ("the defendant testified that she intended to sell only the frame and not the painting"). And if the fact is contested—for example, one witness said the traffic light was green while another said it was red—you probably need to identify them because you will try to show that one is more credible than the other.

The second step is to make an outline that would set out the determinative and explanatory facts in a sequence both persuasive and easily understandable. Sometimes—but not often—the most effective sequence is chronological. More frequently, a topical organization works better because you can use the way you organize the facts to imply the logical relationships between them. In some cases, you might try a topical organization that breaks into a chronological narrative where it is important for the reader to understand the sequence in which events happened. Often, the Statement can be made more accessible by breaking it up with sub-headings that are reprinted verbatim in the table of contents.

4. Start with a punch.   Begin the Statement with a short passage—one or two paragraphs—summarizing your most compelling facts so that the judge understands the heart of your theory. Then tell the whole story, explaining along the way and in detail the facts that you summarized at the beginning. Never begin the Statement with neutral facts, unfavorable facts, or unimportant facts.

The opening passage is the most important part of the Statement. If written well, it puts the judge in a receptive frame of mind; tells the judge what facts to look for later; and creates a lasting impression. The opening passage is usually the hardest part of the Statement to write. But the extra time and effort are an excellent investment.

In the memorandum in Appendix F and in the briefs in Appendices G and H, notice how each Statement begins with a passage like the one described here.

5. Focus on facts that would show that you have satisfied a procedural burden (or that your adversary has failed to do so).   If you must carry a burden of pleading, production, or persuasion, you can emphasize in the Statement of the Case the facts that you will later use in the

Argument to show that you have discharged the burden. If any of those facts are undisputed, you can point that out:

> Dr. Charbonneau testified without contradiction that Ms. Leyland's injuries could have been caused only by a blow from a long, thin object "about the size and shape of a nightstick." (T. at 97.)

Regardless of which party has a burden, you can also point to inconsistencies in the evidence and things that are missing from the record:

> Although Officer Joyner testified that Ms. Leyland was assaulted by another prisoner in her cell (T. at 178), he could not name or describe that prisoner (T. at 187), and there is no evidence anywhere in the record that another prisoner was at any point assigned to or given access to her cell. Moreover, although the warden of the county jail testified that arresting officers are not normally permitted in cell blocks (T. at 245), Officer Joyner was the sole witness who claimed to have seen an assault in Ms. Leyland's cell.

Who do you think beat up Leyland? Every word in this passage is value-neutral, and none of the evidence is interpreted or characterized. Although it persuades, the passage sounds clinically objective. The writer has merely brought together facts that had been scattered about in the record. And the writer has refrained from stating inferences—such as "Officer Joyner should not be believed"—that should be left for the Argument.

6. Emphasize favorable facts. That can be done through organization. Readers tend to be most attentive at the beginning, less attentive at the end, and least attentive in the middle. It can also be done by describing favorable facts in detail and by omitting unnecessary facts that cloud the picture you want the reader to see. Notice, for example, that the name of the warden is missing from the example above: the essential fact is the warden's official position, and the name would have no effect on the court. Specifics about dates, times, and places can be seductively concrete when you are writing, but to a reader they can also obscure what really happened. Compare these:

At 2:10 A.M., on Tuesday, September 2, 1986, Officer Joyner was told by his dispatcher to investigate a disturbance on the fourth floor of the building at 642 Sutherland Street. (T. at 162.) There he took a complaint from Kenneth Novak, a tenant in apartment 4-C, and, as a result, arrested Ms. Leyland, who lives in apartment 4-E. (T. at 163-65.) Officer Joyner was not

Ms. Leyland was awakened and arrested by Officer Joyner at her apartment shortly after 2 A.M. on the day she was beaten. (T. at 162-67.) A police booking clerk testified that she heard "a man yelling in the parking lot" just before Officer Joyner brought Ms. Leyland into the precinct station. (T. at 145.) The booking clerk also testified that she immediately noticed able to leave the building with Ms. Leyland until 2:45 A.M. because she had been asleep and needed to dress. (T. at 166-67.) Ms. Leyland testified that she was so tired that she fell asleep in the police car during the drive to the precinct station. (T. at 14.) Cynthia Scollard, a police booking clerk, testified that she was on duty at about 3:05 A.M. on September 2, when she heard a commotion in the precinct parking lot. (T. at 145.) Ms. Scollard further testified that she noticed Ms. Leyland's injuries as soon as Officer Joyner turned Ms. Leyland over to her, and that Ms. Leyland appeared to be very tired at the time. (T. at 147-49.)

bleeding from Ms. Leyland's lip and from the side of her head (T. at 147-48), and that Ms. Leyland's face began to swell during booking (T. at 148-49.)

In the passage on the left, the date, the address, the precise times, the booking clerk's name, and the details about Leyland's tired state are all clutter. The passage on the right omits the unnecessary, opening up room to dwell on the details that are truly essential. And the carefully edited quotation in the passage on the right brings the story to life.

7. Neutralize unfavorable facts. The most effective method is to juxtapose an unfavorable fact with other facts that explain, counterbalance, or justify it:

> Even though the booking clerk testified that Ms. Leyland did not complain to her that she had been beaten by Officer Joyner, the booking clerk also testified that Officer Joyner stood next to Ms. Leyland throughout the booking procedure. (T. at 166-69.) Ms. Leyland testified that she had no memory of being booked (T. at 32), and Dr. Charbonneau testified that persons who suffer a head injury like Ms. Leyland's are often "stunned and impassive" immediately afterward. (T. at 104.)

The most effective juxtapositions are often found in sentences structured around an "even though" contrast (like the first sentence in the paragraph above). A far less effective method is to de-emphasize an unfavorable fact by tucking it into an obscure part of the Statement of the Case and summarizing it without much detail. Hiding an unfavorable fact will not make it go away. And if you seem to be trying to ignore the fact, you will not be viewed as credible and reliable. If you do not try to neutralize it, you forfeit an opportunity to persuade.

8. Humanize your client.   Be careful about how you refer to the parties. In an appellate brief, you only cause confusion if you refer to them continually as "appellant" and "appellee" because these designations tell the reader nothing more than who lost below.[6] The procedural designations from the trial court are more clear: "the plaintiff" and "the defendant" in a civil case or, in a criminal case, "the defendant" and "the State" (or "the People," "the Government," or "the Commonwealth"). More still can be conveyed by using some generic factual designation related to the issues: "the buyer" and "the seller" in a commercial dispute or "the employer" and "the employee" in a discrimination case. But, unless it would be confusing, your client's real name is often the best tactical choice. The passages on the preceding pages would lose much of their liveliness if "Ms. Leyland" were reduced to "the plaintiff." The same thing would happen if Officer Joyner were to gain anonymity as "the arresting officer," although in many other cases a depersonalized opposing party would seem easier to dislike ("the insurance company," "the union," "the hospital").

§29.3   Fact Ethics

As you know, a lawyer is forbidden to "[k]nowingly make a false statement of material fact or law" to a court.[1] In §25.4, we explored the consequences of a false statement of law. Courts react just as harshly to false statements of fact.

Three kinds of false statements will incur the fury of a court. One is a flat-out misrepresentation: making a statement about a fact that is unsupported by the actual record. The second is misrepresentation by omission: presenting a version of the record that ignores facts favoring the opposing party.[2] The third is misrepresentation by describing inferences as though they were facts. (In the Statement of the Case, only facts may be described, although, as §29.1 explains, inferences drawn by witnesses and inferences the other side will not dispute are both treated as facts. In the Argument, you may draw inferences from the facts, but they should be presented as that — and argued because the court can reject them and draw contrary inferences.)

Even if it were not unethical, factual misrepresentation never fools a court and hurts only the misrepresenting lawyer and that lawyer's client. Misrepresentations are quickly spotted by opposing attorneys, and once a misrepresentation is pointed out to a court, the entire memorandum or brief is treated with deep suspicion.

---

6. In many courts, you are not permitted to use these designations in the body of the brief, although they will naturally appear on the cover page. *See, e.g.,* Rule 28(d) of the Federal Rules of Appellate Procedure.

§29.3   1. Rule 3.3(a)(1) of the Model Rules of Professional Conduct.

2. "[T]he court is not impressed by a statement of facts which completely ignores the evidence produced by the other side." *Manteca Veal Co. v. Corbari,* 116 Cal. App. 2d 896, 898, 254 P.2d 884, 885 (1st Dist. 1953).

§29.4   The Record

Court rules virtually everywhere require that each fact be cited to a specific page or paragraph in the record — not only when you recite the fact in the Statement of the Case, but also when you analyze it in the Argument.[1] The judge should not have to go back to the Statement to find the citation. (In the fact statement, the type of opening passage described on page 363 is usually considered exempt from this requirement if the facts summarized there will be explained in detail later in the Statement.)

Court rules aside, citations have a persuasive effect of their own. Thorough citations, by their appearance alone, create confidence that every fact recited in the Statement is fully supported in the record, while spotty or absent citations arouse a court's skepticism. And thorough record citations add to your own credibility by creating an impression of carefulness.

The record might include any or all of the following: (1) the pleadings; (2) evidence in the form of transcribed testimony, affidavits, and exhibits; and (3) prior court orders, judicial opinions, and, on appeal, the judgment below. Remember that pleadings are not evidence. (See §26.2.1.) If the issue before the court is whether a burden of pleading has been carried, the pleadings are the only source of "facts," and the "facts" must be described as allegations. You do not, however, have to begin every sentence with "The complaint alleges." It is enough to begin the Statement of the Case with the words "The complaint alleges the following:"

In a motion memorandum, cite to specific documents within the record, such as "Compl. ¶22" (complaint at paragraph 22), "Senten. Hrg. Tr. at 98" (sentencing hearing transcript at page 98), or "Kristen Myers Aff. ¶12 (Feb. 2, 2001)" (Affidavit of Kristen Myers, dated February 2, 2001, at paragraph 12). On appeal, cite to the record as a whole ("R. at 393") or to the joint appendix ("J.A. at 99"). If the full cite is long, a shorter form can be used after the full cite has been given once (see the affidavit cites in Appendix F).

Local rules and custom usually allow some latitude in the use of abbreviations when citing to the record. The ALWD Citation Manual provides record citation guidance in rule 29. The Bluebook does the same in B10 and BT1 and table 8. In addition, every jurisdiction has rules and customs of its own. If you use abbreviations that might be unfamiliar to the court, include a footnote near the beginning of the Statement of the Case, explaining what the abbreviations mean. In any event, the citation is placed in a parenthetical:

> The plaintiff alleged only that the goods were not delivered on time. (Compl. ¶22.)

Remember that a citation proves no more than the sentence that precedes it and, if the citation is placed inside a sentence, the citation proves only the portion of the sentence that precedes it.

---

§29.4   1. *See, e.g.,* Rules 28(a)(7) and (e) of the Federal Rules of Appellate Procedure.

Although Officer Joyner wrote in an incident report that Ms. Leyland was injured when she resisted arrest (R. at 98), he testified at trial that she was injured when assaulted by another prisoner in her cell (R. at 178).

As the examples show, the citation ends with a period if it stands alone as a citation sentence, but not if you insert it into a sentence you write.

Exercise I.   What Is a Fact? (Reprise)

Of the eight events listed in §17.1, which can be mentioned in a Statement of the Case?

Exercise II.   Story-Telling

Using a case you have read in another course, develop the facts of the case into a story. Do not change or embellish the facts. Stay strictly faithful to the *substance* of what you read in the case. But develop a story that would move a listener or reader to feel or think that one party or the other should win. Use the techniques described in §29.2.

If your teacher assigns this exercise for class, tell the story there so that the class can offer suggestions for improving the way you tell the story. If this exercise will not be done in class, tell the story to another student and ask that student to suggest improvements.

Exercise III.   Topical Organization v. Chronological Organization

For each Statement of the Case in Appendices F, G, and H, decide whether the organization is topical, chronological, or a combination. For each, is the organization effective or ineffective? Why?

Exercise IV.   Escape from Prison? (Rewriting Statements of the Case)

Orville Bradwyn is being tried for attempted escape from prison. Below is a Statement of the Case for the prosecution, followed by one for the defense. (Citations to the record have been omitted.)

Rewrite each Statement.

For the prosecution:

The defendant is a prisoner at the Simmonsville Penitentiary. On July 6, he was not in the dinner line where he was required to be, and Sgt. Tunmeyer, the prosecution's sole witness, organized a search for him. According to Sgt. Tunmeyer, no prisoner is allowed in the laundry room after 5 P.M., and the defendant was found in the laundry room at 7:39 P.M. The reason for this rule is that the laundry room is an obvious place from which to escape. The prison does the laundry of the state hospital nearby, and hospital trucks pick up hospital laundry directly from the prison laundry room. At 5 P.M., Sgt. Tunmeyer checked the laundry room thoroughly, did not see anyone, and subsequently locked the door. Even though the defendant had been assigned to work in the laundry, he was not on duty when he was found in the laundry. Before and after dinner, prisoners are free to move about outside their cells. When the defendant's cell was checked, many of his personal belongings were found. In fact, the defendant had a reputation for being tidy and was drying all of his clothes when found in the laundry at 7:39 P.M. However, when his cell was checked his radio had been left on, and some material had been left under the covers of his bed to make it look like someone was asleep there.

For the defendant:

Mr. Bradwyn is an inmate at the Simmonsville Penitentiary. At this prison, inmates are free to move about outside the cells before and after dinner, which is from 6:00 to 7:00 P.M. The prisoners are counted each day in the dinner line, and when Mr. Bradwyn was not present, he was considered missing. Prisoners are not allowed in the laundry after 5 P.M. because the laundry room provides an obvious escape route on the truck the state hospital sends at 8 P.M. each night to pick up its laundry. Sgt. Tunmeyer testified that he checked the laundry at 5 P.M. and locked it up without seeing Mr. Bradwyn there.

When Mr. Bradwyn was discovered to be absent from the dinner line, Sgt. Tunmeyer organized a search and found him in the laundry room at 7:39 P.M., where Mr. Bradwyn was drying his prison uniforms. There was no testimony about how Mr. Bradwyn could have entered the laundry room, which Sgt. Tunmeyer claims to have locked. Mr. Bradwyn is one of the prisoners assigned to work in the laundry. Sgt. Tunmeyer admits to past quarrels with Mr. Bradwyn, and that Mr. Bradwyn had filed a complaint against him for beating him. He also admitted that Mr. Bradwyn is an unusually tidy person who does not like other people to touch his things, and that at 7:39 P.M. all of Mr. Bradwyn's clothing was in a dryer.

The state has not introduced any evidence that Mr. Bradwyn was not on duty earlier in the day. Nor has it introduced any evidence that Mr. Bradwyn could not have been locked in the laundry room accidentally by Sgt. Tunmeyer at 5 P.M.

Exercise V.   Drafting Statements of the Case

Draft two Statements of the Case — one favoring each party — using the facts and authority either from an exercise designated by your teacher in either of Chapter 15 or Chapter 16 or from a writing assignment that you have previously completed in this course.

30 Questions Presented

§30.1 The Purpose and Structure of a Question Presented

A Question Presented has two functions. First, it defines the decision that the court is asked to make. And second, within limits, you can use the Question to persuade by framing it in terms of the facts at the core of your theory. If the Question defines the decision objectively, it does not perform the second function of a persuasive Question Presented. And if it argues the case, it does not fulfill the first. The solution is to persuade through juxtaposition and careful word choice — just as you do in a Statement of the Case, but much more concisely.

On whether a Question Presented is appropriate for a motion memorandum, see page 343. You will understand this chapter more easily if you read the Questions Presented in the briefs in Appendices G and H.

Structurally, a Question Presented is an inquiry plus a list of the most determinative facts and an allusion to the body of law that would govern the result:

> Is the manufacturer of an acoustical keyboard liable under an implied warranty of fitness for purpose to a purchaser in whose hands the keyboard exploded the first time it was plugged in?

The determinative facts and the allusion to the governing body of law define the issue so that, as a matter of legal inquiry, it becomes the question "presented" by the situation. "Is a manufacturer liable to a purchaser?" may be a question, but it is not a Question Presented.

The inquiry can begin with whatever verb is most appropriate to the issue:

> Does the First Amendment allow . . . ?

> Is the manufacturer of an acoustical keyboard liable . . . ?

Or the inquiry can instead begin with the word *whether* — even though the result is not a grammatically complete sentence:

> Whether the First Amendment allows . . .

> Whether the manufacturer of an acoustical keyboard is liable . . .

But "whether" Questions often strike the reader as weaker and more tedious than Questions that begin with a verb.

Facts that do not fit naturally into the inquiry can be attached at the end in clauses beginning with "where" or "when":

> Is the manufacturer of an acoustical keyboard absolved of liability under an implied warranty of fitness for purpose where an ordinary consumer bought it in pieces from a street vendor and attempted to reassemble it himself even though the words "Do Not Open or Attempt to Repair This Product" were engraved on the outside?

The inquiry is best placed first because a list of determinative facts makes little sense until the reader knows the inquiry to which those facts are relevant. The following, for example, are *not* easy to understand:

facts before inquiry:	Where an ordinary consumer bought an acoustical keyboard in pieces from a street vendor and attempted to reassemble it himself even though the words "Do Not Open or Attempt to Repair This Product" were engraved on the outside, is the manufacturer absolved of liability under an implied warranty of fitness for purpose?
facts and inquiry intermingled:	Is the manufacturer of an acoustical keyboard, which was bought from a street vendor by an ordinary consumer who attempted to reassemble it himself even though the words "Do Not Open or Attempt to Repair This Product" were engraved on the outside, absolved of liability under an implied warranty of fitness for purpose?

In some cases, even the most determinative facts are so complex that they cannot be reduced to a short list and a reader would drown in a series of "where" clauses. That tends to happen where a set of determinative facts raises several independent issues, and where the facts themselves are difficult to describe concisely. In such cases, lawyers sometimes use a different format, expressing the determinative facts in an introductory paragraph, and then posing the Question or Questions. (An example is the Question Presented in the brief in Appendix G.)

In a persuasive Question Presented, the least confusing way to refer to the parties is generically: "a malpractice insurer," "a prisoner," "an employee," and so forth. Procedural designations are often confusing. "Appellant" and "appellee" tell the court virtually nothing. The same is true of "plaintiff" and "defendant" unless the issue is really procedural or the Question itself makes clear what kind of plaintiff and what kind of defendant are involved. Although most uses of "plaintiff" and "defendant" are confusing, these are not (for the reasons just stated):

> Has a defendant been properly served where the summons was handed to him in a plain manila envelope?

> Does a complaint state a cause of action for personal injuries if it alleges only that the defendant could have rescued the plaintiff but did not?

And in a criminal case it is never confusing to refer to one party as the defendant. (The other party is always the prosecution.) Although a busy judge can be confused when the parties are referred to by name only, it may be tactically wise to try to personalize a party beset by some institutional opponent, if the context will make clear who is who. See the Question Presented in the brief in Appendix G.

Given the relatively few words involved, a persuasive Question Presented can be one of the most difficult drafting jobs in legal writing. The work is best broken into three stages.

First, write out a narrow statement of the inquiry ("Is a prisoner guilty of escape?") and a separate list of the facts that you believe to be most determinative, omitting facts that are merely explanatory or coincidental (see §17.2). Second, tinker with the list, perhaps while writing and rewriting the other components of the memorandum or brief. Add or subtract facts as you come to understand the issue better, and refine the list's wording as you learn the possibilities and limitations of each fact. Third, work out a concise phrasing of the list and merge it into the inquiry in a single sentence. The Question Presented is often the last part of a document to reach its final form.

§30.2 How to Evaluate Your Questions Presented for Persuasiveness

Frank Cooper suggested six standards[1] for judging the effectiveness of a Question Presented:

1. The issue must be stated in terms of the facts of the case [rather than in terms of assumed conclusions of law or fact].

§30.2 1. Frank E. Cooper, *Writing in Law Practice* 80 (Bobbs-Merrill 1963).

2. The statement must eliminate all unnecessary detail.
3. It must be readily comprehensible on first reading.
4. It must eschew self-evident conclusions.
5. It should be so stated that the opponent has no choice but to accept it as an accurate statement of the question.
6. It should be subtly persuasive.

We can add one more:

7. It should clearly define the decision the court has been asked to make.

To see these principles at work, consider a case in which a stockbroker gets tired of his work and decides to do something meaningful. He persuades a gourmet bakery to take him on as an apprentice baker. The bakery has perfected a method — which it keeps secret — of adding a citrus taste to croissants. As a precaution, the bakery requires its employees to sign a covenant not to compete with the bakery for three years in either of the two urban counties in an otherwise rural state. After a short time, the stockbroker quits and forms his own company to bake and sell gourmet baked goods. The bakery where he apprenticed sues for an injunction to prohibit that. In the state where this arises, a covenant not to compete is enforceable if the prohibition on competition is "reasonably limited" in duration and geographic area; if it "does not exceed that reasonably necessary for protection of the employer's business"; if it "is not unreasonably restrictive" of the employee's rights; and if it does not violate public policy.[2]

The bakery's attorney might draft this Question Presented:

> Should a successful stockbroker who is entering the baking business be enjoined from violating a three-year covenant not to compete, where he was trained as a baker entirely by the plaintiff, had access to the secret recipe for the plaintiff's biggest-selling product, and has now set himself up in business as the plaintiff's only competitor in a specialized two-county gourmet baked goods market?

From the other side might come a very different Question:

> Is it inequitable to enjoin an apprentice baker from working "in any baking capacity" for three years in an area that includes three-quarters of the state's population, where the plaintiff's only fear of potential injury is that, in starting his own business, the apprentice might use a croissant recipe?

Now let us apply the criteria set out above:

1. State the issue in terms of the facts and not in terms of assumed conclusions of law or fact. Each Question sets out the attorney's

---

2. *American Credit Bureau v. Carter,* 462 P.2d 838, 840 (Ariz. Ct. App. 1960).

theory of the case without arguing it. Even if you do not know much about the legal rules involved in this case, you can predict from the Questions alone a great deal of what will be argued later in the memorandum or brief. The bakery's attorney is certain to argue that the covenant's geographic area is reasonable because of the nature of the market, that its duration is reasonable because of the nature of the product, and that the court should view the apprentice as a stockbroker and financier and not as a person who really makes his living with bread dough in his hands. The apprentice's attorney is equally certain to argue that the covenant is unreasonable in time (three years), substance ("in any baking capacity"), and area (three-quarters of the state's population).

There are three ways to fail this criterion: by omitting some of the core determinative facts; by listing characterizations or factual inferences instead of facts; or by listing conclusions of law instead of facts.

If the baker's attorney had submitted the following Question, the court would have been given an *incomplete set of the most determinative facts*:

> Should an apprentice baker be enjoined from violating a three-year covenant not to compete in the baking business, where the enjoined apprentice was trained as a baker entirely by the plaintiff?

Would this Question persuade you? (Compare it to the bakery's Question on page 374.)

If the baker's attorney had submitted the following Question, some of the "facts" would actually have been *characterizations and factual inferences,* which must be proved later in the document and cannot be assumed here:

> Should an apprentice who deceived the plaintiff into disclosing its hitherto secret recipe, and who has now betrayed his former employer by setting himself up in business, be enjoined from violating a three-year covenant not to compete in the baking business?

Judges ignore Questions that go beyond the solid facts. Here, there is no evidence of deception, and the writer's claim of it is a kind of inference that we call a guess. In the Argument (where it can be proved), the writer might be justified in calling the stockbroker's conduct a betrayal, but in the Question that is just empty rhetoric.

And in the following Question, the "facts" are really *conclusions of law,* which also must be proved later and cannot be assumed here:

> Should the defendant bakery apprentice be enjoined from violating a covenant not to compete where the covenant is reasonably limited in duration and geographic area, where its prohibitions are reasonably necessary to protect the employer's business, where it does not unreasonably restrict the employee's rights, and where it does not violate public policy?

Judges will ignore this, too. Inferences and conclusions cannot be posited as factual givens. They must be *argued* in the Argument. Questions that contain them mean nothing.

If you find characterizations and conclusions in a Question you have written, cut them out and *replace them with the facts that would make them true.* Which facts, for example, make this restraint reasonably necessary to protect the bakery's business? Those facts belong in the Question, and the conclusion of law should come out.

2. Eliminate all unnecessary detail.   There are two ways to get this wrong. One is to list facts that are not among the most determinative.

The other is to add unnecessary specifics about facts that are determinative. In an earlier draft of the bakery's Question, the phrase "was trained as a baker *entirely* by the plaintiff" might have been "was trained as a baker by the plaintiff *and has never received any other instruction or experience in the field.*" Do you see how much clout a single, carefully chosen word ("entirely") can carry (replacing all the italicized words in the earlier version)? Finding the right level of abstraction or compression is not easy. An overly specific formulation of a fact is too detailed to imply the fact's relevance and usually so verbose as to confuse the reader. An overly general formulation often oversimplifies and is too rarefied to open up the picture that you want the reader to see — the picture that captures the decision-maker.

3. Write the Question so that it can be understood when read only once.   Consider this:

> Should this court enjoin the violation of a covenant not to compete, which applied only to the baking industry and included a prohibition on competition that lasted three years, where the defendant was a baking apprentice who has made a considerable income as a stockbroker and continues to derive passive income from his partnership in a brokerage house, where he was trained as a baker by the plaintiff and has never received any other instruction or experience in the field, where he had access to the plaintiff's hitherto secret recipe for a unique form of croissant embodying citrus flavors, where he has now set himself up in business as the plaintiff's only competitor in this field, and where the parties compete in a specialized gourmet baked goods market that extends over two adjacent counties, each of which includes a major city?

Can you understand this in one reading? Can you tell immediately what facts are important? Compare it — phrase by phrase — with the bakery's Question on page 374. There is no difference in meaning. In fact, the only difference is that the Question above is verbose where it should be concise and detailed where it should be abstract and compressed. (Another way to make a Question unreadable is to use an obtuse sentence structure. See the two examples on page 372.)

It takes much writing and rewriting to make the Question understandable in one reading. It is partly a process of finding the most concise phrasing and partly a process of finding the right level of abstraction or compression.

4. Omit self-evident conclusions.   For example:

> Should violation of a covenant not to compete be enjoined where the covenant's restraints are reasonable, where they are reasonably necessary to protect the employer's business . . . ?

The answer to this will always be yes. It is a question about what the law is and not how the court should rule in *this* case.

5. State the Question so that your adversary must accept as accurate each fact listed.   A Question Presented persuades only if based on undeniable descriptions of facts. The Questions on page 374 persuade by listing facts the opposing attorney cannot claim to be untrue or missing from the record, and by describing those facts in words the opposing attorney cannot reasonably claim to be inaccurate. The bakery's attorney, for example, would have reached too far if the bakery's Question had posited that "the injunction covers *only* two counties" because those two counties include three-quarters of the state's population and cannot reasonably be dismissed as "only."

Moreover, in the Questions on page 374, neither attorney has pretended that the other side's strongest facts do not exist. The Questions are two intellectual constructs between which the court must choose, and a court is not likely to choose one that ignores a significant and troubling aspect of the controversy. Thus, the apprentice's attorney must concede that his client suddenly created a company to compete, but he does so in words that suggest that the bakery will not suffer much as a result ("the plaintiff's only fear of potential injury is that, in starting his own business, the apprentice might use a croissant recipe"). The bakery's attorney can hardly ignore the fact that the state's population is concentrated in the two counties covered by the covenant, but she mentions that in a phrase showing why the covenant ought to address that area ("a specialized two-county gourmet baked goods market"). As in a Statement of the Case, the key here is juxtaposition.

6. Make the Question subtly persuasive.   You want a Question that would cause a disinterested but skeptical reader to think, "This lawyer has the winning side." And you want a Question that would make a judge think, "On these facts, I do not want to rule against this lawyer." The Question should overcome a judge's natural tendency to ask "So what?" or "Is this really so bad that I should use the power of the court to interfere?"

Choose your words carefully to create a picture through nuance. Set out your theory clearly and convincingly. And draft the Question in a positive tone to invite the answer you seek. (The reader should want to say "yes" right after the question mark.)

7. Clearly define the decision the court is asked to make.   Do that by asking a Question that alludes to the governing body of law and lists the most determinative facts.

One way of failing this criterion is to ask a Question that *assumes that the reader already knows the case:*

> Should the violation of a covenant not to compete be enjoined, where the defendant is actually a successful stockbroker who was trained entirely by the plaintiff, who had access to the plaintiff's hitherto secret recipe, and who has now set himself up in business as the plaintiff's only competitor?

Did the plaintiff train the defendant to be a stockbroker? Is this a suit to enjoin competition in the stock brokerage industry? What does a recipe have to do with this? Remember that the reader might not yet have read the Statement of the Case and has certainly not yet read the Argument. Many judges use the Question Presented as an introduction to other parts of the memorandum or brief.

Another way of failing this criterion is to *diffuse the reader's attention* through several Questions that really add up to only one (or a very few). The temptation to pose inappropriately multiple Questions is greatest on appeal:

> 1. Did the Superior Court properly enjoin the violation of a covenant not to compete, which was limited to a three-year period in a two-county area?
> 2. Did the Superior Court properly enjoin the violation of a covenant not to compete, where the enjoined former employee had access to the plaintiff's hitherto secret bakery recipe and has now set himself up as the plaintiff's only competitor?
> 3. Did the Superior Court properly enjoin the violation of a covenant not to compete, where the former employee is a successful stock-broker who does not depend on baking for his livelihood?

This is like trying to cut water with a knife.

You should have one Question Presented for each point in your Argument — not more and not less.

Exercise I.   Bank Robbery (Questions Presented)

The following Questions are all from the same case, which involves the federal bank robbery statute (see pages 209-210). Using the criteria in §30.2, evaluate the effectiveness of each Question. (There is a good reason why you are not told which party propounded each Question: if you cannot tell, after reading a Question, which party propounded it, it has no effectiveness at all.)

1. Should the court grant the defendant's motion for judgment of acquittal on a charge of committing robbery by intimidation in violation of 18 U.S.C. §2113(a), where the defendant, although he did not show a weapon or threaten violence, gave a bank teller a note that would put a reasonable person in fear, where the teller did not hesitate to comply with his demand, although she courageously struck him after he took the money she surrendered, and where she testified afterward that she was "shaken up" by this stressful situation?

2. Whether the Government is entitled to put its case to a jury where a bank teller testified that the defendant — who was charged with bank robbery "by intimidation" — handed her a note announcing that he was conducting a "hold-up," where she gave him all the cash at her window, and where she felt "shaken up" after the defendant's capture, in which she assisted.

3. Whether the defendant should be granted a judgment of acquittal on Count 1 of an indictment for bank robbery "by intimidation" where there was uncontroverted evidence that the defendant was pleasant and smiled throughout the alleged robbery; that he made no threatening gestures or statements and carried no visible weapon; and that the teller, after giving him cash, reached over the counter, grabbed him by the tie, and punched him twice in the face.

4. Has the Government failed to make out a prima facie case of bank robbery "by intimidation" where the sole evidence of intimidation is a note, handed to a teller, that read "please give me money — I don't know how to do a hold-up"?

Exercise II.   Drafting Persuasive Questions Presented

Draft two persuasive Questions Presented — one favoring each party — using the facts and authority either from an exercise designated by your teacher in Chapter 15 or Chapter 16 or from a writing assignment that you have previously completed in this course.

IX
APPELLATE BRIEFS

31 Appellate Practice

§31.1 Introduction to Appeals

A *judgment* (or, in equity, a decree) is the document a court makes to terminate a lawsuit and to record the court's final determination of the parties' rights. If either party has been awarded relief, the judgment may include an award of money or an injunction or a declaration of the parties' rights and so on.

An *order,* on the other hand, is a court's command during the lawsuit that something be done or not be done while the litigation is still in progress. Depending on the complexity of the case and how long it remains in litigation, many orders or only a few might be entered before judgment. Some orders may control the discovery process; others may manage the court's calendar or the trial itself; and still others may award parties provisional relief, such as preliminary injunctions.

The document you have learned to call an opinion or a decision is neither a judgment nor an order. You have by now read hundreds of opinions, most of them in the casebooks you study for other courses, but you might never have seen an order or a judgment. The order or judgment is a court's *action,* and the opinion records the *reasons* for that action.

Within the limitations described in §31.4, a party aggrieved by a trial court's judgment or order can appeal to a higher court, where a group of judges will decide whether the trial court's judgment or order was correct or erroneous. The appellate process performs three functions. The most obvious is the correction of errors made by trial courts. A second is to cause the law to be applied uniformly throughout the jurisdiction, to the extent that is practical. And the most intellectually challenging function is the making and clarification of the law itself through precedents that fill gaps in the common law and in statutory interpretation.

In those jurisdictions with two levels, or tiers, of appellate courts, the intermediate court tends to view its goal largely as error correction, although it must also necessarily cause some uniformity in application of the law and, to a lesser extent, engage in law formation and clarification. A court of last resort, on the other hand, generally believes that its task is primarily to make and clarify law. Such a court might be willing to perform the other two functions only where the intermediate court has not merely failed to do so, but failed badly. In the jurisdictions with only one appellate court, of course, that court is responsible for all three appellate functions equally.

Issues of state law can be appealed only once in a one-tiered state and no more than twice in a two-tiered state. In federal courts, there can be no more than two appeals because the federal courts are organized into a two-tiered appellate system. But where an issue of federal law arises in the courts of a state with two appellate tiers, three appeals are possible because the United States Supreme Court has jurisdiction to decide federal issues even if originally raised in a state court. Thus, if a defendant convicted in a California criminal trial believes that his conviction is defective because the trial court misinterpreted the state statute defining the crime (a state issue) and because the trial court erroneously admitted into evidence items seized in violation of the Fourth Amendment to the United States Constitution (a federal issue), the defendant can appeal both issues to the California Court of Appeal. If that court affirms, the defendant may be able to appeal both issues further to the California Supreme Court. If unsuccessful there, the defendant may be able to appeal to the United States Supreme Court, but only on the federal issue because the United States Supreme Court has no jurisdiction over issues of state law.

With some exceptions (explained in §31.4), the dissatisfied party generally has a right to seek review by the appellate court immediately above the trial court. That one appeal should be enough, in most instances, to perform the error-correcting function of the appellate process. In a state with a one-tiered appellate system, this appeal *as of right* will be to the state's supreme court, but in other states and in the federal system, it will be to an intermediate court of appeals.

An appeal to a still higher court will probably be *discretionary* because it will not happen unless a court permits it. Although every litigant should be entitled to one appeal for error-correction purposes, the other two functions of the appellate process are performed best if the higher appellate courts in two-tiered jurisdictions can concentrate their efforts on those issues where law needs to be made or clarified. Thus, the higher appellate courts in two-tiered systems tend to be invested with *discretionary appellate jurisdiction,* which means that they are empowered to choose the appeals they will hear and to turn others aside. A party unhappy with a judgment made by a United States District Court, for example, has a right to have that judgment reviewed by a United States Court of Appeal, but there can be no further appeal to the United States

Supreme Court unless that court gives its permission by granting a would-be appellant[1] a writ of certiorari.

What kinds of issues are important enough to persuade a discretionary appellate court to exercise its jurisdiction? Generally, such a court may be inclined to grant leave to appeal or a writ of certiorari — the terminology differs from jurisdiction to jurisdiction — where the party seeking permission to appeal wants the court to fill a troubling gap in the jurisdiction's law. A gap might be troubling where lower courts have published decisions coming to opposite results on analogous facts or where a significant part of society needs clarification of the law. Some gaps are large, such as where a court is asked to recognize a cause of action that some states have adopted and others have rejected. But even relatively small gaps can be troubling: a court that has recently recognized a particular cause of action, for example, may need to decide several further appeals until all the elements are clearly defined. If, however, local law is settled, clear, and consistently applied, a discretionary appellate court is likely to give permission to appeal only in two instances. The first is where the intermediate appellate court appears to have made an error that would represent an intolerable failure of the intermediate court's error-correction function. And the second is the unusual situation where the discretionary appellate court is receptive to changing the law.

In the Supreme Court of the United States and in the highest court of every state, all the judges meet together to hear and decide appeals. In some intermediate appellate courts, appeals are heard by panels, rather than by the full court. In the United States Courts of Appeals, for example, decisions are made by panels of three judges; only in rare cases can a party who has lost before a panel persuade the full court en banc to review the panel's decision. Ultimately, of course, the losing party can petition — usually unsuccessfully — for review by the United States Supreme Court.

§31.2 *What Happens During an Appeal*

Although practice varies from court to court, these are the significant events in an appeal:

First, the appellant *serves and files whatever document is required by law to commence the appeal.* If the appeal is as of right, the document is a notice of appeal, an uncomplicated paper that is usually no longer than a page and need not specify grounds for the appeal. If leave to appeal is required, the appellant must petition for it, specifying errors and arguing

---

§31.1 1. In this text, "appellant" refers to the party who commences an appeal, and "appellee" to refer to the opposite party. The terms "petitioner" and "respondent" are used in certain types of appeals in some courts. Before writing a brief, check the court's rules for the terms appropriate to your type of appeal. If you cannot find the answer that way, see how the parties are referred to in a reported case in the same court that *procedurally* resembles your own.

their importance. The notice of appeal is short and simple because it is a mere declaration that the appellant is doing what a losing party has a right to do. But the petition for discretionary review *asks* for something and is therefore far more complex. Because the denial of such a petition forecloses appeal, its contents are crucial and must be drafted persuasively. The notice or petition must be served and filed within the time required by law, and the time limits can vary from jurisdiction to jurisdiction. A notice of appeal is filed with the clerk of the court being appealed *from,* rather than the clerk of the court being appealed to, but the contrary is true of a petition for leave to appeal.

The second step in the appeal is the *transmittal of the record* from the court below to the court above. Although one might imagine this to be an easy matter of the clerk of one court locating a file and sending it to the clerk of another court, it happens that way only in cases where the record is very simple. A record can be simple, for example, where the appeal is from an order dismissing a complaint for failure to state a cause of action. There the record might not include much more than the complaint, the papers submitted by both parties in connection with the defendant's motion to dismiss, and the court's order.

Most appeals, however, arise only later in the litigation, and in those cases the preparation and transmittal of the record can delay matters for months and add thousands of dollars to the cost of the appeal. Wherever the trial court has held a hearing or trial, one or more court reporters will have to type up a transcript from stenographic notes, a time-consuming process that can produce literally volumes of material.

The third step — required in some jurisdictions and optional in others — is the assembling of an abbreviated version of the record called the *joint appendix* or the *record appendix.*[1] At the appealing party's expense, it is printed in sufficient quantity that a copy can be given to each judge who will hear the appeal. The appellate judges need the joint appendix because the full record can be gargantuan, and the appellate court will have only one copy of it. Even if all the judges hearing an appeal were to work in the same building, it would be impractical to ask them to share a single copy, which may be bound into several bulky volumes. Moreover, in many appellate courts the judges do not do all of their work in the same building: they have additional chambers near their homes, which may be scattered about a state, a district, or a circuit, and they gather only when scheduled to hear oral arguments and to deliberate. Whether chambers are scattered or located centrally, the judges can work most efficiently if each has a copy of the most important parts of the record, and if the full record is available in the clerk's office as a reserve.

---

§31.2   1. The joint appendix is not the Statement of the Case. Nor is it the type of appendix that you might add to the brief to set out in full those statutes that a court might be asked to construe. The Statement of the Case and a statutory appendix are each only a few pages long, and both are part of the brief. The joint appendix is often larger than the brief, and it is bound separately.

Although rules vary from jurisdiction to jurisdiction, there are generally two methods of assembling the appendix. The parties can agree on a joint appendix, but that does not happen often. More frequently, the appellant designates those portions of the record that she or he wants in the appendix; the appellee counter-designates portions to be added; and the portions are combined and printed in the same sequence in which they appear in the full record.

The fourth step is the *drafting of briefs,* which each attorney files with the appellate court and serves on opposing counsel. For some lawyers, this is the most intellectually challenging part of litigation, and it is the subject of Chapters 32-33.

In a court without discretionary jurisdiction, the fifth step—and the first in which the appellate court becomes actively involved—is *screening.* Until relatively recently, most appeals were given a full adjudication that included oral argument and a formal opinion, whether or not published. Because of geometrically increasing appellate caseloads, that time is gone forever. Now, in most appellate courts, the appellant must struggle to get a full adjudication, and a wise appellee fights to prevent it. If the appeal is not given full treatment, it is shunted onto a summary adjudication track, where there may be no oral argument or formal opinion, where the judges might not even meet to discuss the appeal. The result of that is usually affirmance. Courts that do not have discretionary jurisdiction use screening to ensure that their error-correction function is performed economically while they concentrate on the most important appeals, which are still given full adjudicatory treatment. The factors that motivate a court without discretionary jurisdiction to give an appeal full adjudicatory treatment are not very different from the factors that would cause a discretionary court to accept an appeal that it is not obligated to decide. Screening is done by one or more specially assigned judges, who may be assisted by attorneys employed by the court to study the briefs and the record. In some courts, every appeal is screened, while in others screening occurs only when a party—usually the appellee—requests it. Some courts require the attorneys to meet with a judge in a pre-briefing or pre-argument conference, which is used partly for screening, partly to clarify and limit the issues, and partly to encourage negotiation between the parties. A few courts without discretionary jurisdiction—most notably the United States Court of Appeals for the Second Circuit—refuse to screen (except perhaps in preargument conferences) and require oral argument in every case on the theory that the screening consumes as much judicial effort as it saves.

In virtually all appeals in a discretionary court and in fully adjudicated appeals in a court without discretionary jurisdiction, the next step is *oral argument.* Each attorney is allotted a predetermined period, such as fifteen minutes, to speak in open court with the judges, who might ask many questions or only a few. Oral argument is particularly satisfying work because it is the attorney's only chance to speak directly with the judges about the problems and issues raised by the appeal. Where the judges and the attorneys are perceptive and well-prepared, oral argument can be the most scholarly type of conversation known to the practice of law,[2] and it is the subject of Chapter 34.

After oral argument, the judges confer and discuss the merits of the appeal. In some courts, this conference occurs on the same day as argument; in others, it may happen several days later. One judge is selected to write the court's opinion. In some courts, the assignment is made by chance rotation, but in others it is made by the presiding judge. In the United States Supreme Court, the assignment is made by the most senior judge among the majority. The assigned judge drafts an opinion and circulates it to the other judges, who might suggest changes or might draft and circulate concurring or dissenting opinions of their own. In routine appeals, the draft majority opinion is often quickly approved, and concurrences and dissents may be held to a minimum. But in more complex and troubling cases, views can change, and an opinion originally written as a dissent might be transformed into the court's opinion, while the original majority draft is demoted into a dissent.

If the losing party can appeal further, the whole process may begin again, with a new notice of appeal or petition for some sort of leave to appeal— more likely the latter, as one moves up the appellate ladder.

§31.3   The Roles of the Brief and of Oral Argument

To understand the different roles of the brief and oral argument, you must be able to visualize the effect of increasingly crowded dockets on the work of appellate judges.

Depending on the court, an appellate judge might in a month hear oral arguments and confer with colleagues on several dozen appeals, and in many courts substantially more than a hundred. For each appeal, the judge will have to read at least two briefs and in multiparty cases or public-interest cases[1] a half-dozen briefs or more, together with portions of the record. The judge will have to write majority opinions in a proportion of the appeals not summarily disposed of; on a five-judge court, for example, each judge is assigned one-fifth of the majority opinions. In addition, the judge may feel obligated to write several concurring or dissenting opinions.

---

2. "I can see the Chief Justice as he looked at that moment. [B]efore counsel began to argue, the Chief Justice would nib his pen; and then, when everything was ready, pulling up the sleeves of his gown, he would nod to the counsel who was to address him, as much as to say 'I am ready; now you may go on.' I think I never experienced more intellectual pleasure than in arguing that novel question to a great man who could appreciate it, and take it in; and he did take it in, as a baby takes in its mother's milk." This is how Daniel Webster recalled his oral argument to the Supreme Court, led by Chief Justice John Marshall, in *Gibbons v. Ogden,* 22 U.S. (9 Wheat.) 1 (1824), one of the leading Constitutional cases of the nineteenth century. (The quote is from 1 Charles Warren, *The Supreme Court in United States History* 603 (Little, Brown & Co. 1935).) Although pens have not been "nibbed" since they were made from feathers, modern appellate litigators know every other sensation Webster described.

§31.3   1. In cases that would affect groups that are not parties, the court may grant permission for nonparties to file briefs as amicus curiae (friends of the court).

The judge will also have to read opinions drafted by other judges and at times will write memoranda to colleagues suggesting changes in those opinions. The judge will spend a fair amount of time reading some of the cases and statutes cited to in all these briefs and draft opinions. And the judge may have screening and other administrative responsibilities. With all this work, the typical appellate judge would find it a luxury to spend as much as an hour reading the average brief, and the time available is often no more than half an hour per brief. That is why briefs, although large, must be carefully crafted to reveal their logic while demanding the least possible time and effort from the reader. Judges spend more time, of course, on briefs where the appeal raises deeply troubling issues than on briefs in more routine cases. And a judge who writes an opinion might read the briefs more thoroughly than one who does not.

In a work environment like this, the brief and oral argument are asked to perform different functions. Each is critical, but in a different way.

The brief can best lay out the theory of the appeal by explaining in persuasive detail the authorities and evidence on which a favorable decision should be based. A successful brief not only persuades the judge that your client should win, but it can also be used as a manual explaining to the judge exactly how to make the decision and how to justify it in an opinion. A judge may use the brief for initial screening, to prepare for oral argument, to prepare for the conference with other judges, and while writing the opinion.

The oral argument, on the other hand, can do two things better than the brief can. First, in oral argument the attorney can more immediately motivate the court by focusing on the most important ideas — the few facts, rules, and policies — that most make the attorney's theory of the appeal compelling. Although the brief should show both the forest and the trees, the oral argument can be a bit more powerful at illuminating the forest. (Conversely it is a horrible medium through which to examine the trees.) Second, in oral argument the attorney can try to discover, through the bench's questions, each judge's doubts, and the attorney can on the spot explain exactly why those doubts should not prevent a ruling in the attorney's favor. Oral argument, in fact, is the attorney's only opportunity to learn directly from the judges the precise problems they have with the attorney's theory. Oral argument's greater efficiency at these two things is not a reason to skimp on trying to accomplish them through the brief as well. Oral argument lasts only a few minutes, and memories of it can fade. The brief, on the other hand, has permanence: it is always among the judge's working materials, and it "speaks from the time it is filed and continues through oral argument, conference, and opinion writing."[2]

Briefs and oral argument have assumed these roles more through evolution than by design, as courts have gradually realized how different kinds of information can most efficiently be conveyed. Detail is communicated best in writing, which can be studied. Conversation, on the other hand, both

2. Herbert Funk Goodrich, *A Case on Appeal — A Judge's View*, in *A Case on Appeal* 10-1 (ALI-ABA 1967).

encourages spontaneous dialogue and lends itself to the broad sweep of underlying ideas.

§31.4   Limitations on Appellate Review

You have already learned of one limitation on the scope of appeals: many courts have *discretionary appellate jurisdiction* and use it to avoid deciding large numbers of cases.[1]

In addition, appellate courts will disturb an order or judgment only if it is based on *reversible error.* An appellate court will affirm unless the appellant can point to a specific error by the trial court that the law considers ground for reversal. Be careful of two kinds of situations, neither of which will lead to a reversal. In the first, the result below seems unfortunate, but no error by the court below can be identified. In the absence of reversible error, an appellate court must affirm what the trial court did. That is because an appeal is only a review for the kind of mistake the law categorizes as error. In the second situation, error can be identified, but it did not cause the order or judgment appealed from. Even if the result below was unfortunate, and even if the court below committed error, an appellate court will reverse only if the result below is traceable to the error. Error that affected the result below is called *material* or *prejudicial.* Error without such an effect is called *harmless.*

To identify error, and to figure out whether it was material or harmless, start with the procedural posture in the trial court. For example, assume that the plaintiff has requested a particular jury instruction; that the trial court denied the request and instead gave another instruction; that the jury returned a verdict for the defendant; and that, on the basis of the verdict, the trial judge entered a judgment for the defendant. The issue on appeal cannot be whether the plaintiff should have won below; rather, it is whether the trial court so erroneously instructed the jury that the entire case should be tried again to a jury properly instructed. If the instruction was error, but if the record shows that the error was not so material as to lead the jury astray, the error was harmless and will not be reversed. The error would be harmless, for example, if the evidence in support of the verdict was so overwhelming that a properly instructed jury would have returned the same verdict.

Appellate review is mostly (but not entirely) limited to *issues of law.* A jury's verdict is a purely factual determination and thus not generally reviewable on appeal. Where a case is tried to a judge without a jury, the judge makes findings of fact that correspond to a jury's verdict. Are judicial findings of fact reviewable on appeal? In some appellate courts, they are not. In the appellate opinions you have read for other courses, you may have noticed the stock phrasing used in such courts to introduce a factual finding

---

§31.4   1. See §31.2.

over which an appellant is unhappy: "The trial court found as a fact, not reviewable by us on appeal, that . . ." In other appellate courts, judicial fact finding is reversible — but only if it is "clearly erroneous."[2] This standard is harder on appellants than that applied to a trial judge's conclusions of law, which can be reversed if merely "erroneous."

Appellate review is further limited to *issues preserved below*. An issue is preserved below only if the appellant raised it and only if the court below decided it. Because an appeal is a review for error, an appellate court will not concern itself with matters the lower court did not decide. An issue is waived unless the appellant raises the issue below and seeks a decision there. There are two exceptions to the requirement that error be preserved. The more rigid exception concerns subject matter jurisdiction, defects in which can never be waived because a court should on its own motion refuse to adjudicate a case outside its authority. The more flexible exception concerns "plain error," which is error so fundamental to the process of justice that it cries out to be corrected even if the appellant seemed unconcerned about it when it happened. Be careful: "plain error" cannot be invoked whenever an appellant has been careless below. Only in the rarest of circumstances is an appellate court so shocked that it will save an appellant who, in the court below, did not even try to save himself.

What happens where, in the trial court, a party advanced several different grounds, all in support of the same relief, and where the court granted the relief on one ground and ignored the others? The ignored grounds are not waived: it would have been pointless to press for a decision on them. In fact, if an appellate court rejects the ground adopted by the lower court, the appellate court can still affirm, if it chooses to do so, on one of the grounds ignored by the lower court. A correct result is affirmable even if the lower court accomplished it for the wrong reason.

Appellate review is still further limited to issues that are actually *raised on appeal*. An appellate court does not survey the record below looking for error: in the adversary system, that is the job of the appellant's attorney. If the appellate court has discretionary appellate jurisdiction, an issue is waived unless raised in the petition seeking leave to appeal. In any appellate court, an issue is waived unless raised in the brief. Only very rarely does an appellate court overlook this limitation and itself raise an issue not asserted by a party. This happens most strikingly when the appellant's attorney has not realized that some of the judges are interested in changing rules of law that the parties have taken for granted.

Appellate courts will review only *final* orders and judgments. Although finality generally occurs when the court below has nothing left to adjudicate, in many jurisdictions the law hedges the concept often. One reason is that finality itself is not always easy to recognize. Sometimes an order may plainly be one that does not terminate litigation on a particular issue, but it may so alter the positions of the parties that the practical effect would be final if not reviewed. Another reason is that it is hard to accomplish the

---

2. *See, e.g.,* Rule 52(a) of the Federal Rules of Civil Procedure. This is explained more fully in §33.3.

purpose of the final order rule—economizing everyone's effort and speeding the real end of a lawsuit by reviewing on appeal only the trial court's finished product—without at the same time precluding review of some types of interlocutory orders that ought not be immune from appellate scrutiny. As a result, most jurisdictions have developed, through statutes and case law, a number of exceptions to the final order rule.[3]

Appellate courts generally refuse to consider facts that do not appear in the trial court's record (also called the *record below*). You can determine whether a fact is in the record by focusing on the procedural posture in the trial court. If the order appealed from is one dismissing a complaint for failure to state a cause of action, a fact is in the record if it is alleged in the complaint. That is because, for the purpose of deciding a motion to dismiss a complaint, all facts properly pleaded are treated as though they could be proven. (And, of course, on such a motion the only factual record before the trial court is the complaint itself.) But the situation is different where the motion in the trial court challenged a party's evidence rather than allegations (see §§24.2.1 and 24.2.3). For example, assume that the appeal is from a summary judgment. If a fact appears as an allegation in a pleading but does not appear in any evidentiary form, it is not "a fact in the record" because the motion below tested evidence and not allegations. (If you are confused about the difference between facts, allegations, and evidence, see §17.1.)

There are two exceptions to the rule against considering facts outside the record. One involves the doctrine of judicial notice, through which a court—trial or appellate—will, without evidence, accept as proven certain facts that are beyond dispute. Do not make more of this than it really is. The following are examples of the kinds of indisputable facts of which courts will take judicial notice: A meter equals 39.37 inches. Cleveland is in Cuyahoga County, Ohio. March 15, 2001, was a Thursday.

The other exception is for what are called "legislative facts," which are generalized social, economic, or scientific information that guides a court in the development of law—as opposed to the "case facts" or "adjudicatory facts," which are the specific events that transpired between the parties. Legislative facts can include empirical data on the detrimental effects of racial segregation, or on the national deterioration of groundwater quality, or on the ways consumers use videocassette recorders—all useful in determining public policy. Although the adversary system is not very efficient at collecting legislative facts,[4] appellate courts need them when making or changing law. And although legislative facts can be placed in the trial record, an attorney called in to handle an appeal sometimes needs to put before the appellate court legislative facts not developed in the record

3. For example, under 28 U.S.C. §§ 1291 and 1292, federal appellate courts are authorized to review a variety of interlocutory orders, including orders granting or denying preliminary injunctions. And the Supreme Court has developed a collateral order doctrine "whose reach is limited to trial court orders affecting rights that will be irretrievably lost in the absence of an immediate appeal." *Richardson-Merrell, Inc. v. Koller,* 472 U.S. 424, 430-31 (1985).

4. Legislatures are far more efficient at using the knowledge of experts, collecting and studying empirical research, and weighing conflicting scientific analyses. Courts must rely on individual attorneys, who are rarely able to match the resources of legislative staffs.

below. The appellate attorney might include in the brief published empirical research that complements but does not crowd out the legal analysis that is the core of argument.[5] Empirical material added on appeal is not set out in the Statement of the Case, because it is not part of the record below. Rather, it appears, with citations, in the Argument, most often in support of policy contentions.

The law presumes an order or judgment to be correct unless an appellant demonstrates that the appropriate *standard of review* has been violated. The standard of review will vary from one kind of appeal to another. Think of it as a formula of deference. Depending on the type of decision made below, the appellate court may defer — to a specified degree — to the decision of the trial court judge. Some types of decisions, for example, will be reversed if "erroneous"; others only if "clearly erroneous"; and yet others only if "an abuse of discretion." (Standards of review are explained in detail in §33.3.)

Finally, appellate courts are temperamentally "affirmance-prone." Unless deeply troubled by what happened below, an appellate judge will be inclined to affirm for several reasons. The trial judge handled the problem first-hand and might know more than distant appellate judges reading a cold transcript of the testimony. Because many trial decisions must be made instantly "in the heat of battle," it is unrealistic to expect perfection from a trial judge. Every reversal disturbs the status quo, and circumspect people like judges are not comfortable disturbing the status quo unless it is truly necessary. And reversals impose tangible costs, which can be large, such as retrials.

---

5. A brief that uses a fair amount of empirical material is called a "Brandeis brief," after the successful one submitted by Louis D. Brandeis in *Muller v. Oregon,* 208 U.S. 412 (1908).

32

Appellate Briefs

§32.1 Appellate Brief Format

This chapter describes the format of an appellate brief and how judges read appellate briefs. Chapter 31 explains how appeals work. Chapter 33 explains how to develop a theory of the appeal, write the brief, and handle the standard of review. In addition, Chapters 24-26 explain generally how to develop persuasive theories and arguments and how to handle procedural postures. Many of the skills used in writing an office memorandum are valuable here as well: organizing proof of a conclusion of law (Chapters 10-13), selecting authority (Chapter 14), working with precedent and statutes (Chapters 15-16), analyzing facts (Chapter 17), paragraphing (Chapter 18), using an effective style (Chapter 19), and citing and quoting properly (Chapter 20).

Although rules on format differ from court to court, the required structure might commonly include the following:[1]

1. a cover page containing a caption and other information that might be required by local rules;
2. a Table of Contents (sometimes called an Index);
3. a Table of Authorities;
4. where the appeal rests on the interpretation of a constitutional provision, statute, administrative regulation, or court rule, a reprinting of the relevant material;

---

§32.1 1. Some courts require additional material, such as a statement specifying how the court acquired jurisdiction over the appeal in question. And some courts restrict the material that may appear in an appendix to a brief.

5.   a Preliminary Statement;
6.   a Question Presented or Questions Presented;
7.   a Statement of the Case;
8.   a Summary of Argument;
9.   an Argument, broken up with point headings;
10. a Conclusion; and
11. an indorsement.

As you read the description below of each of these components, compare the sample briefs in Appendices G and H.

The **cover page** includes the caption, followed by the document's title (such as "BRIEF FOR APPELLANT") and the name, address, and telephone number of the attorney submitting the brief. The caption includes the name of the appellate court, the appellate court's docket number, and the names of the parties and their procedural designations (appellant, appellee, etc.) in the appellate court. Many courts require that the caption also include the parties' procedural designations in the trial court.[2] In federal appellate courts, the appellant is listed first in the caption, but in most state appellate courts the parties appear in the same order in which their names appeared in captions in the trial court. The cover page does not have a page number.

The **Table of Contents** begins on the page after the cover page. It lists all of the components of the brief (except the cover page and the Table of Contents itself); reproduces the point headings and sub-headings from the Argument; and sets out the page on which each component, point, or sub-point begins. Because the point headings and sub-headings are reproduced verbatim in the Table of Contents, a reader can look there for an outline of the argument and for quick grasp of the attorney's theory of the appeal. When read together in the Table of Contents, the point headings and sub-headings should express the theory persuasively and coherently.

The **Table of Authorities** appears on the first page after the Table of Contents. It indexes the cases, statutes, constitutional provisions, court rules, administrative regulations, treatises, and law review articles cited in the argument, together with references to the pages in the brief where each authority is cited. In the Table, every authority is listed in a complete citation conforming to citation rules, and an asterisk is placed to the left of those citations that form the core of your theory. A footnote identifies those citations as "authorities chiefly relied on" or similar words to the same effect.

The Table of Authorities is broken down into three sections headed "Cases," "Statutes," and "Miscellaneous." Cases are listed in alphabetical

---

2. In a criminal case, the prosecution's *trial court* procedural designation is always implied and never expressed. For the accused, the trial court procedural designation is, of course, "defendant"—as in "Merritt Bresnahan, defendant." But it would seem silly to write "People of the State of New York, Prosecution." Phrases like "State v. Bresnahan," "People v. Bresnahan," "Commonwealth v. Bresnahan," and "United States v. Bresnahan" unambiguously communicate that Bresnahan is being prosecuted by whatever government customarily uses the designation that precedes the "v."

order. If constitutional provisions, court rules, or administrative regulations are cited, they are listed with statutes, and the heading is enlarged to accommodate them. (In a brief where all of these materials are cited, the heading would read "Constitutional Provisions, Statutes, Court Rules, and Administrative Regulations.") Under the heading, the citations appear in the following order: federal constitutional provisions, state constitutional provisions, federal statutes, state statutes, court rules, federal administrative regulations, state administrative regulations. "Miscellaneous" is reserved for secondary authority, such as restatements, treatises, and law review articles, and they are listed there in that order.

Both the Table of Contents and the Table of Authorities should be set up on the page so that they are easy to use. In the Table of Authorities, for example, the authorities and the briefs page numbers should be separated so that the difference is immediately obvious. Imagine a Table filled with entries like this:

> *S. Burlington County NAACP v. Township of Mt. Laurel*, 67 N.J. 151, 336 A.2d 713 (1975) 9, 12
>
> *Tidewater Oil Co. v. Mayor of Carteret*, 44 N.J. 338, 209 A.2d 105 (1965) 10, 15
>
> *Village of Euclid v. Ambler Realty Co.*, 272 U.S. 365 (1926) 8, 14

As a reader, you would probably find the following a bit easier on the eye:

> *S. Burlington County NAACP v. Township of Mt. Laurel*, 67 N.J. 151, 336 A.2d 713 (1975) 9, 12
>
> *Tidewater Oil Co. v. Mayor of Carteret*, 44 N.J. 338, 209 A.2d 105 (1965) 10, 15
>
> *Village of Euclid v. Ambler Realty Co.*, 272 U.S. 365 (1926) 8, 14

For pagination purposes, a brief is broken down into two parts. The two Tables (sometimes called the "front matter") are paginated together in lowercase roman numerals. The rest of the brief (the "body") is paginated separately in arabic numbers, beginning with "1," on the first page after the Tables. Although this may seem odd, it has a very practical purpose. Because the Tables must include page references to the body, the body is typed before the Tables are. And because you cannot know how many pages the Tables will occupy until they are typed, the body must begin on page 1. The only efficient solution is to use two separate paginations: lowercase roman for the Tables and arabic for the body.

The **Constitutional Provisions, Statutes, Regulations, and Court Rules Involved** is the easiest part of the brief to draft. It is a place where the court can learn two things.

The first is a list of the codified or promulgated law (as opposed to precedent) that is *critical* to the decision the court is asked to make. A provision is critical to the decision if the parties disagree about its meaning and if the court cannot dispose of the appeal without resolving the disagreement. *A court rule that merely provides for the type of motion made below is not critical to the decision* unless the parties disagree about the rule's meaning and the court has been asked to resolve the disagreement. Although custom requires the use of the misleading word "Involved" in the heading to this portion of the brief, the only provisions printed under the heading are those that are *at the heart of* the issues before the court. They are much more than "Involved."

The second thing the court can learn from this part of the brief is either the precise wording of those relevant portions or—if the relevant portions are extensive—an indication that they are reproduced in an appendix to the brief. If the material is complicated enough to warrant an appendix, the reference to it could read something like this:

> The following statutes and court rules are set out in the Appendix: Sections 362 and 363 of title I of the Bankruptcy Reform Act of 1978, *as amended,* 11 U.S.C. §§ 362, 363 (2000), together with Bankruptcy Rules 1002 and 1003.

On the other hand, if the provisions are short, this portion of the brief might be written in a manner somewhat like the following:

> The First Amendment to the United States Constitution provides, in pertinent part, as follows:
>
> > Congress shall make no law . . . abridging the freedom of speech or of the press; or the right of the people . . . to petition the Government for a redress of grievances.

A reasonable editing of the relevant provisions aids the court. Be careful to indicate deletions, as you would with any other quote.

Phrase the heading of this section of the brief to fit its content. The bankruptcy example above would appear under the heading, "Statutes and Court Rules Involved," while the heading over the First Amendment would read "Constitutional Provisions Involved."

The **Preliminary Statement** briefly sets out the appeal's procedural posture by identifying the parties (if that is necessary), listing the relevant procedural events, and describing the order or judgment appealed from. If it can be done very concisely, the Preliminary Statement might also describe the reasoning of the court below and identify the grounds on which the decision below is challenged on appeal. The point is to tell the court why the matter is before it and to specify the type of decision the court will have to make. That can usually be done in less than a page. Many lawyers add a paragraph summarizing their own arguments. This portion of the brief goes by different names in different courts. Where it is not titled "Preliminary Statement," the heading might read "Proceedings Below,"

"Nature of the Proceedings," or the like. In some courts, the Preliminary Statement is called the "Statement of the Case," and the Statement of the Case — as that term is used in this book — is called a "Statement of Facts."

A persuasive **Question Presented** is explained in Chapter 30.[3]

The **Statement of the Case** is explained in Chapter 29.

A **Summary of the Argument** is what its name implies. The point headings and sub-headings, as they appear in the Table of Contents, outline the argument. But the Summary does more: it condenses the argument into a few paragraphs — usually one paragraph per issue — with more meat in them than can be put into headings. The Summary should not repeat the point headings.

The **Argument** can be divided into points, each of which is a separate and integral theory that, standing alone, would be enough to support a ruling in the client's favor on a question presented. It is unusual in law school briefs for either side to have more than two points, and the appeals assigned often lend themselves to only one point. Points and point headings are explained in Chapter 28.[4]

Although some lawyers use the **Conclusion** to reargue and resummarize the theory of the appeal, the better practice is to limit the conclusion to a one-sentence reiteration of the relief desired, together with an unamplified identification of the ground on which the relief would be based. For example:

> For all the foregoing reasons, the order of the Circuit Court for Albemarle County should be affirmed on the ground that the complaint does not state a cause of action.

A judge who needs to know immediately what you want should be able to find that precisely stated in the Conclusion. This is particularly important where there are cross-appeals:

> For the foregoing reasons, the District Court's order should be affirmed insofar as it enjoins enforcement of Glendale Ordinance 88162, and in all other respects the District Court's order should be reversed.

or where an appellant seeks alternative relief:

> For the foregoing reasons, Mr. Merkle's conviction should be reversed because the Superior Court admitted into evidence a "confession"

---

3. In some cases argued to the Supreme Court of the United States, Questions Presented are not expected to meet criteria 1 and 6 in §30.2. If the controversy is really between two bodies of law (such as "Whether Title IV violates the equal protection clause"), *and* if the events between the parties would not be critical to the Court's decision, the Questions Presented would be framed without lists of determinative facts. (Be careful, though: in some controversies between bodies of law, the facts do matter because they show why a statute either is or is not unconstitutional.)

4. Point headings in briefs to the United States Supreme Court do not necessarily comply with criteria 6 or 8 in §28.2. In part that is because of the reasons explained in note 3 above. And in part it is because a Supreme Court Justice already knows much of what a case is about even before reading the briefs. The Court considers only a few appeals, which it selects (see §31.1) for the purpose of making law.

coerced in violation of his Fifth Amendment rights, or, in the alternative, this matter should be remanded to the Superior Court for resentencing because the original sentence exceeds the statutory maximum.

The **indorsement** is similar to the indorsement in a motion memorandum. (See §27.1.)

Every court has rules governing the contents of briefs and other submitted documents. The rules are designed to make briefs easier for judges to use, and judges understandably become exasperated when the rules are ignored. Egregious violations of court rules can result in the court's striking the brief, in financial penalties imposed on the attorney, and even in dismissal of the appeal.

§32.2 How Judges Read Appellate Briefs

How does a judge read a brief? The answer may vary considerably from judge to judge, but the following is not unusual:

> [B]efore the oral argument I read over the briefs and some material parts of the records, in somewhat cursory fashion, enough to know what the points in the case are and what the positions of the opposing parties are. When the oral argument is over, the answer to the controversy is sometimes indisputably clear. But in most cases it is not and a real study is in order. Usually I first read both parties' statements of the questions presented; then I read the appellant's statement of the general nature of the controversy. Then I look at his outline of argument to see what points he makes. Then I look at the appellee's outline of argument to see what he is going to do in reply. Then I go to the joint appendix to see what the trial court or the administrative agency did. Then I read the appellant's statement of the facts and the appellee's statement. Thereafter I examine the two briefs one point at a time, first the appellant's and then the appellee's, on the first point; then both briefs on the second point, etc. If the point is an obvious one, or if one side or the other seems to be wholly without strength on it, I do not spend too much time on that point in my first study. On the really contested points I study both sides, read the cases, and, if facts are critical check the record references. The briefs on the critical points are often reread and reread.[1]

Other judges might read the parts of a brief in a different sequence — perhaps reading the point headings before anything else — and a given judge might vary the sequence from case to case. But the following observations generally describe the use to which a brief is put:

First, you must write for several different readers. Depending on the court, an appeal might be decided by three to nine judges. And briefs are also read by law clerks or research attorneys who assist judges by studying the briefs and recommending decisions.

---

§32.2 1. E. Barrett Prettyman, *Some Observations Concerning Appellate Advocacy*, 39 Va. L. Rev. 285, 296 (1953).

Second, briefs — like memos — are not read from beginning to end at a single sitting. They are read in chunks, at different times, depending on the needs of the reader. (You probably read an appliance or automobile owner's manual in pretty much the same way, and — as explained in §25.1 — a brief is a manual for making a decision.)

Third, a brief is read for differing reasons, depending on who is reading and when, and the brief must be constructed to satisfy all of these uses without frustrating the reader. If screening is done after briefs are filed (see §31.2), that is the first purpose to which a brief will be put. The judges will also either scan or study the brief in preparation for oral argument, and afterward they will read it again to decide how to vote. One judge will be assigned to write the court's opinion, and while doing that will reread various portions of the brief several times, looking for the detail needed to justify and explain the decision. And all along the way, the judges will be assisted by law clerks who check up on the details of the brief while the judges focus on the broader principles. Each segment of the brief must be written to satisfy all of these purposes.

Finally, a brief must include several different places where a judge can "enter" the brief by learning what the appeal is about. A judge will go first to a part of the brief that reveals the fundamental issues in the appeal and your theory on each issue. A judge ought to be able to find that material plainly set out in four different places: the point headings and sub-headings (collected in the Table of Contents); the Questions Presented; the Summary of Argument; and the Statement of the Case (read together with the Preliminary Statement). Each judge has a favorite starting place. Not only do you have no way of knowing when you write the brief where a given judge prefers to begin, but you are writing for several judges and must accommodate them all. Thus, you must draft these four components so that each can separately be a self-sufficient and self-explanatory entry point for any predictable reader.

33 Writing the Appellate Brief

§33.1 Developing a Theory of the Appeal

In Chapter 24, you learned that a theory is attractive only if it is solidly built on the record and the law, explains away unfavorable facts, is framed in terms of basic fairness to the parties, and appeals to logic and common sense. An effective appellate theory, however, has some additional qualities.

First, a persuasive theory of the appeal is grounded on the procedural posture below and the standard of review in ways described in §33.3. For the attorney urging reversal, the theory is one of *error,* while for the attorney defending the result below, the theory is one of *the absence of error.* And neither error nor its absence can be explained without taking into account the procedural posture below and the standard of review.

Second, a persuasive appellate theory does not ignore any of the limitations on appellate review described in §31.4. An appellate court will reject a theory that would violate restrictions on the court's own power to act.

Third, a persuasive appellate theory goes beyond a technical analysis and addresses the judges' concern about a fair and just result. An appellant must show both error and injustice: "If you can convince the appellate judges that the court below is wrong as an intellectual matter, but leave them with the impression that no worthwhile damage was done, the prior result will be affirmed."[1] Although an appellee might succeed by showing either an

---

§33.1 1. Edward J. Lampron, *Observations on Appellate Advocacy,* 14 N.H. B.J. (No. 3) at 105, 106 (Winter 1973).

absence of error or an absence of harm, the wiser strategy is to try to show both, if that can credibly be argued.

Fourth, a persuasive appellate theory is soundly grounded in public policy. Judges engaged in law formation or clarification are understandably concerned about the wider consequences of what they do. How would the precedent the court will create in your case affect others in the future?

Fifth, a persuasive appellate theory asks the court to make no more law than is necessary to the attorney's goal. Most judges do not believe that their purpose on the bench is to change society in fundamental ways, and you will have a better chance to win if your theory asks only for those changes that are truly necessary to the result you want.

Finally, a persuasive appellant's theory raises no more than two, three, or at the very most four claims of error. A theory is damaged, not strengthened, by adding additional but weaker grounds to the two or three best ones available. The weaker grounds by their mere assertion cheapen the stronger ones and take up room in the brief that is better used to more fully develop the grounds most likely to cause reversal. Good theory development requires the good judgment to choose the strongest grounds, the self-discipline to focus the court's attention on them alone, and the courage to ignore other grounds that may seem tempting but, in the end, are unlikely to persuade.

§33.2   The Process of Writing a Brief

Before you begin to write, digest the record, do a significant amount — but *not all* — of the research, and develop the basic shape of your theory.

Digesting the record is more than merely reading it: study the record to identify potential reversible error by the trial court and to find every fact that could be used either to prove error or to defend what the trial court did. Look for both kinds of facts — regardless of whom you represent. Facts favorable to your position will, of course, become ammunition. But your theory must also show the appellate court why and how the facts that run against you should not become determinative.

Before starting to write, do enough research to have all the ingredients for your theory. That includes all the major authorities on each issue, as well as enough of the lesser authorities for you to have a good handle on relevant policy, on the procedural posture that governed the decision below, and on the standard of review in the appellate court (explained in §33.3). But you do not need to find everything in the library on your issue before you begin to write. In fact, if you try to do that, your brief will probably suffer. Remember the inseparability of writing and thinking: when you begin to write, you will understand more about the kinds of details from authorities that you will need to fill out the Argument (see §14.7).

Just as a judge does not read a brief from beginning to end, neither does a lawyer write it that way. The Table of Contents and Table of Authorities are always done last, after the rest of the brief has already been typed (see §32.1). The order in which the other parts are written differs from lawyer to lawyer and from appeal to appeal because one lawyer's work habits are not necessarily effective for someone else and because an effective lawyer adapts to the individual task at hand. Eventually, you will settle into a range of work habits that are effective for you, and your first brief is an opportunity to begin to define yourself in that way.

To help you start, consider two very different methods of writing a brief.

Order in Which a First Draft Might Be Written	
Model I	*Model II*
1. point headings	1. Questions Presented
2. Argument	2. Statement of the Case
3. Statement of the Case	3. point headings
4. Questions Presented	4. Argument
5. rest of brief	5. rest of brief

A lawyer who uses Model I outlines the Argument by composing the point headings and sub-headings and by listing under each heading the material to be covered there when the Argument is written. The logical next step is drafting the Argument itself. This lawyer might draft the Statement of the Case after the Argument on the ground that the value of specific facts is not fully understood until after the Argument is written. The Questions Presented would be written afterward because the lawyer identifies the most determinative facts — the ones recited in the Questions — while working out the Argument and the Statement of the Case.

Conversely, a lawyer using Model II would begin the first draft by writing the Questions Presented on the theory that the other parts of the brief will be more focused if the issues are first precisely defined. A lawyer who uses this model writes the Statement of the Case next, using it to work out the details of the theory of the appeal (which the Model I lawyer does while writing the Argument). Both lawyers draft the point headings before the Argument because the Argument is easier to write in segments (which the headings create).

A lawyer with flexible work habits might use Model I in an appeal where the authority and issues are difficult and complex and Model II in a more fact-sensitive appeal. Some lawyers write the Question Presented and the Statement of the Case (and sometimes even the Argument) simultaneously, moving back and forth from one pad to another (or from one word processing disk file to another).

Start making practice oral arguments while you are writing the brief. It might seem logical to finish writing the brief and then work on the oral argument. After all, in court you submit the brief long before making the oral argument. But when we talk about a complicated subject, often we find ourselves saying surprisingly interesting and perceptive things. The act of talking can help us understand the subject better. That is because many people learn not just by reading and listening, but also by talking and doing. Some lawyers find it useful to begin work on the oral argument before completing the brief. They find that planning the oral argument sharply focuses their attention on the central problems in the appeal. And when they make practice oral arguments to colleagues, they find themselves unexpectedly saying things that would work well in the brief. So you may be able to write a better brief if you start practicing oral argument while you are still writing.

Before writing each subsequent draft, work on something else for a while or take a break to put the brief out of your thoughts. Come back to it in a frame of mind that enables you to put yourself in the judge's position: If you were a skeptical judge, would you be persuaded? Is the brief clear and easy to read? Does it teach you the appeal and show you how to make the decision? Reverting to your role as writer, have you organized the Argument around some variation of the paradigm formula explained in Chapters 10-13 and in §26.3? Or do you begin applying a rule to the facts before you have finished proving it (a sure sign that your organization is out of control)? At the other extreme, have you invested so much energy in proving a rule that you have forgotten to show the court how the rule governs the facts of your appeal? (When reviewing the Argument in general, see the checklist on organization in §13.2.) If a particular rule is not clearly expressed in the authorities, have you stated it yourself and then proved it with a synthesis? Where a gap in the law must be filled, have you defined the gap and explained the extent of local law before you begin to rely on persuasive authority? Have you used argument techniques (§25.3) and fact description tactics (§29.2)? Do your Point Headings and Questions Presented satisfy the criteria in §§28.2 and 30.2? Throughout the brief, ask yourself the questions in the paragraphing, style, and quotation checklists in Chapters 18, 19, and 20.

It is a good idea — even before you begin research — to set up a schedule with a series of deadlines. Start from the date on which the brief is due, and figure out how many days it will take to have the final draft typed, proofread, and photocopied. Then set a deadline on which those tasks will begin and all rewriting must stop. Figure out how long it will take to turn a second or third draft into a final draft and so on, working your way backward in time to deadlines where each draft must be finished and, for the first draft, where each component must be done. Writing a brief is a big job, and writing it in the time available requires self-discipline from you.

§33.3 Handling the Standard of Review and the Procedural Posture Below

(Before reading this section, you might review Chapter 26 on procedural postures.)

On appeal the question is not whether the appellant should have won in the trial court, but instead whether the relevant standard of review was violated in the particular ruling appealed from. For that reason, judges become quite annoyed with attorneys who write and speak as though there were no standards of review. In fact, the appellant's goal is to show that the standard of review has been violated, and the appellee's goal is to show that it has not.

How much error does it take to cause reversal? That depends on the appellate court and the procedural posture below. The appellate court matters because standards of review differ somewhat from one court to another. The procedural posture matters because different standards are applied to different rulings by the court below.

Many rulings of law—such as orders dismissing pleadings, summary judgments, directed verdicts, jury instructions, and judgments notwithstanding the verdict—are evaluated on appeal "de novo."[1] For appeals from these rulings, the appellate court does not use a standard that defers in any way to the trial court. Instead, the appellate court measures error simply by asking itself whether it would have done what the trial court did. The appellate court can do that because all of these rulings present pure questions *of law*. They do not require the trial judge to determine facts or exercise discretion.

Most law school appellate advocacy assignments involve de novo standards of review. If that is true of your assignment, you probably will not have much difficulty arguing within the standard properly. A de novo standard is neutral, like a pane of clear glass through which light passes without distortion. As you will see in a moment, the other standards are like filters and lenses that modify the image.

If the jurisdiction permits a judge's findings *of fact* to be challenged on appeal,[2] the appellate court will apply a higher standard, one which grants a certain amount of deference to what the trial court has done. In federal appeals, for example, a judge's fact-finding will be reversed only if it is "clearly erroneous."[3]

And on an issue where the lower court has *discretion,* the result below will be reversed only for an "abuse of discretion," which, again, represents a degree of deference to the trial court. A trial court has a wide range of discretion on issues of equity and on issues concerning management of the progress of the litigation, such as rulings on discovery motions and on the conduct of the trial.

---

§33.3 1. "De novo" is the term used in federal courts for this type of standard. Many states use other but synonymous phrases, such as "independent and nondeferential review."

2. See §31.4.

3. *See, e.g.,* Rule 52(a) of the Federal Rules of Civil Procedure.

The diagram below illustrates how standards of review work and how they are related to procedural tests in trial courts. (Read the diagram *from the bottom up.*)

4

Because the granting or denial of a preliminary injunction is a discretionary decision in a trial court, the appellate court will reverse only if the trial court abused its discretion. (*This is the standard of review.*)

↑

3

Plaintiff wins the motion, and defendant appeals.

↑

APPELLATE COURT

TRIAL COURT

1

Plaintiff moves for a preliminary injunction in the trial court.

⟶

2

The trial court will grant a preliminary injunction only if the plaintiff is threatened with irreparable harm, is likely to succeed on the merits, will suffer more if the injunction is denied than the defendant would if the motion were granted, and seeks relief not adverse to the public interest. (*This is the procedural test in the trial court.*)

The only way to find out which standard controls a given appellate issue is to research local law in the same manner that you would research rules governing the procedural posture in a trial court.[4] Look for authority that tells you not only what the standard is, but also what it means and how it works.

4. See §26.4. You can add the term "standard of review" (or "standard review") to a computer inquiry that you have already used to find substantive cases. But do this only after you have found the substantive cases you need. If you look for substantive cases and standards of review in the same search, the standard of review term in your inquiry might exclude valuable substantive cases.

Where a court mentions the standard of review in a decision, it usually does so immediately after reciting the facts and immediately before beginning the legal analysis. This is an example of the type of language you will find:

> A dismissal for failure to state a claim pursuant to Fed. R. Civ. P. 12 is a ruling on a question of law and as such is reviewed de novo. [Citation omitted.] Review is limited to the contents of the complaint.[5]

Here we learn what the standard is ("de novo"), and we learn a little — but certainly not everything — about how the standard operates ("Review is limited to the contents of the complaint"). Occasionally, a court will tell you much more about how the standard is used:

> "In reviewing the [National Labor Relations] Board's decision, we must scrutinize the entire record, 'including the evidence opposed to the Board's view from which conflicting inferences reasonably could be drawn.'" [Citation omitted.] Nevertheless, this court will defer to the Board's judgment and the Board's factual findings shall be conclusive if supported by substantial evidence on the record considered as a whole. [Citation omitted.] This "court may not substitute its judgment for that of the Board when the choice is 'between two fairly conflicting views, even though the court would justifiably have made a different choice had the matter been before it de novo.'" [Citation omitted.] We shall also defer to the Board's inferences in areas where the Board is considered to have "specialized evidence and expertise." [Citation omitted.][6]

And the court might explain at the same time both the standard of review and the rules governing the procedural posture in the trial court:

> The grant or denial of a motion for preliminary injunction is a decision within the discretion of the trial court. [Citation omitted.] Appellate review . . . is very narrow. [Citation omitted.] Accordingly, a district court's decision will be reversed only where there is a clear abuse of discretion. [Citation omitted.] That discretion is guided by four requirements for preliminary injunctive relief: (1) a substantial likelihood that the movants will ultimately prevail on the merits; (2) that they will suffer irreparable injury if the injunction is not issued; (3) that the threatened injury to the movants outweighs the potential harm to the opposing party and (4) that the injunction, if issued, will not be adverse to the public interest. [Citation omitted.][7]

Occasionally, you will come across an issue that is subject to a bifurcated or even (as in the example below) a trifurcated standard of review. Each portion of this test for laches has a different standard of review:

> Our standard of review on the laches issue has various components. We review factual findings such as length of delay and prejudice under the clearly erroneous standard; we review the district court's balancing of the equities for abuse of discretion; and our review of legal precepts applied by the district

---

5. *Kruso v. International Tel. & Tel. Corp.*, 872 F.2d 1416, 1421 (9th Cir. 1989).
6. *NLRB v. Emsing's Supermarket, Inc.*, 872 F.2d 1279, 1283-84 (7th Cir. 1989).
7. *Haitian Refugee Center, Inc. v. Nelson*, 872 F.2d 1555, 1561-62 (11th Cir. 1989).

court in determining that the delay was excusable is plenary. [Citation omitted.][8]

How do you handle the standard of review in a brief? Do three things:

First, set out the relevant standard of review at or near the beginning of the Argument section of the brief (or, if you have more than one point, each point's standard of review can be set out shortly after the point heading).[9] While doing so, identify the procedural posture below and invoke the procedural test that governs it. And — if it can be done succinctly — tell the court how the standard was violated (if you are the appellant) or how it was not (if you are the appellee). For example, from an appellant's brief:

> This is an appeal from a summary judgment, which is reviewed de novo in this court. [Citation omitted.] Summary judgment should occur only where there is no genuine issue as to any material fact and the movant is entitled to judgment as a matter of law. [Citation omitted.] In this case, the movant was not entitled to judgment as a matter of law.

This passage tells us that the standard is de novo, and that the appellant's theory of error is that the second element of the test for summary judgment was not satisfied. (The writer does not say that there was a genuine dispute as to a material fact, which means that only one element of the summary judgment test is at issue.)

An appellee might write the paragraph above differently. In the second sentence, an appellee might write "is appropriate where" instead of "should occur only where." (Why?) And in place of the last sentence, an appellee might write "Here, the appellant concedes that there was no issue as to a material fact, and the record below amply demonstrates that the appellee was entitled to judgment as a matter of law."

A good place to put this material is between a point heading and the first sub-heading. Cite to local authority to prove the procedural rule that governed the trial court and the standard of review on appeal. Unless the law is unclear, a conclusory proof is usually sufficient because these rules are the type with which an appellate court would be routinely familiar. (Notice how this is handled in the Appendix G and H briefs.)

Second, argue *through* the standard of review. If, for example, you are appealing from a decision committed to a trial court's discretion, show throughout rule application (see Chapter 10) that the trial court abused its discretion. If you are the appellee in such a case, show the opposite. It is not enough merely to state the standard of review at the beginning and then ignore it for the rest of the Argument. Instead, use it and corollary

---

8. *Bermuda Express, N.V. v. M/V Litsa*, 872 F.2d 554, 557 (3d Cir. 1989).

9. This is required in federal appeals and in several states. For example, see Fed. R. App. P. 28(a)(9)(B) (The appellant's argument "must contain . . . for each issue a concise statement of the applicable standard of review (which may appear in the discussion of the issue or under a separate heading placed before the discussion of the issues)."). Rule 28(b) permits the appellee to omit this statement "unless the appellee is dissatisfied with the statement of the appellant."

rules wherever they are relevant, weaving the substantive and procedural law together to show either error (if you seek reversal) or the absence of it (if you urge affirmance).

But a de novo standard need not be referred to throughout the Argument unless the very neutrality of the de novo standard helps your case. Because the de novo standard grants no deference at all to the trial court, arguments can be based entirely on the substantive law once the court has been told that a de novo standard is in effect.

Third, throughout the brief (and in oral argument), describe the facts just as they were in the procedural posture in the trial court. (That is because the standard of review is geared to the procedural posture below.) If the appeal is from the dismissal of a complaint, for example, describe the facts as allegations ("the complaint alleges that the defendant struck the plaintiff"). Describe them as evidence ("Smith testified that the defendant struck the plaintiff") if the appeal is from a judgment resulting from a motion challenging the quality of evidence (see §26.2.3) or from an order resulting from a case management motion (see §26.2.4). But if the facts are undisputed, describe the facts as truth ("the defendant struck the plaintiff").

If you are unsure of how to do any of these things, take a look at several opinions in which the court for which you are writing has used the same standard of review in appeals from the same procedural posture involved in your case. Chances are that you will see them invoked near the beginning of the opinion and used at logically appropriate spots thereafter. Look for a definition of the standard, and try to learn its relationship to other procedural rules and get a feel for the court's expectations about how the standard should be used.

X
INTO THE COURTROOM

34 Oral Argument

§34.1 Your Three Goals at Oral Argument

First, you want to engage the judges' attention by getting them *interested* in your case and *motivated* to rule in your favor. They will hear many other arguments on the same day, and they will read many other briefs in the week they read yours. They will forget your theory of the appeal unless you touch their natural desire to do the right thing.

Second, you want to focus the judges' attention on *the few aspects of your case that are most determinative:* the one or two issues that are fundamental, the facts that are most prominent in your theory, the rule or rules for which a decision in your favor would become precedent, and the policy considerations that most compel the result for which you argue. Judges expect oral argument to help them find the heart of the dispute. That is because—as you have already learned—oral argument works best when it concentrates on the few large ideas that are most relevant, while details are best left to the briefs (see §31.3).

Third, you want *access to the court's thinking.* Ideally, you want to discover each doubt the judges have about your theory and every confusion they entertain about any part of your case—all so you can satisfy doubt and clear up confusion. And you want to learn which issues the judges think are most important: if those are profitable issues for you, you can concentrate on them, and if they are the wrong issues, you can try to persuade the court of that. The only way you can get access to the court's thinking is through the questions you are asked when the judges interrupt you. In fact, you go to court *for the express purpose of being interrupted* because the most effective thing you can do in oral argument is to

415

persuade through your answers to the judges' questions. And when the judges interrupt, they are usually not trying to debate with you. For the most part, they are telling you what troubles them and asking you to help them make the decision.

§34.2   The Structure of an Oral Argument

The appellant typically begins by reminding the court of the nature of the case, the facts most essential to the appellant's theory, the procedural history, and the issue before the court. This is a reasonably effective opening:

Good morning, Your Honors. I am Clyde Farnsworth, representing Merritt Bresnahan, the appellant here and the defendant below. This is an appeal from a criminal conviction.

> An alternative start would be "May it please the court. I am . . ." Usually, it would help to name the crime, but the attorney delays that so he can define his client first.

Ms. Bresnahan suffers from a medical condition known as gender dysphoria syndrome. A person with this condition is psychologically of one gender but was born with the reproductive organs of the other gender. Psychotherapy has been shown to have no effect on this disorder. But the suffering it causes is so profound that clinics at leading hospitals must resort to sex reassignment surgery to alleviate the condition. And wise medical practice requires hat before so radical a step, the patient must dress and live as a person of the psychological gender for a long period.

> This recitation is pared to the bone, but it brings out all the facts that are most determinative for a decision in the attorney's favor. The attorney has a duty to point out the most adverse facts as well. That can be done through juxtaposition, as in a written fact statement. Here it is done through implication: has the surgery yet been performed? What does that mean about the defendant's physical state?

On her doctor's orders, Ms. Bresnahan was so dressed when she was arrested for violating section 240.35 of the Penal Law, which punishes anyone who — in the words of the statute — is "in any way disguised by unusual or unnatural attire" and "loiters, remains, or congregates in a public place" with others similarly attired. When arrested, Ms. Bresnahan was walking to lunch in the financial district of Manhattan with two other people who suffer from the same disease.

> This is one of the few situations where words should be quoted in an oral argument: they are the very words the court must interpret.

416

By appropriate motions in the trial court, Ms. Bresnahan sought dismissal of the charge on the grounds that her conduct could not violate the statute, and that, if it did, the statute would invade, among other things, her constitutional right to privacy. Review in this court is de novo. Even though the People concede that Ms. Bresnahan was following her doctor's orders according to accepted medical treatment, the trial court denied the motions and convicted her.

This is the procedural posture below. The appellate court needs to know it because it determines the standard of review.

Notice how the facts are used once again to set up the theory.

The questions before this court are whether the legislature really meant to punish people like Ms. Bresnahan, and, if the legislature did, whether her constitutional right to privacy nevertheless protects her freedom to choose her own clothing.

The statement of the issues leads into the argument that follows.

The legislature did not intend . . .

The sequence need not be as it is here. For example, it might be more effective in another case to state the procedural history or the issue, or both, before the facts. But the facts are what make this opening compelling, and they usually provide the energy in a compelling start. One of the leading appellate advocates of the twentieth century said that "in an appellate court the statement of the facts is not merely a part of the argument, it is more often than not the argument itself. A case well stated is a case far more than half argued."[1] Some courts, however, study the briefs so carefully before argument that they consider a fact recitation to be a waste of time, and in those courts attorneys are discouraged — either informally or through the courts' rules — from opening with the facts.

If you represent the appellee, your opening should be designed to show the court vividly how your theory differs from the appellant's:

> If the court please, I am Allan Kuusinen, for the People.
>
> The defendant concedes that he is and was anatomically male but had dressed up as a woman to disguise that fact. When arrested, he was walking down the street with two other men who were similarly disguised. They could have committed any of a number of crimes and left their victims utterly unable to identify them.
>
> That is exactly the danger the legislature meant to prevent. And because the legislature's goal is reasonable, section 240.35 does not violate the defendant's constitutional right to privacy.

§34.2   1. John W. Davis, *The Argument of an Appeal,* 26 A.B.A. J. 895, 896 (1940).

Usually, the body of the argument begins most effectively with a statement of the rule or rules on which your conclusion rests. If two or more separate conclusions are being urged, the transition from one to another should be clear to the listener:

> . . . Thus, section 240.35 was never intended to punish a patient for complying with an accepted medical treatment.
>
> The second question before the Court is whether section 240.35, if it has the meaning urged by the People, violates Ms. Bresnahan's constitutional right to privacy. . . .

Except in the opening, an appellee's argument does not differ much structurally from an appellant's. Although some of what an appellee says grows out of notes taken while the appellant argues, most of an appellee's argument can be planned in advance. From the appellant's brief, the appellee knows before argument the theory the appellant will advance.

Unless the bench is "cold,"[2] the judges' questions may so occupy you that you are surprised to find that your time is about to or already has run out. (Your time is finished when the chief or presiding judge, in a firm tone, says "Thank you.") When your time has expired, conclude with a brief sentence in which you specify the relief you seek ("Therefore, the judgment below should be affirmed because . . ."). If you are in the midst of answering a question when your time runs out, ask for permission to finish the answer and, if permitted, finish quickly and concisely. If, on the other hand, the judges continue to ask you questions after your time expires, answer them fully: the court has impliedly enlarged your time. If you complete your argument before your time expires, conclude anyway, pause to see whether you will be asked further questions, and, if not, sit down. Whatever the situation, you can signal your intent to finish by using an introductory phrase such as "In conclusion, . . ."

If the appellant has reserved one or two minutes for rebuttal,[3] the appellant can use that time, after the appellee's argument, in order to reply. A court considers its time wasted if an appellant uses rebuttal to reiterate arguments already made or to raise new arguments for the first time. Rebuttal should be used instead to correct significantly inaccurate or misleadingly incomplete statements made by the appellee, and preferably not more than one or two of those. If the appellee's misstatements are trivial, an appellant looks petty correcting them. If it turns out that there is no need for rebuttal, an appellant makes a confident impression by waiving it. A rebuttal ends with a sentence reminding the court of the relief sought.

---

2. A "hot" bench is one that erupts with questions. A "cold" bench is one that listens impassively.

3. The time reserved is subtracted from the time allowed for the appellant's main argument. You can reserve time by telling the court after you introduce yourself in the opening to your main argument.

§34.3   Questions from the Bench

Some questions are neutral requests for information about the record, the law, the procedural posture, or the theory of the appeal. Some are challenges, asking you how you would overcome an adverse policy or equity argument or a contrary interpretation of authority or the record. Some are expressed as concerns: the judge asks how a particular problem in the case can be resolved. Some questions are openly friendly, usually asking the attorney to focus on an aspect of the case that the judge believes to be particularly persuasive. And some questions are neutral prompts, suggesting that whatever the attorney is discussing at the time can be dispensed with in favor of more relevant material. Some questions are asked because the answer is crucial to the judge's thinking. Others grow out of the spontaneity of the moment, and the answer may have little or no impact on the decision.

When you hear a question, listen to it carefully, and do not be afraid to pause for a moment to think before answering. (Never interrupt a question.) Try to figure out the question's purpose and exactly what is troubling the judge. Then craft your answer to satisfy the skepticism or curiosity implied by the question. In the answer, do not give too little or too much. It is a mistake to give a one-sentence reply to a question that a judge plainly considers to be the crux of the case, but it is also a mistake to spend three minutes resolving a straightforward request for simple information.

Do not leap to large assumptions about a judge's predispositions from the questions the judge asks. A neutral judge might ask challenging questions just to see whether your theory will hold up. A friendly judge might ask challenging questions to cause you to argue matters that the judge believes might persuade others on the bench. And an adverse judge might ask friendly or neutral questions out of politeness and a sense of fairness.

In any event, answer the question on the spot. Do not promise to get back to it later at a place in your outline where you had already planned to discuss the subject: other questions may prevent you from getting that far, and the answer will be most persuasive immediately after the question is asked. Even if a question asks you to discuss an entire issue earlier than you had planned, do it and rearrange the order of your presentation to accommodate the judge's needs. Later, when you reach the spot where you had intended to discuss the issue, simply skip what you have already covered.[1]

In answering, state your conclusion first and your reasoning second. As you have seen in so many ways, the law-trained mind most easily

---

§34.3   1. In some schools, students are assigned to coauthor briefs, usually in teams of two, and to split the oral argument. If your school follows this practice, you may be asked questions about material that your colleague intends to argue. Do not respond by saying that your colleague will answer the question. Judges resent that, and you should know enough of the other student's material to be able to give at least a summary answer. If you are arguing first, your colleague can, during her or his allotted time, elaborate on your summary. Courts, by the way, discourage lawyers from splitting arguments, in part because of this problem.

understands discourse that lays out a conclusion before proving it. If you get wrapped up in a lot of preliminary material before producing a conclusion, the conclusion can be obscured or even lost, and you will create the appearance of being unhelpful or even evasive.

Answer the question you are asked, not one you would rather have been asked. The only way you can persuade is by facing directly the problems raised by the question and by showing the judge why those problems should not prevent a decision in your favor. *In every fully litigated case, each side has points of weakness.* If your side of your case did not have them, your adversary would have given up long ago. Where a judge has truly identified a point of weakness, face it and give a realistic counter- argument. Here are three different samples:

> I agree, Your Honor, that in that hypothetical the police would have had probable cause, but the facts of the hypothetical are not the facts of this case. . . .

> Yes, *Soares* did so hold, but later rulings of this court have impliedly undermined *Soares*. . . .

> Certainly, the record does reflect two isolated events that might be construed as evidence of good faith by the defendant, but the record also includes many, many events, stretching over several years, that show exactly the opposite. . . .

Hedging and lack of candor are ways of avoiding what you must do, and they harm your credibility with the court. (If you can surround yourself with an aura of honesty and forthrightness, your arguments will be all the more persuasive.)

During the answer, build a bridge to the rest of your argument. If the question causes you to make part of your planned argument out of order, you can return to your argument at a point that is logically related to the answer. If the answer covers material that you had not planned to speak about, use the answer to lead back to your planned argument. If this is done smoothly, it may be hard for a listener to tell where the answer has ended and the planned presentation has picked up again. Bridge-building helps you redirect the argument back to your theory of the appeal so you can show the court how your theory, as a coherent whole, satisfies each concern raised from the bench. It is, after all, the theory that you are selling.

You will be better able to manage questions if you develop what one judge calls "controlled flexibility": "a relaxed resilience allowing one to respond to a judge's question, coupled with an internal gyro compass enabling one to return gracefully to a charted course."[2]

If you are asked a question to which you do not know the answer, the best thing to say is exactly that. Judges are skilled interrogators, and you will quickly be found out if you try to fake your way through an answer. If you once knew the answer, you might feel a little better saying something

---

2. Frank Morey Coffin, *The Ways of a Judge* 131 (Houghton Mifflin 1980).

like "I'm sorry, Your Honor, but I don't recall." Judges know that you are human, and, unless the point you do not know is a big one, you gain credibility by admitting that you cannot answer.

If you think you understand the question but are not certain, signal that in your answer so that the judge can help you out in case you have missed the gist of the question:

> If your Honor is asking about the possibility that the issue has not been preserved for review—and please correct me if I've misunderstood—trial counsel made a timely objection and moved for . . .

If you plainly do not understand the question, ask for clarification:

> I'm sorry, Your Honor; are you asking about whether the order appealed from is final?

This is one of the very few kinds of questions that *you* might ask during an oral argument.

If a judge asks about a case or a statute about which you have forgotten something, it is appropriate to ask for help:

> I'm sorry, Your Honor, but did *Mansfield* precede the holding in *Soares?*

§34.4 Delivery, Affect, and Style

The most effective way to present arguments is in a tone of what has been called "respectful intellectual equality":[1]

> [I]f the lawyer approaches a court with an appreciation so great that it amounts to awe, perhaps verging on fear, he will not be able effectively to stand up to the court's questioning. . . . It is just as important, however, not to talk down to a court, no matter how much the individual advocate may be more generously endowed with quick perception. . . . The only proper attitude is that of a respectful intellectual equality. The "respectful" part approximates the quantum and type of respect that a younger [person] should show when speaking to an older one. . . . It is not inconsistent with this element of respect, however, for the advocate to argue an appeal on the basis that it is a discussion among equals. . . . Counsel must stand up to the judges quite as he would stand up to the senior members of his own firm. If he permits himself to be overawed . . . , then he—and his case—are well on their way to being lost.[2]

---

§34.4 1. Frederick Bernays Wiener, *Oral Advocacy,* 62 Harv. L. Rev. 56, 72-74 (1948).
2. *Id.*

Although the judges' power is their authority to decide your case, it is their *need* to decide the case that—paradoxically—causes them to look to you for intellectual leadership.

What works best in this situation is not a speech, but a *conversation* in which you take the initiative, talking *with* the judges—not at them. It is a peculiar species of conversation, limited by the formalities of the occasion and by a focus on the decision the bench must make, but it is a conversation nonetheless. If you do the following, you can create for yourself a persuasive presence that helps you to reach and engage the bench:

Look straight at the judges—preferably making eye contact—throughout the argument. Look at your notes only to remind yourself of the next subject for discussion, and even then get your eyes off your notes and back to the bench as quickly as possible. Whenever you look away from the judges, their attention can wander to other thoughts, partially tuning you out. And judges become annoyed with lawyers who read their arguments to the court.[3]

Stand up straight and do not distract the court with restless or anxious movement. Do not play with a pen, shuffle your papers around frequently, put your hands in your pockets, or sway forward and back. Limit your gestures to those that naturally punctuate your argument. A visually busy lawyer radiates nervousness, rather than the confidence needed to establish psychological leadership. Every lawyer—even the most experienced—is nervous before making an oral argument, but that anxiety tends to disappear once the attorney becomes engaged in the conversation. (For beginners, the moment of engagement—when you are so caught up in the work that you forget to be nervous—might not come for several minutes into the argument. But with each succeeding performance that moment will move closer and closer toward the opening, until eventually it coincides with the words "May it please the court" or "Good morning, Your Honors.")

Speak loudly enough that the judges do not have to strain to hear you. If you are soft-spoken by nature, breathe in deeply before you begin and exhale while speaking your first words. Do this again whenever your voice falters. Make your lungs do the work, not your throat muscles. You will be surprised at how well your voice can carry. (If you already have a powerful voice, do not get carried away: nobody likes to listen to shouting.)

Use the tone and volume of your voice to emphasize the more important things you say. A monotone becomes monotonous. Pause before or after your most important remarks.

Communicate tenacity and what one judge has called "disciplined earnestness": "a communicated sense of conviction that pushes a case to the limits of its strength but not beyond. One somehow brings together one's words and body language, facial expression and eye contact, to radiate a sense of conviction without making every point a life-and-death issue."[4]

---

3. See U.S. Sup. Ct. R. 28.1 ("Oral argument read from a prepared text is not favored") and Fed. R. App. P. 34(c) ("Counsel must not read at length from briefs, records, or authorities").
4. Frank Morey Coffin, *The Ways of a Judge* 132 (Houghton Mifflin 1980).

Unless asked, avoid multitudes of detail in discussing authority. Because oral argument works best when focused on the big ideas in the appeal, you are better off concentrating instead on rules of law, policy arguments, and broad descriptions of authority. Citations and the minutiae of authority are very hard to follow when delivered orally, and they ought to be in your brief anyway. If your case is built on a synthesis of authority, describe it generally ("the majority of jurisdictions," "the recent trend of cases in other states," "seven of the federal circuits," "this court has previously held"). But if there is controlling authority, that itself is a big idea and deserves attention, especially where you are asking a court to construe an unsettled statute or to overrule precedent. But even then, do not give the full citation: the name and sometimes the year of a case are enough. And if you must quote—as you might with a crucial statute or holding—limit yourself to the half-dozen or so essential words that the court must interpret.

Know your record thoroughly, use it to its full advantage, and do not discuss "facts" outside the record. And—as with authority—do not supply unnecessary detail unless asked for it. Concentrate on the few facts that are most determinative, and mention along the way one or two facts that most bring the story to life. Some facts do not logically have legal significance, but they help the judges "see" the story and put the case into a realistic perspective. For example, in the appellant's opening in §34.2, it is certainly not legally determinative that, when arrested, the defendant "was walking to lunch in the financial district of Manhattan with two other people who suffer from the same disease," but it helps the court visualize the defendant's theory that the conviction appealed from represents a preposterous application of a statute.

§34.5 Formalities and Customs of the Courtroom

Dress not merely for business, but in conservative clothing that conveys the impression that you are a careful and reliable professional.

Stand at the lectern throughout your argument. Do not stroll out from behind it unless you must go to your materials in order to answer a question.

In court, lawyers do not speak to each other. They speak only to the bench and—when the bench gives permission—to witnesses and juries. But because there are no witnesses or juries in appellate courts, you will speak only to the judges.

The dignity of the occasion will be demeaned if you speak in slang, in emotional rhetoric, or in terms that unnecessarily personalize the attorneys or judges. Even when discussing your adversary's arguments, refer to them as the party's, rather than as the lawyer's. There is a world of tonal difference between "The plaintiff mistakenly relies . . ." and "Mr. Maggione has mistakenly told you . . ." Similarly, do not speak to the bench in flattering language. Judges are satisfied with respect; they are offended by obsequiousness.

While your adversary argues, listen attentively and without facial expressions that could convey your opinion of what is transpiring. Make whatever notes you will need to help you respond in your own argument (if you are the appellee) or in rebuttal (if you are the appellant). Do not interrupt your adversary's argument.

§34.6   Preparation for Oral Argument

Prepare two versions of the same presentation. One version should include the material that you *must* argue — in other words, the core of your case — and, when delivered without interruption, it should fill no more than 30 or 35 percent of the time you are allowed. The other version is an expanded development of the first. It includes the first version, as well as supplemental material that makes the core of your case more persuasive, and, without interruption, it should fill about 80 or 90 percent of the available time. You will know within the first three or four minutes of the argument whether the bench is hot or cold. If it is hot, you can deliver the core presentation and work the supplemental material into your answers. If the bench is cold, you can deliver the expanded argument.

There are many ways to prepare notes to use at the lectern. After you have argued several times, you will figure out which type and style of notes work best for you. But the consensus of experienced advocates is that you are better off with the fewest notes because you will need them only to remind you of the subjects you intend to cover and of a few key phrases that you intend to use. In fact, if you are well prepared, you will know your case so well that a single page on a legal-size pad will often be sufficient. If, in preparing the argument, you come up with an excellent phrasing for a difficult concept, you might write down those few words to remind yourself to use them. Otherwise, your notes should be only a list of subjects to cover.

You can outline both versions of your argument on a single page divided by a vertical line. For example, the lawyer who wrote the appellant's brief in Appendix G might be able to make an oral argument from a very condensed page of notes like the one on the next page.

Some advocates take to the lectern notecards with synopses of the record and of the major relevant cases. You might or might not find such synopses helpful. If you already know your case thoroughly, the cards may only get in your way.

Take the record and each brief to the podium as well, in case you are asked about their contents. Especially with the record, use tabs to mark for quick reference passages that the judges might want explained.

Plan your argument by weaving together policy, the facts, and the controlling rules of law into the seamless theory enunciated in your brief. Show how policy and the facts compel your conclusion, while the technical law can be used to justify it. If the standard of review and the procedural posture below place burdens on you, be sure to show the court how you have carried those burdens. If the burdens rest on your adversary, show instead how your adversary has failed to carry them. Remember that you cannot cover all the arguments you made in the brief: focus on the most important material.

core	_suppl_

facts
   medical condition
   treatment (no psythrpy)
   how arrested
   motions below	

issues
  1. "wh'r leg're really meant to punish people like B"
  2. if yes, rt to priv	

statutory issue 1. not disguised "med prof'n considers her clothing to be an accurate communication of the state of her gender"	how gender determined "no magic moment" when becomes fem
2. modern med treatment	hosps & clinics accepted trtmt kind of pain
3. history	farm revolt sim statutes gap in auth
rt to priv issue	
1. scope of rt	clothing cases
2. no comp'g st int	fund rt st's crime cont theory
3. even if comp'g, ovrbrd	lesser restrict
4. not "rat'l basis"	no cause/effect
summary	

Make a ruthless list of every weakness in your case and every question that you would be tempted to ask if you were a judge—and prepare an answer to each of those questions. Remember that you are not just trying to win a case; you are helping the judges make law. What rule will a decision in your favor stand for? (It would become precedent.) The judges will care deeply about policy concerns. If they do as you ask, how will the law in the future treat facts that are similar to—but not exactly the same as—yours? What would be the practical effects in the courts, in the economy, and in society as a whole? Why is the rule you advocate better than the one your adversary urges? (If you are having a hard time imagining hard questions that you might be asked, study your adversary's brief and the precedents that are contrary to your position.)

Try also to predict which concessions you will be asked to make. Figure out which concessions you cannot afford to make and which you will have to in order to protect the reasonability of the rest of your case. If you think about this for the first time when you are actually asked to make the concession, a very large part of your case could easily disappear in a snap misjudgment.

Practice making your argument to a person who will ask you tough questions but who knows little about your theory of the appeal. If the person mooting you knows too much about your theory, the experience will be unrealistic.

Finally, go to the library the day before you argue. The time between submission of the brief and oral argument might equal up to a month in law school courses and perhaps several months in the practice of law. Check the *Shepard's* supplements to see whether controlling statutes have been amended or repealed, whether one of the key cases has been overruled, and whether any of the recent precedents has been reversed or affirmed. You need not check every citation in your brief, but you do not want to discover in the courtroom that some important texture of the law has changed.

§34.7   State v. Dobbs and Zachrisson: *An Oral Argument Dissected*

To help you understand how oral argument influences judicial decision-making, this chapter concludes with a dissection of the arguments in a real appeal,[1] comparing them to the decision subsequently made by the court to whom the arguments were addressed.

In the city where this case arose, Dobbs operated an illegal book-making business in one neighborhood, and Zachrisson ran a similar enterprise in another area. Dobbs and Zachrisson were each indicted on 16 counts of

§34.7   1. The names of the parties, judges, and attorneys and the citations to local authority have all been changed. The wording of the local statutes has been altered slightly for clarity. To make the story easier to follow, many of the facts have been simplified, but not in ways that are relevant to the court's analysis. Some of the people described here are composites from a larger cast of characters in the original appeal.

bribery and one count of conspiracy to bribe. (They were not indicted for illegal gambling, perhaps because the police lacked the evidence required by the gambling statute.) At trial, a police officer named Porfier testified that Zachrisson had given her money for not enforcing the law against him and Dobbs and arresting their competitors instead. The prosecution also introduced tape recordings of conversations between Porfier and the defendants. Dobbs and Zachrisson testified in their own defense, but a jury convicted on all 34 counts.

At trial, Zachrisson and Dobbs each asserted the defenses of entrapment and coercion, which are separately defined in the state's Criminal Code:

§ 32. Defense of Entrapment

In a prosecution for any crime, it is an affirmative defense that the defendant engaged in the prohibited conduct because he was induced or encouraged to do so by a public servant, or by a person acting under a public servant's direction, where the public servant or the person acting under his direction acted for the purpose of obtaining evidence against the defendant for the purpose of a criminal prosecution, and where the methods used to obtain that evidence created a substantial risk that the crime would be committed by a person not otherwise disposed to commit it. Conduct that merely provides a defendant with an opportunity to commit a crime is not entrapment.

§ 963. Bribery; Defense of Coercion

(a) In a prosecution for bribery, it is a defense that the defendant conferred a prohibited benefit on a public servant as a result of that public servant's coercion of the defendant.

(b) For the purposes of this section, a public servant coerces a defendant by instilling in the defendant a fear that, if the defendant does not comply with the public servant's wishes, the public servant will cause physical injury to the defendant or another, cause damage to property of the defendant or another, cause criminal charges to be brought against the defendant or another, or otherwise abuse the public servant's power as an official of the government.

Porfier testified that initially she approached Zachrisson in an attempt to recruit him and perhaps other bookies as informants. She suggested that Zachrisson set up a meeting with any other bookies that Zachrisson thought might be interested. Zachrisson suggested Dobbs. A meeting of the three of them was arranged, but Dobbs did not show up. At this and other meetings, Porfier wore a "body wire" (a hidden microphone that transmits to a nearby tape recorder). Zachrisson told Porfier that he needed police protection from aggressive bookies with mob connections who were moving into his territory. The jury heard a tape recording of Zachrisson telling Porfier that if she made it easier for him to make a profit, he could "send some money your way." Porfier told him that she would have to think it over, and that he should find out whether Dobbs wanted to make the same arrangement.

A week or so later, Zachrisson and Porfier met again. Porfier told Zachrisson that she would accept money from Zachrisson and Dobbs, that she would not arrest them or their employees, and that she would arrest their competitors. Zachrisson told her that Dobbs was "interested." Zachrisson began making periodic payments to Porfier of $100 to $200 (all of which Porfier turned over to the police department). Zachrisson and Dobbs continued their operations without police interference, and some of their competitors were arrested.

A few months after this arrangement began, Zachrisson told Porfier that he and Dobbs—whom Porfier had still not yet met—wanted to expand their gambling enterprises and were willing to bring in Porfier as a silent partner. Zachrisson told Porfier that she would receive a percentage of the profits in exchange for police protection for Zachrisson and Dobbs. Porfier and Zachrisson met one more time, and that was the only meeting attended by Dobbs. Dobbs stated that he agreed with Zachrisson's goals, but Porfier did not start receiving a share of the profits until a few weeks later.

Zachrisson testified that he paid Porfier because he was afraid that he would be arrested if he did not, and he presented evidence that during the time these payments were being made he had complained to others that Porfier was "shaking me down." Dobbs testified that Porfier had threatened to put him out of business if he did not agree to pay her off.

Both defendants moved for directed verdicts of acquittal on the grounds that the evidence of coercion and entrapment was so clear that those issues had ceased to be questions of fact for the jury. (If this confuses you, see §26.2.3.) The trial court denied the motions. On appeal to the state's supreme court, both defendants argued in their briefs that their convictions should be reversed because the motions should have been granted.

Dobbs asserted two additional grounds for reversal. First, he argued that the trial court committed reversible error in instructing the jury that if they convicted him of conspiracy, they could also convict him of bribery because of the acts of a co-conspirator (Zachrisson). There was no evidence that Dobbs gave any money to Porfier directly, but the trial court instructed the jury that Dobbs could be found guilty of bribery for the payments made by Zachrisson if the jury concluded beyond a reasonable doubt that Dobbs and Zachrisson had conspired to bribe Porfier.

Second, Dobbs argued that his rights to a speedy trial had been violated because the trial did not occur until 18 months after indictment. There are two separate rights to a speedy trial. One is provided by the Sixth Amendment to the United States Constitution ("an accused shall enjoy the right to a speedy and public trial"), which applies to state prosecutions as a result of the due process clause of the Fourteenth Amendment. The other right is provided by section 27 of the state's Criminal Procedure Code, which provides that an indictment must be dismissed if the prosecution is not ready for trial within six months after the indictment. (The constitutional test lacks such a clear deadline and in general is much more elastic.) Delay in coming to trial might arise from prosecutorial tardiness, from tardiness on the defense side of the case, from court congestion, or from some combination of these sources. When a defendant moves to dismiss an indictment for lack of a speedy trial, the trial court tries to determine the sources of delay. Delay due to defense tardiness is ignored as "excludable time." (Otherwise, defendants would profit from procrastination by their own attorneys.) Delay caused by prosecutorial tardiness is "chargeable time" because prosecutors are expected to take the initiative in moving cases to trial. You will see in a few moments whether this state treats court congestion delay as excludable or chargeable time. An appellate court will not automatically reverse a conviction where the trial court erroneously denied a speedy trial motion. As you learned in §31.4, reversals occur only for trial court errors that are material or prejudicial.

Reproduced below is a condensation of the transcript of the oral arguments in the state supreme court.[2] Immediately after the transcript is a synopsis of the court's opinion. When you compare the oral arguments to the court's decision, try to understand the cause-and-effect relationship: how do the arguments seem to have influenced what the court did? Without actually interviewing the judges themselves and without reading the court's internal memoranda and the briefs submitted by the parties, we cannot reconstruct with certainty the process through which the court reached its decision, but some tentative conclusions are possible.

THE CHIEF JUDGE: Mr. Womack?

WOMACK [for Zachrisson]: May it please the court. I will argue the issues of coercion and entrapment. My brief sets out the statutory definition of coercion in a bribery case. The evidence at trial was that Zachrisson, after he had made one or two payments, went to a friend of his and reported, in the friend's words, that he was being " The friend then went to a judge in a neighboring county and reported that Zachrisson was being "shaken down" by the police, that over a period of months the police had been intimidating Zachrisson and asking him for money in exchange for favors. You can't read the summary of the meetings here and not be convinced that the police were the principal participants, instigators and initiators of all the activity that lead up to the money changing hands. I think there is a question of law as to whether this was voluntary.

What do you think of this opening? Does it suggest immediately that what happened in the trial court should make us uncomfortable? How would you have improved it?

2. Those portions of the oral arguments that are most closely related to the state supreme court's decision are reproduced here, and the rest omitted. For the most part, the words in the transcript are the words actually spoken by the attorneys and the judges, but some phrasing has been altered slightly to help you understand what happened and to smooth over transitions from one part of the argument to another.

JUDGE BECENTI: The police denied it, didn't they?

WOMACK: Yes.

JUDGE BECENTI: Doesn't that make it a question of fact, to be resolved by a jury?

WOMACK: No, I think entrapment can be decided on the undisputed, undeniable facts here.

JUDGE BECENTI: As a matter of law?

WOMACK: As a matter of law. Porfier has known the defendants for approximately six years, knew that they were small-time gamblers, knew that they were involved with after-hours bars, having dealings with them over a year and a half period. Those are misdemeanors, but bribery is a felony. The testimony was that everybody knew the defendants were gamblers. Yet the police spent all that time, seeing them on a regular basis and never arrested them for any gambling offenses.

JUDGE BECENTI: They investigated organized crime and gambling, didn't they — an ongoing thing?

WOMACK: If they were investigating organized crime, what came of it? Why did it take them almost two years to get the defendants for bribery?

JUDGE STEIN: Doesn't that argument cut both ways because if it took that long the coercion wasn't very effective?

WOMACK: I disagree. Porfier exacted promises of a hundred dollars a week from these defendants. Porfier manufactured a crime. She got very little money from Zachrisson and then pressured him to introduce her to Dobbs. And that in itself was improper conduct.

JUDGE BECENTI: You'd have to argue that that's entrapment as a matter of law, wouldn't you? The facts were decided against you in the trial court, and we're bound by that.

WOMACK: Yes, I would argue that it was entrapment as a matter of law and that coercion was proved. Porfier engaged in improper conduct because she decided that she wanted to get the defendants for a

The state supreme court can reach the questions of coercion and entrapment only if there are issues of law and not of fact (see §26.4). In a trial court, what might seem to be a fact issue can at times be converted into a law issue through one of the motions described in §26.2.3. That is what these defendants tried to do through their motions for directed verdicts. Trial and appellate judges are inclined to let juries decide matters like these as fact issues unless there is a good reason not to. Here, is the court being given a good reason?

Generally, rhetorical questions do not persuade. It is more effective to lay out each step of the argument.

Is this the most compelling way to describe what happened? Can you think of something better?

Do you find this theory persuasive? If you do not, is that because the theory is faulty or because it is not being adequately supported by the facts and law at the attorney's disposal?

higher crime than gambling. And in this way Zachrisson's reluctance to commit the crime was overcome by persistence. I believe in this case that's obvious. Zachrisson resisted making payments, and the payments did not begin until long after the demands had started. Profier just kept going because she wasn't satisfied with arresting the defendants on petty gambling charges.

JUDGE STEIN: Is there anything wrong about that, as long as it doesn't amount to entrapment? If something is going on, is there any reason why police can't wait before arresting until they accumulate more evidence?

WOMACK: No, Your Honor, if it's indeed going on, but in this case it wasn't going on when Porfier first got involved. I see my time is up. Thank you.

THE CHIEF JUDGE: Ms. Underwood?

UNDERWOOD [for Dobbs]: Your Honors, Johnny Dobbs met with this police officer only once, and that was after the officer demanded that Dobbs be there. He came only after she made five separate demands that he meet with her. Dobbs met with the officer on one occasion and never saw her again. There was no evidence in this trial that he had anything else to do with Officer Porfier. And at that one meeting, he said only one thing of any substance. When the officer suggested that she should arrest some competing gamblers to shake them down, Dobbs said, "Do we really have to arrest people? I don't want that to happen." He disagreed with the plan proposed. And when somebody said, "Johnny, you're not saying much," he replied, "You don't learn anything by talking." These are not words of joining a conspiracy. These are not words of attempting to bribe anyone. And if this is the only evidence in the case, he cannot be considered to have joined a conspiracy. He certainly didn't do it through his own words. The law is clear and settled that the words of somebody else cannot bind a defendant to a conspiracy. There was no evidence that he ever committed any

Notice how this attorney starts off with her best facts to undermine the bench's confidence that whatever happened in the trial court was probably not unjust. (Remember that appellants have the burden of demonstrating error and that appellate courts are affirmance-prone). This presentation paints a vivid picture with a few, very carefully selected facts. As you read the synopsis of the state supreme court's decision, try to figure out what effect that picture had on the bench.

other act in this whole scheme. On this kind of record, the jury should not have been instructed that they could convict Dobbs of bribery.

In fact, Porfier tried five times to get Dobbs to meet with her. And when he finally did meet with her—and this leads into the issues of coercion and entrapment—the first thing she said was "I can put you out of business; I can go into your neighborhood tomorrow and arrest your people and close you down." These words are coercive as a matter of law. And it is also entrapment as a matter of law because the police officer forced the meeting where she made these coercive statements. Here, the police officer created the crime of bribery . . .

JUDGE ORTIZ [interrupting]: You haven't mentioned your speedy trial issue, which you argue in your brief. You still press it?

UNDERWOOD: Yes, absolutely, every point in the brief. In the trial court we tried to demonstrate—and the court wouldn't permit us—that other cases that had been indicted after Dobbs were tried before him, even though those other defendants were not in jail.

JUDGE ORTIZ: You consistently answered ready?

UNDERWOOD: Every time.

JUDGE ORTIZ: There was an 18-month delay?

UNDERWOOD: Yes, Your Honor.

JUDGE ORTIZ: The only excuse given in the trial court was calendar congestion?

UNDERWOOD: Yes.

JUDGE ORTIZ: And you sought no continuances or adjournments during this period?

UNDERWOOD: Not one.

JUDGE ORTIZ: When you made your motion for speedy trial relief, you claimed both a constitutional violation and a violation of our speedy trial statute?

UNDERWOOD: Yes, both issues raised below . . .

This transition is smooth but also clearly announced so that the bench can follow the attorney's organization.

Notice how the attorney picks up the questions and uses it as a springboard for argument.

Are Judge Ortiz's questions hostile? Or does he seem to be helping the attorney make clear that the delay was not caused by the defense and that the question has been properly preserved for appellate review?

JUDGE BECENTI [interrupting]: Were there extensive plea bargaining negotiations?

UNDERWOOD: Not one minute of it, Your Honor.

JUDGE STEIN: Has there been any showing of prejudice?

UNDERWOOD: Yes, in the human sense, but not in the sense that we couldn't find any evidence.

JUDGE BECENTI: Any lost witnesses, anything like that?

UNDERWOOD: No.

JUDGE STEIN: Were the defendants in jail during this time or were they out on bail?

UNDERWOOD: No, Dobbs was not in jail.

JUDGE STEIN: Have you read our opinion in *Weatherby*?

UNDERWOOD: Yes, Your Honor, I know . . .

JUDGE STEIN [interrupting]: That must not have disappointed you.

UNDERWOOD: Well, . . .

JUDGE ORTIZ [interrupting]: You say this was 18 months?

UNDERWOOD: Yes.

JUDGE ORTIZ: *Weatherby* was 18 and a half months.

UNDERWOOD: Yes, I know, Your Honor.

JUDGE ORTIZ: And Weatherby is now at home.

UNDERWOOD: If the court please, I chose to concentrate today on the other grounds for reversal because I know Your Honors were aware of that, and I feel that that was an argument I didn't need to press any further. I think I've taken all my time. Thank you very much.

THE CHIEF JUDGE: Mr. Lysander?

LYSANDER [for the State]: May it please the cou . . .

JUDGE STEIN [interrupting]: What about *Weatherby*, Mr. Lysander, isn't that dispositive of the speedy trial issue?

LYSANDER: Your Honor, in this case, the speedy trial motion was made orally and not in writing. It was made on the eve of

---

This exchange seems to have sparked the interest of Judges Becenti and Stein. What do you think Judge Ortiz was trying to accomplish?

This is the tough question. And in answering, the attorney tries to put the best appearance on a fact that she must admit.

Any equivocation by the attorney on these matters would be quickly discovered and cause the court to lose confidence in the attorney's candor. These are not facts that are open to reasonable interpretations. Either Dobbs was in jail, for example, or he was not.

Weatherby seems at least superficially to favor Dobbs. If Judges Stein and Ortiz had to make a decision on this issue right now, how do you think they would rule? Why do you think so? As you read the argument for the State and the synopsis of the court's decision, remember the prediction you made here.

As you read the synopsis of the state supreme court's decision, ask yourself whether this might be a diplomatic way of explaining a strategy decision. If so, why would the explanation need to be diplomatic?

Judge Stein has gotten *very* interested in the speedy trial aspect of the case.

Do you think this attorney was prepared to answer questions on the speedy trial issue?

trial and without any prior notice to the prosecution. *Weatherby* is distinguishable because there the issue was raised in the trial court in a way that permitted the prosecution to find out the reason for every delay and to put that reason in the trial court record. That didn't happen here.

JUDGE STEIN: In this appeal, did the prosecution oppose the motion in the trial court on the ground that it needed an opportunity to prove that each delay was justified?

LYSANDER: I'm not sure, Your Honor.

JUDGE STEIN: Perhaps the motion should have been made in writing and with prior notice to the prosecution, but if it were not and if the prosecution didn't object to that, I would think that your procedural objection would have been waived.

LYSANDER: Your Honor, this was a pre-*Bachman* case. Before your holding in *State v. Bachman,* both the prosecution and defense were presenting their arguments in trial courts under somewhat lax procedural standards. However, . . .

JUDGE STEIN [interrupting]: But the defendant shouldn't be prejudiced then by that fact, if there were relaxed standards.

LYSANDER: That's correct, Your Honor, but I'm simply saying that the prosecution would be prejudiced in that we were never given the opportunity to have a hearing to develop a complete factual record for the reasons for each delay.

JUDGE STEIN: But wasn't the only excuse advanced trial court congestion?

LYSANDER: The prosecution answered ready for trial for the first time only three months after the indictment, and there was difficulty getting a free courtroom on that date.

JUDGE STEIN: And we held in *Weatherby* that courtroom congestion is no excuse.

LYSANDER: But you also held in *Greenfield* that the trial court's inability to schedule a trial was an excuse. And there has never been an allegation of prejudice

Read coldly in a transcript, this answer might seem flippant. But if it is spoken in the proper tone of voice it becomes exactly the "respectful to Dobbs because of the delay, and Dobbs was the only defendant to raise this issue in the trial court.

JUDGE ORTIZ: But the question is now before us, and it was raised below — although you say it was raised orally instead of on papers —

LYSANDER: That's correct.

JUDGE ORTIZ: The only excuse the prosecution offered is calendar congestion, is that correct?

LYSANDER: That is the only excuse I am aware of, but we never had an opportunity for a hearing, so I do not know what would have developed had there been a hearing.

JUDGE ORTIZ: At the time the motion was made, there was no excuse given other than that?

LYSANDER: No, but as a practical matter, when a motion like that is made on the eve of trial all of a sudden — just before a three-and-a-half-week trial that everybody has been preparing for — on the eve of trial when the defendant suddenly claims his speedy trial rights have been violated, the prosecutor would have to do an investigation in order to be able to account for each and every continuance that happened in the past.

JUDGE STEIN: Was there any request by the prosecutor for additional time to answer the motion — so the prosecutor could develop the record that you're now suggesting could have been developed?

LYSANDER: I don't believe that there was, Your Honor, but if there had been, that would have defeated the ends of getting the trial completed as soon as possible. [pauses] Concerning the question of whether the defendants were entrapped by the police. . . .

intellectual quality" that persuades. We can never know how much the court was influenced by this answer (or by the prosecution's brief), but compare the answer to the court's decision on this issue.

Has this attorney had any effect at all on Judges Ortiz and Stein? When you read the synopsis of the court's decision, notice how they vote.

(The remainder of the State's argument is omitted.)

STATE v. DOBBS AND ZACHRISSON

BECENTI, J. Dobbs's bribery convictions are reversed, his conspiracy conviction is affirmed, and all of Zachrisson's convictions are affirmed.

Dobbs's bribery convictions are reversed because the trial court erroneously instructed the jury that they could convict him of bribery for the payments made by Zachrisson. There was no evidence that Dobbs actually made any bribe payments. Guilt of a substantive offense like bribery may not be predicated solely on a defendant's participation in an underlying conspiracy.

A conspirator is not necessarily an accessory to a crime committed in furtherance of the conspiracy. Under section 129 of the Criminal Code a person is criminally responsible, as an accessory, for the act of another if the person "solicits, requests, commands, importunes, or intentionally aids" the other person to engage in that offense. Conspicuously absent from the statute is any reference to one who conspires to commit an offense. That omission cannot be supplied by construction. It may be true that in some instances a conspirator's conduct will suffice to establish liability as an accessory, but the concepts are different. To permit mere guilt of conspiracy to establish the defendant's guilt of the substantive crime without any evidence of further action on the part of the defendant would be to expand the basis of accessory liability beyond the legislative design. In interpreting our own state's Criminal Code, we decline to follow the rule followed in federal prosecutions.

But we reject Dobbs's further claim that his statutory and constitutional rights to a speedy trial were violated by the delay between his indictment and his trial. Dobbs does not claim to have been prejudiced by the delay in coming to trial. He was not incarcerated, and he does not assert that any of his witnesses disappeared or suffered a fading of memory. *State v. Weatherby* is therefore distinguishable from this appeal. Moreover, when Dobbs moved in the trial court to dismiss for lack of a speedy trial, court congestion was assigned as the reason for the delay, and the prosecution was ready for trial within three months of the indictment. Thus, Dobbs is not entitled to dismissal pursuant to our speedy trial statute, which requires that the prosecution be ready on time but places no corresponding obligation on the trial court. See *State v. Greenfield*.

Finally, defendants urge that the prosecution failed to disprove the bribery defense of coercion beyond a reasonable doubt and that the evidence establishes the affirmative defense of entrapment as a matter of law. The record does not support these contentions. The defendants' motions were correctly denied, and the issues were properly submitted to the jury.

The record before us presents a conflict between the prosecution's version of events and that of the defendants. The defendants asserted that the police officers induced their participation in the bribery scheme and employed coercive tactics to ensure compliance. Although the record does reveal some evidence of conduct that might be construed as harassment, there is also evidence of mutual cooperation. Hence, resolution of the issues was a purely factual matter within the province of the jury.

[There were no dissents.]

APPENDICES

Appendix 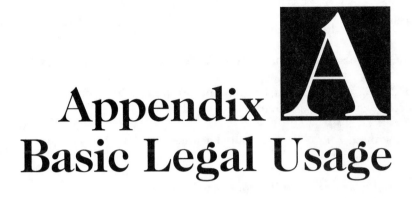A
Basic Legal Usage

Beginners sometimes have trouble with the following words and phrases:

AFFIRM: Precedent can be followed or overruled, but lawyers do not usually say that a precedent has been "affirmed." An appellate court "affirms" when it refuses to reverse the ruling of a lower court *in the same litigation.* See *OVERRULE.*

AND/OR is both ambiguous and awkward. Instead, when writing about a situation where either *and* or *or* might be accurate, use *or* and add to your list an extra item that conveys the meaning of *and:*

   wrong: Under Rule 11 of the Federal Rules of Civil Procedure, sanctions can be imposed on the attorney and/or on the client.

   right: Under Rule 11 of the Federal Rules of Civil Procedure, sanctions can be imposed on the attorney, on the client, or on both.

APPEAL: The past tense is spelled *appealed.*

ARGUE: Lawyers argue, but courts do not. Argument is intended to persuade others. One argues when one lacks the power to decide, and one argues to those who have that power. A court therefore "decides," "holds," "finds," "rules," "concludes," and so on. Individual judges might "argue," but only in dissent.

COUNSEL: Other forms are spelled *counselor, counseling,* and *counseled.*

COURT refers to an institution and not a group of people. The word is therefore used with singular verbs and pronouns.

wrong:	The court have held . . .
	They reversed . . .
right:	The court has held . . .
	It reversed . . .

DICTUM is the singular, and **DICTA** the plural. Do not use a singular verb with *dicta* or a plural verb with *dictum.*

FIND and **FOUND:** When a court "holds," it settles a question of law, but when a court "finds," it decides from the evidence what the facts are. Conclusions of law are not "found."

GUILTY: A guilty defendant has been convicted, in a criminal prosecution, of committing a crime. Cases that end this way are captioned "State v. Smith," "People v. Smith," "Commonwealth v. Smith," or "United States v. Smith." If, in a civil case, Smith loses to a private plaintiff who wants money damages or an injunction or some other type of civil relief, Smith is *liable.* In a civil case, there is no such thing as guilt.

HOLD: See *FIND* and *SAY.*

I: Pronouns identifying the writer are frowned on, except for the use of *we* in judicial opinions. Your goal is to emphasize the ideas under discussion, rather than your own role. "I believe," "we submit," "in our case," and the like are distracting clutter.

INNOCENT: Despite what you hear on the evening news, defendants do not plead "innocent," and juries do not find them "innocent." In a criminal trial, the question is whether the prosecution has proved guilt beyond a reasonable doubt. If it has, the defendant is "guilty." If it has not, the defendant is "not guilty." The jury takes no position on whether the defendant is innocent. "Innocence" has little meaning in criminal law, which cares about whether guilt can be proved and not about whether defendants are guilty or innocent. When a defendant pleads "not guilty," the defendant does not claim to be innocent: instead, the plea is simply a demand that the government prove guilt beyond a reasonable doubt.

IT, when used as a referent, can cause vagueness. See *THIS.*

JUDGMENT: in legal writing, *judgment* is *always* spelled with only one *e.* In a general-purpose, Webster's-type dictionary, you can find "judgement" listed as an acceptable alternative spelling. But the type of judgment described in the first paragraph of page 383; is *always* spelled with only one "e" in the United States (see any *law* dictionary). And out of force of habit, American lawyers customarily use the one-"e" spelling for other meanings of the word.[1]

MOTION, in the procedural sense, is a noun, not a verb. A motion is a request for a court order or a judgment. To get an order or judgment, a lawyer "moves" or "makes a motion." A lawyer does not "motion for an order." (Like everybody else, a lawyer "motions" by making a physical gesture, such as when hailing a taxi.) And a lawyer does not "move *the court* for an order." In that phrase and others like it, "the court" is understood (and need not be stated) because only courts and administrative tribunals can grant orders. And to many readers, adding "the court" looks silly because it evokes other meanings. (For example: The judge wiped away a tear, and it was clear that the witness's story had moved the court. Or: "To what new location are we moving this court?" asked Hercules as he lifted the big granite building with the pillars in front.)

OUR: See **I.**

OVERRULE and **REVERSE** mean different things. On appeal, the judgment or order of the court below in the same case can be *reversed,* but a court *overrules* precedent created in a prior case. In addition, for reasons explained in §14.2, a court cannot overrule the precedent of a higher court, a court of equal rank, or a court in another jurisdiction. (In another context, *overrule* has an entirely different meaning: when a trial judge rejects an attorney's objection to something the opposing attorney has done, the objection is "overruled.")

REVERSE: See *AFFIRM* and *OVERRULE.*

SAY: Statutes do not *say* things, and courts *say* only in dicta. When a court "holds," it is doing and not merely talking, just as a legislature does when it en*acts* a statute. (In statutes, legislatures "provide," "create," "abolish," "prohibit," "penalize," "define," and so forth.) The verb "to hold" has synonyms—"to conclude," "to determine," "to decide," "to reason," "to define," etc.—but "to say" is not one of them. On the other hand, a judge writing a concurrence or dissent does not act for the court, and therefore can accurately be considered to *say* things.

STIPULATE is a term of art and means a formal agreement (or part of one) between the parties to a lawsuit. Judicial opinions cannot "stipulate" (although they might refer to stipulations made by the parties). Nor can statutes or lawyers' briefs "stipulate."

THAT, when used as a referent, can cause vagueness. See *THIS.*

---

1. In Britain, the two-"e" spelling is more common.

THE is sometimes omitted by lawyers, but only before the following party designations: *plaintiff, defendant, appellant, appellee, petitioner,* and *respondent.* Other omissions of "the" make the writer sound semiliterate. And much of the time you will appear more literate if you retain "the" even before party designations. It is fine to title a document "Memorandum of Law in Support of Defendant's Motion for Summary Judgment," but inside the memorandum you are better off writing "The defendant is entitled to summary judgment because the plaintiff has adduced no evidence that could show . . ."

THE COURT: In some students' writing, "the court ruled in *Johanneson . . .*" will be followed by "the court ruled in *Di Prete . . . ,*" even if *Johanneson* was decided by the United States Supreme Court and *Di Prete* by a county trial court. Because opinions are printed in law school casebooks and discussed in law school classrooms without any differentiation within the hierarchy of authority (see §14.2), students are sometimes led into the sloppy habit of writing as though there were only one court in the entire common law world.

THIS and other referents (*IT, THAT, WHICH*) are vague unless the objects or ideas they refer to are immediately clear to the reader. For example:

> On September 9, the supplier threatened to withhold deliveries to the manufacturer, which, due to desperate need, purchased elsewhere at higher cost. The supplier then notified the manufacturer's own customers of the situation. *This* caused the damages for which the manufacturer now seeks recovery.

To what does "this" refer? The communication to the customers? The threat? The timing of the threat? The entire pattern of behavior? How could the meaning be made more clear?

VERBAL is not a synonym for "oral." "Verbal" means "having to do with words"—both spoken and written. A "verbal communication" is one that was made in words and not through gestures and shrieks. An "oral communication" is a spoken one, rather than one made in writing. In popular usage, *verbal* has so often been used as a synonym for "oral" that general-purpose dictionaries have come to accept that usage as an alternative (but not favored) meaning. But law needs clear ways of differentiating between the written and the spoken word and between communication through words and communication through other means. If you have learned about the parol evidence rule and the Statute of Frauds, you have begun to appreciate how critical the differences between written and oral communication can be and how often lawyers must talk about them. Because of the importance those differences are accorded in law, legal usage of *verbal* has not evolved in the same way that popular usage has. (Although "the misuse of *verbal* for *oral* is common, . . . we should not let the distinction between these words be blurred in legal prose."[2]) A lawyer who tells a judge that the parties made a "verbal" contract is apt to be interrupted with a question like "Counselor, do you mean they made an oral contract? Or do you mean that this is a contract expressed in words and not an implied contract inferable from the parties' conduct?"

WE: See *I.*

WHEN and **WHERE** are not used to set out definitions.

wrong:	Burglary is *where* [or *when*] the defendant breaks and enters the dwelling of another, in the nighttime, to commit a felony therein.
right:	Burglary is the breaking and entering of the dwelling of another, in the nighttime, with intent to commit a felony therein.

WHICH, when used as a referent, can cause vagueness. See *THIS.*

---

2. Bryan Garner, *A Dictionary of Modern Legal Usage* 563 (1987).

Appendix **B**
Nine Punctuation
Issues

Punctuation is not decoration. Proper punctuation shows the reader how your sentences are structured, and that makes your writing more clear and the reader's job easier.

Your teacher may mark your work in part by referring to some of the paragraphs in this appendix.

Apostrophes   For many readers, apostrophe mistakes are like hearing fingernails scraping a chalkboard. Start by distinguishing among plurals (more than one); possessives (which show ownership or something similar); and contractions (two words mushed together).

B-1

In a formal memo or brief, do not use contractions, although they are fine in an informal client letter.

Nouns: A plural noun usually ends in an *s* with no apostrophe ("six plaintiffs"). A possessive noun usually ends in an *s* with an apostrophe ("the plaintiff's complaint").

> **wrong:**   Both the legislature and the *court's* have refused to modify the rule.

> **also wrong:**   The defendant appealed the *courts* decision.

Pronouns: Pronouns follow different rules than nouns do and that is where the trouble usually starts. Do not confuse a contraction with a possessive. Be careful with **it, who,** and **they.**

445

it —

> **contraction:** *it's = it is* or *it has* ("it's election day tomorrow")
>
> **possessive:** *its* means that *it* possesses whatever follows ("the state reelected its governor")
>
> **fingernails on chalkboard:** writing *it's* when you mean that *it* possesses something — write *its* instead

who —

> **contraction:** *who's = who is* or *who has* ("who's going to lunch?")
>
> **possessive:** *whose* means that *who* possesses whatever follows ("whose sandwich is this?")
>
> **fingernails on chalkboard:** writing *who's* when you mean that *who* possesses something — write *whose* instead

they —

> **contraction:** *they're = they are* ("they're late")
>
> **possessive:** *their* means that *they* possess whatever follows ("their papers were time-stamped too late")
>
> **fingernails on chalkboard:** writing *they're* when you mean that *they* possess something — write *their* instead

What is wrong with these sentences?

> The courts have limited this precedent to it's facts.
> The courts can impose sanctions on a party who's complaint lacks a basis in law or fact.
> The courts have streamlined they're procedures by adopting a new set of rules.

Here is the basic principle: *Because a pronoun's contraction is formed with an apostrophe, its possessive cannot have an apostrophe.* Otherwise, the contraction and the possessive would look exactly the same.

This diagram might also help you remember:

the contraction	*the possessive*
it's ("it is")	its
who's ("who is")	whose
they're ("they are")	their

Commas and introductory words and phrases   An introductory
phrase is usually set off from the rest of the sentence by a comma. **B-2**
Without the comma, the first example is confusing:

wrong:	Frustrated with all the spyware and viruses on his computer the mouse potato threw it out the window.
right:	Frustrated with all the spyware and viruses on his computer, the mouse potato threw it out the window.

If the introductory word or phrase could have been moved elsewhere in the
sentence and would not have needed a comma there, a comma is not
usually required to set it off at the beginning of the sentence. But you
might want to use a comma anyway for stylistic reasons.

right:	Unfortunately he then sat in front of the television and became a couch potato.
placed elsewhere:	He then sat in front of the television and unfortunately became a couch potato.
also right:	Unfortunately, he then sat in front of the television and became a couch potato.

To prevent confusion, set off a *long* introductory phrase with a comma,
even if it is not required.

Commas both before and after an interruption   If a word, phrase,
or clause should be set off with commas because of the way it **B-3**
interrupts a sentence, one comma should precede it and a second comma
should follow. You need both the "before" comma and the "after" comma.
Do not leave one of them out.

wrong:	Joe who has been granted parole, will be released.
wrong:	Joe, who has been granted parole will be released.
right:	Joe, who has been granted parole, will be released.

B-4 **Commas and independent clauses**   Two independent clauses can be joined together into one sentence with a conjunction (*and, but, or*). When you do that, put a comma before the conjunction.

wrong:	The T-Rex in *Jurassic Park* ate a lawyer and audiences cheered.

This sentence has two independent clauses. Each has a subject ("The T-Rex in *Jurassic Park*" and "audiences"). And each has a verb ("ate" and "cheered"). Each clause could be a separate sentence. That is why they are independent. The conjunction "and" is not enough to join them together. It needs a comma as well:

right:	The T-Rex in *Jurassic Park* ate a lawyer, and audiences cheered.

If what comes after the conjunction does not have a separate subject of its own, do not add a comma:

wrong:	The T-Rex in *Jurassic Park* ate a lawyer, and got indigestion.

"The T-Rex in *Jurassic Park*" is the subject for both "ate a lawyer" and "got indigestion."

right:	The T-Rex in *Jurassic Park* ate a lawyer and got indigestion.

B-5 **Commas and breathing**   Do not add a comma just because a person reading the sentence aloud would run out of breath. No rule of grammar justifies the comma in this sentence:

wrong:	The argument that Napster did not infringe Metallica's copyrights when distributing the band's music over the Internet, is undermined by case law.

If reading the sentence aloud would cause a breathing problem, something is probably wrong with the way the sentence is structured. Try moving the big, complicated part of the sentence to the end:

restructured: Case law undermines the argument that Napster did not infringe Metallica's copyrights when distributing the band's music over the Internet.

Commas and missing words   Do not add a comma just because you have left out a word. No rule of grammar justifies the comma in this sentence: **B-6**

wrong: The court held, abduction by aliens does not excuse failure to attend one's own deposition.

Take out the comma and insert the missing word:

right: The court held that abduction by aliens does not excuse failure to attend one's own deposition.

Punctuation at the end of a quotation   If you add punctuation at the end of a quotation, does it go inside the quotation marks or outside? A comma or a period goes *inside* the quote marks, even if it is your own comma or period and did not appear in the original quotation. But if you add a colon, semicolon, dash, or question mark, put it *outside* the quote marks. **B-7**

right: The defendant may have called the plaintiff "the worst Elvis impersonator in the state," but that is hardly defamatory.

Did the defendant use the comma? Or was it added by the writer? It does not matter. Either way, it goes inside the quote marks.

also right: In fact, it would be futile to try to find defamatory meaning in "the worst Elvis impersonator in the state": our state is so richly endowed with excellent Elvis impersonators that our least talented practitioner might be considered brilliant elsewhere.

Here it does matter where the colon came from. If it was added by the writer, it goes outside the quote marks.

Simple lists and complicated lists — commas and semicolons   Legal writing is full of lists. Lawyers must be able to express lists in ways that are crystal-clear to the reader. In a simple and easily understood list, separate the items with commas. If the list is so complicated that commas will not clearly show where one item ends and the next begins, use semicolons instead. **B-8**

right:	The plaintiff sued, went to trial, and lost.
also right:	The court ordered the corporation dissolved; placed the property under the control of a receiver; and enjoined the defendants from conducting business by interstate telephone, wire, or delivery service.

The second example has a list within a list:

ordered the corporation dissolved;
placed the property under the control of a receiver; and
enjoined the defendants from conducting business by
    interstate telephone,
    wire, or
    delivery service.

Using semicolons for the big list allows you to use commas for the little list that is inside the third item in the big list.

B-9 **Parentheses and enumeration**   Enumeration is the numbering of items in a list. When lawyers and judges state a rule of law, they often enumerate the elements. When you do that, enclose each number completely in parentheses.

wrong:	At common law, a person committed burglary by 1) breaking and 2) entering . . .
right:	At common law, a person committed burglary by (1) breaking and (2) entering. . . .

Appendix C
Sample Office Memorandum

This appendix contains an office memorandum of the type described in Chapter 7.

TO: Theresa Wycoff

FROM: Christine Chopin

DATE: March 1, 1998

FILE: Eli Goslin

RE: constructive trust

ISSUE

Will a constructive trust in favor of Eli Goslin be imposed on the title to his home and only asset, which he deeded over to his nephew after the latter promised to make the remaining three years of payments to prevent foreclosure, where Goslin made no statement at the time that would reveal his reasons for giving the deed, and where the nephew has since then threatened to throw Goslin out of the home?

BRIEF ANSWER

A court is likely to impose a constructive trust in Goslin's favor on the nephew's title to the house. Goslin is able to prove each of the four elements of the New York test for a constructive trust: (1) a confidential or fiduciary relationship between Goslin and his nephew; (2) a promise, implied by the nephew's actions, to hold title while allowing and helping Goslin to live in the house; (3) Goslin's transfer of title to the nephew in reliance on that promise; and (4) unjust enrichment by the nephew if the promise is broken. New York courts have uniformly held these elements to be satisfied where — as happened here — a person in a vulnerable situation deeds the bulk of her or his assets to someone like a trusted relative who pays either nothing or a fraction of the property's fair value.

(This memorandum does not consider an action to set aside the deed on the grounds of fraud, undue influence, or impaired capacity — all of which have already been researched and rejected.)

FACTS

Eli Goslin, the client, is a 74-year-old arthritic widower who has been retired for nine years. He has been married twice, and both wives are deceased. His son is dead, and his daughter lives in Singapore. His only income is from social security.

Until last year, he also had income from an investment, but when that business went bankrupt, he became unable to meet the mortgage payments on his house. The house was Goslin's only asset. He has lived there for 24 years, and when these events occurred, the mortgage had only three more years to run. He has no other place to live.

After Goslin found that he could no longer pay, the mortgage, Herbert Skeffington, a nephew, offered to make the remaining $11,500 in payments as they became due. Within a few days afterward, Goslin, without stating his purpose to anyone, gave a deed to the property to Skeffington and got the bank to agree to transfer the mortgage to him. At the time, the house was worth approximately $95,000 and was unencumbered except for the mortgage

-1-

that Skeffington had offered to pay. Aside from the promise to make mortgage payments, Skeffington gave no value connected to the deed.

Goslin has told us that he made the deed for the following reason: "At the time, it seemed like the right thing to do. He was going to pay the mortgage, and after a certain point—maybe after I'm gone—the place would become his. I didn't think it would end up like this." Skeffington had not asked for a deed, and Goslin arranged for the deed before telling the nephew about it. Goslin knew at the time that Skeffington would not need a deed to make the mortgage payments: the bank would have been willing to accept Skeffington's check if it were accompanied by Goslin's payment stub, or, alternatively, Skeffington could simply have given the money to Goslin, who could in turn have paid the bank.

As far as Goslin knows, Skeffington has made the payments as they have become due.

At the time of the deed, neither party said anything about changing the living arrangements in the house. Goslin continued to live alone there until a few weeks ago, when Skeffington's rental apartment was burned out and he moved, along with his wife and two children, into the house. Goslin neither agreed to nor protested this. A few days later, Skeffington ordered Goslin to move out, which Goslin has refused to do. Since then Skeffington has, at the top of his voice, frequently repeated the demand. While yelling at Goslin, Skeffington has twice, with the heels of his palms, suddenly shoved Goslin in the chest and sent him staggering. Skeffington has threatened to strike Goslin again and to pack up Goslin's belongings and leave them and Goslin on the sidewalk. Skeffington takes the position that his family has no other place to go, and that the house is the only thing he owns.

Skeffington is 36 years old, and throughout Skeffington's life he and Goslin have seen each other at least monthly at family get-togethers, including each other's weddings. Seventeen years ago, Goslin contributed $3,200 to Skeffington's college tuition. The two of them have never discussed whether this was to be treated as a gift or a loan, and Goslin does not recall which he intended or even whether he had an intent at the time. He says that he considered both the tuition money and his nephew's offer to pay the mortgage to be "the sort of thing people in a family do for each other." In any event, except for the mortgage payments, the nephew has never given Goslin money directly or indirectly, and he has not announced an intention to compensate Goslin for the tuition money.

DISCUSSION

A constructive trust will be imposed where the record shows "(1) a confidential or fiduciary relation, (2) a promise, (3) a transfer in reliance thereon, and (4) unjust enrichment." *McGrath v. Hilding,* 363 N.E.2d 328, 330 (N.Y. 1977) (citations omitted).

Confidential or Fiduciary Relationship

Goslin's relationship with his nephew satisfies the first element.

A confidential or fiduciary relationship exists where one person is willing to entrust important matters to a second person. A relationship between an aunt and a niece has been held to be a confidential one for the purpose of a constructive trust where the aunt turned over a substantial amount of her finances to the niece and relied on the niece's care while ill. *Tebin v. Moldock,* 241 N.Y.S.2d

-2-

The conclusion was stated in the first sentence of the Brief Answer. The first sentence in the Discussion states the rule, which is proved conclusorily (§11.2) and will lead to an umbrella-paradigmed explanation (Chapter 12). Headings show where each element is discussed. Under the first heading, the first sentence states the first element's subconclusion (§12.2), and the second sentence states its supporting rule.

A substantiating proof of the rule (§11.3), synthesizing two holdings, *Tebin* and *Sharp* (§15.5).

A counter-analysis (§10.2), smoothly introduced. It would have been awkward to begin "Skeffington's lawyer might argue . . ."

629, 637-39 (1st Dep't 1963), *modified on other grounds,* 200 N.E.2d 216 (N.Y. 1964). A confidential relationship can exist even between an unsuccessful suitor and the woman who has refused to marry him where she accepts from him a deed to his farm and home. *Sharp v. Kosmalski,* 351 N.E.2d 721, 723 (N.Y. 1976).

Although a confidential relationship might not exist between an uncle and a nephew if contact has been rare and if both viewed the relationship as merely technical, that is not true here. Goslin and his nephew have seen each other at least monthly since the nephew was a boy; they attended each other's weddings, frequent family social activities, and other events; and Goslin contributed to the nephew's college tuition.

Implied Promise by the Transferee

The sub-conclusion for the second element.

The supporting rule, synthesized from several cases. Because it is at least a little surprising, it needs an extended explanation and proof. Some corollary rules explain the meaning of "All that is required is a promise." (The first corollary rule tells you that the promise need not be written.)

The courts are also likely to find here a promise — even if not stated in words — by the nephew to hold title in name only for Goslin's benefit while doing nothing that might prevent Goslin from continuing to live in his home. All that is required is a promise. It need not be written, and the Statute of Frauds will not prevent a constructive trust. *Sharp,* 351 N.E.2d at 723-24; *Pattison v. Pattison,* 92 N.E.2d 890 (N.Y. 1950); *Foreman v. Foreman,* 167 N.E. 428 (N.Y. 1929). ("Equity in this area has always reached beyond the facade of formal documents, absolute transfers, and even limiting statutes on the law side." *Tebin,* 241 N.Y.S.2d at 638.)

The promise need not even be expressly stated where it "may be implied or inferred from the very transaction itself." *Sharp,* 351 N.E.2d at 723. In *Sharp,* a 56-year-old farmer conveyed his farm to a 40-year-old woman who had declined his offer of marriage. After the transfer, the woman ordered the farmer off the property. Although the record contained no evidence of a promise in words, the Court of Appeals held that an understood promise was inherent in the actions of both parties because

> it is inconceivable that plaintiff would convey all of his interest in property which was not only his abode but the very means of his livelihood without at least tacit consent upon the part of the defendant that she would permit him to continue to live on and operate the farm.

Id. at 724.

In family relationships, New York courts have been extremely reluctant to accept a transferee's claim, under suspect circumstances, that a transfer was an absolute gift. For example, in *Sinclair v. Purdy,* 139 N.E. 255 (N.Y. 1923), a brother, who was employed as a court clerk and was continually being asked to pledge his property for other people's bail, deeded it over to his sister, receiving nothing in return. The Court of Appeals held that the circumstances implied a promise, and Judge Cardozo wrote for the court that

> [h]ere was a man transferring to his sister the only property he had in the world. . . . Even if we were to accept her statement that there was no distinct promise to hold it for his benefit, the exaction of such a promise, in view of the relation, might well have seemed to be superfluous.

Id. at 258.

Rule application begins (§10.2). This element is the heart of Goslin's controversy, and

The courts are likely to consider Goslin's circumstances to be at least comparable to those of the farmer in *Sharp* and the brother in *Sinclair.* Goslin owned nothing of substance other than his home. At the time of the transfer, he had been retired for nine years, and his only income was from social security. His income had just been reduced because of the bankruptcy of a small business in which he had had an interest. The house itself was worth approximately $95,000 at the time of the transfer, and the three years of mortgage payments remaining totalled $11,500. Even Skeffington's promise to make the mortgage payments cannot be considered a payment to Goslin because, if Skeffington really took clear title, the mortgage payments would benefit him and not Goslin. In addition, seventeen years ago, the nephew had received $3,200 from Goslin for college tuition, and he had not returned any of it. Although the parties have never talked with each other about whether the tuition money was a gift or a loan, the courts are likely to consider the label unimportant and instead focus on mutual family responsibilities. Accordingly, the courts are not likely to conclude that Goslin intended to make an absolute gift of his house. Instead, they will more probably hold that Goslin and his nephew had an unstated understanding that the nephew's mortgage payments were to reciprocate Goslin's contributions to the nephew's college tuition.

> the reader needs an extended explanation of why the rule will be applied this way. The rule application centers on analogies to *Sharp* and *Sinclair* (§15.3).

The courts will probably so hold even though the nephew could have made the mortgage payments without having received a deed. Of all the facts here, the most troubling is the lack of any need to deed the house over to the nephew. For example, the bank would have accepted the nephew's check, as long as it was accompanied by a stub from Goslin's payment book, and the stub could have been filled out by Goslin or his nephew. Or the nephew could have simply given Goslin the money and let him make the payments.

> A counter-analysis. Again, notice how it is introduced.

But under the case law, the lack of a need for a transfer is irrelevant. The farmer in *Sharp,* for example, seems to have given a deed for purely sentimental reasons, but the Court of Appeals considered it to be subject to a constructive trust anyway. *Sharp* can most reasonably be interpreted to stand for the proposition that, no matter how quixotic a transferor's purpose may have been, a promise of some kind will be implied where the parties have a family or other emotionally charged relationship and where the property transferred is the bulk of the transferor's assets. Although Goslin did not have the same practical need to make a transfer that the court clerk had in *Sinclair,* the Court of Appeals did not treat the court clerk's need as essential in that decision.

> The counter-analysis weaves *Sharp* and *Sinclair* together to show you what they have in common. This is a form of synthesis (§15.5).

Transfer in Reliance on the Promise

The transfer itself is not in dispute here, and, for the reasons described above, Goslin should be able to prove that he granted the deed in reliance on his nephew's promise.

> The nephew must concede part of this element, and the rest is proved through the explanations of the first two elements.

Unjust Enrichment

Goslin should also be able to establish the fourth element, which has been described variously as "unjust enrichment under cover of the relation of confidence, "*Sinclair,* 139 N.E. at 258; as a situation where "property has been acquired in such circumstances that the holder of the legal title may not in good conscience retain the beneficial interest," *Sharp,* 351 N.E.2d at 723; and as circumstances where "discernible promises, made in a confidential relationship, have been broken or repudiated, and the trusted one will be unjustly enriched by reason of the breaches;" *Tebin,* 241 N.Y.S.2d at 634.

> The sub-conclusion for the final element. The rule is proved through a conclusory synthesis of three holdings. It can be conclusory because a reader can easily accept it. But a surprise is in a corollary rule, which dispenses

with any need to prove fraudulent intent. That gets more explanation through *Sharp, Tebin,* and *Ferano.*

In *Sharp* and in *Tebin,* the courts held that a plaintiff need not prove that the party who accepted the transfer did so with a fraudulent intent. "A constructive trust may be imposed even though the transferee fully intended to perform his promise at the time of the conveyance." *Ferano v. Stephanelli,* 183 N.Y.S.2d 707, 711 (1st Dep't 1959). It is enough to show that the entrusted party has breached the promise on which the grantor relied.

Rule application.

Here, the nephew took a deed upon promising to make three years of mortgage payments and without paying anything for Goslin's sizeable equity. On these facts, the courts are likely to decide that the nephew has tried to pervert into a windfall his assumption of a family responsibility. (The nephew's offer to pay the remaining mortgage could have been seen by both parties as reciprocation for Goslin's help in putting the nephew through college, although that is not necessary to a ruling in Goslin's favor.)

CONCLUSION

Goslin can demonstrate all the elements of a constructive trust. He had a relationship of confidence with Skeffington because they are uncle and nephew and have acted that way for years. The most reasonable interpretation of the facts is that both parties understood an implied agreement that Skeffington would take title in name only and for the purpose of protecting the house for Goslin's use. The deed was a transfer of Goslin's home and only asset and could have been made only in reliance on that promise. And without a constructive trust, Skeffington would be unjustly enriched because he would have clear title to a $95,000 asset in exchange for $11,500 in mortgage payments.

All of the elements of a constructive trust are therefore established, and a court is likely to impose one.

Appendix **D**
Sample Client Advice Letter

This appendix contains a client advice letter of the type described in Chapter 21.

The client is Ada Warren of Lincoln Notch, Vermont. She is in her late fifties. When the Lincoln Creamery fell on hard times a few years ago, she lost her job as office manager and lived thereafter on savings. When her cousin Virgil died last year, she inherited his farm near Grafton, which she sold to a Boston developer for a half million dollars. She then booked a cruise on the Pride of Seaside, a six-cabin sailing yacht.

Huber & Stanislaw
Attorneys at Law
6 Front Street
Seaside, ME 01203
(603) 555-1111

March 14, 2001

Ada Warren
22 Green Mountain Road
Lincoln Notch, VT 05862

Dear Ms. Warren:

As I promised when we met last week, I have researched your rights against
Seaside Cruises and the state Marine Police. I believe that you probably
would win a lawsuit against Seaside but lose a suit against the police. In
the second half of this letter, I'll explain why.

After you and I spoke last week, I examined the police logs and talked
to some of the passengers. I was able to get some information (though not much)
from the police officers and the captain of the Pride of Seaside. My advice later
in this letter is based on my understanding of the facts, which are described
in the next few paragraphs. If I have gotten any of the facts wrong, please
tell me so that I can determine whether the law would treat the situation
differently.

Facts

You boarded the Pride of Seaside at 8:30 in the evening. The boat left
the dock at 9:00 P.M., and you went below at about 9:30, drew your cabin
curtains, and were asleep by about 10:15. You had felt ill earlier in the evening
and had wanted to rest. At 10:40 P.M., the boat was boarded by Officers
Magrane and Kroyer of the State Marine Police, who suspected that a sailor had
marijuana hidden behind his bunk. They found what they were looking
for, arrested the sailor, and ordered the captain to sail to the Marine Police dock.
There, the boat was impounded and the sailor was taken away by the police.
The other passengers and the rest of the crew were awakened by the ruckus and
came on deck, where they were told by Officer Kroyer that they would have
to leave the boat. Officer Magrane drove the passengers (except you) in a
Marine Police van to a hotel, where they slept.

Neither the crew nor the police searched the boat to make sure no one
else was aboard. The police officers admit that they did not ask for a list
of passengers. They and the boat captain say that the crew did not offer
a passenger list to the police or compare the passengers on deck with the boat's
passenger manifest. The police say they thought it was the crew's responsibility
to get everyone off the boat. The captain says that he thought the police
were doing that. You slept soundly through the night. At 12:15 A.M., Officer
Kroyer sealed the boat. He locked every outer door and hatch — including
the door separating the main deck from the passageway on which the
passengers' cabins were situated — removed the gangway, locked it in a shed,
and went home. As a result, even though your cabin was unlocked, you
would not have been able to get to the deck because all the doors and hatches
were locked from the outside, and even if you had been able to get to the
deck, you would not have been able to walk off the boat.

-1-

No one else was at the dock until Officer Tedescu arrived at about 6:30 on Saturday morning. Tedescu found a note from Kroyer that the boat had been impounded but that it had not yet been searched (except for the sailor's bunk). He rolled out the gangway, walked on board, and at 6:45 unlocked the door to the passageway outside your cabin. You had slept soundly through the night. You awoke at about 7:00 A.M., opened your cabin door, and found Officer Tedescu standing in the passageway. Officer Tedescu explained what had happened, and you suddenly felt light-headed and fell to the floor of the passageway. In his written report, Officer Tedescu used the word "fainted" to describe this. You revived in a moment or two, and he drove you to a hospital, where an emergency room physician decided that you needed no treatment.

You were shocked at the indignity of learning that you had spent the night locked up in a police boat yard rather than cruising at sea as you thought you had been. For you, this was the same as being locked up in a jail cell overnight. Both are shameful, treating you like a criminal. Except for collapsing or fainting, you did not suffer physically from these events. Seaside Cruises has refused to refund the $3,500 that you paid for this two-week cruise. As I understand it, they have not provided any passenger with a refund.

Possible Lawsuits

When we met last week, you said that you are not sure that legal action would be worth the effort, but that you feel taken advantage of and wanted to know what your rights are. I will explain what I think would happen if you were to sue Seaside Cruises and the Marine Police.

Seaside Cruises: The law considers Seaside to be a common carrier. Airlines, railroads, and bus companies are also common carriers. Common carriers owe a very high degree of care to their passengers, including the duty to rescue a passenger from harm. Based on the facts we have at this point, I think you would probably win on this claim. Seaside's employees should have made sure you were off the boat before it was locked up or at least have told the police that you were aboard.

> Common carriers are explained in a nontechnical way so the client will understand.

But it is harder to predict how much money a jury would award on this claim. It might be small on the ground that you were unaware at the time that you were locked into the boat. Or it might be larger if the jury can appreciate the depth of the indignity.

On the other hand, Seaside Cruises does owe you a refund of $3,500. You paid for a service (a cruise) that Seaside did not provide. The law is clear that they are not entitled to keep the money, even though the cruise was prevented by police seizure of their boat.

> Notice the difference in degrees of optimism between the two predictions.

You can bring both claims against Seaside — for the refund and for failing to get you off the boat — in a single lawsuit.

The Marine Police: If you were to sue the state for false imprisonment, I believe that you would not succeed. In this state, a false imprisonment claim can succeed only if the person confined knew of the confinement while it was occurring or was harmed by it. The law defines "harm" in this sense as economic loss or physical injury.

> Here the prediction is negative.

You did suffer an economic loss (the $3,500 that Seaside has not refunded), but not because you were locked in the boat. If the police had driven you to a hotel, Seaside still would have refused to refund the money.

Because you learned of your confinement only after Officer Tedescu had unlocked the boat, the only way of succeeding in a suit against the police would be to show that the confinement caused you physical injury. The only physical injury is your collapse when Officer Tedescu told you that you had been confined. There are two problems here. First, a jury could conclude that you collapsed because you were still ill from the night before.

This is the difficult point. Will the client understand it?

Second, in a case called *Osborne v. Floyd,* our state supreme court recently decided that the physical injury must be caused by the confinement itself. It is not enough for the harm to be caused by knowledge of the confinement. In *Osborne,* a man was comatose and unaware he had been locked into a cellar. His medical condition did not deteriorate before rescuers broke down the door. But after he regained consciousness and learned what had happened, he experienced nightmares. The court held that the nightmares were not sufficient and an injury would have to be physical for him to recover. I think the

A useful thing to say with bad news.

courts would treat your collapsing onto the floor the same way, especially because the emergency room physician decided that you needed no medical treatment. I wish this weren't so, but unfortunately, it is.

Let's talk further in a few days. Originally, you asked what your rights are in this situation. If, after thinking this over, you are interested in suing Seaside Cruises, I can explain what a lawsuit would cost so you can decide whether to go ahead. It might be possible to reduce the expense of suing if other passengers join with you and sue to get the refunds they are entitled to. Please call my office when you feel ready.

Sincerely,

Gary Stanislaw

-3-

Appendix E
Sample Demand Letter

This appendix contains a sample demand letter of the type described in Chapter 22.

The lawyer who wrote the letter represents a tenant whose landlord is refusing to renew the lease. The apartment is covered by a statute that regulates tenancies because of a housing shortage. (Outside large urban areas, these statutes are rare.)

The tenant's lawyer has written the letter for two audiences: the landlord and any lawyer whose advice the landlord might seek. The tenant's lawyer does not know whether the landlord has a lawyer already or who that lawyer might be. But there is a good chance the landlord will ask some lawyer's advice before deciding what to do. The letter is written in straightforward language that a typical landlord could easily understand. But it is also written in precise language that would be meaningful to any lawyer the landlord might consult.

The tenant's lawyer makes assertions about the law that the landlord's lawyer would not accept unless they were supported by legal authority. Putting citations into the text of the letter would make it harder for the landlord to read. The tenant's lawyer's solution was to put the citations in footnotes, where they are obvious to a lawyer reader but do not interfere with the letter's readability. That might or might not work in other demand letters, but it is appropriate here.

If this letter had been written directly to another lawyer — in other words, if it were not addressed to a layperson like the landlord — the letter would need to explain *how* the cases cited in the footnotes support the assertions in the text of the letter. A demand letter addressed to another lawyer sometimes reads like a mini-memorandum. But here the primary audience is the landlord. That kind of reader is often most persuaded by fact analogies rather than nuanced interpretation of precedent. In this letter, can you identify fact analogies designed to show the landlord that the position he has taken is wrong?

The lawyer who wrote the letter had two goals. The more important one was to convince the landlord that the tenant has a right to remain. The other goal was to persuade the landlord to sign a lease so that the tenant could prove his tenancy, if he ever needs to.

Clyde Farnsworth, Esq.
32 Fontanka Street
Bedford Falls, NY 14218

June 28, 2004

Frank Alston
Alston Properties
396 Gilliam Way
Bedford Falls, NY 14218

RE: Mateo Flores
Apt. 4-B
440 Gilliam Way

Dear Mr. Alston:

I represent Mr. Flores. I am writing to explain why he will continue to be a tenant in Apartment 4-B for at least the next three years.

As you know, the apartment is covered by statutes regulating rent and guaranteeing tenants lease renewals if they want them. State law requires you to send Mr. Flores a notice offering him a renewal of his lease, and if he signs the form and returns it to you within 60 days, his lease must be renewed.[1]

For two reasons, the law considers Mr. Flores's lease to have been renewed for three years, even though you refuse to sign a written lease that would document that. He does not need both reasons. Either reason, standing alone, entitles him to a renewal lease.

The first reason is that your renewal notice is dated April 12. If you have a post office receipt proving that you mailed it the same day, sixty days later would be June 11. Because June 11 was a Sunday, the deadline would be the next business day, June 12. Mr. Flores has a postal receipt proving that he mailed his tenant's response to you on June 12. (If your postal receipt shows that you mailed the renewal notice *after* April 12, the deadline would be even later than June 12.)

The law considers the date on which a tenant mails his response to be the date on which it is returned. It is not necessary for you to receive it by the deadline. Mr. Flores only needs to mail it by then — which he did.

The second reason is this: the courts have decided that even where a tenant returns the form late, the tenant is entitled to a renewal lease. That has happened where the tenant mailed the response *twelve* days late.[2] And five days late.[3] And two days late.[4] The courts have held that the only way a landlord can overcome this is to prove that the landlord signed a lease for the apartment with someone else or in some other way prejudiced himself before receiving the tenant's response.[5] But the courts will not even let you do that because Mr. Flores informed your secretary on June 12 that he was renewing his lease and mailing his tenant's response to you on that day.

---

1. N.Y. Emerg. Tenant Prof. Reg. § 2503.5(a) (2004).

2. *Glen Arms Group v. Diaz*, 2001 N.Y. Misc. LEXIS 662 (Dist. Ct., Nassau County 2001).

3. *Gordon v. Barash*, 67 Misc. 2d 764, 325 N.Y.S.2d 213 (Civ. Ct., N.Y. County 1971).

4. *Baja Realty v. Karoussos*, 120 Misc. 2d 824, 467 N.Y.S.2d 505 (App. T., 1st Dept. 1983).

5. *J.N.A. Realty Co. v. Cross Bay Chelsea*, 42 N.Y.2d 392, 366 N.E.2d 1313 (1977); *Sy Jack Realty Co. v. Pegament Syosset Corp.*, 27 N.Y.2d 449, 267 N.E.2d 462, 318 N.Y.S.2d 720 (1971); *67 8th Ave. Assocs. v. Hochstadt*, 88 A.D.2d 843, 451 N.Y.2d 408 (1982).

Thus, Mr. Flores has a right to remain in the apartment at least until July 11, 2007, which is three years from the date his current lease expires. If you do not sign a new lease for that period, the terms of his current lease remain in effect until July 11, 2007.

Mr. Flores has always paid his rent on time and has been a careful and responsible tenant. For example, he is a licensed electrician, and when the apartment complex suffered an electrical outage two months ago, he spent an entire weekend helping your employees diagnose and resolve the problem. He did not ask to be paid for this and was only glad to help. I ask that you sign a new lease. But if you do not, the law will treat the old lease as remaining in effect until July 11, 2007.

Yours,

Clyde Farnsworth

Appendix **F**
Sample Motion
Memorandum

This appendix contains a motion memorandum of the type described in Chapter 27. A preschool has sued a commercial painter in negligence. This is the preschool's memo in support of its motion for summary judgment.

For the preschool, winning this motion is in many ways harder than it looks. First, no reported case in any state has determined whether a painter is liable on facts like these. Judges are much more comfortable applying settled precedent than engaging in the risky business of filling gaps in the law in ways that require people to change their behavior.

Second, what this painter did is not unusual. If the law fills this gap as the preschool would like, a lot of behavior previously deemed blameless would suddenly become tortious. Maybe that should happen, but judges will think long and hard before doing it.

Third, as a plaintiff the preschool must in this motion persuade the court that the defendant is completely defenseless: that he has no affirmative defenses and does not have enough evidence to create a triable issue on any of the elements that the preschool must prove. That is hard to do, and this is perhaps the hardest kind of summary judgment for a movant to win.

Finally, courts hesitate in general to grant summary judgments to negligence plaintiffs, preferring that juries decide whether open-texture tests like negligence have been satisfied. (Courts much more easily grant summary judgments to negligence defendants.)

If, despite all this, you finish reading the memo eager, as a judge, to grant summary judgment to the preschool, then the memo has done its job.

For simplicity as a sample, the memo does not address other theories the preschool might have pursued, such as gross negligence and strict liability for extrahazardous activities claims against the painter.

SUPERIOR COURT OF CONNECTICUT
JUDICIAL DISTRICT OF NEW LONDON

TULTA PRESCHOOL, INC.,

Plaintiff

-against-   No. CV05-8956

MICHAEL D. RAUCHER, dba
RAUCHER PAINTING CONTRACTORS

Defendant

MEMORANDUM IN SUPPORT OF
PLAINTIFF'S MOTION FOR
PARTIAL SUMMARY JUDGMENT

Petra Diaz, Esq.
Attorney for Plaintiff
94 Front Street
Coff's Harbor, CT 14218
(203) 555-1111

CONTENTS

INTRODUCTION

The plaintiff, Tulta Preschool, Inc., teaches children from two to five years of age in Coff's Harbor, Connecticut. The defendant, Michael D. Raucher, is a commercial painter doing business as Raucher Painting Contractors.

Mr. Raucher contaminated Tulta Preschool's building and grounds by power-sanding toxic lead-based paint off the exterior of an adjacent building. Lead paint dust and chips are dangerous, especially to small children. Tulta Preschool was forced to close and could not reopen until its building and land had been cleaned according to government regulations at a cost of $34,550. Tulta also had to refund $17,992 in tuition for the period when it was closed, and its reputation and value as a business have been injured severely.

In this motion, Tulta Preschool seeks partial summary judgment determining that Mr. Raucher is liable to Tulta. If the motion is granted, the only issue for trial would be the size of the damages award.

STATEMENT OF THE CASE

This is the opening paragraph described on p. 363. It is intended to motivate the judge from the very first sentence. (See the note in the margin on pp. 503-504.) How does this Statement of the Case satisfy the other criteria on pp. 360-366?

Lead is a poison. If it gets into a child's body, it can cause permanent brain and neurological damage, leading to learning disabilities, behavioral problems, or reduced IQ. (Aff. Leonard Crosetti, M.D., ¶3 (Feb. 23, 2001).) Lead can also impair a child's ability to process vitamin D and to make red blood cells, and it can irreversibly damage the kidney (id. ¶5). The most common source of lead poisoning is microscopic lead paint dust that cannot be detected through visual inspection (id. ¶2). If the floor inside a building or the soil outside is contaminated with lead dust, young children can literally eat lead because they frequently and unexpectedly put their hands and other things in their mouths while playing (id. ¶3). If a young child sees a paint chip, that chip might also end up in the child's mouth and be sucked on or swallowed whole (id.).

Within 135 feet of a neighboring preschool, Mr. Raucher power-sanded toxic lead paint off every inch of the wood exterior of an antique store at 32 Seabank Road, including all the siding and trim and an intricate turn-of-the-century wood porch. (Depo. Michael Raucher 18:11-18:23 (Nov. 18, 2000).) He did nothing to prevent paint chips and dust from flying onto Tulta Preschool's grounds (id. at 19), and, helped by the wind, they did exactly that. (Aff. Jane Greenburg ¶9 (Feb. 24, 2001).)

Mr. Raucher and Lead Paint

The store was built in 1901. (Aff. Petra Diaz ¶8 (Feb. 27, 2001).) At that time and until the 1950's, most paint contained significant amounts of lead, and some paint was as much as 50% lead (Greenburg aff. ¶6). Lead paint might be found in or on any building that existed before 1978, when the sale of lead paint was prohibited, but it is most frequently found in those built before the 1950s (id.). Mr. Raucher admits that he knew the store's approximate age from its building style and details (Raucher depo. 6:2-6:16).

Sanding prepares a worn paint surface to be repainted (Raucher depo. 11:2-12:25). Mr. Raucher believed at the time he began to sand that much of the building had probably never been stripped of the paint it had accumulated over the years, and that he would in many places be removing all the paint that had ever been applied to the store, right down to the original coat from 1901 (id. at 12).

-1-

Before beginning to sand, Mr. Raucher could have had some paint chips tested for lead at a local lab for $45 per chip (Greenburg aff. ¶26). For $250 to $400, he could have hired a technician to examine virtually all the store's outside surfaces for lead with a hand-held x-ray gun (*id.*). For as little as $15, he could have bought in any hardware or paint store a limited testing kit that would have given him some confirmation of the presence of lead (*id.*).

Mr. Raucher did none of these things. And he did nothing to encourage the store owner to test for lead before Mr. Raucher began work (Raucher depo. 86:16). In fact, he has never tested any paint for lead or encouraged any customer to do so (*id.* 87:19). He believes that no painter he knows has ever done any of these things (*id.* at 89-4).

There are well understood methods of safely removing or encapsulating lead paint. It can be wet-sanded by hand, which is time-consuming but spreads little dust and paint chips (Greenburg aff. ¶8). Or the paint can be stripped following abatement procedures with a work area shrouded in impermeable plastic barriers, which is very expensive but, when done properly, leaves no dust or chips behind (*id.* ¶7). Or the paint can be enclosed inside something new, like aluminum siding, which also leaves no dust or chips but can diminish the architectural character of an old building (*id.* 9).

Mr. Raucher has not learned how to do any of this, and he believes that no painter of his acquaintance has, either (Raucher depo. at 67). But he has seen newspaper stories and television commentary about the dangers of lead paint, and he knows that lead paint can no longer legally be sold because it is considered dangerous (Raucher depo. 42:6, 52:9).

Mr. Raucher believes that concerns about lead are "all exaggerated" because "I've been painting and sanding all my life, and there's nothing wrong with me or with any of the other painters in Coff's Harbor" (*id.* 67:18-67:22). At his deposition, he elaborated as follows:

Q: Why do you keep on power-sanding old paint, after what you've read in the newspaper and seen on TV?

A: People aren't going to pay for all this expensive stuff, and most painters aren't going to learn how to do it. People expect to pay three or four thousand dollars maximum to repaint a house, and painters expect to do the job the way they've always done it, with power-sanders and tarps — and not wearing white hazardous materials suits and trapping every last chip in plastic sheets to be taken away to hazardous waste dumps and all the other crazy things you're talking about. I'm a painter. My job is to sand and paint. That's what painters do.

Id. 68:19-69:14

A Preschool Contaminated with Lead

Mr. Raucher power-sanded 32 Seabank Road during a school vacation week. (Aff. Sharon Williams ¶4 (Feb. 20, 2001.) No one was at Tulta Preschool at the time (*id.*). When some Tulta teachers arrived the following Monday, they noticed "a film of blue dust over most things on that side of the school, plus scattered bunches of blue chips" (*id.* ¶10). They also noticed that every inch of the exterior of 32 Seabank had been stripped of paint down to the bare wood (*id.* ¶11).

The teachers stopped all the arriving children in the parking lot and immediately sent them home (*id.* ¶13). Many parents were forced to leave their

-2-

469

jobs and come home to care for their children (*id.* ¶14). Some parents missed more than a week of work (*id.* ¶15).

Environmental Assessments, Inc. tested Tulta Preschool's soil, walkways, and various interior surfaces (Greenburg aff. ¶12). Dust had entered the building through air-conditioning vents and had been spread inside by a ventilation fan (*id.* ¶19). Most of the interior and exterior surfaces tested by Environmental Assessments contained lead dust in amounts exceeding the guidelines promulgated for soil by the U.S. Environmental Protection Agency (EPA) and for interior floors the U.S. Department of Housing and Urban Development (HUD) (*id.* ¶23).

To restore Tulta Preschool to a safe condition, an abatement company had to clean up visible dust and chips, scrub with a deleading solution most hard surfaces outside and many inside, remove and replace the top layer of soil wherever grass was not already growing (such as under swings), and build a solid fence between the two properties so that additional dust and chips would not later blow onto Tulta Preschool's grounds (Williams ¶28). Everything removed by the abatement company, including soil, had to be taken to a toxic waste dump (Greenburg aff. ¶19).

The cost of testing and abatement totalled $34,550 (*id.* ¶31). Tulta Preschool also had to refund tuition for the period when it was closed in a total amount of $17,992 (*id.* ¶33). Applications for the following year were many fewer than normal, and Tulta Preschool has acquired a reputation as "the place where that lead paint thing happened" (*id.* ¶36).

Lead poisoning symptoms develop so gradually and sporadically that parents and others frequently do not recognize them as symptoms and instead assume that "that is just the way this child is" (Crosetti aff. ¶14). According to Dr. Leonard Crosetti, a lead-specialist pediatrician ready to testify in this case, the reduction of quality of life for a lead-poisoned child can last a lifetime. (*id.* ¶11). (Annexed to Dr. Crosetti's affidavit are 14 articles from medical journals showing that Dr. Crosetti's observations reflect medical research on this question.)

ARGUMENT

Tulta Preschool Should be granted a Partial summary judgment determining that Mr. Raucher Negligently caused Tulta Preschool's injuries.

This is the opening paragraph described on p. 314.

"[L]ead is the number one environmental poison for children," the New York state legislature determined when amending its Lead Poisoning Prevention Act. "Environmental exposure to even low levels of lead increases a child's risk of developing permanent learning disabilities, reduced concentration and attentiveness, and behavior problems. These problems may persist and adversely affect the child's chances for success in school and life. Higher levels of lead can cause mental retardation, kidney disease, liver damage and even death." N.Y. Laws 1992, ch. 485, § 1 (1993).

In New York City, there was a public uproar when city workers sandblasted toxic lead paint off a bridge above a residential neighborhood. The mayor appointed a task force to choose a different method of paint removal, but even

-3-

that was enjoined because the people affected — those who lived in the shadow of the bridge — had not been given sufficient opportunity to be heard. *Williamsburg Around the Bridge Block Ass'n v. Giuliani,* 644 N.Y.S.2d 252 (1st Dep't 1996).

If Coff's Harbor were to have a seaside village's equivalent of the Williamsburg Bridge fiasco, it would be what Mr. Raucher did to the building adjacent to Tulta Preschool. The evidence of that is so overwhelming that Tulta Preschool should be granted summary judgment on the question of liability, leaving for trial only the computation of damages.

Here begins the umbrella paradigm diagrammed on p. 338. Motivating arguments were made above — in the first and second paragraphs of the Argument.

Summary judgment "shall be rendered if . . . there is no genuine issue as to any material fact and . . . the moving party is entitled to judgment as a matter of law." *Appleton v. Board of Educ.,* 254 Conn. 205, 209, 757 A.2d 1059, 1062 (2000) (quoting Practice Book 384). The elements of negligence "are well established: duty; breach of that duty; causation; and actual injury." *RK Constructors, Inc. v. Fusco Corp.,* 231 Conn. 381, 384, 650 A.2d 153, 155 (1994). Although no reported case in any state has determined whether a painter commits negligence on facts like these, there is ample reason to hold Mr. Raucher liable.

> A.   *Mr. Raucher has no evidence contradicting Tulta's on the elements of negligence, and therefore no material fact regarding liability is genuinely in dispute.*

The party resisting summary judgment "must provide an evidentiary foundation to demonstrate the existence of a genuine issue of material fact." *Appleton,* 254 Conn. at 209, 757 A.2d at 1062. It is not enough for the resisting party to claim that its version of a fact is true. The resisting party must demonstrate that there is a genuine issue by submitting admissible evidence that could be believed by a reasonable fact-finder. *Miles v. Foley,* 253 Conn. 381, 385, 752 A.2d 503, 506 (2000).

Mr. Raucher admits to power-sanding the building at 32 Seabank Road. He has no evidence that Environmental Assessment's testing was inaccurate. He does not deny that Tulta Preschool's property was abated, or that the school was closed during the period of the abatement, or that Tulta refunded tuition for that period.

Mr. Raucher does contend that lead paint is not really dangerous because "I've been painting and sanding all my life, and there's nothing wrong with me or with any of the other painters in Coff's Harbor" (Raucher depo. 67:18-67:22). This is a lay opinion, not evidence admissible at trial, and it does not create a genuine issue. "Only evidence that would be admissible at trial may be used to support or oppose a motion for summary judgment." *Home Ins.,* 235 Conn. at 202-03, 663 A.2d at 1008. Mr. Raucher is not a physician and is not qualified to determine whether he or anybody else has been lead-poisoned or whether lead is medically dangerous to small children, which is the crux of this case.

Even if he were so qualified, his opinion could not be accepted by a rational jury. The scientific evidence unanimously contradicts it (Crosetti aff. 2-19 and attached exhibits). And although lead is far more dangerous to children than to adults, courts have recognized, at least since *Dandurand v. Hydrox Co.,* 222 Ill. App. 267, 278 (1921), that painters themselves are in danger of lead poisoning. The children of painters are also in danger because lead dust can attach itself to work clothing and from there be distributed around a painter's home and family car. *Weaver v. Royal Ins. Co.,* 674 A.2d 975 (N.H. 1996).

-4-

*B.   Mr. Raucher should be held to the duty of care of a skilled
lead paint abator working in the vicinity of children.*

Notice how two cases below are synthesized to support the duty formulation specified in the heading. This is paradigmed proof of the first element of negligence.

If a general contractor — the kind that builds and remodels houses — contracts to dig a well, the contractor will be held to "that degree of care which a skilled well driller of ordinary prudence would have exercised under the same or similar conditions." *Sasso v. Ayotte,* 155 Conn. 525, 529, 235 A.2d 636, 637 (1967). In *Sasso,* the general contractor dug a well in such a way that overflow from a septic tank came through the house's fresh water taps. The general contractor made mistakes that a skilled well driller would not have made, and the general contractor was held liable.

A skilled remover of toxic lead paint is a lead abatement contractor, who will follow abatement procedures recognized by HUD including isolating the work area in plastic shrouds to contain the paint being removed. If a painter undertakes to strip toxic lead paint, the painter should be held to the standard of care that an abator would in the same circumstances. If the painter causes injury that a skilled abator would have prevented, the painter should be liable.

But the standard to which Mr. Raucher should be held is even higher than that. Children often do not recognize danger, and they can do unanticipated things very suddenly. "One is required to exercise greater care where the presence of children is reasonably to be expected." *Scorpion v. American-Republican, Inc.,* 131 Conn. 42, 45, 37 A.2d 802, 804 (1944). The *Scorpion* defendant was a newspaper company that left its editions bound in wire on sidewalks, where "newsboys" unbound and delivered them. An eight-year-old child injured her eye on wire left as litter on a residential sidewalk, and the newspaper was held liable because it should have known that children use residential sidewalks, and that many children would not realize that they could hurt themselves while handling the wire.

A counter-argument.

When Mr. Raucher claims that he only did what painters have always done and what other painters would do with the same building, he misconstrues the standard of care by which his conduct should be judged. He did more than remove paint, which is something that painters do and know how to do. He removed toxic lead paint, which requires special skills and knowledge if it is to be done safely.

Enactments are used to support a policy argument.

Our statutes are evidence of the gravity of this situation. The owner of "any dwelling" where a child six years or younger lives "shall abate or manage" paint, plaster, or anything else that contains toxic levels of lead. Conn. Gen. Stats. § 19a111c (1997). And local health directors in this state are authorized to relocate families from their homes when anyone in the family has a lead blood level above a point specified by statute. Conn. Gen. Stats. § 19a-111 (1997).

*C.   The evidence unequivocally shows that Mr. Raucher
breached the duty of care of a skilled lead paint abator
working in the vicinity of children, and that his breach
proximately caused Tulta Preschool's injuries.*

Using relatively inexpensive testing methods, Mr. Raucher could have determined that the exterior paint on the building at 32 Seabank Road was toxic. Lead paint dust and chips would not have contaminated Tulta Preschool if Mr. Raucher had wet sanded by hand, abated according to HUD procedures, or encapsulated the paint. Although the job would have become much more expensive, Mr. Raucher could have learned how to do any of these things

-5-

himself, or he could have hired a qualified abatement company to do one of them as a subcontractor. But instead he power-sanded lead paint and contaminated Tulta Preschool, which had to be closed until, at great expense, it could be deleaded.

Like the general contractor who dug a well in *Sasso,* Mr. Raucher created an environmental hazard by ignoring what specialists know how to do. The general contractor was held liable, and so should Mr. Raucher. And like the newspaper company that left wire on the sidewalk in *Scorpion,* Mr. Raucher left substances particularly dangerous to children in places where children could find them without understanding their danger. In his case, the endangered were 130 children who have not yet reached the age of kindergarten. The newspaper was held liable, and so should Mr. Raucher.

It is not a defense to say that Mr. Raucher was not working on Tulta's property and is therefore not responsible for what happened there. When a person in control of land projects a dangerous situation onto neighboring property, that person is liable for the resulting injuries. *Spagnolo v. Lanza,* 110 Conn. 170, 147 A. 594 (1929). No case holds that this kind of liability is imposed only on landowners. As Mr. Raucher's own conduct demonstrates, anybody in control of land, even if only for a few days to paint a building, has the capacity to create an environmental disaster on adjoining property.

Analogies.

A counter-argument.

CONCLUSION

Tulta Preschool should be granted partial summary judgment determining that Mr. Raucher is liable in negligence. Mr. Raucher owed a duty of reasonable care to Tulta to avoid contaminating Tulta's property with lead paint dust and chips and to avoid creating a risk of lead poisoning in the vicinity of his work site. There is abundant evidence that he breached that duty, at great expense to Tulta and to Tulta's reputation, and that only the coincidence that he powersanded during a school vacation week prevented him from immediately injuring the health of 130 children as well. There is no evidence, admissible at trial, to the contrary, and therefore no rational jury can return a verdict against the preschool on the question of liability.

Respectfully Submitted,

Petra Diaz, Esq.

Petra Diaz, Esq.
Attorney for Plaintiffs
94 Front Street
Coff's Harbor, CT 14218
(203) 555-1111

Appendix G
Sample Appellant's Brief

This Appendix contains the appellant's brief from a hypothetical appeal. Appendix H contains the appellee's brief from the same appeal. Each brief has been limited to only two of the issues that could have been raised on these facts.[1] The material that remains is substantial enough to give you realistic examples of how various tasks might be handled in a brief you would be assigned to write.

The briefs in this appendix and in Appendix H illustrate *two-issue briefs*. In many appellate advocacy and moot court programs, students write briefs in teams of two, each student writing on one of the issues.

If you are writing a *one-issue* brief, *do not expect yourself to produce a document equal to the entirety of one of these briefs.* Instead, simply ignore one of the two issues here. In each brief, Point I argues a statutory issue and Point II argues a constitutional issue. *If you are writing a one-issue brief, pick one of these issues and, as you read the briefs, ignore the other issue.* Unless you are studying constitutional law now or are writing a brief on a constitutional issue, you might find the statutory issue more helpful and a better illustration of good appellate writing.

These briefs come with three caveats.

First, do not imitate something in these briefs without understanding why it was done here and without deciding whether it would be effective in an appeal for which you are writing a brief. If, for example, you like the style of the Questions Presented in one of these briefs, consider the possibility that that style might not work as well with your theory and with the

---

1. In addition to the grounds asserted here, a defendant in a similar case might also argue that the statute involved is unconstitutionally vague and that it violates the Fourteenth Amendment right to equal protection.

facts and law of your appeal. You are learning how to make writing decisions to develop professional self-sufficiency. That cannot be learned by imitating a sample brief unquestioningly.

The second caveat concerns differences in brief format from jurisdiction to jurisdiction. This brief and the brief in Appendix H follow a format that homogenizes the rules of many jurisdictions. Every jurisdiction's rules have at least a few local idiosyncrasies that would seem quirky elsewhere. Although these briefs were written for a hypothetical appeal set in New York, the idiosyncrasies of New York format have been eliminated from what you will read.[2] That is because sample briefs ought to illustrate those brief-writing practices that are most common nationally. If you are asked to follow local format rules with which these briefs would be inconsistent — and your teacher will tell you if that is so — observe those rules despite what you see here.

Finally, citations in briefs submitted to New York courts must include official New York reporters, and both the ALWD Citation Manual and the Bluebook endorse that practice. See ALWD Citation Manual rules 12.4 and 12.6(e) and Appendix 2, and Bluebook B5.1.3 and rules 10.3.1 and 10.4. That might not be true in another state.

---

2. For example, in New York, the non-appealing party is called the "respondent," even though the appealing party is the "appellant." (See N.Y. Civ. Prac. L. § 5511.) The common practice elsewhere, however, is that the non-appealing party is a "respondent" only when the appealing party is a "petitioner," and an "appellant" is always opposed by an "appellee." The briefs in these appendices follow national (and not New York) practice in this and in several other respects.

COURT OF APPEALS OF THE STATE OF NEW YORK

THE PEOPLE OF THE STATE OF NEW YORK,

Appellee

-against-

MERRITT BRESNAHAN,

Defendant-Appellant

No. 09-541

BRIEF FOR DEFENDANT-APPELLANT

Clyde Farnsworth, Esq.
Attorney for Defendant-Appellant
32 Fontanka Street
Bedford Falls, NY 14218
(914) 555 - 1111

CONTENTS

TABLE OF AUTHORITIES

Cases

---

*Authorities chiefly relied on are marked with an asterisk.

Statutes

Miscellaneous

STATUTE INVOLVED

Section 240.35(4) of the New York Penal Law provides as follows:

A person is guilty of loitering when he . . .

4. Being masked or in any manner disguised by unusual or unnatural attire or facial alteration, loiters, remains or congregates in a public place with other persons so masked or disguised, or knowingly permits or aids persons so masked or disguised to congregate in a public place; except that such conduct is not unlawful when it occurs in connection with a masquerade party or like entertainment if, when such entertainment is held in a city which has promulgated regulations in connection with such affairs, permission is first obtained from the police or other appropriate authorities. . . .

Loitering is a violation.

PRELIMINARY STATEMENT

Merritt Bresnahan appeals from a conviction for loitering under § 240.35(4) of the Penal Law. Before trial, she moved to dismiss on the ground that § 240.35(4) violates her right to privacy under the United States Constitution. The Criminal Court of New York City and County reserved decision until the end of trial. After the close of the evidence, Ms. Bresnahan additionally moved for a trial order of dismissal on the ground that the People had not introduced legally sufficient evidence that she had been — as a conviction under § 240.35(4) would require — "masked or in any manner disguised by unusual or unnatural attire or facial alteration." The Criminal Court denied both motions, convicted Ms. Bresnahan of violating § 240.35(4), and sentenced her to a fine of $200. Ms. Bresnahan appealed the denial of the two motions. Appellate Term and the Appellate Division affirmed, and this appeal followed.

QUESTIONS PRESENTED

Merritt Bresnahan suffers from gender dysphoria syndrome, a chronic and potentially disabling disorder in which the patient experiences unremitting anguish from a belief that the reproductive organs from birth are not those of the patient's true gender. Psychotherapy has no effect on this disorder, and the only medically accepted treatment is sex reassignment surgery, preceded by a long period of hormonal injections. Responsible medical practice includes requiring such a patient to dress, during the hormonal, pre-operative phase of treatment, in the clothing of the gender that matches the patient's belief. Ms. Bresnahan was so dressed, as prescribed by her doctors, at the time she was arrested for loitering under Penal Law § 240.35(4). She was charged with no other offense. The questions presented on appeal are the following:

1. Whether the trial court should have granted Ms. Bresnahan's motion for a trial order of dismissal, where the sole evidence that she was "masked or . . . disguised" showed only that she was dressed exactly as her doctors had prescribed.

2. Whether the trial court should have granted Ms. Bresnahan's motion to dismiss the information on the ground that section 240.35(4) violates her right to privacy under the United States Constitution.

-1-

This is an alternative format for a Question Presented (see pp. 372-373).

STATEMENT OF THE CASE

The opening paragraph that summarizes the theory (see p. 363 and p. 367).

At trial, Ms. Bresnahan's doctors testified without contradiction that she suffers from gender dysphoria syndrome; that she has been compelled to enter a long-term treatment program at the Gender Identity Clinic at Murray Hill Hospital; and that her prescribed medical treatment requires her to wear female clothing. (R. at 81 - 96, 388 - 406, 409 - 44.) She was arrested for doing exactly that.

At Murray Hill Hospital, Ms. Bresnahan has been under the treatment of a physician and a psychotherapist. Both specialize in treating this disorder, and both testified at trial. They supplied all of the medical evidence before the trial court. The People called no expert witnesses.

Gender Dysphoria Syndrome

Gender dysphoria syndrome, also known as transsexualism, is a chronic disorder in which the patient suffers from "an unrelenting and uncontrollable feeling that she or he is not the gender that matched the reproductive organs assigned at birth." (R. at 389.) Transsexuals find their reproductive organs to be "repugnant" (R. at 391); often are unable to maintain normal social relationships (R. at 390); suffer from "drastic depressions precipitated by loathing their own bodies" (R. at 392); and, in some cases, become at risk to suicide or mutilation of their own bodies (*id.*). The cause of the disorder is unknown (R. at 398), and psychotherapy cannot provide effective treatment. (R. at 396.) A transsexual is not a homosexual or a transvestite. (R. at 400.) The syndrome becomes apparent in early childhood, often at about four years of age, and the child's gestures and play habits are uniformly of the opposite gender. (R. at 401 - 02.) As a result, the child "suffers merciless teasing and rejection, which continues in more sophisticated form throughout adulthood." (R. at 402.) Because a transsexual "despises his or her own body and is in turn found disgusting by others, such a person is among the most unhappy patients a psychotherapist can treat." (R. at 403.)

Treatment for Gender Dysphoria Syndrome

All this medical detail is intended to help the court visualize the case as a medical problem. The theory thus implied is that medicine is doing what we would want it to do, and that the criminal law should find other problems to worry about.

The trial court heard descriptions of the treatment programs at nine gender identity clinics in North America and Europe. Each such clinic prescribes treatment along the following pattern:

The patient is first given "an exhaustive psychological workup to confirm the diagnosis." (R. at 419.) Then, over a period of six months to two years, the patient is given hormonal injections which alter the body's appearance. (*Id.*) During this period, a clinic typically requires the patient to "live and dress as the gender the patient believes him- or herself to be," and, if the patient does not satisfy this requirement, treatment is stopped "because sex reassignment surgery would not then be indicated as a permanent change in the patient's life." (R. at 419 - 20.)

At an appropriate point, the patient is provided with sex reassignment surgery, in which the original sexual organs are replaced with those that are consistent with the patient's "psychological gender." (R. at 422.) After such surgery, a transsexual who was, for example, born with male reproductive organs would have "an internal sexual structure like that of a woman who has undergone a total hysterectomy and ovariectomy, which is not unusual in naturally born women after a certain age." (R. at 423 - 24.) Medically, such a transsexual would at this point be

-2-

considered a female (R. at 423), although there may be later procedures and continued hormonal treatment. (R. at 425 - 26.)

Sex reassignment surgery is only one of "several stages in a sex role assimilation, and it must be preceded by a complete psychological and social assimilation." (R. at 427.) The surgery is thus "not viewed medically as a sex change operation" because a substantial amount of gender has already been transformed before the surgery takes place. (R. at 426.)

After completion of treatment the typical patient "lives a far happier life" as a result of the elimination of the patient's inner conflict and of the elimination of conflict between the patient and others unable to tolerate the disorder. (R. at 406.)

It is "irresponsible" medical practice to provide physical treatment without at the same time requiring "cross-dressing" because of the need to ensure that the patient is able to live the life to which surgery will irreversibly commit her. (R. at 326, 399.) There are two additional benefits: to prepare the patient for surgery (R. at 341 - 43, 432 - 36) and to relieve some of the patient's suffering until hormonal therapy has made surgery possible (R. at 347 - 49, 401 - 04).

Both doctors testified that medicine considered Ms. Bresnahan, at the time of her arrest, to be dressed in clothing appropriate to her state of gender because gender is determined by hormonal composition and psychological condition, as well as by reproductive organs and chromosomes. (R. at 344, 405 - 06, 443.) They had informed Ms. Bresnahan of this fact and prescribed cross-dressing for her. (R. at 349, 405 - 06, 440 - 42.)

Ms. Bresnahan testified that she had been so informed and was cross-dressing "under doctor's orders." (R. at 176 - 80.) She had dressed exclusively in female clothing and lived as a woman since the age of 16 because of a belief, held since her earliest childhood memories, that she was born female. (R. at 173, 178 - 79.) She testified in detail about her childhood play toys considered feminine as well as several years of conflict with parents, other children, and school authorities "because of my femininity." (R. at 182 - 96.) Her office colleagues accepted her as a woman (R. at 199) and at the time she was arrested, she was on her way to lunch, accompanied by two other transsexuals who also work in the financial district of Manhattan. (R. at 203.)

The Arrest

At the time of the arrest, Ms. Bresnahan was employed as a financial analyst for a stock brokerage firm. (R. at 170.) She was arrested on the street one block from her office, was strip-searched at a police station, and was later compelled to explain to her supervisor the reason why she had not returned from lunch on the afternoon she was arrested. (R. at 202 - 07.) Her psychotherapist confirmed that Ms. Bresnahan had experienced a "profound" depression after the arrest, and that her treatment plan had to be extended approximately six months as a result. (R. at 407 - 09.) Ms. Bresnahan testified that for several days after the arrest she felt unable to return to her office (R. at 208) and that she no longer felt safe in public (R. at 210 - 11).

No Evidence of Crimes Aided by Gender Disguises

The People submitted no evidence of any pattern of robbery, theft, or other crimes committed by groups of people disguising their gender.

-3-

The reader should be able to see a picture of a useful member of society who has been victimized by the machinery of justice for no rational reason.

The absence of a particular kind of evidence can itself be a fact.

SUMMARY OF ARGUMENT

The People did not produce evidence legally sufficient to demonstrate a violation of Penal Law § 240.35(4), and the Criminal Court therefore erred in denying Ms. Bresnahan's motion for a trial order of dismissal. The Criminal Court heard extensive and uncontradicted expert testimony that Ms. Bresnahan suffers from a disease that requires her to dress as she did when arrested. An examination of the statute's history and that of similar statutes elsewhere shows that the Legislature's real purpose was to deter political violence by groups of masked or disguised individuals. Moreover, a cross-dressing transsexual is not disguised at all because the weight of scientific opinion, recognized in the case law, is that cross-dressing accurately informs the bystander of the patient's state of gender. No reported decision anywhere in the United States has held that a statute like § 240.35(4) can be enforced against a cross-dressing transsexual. Whenever courts in other jurisdictions have been asked to use similar statutes to punish persons with gender dysphoria syndrome, the courts have either declared the statutes unconstitutional or have held that they are not violated by transsexuals.

In addition, the Criminal Court should have granted Ms. Bresnahan's motion to dismiss the information on the ground that § 240.35(4) violates her constitutional right to privacy. The right to privacy can be invaded only where (1) the People can demonstrate a compelling state interest and (2) the invasion is no larger than necessary to accomplish that interest. Here, the only interests advanced by the People are a desire to prevent the use of disguises in crimes committed by gangs and an interest in preventing groups of disguised males from gaining access to women's washrooms. These interests are not compelling, and even if they were, they support no intrusion greater than a statute that limits its punishment to persons who appear together in public disguised *for a criminal purpose*. Section 240.35(4) instead punishes all persons who appear together in public with their identities obscured, no matter how innocent the purpose.

Even if a compelling state interest were not required, § 240.35(4) cannot be sustained under the lesser "rational basis" test. The People have not introduced any evidence that § 240.35(4) is connected to any verifiable danger to the public. Although § 240.35(4) is claimed to be justifiable as a crime control measure, even under the rational basis standard there is no basis for an assumption that people who cross-dress for medical reasons will also do so to commit crimes.

ARGUMENT

I.

The Criminal Court should have granted Ms. Bresnahan's Motion for a Trial Order of Dismissal because the People Failed to Introduce Legally Sufficient Evidence that she had been "Masked or . . . Disguised" in the sense required by Penal Law § 240.35(4).

The trial court heard uncontroverted evidence that Ms. Bresnahan suffers from gender dysphoria syndrome and that she was arrested while dressed exactly as her doctors had prescribed for her. (R. at 368.) Their treatment plan

The conclusion for Point I. Only one element of the offense is in dispute.

A summary of the motivating arguments, inserted before the justifying arguments begin (see p. 314).

-4-

486

followed accepted medical practice, and she was compelled to enter treatment because of a medical condition that caused her profound suffering. The People prosecuted her because they consider her conduct to be a threat to society. But the history of § 240.35(4) and of like statutes in other states demonstrates that the Legislature did not intend that people wearing clothing medically appropriate for them would be punished for being "masked or . . . disguised."

The rule.

A determination that the evidence was legally sufficient will be affirmed on appeal if, after resolving factual inferences in favor of the People, a rational trier of fact could have found all the elements of the offense proved beyond a reasonable doubt. *People v. Acosta,* 80 N.Y.2d 665, 672, 609 N.E.2d 518, 522, 593 N.Y.S.2d 978, 982 (1993). But even when viewing the record in the light most favorable to the People, the evidence here is legally insufficient because the Legislature did not intend section 240.35(4) to punish the conduct proved in the trial court.

The standard of review (§33.3).

A.   *Section 240.35(4) is derived from legislation designed to protect the public from violent criminals in disguise.*

Everything under sub-heading A is rule proof.

Section 240.35(4) is descended from a statute enacted in 1845 after an insurrection that had broken out among Hudson Valley tenant farmers who were unable to pay their rents and had begun to disguise themselves as Indians and women for the purpose of murdering officials serving them with writs. *People v. Simmons,* 79 Misc. 2d 249, 253, 357 N.Y.S.2d 362, 366 (Crim. Ct., Kings County 1974) (dicta). The original legislation was entitled "An Act to Prevent Persons Appearing Disguised *and Armed*" (emphasis added), and, among other things, it provided that

Compare the image of these murders with the image of Bresnahan's arrest, in business clothing, in the financial district of Manhattan. What effect do you think this will have on the judicial reader (§24.7)?

> Every person who, having his face painted, discolored or concealed or being otherwise disguised in a manner calculated to prevent him from being identified, shall appear in any road or public highway, or in any field, lot, wood or enclosure, may be pursued and arrested. . . .

1845 N.Y. Laws, ch. 3 § 1.

In 1881, this provision was codified in the former Code of Criminal Procedure, which defined a vagrant as "[a] person who, having his face painted, discolored, covered or concealed, or being otherwise disguised, in a manner calculated to prevent his being identified, appears in a road or public highway, or in a field, lot, wood, or enclosure." N.Y. Code Crim. Proc. § 887(7) (McKinney 1958). A parallel provision, more closely resembling the section at issue in this appeal, appeared later in the former Penal Law at §§ 710-711 (McKinney 1944). Section 240.35(4) appeared in its present form when the current Penal Law was enacted. 1965 N.Y. Laws, ch. 1030. Section 887(7) of the prior Code of Criminal Procedure was deleted shortly thereafter. 1967 N.Y. Laws, ch. 681.

The history of the statute is one of the tools for determining the intent of the legislature (§16.1).

Only one reported opinion interprets § 240.35(4), and only three reported cases interpret any of the predecessor statutes. In the earliest, a trial court concluded that § 887(7) of the former Code of Criminal Procedure was not violated by a man who stood in front of a theater, advertising the entertainment within while wearing a dress, wig, slippers, and makeup. *People v.*

Defining a gap in local law that will be filled through a comparison with parallel statutes in other jurisdictions (§17.1). On the process of gap-filling, see §14.5.

Luechini, 75 Misc. 614, 136 N.Y.S. 319 (Erie County Ct. 1912). The court noted that, if this behavior were considered criminal,

> there is no reason why the disguised circus "barker," the midway "ballyhoo," or even the masquerader at the ball could not be convicted of vagrancy under this statute, . . . and such a conviction, although perhaps it might be deemed righteous by many, would be going far beyond anything conceived by the legislature.

Distinguishing adverse authority (§25.5). If this writer had said nothing about *Gillespi* and *Archibald,* the court could have decided that it was bound by these two cases. (Compare the way the prosecution argues them in App. H. See pp. 506-508.)

Id. at 616, 136 N.Y.S. at 320-21.

Both of the other two cases interpreting predecessor statutes are distinguishable from this appeal. In *People v. Gillespi,* 15 N.Y.2d 529, 202 N.E.2d 565, 254 N.Y.S.2d 121, *amended,* 15 N.Y.2d 675, 204 N.E.2d 211, 255 N.Y.S.2d 884 (1964), and *People v. Archibald,* 27 N.Y.2d 504, 260 N.E.2d 871, 312 N.Y.S.2d 678 (1970), this Court, without opinion, affirmed convictions, under section 887(7) of the former Code of Criminal Procedure, of defendants who appeared in public in female clothing where there was no evidence that they were anything other than unequivocally male. There was certainly no evidence in either case that the defendant was, at the time of the offense, wearing clothing considered by the weight of scientific opinion to be appropriate to that defendant's gender. Instead, the evidence in both cases established that the defendants had concealed their true identities by disguising their true genders. In contrast, Ms. Bresnahan provided the trial court with abundant and uncontroverted evidence that she has for some years worn female clothing at all times, that the weight of scientific opinion considers female clothing to be appropriate to the medically determined state of her gender at the time of her arrest, that she had been informed of that fact by both a physician and a psychotherapist, and that both doctors had prescribed the wearing of female clothing at all times as part of a pre-operative treatment plan (R. at 318-52, 395-406, 418-14).

The only reported case interpreting § 240.35(4) was not a criminal prosecution. A Ku Klux Klan group sued after a police department refused to grant a parade permit on the ground that the wearing of Klan hoods would violate the statute. *Church of the American Knights of the Ku Klux Klan v. Kerik,* 356 F.3d 197 (2d Cir. 2004). The court analyzed the statute primarily to determine that the statutory history (described above) showed a legislative intent to prevent public assemblies of disguised people in situations that posed the risk of violence. *Id.* at 203-06.

By this point, the reader should be satisfied that there is a gap in local law. The foundation is now complete (§14.5.1), and the writer can begin to compare section 240.35(4) with parallel statutes elsewhere (§14.5.2).

A few other states have at times maintained statutes similar to § 240.35(4). Although no reported decision determines whether any of these statutes can be violated by a transsexual's wearing of medically prescribed clothing, the context in which all of them were enacted plainly shows that they were meant to punish people who used disguises to facilitate political violence. In that way, they are remarkably similar to the antecedents of Penal Law § 240.35(4).

For example, the former Texas Penal Code provided that "[i]f any person shall go into or near any public place masked or disguised in such manner as to hide his identity or render same difficult to determine, he or she shall be guilty of a misdemeanor, . . . provided this article shall not apply to private or public functions, festivals or events not fostered or presented *by any secret society or organization.*" Tex. Penal Code § 454a, repealed by 1973 Tex. Gen. Laws, ch. 399 (emphasis added). This section was enacted in 1925, at a peak

-6-

of Ku Klux Klan violence, together with other sections entitled "Masked individuals parading on public highway" (§ 454f). "Masked person entering church" (§ 454d), "Masked person entering house" (§ 454c), and "Masked persons assaulting . . ." (§ 454e). 1925 Tex. Gen. Laws, ch. 63.

The Georgia Anti-Mask Act provides that "[a] person is guilty of a misdemeanor when he wears a mask, hood, or device by which any portion of the face is so hidden, concealed, or covered as to conceal the identity of the wearer" when that person is in a public place or on another's property without written permission. Ga. Code Ann. § 16-11-38(a) (1999). The statute provides exemptions for circumstances like Halloween, theater performances, and Mardi Gras. *Id.* § 16-11-38(b). Noting that the statute was aimed at "mask-wearing Klansmen and other 'hate' organizations," the Georgia courts have held that the statute is violated only where the mask wearer intends to conceal her or his identity and "knows or reasonably should know that the conduct provokes a reasonable apprehension of intimidation, threats or violence." *State v. Miller,* 398 S.E.2d 547, 550, 552 (Ga. 1990).

A similar statute in Oklahoma criminalizes the act of wearing "a mask, hood or covering, which conceals the identity of the wearer." Okla. Stat. Ann. tit. 21, § 1301 (1983). This section was enacted just before — and apparently for the same reason as — former § 454a of the Texas Penal Code. 1923-24 Okla. Sess. Laws, ch. 2. When enacting § 1301, the Oklahoma legislature also made it criminal for a masked or disguised person to demand entry to a house, Okla. Stat. Ann. tit. 21, § 1302 (1983 Suppl. 2000), and made it an aggravated offense to commit assault while masked or disguised, § 1303 (Suppl. 2000).

> These statutory comparisons strongly suggest that the policy behind section 240.35(4) would not be furthered by convicting Bresnahan.

A California statute punishes persons who "wear any mask, false whiskers, or any personal disguise (whether complete or partial) for the purpose of . . . [e]vading or escaping discovery, recognition, or identification in the commission of any public offense [or c]oncealment, flight, or escape, when charged with, arrested for, or convicted of, any public offense. . . ." Cal. Penal Code § 185 (West 1999). This statute was enacted during another period of widespread Ku Klux Klan violence. 1873-74 Cal. Stat., ch. 614.

A few municipalities have enacted ordinances prohibiting persons from appearing in public in clothing customarily worn by the other gender. Only four reported cases have construed ordinances of this type on facts comparable to this appeal. In one of them, the Illinois Supreme Court ruled — for reasons set out in Point II of this brief — that an ordinance penalizing "[a]ny person who shall appear in a public place . . . in a dress not belonging to his or her sex, with intent to conceal his or her sex" could not constitutionally be enforced against transsexuals. *City of Chicago v. Wilson,* 389 N.E.2d 522, 523 (Ill. 1978) (quoting Chi. Mun. Code § 192-8). Enforcement of a similar Houston ordinance was enjoined on the same grounds. *Doe v. McConn,* 489 F. Supp. 76 (S.D. Tex. 1980). A comparable Cincinnati ordinance was declared unconstitutional for violating First Amendment rights. *City of Cincinnati v. Adams,* 330 N.E.2d 463 (Ohio Mun. Ct. 1974). In the remaining decision, the trial court declined to hold the ordinance unconstitutional but instead decided that a transsexual lacks the capacity to develop the *mens rea* required for a violation. *City of Columbus v. Zanders,* 266 N.E.2d 602 (Ohio Mun. Ct. 1970).

The material under sub-heading B continues rule proof through even more explicit policy arguments. Much of the policy relates to Bresnahan's own medical condition. The reader is thus sensitized to the rule application that begins under sub-heading C (which is one of the reasons why this material was organized in this way).

B.   A necessary and lawful medical treatment would become impossible in this State if a transsexual, dressing as medically prescribed, can be held to have violated § 240.35(4).

This state has recognized and protected sex reassignment surgery. A health insurer in this state cannot escape liability for the costs of sex reassignment surgery on the ground that it is merely "cosmetic" and not a needed medical procedure. *Davidson v. Aetna Life & Casualty Ins. Co.,* 101 Misc. 2d 1, 420 N.Y.S.2d 450 (Sup. Ct., N.Y. County 1979). Discrimination against transsexuals in housing is illegal. N.Y. Exec. Law § 296(5)(b)(2); *Hispanic AIDS Forum v. Estate of Joseph Bruno,* 6 Misc. 3d 960; 839 N.Y.S.2d 691 (Sup. Ct., N.Y. County 2007). A professional sports organization that discriminates against a transsexual athlete can be held liable under the New York Human Rights Law. N.Y. Exec. Law §§ 290-301 (McKinney 1993); *Richards v. United States Tennis Ass'n,* 93 Misc. 2d 713, 400 N.Y.S.2d 267 (Sup. Ct., N.Y. County 1977). Under § 8-107(1) of the New York City Administrative Code, a transsexual is protected against employment discrimination. *Maffei v. Kolaeton Indus., Inc.,* 164 Misc. 2d 547, 626 N.Y.S.2d 391 (Sup. Ct., N.Y. County 1995).

Gender dysphoria syndrome is also known as gender identity disorder and is recognized under that name in the Diagnostic and Statistical Manual used throughout psychotherapy. American Psychiatric Association, *Diagnostic and Statistical Manual of Mental Disorders* 532-533 (4th ed 1994). The Criminal Court heard extensive and uncontradicted expert testimony to the effect that sex reassignment surgery is the only successful treatment for gender dysphoria syndrome, but that such surgery must be preceded by an extended period in which the patient dresses according to her psychological sex (R. at 318-52, 395-406, 418-44). The same view is also reflected in the case law. For example, see *City of Chicago v. Wilson,* 389 N.E.2d 522, 524-25 (Ill. 1978); *City of Columbus v. Zanders,* 266 N.E.2d 602, 604-06 (Ohio Mun. Ct. 1970). In *Davidson v. Aetna Life & Casualty,* the court noted that

> The overall process of sex-reassignment surgery is both long and arduous. . . . Among the requirements [for treatment at the Johns Hopkins Hospital Gender Identity] Clinic is that the patient has lived in the female role for a minimum of one year, proving to her own satisfaction and to others her ability to be rehabilitated gainfully in society as a female and to function satisfactorily emotionally, vocationally and socially as a female. . . . The Clinic further states that the operation cannot be looked upon as a sex change operation; rather it is simply the final anatomical step in a gender role assimilation of which the psychological and social steps have already been carried out.

101 Misc. 2d at 4, 420 N.Y.S.2d at 452. As the Criminal Court was informed through expert medical testimony, the practice of pre-operative "cross-dressing" is necessary for three reasons. The first is to test the patient's determination and ability to live fully as her psychological gender before surgery irreversibly commits her to it. (R. at 326, 399.) The second is to prepare her for the drastic and final step of surgery (R. at 341-43, 423-26). And the third is simply to relieve some of the patient's suffering until hormone therapy has made surgery possible. (R. at 347-49, 401-04.)

-8-

C. *Because Ms. Bresnahan wore clothing that was medically*
    appropriate for her and did so under medical advice,
    she was not "masked or . . . disguised."

A cross-dressing transsexual is not disguised. This is not a defendant who lives daily life as a man but had at the time of arrest concealed his identity by dressing as a woman. Ms. Bresnahan's identity is that of a woman. Her friends, neighbors, and colleagues know her as a woman. Medicine considers her primarily to be a woman. And at the time of arrest she was dressed as a woman.

As explained above, the weight of scientific opinion is that cross-dressing accurately informs the bystander of a transsexual's gender. That is recognized in the case law, and there was abundant evidence of it at trial. The People introduced no expert evidence to the contrary. The trial court should not have been permitted to draw a factual inference that Ms. Bresnahan was or is male. And without such an inference the evidence was legally insufficient to support the verdict, even under the deferential standard of review used on appeal.

No reported decision anywhere in the United States has held that a statute like § 240.35(4) can be enforced against a cross-dressing transexual. And the law has established a policy — through the amendment of birth certificates and through interpretation of health insurance contracts — of assisting persons afflicted with gender dysphoria syndrome to obtain treatment through sex reassignment surgery. That policy would be subverted if section 240.35(4) were interpreted to prohibit the necessary and inoffensive pre-operative procedure of cross-dressing.

This Court has more than once noted that it "will not blindly apply the words of a statute to arrive at an unreasonable or absurd result. If the statute is so broadly drawn as to include the case before the court, yet reason and statutory purpose show it was obviously not intended to include that case, the court is justified in making an exception through implication." *Williams v. Williams,* 23 N.Y.2d 592, 599, 246 N.E.2d 333, 337, 298 N.Y.S.2d 473, 479 (1969) (citations omitted). "It is, moreover, always presumed that no unjust or unreasonable result was intended and the statute must be construed consonant with that presumption." *Zappone v. Home Ins. Co.,* 55 N.Y.2d 131, 137, 432 N.E.2d 783, 786, 447 N.Y.S.2d 911, 914 (1982).

Thus, even viewing the evidence in the light most favorable to the prosecution, the People failed to make out a prima facie case that Ms. Bresnahan was "masked or in any manner disguised," and the Criminal Court therefore committed reversible error in denying her motion for a trial order of dismissal.

II.
The Criminal Court should have granted Ms. Bresnahan's motion to dismiss the information because penal law § 240.35(4) violates her right to privacy under the United States Constitution.

This court reviews determinations on the constitutionality of statutes de novo, with no deference to the decisions appealed from. *People v. Uplinger,* 58 N.Y.2d 936, 447 N.E.2d 62, 460 N.Y.S.2d 514 (1983).

Rule application begins.

The writer argues that the prosecution's case flunks the standard of review. Rule application is the place to do this.

Some canons of construction.

Summing up to complete Point I.

The conclusion for Point II.

The standard of review (§32.3).

The organization of
this point is more
complicated than
that of Point I
because the law
involved is more
complex. The writer
must prove two dif-
ferent rules. The
first is stated in sub-
heading A and
proved through the
material under
that sub-heading.
The other is stated
in sub-heading B
and proved there.

The rule of
sub-heading A is
proved through a
synthesis of *Onofre,
Stanley, Eisenstadt,
Uplinger,* and other
cases (§15.5).

A.   *The constitutional right to privacy includes the right to
choose one's own clothing.*

The right to privacy "is a right of independence in making certain kinds of
important decisions . . . undeterred by governmental restraint." *People v.
Onofre,* 51 N.Y.2d 476, 485, 415 N.E.2d 936, 939, 434 N.Y.S.2d 947, 949 (1980).

Pointing to *Stanley v. Georgia,* 394 U.S. 557 (1969), and *Eisenstadt v. Baird,*
405 U.S. 438 (1972), this Court concluded that the United States Supreme Court
has not limited the right to privacy to situations of "marital intimacy" or
"procreative choice." *Onofre,* 51 N.Y.2d at 487, 415 N.E.2d at 939-40, 434
N.Y.S.2d at 950. In *Stanley,* the Supreme Court held that the right to privacy is
violated by a statute that criminalizes the possession of obscene materials in
one's own home. In both *Stanley,* 394 U.S. at 564, and *Eisenstadt,* 405 U.S. at
453-54 n.10, the Court quoted with approval Justice Brandeis's dissent in
Olmstead v. United States, 277 U.S. 438 (1928), where he noted that "[t]he
makers of our Constitution . . . conferred, as against the Government, the right
to be let alone — the most comprehensive of rights and the right most valued by
civilized man" (emphasis added).

This Court held in *Uplinger* that the right to privacy was violated by
§ 240.35(3) of the Penal Law, another subdivision of the same loitering statute
at issue in the present appeal. Section 240.35(3) had penalized loitering "in a
public place for the purpose of engaging, or soliciting another person to engage,
in deviate sexual intercourse or other sexual behavior of a deviate nature,"
and this Court ruled that the state cannot constitutionally punish loitering
which neither is done for a criminal purpose nor is "offensive or annoying
to others." *Id.,* 58 N.Y.2d at 938, 447 N.E.2d at 63, 460 N.Y.S.2 at 515.

The United States Supreme Court has assumed that the constitutional right to
privacy includes "matters of personal appearance," *Kelley v. Johnson,* 425 U.S.
238, 244 (1976). The issue in *Kelley* was whether a police department could
establish hair-grooming regulations for its officers. In holding that the department had demonstrated a sufficiently strong governmental interest to overcome
the officers' assumed privacy rights, the Court noted that it perceived a
"highly significant" distinction between the privacy rights of police officers
to an appearance of their own choosing, on one hand, and, on the other, privacy
rights of persons not employed by a uniformed police department. *Id.* at 245.
Relying on *Kelley,* the Illinois Supreme Court ruled that an ordinance punishing
any person appearing in public "in a dress not belonging to his or her sex, with
intent to conceal his or her sex" cannot constitutionally be enforced against
transsexuals. *City of Chicago v. Wilson,* 389 N.E.2d 522, 523 (Ill. 1978)
(quoting Chi. Mun. Code § 192-8). The defendants in *Wilson* were — like Ms.
Bresnahan — transsexuals, and (as explained below) the issues presented to the
Illinois Supreme Court were the same right-to-privacy issues raised in this
appeal.

B.   *The right to privacy is a fundamental right and can be invaded only
where the People can demonstrate a compelling state
interest and only where the invasion is no larger than necessary
to accomplish that interest.*

Another proof
through a
synthesis — this
time of *Carey, Roe,*
and *Griswold.*

It is settled law that the right to privacy is a fundamental right. *Carey v.
Population Services Int'l,* 431 U.S. 678, 684-86 (1977); *Roe v. Wade,* 410 U.S.

-10-

113, 147-64 (1973); *Griswold v. Connecticut,* 381 U.S. 479, 485 (1965). The Supreme Court has repeatedly held that a state can invade the right to privacy, or any other fundamental right, only where it can demonstrate a compelling state interest requiring such an invasion. *Carey,* 431 U.S. at 685 - 86; *Roe,* 410 U.S. at 147-65; *Griswold,* 381 U.S. at 485. Even where a state can show a compelling interest that could justify some limitation on the right to privacy or another fundamental right, any such limitation must "be narrowly drawn to express only those interests." *Carey,* 431 U.S. at 686.

In *Carey,* for example, the Supreme Court struck down § 6811(8) of the New York Education Law, which made it criminal, among other things, to advertise the sale of contraceptives and to distribute even nonprescription contraceptives without first obtaining a pharmacist's license. The state argued that the prohibition on advertising was justified because contraceptive advertisements would offend and embarrass large portions of the public and would encourage sexual activity among young people, but the Court held instead that neither of these considerations could be considered compelling in the face of First Amendment rights and the right to privacy. *Id.* at 700-02. The state argued further that the prohibition on distribution of contraceptives by nonpharmacists was justified by the state's interests in promoting quality control, protecting the health of the user, and preventing minors from selling contraceptives, but the Court held these concerns were neither compelling nor (excepting the last) even likely to be achieved by the state's invasion of contraceptive users' right to privacy. *Id.* at 686-91.

All of this has been left in place by *Planned Parenthood v. Casey,* 505 U.S. 833 (1992). That decision "reaffirmed" *Roe. Planned Parenthood* at 846, 855-69. And it cited with approval *Carey, Eisenstadt,* and *Griswold. Planned Parenthood* at 848-58. Although the *Planned Parenthood* court adopted an undue burden test, rather than the compelling state interest test, in abandoning the trimester framework set out in *Roe,* it did so only in an attempt to balance what *Roe* itself called "the State's important and legitimate interest in protecting the potentiality of human life." *Planned Parenthood* at 871 (quoting *Roe*). There is no equivalent competing interest in a case, like the present one, where a person is prosecuted merely for wearing clothing prescribed by doctors. The *Planned Parenthood* opinion spoke at length of the Court's awareness that its own "legitimacy" could be damaged if "frequent overruling" were to "overtax the country's belief in the Court's good faith." *Id.* at 864-65. For those reasons, the compelling state interest test still governs privacy law outside the context of abortion, and it is likely to continue doing so.

> A counter-argument (§24.5).

C.   *Section 240.35(4) is not supported by a compelling state interest.*

Here, the only compelling interests claimed by the People are, first, a desire to prevent the use of gender and other disguises in crimes committed by groups of people and, second, an interest in preventing groups of disguised males from gaining access to women's washrooms and other areas where women may be vulnerable. There is no evidence anywhere in the record to suggest that in modern times police anywhere in New York State have encountered difficulties apprehending groups of criminals who have disguised themselves in clothing of the opposite gender. Nor is there any evidence in the record of even a single crime in this state committed by a group of men who got into a women's washroom or the like disguised as women.

> Rule application begins here and continues under sub-heading D. (Remember that the rules in Point II measure whether a statute is constitutional. They are applied to the statute as though the statute were a fact.)

These same interests were cited by the city of Chicago in an unsuccessful attempt to justify an ordinance similar to § 240.35(4), but the Illinois Supreme Court held them to be so insubstantial that they could not even meet the lesser standard of providing a rational basis for the city's invasion of constitutional privacy rights. *City of Chicago v. Wilson,* 389 N.E.2d at 523-25. In *Wilson,* transsexuals had been arrested, even though their pre-operative treatment called for them to cross-dress. The court found the record there as barren as the record here of evidence that could substantiate even a rational basis, much less a compelling state interest, and — in the only reported decision on the privacy issue posed by the present appeal — the Illinois Supreme Court held that, "as applied to the defendants here," the Chicago ordinance created an "unconstitutional infringement of their liberty interest," *id.* at 525.

An argument in the alternative: just in case the court disagrees with subheading C, the writer argues that Bresnahan should win anyway on another ground (§25.5).

D.   *Even if one of the interests advanced by the People were deemed compelling, § 240.35(4) nevertheless invades privacy rights more than would be necessary to satisfy such an interest.*

Even if a government's interest is compelling, it must choose the least restrictive means to accomplish it. In deciding right-to-privacy cases, the courts have often looked for guidance to decisions applying First Amendment and other fundamental rights. For instance, in *Griswold,* 381 U.S. at 485, where it determined that Connecticut's complete prohibition on the use of contraceptives violated the right to privacy because it could not be supported by a compelling state interest, the Supreme Court quoted with approval *NAACP v. Alabama,* 377 U.S. 288, 307 (1964), a First Amendment freedom of association case, for the principle that a "governmental purpose to control or prevent activities constitutionally subject to state regulation may not be achieved by means which sweep unnecessarily broadly and thereby invade the area of protected freedoms." In *United Mine Workers v. Illinois State Bar Ass'n,* 389 U.S. 217, 222 (1967), another freedom of association case, the Court noted that it has "repeatedly held that laws which actually affect the exercise of these vital rights cannot be sustained merely because they were enacted for the purpose of dealing with some evil within the State's legislative competence, or even because the laws do in fact provide a *helpful* means of dealing with such an evil" (emphasis added).

Section 240.35(4) is not the least restrictive alternative to achieve either of the purposes advanced by the People, and the statute is therefore defectively overbroad. Even if this Court were to conclude that the state has a compelling interest in preventing the use of gender disguises in crimes committed by groups of people, that conclusion could sustain only a statute that limits its punishment to persons who appear together in public disguised *for a criminal purpose,* and § 240.35(4) is not so limited. Instead, it punishes *all* persons who appear in public with their identities obscured, no matter how innocent the purpose. Here, there was ample and uncontradicted evidence that Ms. Bresnahan dressed as she did as a result of the requirements of a widely recognized medical treatment program. As explained in Point I of this brief, the law in New York and elsewhere has made adjustments to further the objectives of this kind of treatment by amending birth certificates and requiring reimbursement under properly drawn health insurance contracts where persons suffering from gender dysphoria syndrome are forced to go through the same type of medical treatment that led to Ms. Bresnahan's arrest. No valid governmental purpose is advanced by restricting a transsexual's choice of attire,

-12-

494

and the statute could have been drafted to avoid such an imposition on her liberty.

    E.   Even if a compeling state interest were not required,
§ 240.35(4) cannot survive scrutiny under the lesser
"rational basis" test.

As explained above, the Illinois Supreme Court has ruled that an ordinance similar to the statute here at issue cannot constitutionally be enforced against transsexuals. In *City of Chicago v. Wilson,* 389 N.E.2d 522 (Ill. 1978), the city claimed both of the purposes asserted by the People in the present appeal, together with two others: "to protect citizens from being misled or defrauded" and "to prevent inherently anti-social conduct which is contrary to the accepted norms." *Id.* at 524. The Illinois court determined that none of these rationales could meet even the lesser rational basis test applicable where a constitutionally protected right is not deemed fundamental or, in equal protection cases, where discrimination is not based on a suspect classification.

A governmental purpose satisfies the rational basis or rational connection test where "there is an evil at hand for correction, and . . . it might be thought that the particular legislative measure was a rational way to correct it." *Williamson v. Lee Optical Co.,* 348 U.S. 483, 488 (1955). But here the People have not introduced any evidence that § 240.35(4) is connected to any verifiable danger to the public. Although § 240.35(4) is claimed to be justifiable as a crime control measure, the Illinois Supreme Court concluded that even under the rational basis standard "we cannot assume that individuals who cross-dress for purposes of therapy are prone to commit crimes." *City of Chicago v. Wilson,* 389 N.E.2d at 525.

Nor can § 240.35(4) be justified by a desire to promote a particular standard of sexual morality. Not only was such a purpose unpersuasive in *City of Chicago v. Wilson,* but it would be inconsistent with the law's policy, described in Point I of this brief, of encouraging treatment of gender dysphoria syndrome through sex reassignment therapy. And this Court expressly rejected just such a purpose in *People v. Onofre,* 51 N.Y.2d at 489, 415 N.E.2d at 942, 434 N.Y.S.2d at 952.

Finally, in *Kelley v. Johnson,* 425 U.S. 238, 245 (1976), the Supreme Court permitted a police department to regulate the appearance of its officers but noted that there is a "highly significant" difference between the broad rights of "the citizenry in general" and the narrower rights of public employees. Setting aside situations involving public employees, prison inmates, and nude or obscene behavior, no case since *Kelley* has held that government can regulate a private person's choice of clothing.

    F.   Section 240.35(4) violates Ms. Bresnahan's constitutional
right to privacy.

For the reasons set out above, the purposes advanced by the People do not arise to a compelling state interest. Even if they did, under the cases described above, section 240.35(4) nevertheless cannot be enforced against transsexuals because it does not accomplish those purposes in the least restrictive manner. The required "[p]recision of regulation," *NAACP v. Button,* 371 U.S. 415, 438 (1963), could be achieved only by a statute that would

Sidenotes:

Another argument in the alternative: just in case the court rejects the rule in sub-heading B, the writer argues that Bresnahan should win under the alternative and less favorable test.

A counter-argument.

Another counter-argument.

Because Point II is complex, this summing up is complicated enough to deserve its own sub-heading.

-13-

punish appearing in public in prohibited attire for a criminal purpose. Moreover, enforcement of section 240.35(4) against transsexuals cannot survive scrutiny even under the lesser rational basis test.

For three reasons, the right-to-privacy question in this appeal is not governed by this Court's decisions in *People v. Gillespi,* 15 N.Y.2d 529, 202 N.E.2d 565, 254 N.Y.S.2d 121, *amended,* 15 N.Y.2d 675, 204 N.E.2d 211, 255 N.Y.S.2d 884 (1964), and *People v. Archibald,* 27 N.Y.2d 504, 260 N.E.2d 871, 312 N.Y.S.2d 678 (1970), where constitutional challenges to a predecessor statute of section 240.35(4) were turned aside. First, in neither case did a defendant challenge the statute for violating the constitutional right to privacy. In *Gillespi,* this court was asked to decide only whether the statute was unconstitutionally vague and an unreasonable and arbitrary exercise of police power. In *Archibald,* the appeal was based only on due process and First Amendment grounds. Second, even if those defendants had raised some type of privacy issue, they could not have raised the question presently before the court. In neither case was there any evidence that a defendant suffered from gender dysphoria syndrome or any other medical condition that would have required attire that might be deemed to violate the statute. Third, even if *Archibald* and *Gillespi* had determined precisely the privacy issues presently before the court, those cases would have been impliedly overruled by this Court's later decisions in *People v. Onofre,* setting out this Court's perception of the right to privacy, and *People v. Uplinger,* striking down, on the basis of that perception, another subdivision of the same loitering statute at issue in this appeal.

The Second Circuit's decision in *Church of the American Knights of the Ku Klux Klan v. Kerik,* 356 F.3d 197 (2d Cir. 2004), also is not relevant to the right-to-privacy issue. The Second Circuit did not decide whether § 240.35(4) violates the right to privacy. Instead, it determined only that the statute does not violate the First Amendment, a matter that has not been raised in this appeal.

Thus, the Criminal Court should have granted Ms. Bresnahan's motion to dismiss the information on the ground that § 240.35(4) violates her constitutional right to privacy.

CONCLUSION

For all the foregoing reasons, Ms. Bresnahan's conviction should be reversed, and the information dismissed.

Clyde Farnsworth, Esq.
Attorney for Defendant-Appellant
32 Fontanka Street
Bedford Falls, NY 14218
(914) 555-1111

A counter-argument. These cases were discussed in Point I to show that they do not preclude an interpretation of the statute that favors Bresnahan. Here, they are discussed again to show that they do not preclude a favorable constitutional ruling. Notice how Archibald *and* Gillespi *are distinguished.*

Appendix H
Sample Appellee's Brief

This brief responds to the appellant's brief that appears in Appendix G. See the introductory note on pages 475-476.

COURT OF APPEALS OF THE STATE OF NEW YORK

THE PEOPLE OF THE STATE OF NEW YORK,

Appellee

-against-

MERRITT BRESNAHAN,

Defendant-Appellant

No. 09-541

BRIEF FOR APPELLEE

Hon. Martha Bosley
District Attorney
New York County

BY: Allan Kuusinen, Esq.
Asst. District Attorney
1 Hogan Place
New York, NY 10013
(212) 555-1111

CONTENTS

TABLE OF AUTHORITIES

Cases

*Authorities chiefly relied on are marked with an asterisk.

-ii-

Statutes

STATUTE INVOLVED

Section 240.35(4) of the New York Penal Law provides as follows:

A person is guilty of loitering when he . . .

    4. Being masked or in any manner disguised by unusual or unnatural attire or facial alteration, loiters, remains or congregates in a public place with other persons so masked or disguised, or knowingly permits or aids persons so masked or disguised to congregate in a public place; except that such conduct is not unlawful when it occurs in connection with a masquerade party or like entertainment if, when such entertainment is held in a city which has promulgated regulations in connection with such affairs, permission is first obtained from the police or other appropriate authorities. . . .

    Loitering is a violation.

PRELIMINARY STATEMENT

The defendant was convicted in New York City Criminal Court, New York County, of loitering in violation of Penal Law § 240.35(4). Before trial, the defendant moved, pursuant to Criminal Procedure Law §§ 170.30(1)(a) and 170.35(1)(c), for an order dismissing the information on the ground that Penal Law § 240.35(4) violates his right to privacy under the United States Constitution, and the Criminal Court reserved decision on this motion until the end of trial. After the close of evidence at trial, the defendant moved for a trial order of dismissal, pursuant to Criminal Procedure Law §§ 290.10 and 320.20, alleging an absence of legally sufficient evidence that he had been "masked or in any manner disguised by unusual or unnatural attire" in the sense prohibited by § 240.35(4). Ruling from the bench, the Criminal Court denied both motions, convicted the defendant, and sentenced him to a fine of $200. Appellate Term and the Appellate Division both affirmed without opinion, and this appeal followed.

QUESTIONS PRESENTED

Is a person "masked or in any manner disguised by unusual or unnatural attire," within the meaning of Penal Law § 240.35(4), when his chromosomes and sexual organs are all male but he assumes a female voice and gestures and wears a skirt, blouse, high-heeled shoes, and stockings — all for the admitted purpose of causing others to believe he is a woman?

Does the constitutional right to privacy permit a state to penalize congregating in public by three or more men dressing as and imitating women where men so disguised could gain entrance to women's washrooms and similar places, and where a victim of a crime committed by such men could mistakenly identify them to the police as women?

STATEMENT OF THE CASE

The Defendant's Disguise

When arrested the defendant was wearing a blouse, a skirt, high-heeled shoes, stockings, and women's undergarments. (R. at 109, 187.) He was

These two paragraphs summarize the

-1-

prosecution's
theory (see p. 363).
The record cites are
included here
(despite what is
said in the first
paragraph of §29.4)
because the
prosecution states
these facts
completely here
and will not
describe them
more fully later in
the Statement of
the Case.

standing on a street corner in the company of two other men similarly dressed.
(R. at 108 - 10, 114, 193 - 94.) When arrested and at trial, the defendant
had a penis, testicles, and a scrotum. (R. at 110, 189, 373, 449.) That was
also true of his two companions, who pleaded guilty at arraignment and are
not parties to this appeal. (R. at 3 - 5, 114 - 15.)

The arresting officer at first believed the defendant and his companions to
be women (R. at 101), and the defendant admitted that his purpose in dressing
as he did was to create exactly this impression (R. at 213). The arresting
officer testified that the defendant and his companions convincingly affected
feminine voices, inflections, gestures, and walks (R. at 98 - 101) and "would
have succeeded in fooling me" if the officer had not overhead one of them
make a remark the substance of which was not testified to because of a
defense objection (R. at 98, 103). When arrested, the defendant was not
travelling to or from a masquerade party. (R. at 209.)

The Medical Evidence

From out of the
mass of medical
details, the
prosecution pulls
facts that create a
different picture
from the one
painted in the
defendant's brief.

Notice how this
sentence juxtaposes
two related facts to
neutralize the one
that would
otherwise harm the
prosecution
(see p. 365).

The defendant's own witnesses admitted that he had never had a
vagina, uterus, or ovaries. (R. at 373, 449.) They also admitted that regardless
of any medical treatment that may be performed on him in the future, he
would never have ovaries or a uterus, but that he would have male
chromosomes for the rest of his life. (R. at 374 - 75, 448.)

The defendant claimed that he planned to undergo surgery to remove his
penis, testicles, and scrotum and replace them with an artificially constructed
vagina (R. at 197), but he and his doctors all admitted that such an operation
had not yet occurred. (R. at 189, 197, 373, 449.) Although both doctors
testified that they had advised the defendant to wear female clothing before
surgery (R. at 349, 405 - 06, 440 - 42), they and the defendant all admitted that
the three of them had known all along that such conduct could lead to legal
difficulties. (R. 179 - 80, 406, 442.) The doctors also admitted that their
pre-operative treatment plan would not be "significantly" disturbed if a
patient like the defendant were to refrain, before surgery, from appearing in
public with two or more other men in female dress. (R. at 408, 449.)

SUMMARY OF ARGUMENT

The Criminal Court properly denied the defendant's motion for a trial
order of dismissal. The only element in dispute involved the question of whether
the defendant was "in any manner disguised by unusual or unnatural attire."
Here, the defendant and his co-defendants dressed as women, and the arresting
officer testified that he at first believed them to be women. The defendant's own
experts testified that his reproductive organs were male. Nothing in the statute
requires the People to prove that a defendant had disguised himself in order
to commit some unlawful or antisocial act. In fact, this Court has twice held that
§ 240.35(4)'s predecessor statutes did not require the People to prove a malicious
intent, and that even the most innocent of reasons will not excuse going out
in public disguised in unnatural attire among a group similarly disguised.

Section 240.35(4) does not interfere with the defendant's medical treatment
because it does not prohibit an individual male from appearing in public dressed
in female clothing. The statute instead prohibits three or more persons from
appearing in public disguised and in concert, and it does so because in a
crime-ridden society groups of disguised people can be dangerous. A disguise
such as the one used by the defendant can be so convincing that a victim

-2-

may firmly believe that she or he has been robbed by women even though the criminals were in fact men. Not only does the disguise prevent identification of criminals, but a group disguised in the way these defendants were can gain admission to confined areas, such as washrooms, where women are particularly vulnerable to attack.

Section 240.35(4) does not violate the defendant's constitutional right to privacy, and the Criminal Court properly denied his motion to dismiss the information. The United States Supreme Court has held that a state can regulate attire without offending the constitutional right to privacy unless the party challenging the regulation can show that there is no rational connection between that regulation and some form of public good. Only in matters of marriage, procreation, contraception, abortion, child rearing, education, and family relationships must a state demonstrate a compelling state interest, and none of those categories include any sort of right for a group of men to disguise themselves as women.

The defendant has not shown that § 240.35(4) lacks a rational relationship to a public need. Under the rational connection or rational basis test, a statute is constitutional even if not perfectly consistent with the Legislature's goals. This Court has affirmed convictions under § 240.35(4)'s predecessor statute, and those convictions were attacked on the same constitutional grounds asserted by the defendant here. Even if the men in this appeal were not disguised in order to commit crimes, the Legislature is entitled under the Constitution to regulate together both the truly dangerous and the apparently dangerous, particularly where even the apparently dangerous strikes the public as immoral.

ARGUMENT

I.

The Criminal Court properly denied the defendant's motion for a trial order of dismissal because there was legally sufficient evidence substantiating each element of loitering, as defined by penal law § 240.35(4)

The defendant's expert medical witnesses conceded that, both at the time of trial and of the offense, he had male chromosomes and genitalia and did not have a vagina or ovaries. After denying the defendant's motion for a trial order of dismissal, the trial judge found as a fact that the defendant was, at the time of the offense, a male. When arrested he was wearing a blouse, a skirt, high-heeled shoes, stockings, and women's undergarments. When a determination that the evidence was legally sufficient is challenged on appeal, the People are entitled to all favorable and permitted factual inferences. *People v. Acosta*, 80 N.Y. 665, 672, 609 N.E.2d 518, 522, 593 N.Y.S.2d 978, 982 (1993). And it was both permissible and reasonable for the trial judge to infer that the defendant had disguised himself by dressing in female clothing. When the sufficiency of the evidence is challenged, the conviction must be affirmed — as this one should be — if a rational trier of fact *could* have found all the elements of the offense proved beyond a reasonable doubt. *Id.*

> A. *The only element in dispute raised the question of whether the defendant was "in any manner disguised by unusual or unnatural attire."*

Under § 240.35(4), a defendant is guilty of loitering if he (1) is "in any manner disguised by unusual or unnatural attire," (2) "loiters, remains or

-3-

The conclusion for Point I.

Summing up the theory while emphasizing motivating arguments (see p. 309).

The standard of review (§33.3)

The prosecution's theory depends on a narrow definition of the issue.

<table>
<tr><td>

This is the overall rule, but it is not the one at the core of the prosecution's theory in Point I

</td><td>

congregates in a public place," and (3) does so "with other persons so . . . disguised." Nothing in the statute requires the People to prove that a defendant disguised himself for the purpose of committing some unlawful or antisocial act. As explained below, this Court has twice held that under § 240.35(4)'s predecessor statutes the People need not prove a malicious intent. *People v. Archibald*, 27 N.Y.2d 504, 260 N.E.2d 871, 312 N.Y.S.2d 678 (1970); *People v. Gillespi*, 15 N.Y.2d 529, 202 N.E.2d 565, 254 N.Y.S.2d 121, *amended*, 15 N.Y.2d 675, 204 N.E.2d 211, 255 N.Y.S.2d 884 (1964). Section 240.35(4) provides an exception where permission has been obtained from "the police or other appropriate authorities" for a "masquerade party or other like entertainment."

The defendant concedes every element of the offense but one. He admits that when arrested he was wearing female clothing and was standing on a street corner, and that the two persons with him when he was arrested have the same kinds of sexual organs he does and were wearing clothing similar to his. He does not maintain that he was so dressed in connection with an officially sanctioned masquerade party "or like entertainment." Instead, he claims that he was not "disguised by unusual or unnatural attire" because at the time of his arrest he had plans to have a sex change operation and become a woman at some date in the future.

</td></tr>
<tr><td>

This resolves the only element in dispute and is therefore the governing rule.

</td><td>

    B.   *Under this Court's precedents, a defendant is*
        "disguised by unusual or unnatural attire"
        when wearing clothing that misleads the
        public about the defendant's true gender.

</td></tr>
<tr><td>

Rule proof begins.

</td><td>

This Court held in *Archibald* and in *Gillespi* that even the most innocent of reasons will not excuse disguising one's self with attire normally used by the opposite gender and going about in public with others similarly clothed. The defendant in *Archibald* was arrested on a subway platform while returning home from a masquerade party and wearing a dress, a wig, high-heeled shoes, makeup, and women's undergarments. He was convicted under § 887(7) of the prior Code of Criminal Procedure (repealed by 1967 N.Y. Laws, ch. 681), which made no exception for masquerade parties and which provided that a person could be sentenced as a vagrant if he appeared in public "disguised, in a manner calculated to prevent his being identified," N.Y. Code Crim. Proc. § 887(7) (McKinney 1958). Relying on the straightforward wording of the statute, the Appellate Term rejected the defendant's contention that "the People must prove a specific intention of employing the disguise to commit some illegal act." *People v. Archibald*, 58 Misc. 2d 862, 863, 296 N.Y.S.2d 834, 836 (1968). This Court affirmed without opinion but citing to *Gillespi*.

The defendants in *Gillespi* were also convicted under former Code of Criminal Procedure § 887(7) for dressing like the defendant in this case. They argued on appeal that the statute was unconstitutional, that evidence that a man wore a woman's clothing is not sufficient proof that he was "disguised," and that such a conviction could not be sustained without evidence of intent to mislead for a criminal purpose. This court nevertheless affirmed.

The only other reported New York case on this question is a trial court decision from 1912, *People v. Luechini*, 75 Misc. 614, 136 N.Y.S. 319 (Erie County Ct.), which held for the defendant but which has been impliedly overruled in substance by this Court's later decisions in *Archibald* and *Gillespi*. Only one other court in the United States, a municipal court in Ohio, has issued a reported decision adopting a position similar to the one urged by the defendant

</td></tr>
</table>

-4-

on this question, and that decision — *City of Columbus v. Zanders,* 266 N.E.2d 602 (Ohio Mun. Ct. 1970) — was based on a theory of diminished mental capacity that is not recognized in New York law. See N.Y. Penal Law §§ 15.00-15.25 (McKinney 1998).

Moreover, the Legislature could have placed words in § 240.35(4) requiring proof of a criminal purpose or creating an exception for disguises used by transsexuals, but it did neither of those things. "[W]here as here the statute describes the particular situation in which it is to apply, 'an irrefutable inference must be drawn that what is omitted or not included was intended to be omitted or excluded.' " *Patrolmen's Benevolent Ass'n v. City of New York,* 41 N.Y.2d 205, 208-09, 359 N.E.2d 1338, 1341, 391 N.Y.S.2d 544, 546 (1976) (quoting Consol. Laws of N.Y., Book 1, Statutes, § 240 (McKinney 1971)).

A canon of construction (§16.1).

Section 240.35(4) unambiguously penalizes the act of appearing in public "disguised by . . . unnatural attire" with others "so . . . disguised." "[W]here the statutory language is clear and unambiguous, the court should construe it so as to give effect to the plain meaning of the words used." *Patrolmen's Benevolent Ass'n,* 41 N.Y.2d at 208, 359 N.E.2d at 1340, 391 N.Y.S.2d at 546. Although the consequences of a particular interpretation may be important where a statute lends itself to two different meanings, "[i]f the construction to be accorded a statute is clearly indicated, it is to be adopted by the courts regardless of consequences." *Town of Smithtown v. Moore,* 11 N.Y.2d 238, 244, 183 N.E.2d 66, 69, 228 N.Y.S.2d 657, 661 (1962). The plain meaning of § 240.35(4) is "clearly indicated" by the words the Legislature did use, and, although no legislative committee reports or similar documents explain the purpose of § 240.35(4), there are good reasons for drafting the statute as the Legislature did.

Another canon.

And another.

The Second Circuit has held that § 240.35(4) was "indisputably aimed at deterring violence and facilitating the apprehension of wrongdoers." *Church of the American Knights of the Ku Klux Klan v. Kerik,* 356 F.3d 197, 205 (2004). After reviewing the statute's history, the court concluded that the legislature's purpose was both narrow and proper. That purpose was to prevent the increased risk to the safety of others created when groups of people go out in public with their true identities so convincingly disguised that — as the state's governor put it in recommending adoption of the original 1845 statute — after a crime "has been perpetrated [and] the disguise is laid aside, . . . even eyewitnesses upon the spot may not be able to identify the guilty." *Id.* at 204 (quoting Gov. Silas Wright).

Policy is now used to complete proof of the rule. Because the court has been asked to make law here, policy arguments and motivating arguments tend to merge (see pp. 309-313).

Section 240.35(4) is a necessary and reasonable regulation of public behavior. It does not prohibit an individual male from dressing up in female clothing and then appearing in public — as shocking as that behavior might be to a large proportion of the population. It does not even forbid several males from doing that at the same time, as long as the clothing does not create an illusion so complete as to obscure their true identities. The statute instead prohibits three or more persons from appearing in public disguised and in concert, and it does so because of the serious danger such behavior poses for others.

The difficulties of law enforcement would be magnified if a crime-ridden society were to permit the appearance in public of groups of people who cannot readily be identified, and for that reason legislatures in other states have enacted statutes similar to § 240.35(4). For example, see Cal. Penal Code § 185 (West 1998); Ga. Code Ann. § 16-11-38(a) (1998); Okla. Stat. Ann. tit. 21, § 1301 (West 1983). In this state and elsewhere, the law of conspiracy is based on the concept that a greater public danger is created when criminals act together than where they act individually. The danger is multiplied where a disguise not only prevents identification of criminals after a robbery or other crime, but where the illusion created by the disguise is so convincing that a victim may firmly believe that she or he has been robbed by women although in fact the

-5-

criminals were men. Moreover, where the disguise misleads the observer as to the true gender of a group of males, that group can gain admission to confined areas, such as washrooms, where women can be attacked. If the defendant's interpretation of § 240.35(4) were to prevail in this Court, any three people who can demonstrate an interest in a sex change operation would be licensed to disguise their true identities and put the public at risk.

Rule application begins.

C.   *The People presented legally sufficient evidence that this defendant was "disguised by unusual or unnatural attire."*

The standard of review is used to tilt rule application favorably to the prosecution.

In reviewing trial evidence for legal sufficiency, the evidence must be viewed in the light most favorable to the People. *People v. Malizia,* 62 N.Y.2d 755, 465 N.E.2d 364, 476 N.Y.S.2d 825 (1984). Here, the defendant was disguised. He and his codefendants dressed as women, and the arresting officer testified that he at first believed them to be women. (R. at 101.) Although the defendant's own experts testified that medical science sympathizes with his psychological confusion (R. at 344, 432), they admitted that his reproductive organs remain male (R. at 373, 449).

Even after sex reassignment surgery (which the defendant has not yet had), New York law does not recognize that a man can become a woman. One trial court has held that a health insurer can be made to pay for a sex change operation if it is not explicitly excluded in the insurance policy, *Davidson v. Aetna Life & Casualty Ins. Co.,* 101 Misc. 2d 1, 420 N.Y.S.2d 450 (Sup. Ct., N.Y. County 1979), but that court held only that the operation could alleviate psychological suffering, not that it could produce a woman. Another trial court held that for practical purposes, such as sports competitions, a post-operative transsexual can be considered the equivalent of a woman, *Richards v. United States Tennis Ass'n,* 93 Misc. 2d 713, 400 N.Y.S.2d 267 (Sup. Ct., N.Y. County 1977), but that decision remains the opinion of a single trial court unreviewed on appeal.

Although the New York City Board of Health will issue an amended birth certificate to a post-surgery transsexual, deleting any reference to sex and incorporating a court-ordered change of name, courts have repeatedly refused to compel the Board to issue birth certificates that replace the birth sex with another, even after sex reassignment surgery. *Anonymous v. Mellon,* 91 Misc. 2d 375, 398 N.Y.S.2d 99 (Sup. Ct., N.Y. County 1977); *Hartin v. Director of Bureau of Records & Statistics,* 75 Misc. 2d 229, 347 N.Y.S.2d 515 (Sup. Ct., N.Y. County 1973); *Anonymous v. Weiner,* 50 Misc. 2d 380, 270 N.Y.S.2d 319 (Sup. Ct., N.Y. County 1966). These courts have acquiesced in the Board of Health's adoption of a report by the New York Academy of Science, which found that, even after surgery, "male-to-female transsexuals are still chromosomally males while ostensibly females," and which warned that a post-operative transsexual's desire for "concealment of a change of sex . . . is outweighed by the public interest for protection against fraud." *Weiner,* 50 Misc. 2d at 382-83, 270 N.Y.S.2d at 322 (quoting the Academy report).

Thus, New York has not established a public policy protecting the aspirations of transsexuals. The legislature has enacted no statute that could be interpreted to reflect such a policy. The precedent favoring transsexuals comes entirely from trial courts, and nearly all of it is limited in scope. Only one New York appellate case decided a transsexual issue. This Court affirmed the refusal of the Commissioner of Social Services to pay for a sex change operation desired by an indigent transsexual. *Denise R. v. Lavine,* 39 N.Y.2d 279, 347 N.E.2d 893, 383 N.Y.S.2d 568 (1976).

-6-

Nor have other states taken the position that medical treatment can legally change a person's sex. That is most apparent in two situations where a person's sex is essential to determining legal rights: in interpreting employment discrimination statutes and in the determining capacity to marry.

One trial court has held that a New York City ordinance protects a *post*-surgery transsexual against employment discrimination, *Maffei v. Kolaeton Indus., Inc.,* 164 Misc. 2d 547, 626 N.Y.S.2d 391 (Sup. Ct., N.Y. County 1995). That court did not hold that sex reassignment surgery can medically or legally change the sex a person was born with. Courts elsewhere have held that post-surgery transsexuals are not protected by antidiscrimination statutes. *Ulane v. Eastern Airlines, Inc.,* 742 F.2d 1081 (7th Cir. 1984); *In re Grossman,* 316 A.2d 39 (N.J. Super. Ct. 1974).

The defendant in this appeal has not yet received sex reassignment surgery. Most reported cases have held that *pre*-surgery transsexuals are not considered women or are not otherwise protected under the various federal and state statutes that prohibit discrimination in employment. *Kirkpatrick v. Seligman & Latz, Inc.,* 636 F.2d 1047 (5th Cir. 1981); *Sommers v. Budget Marketing, Inc.,* 667 F.2d 748 (8th Cir. 1982); *Holloway v. Arthur Andersen & Co.,* 566 F.2d 659 (9th Cir. 1977); *Etsitty v. Utah Transit Authority,* 502 F.3d 1215 (10th Cir. 2007); *Voyles v. Ralph K. Davies Med. Ctr.,* 403 F. Supp. 456 (N.D. Cal. 1975), *aff'd,* 570 F.2d 354 (9th Cir. 1978); *Powell v. Read's, Inc.,* 436 F. Supp. 369 (D. Md. 1977); *Dobre v. Amtrak,* 850 F. Supp. 284 (E.D. Pa. 1993); *Sommers v. Iowa Civil Rights Comm'n,* 337 N.W.2d 470 (Iowa 1983); *Goins v. West Group,* 635 N.W.2d 717 (Minn. 2001); *Doe v. Boeing Co.,* 846 P.2d 531 (Wash. 1993). In these cases, a pre-surgery transsexual's cross-dressing disguise caused so much difficulty with restrooms and other aspects of the workplace that the transsexual was fired.

Although no other federal Circuit has done so, the Sixth Circuit has held that an employment discrimination statute is violated when an employer treats an employee born male adversely because he wears a dress on or off duty. *Barnes v. City of Cincinnati,* 401 F.3d 729 (2005); *Smith v. City of Salem,* 378 F.3d 566 (2004). The New Jersey Superior Court agreed in *Enriquez v. West Jersey Health Systems,* 777 A.2d 365 (2001). These courts held that an employer engages in "sexual stereotyping" by assuming that men should not wear dresses. None of these cases, however, held that a transsexual has changed sex and become a woman. In fact, inherent in their holdings is the idea that the employees are still men. And *Enriquez* referred to the plaintiff as "he."

Typically in the reported capacity-to-marry cases, a person born male undergoes sex reassignment surgery and either goes through a marriage ceremony or tries to do so. In one case, the supposed husband died, and a post-surgery transsexual brought a wrongful death action claiming to be a surviving spouse. Texas courts dismissed on the ground that the post-surgery transsexual was still biologically male — having male chromosomes and lacking a womb, cervix, and ovaries — and therefore lacked the capacity to marry another male. *Littleton v. Prange,* 9 S.W.3d 223, 230 (Tex. Ct. App., 4th Dist. 1999). On similar facts, the Kansas Supreme Court reached the same conclusion in *In re Gardiner,* 273 Kan. 191, 42 P.3d 120 (2002). An Ohio trial court held on the same grounds that a post-surgery transsexual had not become female and therefore could not be issued a license to marry another man. *In re Ladrach,* 513 N.E.2d 828 (Ohio Prob. Ct. 1987). Where a post-surgery transsexual had a marriage ceremony with another man and later sued for support, a New Jersey appellate court concluded that sex reassignment surgery could convert a man into a woman — but that a *pre*-surgery transsexual is unquestionably male. *M.T. v. J.T.,* 355 A.2d 204 (N.J. Super. Ct. 1976).

-7-

Two New York annulment cases have considered capacity to marry. In one, a person who had been born female had surgery to gain characteristics of a man and then purportedly married a woman. The marriage was found to a nullity because surgery had not medically given the transsexual a new sex. *B. v. B.,* 78 Misc. 2d 112, 355 N.Y.S.2d 712 (Sup. Ct., Kings County 1974). The other case involved a *pre*-surgery transsexual like the defendant in the appeal now before this court, and the court there held that the transsexual still had the sex he was born with. *Anonymous v. Anonymous,* 67 Misc. 2d 982, 325 N.Y.S.2d 499 (Sup. Ct., Queens County 1971).

Thus, there was legally sufficient evidence before the Criminal Court substantiating every element of the offense defined by § 240.35(4), and that court therefore properly denied the defendant's motion for a trial order of dismissal.

II.

The Criminal Court properly denied the defendant's motion to dismiss the information because penal law § 240.35(4) does not violate the United States Constitutional right to privacy.

The conclusion for Point II.

Review is de novo where the constitutionality of a statute is at issue. *People v. Uplinger,* 58 N.Y.2d 936, 447 N.E.2d 62, 460 N.Y.S.2d 514 (1983).

The standard of review.

A. *Section 240.35(4) would violate the constitutional right to privacy only if the defendant could demonstrate that it is not rationally connected to any need for public protection.*

The rule.

The United States Supreme Court has held that a state can regulate attire without offending the constitutional right to privacy so long as there is a rational connection between that regulation and some form of protection provided to the public. In the leading decision on the question, the Court distinguished an interest in controlling one's own appearance from the more well-established right to control one's body, and it concluded that the Constitution allows a government more freedom to regulate appearance than "certain basic matters of procreation, marriage, and family life." *Kelley v. Johnson,* 425 U.S. 238, 244 (1976). There, the Court ruled that a state has the power to regulate an individual's appearance unless that individual can demonstrate that the state's regulation "is so irrational that it may be branded 'arbitrary' and therefore a deprivation of [the individual's] 'liberty' interest in freedom to choose his own" appearance. *Id.* at 248.

Rule proof begins.

A compelling state interest is not required here because the right to dress as one pleases — if it is a right at all — is not one of the fundamental rights at the core of freedoms protected through a constitutional right to privacy. Under *Griswold v. Connecticut,* 381 U.S. 479 (1965), *Roe v. Wade,* 410 U.S. 113 (1973), and their progeny, a state was able to regulate an individual's decisions concerning procreation and allied questions only if the state could demonstrate that it has a compelling interest in doing so and that its means of regulation are the least restrictive manner of satisfying that interest. But in *Bowers v. Hardwick,* 478 U.S. 186, 190 (1986), which determined that a homosexual's right to privacy was not violated by a state sodomy statute, the Court interpreted its right-to-privacy precedents to require a compelling state interest only in matters of marriage, procreation, contraception, abortion, child rearing,

The beginning of many counter-arguments needed to dispose of the competing test. Much synthesis goes on here.

-8-

510

education, and family relationships. And although the Supreme Court might have "reaffirmed" that line of cases in *Planned Parenthood v. Casey,* 505 U.S. 833, 845 (1992), it also refused to enforce a compelling state interest test in abortion cases—thus impliedly questioning the use of that test in any right-to-privacy case. Moreover, in the only reported decision to consider whether a statute like section 240.35(4) violates the constitutional right to privacy, the Illinois Supreme Court did not require a compelling state interest and instead applied the rational connection test. *City of Chicago v. Wilson,* 389 N.E.2d 522 (Ill. 1978).

Even if *Griswold* and its progeny had not been weakened by *Planned Parenthood,* they never required a compelling state interest outside the context of reproduction. In *Bowers,* the Supreme Court held that "[n]o connection between family, marriage, or procreation on the one hand and homosexual activity on the other has been demonstrated." *Id.* at 191. Nor is there any connection between family, marriage, or procreation on one hand and men disguising themselves as women on the other. In *Kelley,* the Court even declined to determine whether the Fourteenth Amendment—and presumably the right to privacy inherent therein—actually provides a right to wear whatever one wants. *Id.* at 244. Instead, the Court merely assumed the existence of such a right because the regulation there at issue was so plainly supported by a rational connection to the public interest that the more difficult question of whether such a right exists at all could be deferred to another day. *Id.*

The defendant mistakenly relies on *People v. Onofre,* 51 N.Y.2d 476, 415 N.E.2d 936, 434 N.Y.S.2d 947 (1980). *Onofre* was impliedly overruled by the Supreme Court in *Bowers* because the New York sodomy statute struck down in *Onofre* was in every substantive way identical to the Georgia sodomy statute upheld by the Supreme Court in *Bowers.* Moreover, *Onofre* was not premised on any provision of the New York State Constitution, and *Bowers* condemns the ever-expanding federal right-to-privacy theory enunciated in *Onofre,* 478 U.S. at 194-95.

> B.   *The defendant has not shown that § 240.35(4) lacks a*
>   *rational connection to some need for public protection.*

Rule application begins.

Under the rational connection or rational basis test, a "law need not be in every respect logically consistent with its aims to be constitutional. It is enough that there is an evil at hand for correction, and that it might be thought that the particular legislative measure was a rational way to correct it." *Williamson v. Lee Optical, Inc.,* 348 U.S. 483, 487-88 (1955). In *Williamson,* the Court held that an Oklahoma statute was constitutional because none of the rights asserted against it were fundamental and because it had a rational connection to an identifiable risk to the public. Among other things, the statute prohibited opticians (who grind lenses and fit frames) from selling eyeglasses except on a prescription written by an optometrist or an ophthalmologist, both of whom have at least diagnostic training and the latter medical training as well. Although the Court recognized that the Oklahoma statute "may exact a needless, wasteful requirement in many cases," it found a rational connection, sufficient to justify the statute, because "in *some* cases the directions contained in the prescription are essential" and the "legislature *might* have concluded" that wastefulness on many occasions is balanced by what is essential on others. *Id.* at 487 (emphasis added). Thus, the essence of the test is deference to the legislature, as "it is for the legislature, not the courts, to balance the advantages and disadvantages" of a statute that need be supported only by a rational connection to a public need.

So, too, in *Kelley,* the Court upheld a police department's regulation of its officers' hair grooming. The Court pointed to the public's interest in being served by police officers neatly and uniformly attired and groomed, and it concluded that governmental decisions of this kind are "entitled to the same sort of presumption of legislative validity as are state choices designed to promote other aims" within the state's general authority. *Id.* at 247. The Court held it to be reversible error to evaluate such a challenge on the basis of "whether the State can 'establish' a 'genuine public need' for the specific regulation" because the true test is whether the party challenging the regulation "can demonstrate that there is no rational connection between the regulation . . . and the promotion of safety of persons and property." *Id.* In *Bowers,* the Supreme Court went even further and held that a legislature can have a rational basis to proscribe conduct simply because the public perceives it to be "immoral and unacceptable."

The defendant has not carried such a burden in this appeal. This Court has affirmed convictions under section 240.35(4)'s predecessor statute, *People v. Archibald,* 27 N.Y.2d 504, 260 N.E.2d 871, 312 N.Y.S.2d 678 (1970); *People v. Gillespi,* 15 N.Y.2d 529, 202 N.E.2d 565, 254 N.Y.S.2d 121, *amended,* 15 N.Y.2d 675, 204 N.E.2d 211, 255 N.Y.S.2d 884 (1964). The Second Circuit has held that § 240.35(4) does not violate the First Amendment, *Church of the American Knights of the Ku Klux Klan v. Kerik,* 356 F.3d 197, 205 (2004), and other states have similar enactments, Cal. Penal Code § 185 (West 1988); Okla. Stat. Ann. tit. 21, § 1301 (West 1983) — all because of the danger that would be created if groups of people were permitted to disguise their identities in public without any supervision by the police and because of the deeply held public belief that it is immoral for a person to disguise her or his true gender. In a modern society that is more mobile and anonymous than ever before, it would be cause for insecurity among public and police if potential crime victims could not be confident that groups of strangers met on the street and elsewhere are in fact who and what they appear to be.

Policy and
motivating
arguments
combine.

The type of disguise chosen by the defendant in this appeal is a particular cause for governmental concern. It is immediately clear that people who disguise themselves with ski masks or the like are involved in something suspicious, even if those people are not identifiable. Here, however, the defendant and his companions so convincingly dressed themselves up as women that the arresting officer did not at first recognize them to be men (R. at 101). They could have gained entrance to a women's washroom, to the dressing rooms in apparel stores, and to other areas where women would be vunerable to harassment or attack. They could also have committed a crime while deceiving the victim into believing that the perpetrators were women and not men. Even if these particular men were not disguised in order to commit crimes, the Legislature is entitled — under the rule articulated in *Williamson* and like cases — to "balance the advantages and disadvantages" and to regulate together both the truly dangerous and the apparently dangerous where the Legislature deems that necessary to protect the public and particularly where even the apparently dangerous strikes the public as immoral.

A counter-
argument.

Although the Illinois Supreme Court, in *City of Chicago v. Wilson,* 389 N.E.2d 522 (Ill. 1978), held that an ordinance similar to § 240.35(4) could not be enforced against transsexuals, there are two reasons why that holding should not be persuasive in the instant appeal. The first is that, although the *City of Chicago* court applied a rational connection test to the challenged statute, it incorrectly placed the burden of proof on the government, rather than on the party

-10-

challenging the ordinance. The court reasoned that "the State is not relieved from showing some justification for its intrusion," *id.* at 524, and it concluded that "[i]nasmuch as the city has offered no evidence to substantiate its reasons for infringing on the defendants' choice of dress . . . we do find that § 192-8 as applied to the defendants is an unconstitutional infringement of their liberty interest," *id.* at 525. In *Kelley,* the Supreme Court held this approach to be error, and it there reversed a lower court that had done the same thing. The second reason is that the statute at issue in *City of Chicago* was a far more drastic one than § 240.35(4). Section 192-8 of the Chicago Municipal Code punished any person who appeared in public "in a dress not belonging to his or her sex," even when that person was alone. Section 240.35(4) does not do that: its scope is limited to the more dangerous situation in which people appear in public both disguised *and* in groups.

Not only is § 240.35(4) narrowly drawn, but a conviction under it does not create a criminal record because the offense it defines is a violation and not a crime. N.Y. Penal Law §§ 10.00(1), (3), (6) (McKinney 1998); N.Y. Crim. Proc. Law § 160.60 (McKinney 1992). Moreover, the impact of § 240.35(4) on the defendant in this appeal is not very substantial. The statute does not prohibit him from dressing as a woman before he has a sex change operation. It punishes him only for so dressing in public with two or more other men who are doing the same thing. Both the defendant's physician and the defendant's psychiatrist testified that if he were to refrain before his surgery from going out in public with other men dressed as women, there would be no "significant" detrimental effect on his pre-operative therapy (R. at 408, 449).

Thus, § 240.35(4) does not violate the defendant's right to privacy under the United States Constitution, and the Criminal Court properly denied his motion to dismiss the information.

CONCLUSION

For all the foregoing reasons, the defendant's conviction should be affirmed.

> Hon. Martha Bosley
> District Attorney
> New York County
>
> BY: Allan Kuusinen, Esq.
> Asst. District Attorney
> 1 Hogan Place
> New York, NY 10013
> (212) 555-1111

Index